# BED AND BREAKFAST

## IN NEW ENGLAND

***Praise for the previous edition:***

*"Best of genre. Thoroughly researched and accurate."*
**—Thorncroft Inn, Vineyard Haven, Massachusetts**

*"You made our host homes come alive."*
**—Bed and Breakfast Associates Bay Colony**

*"Gives all the answers to questions people ask when they call for reservations—even whether anyone in residence smokes."*
**—Jeanne Lewis, Fairfield-by-the-Sea, Westerly, Rhode Island**

*"After we discovered your book, we tried our first B&B in New York. Our hosts and their wonderful hospitality were just as you described."*
**—P.J. Fetterman, Cambridge, Pennsylvania**

*". . . delightful, accurate, interesting, helpful . . . a pleasure to read and poke through."*
**—Jane Hence, Essex, Connecticut**

*"A really needed B&B book! The way you did it tells people exactly what they like to know. And it's a good book to read for entertainment."*
**—Martha Dorais, New Hampshire**

*"The little anecdotes you've selected to clarify and describe accommodations and hosts do much to show how comfortable and relaxing staying in a B&B home can be."*
**—Elaine Borowick, West Hyannisport, Massachusetts**

*"Splendid."* **—Helen Ellison, Shore Inne, Groton Long Point, Connecticut**

*"A winner."* **—Kit Shane, Bloomington, Indiana**

*"Because of* Bed and Breakfast in the Northeast *we now hear from all parts of the country."*
**—Boston Bed and Breakfast**

*"The book makes B&B contagious."* **—Rae Eastman, West Cornwall, Connecticut**

Other books by Bernice Chesler

Editor and Coordinator
*The ZOOM Catalog*
*Do a ZOOMdo*
*People You'd Like to Know*

Coauthor
*The Family Guide to Cape Cod*

Author
*In and Out of Boston with (or without) Children*
*Mainstreaming through the Media*
*Bed & Breakfast Coast to Coast*
*Bed and Breakfast in the Mid-Atlantic States*

# BED AND BREAKFAST
## IN NEW ENGLAND

*by* Bernice Chesler

*A Voyager Book*

The Globe Pequot Press

Chester, Connecticut 06412

Cover photo by Sean Kernon
Cover design by Barbara Marks



Prior to revision, some of the material in this book appeared in *bed and Breakfast in the Northeast.*

**Library of Congress Cataloging-in-Publication Data**

Chesler, Bernice.
Bed and breakfast in New England.

(A Voyager book)
Includes index.
1. Bed and breakfast accommodations—New England—Guide-books. I. Title. II. Series: Voyager book (Chester, Conn.)
TX907.C55286 1987 647′.947403 87–8499
ISBN 0–87106–754–4 (pbk.)

Manufactured in the United States of America
First Edition/First Printing

# CONTENTS

*to David*

# INTRODUCTION

"We almost hesitate to rave too much because we want to be able to find an opening next time. It was the highlight of our trip."

—B&B guests

Thousands of letters and interviews and hundreds of stays later, the 500-page *Bed and Breakfast in the Northeast*, my first B&B book, has become two separate volumes, *Bed and Breakfast in New England* and *Bed and Breakfast in the Mid-Atlantic States* (from New York and Pennsylvania south to Virginia and West Virginia).

As the number of B&Bs continues to multiply, it seems that the need for information has also increased. Readers have expressed thanks for knowing facts that are usually gathered only by phone calls to each and every place that "sounds pretty good." And it seems that first-timers and experienced B&B travelers alike appreciate the opportunity to "meet" hosts in print.

Before my full-time B&B research, I interviewed many caring and sharing people throughout the country for documentary films, articles, and books, but it is hard to recall another project that involves individuals who *all* love what they are doing. As a matter of fact, their enthusiasm is quite contagious. "One out of every five guests leaves with the dream of opening their own B&B," according to one Vermont host. Most B&Bs find that they are a model for dreamers.

Now that bed and breakfast, long established in Europe, has finally been accepted in this country, B&B here has come to mean many different things to different people. It can be a money saver, particularly in big cities and resorts. In some locations a few have opened with lavish and expensive accommodations. B&B is also chosen for peace and quiet; for company; for pampering; for food; for a convenient or an off-the-beaten path location; for an opportunity to meet new people; for a home away from home. B&B hosts can be a great resource for information about an area's attractions, restaurants, back roads, history, housing, jobs, people. Whatever, wherever, the best always have hospitality that can't be beat.

Although the popularization of B&B has reached the point where B&B package rates are now offered by some hotels and motels as well as by smaller facilities that are managed but not owner-occupied, I still like the traditional interpretation: a home setting with an owner in residence; a maximum of about ten rooms; no bar on the premises; a common room available to guests; breakfast included in the rate; dinner served, if at all, only occasionally and only to B&B guests. On the following pages you will be introduced to avocational hosts with one or more extra rooms; to hosts in business—"an enjoyable people business," they say; and to part-time anonymous-to-the-public hosts who prefer to let a reservation service arrange bookings. In addition, the extensive list of 300 reservation services gives you access to at least 15,000 (possibly 20,000) B&Bs throughout the United States and Canada.

B&B conversations, however brief, are usually remembered more than the color of the wallpaper. Still, with current interest in interior design, architecture, food, and innkeeping, it turns out that many creative hosts become casual or formal consultants to guests. Hence you'll find the additional of symbols that refer to potential advice or recipe sharing.

Each writeup gives bed sizes and the floor location of guest rooms. A bath may be private or shared, full or with tub or shower only. Details, details—all spelled out. If a "no smoking" rule (under "Restrictions") is of interest, also check "In residence" to see if any member of the household smokes. For guests with allergies, there's information about pets in residence. Both the hour of the morning meal as well as a typical menu are in each description. Specific rates, rather than a range, are listed. Is the B&B near shops or the highway, or up and away on the mountainside? The setting is under "Location." Are you on business? Do you want a family place? One that is better for honeymooners? It's all here.

Information is as up-to-date as possible. Ellen Madison's cat reappeared just before the books went to press. The B&B that was sold suddenly because "an offer came that we couldn't refuse" has been withdrawn—until the hosts finish their property search currently being conducted in a mobile home. Other successful hosts have been known to add a room; change the bed size; change the menu or decor; and, yes, change the rates too.

In order to produce such personalized books, there is a processing fee for the full description of each selection I make. There is no charge for a place on the comprehensive list of reservation services throughout North America.

My thanks go to Leona DeMartino for her terrific assistance at the beginning stages of compilation. Ann Meyers brought considerable expertise and dedication to the project. Her curiosity (and humor) refined many points—including the typo that announced that there was a complimentary wino in every room of one B&B. It's a pleasure to have Jay Howland as editor; she knows as much (everything) about B&B and my writing quirks as about editing. My thanks, too, to the Tourism Division of the Canadian Consulate General in Boston, Massachusetts. And again it is true that without David, my husband, there wouldn't be any books. He plans all our trips by plane, car, and bicycle. He listens to the extraordinary letter of the day, offers judgment when I solicit objectivity, keeps the household going, and acts as my computer expert in residence.

Suggestions about people and places are welcome for consideration in the next edition. Please address them to me at The Globe Pequot Press, Box Q, Old Chester Road, Chester, CT 06412.

Bernice Chesler

# ANSWERS TO FREQUENTLY ASKED QUESTIONS

**What is bed and breakfast?**

It is a package arrangement that includes overnight accommodations and breakfast. Although there are many embellishments (amenities) offered at some American B&Bs, the keynote is hospitality. Think of it as a people-to-people program.

B&Bs range from simple to elegant. A B&B may be a private home with an extra room or a business—"home on a larger scale"—sometimes called a B&B inn. As at home, nothing is standardized. Every room is different. Many are freshly and imaginatively decorated. Some are suites, or they might be in a private wing or a converted carriage house. Most are not just clean; they are immaculate.

**Are baths shared?**

Some are. But depending on the number of guests, a shared bath could be private for you. It may adjoin the room or be down the hall; sometimes it is up or down the stairs. Trend: In high demand areas where B&Bs have signs and advertise, Americans, even those who are used to European shared-bath arrangements, are requesting—and willing to pay extra for—a private bath. Yet there are hosts in older homes who have no interest in adding baths, who find no problem with shared baths, and who even suggest that "a certain type of guest—all very nice" do not care whether baths are private or shared.

**Do you have to get up for breakfast?**

Again, no one rule. Check each description in this book for the various arrangements. More than one guest has been enticed by the aroma of fresh muffins. More than one guest has helped himself to breakfast after the host has left for work. If you are on business or want to catch the morning ferry, eat-and-run is just fine. If, however, cuisine is a feature, plan on appearing at the specified time!

Vacationers (not skiers) find breakfast a very social time. One hostess says that even when guests say they want to be on the road early, they often linger over breakfast for hours. If hosts join you, please understand when they leave the table after a while.

**Is B&B like a hotel?**

Not at all! It's not intended to be. You are greeted by a member of the family, an assistant, a neighbor, or, occasionally, by a note.

Perhaps one Connecticut host put it best: "We seem to live in an era when the human touch is becoming a lost pleasure. We will never threaten Hilton, Marriott, or Holiday Inns. How many times have you written a thank-you note to (or hugged) them?"

Depending on the size and layout of the B&B, it may not provide the privacy—or the loneliness—of a hotel. There's no elevator service and rarely is there an ice machine down the hall. Television is not an important feature. Neither is a phone in the room. (Exception: One reservation service, noting the increased number of business guests, has suggested that their listed B&Bs install telephone jacks in guest rooms. A new trend?)

**How much do they cost?**

As little as $15 a person for the night. Many are in the $35–$50 range (including breakfast) for two people. Rural regions tend to be less expensive. With soaring real estate prices and the public's desire for more amenities, a few have topped the $100 mark. The season and location can affect the rate. Some hosts who have lived in the B&B for years are happy to charge less, believing that the traveler should be able to find reasonably priced accommodations. Because of all these variables the rate may or may not be indicative of facilities. A B&B is almost always less—often much less—expensive than a hotel in the same area, and for just economic comparison, breakfast should be taken into account.

**Other money thoughts:**

Unless credit cards are in the B&B description, please do not expect hosts to accept them. Ask if personal checks are acceptable. Most small places prefer cash or travelers' checks. And it's a good idea to check on deposit requirements; refund policies differ. Required local or state taxes vary from place to place, and are usually not included in the listed rates.

Consider paying upon arrival rather than waiting until departure time. The goodbyes can be that much smoother, and you really do feel as if you have visited friends.

To tip—or not? Not usually in a private home, but if there are helpful children in the family, they appreciate being remembered. In a B&B inn, treat staff as you would in a hotel.

**How do B&Bs on this side of the Atlantic differ from those in the British Isles or other European countries?**

The idea of B&B and away-you-go is not necessarily the norm in North America. Although there are B&Bs with just one room and many where you are expected to leave for the day following breakfast, guests are often invited to spend more time "at home"—by the pool or fireplace, on the hiking trails or borrowed bicycles. Even hosts are amazed at what they do when they get involved in others' lives! They worry about late arrivals. They have been known to drive someone to a job appointment or do laundry for a businessman whose schedule changed or prevail upon the local auto mechanic when the garage was closed.

Another major difference is the concept of a reservation service, which is responsible for the enormous numbers of part-time hosts here.

**What is a reservation service?**

In the B&B world, it is primarily an American creation, a phenomenon really. For hosts, it's a private way of going public because the host remains anonymous until the service (agency) matches host and guest. No signs are on the house or building. This unique system also allows hosts in private homes to have an irregular hosting schedule.

For more information about reservation services, please see page 469.

**Who are the hosts?**

Singles, couples, maybe three friends in business together, or families. Parents and even grandparents of grown children. Retirees. Natives and transplants. People who know how to help and when to leave you alone. People who are sensitive to the wishes of nonsmokers. Sharers all. They represent hundreds of occupations—politicians, lawyers, doctors, business people, mid-life career changers, farmers, artists, housewives, hotel executives too. A sociologist or an architect could probably make quite a study with the variety of people and their backgrounds and settings.

**Who goes to B&Bs?**

The endless list includes travelers who are alone or in small groups; travelers who are with or without children, with or without pets; travelers on business or in an area for professional reasons. Vacationers. College shoppers. Parents of college students and summer campers. International visitors. Conventiongoers. Honeymooners. Retirees. Relatives of hospitalized patients. Transferees. House hunters. Most are people who are looking for a touch of home. Some want to be pampered. Some are looking for a bargain. Budgets aside, most guests intentionally choose B&B—preferring the guest book to the registration desk.

**Are all B&Bs "palaces"?**

The Virginian who asked me that question had the idea that every place is antique-filled, magazine-picture-perfect with canopied beds. There *are* plenty of those. And there are *some* (not thousands, maybe not even hundreds) with working fireplaces in guest rooms or a hot tub. Many B&Bs are on the National Register of Historic Places. A B&B may be a collector's or decorator's dream. It may be a penthouse or surrounded by rolling acreage. Others that lack lounging space in "cozy rooms" can be counted on for a warm welcome, perhaps a porch, yard, or wood stove. It is the variety and personalized touches that make each B&B so different. This book is written so that you know whether to expect pure luxury, "just plain home" that is sparkling clean and maybe freshly decorated, fine antiques, or "Mother's attic."

**Is B&B for everyone?**

"What do you mean, a private home? I just want a bed!" That's exactly how some travelers have been introduced to B&B; now they opt for personalized travel everywhere. As you can see by the writeups in this book, many B&Bs are perfect getaway spots—just right for unwinding and a change of pace. However, if you seek total anonymity, B&B probably isn't for you.

One Vermont host said, "Guests who come to B&Bs screen themselves: They are outgoing, want to be sociable and learn about you and the area; are easy to please and most grateful for anything you go out of your way to do for them. They are willing to risk the unknown."

Recommendation: Tell the host if this is your first time at a B&B. When making the reservation, if privacy is a real concern, say that too. Hosts' listening skills are usually well tuned.

Among all the wonderful guests, a few hosts can recall the occasional "memorable" demanding guest; sometimes I think that it is the same person going from B&B to B&B. And I have heard of a first-timer who appeared with considerable luggage—cumbersome, indeed, on the narrow steep stairs to the third floor of the historic house.

Charm. "Tell me," said the older guest, "what's so charming about a tub on legs? I was so glad when built-ins finally became the fashion." Tastes and interpretations differ. Conclusion: If you must have things exactly as they are in the hotel you usually go to, go to the hotel!

**Because B&Bs are private residences, can we be more casual about cancellations?**

Sorry, on the contrary. Hosts plan their lives around your arrival and stay. They may pick (or buy) flowers for your room, prepare certain foods, and schedule appointments according to your reservation. Remember, too, that they may have turned away others. It may or may not be possible to fill the vacancy that a cancellation creates. As a result, many B&Bs have deposit requirements and specific cancellation policies.

**Why don't some B&Bs answer the phone during normal business hours?**

If they are solo or if they are without paid help, they may be doing an errand. One hostess observed that the phone rings whenever she is taking a bath. Please remember that most hosts wear many hats—from cleaning person to desk clerk, from chef to fire tender. Some have other jobs. Some have been known to put out a "No Vacancy" sign when they need time for themselves or have visiting family. Much may depend on whether the B&B is a full-fledged business or an avocation. If you do call in the evening, heed the words of a city host: "It's our home. B&B guests know not to call late at night."

**Why do all these people choose to host "strangers"?**

Many of the descriptions in this book will satisfy your curiosity. Lifestyle. That's the word that crops up over and over again. B&B provides an avenue for meeting people that the hosts wouldn't meet in any other way. Few in private homes host to make a living. Some do it to be able to buy the old place. Other hosts use it to defray expenses. A few contribute B&B fees to their favorite charity. Now that B&B is so popular, there are B&B inns that have opened as a business. (In this book, B&B inns are limited to small, owner-occupied places.)

**Compared with Europe, rates seem high. Is B&B a big money maker?**

If we could shape the calendar so that it had a week of Saturdays or a year of Northeast Octobers, then B&B might be considered a lucrative undertaking. Experienced hosts will tell you that business can be quite seasonal and uneven. They also quickly learn that, depending on the number of rooms they have and the occupancy rate, it helps to have another source of income. "I have to have another job to support my innkeeping habit," replied one exuberant hostess. The casual traveler does not see the long list of hidden expenses. If there are more than a couple of rooms, local ordinances can go as far as requiring a restaurant stove or other expensive equipment. One-nighters are not necessarily profitable if you consider what it takes to ready a room on a daily basis. It can take three to five years to get established. Many a restorer hangs out the welcome sign only to find that the hideaway has to be marketed.

**Help! Our town fathers don't know what a B&B is.**

Bed and breakfast doesn't fit into any category on the books of most lawmakers; zoning can be an issue. More than one lawyer has used my B&B books to illustrate the concept. The most convincing argument, of course, is a B&B stay. As each community and each state defines B&B, they hear about the economic benefits and the public relations for an area. Continent-wide, many larger and historic properties are being restored and maintained, thanks to bed and breakfast.

Even when B&B is established, there are concerns: In a few communities where the idea was slow in starting, some think that too many private homes have been converted to inns. (Pockets of the country where B&B has not taken hold can't imagine having such a problem.) In 1986 cooked breakfasts were an issue at a Nantucket town meeting; one hostess who had hosted for 13 years declared that she had not yet lost a guest who had eaten her homemade muffins (baked in an impeccable kitchen).

**If you like people and enjoy company and cooking, isn't that enough experience to host?**

It helps. But experienced hosts have all commented on the time and work involved. Guests who ask, "Is this all you do?" would be surprised to realize that there *is* more to hosting than serving tea and meeting interesting people. Even I have fallen into the trap of multiplying a full house by the nightly rate, only to hear my husband say, "Never mind, that's 600 sheets!"

**What do you recommend to people who dream about having their own B&B?**

Attend a workshop or seminar given by adult education centers, state extension departments, innkeepers, or reservation services. Find some way to try hosting: Apprentice, even for a weekend, or sign up with a reservation service and host in your own home.

Every host in this book enjoys what they call "the great emotional rewards of a stimulating occupation." Some remind couples who wish to make hosting a vocation that it helps to have a strong marriage. One who encourages prospective innkeepers to "Just do it!" adds, "But be aware that you have to be more gregarious than private. You have to learn to carve time out for yourself. Hosting requires a broad range of talents (knowledge of plumbing helps), a lot of flexibility, an incredible amount of stamina, and perseverance. Did I mention you might need some capital?"

*Author's note:* The mail indicates that this book has a fringe benefit. From Mississippi, from Michigan, and from Massachusetts too have come notes from hosts who were inspired by the profiles. And hosts report that guests stay up reading about all these wonderful people. Category: "You never know."

**What do you do with all the letters you receive?**

Hosts who wish to be included receive a response. Because it isn't possible for any one person to sleep in all these beds, the (thousands of) guests' letters—even the handful of complaints—are a big help.

Every host in this book has subscribed to more than the standards of cleanliness, comfort, and congeniality. There's another *c*: commitment. A popular (and enthusiastic) New York host suggested that we could add "confinement" and "confusion" to the list!

**What are some of your favorite B&Bs?**

Even when you stay in hundreds, you tend to remember the hosts more than the place. It is true that each one is special in its own way. We have enjoyed rather luxurious settings and some casual places too. There's the antique dealer in Virginia who slept in the barn with her horse that was due to deliver; the hostess came in each morning to whip up a wonderful farm breakfast for us. The horticulturist, a septuagenarian whom we could hardly keep up with as she toured us through her spectacular gardens. We have arrived on bicycles and been greeted with the offer of a car to go to dinner. There's the couple who built their own solar house. Multifaceted retirees. The history buffs who filled us in on the area and recommended back roads. The literary buffs who suggested good books. Hosts in a lovely residential section just minutes off the highway. Hosts we have laughed with. Yes, even some we have cried with too. Great chefs. People who are involved in their communities and trying to make this a better world. People whose home has been a labor of love, sharing it with others.

**Where do you see B&B going from here? Is it a fad?**

There's still a lot of growing to be done. I call it the antique shop syndrome. One comes and paves the way. More open. And the idea spreads. The place to stay can be the reason to go. It's wonderful.

# BED AND BREAKFAST
## IN NEW ENGLAND

**KEY**

 Recipes shared, often for house specialties.

 Inquiries welcomed about restoration and/or decorating. Symbol indicates that host is willing to share experiences with guests. Tips range from a before-and-after album to rebuilding advice, from furniture refinishing to curtain making. Expertise of hosts ranges from learn-by-doing to professional.

 How-To B&B workshop, seminar or apprentice program offered.

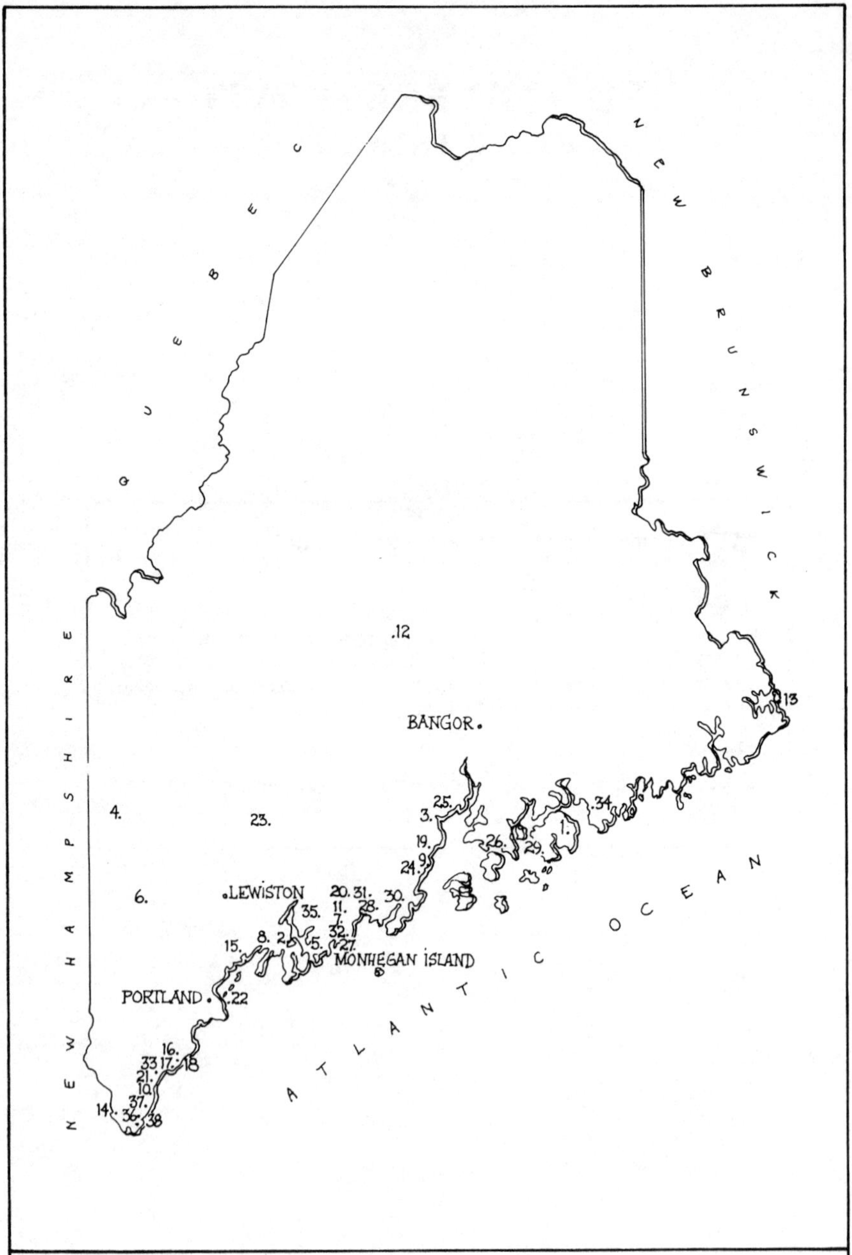


*The numbers on this map indicate the locations of B&Bs described in detail in this chapter.*

# MAINE

# Maine Reservation Services

## Bed & Breakfast Down East, Ltd.

Box 547, Macomber Mill Road, Eastbrook, ME 04634
**Phone:** 207/565-3517. Monday through Friday, 8:30-8:30; 8-1 Saturday.
**Listings:** 150 in about 80 communities. "They are all over the state in every possible setting—oceanfront, lakeside, beach, mountain, rural, coastal village, city, suburban, inland village, on farms, aboard a boat, wilderness lodge, and in a lighthouse keeper's cottage." Mostly hosted private residences. A few inns. Directory ($3) organized according to region with full description and detail.

Many of Sally Godfrey's hosts have listed with her since she began the highly personalized service in 1983. She knows all her (varied) hosts and has visited their homes; she matches travelers with compatible hosts in surroundings of comfort and hospitality.

**Reservations:** At least 2-3 weeks advance notice preferred. Most hosts will take one-night stays. Some, particularly in busier resort areas, insist on two- or three-night minimum stays on weekends in the summer. Also available through travel agents.
**Plus:** Some homes offer babysitting, laundry, or other services. Some will pack lunches. "Most offer the spectacular Maine scenery, clean air, peace and quiet."
**Rates:** $30-$50 single, $35-$100 double. Some family and weekly rates. $20 deposit per room per night. $10 processing fee charged for cancellations with more than a week's notice. With less notice, a refund is at the host's discretion. MasterCard, VISA, and AMEX accepted.

## Bed & Breakfast of Maine

32 Colonial Village, Falmouth, ME 04105
**Phone:** 207/781-4528. Live 6-11 weekday evenings, all day on weekends. Answering machine at other times. Closed December 24-January 2 and during a three-week period in the winter or spring.
**Listings:** 55 in 27 communities. All hosted private residence. One inn. Located mostly along 250 miles of coast, but few are actually on the waterfront. About 10 listings in mountains and near lakes, a couple in Portland. Directory ($1) is about six pages of descriptions with rates.

Most of Peg Tierney's homes have been listed with her for four years, are historic, and offer a full breakfast. "My hosts must have clean and pretty homes, but in addition they *must* offer friendly hospitality. My guest response cards give a clear indication of this. When guests call for bookings, I often assist them in planning their trips."

**Reservations:** Two weeks' advance notice preferred. Minimum stay required in resort areas in July and August. Available through travel agents. Short-term (1-2 weeks) hosted housing available.
**Rates:** $28-$50 single, $35-$75 double. Some weekly rates available. $25 deposit required in most cases; two hosts require first night's rate. Cancellations made within 72 hours of reservations receive refund less a $10 service charge. MasterCard and VISA accepted.

## Christian Hospitality

This service has hosts in Bailey's Island, Bath, and Belfast. Please see page 287.

## Pineapple Hospitality

This service has hosts in the Augusta area, Bar Harbor area, Bath, Belfast, Boothbay Harbor area, Bridgton, Bucksport, near Sanford, Fryeburg, Ogunquit, Portland, Readfield, and in Scarborough,

Sheepscot, Southwest Harbor, Waldoboro, Wells Beach, and Wiscasset. Please see page 214.

## Maine B&Bs

### The Atlantean Inn

11 Atlantic Avenue, Bar Harbor, ME 04609
**Phone:** 207/288-3270
**Location:** On a quiet street, a short walk away from the heart of Bar Harbor, two miles from Acadia National Park on Mount Desert Island.
**Hosts:** Lucille and Joseph Striefel
**Open:** Year round. Two-night minimum reservation.

Joe and Lucie, parents of a growing family, have lived in this large 1903 Tudor home for thirteen years. It has always provided lodging for travelers, but breakfast was added to its offerings just a couple of years ago. Then the newspaper was provided at the table—for only two days. "Now guests talk to one another at breakfast and very often they end up spending the day together."

Lucie calls Joe "the athletic director" because he's the one who gives the windsurfing lessons and oversees the sports equipment. Joe, a national flatwater kayaking champion, is training for the Olympics again.

They have filled their home with plants and flowers and antique oak furnishings. The two of them have done all the restoration work. "What you need is a lot of patience," is the advice they give to guests who inquire about what it takes. Their knowledge extends to suggestions for Acadia National Park trails and waterfalls that are relatively undiscovered.

**Restrictions:** Children 14 and over accepted. No pets nor smoking.
**Bed and bath:** Eight rooms, each with a private bath. Two rooms with king-sized bed and fireplace, two with two doubles and fireplace. Four rooms have one double bed in each. Cot available.
**Breakfast:** Served at 9 in large dining room, sometimes outside. A full meal could include blueberry pancakes, waffles, or an omelet.

**Plus:** Use of 1880 solid oak billiard table. Library with large-screen television. Fresh garden flowers in rooms. Thick towels. Picnic table and lounge chairs in the "largest yard in Bar Harbor." (In 1986 750 tulip and daffodils bloomed there.) Hourly charge for sports equipment including windsurfers (lessons available too), sailboats, mountain bikes, kayaks, canoes. Will meet guests at Bar Harbor airport. Laundry facilities. Dinners for overnight guests (only) can be arranged.
**Rates:** $55-$95 according to size of room. Extra person $10. MasterCard and VISA accepted.

## Nannau-Seaside B&B

P.O. Box 710, Lower Main Street, Bar Harbor, ME 04609
**Phone:** 207/288-5575
**Location:** A mile from Bar Harbor, down a long private driveway in a quiet wooded area adjoining Acadia National Park. Access to a private beach and lovely winding trails from the back door.
**Hosts:** Ron Evers and Vikki Erickson Evers
**Open:** May-October. Weekends only in the winter.

If you have ever wanted to stay in one of the area's famed summer cottages, here is your chance. From the grand front hall your eyes focus ahead to the enormous full length window and its views of the ocean. To the left is the living room with huge fireplace (with crackling fire many mornings and most nights) and walls of a wonderful shade of coral.

With prompting, Ron and Vikki will share their unlikely experience of taking a hike in Acadia National Park in 1983, seeing an empty house without a "for sale" sign, and finally buying the place that was "way too big for the two of us." They found the blueprints in a third-floor closet, so know just how untouched, except for some kitchen renovation, it was.

They are the first residents to live year round in the house built in 1904. Vikki, an art-history major turned researcher and fine wallpaperer, and Ron, now a carpenter, are doing all the restoration work except the plumbing. After finding an original block-print wallpaper fragment in two rooms, they were thrilled to learn that hand-printed William Morris papers are still made in England. The hosts have been granted National Registry status. The perennial gardens are being reclaimed. Period furnishings will come in time too. (Vikki is a good source for auction and yard sale information.)

Most guests return from their walk to the beach with treasures, smooth flat rocks. "Wax them and they'll look like wet ones," Ron advises. He and Vikki can also tell you about hikes where you can swim on top of a mountain or enjoy the spectacular scenery away from the summer crowds.

**In residence:** Misty, their eight-year-old mixed terrier. Mr. T., their three-year-old cat.
**Bed and bath:** Three rooms. All have ocean views. One has private bath. Two second-floor rooms, each with a queen-sized bed, bay window, and fireplace. Third-floor room has extra-long double bed.
**Breakfast:** 8-10, but served earlier by arrangement for guests departing on the ferry or whale-watching expeditions. Ron's freshly made pastry might be croissants or Danish. Fresh fruit, juice, eggs, cereals, and hot beverage.
**Plus:** Screened porch. A pot of tea or coffee in the evening. Ron brews his own beer and is usually happy to share a glass and recipes. Will meet guests at ferry. Refrigerator space available.
**Rates:** Second-floor rooms $55 with shared bath, $65 private. Third-floor room is $45. All rates are $5 less for a single. Extra person $10.

## Glad II

60 Pearl Street, Bath, ME 04530
**Phone:** 207/443-1191
**Location:** At beginning of "down east" Maine, in historic area, 45 minutes north of Portland, on the Kennebec River. Ten minutes to Bowdoin College, 20 to Freeport, 40 to Boothbay Harbor.
**Host:** Gladys Lansky
**Open:** Year round, reservations appreciated.

"I worked for a large insurance company in New York City, and I also gave piano lessons for many years. I have stayed in B&Bs and can't think of a nicer thing to do. Since coming here and opening in 1984, it has proven to be exactly what I had hoped for."

Once you meet Gladys, you'll share her excitement about her new community. She is conducting a one-woman campaign to change its pass-through image. As a result, many guests spend hours, even whole days, at the Maritime Museum, by including a visit to the working shipyard, reached in the summer by a boat ride down the river. She'll suggest beaches, a state park with varied topography, classical music performances, local band concerts, and festivals. Her only regret? Not having taken "before" pictures of the layers of wallpaper. She has painted the walls of the Victorian house white, and added cheery primary color accents and a blend of furnishings that individualize each room.

**In residence:** Two dogs, both lovers: elderly Herkimer Peabody, age 16, and Nicholas the Naughty, 13 months, "a gangling teenager—specializes in shoelaces."
**Restrictions:** No pets, and please, no smokers.
**Foreign languages spoken:** "A bit of French and Spanish."
**Bed and bath:** Three second-floor carpeted rooms. Two shared baths. One large room with double bed, another large with two twin wicker beds. One small with two twin brass beds.
**Breakfast:** Available until 10. Juice, fruit, cereal, homemade muffins and jam, beverage. Served in dining room or on screened-in porch.
**Plus:** Grand piano, cable television, Cinemax. Air-conditioned parlor. Bedroom window fans. Porch. Champagne for honeymooners. Babysitting sometimes.
**Rates:** Single $35, double $40 for large rooms. Smaller room, single $30, double $35. Seventh night free with one-week stay.

## Sebastian & friends

2 Raymond Court, Bath, ME 04530
**Phone:** 207/443-4787
**Location:** Five minutes off Route 1, three blocks to shops, restaurants, waterfront park, Maine Maritime Museum, and Bath Iron Works. Half hour to beaches.
**Host:** Claire den Hartog
**Open:** Year round. Reservations preferred; requested for wintertime. Two-day minimum preferred.

Claire made major changes when she moved here in 1981 after selling real estate for ten years in Massachusetts, "where there is more snow than we have here with our river location." She loves the idea of combining all her interests under one roof. Guests are staying at a B&B, an antique shop, and the 1950 Greek Revival home of a renovation and decorating consultant. You are welcome to stay put and relax, to visit nearby attractions along the coast, and, always, to make yourself at home. People have come from all over the world. One group brought a turkey and all the fixings for Thanksgiving and eventually bought a house in the area.

**In residence:** Two cats. Sebastian, the Siamese, owns the business, and Sammy girl. ("Both will be kept out of the way, if necessary.")
**Restrictions:** "My facilities are not adequate for children because of the layout of rooms." Nonsmokers please.
**Foreign languages spoken:** French and "small amount of German."
**Bed and bath:** Two south-facing rooms share a bath. The one with a view of river has twin beds; other has double bed.
**Breakfast:** Available 7-9. Continental served with linen and silver in cheerful dining room; by wood stove in winter. Music, if desired.
**Plus:** Sherry usually offered in evening. Help-yourself to tea or coffee. Heaps of towels, nice soaps, flowers, candles. Good reading light. Deck chairs. Use of refrigerator.
**Rates:** $35 single, $40 double.

From a Hyannis, Massachusetts guest, ". . . warm and charming. Guest rooms are large and sunny. They even had fresh flowers."

## The Horatio Johnson House

36 Church Street, Belfast, ME 04915
**Phone:** 207/338-5153
**Location:** In the historic district, a neighborhood of lovely old homes in a small town experiencing a renaissance. A five-minute walk to downtown retail shops, antique centers, restaurants, and waterfront; 17 miles north of Camden. Half mile from the intersection of Routes 1 and 3.
**Hosts:** Helen and Gene Kirby
**Open:** Year round. Reservations recommended.

"In 1984 we decided to remodel our 1842 home into a comfortably furnished B&B that would reflect American hospitality to travelers arriving by land, sea, air, or stagecoach."

Helen was a university administrative assistant and Gene a superintendent of a Massachusetts vocational school "in our other life." Here, in the former home of a 19th-century dry-goods merchant, Horatio Johnson, Gene makes frames and refinishes furniture, and Helen runs a small antique shop in back. (Antique linens are among her favorite items.) They've established an herb garden too.

Their suggested walking tour includes architectural gems and the Paul Revere bell in town. At "home," you might inquire about the punched tin kitchen cabinet doors Gene made. (The kitchen is complete with wood stove, beamed ceiling, and hanging baskets.) The Kirbys share all their expertise and can tell you about making a bathroom out of three closets or teach you the ways of counted cross stitching—all in a very relaxed welcoming atmosphere.

**In residence:** One host smokes.
**Restrictions:** No guests' pets.
**Bed and bath:** Three rooms. One with twin beds and a private bath. A room with a double-sized brass and iron bed shares a full bath with a room with twin brass and iron beds. Cot available.
**Breakfast:** Very full. Available after 7:30. Freshly squeezed orange juice, French toast or Belgian waffles, eggs, bacon, homemade muffins, beverages. Leisurely. Usually joined by hosts.
**Plus:** Late-afternoon or evening tea or coffee. Tour of the house.
**Rates:** $35 double occupancy with shared bath, $40 with private bath.

## The Chapman Inn

P.O. Box 206, Corner Church & Broad Streets, Bethel, ME 04217
**Phone:** 207/824-2657
**Location:** In town, facing the Bethel Green, in a historic district. Ten minutes to Sunday River and Mt. Abram ski areas, 40 minutes to Mount Washington. Across the street from cross-country trails.
**Hosts:** Robin and Doug Zinchuk
**Open:** Year round. Reservations recommended for winter weekends, foliage season, and summer months.

The 1860 Federal-style home was originally built by a sea captain. It has been a boardinghouse, a tavern, and the home of composer/conductor William Rogers Chapman, a founder of the Maine Music Festival and a leader in New York music circles. The Zinchuks bought it in 1984. Douglas, a former painting contractor, did all the renovations. Robin decorated with a country theme, furnishing with older furniture, "but nothing that children should be afraid to touch. We share our living room with guests and have a casual and homey atmosphere."

Together they had had a general store in North Paris, 20 miles away. Now Robin sings in the church choir in "our historic town chosen for a Hallmark Christmas card commercial" and is part-time executive director of the Bethel Area Chamber of Commerce. Doug is part-time chef and full-time maintenance person at the inn. In the fall of 1986, after their third child was born, the Zinchuks moved to a nearby house and enlisted the assistance of the Szosteks as managers in residence.

**In residence:** Fran and Kathleen Szostek.
**Restrictions:** Some pets allowed. No smoking in dining area.
**Bed and bath:** Eight rooms. Two two-room first-floor suites, each with kitchen and private bath. Second- and third-floor rooms that share two baths (one room also has half-bath) have either a double bed or both a double and a single bed.
**Breakfast:** 7-9. Served family style. Fresh fruits, whole grains, whole-grain muffins, pancakes, or French toast or eggs. No meat. Will accommodate special diets.
**Plus:** Bedroom fans. Thick towels. Evening tea or on cold days, homemade soups. Barn converted to game room, TV room, two electric saunas. No charge for use of canoe and beach chairs on pond, four miles away. Dinner ($5-$8 per person) by special arrangement for groups. Babysitting with advance request. Kitchen and laundry privileges sometimes arranged. Directions to a favorite place, Step Falls.
**Rates:** $30 single, $40 double ($10 more for suites). $10 additional for adults in same room, $5 for child, $5 for cot or crib. AMEX, VISA, MasterCard accepted.

> "I am a pastry chef . . . in York Harbor, Maine. I must tell you of my wonderful vacation this past winter. . . . They made us feel right at home. . . . After a hectic seasonal work schedule, I enjoyed the peace and solitude as well as the charm of the house."

## The Douglass Place

Route #2, Box 90, Bethel, ME 04217
**Phone:** 207/824-2229
**Location:** On Route 2, a little over a mile north of the village; 72 miles from Portland, 180 miles to Montreal. Six miles to Maine downhill ski areas, 30 miles to foot of Mount Washington in New Hampshire. Great area for antiquing, hiking, fall foliage.
**Hosts:** Dana and Barbara Douglass
**Open:** Year round. Two-night minimum stay on holidays and weekends, December 15-March 15.

Good timing! Barbara had thought about her B&B stays in the British Isles. And she thought the idea might be a good solution toward meeting the terrific oil bills. "And it has proved thus!" Barbara retired in the summer of 1982 from 25 years as a social worker. The first B&B guests arrived in August. "Sharing this home is a marvelous way to meet travelers." Whether they come for antiquing, skiing, hiking, or foliage, most visitors seem to turn in early.

Dana is a semiretired surveyor. The Douglasses bought this house in 1950 and brought up four daughters here. They are the only other family to live in it since the original Twitchell family built their first home in the early 1790s. By 1890, Twitchell descendants were prosperous farmers and they put on a Victorian addition. Later the 20-room home was a summer boardinghouse operated by the Twitchell sisters. Barbara appreciates "this house that lends itself—inside and out—to partying. I love parties."

**In residence:** Husband occasionally smokes ("Shouldn't!").
**Foreign language spoken:** A little French.
**Bed and bath:** Five bedrooms with twin beds share two full second-floor baths, one with shower, plus a half-bath downstairs. In addition, a large second-floor living room includes sleep sofa, twin bed, and TV. Cot and crib available.
**Breakfast:** Continental 7-9:30. Includes homemade muffins and preserves. Tends to be leisurely except for skiers.
**Plus:** Attractive gazebo. Fresh flowers in season. Tour of huge pegged barn. Game room with piano and pool table.
**Rates:** $26 single, $35 double. Cots $15. Crib $5.

"What a joy to stay at the Douglasses', my old ancestral home. It is changed just enough to make it convenient and comfortable. And what delightful hosts! I visit at least once a year."

—Roxanne Twitchell Sly, Princeton, New Jersey.

## Kenniston Hill Inn

Route 27, Boothbay, ME 04537
**Phone:** 207/633-2159
**Location:** Two miles north of bustling Boothbay harbor, set back from the road on a hill, and surrounded by maple and oak trees.
**Hosts:** Paul and Ellen Morissette
**Open:** April-December. Reservations recommended July-October.

After a quarter century of being a renowned Vermont restaurant owner and chef, Paul decided to become an innkeeper. Ellen put her decorating skills to work with antiques, wallpapers, handmade quilts, fresh flowers, and plenty of books and magazines.

Their 200 year-old center chimney colonial, named for the original owners, is Boothbay's oldest house. It had become four apartments when the Morrisettes restored it to an inn in 1983. Now the grandparents of two share their love of gardening, cooking, traveling—and refinishing and restoring too—with guests.

The owners aren't the only ones who are enthusiastic about Kenniston Hill. Several other B&Bkeepers, in addition to well-traveled guests, have commented on this charming place and its wonderful hosts.

**Restrictions:** Children under 10 only in the carriage-house room. Sorry, no pets. Smoking allowed on first floor and porches. Check-in time after 2 p.m.; check-out by 11 a.m.
**Bed and bath:** Nine rooms on first and second floors. Arrangements include four rooms with working fireplaces and adjoining private full baths, three rooms with king-sized beds, three with queen-sized, and three with doubles. One first-floor double-bedded room also has a private entrance. Two of the rooms, each with a double bed, share one bath. Cot available.
**Breakfast:** Memorable. Beautifully and bountifully served at 9 in the gracious dining room overlooking fields and gardens, or by a roaring fire in living room. Fresh fruit, juice, a specialty that could be vegetable frittatta, zucchini walnut pancakes, peaches and

cream, French toast, or bacon and potato cheese pie. Homemade blueberry, bran, or oatmeal muffins, and, yes, brandy.
**Plus:** Beverages in evening. Tour of house to see the beamed ceilings, very large fireplaces, decor that differs in each room. Front porch with rockers overlooking town and gardens. Adjoining woods for walking and picnics. Bordering country club property for golf and cross-country skiing. Croquet. Bicycles for guests' use.
**Rates:** $70 king or queen bed, working fireplace, private bath. $60 without fireplace. $50 shared bath. April, May, November, December $10 less. Singles $10 less. Additional person in room $10. MasterCard and VISA accepted.

## The 1859 Guest House

60 South High Street, Bridgton, ME 04009
**Phone:** 207/647-2508
**Location:** On the corner of Route 302, "the only east-west highway from the Maine coast to New Hampshire." In antiquing and lake country. Five miles from Pleasant Mountain ski area.
**Hosts:** Dr. William and Mrs. Mary Zeller
**Open:** Year round, except for December. Reservations required.

"Often we find that we have mutual acquaintances." The first B&B in the area is also the gathering place for the garden club, church groups, benefit musicales, and luncheons. Mrs. Zeller has a history of community involvement. Recently she received a National Congress for Negro Women's award for her efforts with a successful Connecticut inner-city educational program.

Although the Zellers have lived in six states, they know this region from 15 summers on a nearby lake. They settled in Bridgton in 1981 and painted, papered, refinished floors and the stair railing (all themselves). Their Empire and Victorian furnishings are family pieces, but the clock collection is Dr. Zeller's. The foundation of their house (and what was a tavern) was put in in 1821. After a fire the present house and barn were built in 1859.

"When someone asks about 'something different' to see, we recommend a ten-minute 'mountain climb' just 11 miles away, to the top of 'the largest free-standing boulder in the world,' where there is a 360-degree view of the White Mountains, lakes, towns, woods, and meadows."

**Restrictions:** Sorry, no pets allowed.
**Bed and bath:** Three rooms. Two with twin beds, one with a double. One shared guest bath. Floor mattress and crib available.
**Breakfast:** At guests' convenience. Mary says grace before the full meal which includes hot or cold cereal, homemade coffee cake and jellies, maybe Pennsylvania scrapple or waffles or pancakes with Maine maple syrup. Served with china and silver on porch in warm weather or in the inviting fireplaced kitchen at a table made from a door from the old barn. The Zellers often join guests for coffee.
**Plus:** Those clocks! All 100 of them. Dr. Zeller is happy to talk about his collection. Porch. Television.
**Rates:** $40 per couple. $20 single. $5 for a crib or floor mattress.

## The Noble House

P.O. Box 86, 37 Highland Road, Bridgton, ME 04009
**Phone:** 207/647-3733
**Location:** On scenic Highland Lake. On rolling green acreage with oak, sugar maple, and pine trees. Within walking distance of antique shops in the village. Five miles from Pleasant Mountain ski area, 30 minutes from outlet shopping in North Conway, N.H., less than an hour to L. L. Bean.
**Hosts:** Dick and Jane Starets and family
**Open:** Year round. Two-day minimum stay preferred June-October weekends.

Just about everyone in town knows the Noble House, built around 1903 by a senator. When Jane and Dick bought it from Dr. Noble, the town dentist of 40 years, and his wife, little restoration was needed in the main house. Jane is responsible for decor that includes wicker, antiques, comforters, and color-coordinated guest rooms. The Starets' barn conversion is recorded in a fascinating before-and-after album.

Since coming from California in 1984 they have created a family project that has been extolled in many guests' letters to me. From Florida, "A fulfillment of how I thought New England would be." From Kansas, ". . . just the right atmosphere."

Jane has been a special-education teacher in three states. Dick is an airline pilot. Son Rich is responsible for the calligraphy on their brochure. Beyond B&B, the Staretses find time for involvement in ending world hunger and for family outings, skiing, and canoeing. They are familiar with attractions from the Shaker Museum and Village to water slides, from foliage routes to craft and antique shops.

**In residence:** Sons Rich, 18; Tim, 16; and Jonathan, 6. Heather, 15, is home from school in the summer.
**Restrictions:** No pets. No smoking inside, but permitted on porches.
**Bed and bath:** Eight rooms. Queen-sized four-poster or double bed in three second-floor rooms that share a large full bath and porch. Huge third-floor suite with two twin beds and a double bed, private bath with shower. In converted barn, two adjoining ground-level rooms; one with full bed and whirlpool bath and one with two twin beds, private bath with shower. Honeymoon suite has queen-sized brass bed, view of the lake, whirlpool bath. Rollaway bed and bassinet available.
**Breakfast:** At 8:30 or a time requested by the guests. Freshly squeezed orange juice, fruit in season, homemade bread, and Noble House eggs. Cheese strata, blueberry or whole-wheat pancakes with pure maple syrup. Served at elegantly set table in Victorian dining room with working fireplace.
**Plus:** Grand piano, antique organ and fireplace in the front parlor. Exercise room. Porch rockers. Hammock for two. Cream sherry. Champagne for honeymooners. The lake for canoeing, swimming, ice skating. Babysitting possibilities. Berry and apple picking nearby in season.
**Rates:** Memorial Day-October 15, $45-$55 single and $55-$75 double. Off-season, Sunday-Thursday or two-day weekend stays, $40-$50 single, $50-$68 double. Additional adult in room $15, child $10. Bassinet—no charge.

## Bed & Breakfast of Maine Host #31

Bristol Mills, ME
**Location:** On 180 acres. Set back from the road. One mile from Route 130. Seven miles from Damariscotta, a mile from the ocean and working harbor, six miles to small sandy beach. Fifteen-minute drive to Pemaquid Point Lighthouse, museum, lobster restaurant, and rocky coast.
**Reservations:** Available year round through Bed & Breakfast of Maine, page 6.

This is the place for peace and quiet, for picture-taking, for being on the farm yet near the ocean, and for meeting an exuberant young couple who are working toward self-sufficiency.

"Our scenic little flock out in back includes a Nubian dairy goat who loves attention. Muffie, an angora goat, is 18 inches tall, has horns and looks like a runaway dustmop. She produces mohair which I use for spinning and weaving. There are four geese who stand in the driveway and won't let cars by; guests find that amusing but I don't! A black rabbit hops freely on the lawn during the summer. . . .

"We bought this 1800 Federal home two years ago, all tastefully restored (thank goodness) by the previous owners. It is white with green shutters, surrounded by huge trees, stone walls, acres of manicured lawn, garden and red outbuildings. It is furnished with Oriental rugs, period antiques, old maps and sheep prints. We live right behind the house in a converted workshop. We are very active in the Maine Farm Vacation Association and think farming and B&B go together. Guests love to collect their own eggs before breakfast; that arrangement was particularly exciting one morning when the hens had a molt and stopped laying!"

**In residence:** Six rare Cotswold sheep (which wear covers to keep valuable fleece clean), two horses, four geese, a rabbit, and chickens. A couple of barn cats. A friendly, well-trained German shepherd.
**Restrictions:** Children should be at least 12. No guests' pets and no smoking.
**Foreign languages spoken:** Some French and some Italian.
**Bed and bath:** Five rooms. Two (one with a private entrance) on first floor, each with queen-sized bed and private bath with shower. Second-floor rooms with a double, a queen-sized bed, or two twins share two baths. Cot available.
**Breakfast:** 7-9. Blueberry pancakes with maple syrup, scrambled eggs with cheese, link sausage, juice, and coffee. Syrup, eggs, and sausage are produced on the farm. Served in the breakfast room overlooking old-fashioned English perennial garden.
**Plus:** Canoe for use on pond here. Hiking and cross-country ski trails. Afternoon beverages and cookies. Mints. Thick towels. Flowers in rooms. Tour of house and farm. Picnic tables and barbecue grills. Suggestions of dinner at lobster coop, ten minutes away in fishing village. Sheep shearing in April and October. Daily opportunities to observe spinning, weaving, and dyeing.

**Rates:** Double occupancy. $50 shared bath, $60 private bath. $10 cot. Reduced rates, November-May.

## Middaugh Bed & Breakfast

36 Elm Street, Topsham, ME 04086
**Phone:** 207-725-2562
**Location:** In the historic village. Half-mile from the center of town, one mile to downtown Brunswick. The yard adjoins the Topsham Fairgrounds.
**Hosts:** Barbara and Richard Middaugh
**Open:** Year round. Reservations preferred.

There's a family atmosphere in this 150-year-old Federal/Greek Revival house, which has been a B&B since the Chamber of Commerce put out a call for hosts in 1983. "Guests are welcome to share our family room or they can entertain or relax in the privacy of our living room."

Originally built for a town merchant, the house is on the National Register of Historic Places. It is decorated with traditional furnishings and Federal colors.

Before moving here seven years ago, Barbara was a financial counselor. Rich is a lieutenant commander in the navy.

**In residence:** Ryan, five, and Colin, two. Two middle-aged dogs that will greet guests and then go away if not encouraged to stay; Tasha, very affectionate white mutt, and Bits, collie.
**Restrictions:** Children welcome. Sorry, no guests' pets. Smoking discouraged, but permitted downstairs only.
**Foreign language spoken:** A little Spanish.
**Bed and bath:** Two large upstairs rooms with queen-size beds, one with four-poster. Private baths for both.
**Breakfast:** 7:30-9. Sometimes Rich bakes on weekends. Continental with homemade muffins, jams, and jellies. Served on sun porch in summer and in dining room in winter with china that matches the stenciled walls and curtains.
**Plus:** Beverages in the afternoon. Large yard. Fresh flowers from gardens. Will meet bus in Brunswick. Babysitting sometimes. Kitchen privileges on request.
**Rates:** $40-$50. Up to age five, free. Ages 5-12, $5 extra. Over 12, $10 extra.

## The Walker Wilson House

2 Melcher Place, Topsham, ME 04086
**Phone:** 207/729-0715
**Location:** Ten minutes north of Freeport, 1.3 miles from Bowdoin College campus, half-mile from downtown Brunswick, 30 minutes north of Portland.
**Open:** Year round. Reservations requested. August-November are the busiest months.
**Hosts:** Skip and Annie O'Rourke

The "someday" possibility became a reality within a weekend, all because the restauranteur and home restorer/builder from Connecticut took a ride and saw this house, a 1803 Federal that had been beautifully restored in the 1950s by a Williamsburg curator. Three months after moving here in July 1985, they hung out the hand-carved sign and found out that "people are even nicer than we thought." It's reciprocal; some guests who come for specific area attractions discover auctions and a very good restaurant, thanks to the O'Rourkes.

Named after the original owners, Walker and Wilson, the gracious classic has a warm inviting interior with a fireplace in every room, fine detailed interior woodwork, and antique furnishings. It is on the National Register of Historic Places.

**In residence** (with parents in attached apartment): Matthew Cawley, born August 22, 1986. Spatziee, the cat.
**Restrictions:** No guests' pets. No smoking upstairs.
**Bed and bath:** All three rooms have sitting areas. One with two twin beds and sink shares a bath with one that has a queen-sized bed and sink. The double-bedded room shares a bath with the hosts. Cot and crib available.
**Breakfast:** Generally 8-9, but flexible. Possibly eggs, waffles, or souffles, with homemade biscuits, muffins, or coffee cakes. Served on china with sterling in elegant dining room with fireplace.
**Plus:** Flannel sheets in winter. Robes in each room. Thick towels. Will meet guests at limo drop-off or bus stop in Brunswick. Extensive collection of books, magazines in every room. TV, VCR.
**Rates:** $50-$60 double occupancy. $10 for extra person.

## Edgecombe-Coles House

H.C.R. 60, Box 3010, 64 High Street, Camden, ME 04843
**Phone:** 207/236-2336
**Location:** On Route 1, overlooking the ocean. A half-mile north of the center of Camden.
**Hosts:** Louise and Terry Price
**Open:** Year round. Minimum two-day stay on summer weekends. Reservations required for weekdays November-May.

What was a New England farmhouse, a summer cottage added on to in the Victorian era, started out as the property of a wealthy Chicagoan. Through many changes, the farmhouse became the gatehouse to a mansion that is no more.

Terry, an engineer/designer, and Louise, an illustrator/designer, had already restored 12 houses in California. Since relocating to Camden, they have not only worked on this house and opened it as a B&B, but spend their winters restoring old houses to sell in the spring.

Because they are avid collectors, the Edgecombe-Coles House is filled with various types and styles of antique furniture, Oriental rugs, and original art. The Prices have hosted artists, photographers, and celebrities, some people who "require lots of attention and others who wish privacy." Their list of favorite places includes Ducktrap Beach, Pemaquid Lighthouse, and Camden Hills State Park.

**In residence:** Sheba and Szeszy, two show dogs not allowed in guest areas.
**Restrictions:** Minimum age for children is eight. Pets allowed with prior arrangement. In keeping with a good neighbor policy, guests are asked not to walk on the private road in the back of the house.
**Bed and bath:** Six second-floor rooms. Three have private baths. One with king-sized brass bed and working fireplace has spectacular view of Penobscot Bay. Ocean view from room with queen-sized bed as well as from deck of suite with two bedrooms, one with queen-sized bed and the other with double bed. Room with two twin four-poster beds and garden view adjoins bath shared with room that has a double brass bed. Cot available.
**Breakfast:** Coffee available at 7:30, breakfast at 8:30, unless otherwise arranged. Usually have a choice of three juices, fresh fruit, home-baked muffins and bread, eggs, bacon or sausage, homemade jams, tea, coffee. Some days Terry makes omelets, sour-cream blue-

berry pancakes, waffles, or Dutch babies. After serving, hosts join guests at dining room table.
**Plus:** Fireplaces in dining and living rooms. Deck with ocean views. Chocolates and flowers. Thick towels, imported soaps, shampoo, bath foam, shower caps, mending kits. Champagne for honeymooners, birthdays, or anniversaries. Afternoon beverages. Window fans. Tour of house. Option of dinner ($12-$14) on Thanksgiving and Christmas or during severe weather. Will meet guests at bus stop in Camden or at Rockland/Owls Head Airport. Local service will pick up laundry daily and return next day.
**Rates:** Late June through October, double or twin $65, queen $75, suite $85, king $105. Rest of year, double or twin $55, queen $65, suite $65, king $75. Additional person in room $20. MasterCard, VISA, AMEX, and Diners Card accepted.

## Goodspeed's Guest House

60E Mountain Street, Camden, ME 04843
**Phone:** 207/236-8077
**Location:** Quiet. Five blocks up the hill from the harbor with view of mountains from large back garden. Bordered by an interesting place for a walk, one of the original town's original graveyards. Two blocks from entrance to Mount Battie hiking trail.
**Hosts:** Don and Linda Goodspeed
**Open:** May-October. Reservations suggested mid-July through Labor Day.

Old-house restoration, antique furniture, antique clocks, sailing, windsurfing, skiing, and hiking. That's the list of pursued interests for Don and Linda, parents of two grown daughters.

After 25 IBM years spent in eight states and in Europe, including four in Paris ("where we got hooked on B&B as the only way to travel"), they vacationed in Maine, decided on their mid-life career change, and bought the soon-to-be guest house in one hour. Don tackled ten layers of wallpaper, sanded and refinished spruce and pine floors, cleaned the stained glass windows, and moved the kitchen of the 1879 farmhouse that had an attached barn added in 1882. Since the Goodspeeds opened here in 1981, daughter Lisa acted as manager for two seasons, and now she is out of college and with the Marriott Hotel chain. Don does free-lance computer consulting.

**In residence:** One (Linda) who smokes.
**Restrictions:** Children should be at least 10. Guests are allowed to smoke in sitting room or on outside deck only.
**Foreign language spoken:** French.
**Bed and bath:** Eight rooms on three levels. One with private outside deck entry. Six rooms have double beds, one has extra-long twin beds, one a single twin bed. Sinks in many of the rooms. One room with private bath; others share a bath (may be shower only, no tub) with one other room. Beds include carved oak, wicker headboard, iron and brass, and canopied style. All rooms are papered with period patterns. Cot available in four rooms.
**Breakfast:** 7:30-9:30. Freshly squeezed orange juice, homemade bakery and muffins, freshly-brewed coffee. Served in dining room (decorated with some of the clocks) or outside on south-side flower-filled deck. Hosts there with ever-present coffee-pot in hand.
**Plus:** Lemonade upon arrival. Line-dried sheets. Ceiling fans. Fresh flowers. Books and games in sitting rooms. Garden for relaxation. Tours of house. Off-street parking. Will meet guests at bus. Occasionally there are spontaneous lobster parties with guests.
**Rates:** Mid-July-Labor Day, single $45, double $59, with deck $69, with bath $69. Off-season rates $10 less. Cot for child $10, rollaway for adult $15.

> From New York: "The decor of this turn-of-the-century home has got to be out of *House Beautiful*. . . . Cleanliness, charm and hospitality . . . responsible for the most enjoyable vacation of our lives."

## Maine Stay

22 High Street, Camden, ME 04843
**Phone:** 207/236-9636
**Location:** On Route 1, three blocks from Camden Harbor and village, 97 miles from Portland, and 200 miles from Boston.
**Hosts:** Sally and Bob Tierney, Pat and Bruce Hunt
**Open:** Year round. Two-night minimum reservation on holiday weekends.

While vacationing along the Maine coast in 1982, two sisters and their husbands saw this house for sale. It was the right time in their lives to make a change and that's exactly what they did. Before they became innkeepers, Sally taught high school English and French, Bob was with the state department in Washington, D.C. and the Far East, and Pat and Bruce had corporate professional lives in California. While at least one of them is "around" to welcome guests, the shared responsibility allows them to be involved in community and sports, particularly sailing.

The stately 1813 colonial home has twin parlors, a red-carpeted stairway, antique and period furnishings including some pieces from Hong Kong and Japan. "None of us has degrees in interior design, but we thoroughly enjoyed choosing the varied decor and doing the work ourselves." The house was on the 1985 Camden House and Garden Tour.

The hosts observe that though each guest is different, "those who stay here share a common interest in the history and charm of old houses, and a respect for their fellow guest." A favorite recommendation: A trip to the top of Mount Battie to enjoy the view or to picnic.

**Restrictions:** Six is the minimum age for children. Smoking allowed in downstairs parlor or on outside deck.
**Foreign language spoken:** French.
**Bed and bath:** Eight rooms. Five with double beds, two with two twin beds, one with a single. Five rooms on second floor share two full baths. On the third floor, guests share one very large skylit bath. Beds include mahogany, maple, oak with high headboard, and antique brass. Each room has a different flavor—from French country stenciling and Laura Ashley prints to wallpaper dating back to 1930.
**Breakfast:** 8-9:30. Varies but could include freshly squeezed juice, fruit with yogurt and home-made granola, sausage made by local grocer, homemade cinnamon caramel nut rolls, scones, muffins or coffee cake. Served at large dining room table or on adjoining deck with mountain views. Hosts often join guests for coffee.
**Plus:** Afternoon tea, wine or sherry, tours of house. Will meet guests at Rockland Airport or Greyhound bus stop in Camden. Fans available. Use of refrigerator, decks, barn for bikes or camping equipment. A "welcome back" note and wine or candy for returnees.
**Rates:** Late May through October, double $50-55, single $35. Rest of year: double $40-$45, single $30. $15 for extra person in room. Ten percent discount for families reserving two rooms. MasterCard and VISA for phone confirmations only.

## Cape Neddick House

Rt. 1, Box 70, Cape Neddick, ME 03902
**Phone:** 207/363-2500
**Location:** On Route 1, four miles down the road from the York-Ogunquit exit of Route 95. Minutes from beaches, boutiques, historical sites, antique shops, factory outlets, and cross-country ski trails.
**Hosts:** John, Dianne, Christine, and Jennifer Goodwin
**Open:** Year round. Two-day minimum stay on holiday weekends and weekends during July, August, and October.

There are refinished random-width pine floors and white ruffled bedroom curtains. The marble-topped commodes, the high headboards, and the pitchers and bowls are all Goodwin heirlooms. What makes the rest of this story so different is often part of the breakfast conversation. John inherited the family homestead from his bachelor uncle, who had lived here alone for about fifty years. The plan was to clean out the house and sell it. But the heirlooms—treasures dating back a couple of centuries—were found under eaves, in trunks, in the basement, and in what was the town's original post office. Two years, nine additional rooms, and many dollars later, Dianne left her position as a geriatric nurse and John his as a crane operator, and they moved from Connecticut with their two daughters "in a wagon train of U-Hauls to the uncharted land and new world of Maine."

In less than a year after the move, Dianne became a director of the Yorks Chamber of Commerce. She leads visitors to places such as Mount Agamenticus (where you can see hawks' nests and have a view of Mount Washington and the coast). She has an antiques business in the barn and invites guests to visit craftspeople with studios in the former post office. Her printed recipes are for sale. She does her own chair caning and basket weaving. John has gone into the demolition business.

**In residence:** Daughters Christine, 16, and Jennifer, 15. Fritzie and PeeWee, mother and son barn cats that visit indoors. Daughters' horses, Snowball (Arabian) and Ginger (quarter horse).
**Restrictions:** Children should be at least nine. No guests' pets. Smoking is allowed downstairs in common rooms only.
**Foreign language spoken:** Elementary French.

**Bed and bath:** Six guest rooms, all on the second floor. All have double beds. One has an additional single bed and accommodates three. The three shared bathrooms are all new with fiberglass tub and showers and tile floors.
**Breakfast:** 8:30-9:30. Fresh fruit is cut, fluted, or sliced and garnished with mint, lemon balm, or even Johnny jump-ups from the herb and flower garden. Then you might have cinnamon popovers with wild-raspberry jam, native-blueberry muffins, apple fritters, and ham and apple biscuits or baked peach pancakes. Table is set with linens and china. Served in summer on the cypress deck with view of the country scene complete with wildflowers, woodlands, birds, and horses.
**Plus:** Late-afternoon refreshments, relaxation and conversation in the parlor and living room or on deck. Two rooms have air conditioners. Lawn games. Occasionally, very complete dinner cooked on original Glenwood stove. Theme weekends in the planning stage include maple sugaring tours and cooking sessions. Scrapbook of local attractions and activities.
**Rates:** $55 June 15-September 1; $45 September 2-October 12; $40 at other times. Additional person in room, $10. Singles $5 less. Extra charge for air conditioner.

From New York: "In all my visits to Maine, I have never experienced the down-east hospitality that I did with the Goodwin family. . . . Breakfast could melt the heart of even the grumpiest morning person."

## Brannon-Bunker Inn

HCR 64, Box 045C, Route 129, Damariscotta, ME 04543
**Phone:** 207/563-5941
**Location:** Rural but just a five-minute drive from Route 1. Close to Damariscotta, Boothbay Harbor, Wiscasset, Bath, and Camden-Rockland activities.
**Hosts:** Joe and Jeanne Hovance
**Open:** Year round. Advance reservations preferred.

"After visiting Maine for eight years, we began to look into getting into the business of B&B since we always enjoyed traveling that way." And so in 1984 the Hovances bought the Brannon-Bunker Inn, one of the first B&Bs in the area.

The fascinating barn-turned-inn attached to a Cape-style house has a wide interior staircase and a low ceiling on the first floor, creating a wonderful gathering area by a huge fieldstone fireplace in the Publyk Room. Actually, the first conversion of the barn was in the 1920s, when it was known as La Hacienda, a dance hall. Later it became an overflow facility for a nearby inn.

Everyone asks the Hovances about their pre-inn lives. Joe was director of an environmental center and historic sites in New Jersey. Now he is host and antique dealer and refinisher. Previously, Jeanne had restored both a Victorian and a Cape home. She redecorated the inn using antique pieces ranging from colonial to mission. She also works with a Maine carpenter on old-house renovations.

The Hovances have discovered a gem of a canoeing place, a stream through beautiful marsh, with flora, birds, and wildlife. They have also discovered that B&B travelers from all over the world are pretty nice people.

**In residence:** Michael, age 14; Beth, age 9; and Jamie, 4.
**Restrictions:** Children of all ages are welcome. Guests' pets are allowed. Smoking is allowed in the Publyk Room.
**Bed and bath:** Seven rooms. The first-floor room is Victorian with a queen-sized bed and private bath. Second-floor rooms consist of an Empire room with double bed, Country Cottage room with double bed, and a shared bath. Two rooms each with two four-poster twin beds and a view of the river share a connecting bath. The carriage house has a three-room suite accessible to the handicapped and includes a double-bedded room, a room with two twin beds, a bath with shower (no tub), and a kitchen/living room.
**Breakfast:** Served from 8-10 in the Publyk Room with view of river. Juice or fruit, homemade muffins, toast, cereal; coffee, tea, or milk. Turns out to be quite leisurely.
**Plus:** Television, games, and books. Picnic table and outdoor seating. Tour of the inn. Kitchen facilities. Babysitting,
**Rates:** $50 double with private bath; $42 double with shared bath; $55 double with private bath and kitchenette. Singles deduct $7.50. $10 for additional person in room. Suite is $55 for two; $90 for four; $300 weekly. November-April $10 less per night. VISA and MasterCard accepted.

## Bed & Breakfast Down East Host #217

Dover-Foxcroft, ME
**Location:** In small scenic village, the county seat, two doors away from church with chiming clock, 40 minutes north of Bangor and from the southern tip of Moosehead Lake; 40 minutes northwest to Squaw Mountain; 15 minutes to Appalachian Trail.
**Reservations:** Available year round through Bed & Breakfast Down East, page 5.

"People come here because they love Maine—the pines, the lakes, the fishing, the foliage. That's why we're here! We've lived in the state all our lives and recently moved up from Portland. Just last week I took my first walk on a nearby trail; we met a bull moose within the first five minutes and away he went, as they do. There are walks to some pretty beautiful places; depending on your route, it can take an hour or all day to get to the fantastic Gulf Hagas Gorge on the Appalachian Trail. Some travelers going from Montreal to Nova Scotia stop here rather than stay on the highway."

After having raised six children, the hosts decided to do B&B. Now the host, a Maine Guide, not only has more time for photography and painting, but because he is a bush pilot, he can arrange to fly guests to some pond or lake, maybe (on a float plane) to Gulf Hagas Gorge area.

Their lovely 12-room 1846 Georgian Colonial, immaculately kept, was the headmaster's house for a local academy.

**In residence:** Daisy, a small, blond cocker spaniel.
**Restrictions:** "We do not encourage young families." Sorry, no guests' pets.
**Bed and bath:** Three large bedrooms. One with a double bed, nonworking fireplace. Two with two twin beds. One and one-half shared baths.
**Breakfast:** Can be as early as 4:30 for fishermen. Full breakfast until 9:30, continental until 10:30. Fresh homemade muffins, pie, and jams, fish in season. Served in large country kitchen.
**Plus:** Window fans. Picnic lunches packed. Dinner may be arranged if local restaurants (including a reknowned one in Victorian home just down the street) are closed. Will pick up at Bangor airport 40 miles away. Flights arranged to some inland places (see above). Inquire about cross-country ski packages.
**Rates:** Single $25, double $35, cot $10.

## Todd House

1 Capen Avenue, Eastport, ME 04631
**Phone:** 207/853-2328
**Location:** At Todd's Head on Passamaquoddy Bay in this coastal fishing village. One guest wrote, "On a promenade . . . where one can see Campobello Island in Canada. It's truly magnificent to be the first to see the sunrise in the United States."
**Host:** Ruth McInnis
**Open:** Year round.

Guests wrote: "It's like an English inn, filled with early American furnishings and memorabilia, and I only wish I could live there permanently. . . . Setting gives one a sense of quietude, yet it's the hostess's hospitality that brings us back."

With advice from the Maine Historic Preservation Commission, Ruth has become a restoration expert. You can almost follow the history of the house through the names of rooms. The Indian Room has a display of Indian artifacts. The Cornerstone Room recalls the chartering of the Masonic Lodge here in 1801.

Until seven years ago, when she returned to Eastport to teach in her home town, Ruth taught in Portland. Todd House is her way of sharing her love of old houses, Eastport, and history. For special places, Ruth is likely to recommend Indian Island, Reversing Falls or "my own back yard with its spectacular sunsets."

**In residence:** Midnight, the cat, "a hit with many guests."
**Restrictions:** Pets allowed if well behaved. Nonsmokers preferred.
**Bed and bath:** Five rooms on two floors with two shared baths. Two with double beds, two with twin beds, one single. Some with working fireplaces, cable TV, sitting areas, and view of water. Two double rooms and the single are on the first floor and are available for handicapped. Two trundle beds available.
**Breakfast:** 7:30-10. Juices, coffee, tea, milk, cereals, homemade muffins. Served at antique table in common room with huge fireplace with bake oven.
**Plus:** Tours of the house and area. Library of books on local history. Will meet guest at the airport or bus. Kitchen privileges. Cookout equipment.
**Rates:** $25 single, $35 smaller double, $40 other doubles. $10 additional person in room. $5 per day discount on stays of more than five days.

From Ohio: "A most felicitous place . . . always a native Mainer stopping by to chat. . . . The rooms are exquisite—all the modern conveniences in a 200-year-old setting. And where does the coffee smell better than 100 feet from the Bay of Fundy?"

## High Meadows

Rt. 101, Eliot, ME 03903
**Phone:** 207/439-0590
**Location:** On a country road hillside surrounded by woods. Six miles to Portsmouth, New Hampshire. Four miles to factory outlets on Route 1. Near beaches and historic sites.
**Host:** Elaine Raymond
**Open:** Year round, except for January, February, and March.

An oft-heard comment: "Everything about High Meadows is special—including Elaine Raymond." That's the impression of many B&B travelers who put High Meadows at the top of their recommendations list.

Guests have been coming since 1981 to this antique-filled home built in 1736 by a merchant shipbuilder and captain. "When you have a visitor from Kansas at the table with someone from Brooklyn, the conversation can really be fun. Yes, they ask about the house and I tell them about camping with the children here in 1960 when there was no water, no electricity, no roadway." For the restoration of all 11 rooms, Elaine designed and planned everything, including the kitchen cabinets made from 200-year-old attic floorboards. She made all the curtains and hooked some of the rugs. "Eventually we took the barn down and had its granite foundation moved closer to the house as a base for the terrace." The gardens are Elaine's; her husband takes care of the lawn and maintenance. Enthusiasm remains high. "I love to entertain, and enjoy people and cooking."

**In residence:** Eden, a golden retriever, and Topaz, a Persian cat.
**Restrictions:** Children should be at least 14. No guests' pets.
**Bed and bath:** Four rooms. The first floor Wedgwood Room has a queen-sized bed and private bath. On the second floor, two rooms each with a double bed and one room with two twin beds share a full bath.

**Breakfast:** Usually 8-9. Fruit compote, juices, homemade muffins or croissants, beverage. In summer, served on large screened-in porch or patio facing the woods.
**Plus:** Beverage in late afternoon or evening. Lovely large terrace always available. Flowers, in season, from the perennial gardens. Living room fireplace that is high, shallow, and draws beautifully. Half-hour walking trail with wild raspberries in July.
**Rates:** $45 shared bath, $60 private bath.

## Harraseeket Inn

162 Main Street, Freeport, ME 04032
**Phone:** 207/865-9377
**Location:** Two blocks north of L. L. Bean and within walking distance of dozens of factory outlet stores. Three miles from South Freeport Harbor, where boats can be rented for fishing or sailing. Within a mile of Wolf Neck Park and the Audubon Sanctuary. Ten miles from Brunswick, Bowdoin College, the U.S. Naval Air Station, and Bailey Island.
**Host:** Paul Gray
**Open:** Year round. Reservations suggested.

> From Rhode Island: "Paul is so in tune with the plumbing in the house that he has the scrambled eggs just about ready as his guests come down the stairs. . . . His sourdough pancakes are almost sinful. . . . The rooms are filled with beautiful antiques. The colors throughout the house are muted and warm."

When Paul, a water engineer and Maine Guide, retired, he began a new career by turning an 1850 Greek Revival farmhouse into a luxury B&B. Designer linens, thick towels, flower arrangements, and tea are all a backdrop for personalized attention—and plenty of conversation, even a good cribbage game.

Born 12 miles from here, Paul knows much about the area. He has a particular interest in fly fishing and upland hunting. And if you want to know what it took to redo the house, he'll give tips and even tell you about the mistakes he learned from.

**In residence:** Three dogs, not allowed in the house. Deuce, a golden cross; Scout and Sal, both Labs.
**Restrictions:** Children welcome if they share two bedded room with their parents. No smoking allowed in public rooms.

**Bed and bath:** Six rooms, some with fireplaces. First-floor room is accessible to the handicapped and has two double beds and a private bath with jacuzzi. Second-floor rooms each have a canopied bed and private bath with either a steam bath or jacuzzi. One has two double beds; others have a queen-sized.
**Breakfast:** Host cooks and serves breakfast in the dining room or the greenhouse or outside on the terrace overlooking the garden. Full buffet includes bacon, homemade muffins, fresh toast or sourdough pancakes, juice, grapefruit, yogurt, cereal, eggs, coffee cake, maybe strawberry shortcake in early July, "whatever the cook feels like." How leisurely? "It takes all morning!"
**Plus:** Central air conditioning. Fireplace in living room. Each room has antique furnishings, cable TV, air conditioning. Cross-country skiing from the door to the Audubon Sanctuary.
**Rates:** Mid-May–December 23, $75-$90; Christmas–mid-May $65-$80.

## The Isaac Randall House

Independence Drive, Freeport, ME 04032
**Phone:** 207/865-4183 or 207/865-9295
**Location:** Off U.S. Route 1, ¼ mile south of village center. Within walking distance of L. L. Bean, yet on a quiet six-acre tract with spring-fed pond and nature trail.
**Hosts:** Glynrose and Jim Friedlander
**Open:** April-December. Reservations strongly recommended July-October.

Where are you? Well, in 1823 it was Isaac and Betsy Randall's home, where they raised eight children. Before the Civil War it was part of the Underground Railway. The barn was a dance hall in the 1920s and 1930s. "If the bottles found in the woods behind the barn are any indication, it might also have been a speakeasy." It has also been an apartment house. After restoring it (1980-1984), the Friedlanders furnished it with antiqucs, Oriental rugs, and lovely old quilts.

Jim was an urban planner in seven states. Glyn was a secretary. They enjoy traveling, reading, and classical and jazz music.

**In residence:** Two cats, Grendel and Dulcinea

**Restrictions:** Smoking is limited to public areas and the consent of other guests.
**Bed and bath:** Eight rooms, six with private bath. Five of the rooms are on first floor. Three rooms can accommodate up to four people each. Queen-sized and/or double beds. Cot and crib available.
**Foreign languages spoken:** French and Spanish.
**Breakfast:** 7:30-10:30. Homemade breads, coffee cakes, granola, blueberry pancakes or French toast with real maple syrup, amaretto coffee, teas, herbal teas, and chocolate. Served by Jim in country kitchen.
**Plus:** Fans (rarely needed) in bedrooms. Wine, cider, soft drinks, and cheese in evening. Tours of house and area. Player piano, cable TV, croquet, horseshoes, library, cards, board games, use of second-floor kitchen and outdoor barbecue. Imported soaps, personalized rooms, candy and fruit. Will meet guests ($15 charge) at Portland airport or bus if notified well in advance. Babysitting. Horses can be accommodated on the property.
**Rates:** June through October $65 double with private bath, $50 shared bath. November through May $55 private bath, $40 shared bath. $5 less for singles. Extra person (over age 12) in room, $10. No credit cards, but personal checks accepted.

## Arundel Meadows Inn

Route 1, Arundel
Mailing address: P.O. Box 1129, Kennebunk, ME 04043
**Phone:** 207/985-3770
**Location:** Three minutes from the center of Kennebunk, ten from Kennebunk Beach and Kennebunkport. Eleven miles from Ogunquit. Situated on 3½ acres of land next to the Kennebunk River.
**Hosts:** Murray R. Yaeger (summer and weekends year round) and Mark Bachelder
**Open:** Year round.

A Maine native returns home! After majoring in hotel management in college, Mark was an administrator with Boston's Parker House, Copley Plaza, Blue Beard's in St. Thomas, and the Hyatt Regency in Cambridge, Massachusetts. After studying with Madeleine Kamman at her Modern Gourmet School, he cooked for her as well as at other Boston area restaurants.

Murray, Mark's partner in this dream of many years, is a faculty member at Boston University's School of Communications and consultant to companies and organizations. You never know who your fellow guests might be at a B&B; here they could include TV performers, network news producers, or magazine editors, all former students of "the prof."

There were many "almosts" before the 1830 farmhouse became their chosen place and was just about rebuilt. The real fun part, of course, was the decorating, for it allowed Murray to utilize his collection of art objects gathered over a long time. The Oriental Room is done in light blue grass cloth and has an Oriental rug, screen and artifacts. Other rooms are color coordinated. Some have antique beds and armoires. Among the many paintings throughout the inn are Murray's own works.

**In residence:** Hildie, "a schnauzer who 'knows' she's a person."
**Restrictions:** Minimum age for children is 12. No guests' pets please.
**Bed and bath:** Six rooms, each with a double bed and private bath. Three have fireplaces. Two have private entrances. The suite consists of two rooms, one with a double bed, the other with twins.
**Breakfast:** 8-10. Cooked by Mark and served by Murray in dining room overlooking the patio. Fresh juice, fruit, croissants in addition to a creation such as brioche, quiche, eggs Benedict, amaretto French toast. A different menu each morning.
**Plus:** Fireplace to relax by. Patio. Afternoon tea featuring pates and homemade sweets. Weekend packages may include dinner.
**Rates:** Double $55; with fireplace $65. With private entrance $60. Suite $65. Each additional guest (up to two) $15.

## The Ocean View

72 Beach Avenue, Kennebunk Beach, ME 04043
**Phone:** 207/967-2750. Winter phone: 207/967-2681
**Location:** Directly on Kennebunk Beach, ¼ mile from center of Kennebunkport. In a neighborhood of private homes.
**Hosts:** Bob, Carole, "and in order of appearance, Mike, Rob, and Chris" Arena
**Open:** April 1-October 31. Minimum stay for reservations made in advance is two days.

"We live in a tourist area. Carole has been working for someone else in the inn business for 11 years. Opening our own place just seemed natural. This property, built here in the 1800s, was all we dreamed about."

They opened in 1985, with Carole still working as manager and accounting at an inn and Bob still employed in Human Resources for a company. Ocean View has always been a guesthouse, but cosmetic work was in order. They were fussy about the selection of mattresses and have decorated to give a light, airy, not overly decorated feeling. Yes, they took before-and-after pictures. Due credit is given to the sons, all athletes, for making the whole project possible. Enthusiastic guests—most of whom say that they, too, have such a dream—comment that the location gives them a feeling of being on a boat.

**In residence:** One member of the family smokes. Chris is 15, Rob and Mike are around when they aren't in college.
**Restrictions:** No pets, please. Smoking in common rooms only. Inquire about arrangements for children.
**Foreign language spoken:** A little French.
**Bed and bath:** Five rooms. Two with private baths; others have a sink in the room and share one full bath. All rooms have an ocean view. On third floor is a "most desired" suite with large room with two double beds, sitting room with futons, and private bath with shower, no tub. Other room with private bath has a queen-sized bed. Rooms that share a bath have, respectively, two twin beds, double bed, queen-sized bed.
**Breakfast:** 8-10. Fresh fruit in season, croissants or brioche with cheese, cheese-filled Danish, blueberry muffins. Served by Carole and Bob at round cafe tables in the breakfast room.
**Plus:** Fresh fruit, coffee, tea, soft drinks always available. TV room, fireplaced living room, front porch and yard. Garden flowers.
**Rates:** April-June 15 and after Labor Day through October, $50 shared bath, $65 private bath. June 15-Labor Day, $65 shared bath, $80 private bath.

*Can't find the community you are going to? Check with a reservation service described at the beginning of this chapter. Through the service, you may be placed (matched) with a welcoming B&B that is near your destination.*

## 1802 House, Bed and Breakfast Inn

P.O. Box 646A, Locke Street, Kennebunkport, ME 04046
**Phone:** 207/967-5632
**Location:** On a side road in a residential historic district within walking distance of Dock Square. Next to an 18-hole golf course. Trolley stop just around the corner.
**Hosts:** Bob and Charlotte Houle
**Open:** July-December. Two-night minimum stay July-October and on all weekends.

When the Houles first came to Kennebunkport in 1975 they found an "honest-to-goodness small town spirit, one that's contagious, with down-to-earth Maine people who have hearts of gold."

The family came from Massachusetts when the government funding was discontinued for Bob's woodworking design workshops. They bought an apartment building; Bob put all of his woodworking talent to work and Charlotte helped with decorating. For three more years it had apartments. Then local residents who were aware of the transformation encouraged the Houles to become B&B hosts.

In a way history is repeating itself. The original part of the building was built by a sea captain in Waterboro in 1802 and brought by oxen to Kennebunkport, where it became the lodging for men who worked on the locks on the Kennebunk River.

The decor is colonial with reproduction furniture and wallpaper. The atmosphere is cozy. Housekeeping is meticulous. "I love the job of managing the inn. Bob loves the custom woodworking opportunities that are endless here. It's gratifying to see the pleasure our guests have received from our efforts."

**In residence:** One pipe smoker, Bob. Laura-Lyn, a teenager, covers the reservation desk when Mom is on errands. Daughter Debra, married and a mother, comes to take over when Mom and Dad need a vacation. Granddaughter Dorian, age five, likes to chat with guests. You may get to meet her uncle, the oldest Houle son—Bruce, a draftsman. And then there's Uncle Bob who is in the Air Force and stationed close to home! You will also be greeted by Laura-Lyn's cat Moxie and Char's apricot poodle, Big Boy.
**Restrictions:** No guests' pets. Children should be at least 12.
**Foreign language spoken:** Some French.

**Bed and bath:** Eight rooms, all with wall-to-wall carpeting, reproduction wallpaper and furnishings, private baths. Some have working fireplaces, including the Honeymoon Suite.
**Breakfast:** Served at 9 at the sound of the ship's bell. Char is chef, and Bob Sr. is a very popular waiter. Could be fresh fruit cup or strawberry yogurt and homemade granola topped with strawberries, plus pineapple French toast with pineapple sauce, or sour-cream scrambled eggs with a delicate flavor of herbs, or walnut pancakes with real maple syrup.
**Plus:** Common room with fireside hearth, books, games, sofas with big pillows. Umbrella tables and chairs. In summer, shower and towels available to beachgoers after checkout. In fall and winter, cross-country skiing followed by mulled cider or hot chocolate.
**Rates:** July 1-December 31, $74 double or twin beds, $84 double with fireplace. Other months: $5 less. $25 for extra person in the room. AMEX, MasterCard, and VISA accepted.

## Bufflehead Cove

P.O. Box 499, Kennebunkport, ME 04046
**Phone:** 207/967-3879
**Location:** On the tip of a peninsula on the tidal Kennebunk River. In view of the village of Kennebunkport and surrounded by five acres of woods and an orchard. "The golf course—near by boat—is on a bend upriver."
**Host:** Harriet Gott
**Open:** Year round. Reservations recommended. Two-day minimum stay on weekends July-October.

Guests from Alaska recall ". . . the shingled house and its veranda overlooking the river to the lush cozy romantic feeling one gets in this peaceful setting. . . . Harriet is by far the most cheerful and sincere hostess we have had the pleasure to meet."

James, a commercial fisherman and lobsterman, is the seventh generation to live in Maine. Harriet, a lifelong resident who spent childhood vacations in the summer hotel her parents owned, loves to help with orientation, to send guests off to discover, and then to hear of their adventures. Sometimes she tells of the old lock up the river and its part in colonial history. "I have been an ongoing college student for years and will continue to be." At low tide she may suggest that you explore Cape Porpoise Islands, easily accessible by foot.

Her flair for flower arranging is evident throughout the former sea captain's house, named for the bufflehead ducks that winter over in the cove. The Gott home for twelve years was an inn called The Maine Riviera in the 1940s and '50s. In redecorating three years ago, Harriet used a lot of stenciling. "My expertise is an eye for design and color." Many a big-city professional has found this a good place to unwind.

**In residence:** Shannon, age 18; Erin, age 12.
**Restrictions:** Pets rarely accepted although exceptions are made. Smoking allowed outside on the property, but not encouraged.
**Foreign language spoken:** Spanish.
**Bed and bath:** Five rooms. Four with double beds, the one with a queen-sized bed and a small daybed has a private balcony. Two rooms have private baths. Others have marble sinks in the room. Two rooms can combine to make a suite. All have river view. Cot available.
**Breakfast:** 8:30. Could include honeyed souffle with fresh fruit or waffles with apple cider raisin sauce, homemade breads, breakfast flan. Served in the dining room or on the porch. If requested, continental breakfast served in room.
**Plus:** Tea always available. Fireplace in spacious beamed living room. Wraparound veranda (good for sunbathing). Private dock on tidal river. Use of kitchen for special parties. Babysitting.
**Rates:** $55-$60 for one night. $5 discount for a two-night stay. The "Nook," a smaller room, is $40.

From Vermont: "My husband and I stayed at Bufflehead Cove when it first opened (in 1984) and returned the following year with our three children. . . . Harriet and Jim are very special people . . . a quiet, private spot . . . delicious breakfast and Harriet is generous with her recipes. We are looking forward to another stay this summer."

## The Captain Lord Mansion

Corner of Pleasant and Green Streets, Kennebunkport
Mailing address: P.O. Box 800, Kennebunkport, ME 04046
**Phone:** 207/967-3141

**Location:** In historic neighborhood of 18th- and early 19th-century houses, overlooking Kennebunk River. Three blocks from Dock Square shops and restaurants.
**Hosts:** Bev Davis and Rick Litchfield
**Open:** Year round. Reservations recommended. Two-night minimum stay on all weekends; holiday minimums vary.

Attention to detail is hallmark to this day. *Colonial Homes* is among the national publications that have recognized the elegant but comfortable decor in this magnificent example of Federal architecture. Built in 1812, The Captain Lord Mansion is now listed in the National Register of Historic Places.

Bev and Rick personally scraped, sanded, painted, wallpapered, plastered, and carpentered from their first day of ownership in 1978 until 1983. Their original hunt took place when Bev was an ad manager for McDonald's and Rick an account manager at an advertising agency. What they found was a boarding house for senior citizens that had inn potential. Today Bev and Rick live just down the street from The Captain Lord Mansion, and they have a staff. Rick greets guests five days a week. He shares the history of the mansion and its furnishings. As San Diego guests remember, "He magically takes you through the mansion's history, telling of the ghost child you might hear near the spiral staircase leading to the cupola."

Bev's touches are visible in constant changes and additions. This year she cross-stitched name plaques and do-not-disturb door knob pillows for each room. Her love of auctions and hand crafts can also be seen in collections for sale in her own gift shop. She dovetails her behind-the-scenes work with mothering the two young Litchfields, Dana and Stacia.

When guests write to me about The Captain Lord Mansion, they mention *everything*—the exquisite furnishings, the charm, lovable Aggie, and the hospitality.

**In residence:** Aggie, their Maine coon cat, known to help escort you to your room.
**Restrictions:** Minimum age for children is 12. Smoking in guest rooms only.
**Bed and bath:** Sixteen rooms, 11 with working fireplaces. All with private baths, all with showers, some with tubs, even original claw-foot ones. All furnished with four-poster beds (12 rooms with queen-sized beds), quality antiques, sitting area.

**Breakfast:** At 8:30 and 9:30, served family style in country kitchen that has original restaurant-sized coal stove (not used). Fresh-baked muffin and sweet bread of the day, soft-boiled eggs, herbal teas, juice, butter, cream cheese, preserves.
**Plus:** Tea in evening, iced in summer. Chocolates in room, boxed fragrance soap, shower cap, sewing kits. Window fans. Lawn chairs in yard. Complimentary cheese and cracker platters for returnees. Thick towels. Will meet at Portland airport and bus.
**Rates:** January–mid-May $59-$119 per room, mid-May through December $79-$129; less mid-week, November, December. Firewood $3 per day, September-June. Deposits required for one- or two-night reservations. MasterCard, VISA, AMEX only for balance, not deposits. Rates vary according to season, weekday, weekend, and whether room has fireplace.

## The Chetwynd House

Chestnut Street, Box 130, Kennebunkport, ME 04046
**Phone:** 207/967-2235
**Location:** In the village within walking distance of everything. Across the street from Kennebunk River marina.
**Host:** Susan Knowles Chetwynd
**Open:** Year round. Reservations recommended. Two-night weekend minimum, three-night holiday minimum.

"Everything about The Chetwynd House was special," said the rather fussy fellow guest we met at another B&B. "To begin with there's a beautifully served exotic breakfast. Then there's high tea. And it's in a great location. And it has Susan."

Since coming here in 1971, Susan, a former English teacher in Connecticut, has become quite knowledgeable about the town's early history and its citizens. In winter, she sometimes joins the natives and dons foul-weather gear for an outdoor look at a dramatic angry ocean. She lives in a tall-windowed blue-shuttered home, originally built around 1840 for a sea captain, the home of artist Abbott Graves in the early 1900s. Its wide pine floorboards are graced with antique and traditional furnishings with blue, Susan's favorite color, tastefully introduced throughout.

"Many a fine friendship began with talk about the favorite dishes served in area restaurants and moved on to the offerings in the art galleries. We talk about our efforts to understand the school of art of black squares and harmony of colored stripes on canvas, and confess we buy paintings of the sea and harbor, and village scenes—and we ponder why that is. We ponder about a lot of things. That's nice."

**Restrictions:** Sorry, no children in season. No pets.
**Foreign languages spoken:** Some French and Italian.
**Bed and bath:** Four rooms. One with king-sized bed, private shower bath. One with double bed, private tub bath. Two with four-posters, one queen-sized and one double, share a shower bath. Extra twin bed available.
**Breakfast:** At 9. Full, year round. Fresh fruits, blueberry muffins, maybe egg dishes, fillet of sole or haddock, crabmeat souffle, quiches, oyster stew (in season), Belgian waffles. A different vegetable offered each day.
**Plus:** Living room/library. Fruit basket in room. High tea at four; by candlelight in winter. Flower-bedecked porch. Many suggestions including "a special beach with dunes and grasses" as well as restaurants established by good chefs previously with other restaurants. Fans, if needed. Tea or hot chocolate. On-site parking.
**Rates:** Per room. June 15-January 1, $85 private bath, $65 semiprivate. Rest of year, exluding holidays, $74 private bath, $59 semiprivate. Off-season 10 percent discount Sunday through Thursday. Extra twin bed $30.

## The Inn at Harbor Head

Pier Road, Cape Porpoise, Kennebunkport
Mailing address: RFD 2, Box 1180, Kennebunkport, ME 04046
**Phone:** 207/967-5564 and 967-4873
**Location:** "On the harbor where gulls wheel and dive and the tide is constantly changing." Two and one-half miles from the center of Kennebunkport in the historic fishing village of Cape Porpoise. "The lighthouse on the horizon is 20 miles south of us. Across the ocean you would land in Spain. We are close to hidden woodland roads, places to find wildflowers, quiet beaches, museums, art galleries, and crafts places . . . fine boutiques and junk shops abound as well."
**Hosts:** Joan and David Sutter
**Open:** Year round. Reservations are a necessity during summer. Two-night minimum most holidays and summer weekends.

It is a rambling shingled place filled with antiques, ambiance, and joy. Many guests take pictures of the stencils and decorating ideas that Joan conceived and executed throughout. Others wrote to me about photographing "the breakfast table before commencing to devour the wonderful meal."

The Sutters (now grandparents of one) moved here 15 years ago with five children, one dog, and two cats. The house was built in 1898 by the father of the Sutters' next door neighbor—in an era when the granite foundation was hauled 40 miles by oxen for $100.

"For years I led the solitary life of an artist with gallery deadlines to meet and children to raise, and David went off to the office to pursue his engineering skills. He still goes to the office, but not until the orange juice is squeezed! . . . When the B&B idea hit us we put up a temporary sign and had our first guest 45 minutes later. Life has never been the same. . . . It has been much more fun than we ever expected."

**In residence:** Rob is at college. His brother and sisters occasionally are here for a weekend. Duffy (short for Gloria McDuff), 12-year-old wire-haired fox terrier, described by one guest as "the secret ingredient that really makes this B&B work."
**Restrictions:** No guests' pets. "Duffy wouldn't like it." Smoking outside only. Children should be at least ten, unless all rooms are booked by one party.
**Bed and bath:** Three rooms, one with adjoining room used occasionally. All private baths, one with shower, no tub. "The Greenery" (very private) on the first floor has brass king-sized bed, hand-painted flowers on furniture, ceiling fan. Second-floor "Ocean Room" with Victorian white brass double bed and a fainting couch. "Harbor Room" has mahogany double four-poster with hand-crocheted bedspread and handpainted murals of harbor, sky, and clouds.
**Breakfast:** Around 9. Freshly squeezed juice in stemmed glasses. Fruit—melon, citrus slices garnished with violets in season, pineapple boats, berries with cream, grapefruit with syrup. Heated plate of sausage, bacon, or ham and oven scrambled eggs, cherry tomatoes with fresh oregano and basil, pecan sticky buns. Next day might be a vegetable medley or Belgian waffles with amaretto-flavored whipped cream or French toast and bacon topped with sliced fruit. At table set with flowers, linen, and silver in dining room with bay window and wood stove or outside on terrace.

**Plus:** Champagne to make mimosas for special occasions. Afternoon beverages with cheese and crackers. Informal tours of house. Will meet at airport. Use of refrigerator. Private dock and floats for sitting or swimming. Boat rentals nearby for exploring the islands. Hammock. Library, games, and puzzles. Classical music always. Turned-down beds. Thick towels. Fruit and chocolates in room.
**Rates:** November-April $60, May and September $65 and $70, June, July, October, and holidays $75-$85. $15 for third person in the room. MasterCard, VISA, AMEX, and DISCOVER accepted.

## The Inn on South Street

P.O. Box 478a, South Street, Kennebunkport, ME 04046
**Phone:** 207/967-4639 or 207/967-5151
**Location:** On a quiet tree-lined street in the historic village area within easy walking distance to shops, restaurants, and beaches.
**Hosts:** Eva and Jacques Downs
**Open:** Year round, except for three weeks in January. Two-night minimum stay late June through October.

"All our children were in college and (after living here for 23 years) I wanted to fix up the house the way it should be and I wanted to share it with others. Seven people is really our limit and we plan to keep it that way to carry out our personal style," Eva told me.

Long letters from guests confirm that the goals have certainly been met. One from a hotel consultant (!) commented, "The structure allows each room substantial privacy." Also, "accommodations are spotless, cheery and comfortable. The old house is beautifully decorated, but it's Eva and Jack that make the Inn special."

Both Eva and Jack grew up in California. They have traveled extensively in Europe and Mexico. She was a social worker in Portland. Jack is a history professor at the University of New England, has authored two books, and frequently is a guest speaker. (The house itself has an interesting history and is on the National Register.) At the inn the conversation might cover any number of topics, including places to sight rare birds or how to locate a summer rental (as one guest did in March, thanks to the Downses).

The decor of this 19th-century Greek Revival home is strongly reminiscent of Kennebunkport's maritime past, particularly the connection with 19th-century China. The Oriental flavor is evident in the foyer, which is dominated by an elaborately carved shrine door. Elsewhere there are period antiques and traditional furnishings.

**In residence:** Son Jonathan (in his twenties) assists in summer months.
**Restrictions:** Children should be at least eight; can accommodate one or two at a time.
**Foreign languages spoken:** Spanish and German fluently, some Russian. Jonathan speaks French.
**Bed and bath:** Three spacious rooms with private baths. Cot available. "Mrs. Perkins" on the first floor has a single and a double bed; both are brass and iron. Second-floor "Gibson Room" has queen-sized brass bed. Third-floor "The Romantic Room" has queen-sized bed and a single sleigh bed, arched Italianate window.
**Breakfast:** Summer 8:30-9. Winter 9-10, but flexible. Home-baked breads, souffle-omelets with fruit sauces or filled pastries or blintzes, juice and fresh fruit in season. Herbs from garden often used. Homemade jams made with local berries. Served in country kitchen with a view of river and ocean; sometimes in garden in warm weather. Option of continental breakfast in room.
**Plus:** Hot coffee at 7 a.m. Afternoon tea, wine, hot cider, or lemonade with family members. Fireplace and antique Franklin stove. Dinner can be arranged for a party wishing to take the whole house. Limo service arranged from airport. Use of refrigerator. Secluded garden for lounging. Balcony off living room. Fresh flowers from Eva's garden. Thick towels. No television. Sometimes surprise snacks. "We offer valet jogging."
**Rates:** Late June through October, $60-$70 for two. Rest of year $55-$60. Fireplace room add $10. Extra person in room $10. Reduced rates for a full week's stay. AMEX accepted.

One guest wrote, "We slept in a comfortable (which to us means firm!) queen-sized bed with an adjacent modern (thank God!) and spacious bathroom. . . . No need to try any other place. . ."

## Old Fort Inn

P.O. Box M33, Old Fort Avenue, Kennebunkport, ME 04046
**Phone:** 207/967-5353
**Location:** On three acres in an area of large summer estates. One block from the ocean in a secluded setting with tall pine, oak, and birch trees.
**Hosts:** Sheila and David Aldrich
**Open:** Mid-April through mid-December. Three-day minimum stay July-Labor Day, Memorial and Columbus Day weekends. Two-day minimum stay mid-September through mid-October.

Sheila had worked for the airlines and David was associated with the oil industry when they came here in 1980. Their property had a large summer inn built on it around 1900. That inn closed in 1962 and was torn down in 1967. The remaining stable and carriage house became a summer club in the 1970s. The Aldriches converted it to their home and B&B business.

In a way, what they offer in this summer resort town is an intimate mini-resort in itself. As guests from Virginia who have been returning for years wrote, "After breakfast, we usually have a tennis game on their professional court, followed by a swim in the fresh-water heated pool."

David gives Sheila credit for "the decor and creative side." All the guest rooms, located in a brick and stone turn-of-the-century carriage house, are either papered in Laura Ashley prints or stenciled, setting the backdrop for the American country style and antiques. When David isn't overseeing construction and maintenance, you'll find him in the antique shop, always ready to discuss the collection of treasures, or personalized professional B&B, or tennis or skiing, or maybe the restoration of antique cars.

**In residence:** Shana, age ten. Two cats, Samantha, a large gray fluffy female, and Bogart, a large sleek black male.
**Restrictions:** Children should be at least seven. Sorry, no guests' pets. No pipe or cigar smoking in the guest rooms.
**Bed and bath:** Twelve large rooms, each with a private bath. A king, queen, two doubles or twins to a room; most are four-posters. Each room has electric heat, wall-to-wall carpeting, color TV, and kitchen unit.
**Breakfast:** 8:30-10. Juice, coffee, several varieties of tea, cocoa, fresh fruit, home-baked fruit bread, croissants, a selection of jams. Buffet in lodge common room. Sheila and David usually join guests.

**Plus:** Pool. Shuffleboard. One hour of free tennis daily. Converted barn common room that has beams, weathered pine wall boards, huge brick fireplace. Bedroom window fans. Babysitting. Laundry facilities. Bicycles for rent.
**Rates:** Double occupancy. Mid June-December 15 $75 queen, $85 queen and one twin, $95 king and twin doubles; $125 for three-room suite. Off-season $60-$95. Additional person in a room $15. Spring and November mid-week package rates. MasterCard, VISA, and AMEX accepted.

## Port Gallery Inn

Corner of Spring and Maine streets, Kennebunkport
Mailing address: P.O. Box 1367, Kennebunkport, ME 04046
**Phone:** 207/967-3728
**Location:** In village center; walk to shops, restaurants, and marinas. Among many homes listed on the National Register.
**Hosts:** Lucy and Francis Morphy
**Open:** Year round. A two-night minimum stay for all holidays.

It started out to be an art gallery. Then Francis's brother suggested that the upstairs bedrooms be used for a B&B. And so it was that the Port Gallery Inn, formerly a private home, opened in 1983.

Francis and Lucy Morphy, brother and sister, moved here from New Jersey in 1981. Lucy and Bud Edwards, their aunt and uncle, also sister and brother, also moved with them to Maine. All four host at the inn at one time or another. (Their home address is two doors away.) Francis and Lucy Morphy dovetail their B&B involvement with a real estate business. Some guests have the family figured out by departure time.

Francis was an antique dealer in New Jersey, and the furnishings, mostly English, came with him to Maine. The paintings throughout the house are done by Lawrence Donnison, a recognized English marine artist who has recently painted some of the sailing ships built in Kennebunkport. The swan motif, a British symbol of welcome, seen as wooden carvings on the porch and in several rooms, links the Morphys to their English grandparents.

If Francis had his druthers, he would replace the Victorian furniture in this Victorian house with gilded Louis XIV pieces. Whatever your taste, you'll find this inn without clutter and immaculately kept.

**Restrictions:** Maximum of one child among guests on any given night.
**Bed and bath:** Seven rooms, all with cross-ventilation. Five with queen-sized beds and private baths (one with shower only). Suite on third floor has one room with a double bed with a sitting room that has two sofa beds; bath with shower.
**Breakfast:** 8:30-9:30. Continental. Buffet style in dining room that seats 8 (15-20 for special events) and on a cozy sun porch that seats 10.
**Plus:** Beverage in evening. Spontaneous classical concerts on the baby grand by Francis or (aunt) Lucy Edwards. Mints and fruit. Color cable TV in each guest room.
**Rates:** Double bed $69, queen $89. Third person in room, $20 each. MasterCard, VISA, and AMEX accepted.

## The Welby Inn

P.O. Box 774, Ocean Avenue, Kennebunkport, ME 04046
**Phone:** 207/967-4655
**Location:** In a quiet residential neighborhood, a five-minute walk to town (Dock Square) or hosts' favorite little beach.
**Hosts:** David Knox and Betsy Rogers-Knox
**Open:** Most of the year. Reservations preferred. Two-day minimum stay in July and August.

Betsy's touch is everywhere, starting with the sign on the lawn. She is a published botanical illustrator who has enhanced every room here with an original illustration. Even the hand-painted tiles in the bathrooms are hers. (Their small gift gallery has paintings and tiles for sale.)

David's touch is everywhere too. He was a captain in the Air Force and then a high school teacher in Vail, Colorado, but lately he has learned everything about the building trade by doing. The gambrel-roofed captain's house, built in 1900, had been a guest house for 38 years when the Knoxes bought it in 1985. They have added five bathrooms and done considerable redecorating. And all because they followed up on a *Down East* magazine ad that they saw during their fifth Maine vacation! Both are marathoners who have "discovered" Monastery Walk and Parson's Beach as special places to visit.

Betsy and David grew up in New England, but Betsy's grandparents come from Welby, England. (Hence the name of the inn.) This blend continues with the Laura Ashley prints, old New England beds, English wardrobes, and old quilts. One Manhattan guest summed it up: "Delightful."

**In residence:** Daughter Jessica Ann, age eight.
**Restrictions:** Children over ten are welcome. Smoking is not encouraged but is allowed in individual guest rooms. Sorry, no pets.
**Bed and bath:** Seven rooms. Five on second floor all with double beds and private baths (showers, no tubs). Two third-floor skylighted rooms share a sitting room and full bath; one room has antique twin sleigh beds, the other a queen-sized bed. Cot available.
**Breakfast:** 8-9. Fresh fruit, juices, coffees, teas, milk. Several varieties of homemade breads, muffins, granola, eggs, quiches. Served by Betsy and Jessica in country-style dining room or on enclosed porch. Informal and quite social. Upon request, continental breakfast in bed.
**Plus:** Homemade amaretto in evening. Mints on the pillow. Flowers in rooms. Thick towels. Fireplaced living room. Guest pantry and bicycles available at no charge.
**Rates:** July-October, $60-70 double occupancy. Other months, $55-$65. $5 less for singles. $15 charge for a third person. AMEX accepted.

## The Red House

Box 540, HC 60, Lincolnville Beach, ME 04849
**Phone:** 207/236-4621
**Location:** On Route 1, four miles north of Camden, half-mile south of Lincolnville Beach on Route 1. Panoramic view of Penobscot Bay.
**Hosts:** Ross and Mary Lou Overcash
**Open:** Year round.

When they lived in the Boston area, where Ross was a college professor and administrator and Mary Lou a Girl Scouts training director, they hosted B&B guests through a reservation service. Since the 1984 move to their vacation area of 20 years, they are meeting more travelers, and Ross has more time for hunting, fishing and gardening. Mary Lou does the cooking and enjoys making cut and pierced lampshades, knitting, and stenciling. Their modified Cape-style house is furnished with antiques, including their collection of salt dishes, cruets, and clocks.

Fresh flowers in the rooms and different table settings each day reflect the care given to visitors. Along with the scenic drive up Mount Battie, their favorite touring suggestion is the magnificently landscaped and terraced Children's Chapel overlooking the ocean in Rockport.

**Restrictions:** No pets. Maximum of two guests in a room.
**Bed and bath:** Two twin-bedded rooms share a guest bath. Both on second floor, one with ocean view.
**Breakfast:** Full breakfast 8-8:30. Earlier on request. Continental after 8:30. Juice, fresh berries in season, sweet breads, homemade preserves and pancakes or French toast, eggs, baked cheese grits. Served in dining room overlooking the bay.
**Plus:** Large yard with comfortable chairs and chaises. Babysitting can be arranged.
**Rates:** $35 for one, $40 for two. $5 discount for AARP members. Off season rates available.

## Oliver Farm Inn

P.O. Box 136, Old Route 1, Nobleboro, ME 04555
**Phone:** 207/563-1527
**Location:** On quiet road, five minutes north of Damariscotta. Midway between Boothbay Harbor and Camden, "where birds instead of alarm clocks awaken you and where moose tracks have been sighted in the garden."
**Host:** Joyce North
**Open:** Mid-June–Mid-October.

Wanted: A place with land and space and peace. Found: 20 acres, after a two-year search.

Joyce's dream of her "piece of Maine" was a rather ramshackle farmhouse that needed considerable restoration. Now, there's a before-and-after-photo record to browse through. Antique iron bedsteads, patchwork quilts, stenciled walls, and every accessory down to the last woven wreath make the project quite complete. Back home in Maryland, Joyce has designed rooms for decorators' showhouses and been an antique dealer. After opening Oliver Farm Inn, she couldn't resist a "For Rent" sign in Damariscotta; Katydid, Joyce's whimsical gift shop there, is her excuse to make regular off-season jaunts to Maine.

Dick is a contractor, and Muffie and Karis, both horse lovers, spend their college summers here.

The Norths had been in residence for just two days when we pedaled up as their first visitors of the season. We met Kai, their exchange student from Germany *and* the local health inspector! The man with clipboard appeared during breakfast and declared that the kitchen was so perfect that Joyce could serve dinners, if she wanted to.

**In residence:** Daughters Muffie and Karis.
**Restrictions:** No pets, please. Smoking outdoors only.
**Foreign languages spoken:** A little French and German.
**Bed and bath:** Five rooms, all carpeted. One on first floor, with a double bed, shared bath. Second floor has two rooms with two double beds in each, two with one double in each, and two shared baths. Crib available.
**Breakfast:** 8-9:30. Sumptuous. Blueberry pancakes, quiche Lorraine, curried goldenrod eggs, cheese omelets, or French toast. Juice or fruit cup, cereal, homemade muffins, freshly ground coffee or tea.
**Plus:** Wine and cheese. Front porch seating. Walking trail through meadow and woods. Will meet guests at the local bus. Dinner by special arrangement. Baby sitting sometimes available.
**Rates:** $35 single, $47 double. $12 for third person.

> From New York: "Charming accommodations . . . and I was sent on my way with a package of freshly baked zucchini bread for a snack on the road."

---

## The Gazebo

---

P.O. Box 668, Route 1, Ogunquit, ME 03907
**Phone:** 207/646-3733
**Location:** On Route 1, one mile north of Ogunquit village center.
**Host:** Tony Fontes
**Open:** Year round except for the month of January.

**Ogunquit**

"Take a left at the Gazebo," residents may say. A local landmark now, the new latticed structure with hanging geraniums in each of its eight archways is a place to read the paper, have coffee, or watch the trolleys go by.

The contented host of this B&B was the supervisor of an airlines complaint department when, one weekend, he realized that going back to that work was not what he wanted to do. "I couldn't bang a nail to begin with, but we gutted and rebuilt and put new plaster throughout this 150-year-old Greek Revival house. You can follow everything that was done in our before-and-after book, even for the very room you stay in." The window treatments—balloon shades, jabots, and swags—are often a source of guests' comments. So, too, is the breakfast, planned with great eye appeal.

The (mostly) young couples who come here have use of the entire house and often say that they feel like they are in grandmother's place.

**In residence:** The host smokes.
**Restrictions:** No pets, please. Children over 12 welcome.
**Bed and bath:** Nine rooms, seven with private baths. Four rooms have private entrances. One room with two twin beds, one suite with queen-sized bed, a double bed in all the others. All antique beds; each room furnished differently.
**Breakfast:** 8-10. Possibilities include stuffed French toast with apricot-orange sauce, homemade turkey sausage, poached pear with raspberry sauce, homemade apple-walnut muffins, ham and egg croquette with tomato basil sauce, eggs Benedict, apple walnut muffins. Served on china and crystal in fireplaced dining room.
**Plus:** In-ground swimming pool. Air conditioning in front bedrooms. Afternoon tea with pate served in breakfast room, around pool, or in gardens. Maps/menus. Upstairs rooms have sun deck. Short walk to beach, trolley to all shops, nearby restaurants, and Perkins Cove.
**Rates:** All per room. April 15-October 15, $65 private bath, $55 shared bath. Suite $75. October 15-April 15, private bath $50, shared bath $40.

## Morning Dove

P.O. Box 1940, 5 Bourne Lane, Ogunquit, ME 03907
**Phone:** 207/646-3891
**Location:** Just off the shore road, away from major traffic, among lovely gardens. Short walk to trolley, beaches, shops, galleries, restaurants, harbor, and famous Ogunquit Playhouse.
**Hosts:** Peter and Eeta Sachon
**Open:** Pretty much year round. Three-day weekend reservation required from the third weekend in June through Labor Day and on holidays. Two-day reservations preferred at other times.

"After years as a flight attendant, I wanted to be at home. B&B combines my experience with people, art (she was an art major in college) and antiques (her mother owned an antique shop).

When Peter is not flying (he is a commercial pilot), he is the official architect, landscaper, and gardener. Eeta arranges his flowers in all the rooms, and is responsible for the decor that gives a light and airy feeling throughout. And if pushed, she'll tell you that she also plays the roles of chef, reservationist, bookkeeper, maid, tour director, mother advisor. . . .

The 1860 farmhouse had always been a private home, but it had been "modernized" through the years. So the Sachons have made many changes inside and out since they bought it three years ago. Two arched windows, two bay windows, and a Palladian window are some of the additions. Among the antiques you will find a spinning wheel, cradle, and collection of old toys.

With all there is to do in the area, Eeta considers Mount Agamenticus a highlight—great for "a romantic picnic, a champagne breakfast, and sunsets too."

**In residence:** Sultan, "our boxer, a real beauty who thinks he's human. He runs the place."
**Restrictions:** Minimum age for children is 12. No more than two people per room.
**Bed and bath:** Six rooms, all decorated with antiques, original paintings, and quilts. Four rooms with private baths, three with showers only, one with tub. First floor—two mahogany twin beds, private exterior entrance. Second floor—one room with queen-sized brass bed, private bath; one room with two twin beds and one small but quiet room with brass double bed share a bath. Third floor—Sea Captain's Room with queen-sized antique pine rope bed, and Grandma's Attic, "our best room," with queen-sized bed.

**Breakfast:** 8:30-10:30. Continental with croissants, muffins, or popovers. Served on bone china and linens on sun porch or in sunny common room.
**Plus:** Living room. Wine served upon arrival. Window and ceiling fans. Games, books, magazines. Huge covered porch. Sunning in large garden. Grill available. Use of refrigerator. Turned-down beds at night; chocolates on pillow. Thick towels.
**Rates:** $45-50 shared bath, $55-60 private bath, third weekend in June-Labor Day. Other times—$40-45 shared bath, $50-55 private bath. Inquire about theme weekends, e.g. romantic getaways, Christmas shopping weekend, or artists' workshops.

From Pennsylvania: "The best part, however, is its proprietors . . . very warm, charming and hospitable."

## Bed & Breakfast of Maine Host #16

Peaks Island, ME
**Location:** Harborside. Reached by ferry that leaves hourly from the Old Port section of Portland. A quick taxi ride or seven-minute walk from ferry landing to B&B.
**Reservations:** Available year round through Bed & Breakfast of Maine, page 6.

How about cross-country skiing on an island? Here's the chance, just 15 minutes out to sea.

"Most guests love hiking and cycling, appreciate the outdoors and are curious about island living. I moved here from Portland in 1983 because I found the perfect house in the perfect location. It is one of the original island houses, built in 1860, was once owned by a fisherman and later became a store and boat repair facility."

The house has the casual and charming island ambiance you have come for. It is uncluttered, with white walls, wood floors, braided rugs, drying herbs, and simple furnishings. If the hostess is out, she leaves a welcoming note that leads you to the kitchen and its gorgeous view of Portland Harbor. Your hostess is an amateur photographer and former graphic arts teacher.

The island is still relatively rural, even with six thousand people in summer, four times the winter population. Try cycling (rentals available in Portland) the five-mile road that encircles the island, or hike along beaches and through pine forests. Rocky cliffs and abundant wildflowers add to the scene. Explore old forts. Examine tide pools. Off-season, of course, the flavor is different—and delicious.

**In residence:** The hostess smokes.
**Restrictions:** No guests' pets.
**Foreign languages spoken:** A little Spanish and French.
**Bed and bath:** Seven rooms share three baths, one with tub and two with showers. Some rooms with water views. Double beds, twin beds, and two mattresses on floor in loft. Cots and crib available.
**Breakfast:** 8-9. Fresh fruit, juice, cereal, toast, rolls or coffee cake, milk, tea or cocoa. Served buffet style in dining room overlooking Portland harbor.
**Plus:** Harborside deck for relaxation and picnicking. Stairs to beach. Fans available. Children's toys. Even a laundromat just a minute away. Restaurants and a food store on the island. Frequent ferry to Portland for dinner, if you'd like.
**Rates:** Single $33 weeknights, $38 Friday or Saturday. Double $38 weeknights, $43 Friday or Saturday. No charge for crib. $12 per night per cot. Reduced rates November-May.

## Menatoma Lodge

Readfield, ME
Summer mailing address: RFD #2, Box 3400, Winthrop, ME 04364
**Phone:** 207/685-9986
Winter contact information: 267 Foreside Road, Falmouth, ME 04105. Telephone: 207/781-5691
**Location:** In a quiet woodsy setting on two-mile-long Lovejoy Pond. Part of a family resort community known as The Birches of Menatoma. On a dirt road in Readfield, two miles in from Routes 17 and 41. Fourteen miles west of the Maine Turnpike in Augusta.
**Hosts:** Laura and Tony Bantly
**Open:** Last of June through Labor Day. "We don't require a minimum stay, but those who only come for one night wish they could stay for two or three."

"Just what I was looking for," said the guest from the Department of Agriculture. Casual, unpretentious, and relaxed. A place where the hostess has to declare that the season is over and, sorry, but they are closing. Upon hearing that she meant it, one guest planned a lobster bake for the final night. Plenty of spontaneity here.

What was for 50 years the main lodge (rec hall) for a luxury summer camp has been the summer residence for the Bantlys since 1981. It's one of those wonderfully built rustic places from the late 1920s with open ceiling and massive beams. The nine-foot fieldstone fireplace is the only source of heat. The second floor is bordered by a ten-foot-wide balcony that overlooks the main eating area. Furnishings are simple and functional.

"With four teenagers and college years approaching, we knew this was a place to share. Our very first guests were two so-called senior-citizen friends who put us all to shame with their endless energy and enthusiasm. (They also sent us off packing when they discovered it was our wedding anniversary and did the dishes themselves.)"

Tony is a manufacturing manager and Laura has been a nursery-school owner-director for 15 years.

**In residence:** One shy black cat and a very quiet female beagle. "Our teens and college students spend much of the summer at our winter residence near Portland where they have jobs. Gram and Laura are usually the anchors. Tony joins us on the weekends."
**Restrictions:** No smoking or drinking.
**Bed and bath:** Three rooms. Shared baths, one with "a quaint little tub on legs and a neat little makeshift shower." Family room on main floor sleeps four (a double bed and bunk beds). Two second-floor rooms; one with double bed and one with double bed, a single, and space for a cot.
**Breakfast:** Generally 8-9. Cereal selection, homemade granola, sometimes blueberry pancakes, frequently hot muffins, occasionally eggs, homemade jellies and jams. Hostess and Gram cook. Everyone seems to help thereafter.
**Plus:** Crackling fire every night. Candles by the fireplace. Use of canoes, ping-pong, games, puzzles. Warm lake swimming. Playing field, basketball court. Tennis courts available at an hourly rate.
**Rates:** Single $25, double $30. Cots, cribs or guest children bunking with our children $5.

From Connecticut: "To enjoy the calls of the loons and to canoe on water disturbed only by the ripples made by my boat was a relaxing experience which surpassed any previous flight from the city."

## Sign of the Unicorn Guest House—Bed & Breakfast

191 Beauchamp Avenue, Box 99, Rockport, ME 04856
**Phone:** 207/236-8789 or 207/236-4042 (answering machine)
**Location:** On a quiet lane overlooking harbor. Within walking distance of restaurants, galleries, performances, Rockport Opera House, photography and art lectures and classes. Ten minutes to lakes for warm-water swimming. Two miles from Camden.
**Host:** Winnie Easton
**Open:** Year round. Usually closed Thanksgiving and Christmas. Two-day minimum stay suggested in July and August.

The Unicorn is an environment—and a unique one at that. For eight years, word of mouth has brought guests who are looking for informality, tranquillity, maybe participatory possibilities, maybe some inspiration in a creative atmosphere.

Original art—by professionals and guests—is displayed. For youngsters there are crayons, building materials, clay, paper. The library has art books, mystery books, children's books, and over 100 cookbooks. Unplanned music making may occur any evening. The grand piano is available, as are recorders, guitar, and harmonicas. Some guests arrive with their own instruments; one summer a young woman came with her harp.

And what if all you want to do is sit on a rock and read? Or walk through a wildlife refuge? That's fine, as long as the hosts are allowed to live up to their motto, "We spoil you rottener than you are." Winnie Easton's welcoming co-host, Howard Jones, is a model maker and Nantucket lightship basket maker. The fun map of Rockport they send you shows how much there is—culturally and recreationally—to do in and around this picturesque village.

Winnie's story links her roles as mother, teacher (of French, music, young children, English), day-camp director, professional photographer, B&B traveler abroad, watercolor and oil student, and now working poet and writer. She is a tutor with Literary Volunteers and a docent at the Farnsworth Art Museum. There's more: The newest hat says "Rockport Realty."

**Restrictions:** Nonsmokers preferred, but considerate (outside on the porch) smokers are welcomed. No guests' pets, please.
**Foreign languages spoken:** French. Winnie is learning Spanish.

**Bed and bath:** Four rooms. Private bath an option for some rooms. One first-floor room has double bed and a twin bed, white carpeting, grand piano. The Great Room has a double bed, a loft with two additional beds, rough sawn pine walls, sliding glass doors overlooking harbor. Upstairs two rooms, one with double bed and one with two twin beds, share a full bath. For large groups (family reunions, wedding parties), a fifth room is available.
**Breakfast:** Full. Yogurt and fresh fruit salad. Maybe blueberry muffins, pancakes, French toast with orange drizzle, long cooked oatmeal, homemade granola, or "eggs with herbs, potatoes, cheese, and onions if you're brave and 'snail sauce' eggs if you're intrepid!" Guest cooks are welcome.
**Plus:** Wine and cheese. Fruit bowl. Air conditioning in bedrooms. Picnic tables and barbecue. Washer, dryer, and kitchen privileges for those staying longer. Hosts enjoy taking guests for scenic rides or to meet artisan friends. Babysitting. Special weekends (birding, watercolor, cooking, jewelry making, French phonics) spring through fall. Antique and auction locations cheerfully shared. Woods for jogging.
**Rates:** Mid May-October $55-$65 per room. $10 extra guest in downstairs rooms. $10 surcharge for private bath. $35 single, shared bath only. Weekly and group rates; long-term arrangements. Off-season rates, $5 less.

## Homeport Inn

Rte. 1, East Main Street, Searsport, ME 04974
**Phone:** 207/548-2259
**Location:** On main road of village, surrounded by beautiful flower gardens and grounds that extend to the seashore.
**Hosts:** Dr. and Mrs. F. George Johnson
**Open:** Year round.

When the Johnsons decided to become innkeepers in 1977, they bought and restored this sea captain's house that is listed on the National Register of Historic Places. Changes are ongoing. There has been an addition to the main house, the carriage house now has guest rooms. Beyond "what's where," hosts find that many questions from guests focus on the lovely home furnished with family heirlooms and period antiques, all shared with guests.

Dr. Johnson is a down-easter who comes back home on weekends from his dentistry practice in Massachusetts. Mrs. Johnson has worked in the health profession. Both are quite familiar with the state. When I asked how long they had been here, they replied, "We are Maine people of Scottish descent."

Dozens of antique shops are in the area. And there's a long list of recreational and cultural opportunities. Within the last few years, the year-round appeal seems to have been discovered by honeymooners.

**In residence:** Dr. Johnson is a pipe smoker. Tina is their Yorkshire terrier and Joshua is a big yellow cat.
**Restrictions:** Sorry, no guests' pets. Smoking allowed on first floor.
**Bed and bath:** Thirteen elegant rooms. Nine have private baths. Queen and double beds, some canopied. Crib available.
**Breakfast:** 8-9. Juice, fresh fruit, freshly baked muffins and breads, Scotch porridge, sausage, bacon, eggs. Served in formal family dining room or on the sun porch, overlooking Penobscot Bay.
**Plus:** Afternoon tea, 2-5. Flower gardens. Packed lunches can be provided. Option of lobster dinners on the shore Wednesday and Sunday, July-September.
**Rates:** $25 single with shared bath, $30 private. $50 for two with shared bath, $55-$65 private. $15 additional person sharing room, $6 if under age 14. Weekly stays and off-season, 5 percent less. MasterCard, AMEX, VISA, Diners Club accepted.

---

## Sedgwick B&B

Box 51, Sedgwick, ME 04676
**Phone:** 207/359-4495
**Location:** Off the beaten track "in a very special part of Maine." On a main rural road. Ten miles south of Blue Hill, one mile from Sedgwick Village. Overlooking Benjamin River and Eggemoggin Reach to Deer Isle. Thirty minutes from Stonington or Castine. One hour to Bar Harbor and Acadia National Park.
**Host:** Kathryn Brunelle
**Open:** Year round. Reservations appreciated.

"A real B&B." A sheaf of letters testifies to that. "She is nonintrusive and respects your privacy. . . . Her lovely manner is reflected throughout her home."

Kathryn, a year-round resident, did social work in Kansas and Connecticut before moving here with her husband in 1979. In addition to managing that marvelous craft coop in Stonington, she is involved in the community. She is passionate about gardening, music, and being on the water.

Her house is filled with charm and warmth and B&B explorer-type guests who book for one or two nights but stay longer. And then they return. And then they write to me about dreaming of returning again.

**In residence:** Two neutered male cats, Marmalade and Max, kept out of B&B unless guests welcome them.
**Restrictions:** Children gladly accepted. Smoking not permitted.
**Foreign language spoken:** "Could limp along in German. I would find it fun, but am not sure guests would."
**Bed and bath:** Two second-floor rooms, queen-sized bed in one, two twin beds in the other. All with log cabin quilts made by Kathryn. Shared full bath. Cot and crib available.
**Breakfast:** 7-9, but flexible. Called the basics by Kathryn, but called "the best in Maine" by a guest from Maryland, and "sumptuous" by two from Massachusetts. Might be yogurt pancakes or crab cakes made with local crabmeat, whole-wheat potato bread or home-made muffins, sweet rolls, blackberry jelly made from her blackberries; in August wild blueberries and raspberries. "A friend down the road keeps me supplied with wonderful, super-fresh eggs . . . I'm a vegetarian and easily accommodate that diet, and others if I have some notice. And I think bad coffee is a capital crime."
**Plus:** Private entrance to guest area. One comfortable parlor designated for guests, but you are welcome anywhere in the house. Tour of house—including wonderful dining room with brick wall, beamed ceiling, hanging herbs, piano, marvelous use of color. Maybe a pot of brewed decaf and fruit for evening nibbling. Fresh bouquets in guest rooms. Walls of books. Magazines. Television. On the five acres are vegetable garden, perennial flowers and wildflowers, woods, a stream, spectacular view. Suggestions, if you ask, for walking places, great sunset spots, the best shoreline for finding sea glass.
**Rates:** $40 double, $35 single. Rollaway $10. No charge for crib.

## Pineapple Hospitality Host #ME 412

Sheepscot, ME
**Location:** Coastal country setting with large lawn, shade trees, on 30 acres. On the Sheepscot River in historic village four miles from Route 1 and Wiscasset. An hour north of Portland, about 12 miles from Boothbay Harbor or Pemaquid Lighthouse.
**Reservations:** Available April-November through Pineapple Hospitality, page 6.

History, charm, and tranquillity. That's what won the hosts over when they came here in 1981 to begin a B&B in the European style. They are antique dealers who are responsible for the stenciling and much of the restoration of their classic 1801 Federal home. Built by a shipbuilder and on the National Register of Historic Places, it is filled with Early American antiques, many for sale. In addition to background about the house and its furnishings, the hosts are well informed about the interesting history of the area.

The host wears a few other hats; he is a pilot and a real estate salesman. The hostess is former physical education teacher. Both enjoy bluegrass music, gardening, skiing, swimming, and fishing—"and guests, each one different."

**In residence:** (Not in guest area) a beagle named Muffin, cats named Sassafras and Inky. Gus and Guilda are the geese.
**Restrictions:** Guests' pets may be allowed if arrangements are made in advance. No smoking in the house.
**Foreign language spoken:** German.
**Bed and bath:** Two second-floor rooms, each with private entrance, double bed, private full bath, working fireplace, water views. Cot available.
**Breakfast:** Fresh fruit, homemade pastries, beverages. Served in the antique-filled dining room. Hosts usually join guests at end of meal.
**Plus:** Lighted tennis courts (no charge) within 200 yards. Five-acre pond with wildlife. River frontage; good swimming. Reversing tidal waterfall. Den with reading library, stereo, and TV. Late-afternoon or evening beverages. Tour of house.
**Rates:** $40 single, $45 double.

## The Barn

Route 220 South (Friendship Street), South Waldoboro
Mailing address: RD #3, P.O. Box 157A, S. Waldoboro, ME 04572
**Phone:** 207/832-5781
**Location:** A very peaceful spot in a charming setting with a long view. "The only humanly inhabited barn along this country road." Not far from a barn depicted in one of Andrew Wyeth's paintings. Six miles from Waldoboro Village. Four miles from Friendship.
**Host:** Helen Power
**Open:** May through October 15. Advance reservations are advisable in the summer and always appreciated.

Pages and pages! Guests extol everything from the wildflowers at the doorstep to the tasteful decor. Helen, too, loves this place, and the open sky and fields, "the blue smile of the firmament."

Since she started B&B in 1980, she has had the pleasure of seeing the growing children of many repeat visitors "and even their new arrivals in some cases." The feeling is mutual. One Rhode Island father wrote, "The strongest point about Helen's place is Helen. She has always provided us with a warm welcome."

First built across the road about 1793, the Barn has been moved, divided, added to, and finally reconstructed into a well-insulated home.

Maine was the home state of Helen's mother. Before Helen, now a grandmother herself, moved here, she was a potter in Boulder, Colorado and then in California, Wyoming, and New York.

**In residence:** Jaime (pronounced Heimie), a shy and reclusive cat with "a Spanish past" lives in the unreconstructed end of the barn. Mr. Oulton is a mechanical engineer who does occasional consulting.
**Restrictions:** No smoking upstairs. Sorry, no pets allowed.
**Foreign languages spoken:** "Could probably struggle with French and German."
**Bed and bath:** Three rooms share one full bath. One large room with double bed,, one medium-sized room with two twin beds, and one small room, Helen's favorite (comfortable but "you cannot swing a cat in it"), with single bed. Cot available. Shared living room upstairs.
**Breakfast:** Time established by guests but 8:00 seems to be the preference. Fruit (maybe blackberries picked that morning in the lane) or juice, sausages or bacon and eggs, sometimes crepes or

omelets; homemade blueberry, rice, or kasha muffins served in old-fashioned cast iron muffin pans; coffee, tea. Served on her own blue and brown pottery in the brick-floored kitchen.
**Plus:** Flowers from Helen's garden. Living room with good library. Thick towels. Wood stoves for heat. Option of picnic baskets filled with accompaniments for lobster procured by you at Helen's favorite nearby place. Comfortable chairs outdoors. Horseshoes.
**Rates:** $36 for two, $30 for one. $10 for a cot in the large double room. The small room is $20.

## The Island House

Box 1006, Clark Point Road, Southwest Harbor, ME 04679
**Phone:** 207/244-5180, after 5 p.m. and before 7 a.m.
**Location:** Across the street from the harbor. Ten-minute walk from village center. Five minutes' walk to lobster docks, Oceanarium and Coast Guard station. Five minutes' drive to Acadia National Park and the open ocean.
**Host:** Ann Gill
**Open:** Year round. Reservations preferred.

Sheep farmers from Australia, students from Germany and Japan, women lawyers and doctors, air traffic controllers, Appalachian Club hikers . . . all have found their way to the "comfortable house with simple charm."

B&B started as a way to make the house work for Ann. "The surprise was to find that I loved it!" The cooking part is so much fun for her that she is planning an Island House Cook Book.

At one point this was the first summer hotel on Mount Desert Island. Old photos, a page from an old register, and an advertising poster show how the place started around 1850 and grew to four stories high. It was separated into two houses in 1912.

The furnishings reflect Ann's childhood years in Southeast Asia and extensive travels. She plays both piano and cello and welcomes musicians for chamber concert evenings.

Ann is a secretary at a genetics research institution in Bar Harbor. Having lived in the area for 18 years, she has her own list of non-touristy hiking trails.

**In residence:** Charlotte, 16, and during the summer, Alyson, home from college. "Our three-year-old Charlie is a wonderful mixture of German shepherd (not the size, but the pelt!) and Norwegian elkhound."
**Restrictions:** Children should be at least a year and sleep through the night. Smoking not encouraged.
**Foreign languages spoken:** Alyson speaks fluent French and passable Greek.
**Bed and bath:** Entire second floor is for guests. Four rooms share a bath on second and another on first floor. One room has two twin beds, one a double bed and nonworking fireplace. Cozy room with sloped ceiling has two twin beds and adjoins room with queen-sized bed. All have pumpkin pine floors, antique washstands, quilts, Ann's dried flower wreaths. Two cots and playpen/crib available.
**Breakfast:** 7:30-9:00, earlier by arrangement, in sunny dining room. Always a special item, perhaps blueberry coffee cake, applesauce muffins, apple-cheese toast, walnut-date French toast, hominy cheese souffle, Swiss eggs, or eggs Florentine. Juices, fruits, dry cereal, toast, coffee, teas. Leisurely. Served by a local friend weekdays May-October, by Ann on weekends. In winter, served around the wood stove in the kitchen. (Coffee pot is on at 5 a.m.)
**Plus:** Beverage upon arrival; help-yourself any time thereafter. Babysitting. Piano. Side porch with swing. Large garden and yard. Flowers in rooms. Option of box lunches on weekends. Will meet at airport.
**Rates:** Single $35, double $45, queen $47 May-October. $30-$38 off-season. Cot $10. Crib $5.

---

## Island Watch

P.O. Box 1359, Freeman Ridge Road, Southwest Harbor, ME 04679
**Phone:** 207/244-7229 or 244-5012
**Location:** Quiet. High atop Freeman Ridge, overlooking great harbors of Southwest Harbor and Mount Desert. Fifteen-minute walk by paved town road and 5-minute walk by graveled woods road to the village. Within walking distance of Seal Cove's narrow graveled Acadia National Park Road with scenic winding trails.
**Host:** Maxine Clark
**Open:** Year round. Minimum stay of two days required during summer months.

The grandmother of four, ranging from age 8 to 17, likes to hike, motorcycle, snowmobile, sail, sew, and cook. Professionally, she is a successful Realtor who knows the area well. She spent her early years on an island, and as a teenager, when her father was a lighthouse keeper, she lived in Bass Harbor Lighthouse.

With its white walls and clear uncluttered spaces, the family-built house uses the great outdoors as its primary decor. The floor-to-ceiling windows give the feeling of living in the tree tops—or even above them. The sunrise was a treat right from here! There are plenty of comfortable chairs in front of the hearth and the length of the living room allows the television set to be quite nonintrusive.

**In residence:** Sonsie, a standard black poodle who is seldom with guests. "Likely to be around are native-born friends who offer sailboat rides, tell fish stories, help with maps. . . ."
**Restrictions:** Minimum age for children is 12. No smoking in bedrooms.
**Bed and bath:** Six rooms. Two, as part of a suite, handicapped accessible. Two have private baths. One with king-sized bed. Others have a double or queen-sized bed. Cot available.
**Breakfast:** 7:30-10. French toast, pancakes, waffles. Homemade breads. Guests help themselves to coffee, juice, and cereal. Eaten at a table that displays the geodetic charts of the area seen from this very spot. Maxine cooks in a marvelous arrangement that allows her simultaneously to work in kitchen, socialize with guests, and point out the Bluenose ferry rounding the tip of the island.
**Plus:** Enormous fieldstone fireplace (built with stones from family farm site). One deck for sunning, one for shade; both for star gazing. Tea and coffee in evening. Will meet guests at Bar Harbor airport. Garage available for bikes, skis, camping equipment, snowmobiles. Barbecue available. Canoe (and jeep transportation too); beautiful canoeing on tidal creeks within the park.
**Rates:** Memorial Day-October 15, per room—private bath $55, shared bath $45. January-February, private bath $45, shared $30. Other months—private $50, shared $35. Extra person beyond two in room $10.

*Can't find the community you are going to? Check with a reservation service described at the beginning of this chapter. Through the service, you may be placed (matched) with a welcoming B&B that is near your destination.*

## Penury Hall

P.O. Box 68, Main Street, Southwest Harbor, ME 04679
**Phone:** 207/244-7102
**Location:** In the village. Just 2¾ miles from Echo Lake and Acadia Mountain Trail.
**Hosts:** Toby and Gretchen Strong
**Open:** Year round except March 15-April 15. Two- night minimum stay June through August.

Turn the old bell on one of the etched-windowed double doors—and you will be warmly greeted by horn-rimmed Toby and, very likely, those two felines who may assist in escorting you to your room.

In summer the porch is blossom-filled by the Tremont town manager, Gretchen. In the winter Penury Hall features "Scrabble spoken here" and a welcome mat for cross-country skiers. Toby's diverse professional experiences include newspaper editing, innkeeping, and a software company.

Ten years ago the Strongs moved here with their two teenage sons. Since then they have been restoring the house, which was built in sections at different times. The oldest part dates back to 1830. It is comfortably furnished. "And don't forget to mention the forest green living room walls with pure white trim." (Everybody does.)

Six years ago, a B&B trip to Cape Breton and Nova Scotia won them over to hosting. Among their guests who have written to me are a single woman who felt part of the family, first-timers who loved B&B, and a winter hiker, a physician, who felt pampered.

**In residence:** Both hosts "are in the process of stopping the habit of smoking." One son during college vacations. Two cats, Patches and Trepid.
**Restrictions:** Mature children welcome.
**Bed and bath:** Three rooms on second floor. One with twin beds, two with double beds. Two shared baths, one with shower and one with tub.
**Breakfast:** 7:30. Juice, fresh fruit, maybe eggs Benedict, blueberry pancakes, omelet, date-walnut French toast, assorted eggs with muffins, homemade jams and jellies, pure maple syrup. Prepared and served by Toby, who usually joins guests.

**Plus:** Wine or tea in afternoon or evening. Sauna. Will meet guests at airport. Laundry facilities. Kitchen privileges during winter and off- season. Use of canoe, windsurfer, 21-foot Day Sailor (rental fee).
**Rates:** Double $40, single $32. Less 10 percent November-April 1.

---

## The Belvedere

163 Main Street, Thomaston, ME 04861
**Phone:** 207/354-8759
**Location:** In historical district of old sea captains' village. Fifteen minutes from Penobscot Bay and ocean beaches, 20 minutes to Camden, 15 to Port Clyde for ferry to Monhegan Island.
**Host:** Barbara Lee
**Open:** May-October.

"The nicest feature is that this Victorian Italianate house, complete with gazebo and widow's walk, has never been renovated, modernized or changed structurally in any way except for the commodes in bathrooms, and stove, dishwasher and refrigerator in kitchen. Old house enthusiasts can see the original iron sink and the cupboards in the two pantries, the large built-in ice box in room off the shed, marble and brass bathroom fixtures, carved staircase and lighted newelpost. I have 1898 pictures of the interior of the house, velvet drapes and all. I just hated to sell the house after my daughters left, so B&B seemed a perfect solution.

"When hesitant potential guests ask to see the room, that always clinches their decision. It has a combination of traditional and antique furnishings. I have made it as personal as possible."

Barbara spent five years in the foreign service in Germany and has lived in the Washington, D.C. area. She is involved with environmental and political issues as well as with the League of Women Voters. Some evenings she or guests play the piano, but after traveling or sightseeing, guests frequently turn in early here.

Although The Belvedere is "the perfect stopover on the way to Bar Harbor," Barbara enjoys suggesting closer places to visit (she loves Monhegan Island)—and even discovering some places and people through her guests.

**In residence:** Two 16-year-old cats, Boogie and Bo Bo. Jessica, "a sweet old mutt from the pound."
**Restrictions:** Smoking permitted in the front parlor. Sorry, no pets.

**Bed and bath:** Three rooms. Two doubles, and one with two twin beds. Two shared baths, upstairs one with tub and downstairs one with shower. Bathrobes provided in each bedroom.
**Breakfast:** Generally 8-9:30 but flexible. Juice, fruit, homemade granola, coffee cakes, breads, muffins, coffee, tea, hot chocolate. Served in chandeliered dining room with bay window. Leisurely.
**Plus:** Beverages and snack. Tour of house up to widow's walk. Piano. Television. Gazebo. Porch. Lots of books. Use of laundry. Will meet guests at Rockland Airport, 15 minutes away.
**Rates:** $37 double, $27 single occupancy. Children 5-14 $5 with cot; under 5, free.

---

## River House B&B

HCR 35, Box 119, Thomaston, ME 04861
**Phone:** 207/354-8936
**Location:** Rural. Three miles from Route 1, on Route 131, south of Thomaston. On eight acres that slope to the St. George River. Eleven miles north of Port Clyde (for Monhegan Island ferry), 6 miles from Rockland, 5 from Owls Head, and 16 from Camden.
**Hosts:** Paul and Betty Koelle
**Open:** Year round. Reservations recommended.

"Monday we're moving from our B&B in Tenants Harbor to a renovated farmhouse and we have some guests who are moving right along with us. The Thomaston house is wonderful for B&B with both a screened porch and a sitting room that have gorgeous views across our meadows down to the river. B&B is really Paul's project, so he'll use the fantastic kitchen in the morning. At other hours, I just might do some of the cooking for the restaurant I'm taking over in Tenants Harbor. And yes, I'm still a Realtor." That's the latest update from Betty, one of those creative enthusiastic people who wears many hats comfortably.

The Koelles, restauranteurs for about 15 years, were recognized in the book *Road Food*. They have also been residents of Oregon, in Paul's forestry days. And Betty is the author of a cookbook.

**Restrictions:** Guests' pets may be allowed; inquire first. Nonsmokers preferred.

**Bed and bath:** Five rooms, two with a river view, share three full and two half baths. One double, one queen, one single, one room with two twin beds and two bunk beds, and one with a queen-sized bed and rollaways.
**Breakfast:** Continental with Paul's coffee cake, muffins, or popovers. Served in a big family-style dining room.
**Rates:** $23 single, $30 double, $42 for four people in a room.

## Medomak House

P.O. Box 663, Friendship Street, Waldoboro, ME 04572
**Phone:** 207/832-4971
**Location:** Within the village of Waldoboro, across from the Medomak River, up on a hill on three acres of land.
**Hosts:** Susan and Adrian Hooydonk
**Open:** June-October.

Ad was a chef with the Holland-American Line when he met Susan, a college student with World Campus Afloat in Bombay, India. Knowing B&B as they did from Holland, it was something they always wanted to do. They came to Maine in 1981, opened Medomak in 1982. Ad teaches at a vocational school in the winter and lobsters in the summer. The whole family appreciates Maine; a favorite place is a "lovely little beach off the beaten path."

Guests from Ohio were happy to tell me about the toys shared by the three Medomak "helpers." From New Jersey and Massachusetts came notes about a memorable stay.

The Hooydonks are continuing to restore and redecorate their Greek Revival home. It was built by one of Waldoboro's leading shipbuilders with two marble mantels, tin ceilings, and lovely door moldings. All guest rooms are furnished with antiques.

**In residence:** Alexis, eight; Jesse, six; Ineke, four. Sasha is a very 11-gentle-year-old dog, a collie/shepherd mixture.
**Restrictions:** Nonsmokers reside; smoking allowed in front parlor, dining room, or outdoors.
**Foreign language spoken:** Dutch.
**Bed and bath:** Private guest entrance to three second-floor rooms that share one new bathroom with shower. All have double beds. Cot and crib available.

**Breakfast:** Available 6-10. Cheeses, fresh fruits, homemade bread, muffins, and eggs from own hen house. Hosts serve in formal dining room.
**Plus:** Beverages in afternoon or evening. Wraparound porch with swings and chairs. Sometimes, option of dinner.
**Rates:** $40 double, $30 single. $10 for extra person in room.

---

## Old Broad Bay Inn and Gallery

P.O. Box 607, Main Street, Waldoboro, ME 04572
**Phone:** 207/832-6668
**Location:** In residential neighborhood, just off U.S. Route 1, in Waldoboro village. Short drive to ferries for Monhegan Island, Islesboro, and Vinal Haven. Close to Audubon wildlife sanctuary.
**Hosts:** Jim and Libby Hopkins
**Open:** Year round. Two-night minimum stay in August.

> "Although we encountered many wonderful people and had pleasant experiences during our drive through Maine and Nova Scotia, our stay at charming Old Broad Bay Inn was the most memorable. . . . Gracious and pleasant hosts . . . delicious breakfast (with fresh flowers on your plate!). . . . Bedroom that can only be described in absolutes. . . . Anyone would adore staying here."—Many guests.

"Rejuvenated!" That's how Libby describes her feeling of coming to Waldoboro "to start afresh." It reminds her of the days in North Carolina summer stock where she ran the art shows at the theater and met one Jim Hopkins, a designer/actor/puppeteer/singer. "It was such a great time in our lives. Almost three decades later, we feel like kids, reliving that dream period."

They were artists with Princeton University, the Educational Testing Service, and the *Wall Street Journal* before arriving in Waldoboro, "a sleepy little town" in 1984 when they settled into their turn-of-the-century house. Already they have seen many creative changes and are part of some of them. Their art workshops are "taking off" and, depending on timing, B&B guests are likely to meet the internationally known workshop leader(s). Jim directs local musical theater and Libby does substitute teaching. Although there are about 100 volumes in Libby's cookbook nook, there is room for at least one more. She is preparing her own, one that will, I trust, convey her passion and zest for cooking.

**In residence:** Mi Tu (Me Too), a people-loving male Shih Tzu.
**Restrictions:** Minimum age for children is 12. Sorry, no guests' pets allowed, but kennel is nearby. No smoking in bedrooms.
**Foreign language spoken:** Some French.
**Bed and bath:** Four rooms, shared baths. First-floor Victorian Room with double bed shares bath with hosts. On second floor, two shared baths for single room with wrought iron bed, a large corner room with lace-canopied four-poster double bed, and a room with two twin beds, shuttered windows.
**Breakfast:** 8-9:30. May be croissants, blueberry muffins, homemade breads; frittata, parmesan baked eggs, ham, bacon, sausage, pancakes, crepes, baked apples, fresh fruit ambrosia. Local farm-fresh eggs. Served on English china on starched white, hand-embroidered tablecloths, in dining room in summer; in large kitchen with a wood stove burning in winter.
**Plus:** Evening tea or sherry. Fresh flowers and fruit in rooms. Robes supplied, English soap, potpourri. TV, games, piano. By arrangement, Friday or Saturday candlelight dinners. Sun deck. Barn gallery and boutique featuring paintings by Maine artists, some antiques and crafts items. Picnic basket lunch arranged. Will meet bus in Waldoboro.
**Rates:** May-October, single $35, Canopy Room $55, Victorian Room $55, twin room $45. Cot $10. Other months, 20 percent off. VISA and MasterCard accepted.

## Bed & Breakfast Down East Host #232

Walpole, ME
**Location:** High on a ridge surrounded by beautiful grounds with flowering shrubs and an orchard of 1200 apple, pear, plum, and cherry trees. Ten miles from Pemaquid Point. A fifteen-minute walk to a golf course. Archeological dig at early settlement nearby.
**Reservations:** Available April 1-November 1 through Bed & Breakfast Down East, page 5. Two-day minumum stay.

Extraordinary. The Federal-style house, built in the late 1700s in Warren, Maine, was moved the twenty miles, piece by piece, to this prepared site in 1960. It took 2½ years to reconstruct with "original" features and great attention to detail—plastered walls, Indian shutters, bullseye glass, seven (some tiled) fireplaces, wide pine floors, the beamed Keeping Room, and latches and hinges too.

"We bought this big house two years ago and wanted to share it! The experience has been wonderfully refreshing; B&B people are ready to enjoy everything. Last week we had guests who were celebrating their anniversary. After we took them to dinner in our 1957 Bentley, we stopped at Pemaquid Point. There, with ice cold champagne and silver wine goblets, they watched the moon rise. Memorable."

The enthusiastic hosts "love everything"—animals, gardening, hunting, decorating, woodworking boating, snowmobiling, old cars, traveling, and B&B. They are Maine natives with a grown family. The host is retired from Civil Service. The hostess is a semi-retired real estate broker.

**In residence:** A host who smokes, but only outdoors. Dubie is a mongrel of dubious origin, "but the friendliest, most intelligent and mannered dog ever."
**Restrictions:** Children should be at least 12. No guests' pets. No smoking indoors.
**Bed and bath:** Two second-floor rooms, each with a queen-sized bed, share a bath. One room with stenciled walls and working fireplace overlooks gardens and stone walls. The other room has colonial decor, overlooks a view that goes on forever. Cot available.
**Breakfast:** 8-9. Breads and muffins are the house specialty. Homemade granola, fruit and vegetables from the garden (in season). Served at the round mahogany table in the dining room with Hepplewhite-style furniture or outdoors on the terrace. Can last up to two hours.
**Plus:** Late-afternoon or evening beverages. Tour of the house and farm. Pine paneled barn that was once a restaurant has wall-to-wall windows, overlooks the orchard, and has television, comfortable chairs, huge deck with western view. Fresh flowers in rooms. Thick towels. B&B seminars conducted for ten people at a time.
**Rates:** $55 double occupancy. $10 extra for the cot.

## Maine Back Roads Bed & Breakfast

Tatnic Road, Wells
Mailing address: RD 1, Box 530A, South Berwick, ME 03908
**Phone:** 207/676-9460

**Location:** Rural. Five miles inland from coastal Route 1 and six miles from beaches. Set on 100 acres of woods and a few fields. Within half hour of Kennebunkport, Ogunquit, and York.
**Hosts:** Joseph Hardy and Alice Schleiderer
**Open:** Year round. Reservations required.

"We are much like the farm family that takes in a traveler for a night's lodging. There's nothing commercial about our B&B." Indeed, in addition to hospitality, they offer a special experience that has been discovered by artists, dowsers, shoppers, skiers, tourists.

Over a five-year period Alice and Joseph designed and built their post-and-beam solar house with four levels, following the natural contours of the south-facing slope and using wood from their own land. It is cool in the summer and warm in the winter, but they do have four wood stoves, including an antique cookstove in the kitchen. The house has wonderful natural light, wood floors and ceilings and black granite masonry walls in dining and living rooms.

This B&B is a great source of information about southern Maine. For a while, Joseph, an educator and native Mainer, had his own historical tour business that explored rural Maine that was and is—everything from shipbuilding sites to marshes and glacial boulders. Now he is an environmental consultant. Alice, originally from California, has a counseling practice.

**In residence:** Daughter Hesper Dawn, age seven, "who loves the company of other children." The "adult's cat" is named "Ashes or Her Royal Fatness." Feathers, "a child's cat," has a good disposition. Max, a husky-type dog, is calm and friendly.
**Restrictions:** Guests' pets are sometimes allowed. No smoking.
**Foreign language spoken:** "Stumbling" French.
**Bed and bath:** A double bed and a twin bed in a very private large second-floor room lined with windows, surrounded by trees. Outdoor entrance from the deck below. Plus fold-out double bed in the living room. Full bath shared with hosts. Crib available.
**Breakfast:** 7-9. Time set the night before to accommodate guests' schedule. Fresh fruit, freshly ground coffee, black or herbal tea, eggs or pancakes with real maple syrup and homemade preserves, cereals including Joseph's homemade granola. Freshly made muffins, biscuits, or cinnamon rolls. All without additives.
**Plus:** Late-afternoon or evening tea. Fresh flowers. Babysitting possibilities. Limited kitchen privileges can be arranged. Deck adjoining guest room. Trails for hiking and cross-country skiing.
**Rates:** $30 single, $40 double. Extra adult $15. Child $10.

## Tatnic B&B

Tatnic Road, Wells
Mailing address: Box 518A, South Berwick, ME 03908
**Phone:** 207/676-2209
**Location:** Half in Wells and half in South Berwick. In a secluded and very quiet spot at the end of a five-mile uphill road off of Route 1. Six miles from Ogunquit's beaches, 15 miles to Kennebunkport and to Dover and Durham in New Hampshire.
**Hosts:** Tin and Jane Smith
**Open:** Year round.

"We built our passive-solar modified shed-roof styled home with the help of all our friends in 1978-1980. It heats with about 3½ cords of wood in the winter. There is no backup heat. Insulation and cross-ventilation keep it cool 'like a cave' in summer. Hot water is solar in summer, heated by wood stove in winter. Even *Better Homes and Gardens* has been here. It's a great example of what you can do yourself with a little forethought and a tight belt."

It's also a great example of a warm inviting environment enhanced by two people who haven't changed their outlook since completing their ambitious project. Tin, in addition to being a talented builder-by-doing, sells greenhouse supplies by mail, is a director of Maine Organic Farmers and Gardeners, and as a marine biologist is working on the establishment of the Laudholm Farm National Estuarine Sanctuary in Wells. Jane loves teaching, creating, and quiltmaking. Since being featured in *Family Circle* magazine for her "Quilt-In-One-Day" presentations, ingenious patterns, and her Teachers' (Quilt) Work Kit, she travels nationwide to give workshops. Still, B&B is an important part of the Smiths' lives. "Guests from all over the world give us energy, ideas, and inspirations."

As in an expanded New England farmhouse, Marie-Louise Smith's solar addition was built in 1986. Tin's mother retired from Marblehead, Massachusetts to join in this joyful lifestyle.

**In residence:** Poppi, a friendly black dog who barks at everyone walking across the short footbridge to the front door. ("Even she's a vegetarian!")
**Restrictions:** Smoking permitted outside.

**Bed and bath:** Two "treetop" bedrooms reached via spiral staircase from two-storied living room. One shared first-floor bath. One large bedroom/study with extra-long double bed and space for two or three cots. Two twin beds in other room. Handmade quilts on beds.
**Breakfast:** Generally at 9. Fresh-baked coffee cakes, quick breads, or muffins. Fresh fruit from the organic garden in season, corn pancakes made with freshly ground flours and served with locally produced maple syrup, homemade granola or fresh eggs. Honey from Tatnic's beehives. Served in dining area overlooking, the beautiful gardens (and hummingbirds, too, when we were last there).
**Plus:** Tree swing. Outdoor furniture (and maybe mosquitoes too). Ideas for a floor plan that has many well-designed built-ins; step-by-step photo album. Directions to Balancing Rock, a two-mile walk into the woods. Kitchen facilities for dinner preparations. Sometimes dinner and/or an evening swim at Ell Pond, seven miles away. Help welcomed in the garden. Quilt-making session (nominal fee) by advance arrangement.
**Rates:** $25 single, $40 double. $10 for each added day bed. Children's special—$55 for one family in one room. MasterCard and VISA accepted.

---

## The Sunset House

---

Route 186, West Gouldsboro
Mailing address: HCR # 60, Box 62, Gouldsboro, ME 04607
**Phone:** 207/963-7156
**Location:** Half-mile from U.S. Route 1, in a quiet seacoast village with sunset views over salt water and sunrise over fresh water. One and one-half hours from Campobello, 45 minutes northeast of Bar Harbor, 10 minutes from Schoodic Point.
**Hosts:** Dan and Ruth Harper
**Open:** Year round. Reservations strongly recommended in summer. Call ahead during the winter, as hosts may be on a brief vacation!

This has always been a family-oriented home ever since it was built in 1898 by a local entrepreneur who had six children. Not until 1976 did it change hands. Then it was purchased by another large family that restored, redecorated, and did B&B when their children grew and left. Ruth and Dan bought it in 1984.

Their own family is, as they say, rather unique. Dan, recently retired, enjoys balancing innkeeping with his young second family. His two grown sons, their wives, and a teenage grandson live in California. He and Ruth, mother, wife and B&B keeper, met 11 years ago at the Hurricane Island Outward Bound School of Maine, were married, moved to California, had two children, then moved back east to start a B&B. Both are widely traveled with many life experiences including prospecting for gold with a mule and rural ambulance attending. "In one morning a breakfast conversation might cover subjects from World War II to modern child rearing. It's a wonderful experience for everyone."

**In residence:** Anastasia, six, and Camden, four.
**Restrictions:** Pets discouraged. Smoking limited to front porch in summer, sitting room in winter.
**Bed and bath:** Seven rooms. Four (three with water view) on second floor share a full bath that has house's best view from the tub. Various bed sizes from twins to queen. Three (two with water view) on third floor share another full bath. Cots and portacribs available.
**Breakfast:** Usually 7:30-9. Fruit in season, eggs, some kind of meat, homemade baked goods such as blueberry muffins, jams, coffee, tea, hot chocolate with real cream. Served in double parlor turned into a dining area, or on front porch in summer.
**Plus:** Afternoon beverages. Shared family living room in summer. Porch. One bedroom turned into guests' sitting area in winter. Fenced yard with play set for smaller children. Pond for swimming and boating (bring your own), skating in winter. Summer picnic basket dinners ($10). Kitchen privileges. Use of laundry ($3/load).
**Rates:** July and August—$40-$45 on second floor, $35-$40 on third. $10 less rest of year. Children under 12 free. $5 additional adult. Single is $5 less per room. MasterCard and VISA accepted.

## The Stacked Arms

RFD 2, Box 146, Birch Point Road, Wiscasset, ME 04578
**Phone:** 207/882-5436
**Location:** On the top of a hill in a quiet neighborhood, one mile from Wiscasset Village. Half hour northeast of Freeport.
**Hosts:** Dee and Karen Maguire; Allie Green, Dee's mother—84 years old.
**Open:** Year round, except January.

Twenty moves in about as many years! The military family lived all over this country and in Central and South America. Major Maguire didn't live to see the long-held idea of settling down after retirement as B&B hosts, but the family has followed through.

Originally their home was a saltbox. Previous owners added to it, and the Maguires added to that. Dee drew the plans. Every room is different. The Brass Room seems to be the most talked about. Another room is very modern. Still another has beds made by a son. It's a homey, comfortable place with collections of crystal, wood carvings, and figurines from various parts of the world.

Even with all this moving, in just a few moments of listening to Dee you can still tell that she was brought up in Georgia. Karen is her adult daughter and major assistant.

**In residence:** Mimi, an apricot miniature poodle.
**Restrictions:** Minimum age for children is five. No smoking in bedrooms; social drinking restricted to bedrooms.
**Foreign languages spoken:** Spanish and some French.
**Bed and bath:** Five rooms. One with twin beds. Four with queen-sized beds and views of mountains or woods. Two shared guest baths. Color-coordinated linens. Cot available.
**Breakfast:** 7-9. Usually fresh fruits or melon, with omelets, poached eggs, sausages, bacon, or blueberry pancakes, home-baked cinnamon loaves, southern biscuits, beverages, homemade jams and jellies. Served in dining room at large family table and several small tables.
**Plus:** Late-afternoon beverages. Pedal boat and canoe available (no extra charge) for use on the one-acre pond. Skating on pond in winter; bring your own skates. Picnic tables, sun deck with table, benches, and chairs. Paths through wooded areas with wildflowers and berries. Ceiling fans in two bedrooms. Fresh flowers in summer; dried arrangements in winter. Picnic lunch by prior arrangement. Will meet at Portland airport and Wiscasset bus.
**Rates:** May-November $55 for two. December-April $45 for two, shared bath; private bath (available in off-season) $55. $15 each extra person. MasterCard and VISA accepted.

## The Wild Rose of York B&B

78 Long Sands Road, York, ME 03909
**Phone:** 207-363-2532
**Location:** One mile from the ocean. On a hill in a quiet area near the center of the historic village. Just down the road from a game preserve with trails for hiking or cross-country skiing. Fifteen minutes from Portsmouth, New Hampshire.
**Hosts:** Fran and Frank Sullivan
**Open:** Year round, except for some times in the winter. Reservations suggested. Two-day minimum stay on holiday weekends.

Captain Rufus Donnell built this columned colonial mansion for his bride in 1814. Fran and Frank thought for years about opening a B&B. Authors of *Budget Dining and Lodging in New England*, they bought this house "for the fun of meeting new people, making them comfortable, and helping them to appreciate an area."

They moved in 1985 from the nearby north shore of Massachusetts, so Fran is still a nurse/counselor on call at the Portsmouth Hospital. In addition, she is an artist and quilter, offers summer art workshops with guest instructors, and has plans to open an art gallery. Frank, a biology professor at Salem State College in Massachusetts, conducts tide pool walks for interested guests. Daughter Julie is a student of interior design.

The mile-long cliff walk in York is a Sullivan summer favorite. Winter brings cross-country skiing and hot soup by the fire.

**In residence:** Daughter Julie, age 19, is home during college vacations. Three outdoor cats, Bojingle, Aurora, and Gregory.
**Restrictions:** Children should be "well behaved." No guests' pets, please.
**Foreign languages spoken:** French and some German understood.
**Bed and bath:** Four rooms. Two with private baths: one has double four-poster and fireplace; the other, a double bed and enclosed sun porch with single bed and room for a cot. One room with a double bed and one with queen-sized share a bath. All rooms have antique beds, quilts, and access to balcony. Cot and crib available.
**Breakfast:** 7-9:30. Juice, fruit-filled crepes, apple nut waffles, peach pancakes, Belgian waffles, a Dutch puff (popover with apples). Fresh fruit, coffee or tea. Served on a glass-top table in bottle-green and white dining room fashioned after a tavern, or on large front porch.

**Plus:** Tea or soda at 4 on porch in summer. Evening sherry. Two large common rooms, fireplaced living room. Piano (spontaneous concerts and sing-alongs encouraged). Library/TV/game room. Window fans. Wraparound porch, partially screened. Hibachis. Umbrella tables. Huge yard with swing, lawn darts, badminton. Sleds. Will meet airport limo at Portsmouth Circle or Portsmouth bus at Route 95.
**Rates:** June 15-October 15, $35 single. Double $44 with shared bath, $48 with private bath. October 15-June 15 $30, $38 $42. $10 extra person in a room. Extra adult on sun porch $20, child $10; under age five, free. Special college student rates.

## Lilac Inn

P.O. Box 1325, Ridge Road, York Beach, ME 03910
**Phone:** 207/363-3930
**Location:** Three-minute walk to Short Sands Beach. Ten-minute drive to Ogunquit, 15 to Portsmouth, 25 to Kennebunkport, an hour to Boston.
**Hosts:** Sue and Jeff Karns
**Open:** May-December. Full weekend stay required on holiday weekends.

"The Lilac Inn is an informal place with a growing boy, cats, dog, touchable antiques, and a warm dose of hospitality. Our guests come to us for the family environment, the nearby beach, and the amusement park that includes a zoo and rides."

The inn is really two houses together with separate entrances. The 1890 Victorian has a center staircase, gingerbread, and Laura Ashley decor. The 1800s Cape has wide floor boards, early door latches, and a staircase made to accommodate the smaller feet of 19th-century residents.

It was on a weekend in coastal Maine, away from their Nantucket Christmas Shop, when the idea of innkeeping came to Sue and Jeff. What followed was a three-year search with lots of career and location changes, including a time in Florida. In 1984 they settled here. Sue is a registered nurse. Jeff is a commercial airline regional manager.

**In residence:** Son Robert, 11. Ted, their cocker spaniel, and two cats, calico Edith and marmalade Rusty.

**Restrictions:** Sorry, no guests' pets.
**Bed and bath:** Five rooms in summer, three with private baths. Three rooms available off-season. The Cape has a first-floor room with a queen-sized and a double bed, private bath. Second-floor room has two double beds and private bath. The Victorian has one room with double bed and private bath. One with a double bed and another with twin beds share a bath. Cots and crib available.
**Breakfast:** 7:30-9:30. Juice, fruit, and entree that could be quiche, crepes, or bourbon French toast. Cocker Ted makes sure that he doesn't miss a morning meal; he has his reserved spot on the dining room rug.
**Plus:** Beverages in afternoon; English tea in winter. Lots of books and magazines. Porch. Tour of the house. Kitchen privileges. Use of picnic table and grill.
**Rates:** July 1-Labor Day $30-$43 single. $55 double with private bath. $38-$44 double with semiprivate bath. $5 per additional person. Off-season $25 single. $45 double with private bath, $30-$35 semiprivate. VISA and MasterCard accepted.

## Bed & Breakfast Down East Host #228

York Harbor, ME
**Location:** Overlooking harbor. A picturesque quiet neighborhood that is a five-minute walk—along winding shore path—to beach. Five miles from Route 95, off Route 1A. Close to shopping outlets, summer theater, antique shops, art galleries.
**Reservations:** Available June through September through Bed & Breakfast Down East, page 5.

All guests rave about the relaxing, warm atmosphere in a wonderful location. The hosts describe their big old Victorian as "homey and simply decorated with some new and many old furnishings passed down to us from our families." Sure, there's plenty to do just minutes away, but if you want to find your own space, the hostess will share directions to some of her niches in the rocks where she sometimes "hides" just to listen to the sea and birds.

The 1883 house, previously owned by the "Stanley Steamer family," was a summer cottage until 15 years ago, when the hosts made it their year-round home. "We renovated from top to bottom, inside and out—and we're still working at it."

The host is a manager at a computer company. The hostess is very involved in community activities, is a hospice volunteer, and finds time for gardening, needlepoint, and photography.

**In residence:** A 15-year-old golden retriever, "a quiet, friendly old gentleman."
**Restrictions:** Adults preferred. Sorry, no guests' pets.
**Bed and bath:** Two second-floor rooms, each with a double bed and private bath. One room has a sitting area facing the ocean.
**Breakfast:** 8-10. Fresh fruit, choice of eggs, sausage, bacon or ham, French toast, pancakes. Homemade breads and jams, beverages. Juice and homemade muffins usually available. A leisurely meal served in the dining room.
**Plus:** Porch. Garden.
**Rates:** $30 single, $40 double.

*Can't find the community you are going to? Check with a reservation service described at the beginning of this chapter. Through the service, you may be placed (matched) with a welcoming B&B that is near your destination.*

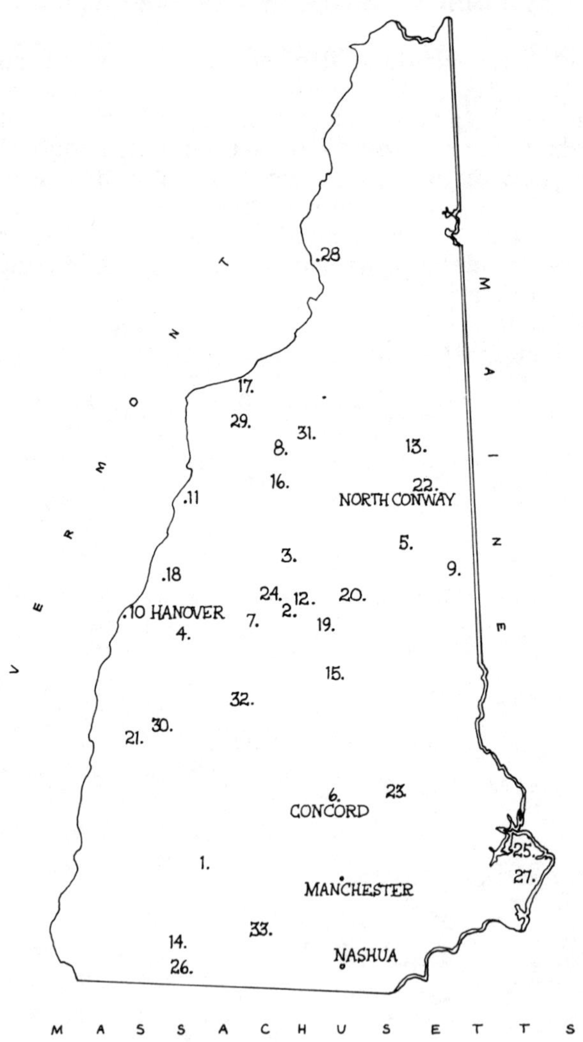


*The numbers on this map indicate the locations of B&Bs described in detail in this chapter.*

## NEW HAMPSHIRE

**Contents**



**KEY**

Recipes shared, often for house specialties.

Inquiries welcomed about restoration and/or decorating. Symbol indicates that host is willing to share experiences with guests. Tips range from a before-and-after album to rebuilding advice, from furniture refinishing to curtain making. Expertise of hosts ranges from learn-by-doing to professional.

How-To B&B workshop, seminar or apprentice program offered.

# New Hampshire Reservation Services

## New Hampshire Bed & Breakfast

RFD #3, Box 53, Laconia, NH 03246
**Phone:** 603/279-8348, Monday-Friday 10-5.

**Listings:** 60. Located throughout the state in and around cities and small towns. Included are restored colonials, farms, lakefront and mountain view homes. Mostly hosted private residences and a few small inns. Directory ($1).

Martha Dorais has been offering "a little of everything" for five years. Most homes offer a full breakfast. Some offer cross-country skiing, tennis courts, and swimming pools on the premises. "Reservations made efficiently with a dash of humor. Our motto is 'The Friendly Way To Travel.' "

**Reservations:** Two-day minimum stay required on holiday weekends. Also available through travel agents. Short-term (one month plus) hosted housing available.
**Rates:** $25-$50 single, $35-$65 double. Family and weekly rates available. Thirty percent and credit card number required as deposit. If cancellation received seven days prior to arrival, full refund, less a $10 service charge, is made. Credit cards accepted only to guarantee reservations.

## Christian Hospitality

This service has hosts in Keene, Jefferson, Northwood, Tilton, and Westwood. Please see page 287.

## Pineapple Hospitality

This service has hosts in Exeter, Franklin, East Hebron, Jefferson, Meredith, Milton Mills, Northwood, North Conway, and Strafford. Please see page 214.

# New Hampshire B&Bs

## The Steele Homestead Inn

R.R. #1, Box 78, Antrim, NH 03440
**Phone:** 603/588-6772
**Location:** On a quiet country road in Monadnock region. Twenty-two miles west of Concord and east of Keene. Surrounded by lawns and gardens, bordered by woods and a river. Near Crotched Mountain, Pat's Peak, Temple ski areas. Minutes to lake swimming.
**Hosts:** Barbara and Carl Beehner
**Open:** Year round except for two weeks in May and November. Two-night minimum on holiday weekends, and local colleges' open house and graduation weekends.

From Florida: "The minute I stepped inside, I promptly fell in love with the warmth of the inn. It is spotless and filled with authentic and unusual early American antiques."

The Beehners' antiques were collected over a 30-year period and include a grandfather's clock, Bennington pottery, molds, glass, tools, and pulleys. They were brought from California in 1983 when Barbara and Carl left their positions as office manager and marketing director to restore the 1810 Federal house with the help of local craftspeople. The front hall duplication of Moses Eaton stenciling really does look "old."

**Restrictions:** Sorry, no pets. Smoking downstairs only. Prefer no eating in bedrooms. Maximum of three people in one room.

**Bed and bath:** Four second-floor rooms with sitting areas. Of the two with private full baths, one has king-sized, the other a queen-sized bed; both have working fireplaces. The Brass Room with a double and a twin bed shares a full bath with The Pine Room, which has two twin beds. Cot and crib available.
**Breakfast:** 8-9. A brunch. Various egg or eggless dishes, bacon, sausage, ham, Canadian bacon. Juice, fresh fruit in season, homemade sweet rolls, coffee cakes, breads, and biscuits. Special diets accommodated. Served in cheerful fireplaced dining room at table set with sterling and china.
**Plus:** Early evening beverages with hors d'oeuvres. Parlor with games, books, puzzles. Croquet. Shuffleboard court. Turned-down beds. Chocolate depicting season on pillow. Bedroom fans. Beach towels. Directions to a preserved mill town and barn herb shop. Will pick up guests at private Hawthorne airport landing.
**Rates:** $58 single, $65 double, private bath. $45 single, $50 double, shared bath. Extended stay discounts. $15 crib. $10 cot. MasterCard and VISA accepted.

From Massachusetts: "The kitchen belongs in some decorating book. . . . Breakfasts are not only delicious but inventive. . . . From the time we arrived until we left we had pure pleasure (even with our kids)."

## Cheney House

Box 683, 40 Highland Street, Ashland, NH 03217
**Phone:** 603/968-7968
**Location:** On a lovely street, across from a pasture and stone wall. Within walking distance of village center and tennis. One mile from town beach on Squam Lake. Twenty minutes from White Mountains and Lake Winnipesaukee.
**Hosts:** Michael and Daryl Mooney
**Open:** May through October. Two-day minimum July Fourth and Columbus Day weekends.

There are good reasons for the professional style that makes the gracious hosting here look so easy. Mike has been in hotel management for 15 years; and before moving into this home the Mooneys together managed a Dartmouth College conference center for 4 years, with Daryl being chef. Before that, Daryl was a home-economics teacher and home decorator.

Since 1976 the Mooneys have worked on the gardens, restored the hardwood floors, and tastefully decorated the 1895 brick Victorian with country furniture and crafts.

An acquaintance who enjoys cycling, swimming, sightseeing, and B&Bs rates the Cheney House at the top: "It's a beautifully restored place with a great family. The rooms are big and really nice. The breakfast is delicious and endless."

**In residence:** "Our children are at a wonderful age. Cameron is seven. Shannon is four."
**Restrictions:** Nonsmokers preferred. No pets please.
**Bed and bath:** Three second-floor rooms, each with a double bed, share one full bath.
**Breakfast:** 7:30-8:30. Menu could be fresh fruit, peach pancakes, and cinnamon rolls or juice with oven popovers stuffed with eggs. "Our own eggs, creamery butter and (usually) local syrup." Served formally in the unique and beautiful front hall, which has wainscoting, stained glass, and fireplace.
**Plus:** If you'd like, gather your own breakfast eggs from the flock of hens. Fresh flowers in rooms. A Cheney House suggestion sheet for a day trip around Lake Winnipesaukee.
**Rates:** $38 single, $42 double.

## Mountain Fare Inn

Box 553, Mad River Road, Campton, NH 03223
**Phone:** 603/726-4283
**Location:** In a small White Mountain village surrounded by a six-acre field which is all white in winter and full of gardens in summer. Ten miles from Waterville Valley ski area, 20 north of Laconia/Lake Winnipesaukee area, 20 south of Franconia Notch.
**Hosts:** Susan and Nicholas Preston
**Open:** Year round. Two-night minimum stay on weekends during the fall and winter. Serious skiers and teams particularly welcome in winter.

Warning. The energy in this multigabled house is contagious. There's a love of the outdoors and the active life, and of people. And good wholesome food. Even quiet nights by the fire. Suzi tells the Prestons' story:

"Nick and I are ski professionals. Nick has directed Waterville's freestyle ski program (for teenagers) since 1980. I coach on weekends. Several of our skiers compete on an international level. A few years ago when we were boarders in this former inn, it was for sale. We found an old brochure that made us realize what potential it had. So, after much renovation (ongoing), here we are—out on the mountain before eight in winter, but with guests for mornings in other seasons. I love breakfast! And we love this simple and lovely house decorated with a mixture of family heirlooms, country furniture, printed fabrics, and a special collection of wildlife art prints. All kinds of truly great people pass through here."

**In residence:** Wesley, age 6½, and Timothy, age 3. Dawa and Rascal are outdoor cats who like to sneak in whenever the door opens in winter.
**Restrictions:** Guests' pets (with advance notice) may be allowed in spring or summer. No smoking or ski boots indoors.
**Foreign language spoken:** A little French ("and lots of ski and garden dialect").
**Bed and bath:** Nine rooms of various sizes on two floors. Six with private baths. All sorts of combinations possible with twin, double, and bunk beds. Extra beds and cribs available.
**Breakfast:** 7:30-9. (Starts at 7 in winter.) After 9, coffee and muffins. Orange juice, a cereal bar, fruit, and yogurt or cottage cheese. Blueberry pancakes, eggs and muffins, or French toast. Hot beverages. Herbs and flowers from garden. Served in dining room with its picture windows, antique snowshoes and skis, and piano.
**Plus:** Snacks and beverages in late afternoon and evening. Theme weekends, e.g. music, women, cycling, reunions. Dinner is an option winter weekends and school vacation periods ($10-$13 per adult). Picnics packed too. Guest refrigerator. Back deck with mountain views. Ski lockers and tuning benches. Cross-country in the field. In summer, volleyball, croquet, and soccer. Bedroom window fans. With advance notice, babysitting can be arranged.
**Rates:** Per Person. $27 single, $24 double, $20 triple, $18 quad with private bath. Shared bath $2 less per person. Fifteen percent less nonholiday midweek (except September 15-October 15). $10 per child 6-12 sharing parents' room, $5 if 1-5. No charge for infants. Senior citizens $4 less except foliage and ski season weekends.

## The "Inn" on Canaan Street

RD #1, Box 92, Canaan Street, Canaan, NH 03741
**Phone:** 603/523-7310
**Location:** At the foot of Mount Cardigan on 14 acres. Five minutes off Route 4, way uphill to historic district (1788) on Canaan Street Lake. Twenty-five minutes from Dartmouth College.
**Hosts:** Lee and Louise Kremzner
**Open:** Year round. Reservations required. Two-night minimum stay on holiday weekends.

Guests are always asking, "How did you ever find this lovely place?" It's located on a street that is in the Federal Register. Decorated for comfort and charm, it's the home of a Columbia professor emeritus and his wife, a former nutritionist/consumer publicist. The enthusiastic couple restored the "Federal but country style house" four years ago, following a search for a place in an area they love. Now they are developing an herb garden, thinking of a cookbook, and finding time to fish, canoe, hike and swim.

"Pampered guests" come for relaxation, Dartmouth's Hopkins Center performances, food (Louise owns over 400 cookbooks), the views—and all the lake has to offer.

**Restrictions:** Children should be at least seven. Sorry, no guests' pets. Smoking in designated areas.
**Foreign languages spoken:** German and a little French.
**Bed and bath:** Five second-floor rooms, two with private baths. Three with twin beds, two with a double. Three rooms share one huge elegant bathroom. Cot available.
**Breakfast:** 8-9:30. Juice, fruit in season, breads for toasting, homemade sweet breads, muffins or popovers, jams and jellies. Blueberry pancakes, eggs and bacon country style, or omelets. Served in Garden Room that opens onto porch.
**Plus:** Sherry. Fruit in rooms. Swimming, canoeing (no charge for canoe), and cross-country skiing right here. Theme weekends (antiques, auction, gardening, cooking). Dinner ($12.50-$16) and picnic baskets by reservation only. Library, games, movies, ping-pong, croquet, badminton.

**Rates:** $55 single. $58 double with shared bath, $65 with private bath. $125 two bedrooms as a suite with private bath. $15 for a third person in a room. Lower rates for two-night or extended stays.

> A guest wrote: "We arrived during a pounding blizzard and at once were made to feel like Charles and Diana!"

## New Hampshire Bed & Breakfast Host #107

Chocorua Village, NH
**Location:** On a hilltop, set on 20 acres with spectacular views of Ossipee Lake and mountains. Fifteen miles south of North Conway, factory outlets, and the oldest summer stock theater in New Hampshire. Near lake for swimming, canoeing, auctions.
**Reservations:** Available May-October through New Hampshire Bed & Breakfast, page 85.

One of the first guests at this B&B was so pleased with her visit that she decided a weekend here would be the perfect Christmas gift for her daughter and son-in-law. Since then many guests have not only returned but brought their friends.

Because of their marvelous experiences with homestays abroad, the host couple decided to host here in the gracious Georgian colonial they purchased seven years ago. They were familiar with the area from frequent visits to their New Hampshire vacation home. The host is an engineer. He and his wife enjoy restoring antiques, gardening, and traveling.

**In residence:** Their youngest daughter when home from college and any one of their older children, who visit often.
**Restrictions:** Children should be at least eight. No guests' pets. Smoking not permitted in bedrooms.
**Bed and bath:** Three second-floor rooms share two full guest baths. One room with double bed and fireplace. One with two antique four-poster twin beds and an adjoining one with a single bed. All rooms stenciled by hostess and one of her daughters.
**Breakfast:** 7:30-9:30. Juice or fruit cup, homemade muffins with bacon and eggs, or pancakes or French toast with sausage. Served by hostess in a countrylike breakfast room or in fireplaced dining room with a view of lake and mountains.

**Plus:** Plenty of privacy. Large screened porch. Large fireplaced living room with piano, television, many books and games. Clay tennis court, badminton, croquet, horseshoes. Walking trails through the woods on the property. Hot mulled cider or other beverage in late afternoon or evening.
**Rates:** $40 single, $50 double. Cot $10.

## The Farmhouse—Bed & Breakfast

P.O. Box 14, Page Hill Road, Chocorua Village, NH 03817
**Phone:** 603/323-8707
**Location:** Fifteen minutes south of Conway, N.H., just west of Routes 16 and 113. Trailways bus from Boston stops in the village. Short walk to farm.
**Hosts:** John and Kathie Dyrenforth
**Open:** Year round.

"When the former owner sent six sons to World War II, she found she had lots of time and space for guests. Thirty years later we found her sign in the woodshed, put it up, and it worked! We have now had guests for eight exhilarating years."

Many of those guests tell Kathie (a former teacher) and John (who still teaches) that they feel that they are at grandmother's house—a big old beautiful homestead among giant maples in a quiet village. The tasteful "some old-fashioned, some antique" furnishings belie the house's origin. Around 1860 the original part of the farmhouse was moved to this site by a young man for his bride. It had been a blacksmith shop on a nearby riverbank before, and as Kathie says, "this young bride worked her magic."

Guests come for the natural scenic beauty of the lakes and White Mountains, auctions, shopping, and antiquing. Right here there's hiking or cross-country skiing on seven acres with pasture, woodlands, and brooks. March is the time for seeing the small sugarhouse in operation—and leaving with the gifts of a cookbook and your very own sample of maple syrup.

**In residence:** David, age nine, an experienced host. Tom at age three "thinks all guests come to see him."
**Restrictions:** Well-behaved children are welcome. Pets are not encouraged.

**Bed and bath:** Four second-floor corner rooms share two baths. Three rooms have double beds, one with twin beds. Children may stay in their own sleeping bags in parents' room. One cot available.
**Breakfast:** Available 8-9, but flexible. Very full. Fresh fruits. Own products—eggs with bacon, ham, or sausage. Homemade muffins, breads, pancakes with hosts' own maple syrup. Served in formal dining room around the large antique mahogany table.
**Plus:** Late afternoon or evening tea and cookies, maybe home-brewed cider. Wood stove. Plant-filled screened porch. Use of refrigerator. Swings and sandbox. Babysitting.
**Rates:** $35 single, $45-$50 double. $7.50 for child in own sleeping bag. $10 child in cot. Seventh night free.

## Wyman Farm

R.R. #13, Box 163, Concord, NH 03301
**Phone:** 603/783-4467
**Location:** In Loudon, 15 minutes from Concord center in a rural setting high on a hill. Ten minutes from Shaker Village in Canterbury, an hour from ocean or mountains.
**Hosts:** Judith and Lyford Merrow
**Open:** Year round. Reservations, please.

The hilltop view, peace and quiet, and many varieties of birds are long remembered. In addition there is oral history that starts this way, "The land was bought in English pounds by my great-great-great grandfather in 1782. His son, my great-great grandfather, came here with his bride in 1824." The hostess entered the picture in 1963 when she came for the summer. "And I'm still here, still restoring. I feel I'm taking care of an elderly relative. I love it dearly." The picture-postcard property has provided the inspiration for gardening pursuits and birding. Lyford is in real estate and is an officer in the Volunteer Fire Department.

While working at the New Hampshire Historical Society Judith discovered that tourists were looking for personalized accommodations. She is now the third generation to host in the "continuous architecture" farmhouse, a great place to unwind.

**In residence:** A son, during his college vacations. Two dogs and Charley-the-Cat.

**Restrictions:** Nonsmokers preferred. Well-behaved children are welcome.
**Bed and bath:** Three rooms, each with private entrance and sitting area. One with twin beds, bath with shower. One with double bed, nonworking fireplace, bath with shower. The third room has a canopied double bed, large full bath with antique copper tub, fireplaced parlor.
**Breakfast:** Available from 6:30 on. Full. Could be French toast or golden delight pancakes served with local maple syrup. Oatmeal or other homemade bread.
**Plus:** Color TV in each guest room. Beverages, crackers, fruit, cookies in late afternoon or evening. Screened porch, badminton, croquet. Fields and woodlands for walking and birding. Swimming pond two miles down the road.
**Rates:** $30 single, $40-$45 double.

From Massachusetts: "In all my travels I can say without reservation, Wyman Farm surpasses any other B&B here in the States or overseas—in every respect."

---

## Six Chimneys

SR Box 114, Route 3A, East Hebron, NH 03232
**Phone:** 603/744-2029
**Location:** Near a small town between Bristol and Plymouth. Across the road from (hidden) Newfound Lake; Mount Cardigan on the horizon. Minutes from Tenney Mountain.
**Hosts:** Peter and Lee Fortescue
**Open:** Year round. Two-day minimum stay on holiday and special camp weekends.

"Records of the old stage coach stop show they sold a glass of rum for ten cents. And a bed here could be rented for the same price. With all the changes this 1791 house has seen, we really feel good when someone from New Mexico leaves with the comment that they (at last) have seen the New England they were looking for. Our changes include more baths, a fireplace, and a wood stove. Our furnishings reflect the places we have lived in all over the world."

The Fortescues came here in 1971. Peter is a retired air force colonel who now clerks in the post office. Lee, a former teacher, has terrific off-the-beaten-path day trip suggestions. Their summer visitors are offered the treat of a private sandy beach and picnic facilities, just a mile away.

**In residence:** Abigale, a friendly border collie-spaniel allowed only in the kitchen and den.
**Restrictions:** Sorry, no children under six. No guests' pets. Smoking allowed in the den.
**Bed and bath:** Six second-floor rooms; some are large, some cozy with sloped ceilings. Three with double beds; three with twin beds. Three semiprivate baths. Cot available.
**Breakfast:** 7-9. Fruit, orange juice, eggs and/or French toast, bacon and sausage, homemade cranberry or raspberry muffins and jams, English muffins, local maple syrup. Served in the dining room set with silver and china.
**Plus:** Four common rooms. Ice and glasses provided. Turned-down beds. Dinner ($10-$15 each) on winter weekends by special arrangement. Cards, puzzles, dominos. Croquet, badminton, horseshoes.
**Rates:** $30 single, $35-$38 double. $10 for an extra person.

From New Jersey: "A sheer delight. It's like being a guest in a lovely home. Beautiful antiques and fine food."

## The Bungay Jar

Route 116, Easton
Mailing address: P.O. Box 15, Franconia, NH 03580
**Phone:** 603/823-7775 or 444-2919
**Location:** In Robert Frost's Easton Valley. On a main road, but in the woods of eight acres bordering the White Mountains. Six miles south of Franconia, ten miles southeast of Littleton. Ten minutes from Cannon Mountain, 30 from Loon and Bretton Woods.
**Hosts:** Lee Strimbeck and Kate Kerivan
**Open:** Year round.

Informality reigns in this post-and-beam house reminiscent of the century-old barn from which it was built. Guests have full access to the two-storied, fireplaced living room, sauna, small library, and multiple porches with views of gardens and romantic mountains.

Lee, a patent attorney, and Kate, landscape architect for the city of Manchester, find that even those who come with grandiose plans are mesmerized by the view. "They sleep late and feel very unhurried. We're fairly remote. Only 42 families live in Easton." The hosts' own interests include hiking, scuba diving, sailing, and travel.

**In residence:** Kyle, their young son. Hugo, a standard poodle.
**Restrictions:** Children should be at least six. Sorry, no pets. No smoking in the house.
**Bed and bath:** Four rooms. Two guest baths. One room with queen-sized bed, two with a double in each, one with twin beds. Cot available.
**Breakfast:** Full. Blueberry pancakes with local maple syrup. Muffins with homemade honey and preserves. Served 7-10 by hosts—or sometimes even guests—at a trestle table in the dining area or on porch in summer.
**Plus:** Coffee available any time. Other meals by arrangement. Guests may pack their own lunches and contribute to the cost of dinner. Trails through woods on property to the river. Laundry facilities. Movies on VCR; no television.
**Rates:** $40 single, $60 double. $25 cot.

## Freedom House

Box 478, 1 Maple Street, Freedom, NH 03836
**Phone:** 603/539-4815
**Location:** In a quiet country village by the mill pond. Half hour south of the Conways. Half hour to Wolfeboro.
**Hosts:** Bob and Marjorie Daly
**Open:** Year round.

A genuine Old Home Week and Firemen's Parade is held every August is this friendly New Hampshire town. And now, within walking distance of a lake, the country store, church, town hall, and library, there's a B&B in a white Victorian house with bay windows, gray shutters, an American flag, and a hostess who says that she models "out-of-fashion fashions with and for local residents!" Features include a warm atmosphere and fresh country decor.

Since coming here in 1985, both Bob (retired from the U.S. Coast Guard) and Marjorie (a skilled craftsperson) have immersed themselves in town activities. It's the very change they were seeking after being in Florida resort management. Latest plans call for an antiques co-op in their barn.

**In residence:** Muffin is a friendly and declawed house cat who helps show guests to their rooms.
**Restrictions:** No guests' pets. Smoking restricted to common rooms.
**Bed and bath:** Six rooms. Two shared baths; one with tub, one with shower. Two rooms with two twin beds each. Three with doubles. A third-floor room is a single. Cot available.
**Breakfast:** 7-9. Homemade muffins, pancakes with Freedom's own maple syrup, French toast, farm-fresh eggs, bacon, ham, and sausage. Served in dining room.
**Plus:** Beverages upon arrival. Dinner by advance reservation. Tour of the house.
**Rates:** $27.50 single, $37.50 or $40 double. $10 cot for child in same room. Crib could be rented. MasterCard and VISA accepted.

## Moose Mountain Lodge

Moose Mountain, Etna, NH 03750
**Phone:** 603/643-3529
**Location:** One mile *up* a winding dirt road to a view of the Connecticut River valley below and the Green Mountains beyond. Ten miles to Dartmouth Skiway, 20 to King Ridge, 24 to Suicide Six, 40 to Killington.
**Hosts:** Kay and Peter Shumway
**Open:** June 1-October 31 and December 26-March 21. Two-day minimum stay on weekends, three-day minimum on holiday weekends.

From New York City: "This place is just about as close to heaven as we can get. The food is sumptuous and uncomplicated. The skiing is fabulous and the evenings are always filled with companionship and plenty of laughs. You feel you are staying with friends. This past winter I brought my 70-year-old mother, who can't wait to go back."

The canoeing inn-to-inn program introduces many summer visitors to the Shumways, easy-going folks who have time to listen. "We love to introduce people to the beauty of our trails and the Beaver Pond with its wonderful animal and bird life. After 12 years here, we still enjoy sharing this tranquil place with others."

Originally built as a ski lodge in 1938, the rustic building has furniture, including couches and four-poster beds, made of logs. Guests come looking for peaceful relaxation—and find it.

**In residence:** Ulla, a gray weimaraner, who loves long walks. Kirby, a friendly goat, who hikes and skis with Kay.
**Restrictions:** Smoking limited, please. No pets. Children should be at least five.
**Foreign languages spoken:** French, some Spanish and Swedish.
**Bed and bath:** Twelve rooms with five shared baths. Bed sizes are twin, double, queen; two rooms each have four bunk beds, and one room has a double and two bunks.
**Breakfast:** Huge, leisurely country breakfast 8-9:30. Could include homemade granola, fresh farm eggs, bacon or sausage, hot cereals or pancakes served with the hosts' own maple syrup.
**Plus:** Option of lunch and dinner (extra charge). Hiking and cross-country trails. Equipment for snowshoeing and cross-country skiing (extra charge). Huge porch with panoramic view. No TV.
**Rates:** $45 single, $32 per person double, $26 per person triple, and $21 per person quad. $15 children under 12. MasterCard and VISA accepted.

## Haverhill Inn

Dartmouth College Highway, Haverhill, NH 03765
**Phone:** 603/989-5961
**Location:** On main route N.H. 10, half a mile south of the Common, with a wonderful view of Connecticut River valley and Vermont hills. Half hour north of Dartmouth College. Within an hour's drive of five major ski areas. Antiquing in town.
**Hosts:** Stephen Campbell and Katharine DeBoer
**Open:** Year round except for a few weeks in March during mud season. Two-day minimum stay during fall foliage season.

There really has been a Christmas guest called Dickens. And an ambassador who just dropped in off the road. And plenty of returnees (greeted as long-lost friends) to this gracious 1810 Federal house turned into inn.

A partial list of features includes wide-board floors, painted-grain interior doors, solid panel interior (Indian) window shutters, old kitchen hearth and bake oven, and the warmth of antique furnishings. If you are interested in a complete history of the house, there are two volumes to peruse. For a perspective on the area, there's a collection of antique maps. And for help in planning day trips, there are two hosts who live a balanced (and full) life.

"Since opening in 1981, we've been part of a house tour, and sure, we're glad to show house fans around and describe what we did." They continue their separate professions—Steve is a system manager in the Dartmouth College computer center. Katharine, a concert soprano, teaches voice in her Hanover studio. Her heaviest concert seasons are less busy innkeeping times, so the schedules are complementary.

**In residence:** Two shy cats who aren't allowed in guests' rooms or parlor. Two dogs.
**Restrictions:** Children should be at least eight years old. Smoking in the parlor only.
**Foreign languages spoken:** Katharine speaks reasonable French. Steve knows some Spanish.
**Bed and bath:** Four large rooms. First-floor room has twin canopy beds. Upstairs, one double, one queen-sized, and one with a pair of double beds. Each room has a fireplace and a private bath. Two full baths, two with showers only.
**Breakfast:** 8-9. Always a full meal. Fresh bakery, locally smoked bacon, freshly brewed coffee. Steve is chef. Katharine serves.
**Plus:** Afternoon tea. A decanter of sherry on the hall desk. Other meals prepared for canoeists who participate in a (great) inn-to-inn program. Cross-country ski trails at the door.
**Rates (include tax):** $50 single, $65 for two. $10 additional person (up to two) in the room with two double beds. $10 a day discount after the fourth day.

## The Inn on Golden Pond

P.O. Box 126, Route 3, Holderness, NH 03245
**Phone:** 603/968-7269
**Location:** On 55 acres across the street from Squam Lake, setting for the film *On Golden Pond*. Twenty minutes to White Mountain National Forest, 15 minutes to Tenney Mountain. Four miles from I-93.
**Hosts:** Bill and Bonnie Webb
**Open:** Year round.

From New York: "Bill and Bonnie run an extremely clean, comfortable inn. Bill has a great talent for making everyone feel they are family. Bonnie is an excellent cook. Their bulletin board of area activities is a great time saver. It's so nice to be spoiled when on vacation!"

Bill left his job in guidebook publishing and Bonnie her data processing position when they returned to New England (from California) to live their dream of running a personalized inn where guests feel they are "away." Their country home, built in 1879, is surrounded by stone walls, antique split-rail fences, flowers, bushes, and shade trees.

**In residence:** "A mellow cat named Brandy."
**Restrictions:** Children should be at least 12. No guests' pets. Smoking is discouraged in general and not allowed in the bedrooms.
**Bed and bath:** Eight rooms on second and third floors. All private baths except for two rooms. Twin beds, double, or queen-sized; one room with double and twin-sized beds. Cot available.
**Breakfast:** 8:30-9:30. Homemade bread and muffins, eggs and bacon, fresh fruit, and a specialty such as apple pancakes. Prepared by Bonnie and served by Bill at individual tables in the breakfast room.
**Plus:** Roaring fire (except in warm weather). Picnic tables. Lawn games. A 60-foot screened porch. Swimming (small fee) at town beach just around the corner. Ice and glasses. Homemade mint on pillow. Trails through wooded property.
**Rates:** $40 single, shared bath. $50 single, private bath. $60 double, shared bath. $70 double, private bath. $25 cot for additional person in room. MasterCard and VISA accepted.

## Ellis River House

Box 656, Route 16, Jackson, NH 03846
**Phone:** 603/383-9339
**Location:** Set back from the road, overlooking the river. Ten minutes to Attitash, Wildcat, and Black Mountains and Tuckerman's Ravine. Walking or cross-country skiing distance to Jackson Ski Touring Center.
**Hosts:** Barry and Barbara Lubao
**Open:** Year round. Two-day minimum stay on holidays and ski season weekends.

> From New Hampshire: "Exquisite decor and down-home atmosphere. Country breakfasts fit for royalty. Many little extras that meant so much. The setting was beautiful. We have been taking ski vacations for years and this was, without a doubt, the most enjoyable."

Barry was chief engineer for the Sheraton hotels when the family found this well-maintained farmhouse "sitting on the market waiting for us. Jackson is a wonderful four-season area that is still quaint. Our children attend a grammar school that has a total of 20 students. And it's great to be able to take a dip right here in the river."

The farm is growing and now has pigs, chickens, turkeys, geese, rabbits, and ducks. Changes to come include a greenhouse and hot tub. Barry, chief chef here, has an air-conditioning business, and Barbara makes crafts for sale.

**In residence:** Barry (Jay), age 12, and Jennifer, the unofficial concierge, age 6. Polly, the parakeet, resides in TV room.
**Restrictions:** Children should be at least five. Some pets allowed. Smoking only in the social rooms.
**Foreign language spoken:** Polish.
**Bed and bath:** Five rooms plus suite. Three on second floor share two baths with claw-foot tubs: one room with queen-sized bed, one with queen and a twin, one with double bed. Third-floor room with two double beds and another with a double and twin bed share a full bath. Suite has queen-sized bed, four singles, private balcony, bath with shower. Rollaways available.
**Breakfast:** Usually 7:30-9 in winter, 8-9:30 in summer. Juices, fruit, homemade banana bread, Barry's highly acclaimed cinnamon bread, English muffins. Cereals, eggs, sausage, bacon, French toast or pancakes. Served in the Queen Anne–style dining room.

**Plus:** Sundecks and wraparound screened porch. Piano. Popcorn by the fire. Gather your own breakfast eggs. Playground. Horseshoes. Croquet. Volleyball. Trout fishing. Option of dinner ($14.50) by reservation only.
**Rates:** Per person, double occupancy. $22-$35 depending on season. Highest in September and October. $10 child under 12 in same room as parents. Single rates depend on availability. Suite $175-$225 per night. MasterCard and VISA accepted.

## The Nestlenook Inn

P.O. Box Q, Dinsmore Road, Jackson, NH 03846
**Phone:** 603/383-9443
**Location:** On 65 acres. Off Route 16A through the 150-year-old covered bridge in Jackson village, onto Dinsmore Road. Ten miles north of North Conway.
**Hosts:** Tom, Patti, and Cullen Burns
**Open:** Year round. Reservations required during ski season, foliage season, summer months. Three-day minimum stay for holiday weekends, Christmas, school vacations; two days on weekends.

> From Massachusetts: "A complete getaway. A trip back into time. I escaped into the Sherwood-like forest on foot and horse. I sat by the pool and enjoyed the grandeur of the serene mountain view. . . . The barn area with ducks, horses, pigs, and chickens reminds me of my childhood days in North Carolina and the simple values of farm living. Breakfast is made with farm-fresh eggs that you can gather. Each room, creatively decorated, welcomes you into a relaxing environment. Nestlenook inspired me to write and illustrate a children's book."

> From New York: "Patti and Tom instantly made us feel as though we were long-lost friends in need of a much deserved vacation."

Patti was public relations and marketing director for Faneuil Hall Marketplace and Tom worked in Boston retailing and residential renovation before they took New Hampshire by storm. Since reviving the old inn in 1983, they have established an equestrian center with lessons, clinics, and trail rides, and opened a ski-touring center with 25 kilometers of groomed and tracked trails. A highlight for B&B guests is the evening sleigh ride pulled by two team Belgians over the meadows and through the lantern-lit paths.

**In residence:** Son Cullen is three years old. Rufus, a Chinese shar-pei; Josephine, an elderly cat. A cow named MooMoo. Whammo the Wonder Lamb. Horses, pigs, chickens.
**Restrictions:** Smoking in downstairs common rooms only.
**Bed and bath:** Ten rooms, one on the first floor, each with two twins or a double bed, wash basin; most with private baths. Roll-away and crib available.
**Breakfast:** 8-9:30. Homemade breads (including Tom's beer bread); juice, fruit, cheese; French toast with walnuts, raisins, and cinnamon; eggs; freshly brewed coffee. Served in family-style dining room filled with collectibles.
**Plus:** Seasonal beverages. Video library with over 300 movie classics. Tour of house and farm. Special packages for horseback riding, cross-country skiing, mystery weekends. B&B seminars. Apprentice program.
**Rates:** Per person. Double occupancy. Off-season $23-$25 shared bath, $28-$30 private bath. December-March and mid-June-October $28-$30 shared bath, $30-$35 private bath. Single occupancy $10 more, depends on availability. $10 cot. $5 crib. Children 12 and under $10/$15. MasterCard and VISA accepted.

## The Benjamin Prescott Inn

Route 124 East, Jaffrey, NH 03452
**Phone:** 603/532-6637
**Location:** On the old turnpike road, surrounded by an active dairy farm and meadows, facing Mount Monadnock, 2½ miles from village center.
**Host:** Richard Rettig
**Open:** Year round. Reservations recommended. Two-day minimum stay weekends from May until November.

> From New Hampshire: "The friendliness and warmth given to me was wonderful. And at a time when I needed these creature comforts! Clean, tastefully decorated with a country flair."

It's a restored 1852 Greek Revival farmhouse with warm colonial colors, quilts, and Oriental rugs. Not sparse, not cluttered, but welcoming. Although it is many years since Richard has had an antique shop, the opening of the inn (in 1984) gave him "a good reason to continue buying." (Occasionally he will part with a treasure.) The bear logo has inspired a collection, a subtle touch, in various forms from mechanical to porcelain; a total of 90 were counted by least one young guest.

Richard brings 20 years of experience in the hospitality industry to his newest career. At Franklin College he has been in charge of the food service and given B&B courses; currently he is Special Projects Coordinator.

**In residence:** Pumpkin, a Maine Coon cat born on Halloween.
**Restrictions:** Children should be at least seven. Sorry, no guests' pets.
**Bed and bath:** Eight rooms, all with private baths. Antique beds—king, double, or two twin-sized, with color-coordinated linens and lots of accent pillows.
**Breakfast:** 8:30-9:30. Maybe blueberry pancakes, French toast, or a super cheese casserole. Fresh fruits, homemade breads, bacon and sausage. On the porch, or by the living-room fireplace. Served by Richard, his assistant Herb O'Brien, and college students.
**Plus:** Afternoon or evening beverages. Fireplaced living room. Second-floor sitting room with color TV. Screened porch with wicker furniture. Lounge chairs and picnic table on huge lawns with commanding views. Tour of house. Apprentice program.
**Rates:** $40 single with shared bath, $50 with private bath. $45 double, shared bath; $55 private bath. $20 cot. MasterCard accepted.

## The Galway House

Old Peterborough Road, Box 201K, Jaffrey, NH 03452
**Phone:** 603/532-8083
**Location:** On a quiet woodland road ten minutes from the villages of Jaffrey and Peterborough.
**Hosts:** Joe and Marie Manning
**Open:** Year round except July. Reservations required.

From New Jersey: "Very enjoyable. On maps they showed us back roads for bicycling and trails for hiking that were less crowded during peak fall season. We plan on returning this winter to cross-country ski on the trails leaving from their backyard."

"Since 1980 we've had guests from as close as the next town (while their house was being readied) and as far away as mainland China. Our oversized Cape house was built in 1974 on a 1760s road that was just recently paved."

Joe is semiretired. He and Marie think the people-to-people theme of B&B makes it a great way to travel.

**In residence:** Brigid, age 15. Sean, a gentle yellow Lab.
**Restrictions:** No guests' pets. Smoking downstairs only.
**Bed and bath:** Two second-floor large rooms share a bath. One has a double bed and two twin beds, the other a double and a single bed. Cot and crib available.
**Breakfast:** 7-9. A full country breakfast including juice, hot and cold cereal, pancakes, eggs, homemade muffins, and hot beverages served in the dining room.
**Plus:** Afternoon tea. Ski weekends in winter, foliage weekends in the fall. Will meet guests at Logan Airport (Boston) or the Fitzwilliam bus for an extra fee. Babysitting available. TV. Sun deck. Beaches nearby.
**Rates:** $30 single, $35 double. $10 per extra person.

From Massachusetts: "Warm and friendly hosts on a absolutely quiet back road. Best place I have ever been for a good night's sleep. Rooms large and pleasant."

## Lilac Hill Acres

5 Ingalls Road, Jaffrey, NH 03452
**Phone:** 603/532-7278
**Location:** Two miles from historic Jaffrey center. High on a hill overlooking Gilmore Pond and surrounded by Monadnock, Pack Monadnock, and Temple mountains.
**Hosts:** Frank, Ellen, and Jacqulyn McNeill
**Open:** Year round. Reservations required. Two-day minimum stay on weekends during the fall.

"We were on a foliage tour in 1985 and saw this place for sale. Just like that, we decided that the 1740 house would be the new family homestead and lifestyle. There's always family around. My father, a plasterer who worked on Boston's Music Hall (and his father did the original ornate work there), loves having a farm."

Jacqulyn is at the farm between flights as an airline stewardess. All the McNeills are just as enthusiastic about their move: "We have our own apple orchard, a stocked spring-fed pond that you can swim in, open hay fields, and for the first time, a lot of animals in our lives. Guests feel very relaxed here. They sit on the porch. They read. They become a big kid when they go out in the barn. We provide boots so you can feed the pigs. It's all great."

**In residence:** Geese, horses, pigs, sheep, Black Angus cows, cats, dogs. Grandchildren are occasional visitors.
**Restrictions:** Children should be at least 12. No guests' pets. Smoking in the living room only.
**Bed and bath:** Six rooms on two floors. Three shared baths. Two rooms with a twin bed in each, one with a king-sized and one with a king and a twin. One with a double and one with a king and three twins.
**Breakfast:** 8:30-9:30. Full. Made with their own or locally grown vegetables (and meat). Served in the country kitchen or formal dining room. The record time is four hours!
**Plus:** Fireplace in living room. Tea, hot mulled cider in afternoon or evening. Kitchen privileges. Will meet guests at the airport.
**Rates:** $45 single, $55 double. $25 for each extra person in room.

## MacKissock House

1047 Union Avenue, Laconia, NH 03246
**Phone:** 603/528-4185
**Location:** On a main street. Overlooking Paugus Bay on Lake Winnipesaukee. Four miles from Gunstock ski area. Walking distance to fine and fast-food restaurants.
**Hosts:** Jim and Jane MacKissock
**Open:** Year round.

In the 1920s big-band players were guests here. Now big-band music can be heard on the living-room Victrola, one of the touches of "home" provided by the MacKissocks, a former high-tech researcher and a nutrition consultant. The people-oriented couple followed their instincts and talents, came back to Jim's hometown, restored and redecorated the home originally built in 1915 for a lumberyard owner. In one bedroom they kept a functioning clawfoot tub, and added a shelf now complete with toiletries—

and for special occasions, champagne and two champagne glasses. Elsewhere, there are antique furnishings, some for sale.

"I'll never stay anywhere but a B&B again" is often heard from first-timers at the breakfast table. The MacKissocks have done their part to extend the possibilities; Jim is the first president of Traditional B&B of New Hampshire, an association that promotes B&B travel.

**In residence:** A cat named Jerry.
**Restrictions:** Sorry, no guests' pets.
**Bed and bath:** Four second-floor rooms with antique furnishings. Three rooms with a double bed in each; one with two four-poster twins. Two shared baths with showers, no tub. The bathtub-in-room (see above) is appreciated "for long hot soaks." Crib and cot available.
**Breakfast:** 8-10. Full country breakfast with whole-wheat pancakes and maple syrup, farm eggs, homemade breads, jams, quiche, fresh fruit specialties, gourmet omelets. Prepared by Jim and served by Jane in the formal dining room overlooking the bay or on the veranda.
**Plus:** Tea and coffee are always on; cider in autumn. Flowers in rooms. Quiet reading room with piano and fireplace. Game and TV room. Fans in bedrooms. Guest fruit basket. Porch with rockers. Kitchen privileges.
**Rates:** November-May $38 single, $42 double. June-October $48 single, $52 double. $10 for extra cot. MasterCard, VISA, and AMEX accepted.

## Charpentier B&B

Box 562, Pollard Road, Lincoln, NH 03251
**Phone:** 603/745-8517
**Location:** One mile from I-93 with a scenic view from every window. Located in center of the notches, next to White Mountains attractions. Two miles from Loon Mountain and minutes from Cannon, Bretton Woods, Waterville Valley skiing.
**Hosts:** Dave and Tillie Charpentier
**Open:** Year round. Reservations are suggested.

Dave may be the only B&B host who is executive director of a local chamber of commerce. (Of course the Charpentiers have some suggestions of little-known places to see!) He is also a justice of the peace. Before coming here, the cheerful couple lived in Connecticut and traveled all over the country when Dave was an engineer for 30 years. Most recently, he was president of a subsidiary of Walter Kidde Corporation.

It's three years since they bought and restored the 1800s farmhouse, which was built by the man who brought the logging industry to Lincoln. Furnished with family antiques, and with oil paintings by Dave's mother, it has a candle in every window in winter. In every season, hospitality here is based on the idea that "people on holiday deserve to be pampered."

**In residence:** Meghan, a friendly calico cat, and Sheba, a husky/Lab mix who is very quiet but friendly.
**Restrictions:** Sorry, no guests' pets. No children. Smoking restricted to first-floor porch.
**Bed and bath:** Five second-floor rooms and two third-floor rooms share three baths, one on each floor. Rooms with twin, double, or king-sized beds.
**Breakfast:** 7:30 or 8:30. Scrambled eggs or French toast or pancakes with sausage, ham or bacon. Home fries; quiche; pumpkin, cranberry, or coffee cake, all homemade; popovers, muffins, cinnamon jelly, peach conserve.
**Plus:** Hot cider and homemade goodies in ski season. Ski room for do-your-own tuneups; or, for a small fee, Dave will do it for you.
**Rates:** $40 room, double or twin beds. $50 king. Family room with five beds, $20 per person.

## Beal House Inn

247 West Main Street, Littleton, NH 03561
**Phone:** 603/444-2661
**Location:** Steps from the town center, but quiet. Near Bretton Woods and Cannon Mountain ski areas.
**Hosts:** Doug and Brenda Clickenger
**Open:** Year round. Two-day minimum stay during fall foliage and long holiday weekends.

This is a living antique shop. Except for the sign outside it looks like a typical rambling "added-on-to" upcountry Federal-style home, circa 1833.

It's seven years since the salesman and his cartographer wife came from St. Petersburg, Florida, looking for an inn that would offer a new family lifestyle. What they have now attracts repeaters who make it a point to visit the Clickengers at holiday time; local residents who book their own visitors here; and newcomers who think they have stumbled into a lost era. It's a comfortable home with the mix and match of the current collection of antiques. Everything—the canopied beds, Windsor chairs, mirrors, clocks—is for sale. Browsers find more in the barn shop.

Along with the period papers and handmade quilts has come a style, one that has made their breakfasts (see below) somewhat famous. The family has seen a few changes in the town too; art sales, shops, and trout tournaments are fairly new attractions. If you're looking for a suggestion, "there's an easy hike that leads to a splendid view of Franconia Notch."

**In residence:** College-aged daughters during school vacations. Pepper, a small, friendly, quiet, nonshedding dog.
**Restrictions:** No guests' pets. No cigars. No smoking in the breakfast room during meals.
**Bed and bath:** Fourteen rooms on first and second floors, twelve with private bath. There are two two-room suites. Queen, double, and twin-sized beds available.
**Breakfast:** 8-9:30. Served by candlelight in dining room at tables set with red and white tablecloths, by Clickenger women in long dresses. Homemade breads, popovers, waffles and French toast with pure maple syrup, creamy scrambled eggs served in glass hen dishes, meats, 50 varieties of tea—all prepared by Doug.
**Plus:** Tea, popcorn, cheese and crackers in the late afternoon or evening. Sitting rooms with fireplaces. Books. Games. Glassed-in porch with mountain views. Backyard picnic tables. Woods, lawn, deck, gardens. Limited kitchen privileges.
**Rates:** \$30-\$42 single with shared bath, \$35-\$45 private bath. \$35-\$45 doubles with shared bath, \$40-\$75 private bath. \$8 portacrib or cot. Family rates \$65-\$110. Major credit cards accepted.

## Loch Lyme Lodge

RFD 278, Lyme, NH 03768
**Phone:** 603/795-2141
**Location:** On Route 10, one mile north of the village. On a spring-fed lake surrounded by hills. Eleven miles from Dartmouth College, four miles from Dartmouth Skiway.
**Hosts:** Paul and Judy Barker
**Open:** Mid-September through mid-June. Closed Thanksgiving and Christmas Days. Three-night minimum stay on Columbus holiday weekend. Reservations suggested.

In 1784 Loch Lyme was a farmhouse. By 1923 it had grown and become part of a boys' camp and a lodging place for campers' parents and tourists too. Eventually Judy's parents ran it as a resort. When Judy and Paul left their teaching careers in 1977, they took the resort over, and added B&B in their home, spring through fall.

"Pure B&B is what we offer. A home away from home. Immediately after Labor Day we close the cabins, move from the barn (the location of our summer apartment) into the main Lodge, move all the tables and chairs out of the dining rooms (which become our living room and piano room), and reopen as a 'comfortably furnished, maybe antiques someday' bed and breakfast. We enjoy both seasons, but the fall and winter give us more time to spend with guests, many of whom think that our lifestyle is definitely in the slow lane."

**In residence:** Jon Paul, almost six, loves "having company." Two cats, Beefer and Willie.
**Restrictions:** No guests' pets. Smoking is not encouraged.
**Foreign languages spoken:** Paul speaks Spanish, Judy a little French.
**Bed and bath:** Four second-floor rooms share one full bath. Three rooms have two twin beds each. One has a double. Cots available.
**Breakfast:** Usually 8-9. Full country breakfast served family style on the sun porch. Busy bird feeder in view.
**Plus:** Living room with fireplace. Piano room. Fans available. About 125 acres of woodlands, fields, and lake shore. Skating and night cross-country skiing possibilities. Informal cross-country lessons and tours. Beverages. Babysitting possibilities.
**Rates:** $23 per person, $8 ages 7 and under, $14 ages 8-12. $8-$14 for cots. One-time charge of $4 for crib.

## New Hampshire Bed & Breakfast Host #212

Meredith, NH
**Location:** On a quiet residential road. Five-minute walk to Meredith village, the shores of Lake Winnipesaukee, and Trailways bus stop. Ten miles from I-93. Fifteen minutes to Gunstock ski area.
**Reservations:** Available year round through New Hampshire Bed & Breakfast, page 85.

The sampler in the living room reads, "Let me live in the house by the side of the road and be a friend to man."

The entire modified Cape is decorated in Early American style with primitive antiques, baskets, handmade crafts, quilts, and floor cloths. When the hosts, a surveyor and his wife, came here two years ago they did all the restoration themselves. "Through the pursuit of our dreams, we are into the B&B world."

They have found a little-known ten-mile scenic drive: "The old road is not found on many maps, but has been the subject of a book." Directions happily shared with guests.

**In residence:** A shaggy mixed-breed dog named Myrtle "who assumes that all guests have come to visit her."
**Restrictions:** Children should be at least eight. Well-behaved dogs allowed. No smoking in the bedrooms.
**Bed and bath:** Five second-floor rooms, each with a double bed. One room has a private bath. Two rooms to each of the other baths; one is a full bath, one shower only. All rooms have stenciled walls (some floors stenciled too), antique furnishings, and quilts (some handmade). Two cots available.
**Breakfast:** 8-10. Menu changes daily. "From ham and brie omelet to funnel cakes." A choice of two entrees and two meats, coffee cake or muffins, home fries, toast, juice and coffee. Served at a large table in the country dining room. Hosts may join you for coffee.
**Plus:** Late-afternoon or evening beverage and snack. Living room. Sun porch. Sun deck. Yard. Fattening snacks.
**Rates:** $40 single, $50 double. $10 for a cot.

## Olde Orchard Inn

R.R. Box 256, Moultonboro, NH 03254
**Phone:** 603/476-5004
**Location:** On 12 acres with pond and brook, fronted by granite fence posts, on a quiet country road surrounded by meadows and orchards. One mile from Route 25 and Moultonboro center. Across from Woodshed Restaurant. Within half-hour drive to all Lakes Region attractions; an hour's drive to White Mountains.
**Hosts:** Chuck and Ginger Litzell
**Open:** Year round. Two-night minimum stay during holiday weekends.

Just a mile down a country road from Lake Winnipesaukee is "a wonderful place to visit and a grand place to live." After three decades as a builder in Ohio, Chuck, his wife Ginger, a teacher, and their daughters moved in 1984 to this double (half brick, half clapboard) early 19th-century Cape. Six new tile baths were part of their year-long restoration. They decorated with Williamsburg colors and Oriental rugs. Furnishings are antique and reproduction, with a wing chair in each guest room.

The farm has a tradition of family involvement. The bricks for the house were made by a son of the first owners from clay found in the pasture and dried in a sun kiln by the brook. Chuck has a reproduction furniture business in the barn. The orchards' spring blossoms are beautiful. Guests from around the world come for the mountain views, a sense of history, and a relaxing atmosphere.

**In residence:** Elizabeth, 17, and Sarah, 14. Kilda is a lovable yellow Lab.
**Restrictions:** Sorry, no guests' pets. No smoking.
**Bed and bath:** Five rooms in private wing with private entrance. All private full baths. Three first-floor rooms, one with fireplace. Two second-floor rooms. Four rooms with double beds, one with twin beds. Cot and crib available.
**Breakfast:** 8-9. Omelets, pancakes, or French toast. Fruit, homemade baked goods, buttermilk biscuits, sticky buns, juice, hot beverages. Chuck cooks. Ginger assists. Very leisurely meal.
**Plus:** Guest sitting room with fireplace. Tour of house and farm (barn, orchards, old cemetery). Bedroom fans. Use of refrigerator. Brook fishing. Cross-country skiing.

**Rates:** $55 for two, except for larger room with fireplace, $65. Suite of two rooms, one with double bed, one with twins (two baths) $100 for four. $15 cot. $5 crib. AMEX accepted.

From Washington, D.C.: "A beautifully restored farmhouse. The Litzells' warmth and friendliness made us feel right at home."

## The Inn at Coit Mountain

HCR 63 Box 3, Newport, NH 03773
**Phone:** 1-800/367-2364. In New Hampshire: 603/863-3583.
**Location:** Two miles north of Newport on Route 10 with mountain and river views. Ten miles west of Sunapee.
**Hosts:** Dick and Judi Tatem
**Open:** Year round.

From Massachusetts: "It's a lovely place. And don't forget to mention the light with wide shade directly over one bath tub. The lady of the house used to read there."

"Cozy elegance" is the style today, and maybe always has been here. The 1790 Georgian was purchased in 1878 by the developer of Coney Island and the Long Island Railroad as a wedding present for his daughter. About 25 years later, the 35-foot, two-storied library and the artist's studio (now frame shop) with Palladian window were added. Today, the library with huge granite fireplace is filled with books once again. Rooms are inviting, relaxation a feature.

The creative Tatems have many ideas. Ask about sleigh rides pulled by their Morgan horse or a Victorian weekend complete with poet and magician. A jacuzzi is planned. The print shop is Dick's new business and Judi is still a professional retouch artist. The family came to Newport from rural Connecticut in 1985.

**In residence:** Debbie, age 16; Dan, 13; Melissa, 12. Two red setters, Ted and Becky. One cat named Rascal, a pony and two horses.
**Restrictions:** Sorry, no guests' pets. Smoking allowed in library.
**Bed and bath:** Five rooms, two with working fireplaces. A first-floor room has twin beds, shared bath with shower. On second floor, rooms have king-sized bed, queen-sized, or double bed, and a queen-sized sleep sofa. A bath with footed deep tub, no shower, for each two rooms. Rollaways and crib available.

**Breakfast:** Generally, anytime up to 10:30. Freshly squeezed orange juice, fruits, breads and muffins. Specialty of the day could be eggs Benedict, sherried creamed eggs and mushrooms on toast, pecan waffles with honey butter. Served in fireplaced dining room.
**Plus:** Turned-down beds. Refrigerator in each room. Piano. Two-storied porch. Large yard and garden. Babysitting available. Dinner ($15) by prior arrangement.
**Rates:** $45-$65 single, $55-$75 double. Two rooms used as a suite (with connecting bath) $100 single, $125 double. $10 higher July through October, January and February weekends only. MasterCard and VISA accepted.

---

## The Buttonwood Inn

P.O. Box 3297C, Mt. Surprise Road, North Conway, NH 03860
**Phone:** 603/356-2625
**Location:** Very quiet. On Mount Surprise, on five wooded acres, three miles from the village and Route 16.
**Hosts:** Ann and Hugh Begley
**Open:** Year round except April. Two-night stays preferred for ski season and holiday weekends.

After working with innkeepers while booking tours for a New Jersey bus company, Ann, together with Hugh, a schools' equipment salesman, chose B&B for their next step. Their added-on-to Cape, originally an 1820s farmhouse and in the 1940s a ski lodge, is a 20-room house with wide board floors in the guest rooms. Fresh paint and country print wallpapers and the addition of country antiques were all part of the Begleys' 1984 "sprucing up." A waterfall in the newly done living room was their introduction to country plumbing—and calm plumbers. ("If that don't beat all.") The outdoor swimming pool was installed in 1986.

The Begleys, parents of five grown children, enjoy sports themselves and arrange guided fishing and hunting weekends.

**In residence:** One host who smokes. "Icis the cat and Penny, our retriever-and-Lab-mix dog, delight guests with their antics." Son Walt is around some weekends; grandchildren come during school vacations.
**Restrictions:** Sorry, no guests' pets.

**Bed and bath:** Ten second-floor rooms, some dormered, two with private baths. Eight share three baths. Rooms have double or twin-sized beds. Cot and crib available.
**Breakfast:** 8-9:30, earlier by request. Juices, eggs, bacon, sausage, thick French toast, maple syrup pancakes, English muffins, homemade breads, blueberry muffins in season. Served in dining room at tables set with linen, fresh flowers. Leisurely. Sometimes hosts are assisted by grandson Chris, age six.
**Plus:** Hot buttered rum or mulled cider during ski season. Complimentary bottle of wine upon arrival. Dinner ($12 per person) in ski season. Babysitting. Dryer. Guest refrigerator. TV room and game room. Horseshoes, badminton, croquet. Hiking and cross-country trails from back yard.
**Rates:** Per room. Double occupancy. January-March/July-October weekend and holiday weeks $55-$60 shared bath, $60-$65 private bath. Midweek and off-season $40-$50 shared bath, $45-$55 private bath. $10-$15 third person in room. Under age five free. Reduced rates for three or five nights, and for singles. MasterCard, VISA, and AMEX accepted.

From Texas: "Lovely. Wonderful hosts. A highlight of our trip. Spotlessly clean. Good food. And believe me, all four of us are very choosy."

## The Center Chimney—1787

P.O. Box 1220, River Road, North Conway, NH 03860
**Phone:** 603/356-6788
**Location:** Just off the main street of North Conway, yet woodsy and quiet. Within walking distance to swimming and boating at Saco River, to free ice skating and cross-country skiing, and to shops and restaurants.
**Host:** Farley Whitney
**Open:** Year round. Two-day minimum preferred during holidays.

"Many of my guests are also fascinated with antiques and restoration; we enjoy sharing information. Often I show prints of what this house, one of the oldest in North Conway, used to look like. It has three working fireplaces off the center chimney and wide board floors, comfortable facilities, and a friendly atmosphere! One bed (with new box spring and mattress) is as old as the house. The combination of my years in Stowe, Vermont (working in recreation) and living in Europe inspired me to become innkeeper in 1984. This is a diversified four-season area. Cathedral Ledge (for rock climbing) and Echo State Park, two gems, are just down the road."

**In residence:** Farley smokes but not in presence of nonsmoking guests.
**Restrictions:** Sorry, no pets allowed; boarding nearby.
**Bed and bath:** Four second-floor rooms in guest wing share two full baths. One room with a double bed, one with king-sized, one with three twin beds. Fourth has a double bed, single sleep sofa and sun deck. Cot available.
**Breakfast:** 7:30-10. Home-baked muffins and coffee or tea. Apples in fall. Buffet. Eat in country kitchen, living room, or on patio.
**Plus:** Whirlpool bath available by appointment. Hot cider in winter. Cribbage. Backgammon. Piano. Cable TV. Will meet guests at the bus (direct service to and from Boston's Logan Airport). Window fans in bedrooms.
**Rates:** $20 per person, double occupancy, except room with sun deck $24 per person double. $10 third person in room. $30 single, when available. $5 less during spring and post-foliage/pre-ski season.

## Sunny Side Inn

Seavey Street, North Conway, NH 03860
**Phone:** 603/356-6239
**Location:** In a quiet residential area within walking distance of Mount Cranmore and the center of North Conway.
**Hosts:** Tracy Minnix and Anthony Tulip
**Open:** Year round. Two-night minimum on winter weekends, three nights during major holiday weekends.

A "casual, convenient, affordable place" is the home of the young hosts who, three years ago, left the West and their jobs in natural gas and oil exploration and U.S. Forest Service. Because Tracy's parents have a guest house in Cape May, New Jersey, the hosts came here knowing about the commitment and rewards of a people-oriented business. Sunny Side is an added-on-to farmhouse that "we're always fixing up." It has been an inn since the 1930s and appeals to a wide age range including families and groups.

"We enjoy hiking, rock and ice climbing, cycling, and skiing, and find that many of our guests do too. River rafting seems to be taking hold around here now."

**In residence:** Son Corbett Tulip, a year old.
**Restrictions:** Sorry, no pets.
**Foreign language spoken:** Some Spanish.
**Bed and bath:** Eleven rooms. The three with private baths have a double or double and a twin bed. Other rooms, which share two baths, have a single, a double, two twins, or two double beds. One room can accommodate up to four people.
**Breakfast:** 7-9. Hearty. Fresh fruit, juice, homemade pastry and coffee cakes, beverage. Main course could be whole-grain buttermilk blueberry pancakes, whole-grain French toast, waffles, or cheese strata "with all the trimmings."
**Plus:** Wood stove in dining room by reading nook. Dinners for groups, if arranged in advance. Babysitting. Yard. Garage for ski and bicycle storage.
**Rates:** Shared bath $20 single, $30-$42 double. $47-$55 double with private bath. $15 per extra adult. $10 under age 12. MasterCard and VISA accepted.

## The Aviary

P.O. Box 268, Northwood, NH 03261
**Phone:** 603/942-7755
**Location:** In a quiet, private wooded rural area on the edge of a lake.
**Hosts:** Martha and Tad Comstock
**Open:** Year round. Reservations required. (The hosts' grown children like it here too.)

Guests say: "Superb. Elegant. Peaceful and relaxing. Warm and gracious hosts."

"We are somewhat hidden and unknown. No signs. No traffic." In 1979 Martha designed and decorated this two-storied contemporary house with living areas on top of the sleeping quarters. The exceptional spot is the former site of her grandfather's camp, which was moved across the ice to a new location. Antiques, art work, samplers, and some modern things, too, blend beautifully.

Hosting here is all for the joy of sharing. "People are really wonderful. We've enjoyed them all—from the college students who come for a rest to honeymooners and great-grandparents." Both Martha and Tad have wide interests ranging from photography to sailing, from bridge playing to building.

**Restrictions:** Martha is allergic to smoke. Four-wheel or front-wheel drive is helpful in winter. No snowmobiles allowed. There are no facilities for small children. Sorry, no guests' pets.
**Bed and bath:** Three first-floor rooms. Private bath with shower for room that has queen-sized bed. If other two rooms are both occupied, one with queen-sized bed shares a full bath with room with two twin beds. Cot available.
**Breakfast:** 6-10. Full with eggs, maybe French toast, cereals. Menu additions by whim. A relaxed meal at time selected by guests. Served in breakfast area overlooking the lake, outside on the porch, or occasionally in the formal dining room.
**Plus:** Dock and beach. Maybe use of canoe, rowboat, or Sailfish. Screened porch. Deck. Lawn games. Grill. Fans, if ever needed. Fishing year round. Cross-country skiing. Fireplaced living room. Den with TV.
**Rates:** June 1-October 1 $30 single, $45 double. Off-season $25 single, $35 double. $20 cot.

## Meadow Farm

Jenness Pond Road, Northwood, NH 03261
**Phone:** 603/942-8619, 942-7711
**Location:** Quiet. Lake frontage, 50 acres of field and woods. Five minutes from Route 4; 25 minutes east of Concord and west of University of New Hampshire; 45 minutes to Gunstock ski area.
**Hosts:** Doug and Janet Briggs
**Open:** Year round. Reservations preferred.

From New York: "Our overnight was refreshing and relaxing. An exciting trip back in time in a very old home, yet with modern comforts and a great breakfast after a quiet and very private and comfortable night's sleep. . . . Interesting people to be with."

Off the beaten track is this 1770 center-chimney colonial with old beams, four fireplaces, and original paneling. Since coming here almost ten years ago, Doug and Janet have restored, stenciled, and painted with authentic colors. When they aren't hosting or skiing or gardening, Janet is director of the university program of horsemanship and Doug manufactures and markets equipment for agricultural research.

**In residence:** Son Darrell, age 16. Two dogs, Rainee, a friendly female Doberman, and Nifty, a Jack Russell terrier with lots of personality.
**Restrictions:** Children should be at least three. Pets allowed sometimes. No smoking in bedrooms.
**Bed and bath:** Three rooms. A first-floor single room shares a bath with the hosts. One upstairs room with two twin beds and original beamed ceiling, and another with a double bed, share a full bath. Cot available.
**Breakfast:** 7:30-9. Homemade breads, muffins, and preserves and specialties such as bismarcks, German pancakes, Belgian waffles with New Hampshire maple syrup. Served in keeping room with fireplace and bake oven. Leisurely.
**Plus:** Use of private beach and dock. Pony ride for children. Beverages. Window fans. Fields and woods for cross-country skiing on marked trails. Ten-minute walk to tennis courts.
**Rates:** $30 single, $40-$45 double. $10 cot. Family and weekly rates.

Originally from California: "We were so impressed with them, the area, and the lifestyle, that we decided to move. We now live in the town next to theirs, where we bought an old house and plan on opening a craft/gift shop in the barn."

## Crab Apple Inn

RFD 2, Box 200 B, Plymouth, NH 03264
**Phone:** 603/536-4476
**Location:** Beside a brook at the foot of Tenney Mountain, on Route 25, four miles west of Plymouth, gateway to the White Mountains. Forty miles north of Concord.
**Hosts:** Carolyn and Bill Crenson
**Open:** Year round. Reservations preferred.

The 1835 brick house of Federal design is a beauty inside and out, complete with white picket fence, original glass in windows framed by black shutters, and fan window over the entrance. There's an antique wood stove in the common room, wide pine floors, and period furnishings. The Crensons embellish all this with fresh flowers, sherry-filled decanters, handmade quilts, and lace trimmed sheets.

They had thought about hosting for a long time while Bill was an educational administrator and Carolyn a medical director for developmentally disabled adults. Restoration was done by the previous owners, who had established the B&B. Ever since the Crensons took over during a freezing week (outside) in January 1986, they have offered "gracious B&B in the English tradition."

**In residence:** A small, friendly Lhasa apso named Pekoe, who doesn't shed and loves her position as "inn dog."
**Restrictions:** Children should be at least eight. No guests' pets.
**Bed and bath:** Five guest rooms on second and third floors. Some with fireplaces. Two with private baths. One room with queen-sized canopy bed. Suite with queen sleigh bed and adjoining sitting room convertible to bedroom. Other rooms have a double bed or double and a twin. Cot available.
**Breakfast:** 8-9. Orange juice, fresh seasonal fruit, herbed cheese omelet with ham or sausage, blueberry muffins, English jams, tea, freshly brewed coffee, apples. Served in the common room or on brick patio.
**Plus:** Air conditioning in bedrooms. Ceiling fans in hallway. Down comforters. Beverages. Tour of house. Library. Brick patio. Beautifully landscaped yard with English garden and wooded path through pine grove.
**Rates:** Double occupancy. $50-$60 shared bath, $55-$65 private bath. $15 extra person in room. MasterCard and VISA accepted.

---

## Inn at Strawberry Banke

314 Court Street, Portsmouth, NH 03801
**Phone:** 603/436-7242
**Location:** In the historic district, within walking distance of waterfront, restaurants, shops, and Prescott Park.

**Hosts:** Mark and Kerrianne Constant
**Open:** Year round. Reservations required.

A young couple, still in their twenties, stayed at a guest house on Nantucket and mused about duplicating the setup back in Portsmouth. They returned home on a Wednesday, saw this 1790 colonial (which abuts Strawbery Banke) on Friday, and had their offer accepted that Sunday! Opened in 1981, the inn was in my first B&B book when Kerrianne was pregnant and Mark was working at a restaurant. Kerrianne's update: "The people we meet are wonderful. Portsmouth has become a destination point rather than a pass-through town. Most of our guests are returnees! We have a few more guest rooms now that we added new hosts' quarters. Mark is here full time. I still do some part-time work in fund raising/public relations. And Caitlin is live entertainment at breakfast."

If a floor creaks, that's considered part of the charm by guests who have come to sense a bygone era. Rugs are hooked and Oriental. Furnishings include some colonial reproductions, some antiques. An artist friend's paintings are on display and for sale.

**In residence:** Caitlin, age four. Two dogs—Kemo, a husky, and Maggi, a collie. One cat, Punky Brewster.
**Restrictions:** No infants. No guests' pets. No smoking in guest rooms.
**Bed and bath:** Seven rooms, each with a double bed, on first and second floors. Three private baths, two shared.
**Breakfast:** Juice, fresh fruit muffins, and coffee served in the sun room.
**Plus:** Sherry in living room. Strawberry candies on pillow. Small secluded yard and garden with wrought-iron furniture overlooking rose trellises. Bicycles loaned to guests.
**Rates:** $35 single, $50 double, $65 triple. MasterCard and VISA accepted.

## Grassy Pond House

Rindge, NH 03461
**Phone:** 603/899-5166/5167
**Location:** Secluded, in 150 acres of woods and fields on an unspoiled lake. Within walking distance of groomed cross-country

trails and Cathedral of the Pines. Three miles from the junction of U.S. Route 202 and N.H. 119.
**Hosts:** Carmen Linares and Robert Multer
**Open:** Year round. Reservations required. Two-night minimum stay October 5-20.

The site of Rindge's first sawmill, whose dam is now maintained by beavers, is the home of enthusiastic students of New England's historic building styles and furnishings. Between them, the hosts do all the "building trades" including gardening and forestry. They have done most of the restoration work on their Greek Revival house, which was built in 1830 and expanded in 1960. For relaxation, they prowl historic sites, antiques shops, and auctions.

"Our house, which was built on land purchased in 1781 for '60 pounds in gold and silver,' is a place where you can put your feet on the couch, read by the fire, stroll on the grounds. It is comfortable and nonthreatening, clean and bright," with antique beds in carefully appointed guest rooms. Everything from a mantel to a bench or quilt has a story.

In addition to full-time B&B hosting, Carmen, with a degree in psychology, remains a management consultant-trainer, and chemical engineer Bob continues his solar energy practice.

**In residence:** Lilly, a Maine coon cat, who is kept away from guests' bedrooms and guests who are not fond of cats.
**Restrictions:** Children should be at least 14. No guests' pets. No smoking inside the house.
**Foreign languages spoken:** Spanish and "a trace of Japanese."
**Bed and bath:** Three first-floor rooms with private guest entrance. One room with double bed and one with two twins adjoin a shared bath. One double-bedded room with full bath.
**Breakfast:** A hit. Usually 8-9. Buckwheat pancakes, French toast, pecan waffles, baked apples, fresh fruits, freshly ground Columbian or decaf coffee, local maple syrup. In the dining room with view of the pond. Bob and Carmen join guests.
**Plus:** Beverages and fresh fruit always available. Thermostat in each room. Wool blankets. Paths through field and woods. Thick towels. TV, audio cassette player, games, books, magazines in common room.
**Rates:** $35 single, $55 double with shared bath. $65 double with private bath.

## Tokfarm Inn

Box 229, Wood Avenue, Rindge, NH 03461
**Phone:** 603/899-6646
**Location:** On a country lane, 5 miles from Rindge village and Cathedral of the Pines, 12 miles from Fitzwilliam. Mount Monadnock is nearby. Near antiquing and Franklin Pierce College.
**Host:** Mrs. E. Nottingham
**Open:** July 1-November 30. Reservations preferred. Two-day minimum stay during foliage season.

"The most noise here is the chirping of birds in the morning and/or the wind in the trees when it's windy."

It's a 150-year old farmhouse originally built as a private home, extended over the years to a 23-room inn on the Boston-to-Keene stagecoach road. Bought by the Nottinghams as a summer place 45 years ago, it is now a much smaller, casual and comfortable B&B as well as an active 100-acre tree farm. (About Thanksgiving time, come choose and cut your Christmas tree.) The tri-state viewing site is a great vantage point for watching sunsets or fireflies.

Mrs. Nottingham's experiences are indeed diverse. Born in Holland, educated in Canada, she was one of the first ten women to receive an MBA. For ten years, she and her MIT professor husband ran a ski lodge in Stowe, Vermont. At times she can be talked into showing slides and home movies of the exotic and not-so-exotic places she has been to.

**In residence:** One cat.
**Restrictions:** Minimum age is 16. No pets. No smoking.
**Foreign languages spoken:** German, Dutch, French, and Spanish.
**Bed and bath:** Six rooms (never all booked at one time). Two shared baths. Every bed size from single to king available.
**Breakfast:** 8-9. Continental in a remodeled farm kitchen.
**Plus:** Lounge area with Franklin fireplace. TV. Private guest entrance. Spring-fed pond. Hiking trails. Wild blueberry picking.
**Rates:** $17 single, $33-$38 twin or double, $45 king ($48 with extra bed).

## Rock Ledge Manor Bed and Breakfast

1413 Ocean Boulevard, Rt. 1A, Rye, NH 03870
**Phone:** 603/431-1413
**Location:** On the ocean with view of Isles of Shoals. Five miles to Portsmouth, 25 to York or Ogunquit, Maine. Within 20 minutes of Hampton, Exeter, and University of New Hampshire.
**Hosts:** Norman and Janice Marineau
**Open:** Year round. Reservations recommended.

From Illinois: "Beautiful home. Fantastic location. Rooms immaculate and charmingly appointed. Warm hosts. Breakfast was an occasion."

Many guests walk the coastline before the memorable breakfast at this prime location that was part of an old "gingerbread" resort colony built around 1880. Until the Marineaus opened here five years ago, they were apartment-house owners and caterers with personal interests in the arts, running, and racquetball. Now most of their energy goes toward making this property the landmark it once was. A huge stack of letters written to me lauds their efforts.

**Restrictions:** Children should be at least 11. No smoking. No guests' pets.
**Foreign language spoken:** French.
**Bed and bath:** Four double-bedded rooms, two with full private bath and two with private half-bath and shared shower. All rooms have ocean views. Cots available.
**Breakfast:** 8-9. Brunchlike menu could include crepes, meats, vegetables. Served in a mahogany-ceilinged breakfast room that overlooks the ocean. Table set with linens.
**Plus:** Air conditioning or ceiling fans. Sunbathing area on property. Adjoining beaches. Porch. Library/music room, sun room. All-day parking, even after checkout.
**Rates:** $45-$50 single, $50-$55 double. $15 Cots.

*Can't find the community you are going to? Check with a reservation service described at the beginning of this chapter. Through the service, you may be placed (matched) with a welcoming B&B that is near your destination.*

## Province Inn

Box 309, Province Road, Bow Lake, Strafford, NH 03884
**Phone:** 603/664-2457
**Location:** A pastoral setting on a cove of a quiet lake, with 120 wooded acres, hiking trails, and waterfall. Restaurants, country stores, and antiquing nearby. About a half hour to Portsmouth or University of New Hampshire; an hour to White Mountains.
**Hosts:** Steve and Corky Garboski
**Open:** Year round.

The setting may be perfect for a country wedding, but this personalized B&B comes complete with a justice of the peace, the hostess. Corky is also an airline stewardess and an ice skating instructor. Steve, a former Olympic class bicyclist, is an airline pilot. The Garboskis combined all their interests and expanded their skills in 1984 when they bought and restored their 18th-century center-chimney colonial, furnishing the living room with Victorian furniture and swags, the den in casual style.

The extensive facilities here (see "Plus" below) make it almost a miniresort—without crowds. "We love our cove, the home of several beavers and a large heron." For nightlife, the hosts suggest summer theater or, on weekends, dancing and sing-alongs at the local country club, five miles away.

**In residence:** In hosts' wing of house, Bethany, age two. Ralph is a playful Welsh corgi who guides guests to the waterfall; Thai Kitty, a Siamese cat, has been known to sleep at the foot of a guest's bed or knock on the window to be let in.
**Restrictions:** Children in a crib share room with parents; otherwise maximum of two persons per room. Sorry, no guests' pets.
**Bed and bath:** Four second-floor rooms share two full baths plus one half one. Three rooms with double beds, one with twin beds. Two rooms have nonworking fireplaces. Crib available.
**Breakfast:** 8-10, or by special arrangement. Home-baked muffins and breads, whole-wheat date bar, fresh fruit, hot and cold cereals, beverages. Buffet style in fireplaced Keeping Room. Hosts usually join guests for breakfast.
**Plus:** Enclosed heated swimming pool. Lighted tennis courts. Use of canoes, Sunfish, sailboat, windsurfers, and bicycles. Cross-country skiing on 40 miles of groomed trails. Fireplaces. Gluhwein (hot spiced wine) served in winter. Snacks. Fruit. Fresh flowers in sea-

son. Guest refrigerator. Barbecue. Babysitting possibility. Nine-hole golf course 5 miles away.
**Rates:** $48 per room. $5 crib. Off-season and midweek, children use the twin-bedded room at half price.

## Southworth's B&B

Main Street, Sugar Hill, NH 03585
**Phone:** 603/823-5344
**Location:** On Route 117, across from Town Meeting House. Fifteen minutes to Cannon and Loon Mountains and Bretton Woods. About three miles from Franconia.
**Hosts:** Amy and David Southworth
**Open:** Year round. Reservations preferred.

The convenient location of this traditional two-storied house attracts skiers, hikers, and cyclists as well as travelers passing through while "taking in all of New England." All appreciate the hospitality in a homey (and very clean) recently decorated B&B with its country look, antiques, and older furniture.

Although a couple of Southworth generations started the B&B, the senior Southworths are currently in Texas. Until they retire here, Amy and David are greeting guests—and sharing knowledge about the area. In addition to running his home maintenance business, David is an active selectman, fireman, and E.M.T. for the town of Sugar Hill. Amy works with David and may some day have her own sleigh ride business. M&M, her horse-in-training, is in the pasture just across the road.

**In residence:** Shadow, a friendly mixed black Lab.
**Restrictions:** No children or guests' pets. Only two people to a room.
**Bed and bath:** Three bright and cheerful second-floor rooms, each with a double bed, share one large full bath.
**Breakfast:** Coffee and doughnuts or homemade muffins. "Our guests seem to have planned days. Occasionally they just have coffee and go down the road (May through mid-October) for Polly's Pancake Parlor, featured in *Road Food*."
**Plus:** TV room. Games, puzzles, magazines and books. Living room. Bedroom fans. Electric blankets. Flannel sheets in winter.
**Rates:** $35 per room. $5 surcharge for one-night stay.

## Haus Edelweiss Bed & Breakfast

Maple Street, P.O. Box 609, Sunapee, NH 03782
**Phone:** 603/763-2100
**Location:** On a residential street, 500 feet from the public boat landing. Five minutes to Sunapee ski area.
**Hosts:** Alan and Lillian Norton-McGonnigal
**Open:** Year round.

"Alan is the cook and I'm in charge of the business end. We wanted to work together and found this wonderful big freshly decorated Victorian house. B&B is full-time for us, with Alan still doing free-lance photography. We moved here in 1986 from Cape Cod, where we lived after Alan retired from the Air Force and I was a manufacturer's buyer. Our furnishings are an eclectic mix with lots of plants. Since meeting our very first guests, Irish skiers who were ecstatic about our Irish oatmeal and the house itself, we have met many other interesting people—with or without children, antiquers, hikers, artists. B&B is wonderful!"

**In residence:** One who smokes; Lillian's mother. Two dogs—Sam, an apricot miniature poodle, and Sarah, a peek-a-poo. Four third-floor resident cats who do not see guests.
**Restrictions:** Well-mannered pets allowed. No smoking in bedrooms.
**Foreign language spoken:** German.
**Bed and bath:** Five rooms, all with cross-ventilation; one single and four doubles. (Two doubles have permanent day beds.) One double has a private half-bath, other rooms share two full baths. Cot and crib available.
**Breakfast:** Usually 7-9. Traditional—ham/bacon or sausage and eggs with home fries or French toast; Yankee—fish cakes, beans, eggs, and corn bread; Bavarian—cheeses, smoked meats, hard rolls. Homemade bread, rolls, and muffins. Continental jams and jellies. In dining room with candlelit sconces. Or in bed. Or on porch.
**Plus:** Beverages, Bavarian gluhwein (hot mulled wine) in winter. Wood stove in living room. Mints. Evening snacks. Extra pillows.
**Rates:** $25 single, $45 double with shared bath. $50 double with private half-bath. $5 extra person. No charge for children under six; 10 percent discount for students, military, or a stay of more than three days. Over seven days less 15 percent. Package plans available. MasterCard and VISA accepted.

## The Partridge House Inn

P.O. Box 231, Profile Road, Route 3, Twin Mountain, NH 03995
**Phone:** 603/846-2277
**Location:** On main road with views of Mount Washington. Minutes to five notches and to Bretton Woods, Cannon, Loon, Attitash, Black, and Wildcat ski areas. Fifteen minutes from I-93.
**Host:** Janet Partridge
**Open:** Year round. Reservations preferred. Three-day minimum stay during foliage season.

"We planned to have an inn that was elegant enough to make you feel special, but not so elegant that you don't feel at home. People who come here range from honeymooners who might be looking for privacy to those who enjoy the company of other guests. The blend of guests is amazing—senior citizens, young couples, artists, skiers, hikers, families. Somehow everyone who has stayed with us has made this a better place. When I left my job in customer service with Carroll Reed, I certainly never expected innkeeping to be such a rewarding experience."

Paintings by local artists add to the warmth of the 1800s inn, which was renovated in 1985.

**In residence:** Jeremy, age 13, and Josie, age 9. Two white cats, Mr. "C" and Snowball, who become good friends with many guests.
**Restrictions:** No guests' pets. Smoking restricted to sun porch and dining room.
**Foreign language spoken:** French.
**Bed and bath:** Ten rooms, eight with private baths. Three rooms on first floor, five on second, two on third. Some baths are full; some shower only. Rocking chair in each room.
**Breakfast:** 7:30-10. Fruit, juice, apple coffee cake, fruit muffins, homemade breads, jams and jellies, oatmeal, granola, raisin bran, shredded wheat, coffee, tea. Buffet style in dining room with working antique wood stove.
**Plus:** Beverages, cheese and crackers. Sun porch. Piano in library. Common room. Deck. Bath sheets and thick towels. Turned-down service. Double hammock and glider in the yard. Five acres for walking—to the river, beaver bog, and connecting properties.

**Rates:** $45 single, $25 per person double occupancy. $5 additional person in room. Midweek packages, discounts for extended stays. MasterCard and VISA accepted.

A guest wrote: "It was the highlight of our trip."

## Maria W. Atwood Inn

RFD 2, Route 3A, West Franklin, NH 03235
**Phone:** 603/934-3666
**Location:** Within a half hour of Gunstock, Sunapee, and Loon Mountains. About 15 minutes to five lakes including Winnipesaukee. Ten minutes to Tilton School or Proctor Academy.
**Hosts:** Stephen Green and Andy LaBrie
**Open:** Year round.

"The TV Room doesn't get much use here. Of course some people aren't in the mood to talk, but there's something about our big dining-room table that seems to make it the gathering place."

Before renovating this stately brick Federal house "expressly for B&B," Steve had done several other places, including a one-room schoolhouse, some 18th-century Capes, and a chicken coop that is now a manufacturing facility. He left his solar research job in 1984 and teamed up with Andy, who had had more than a dozen years in hotel and restaurant management. Andy, now a Realtor, chose the colonial colors and wallpapers and the antique furnishings, from primitive to formal mahogany. His collection of teddy bears makes quite a hit, particularly with children. The third important person here is Ruth, Steve's mother. She makes breakfasts and inn-sits during the day at "our friendly place that is really a lovely home away from home."

The 1832 building, a conversation piece in itself, has four chimneys, six fireplaces, wide board floors, and Indian shutters. Most guests who request a tour marvel at the match between old and new, so that you can "hardly tell."

**In residence:** One host who smokes. An old English sheep dog named Chauncy.
**Restrictions:** Children should be at least five years old. Sorry, no guests' pets. No smoking in bedrooms.

**Bed and bath:** Eight rooms, each with private shower bath. Double or twin beds or combination of both. One room has four twin beds. Cot available. Most rooms with fireplaces (not used); many with four windows, some with skylights.
**Breakfast:** 8-9. Juice, fresh fruits, meats, eggs, pancakes, or "our yet to be famous" French toast; coffee or tea. Buffet style in formal dining room; weather permitting, on deck or in the gardens.
**Plus:** Two acres of lawns and formal flower gardens. Refreshments on arrival. Short walk down the road to Pemigewasset River. Cross-country skiing and horseback riding nearby.
**Rates:** $45 single, $55 double. $10 additional person in a room. MasterCard, VISA, and AMEX accepted.

## Stepping Stones

RFD 1, Box 208, Bennington Battle Trail, Wilton Center, NH 03086
**Phone:** 603/654-9048
**Location:** Quiet. Across from a reservoir. In the country, two minutes from a picture-book village in the Monadnock Hills. Six miles from Temple Mountain, 20 miles west of Nashua.
**Host:** Ann Carlsmith
**Open:** Year round. Reservations recommended.

> From Massachusetts: "It's a magical older home, peaceful yet inspiring, friendly yet private, comfortable yet beautiful to behold. . . . Many exquisite works of artists and artisans. . . . People travel great distances just to wander the winding paths of the spectacular perennial gardens. . . . A guest is reminded that some people and some places are still extra special."

Many long glowing letters have arrived to praise the garden designer who spends her winters weaving on her many looms. Perhaps you have come for chamber music concerts, weaving lessons, antiquing, or theater, or to rest in the quiet country. When you tear yourself away, Ann can direct you to a back road lined with farms or a 30-foot waterfall. People from all over the world—"people whom I never would have met otherwise"—have found this haven.

**In residence:** Mehitabel, a long-haired gray cat, and Dustin, a 100-pound collie/golden retriever mix.
**Restrictions:** Pets allowed if kept well under control. Smoking not allowed indoors.

**Bed and bath:** Two second-floor bedrooms share a full bath. One with extra-long double bed and a crib, the other with two single beds. Both rooms overlook a private garden, with wooded hills beyond. Down comforters, handwoven throws and rugs.
**Breakfast:** By 10. Belgian waffles or French toast with maple syrup or homemade preserves, sausages, omelets, croissants, homemade muffins and sweet breads, seasonal fruit and orange juice. Served in the solar breakfast room, which has plants, pottery, a wood stove, and a view of garden.
**Plus:** Beverages and ginger cookies. An opportunity to visit gardens and to observe weaving. Window fans. Color TV, stereo, books and magazines in living room.
**Rates:** $25 single, $35 double. $25 child in single bed, $10 infant in crib. Seventh night free.

From Tennessee: "On a scale of 1 to 10, her home ranks 11. (She even shared plants with us to bring home!)"

*Can't find the community you are going to? Check with a reservation service described at the beginning of this chapter. Through the service, you may be placed (matched) with a welcoming B&B that is near your destination.*

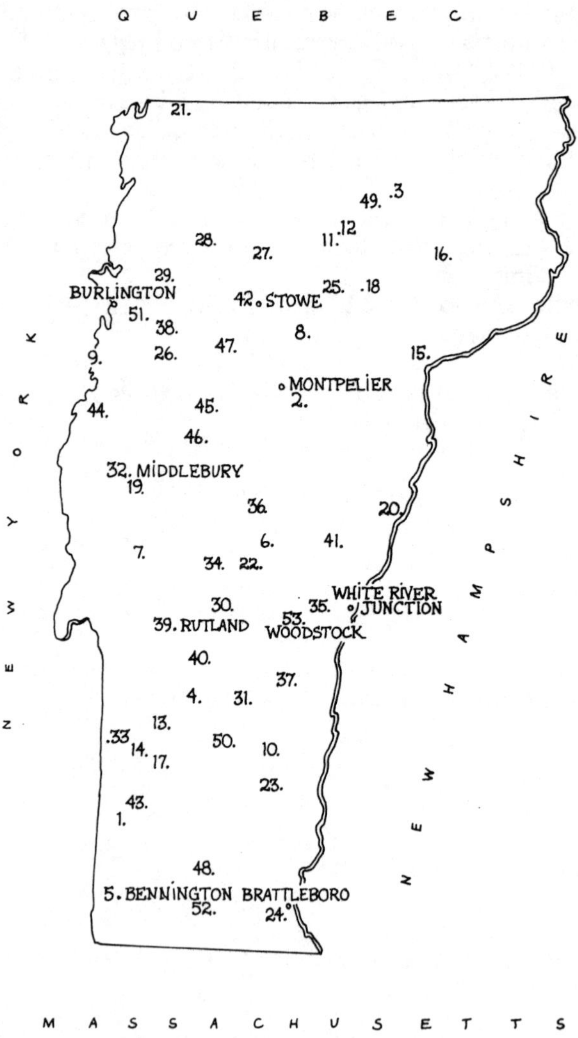


*The numbers on this map indicate the locations of B&Bs described in detail in this chapter.*

## VERMONT

**KEY**

Recipes shared, often for house specialties.

Inquiries welcomed about restoration and/or decorating. Symbol indicates that host is willing to share experiences with guests. Tips range from a before-and-after album to rebuilding advice, from furniture refinishing to curtain making. Expertise of hosts ranges from learn-by-doing to professional.

How-To B&B workshop, seminar or apprentice program offered.

# Vermont Reservation Services

## The American Country Collection

984 Gloucester Place, Schenectady, NY 12309
**Phone:** 518/370-4948. Tuesday-Friday 10-noon; 1-6.

**Listings:** 50 hosted private residences, a few inns. Most New England listings are in southern and central Vermont and in the Berkshires of western Massachusetts. A few are in the Connecticut River Valley sections of Massachusetts and Connecticut. In New York State, most are in the Albany/Saratoga region with a few in the Hudson Valley/Catskill and Leatherstocking areas. Many homes are on the National Register of Historic Places. Range includes budget to luxurious. Directory ($2).

Beverly Walsh's "delightful hosts" are attentive to guests' needs but aware of the need for privacy. They present homemade foods, know their area, and often have attended Beverly's comprehensive workshops about running a B&B.

**Reservations:** Two weeks in advance preferred. Last minute accepted when possible.
**Plus:** Arrangements for B&B-to-B&B trips. Pickup at transportation points provided by some hosts.
**Rates:** $25-$75 single, $30-$85 double. Some family and weekly rates. Deposit is at least one night's lodging; 1/2 of total stay. Refunds made, less $10 service charge, for cancellations received at least seven days before arrival. Within seven days, one night's lodging charged.

## Vermont Bed & Breakfast

P.O. Box One, East Fairfield, VT 05448
**Phone:** 802/827-3827. Monday-Saturday 11-7.

**Listings:** 35 "and growing fast." Mostly private residences. A few inns. Located throughout Vermont, "from lakeside to mountain top, from city to village to farm."

Jane Torbert Zurn's varied listings offer opportunities to experience the "diversity of that state of mind that is Vermont." She took over the service in 1986 with the goal of providing hospitality to all who wish to "come home to Vermont."

**Reservations:** At least 24 hours' notice required. Some hosts have a two-day minimum. Also available through travel agents.
**Plus:** Some unhosted residences available for up to several months. Gift certificates. Combination "B&B and see Vermont" packages. Ski and dining packages.
**Rates:** $25-$70 single, $35-$85 double. Some family and weekly rates. Some have one-night surcharge. $15 booking fee per trip for nonmembers. Annual membership ($25) benefits include no booking fee, a directory, and a newsletter. Minimum one night's lodging required for deposit. Cancellations with less than ten days' notice are charged a minimum of one night's stay at each location plus booking fee. VISA and MasterCard accepted; 4 percent surcharge.

## Christian Hospitality

This service has hosts in Danby, Middletown Springs, Mount Holly, Ripton, Rutland, and Shrewsbury. Please see page 287.

## Pineapple Hospitality

This service has hosts in Brattleboro, Burlington area, Essex Junction, Hyde Park, Middlebury, Pawlet, East Poultney, Rupert, Stowe, and Williamsville. Please see page 214.

# Vermont B&Bs

## Hill Farm Inn

RR 2, Box 2015, Arlington, VT 05250
**Phone:** 802/375-2269
**Location:** At the foot of Mount Equinox, surrounded by 2½ acres of lawns and gardens and farmlands. Between Bennington and Manchester, ½ mile off Route 7A.
**Hosts:** Joanne and George Hardy, Cathy Harper
**Open:** Year round. Reservations preferred. Two-night minimum stay on holiday weekends.

"At least one of us is interested in almost everything." One is Joanne, already a member of the local school board (having come here just three years ago) and a teacher of early childhood education at the community college. Then there's her husband, George, who was a minister and a social worker when they lived in Indiana and Ohio. Cathy, a fun-loving friend from Ohio, left Washington, D.C. where she was an assistant to a member of Congress, to come and help run the inn.

"We are the first people not named Hill to own this property since it was deeded to them in 1775. The prior owner was King George III." Until the Hardys bought it in 1983, some member of the Hill family had been innkeeper here since its opening in 1905. The inn is really two post-and-beam buildings—the main (Federal) building and the guesthouse, a Cape, built around 1790 and completely renovated in 1984.

There is a piano in the living room and a wraparound porch with rockers, but the kitchen is the real heart of the house. Guests find apples in their room, a take-home jar of Joanne's own jam, and at Christmas, a filled stocking. Embroidered pictures, dresser scarves, crocheted rugs, a spinning wheel—all contribute to that comfortable "unwinding" feeling.

**In residence:** Patches, the offspring of an English setter and a traveling hound dog, is usually the first one to welcome guests and the last to say goodbye. Numerous barn cats.
**Restrictions:** Smoking in common rooms only.

**Bed and bath:** Eleven rooms, five with private baths. Three rooms each have a king-sized bed and a twin bed. Double or two twin beds in other rooms. Flowered wallpapers, color-coordinated linens.
**Breakfast:** 7:30-9:30. Juices (tomato is homemade), cereals (including homemade granola), eggs, homemade bran or blueberry muffins, French toast or blueberry pancakes. Served in dining room.
**Plus:** Late-afternoon snacks in winter. Tour of the house. Dinner ($11 for a four-course meal) offered to guests only by advance reservation; served at 6:30. Electric blankets. Fans available. Board games, puzzles, and books. Croquet and badminton. Fishing in the Battenkill River, which winds through the farm. Bounty of garden shared in summer. Will meet Manchester or Arlington bus.
**Rates:** $52 double occupancy with shared bath, $60 double with private bath. Discounts for children 12 and under. Children under two free unless the crib ($5) is needed. MasterCard, VISA, and AMEX accepted.

## Woodruff House

13 East Street, Barre, VT 05641
**Phone:** 802/476-7745
**Location:** Near center of the city, on a quiet old-fashioned park. Half way between Boston and Montreal. Near the state capitol (Montpelier), the largest granite quarries in the world, and Sugarbush, Mount Mansfield, and Stowe ski areas.
**Hosts:** Robert and Terry Somaini
**Open:** Year round.

"Our home is an 1883 Victorian, blueberry with vanilla trim and cranberry shutters, filled with antiques of all styles. It is warm, cozy, a bit Edwardian. Our eclectic collection is ever changing and being added to. Must be experienced to appreciate fully."

Fully appreciated it is! By many who have written in great detail, including wet and soggy cross-country cyclists from California and travelers from Virginia ("pleasantly impressed with the charm of the house, but more so by the hosts who made us feel like one of the family"). From Tallahassee, Florida: "Bob's cooking set a new standard for B&Bs." From Maryland: "Breakfast served with silver, china and crystal on lace tablecloth by candlelight."

Robert, a native Vermonter, is an interior consultant and in sales work. Terry is employed with an accounting firm.

**In residence**: Daughter Katie, age 12.
**Restrictions:** Sorry, no guests' pets. No smoking.
**Bed and bath:** Two guest rooms on first floor. One with double antique sleigh bed and private porch, the other with twin beds and antique furnishings. Shared bath with shower only.
**Breakfast:** At 8 weekdays, 9 weekends in one of two dining rooms. Menu varies from simple to fancy.
**Plus:** Living room on first floor with piano. TV upstairs. Quiet times by the fire. A large wood furnace to keep house warm on long winter nights. Beverage and dessert often served in the evening.
**Rates:** $35 single, $45 double.

## Lafont's Bed & Breakfast

RR 3, Box 90, Barton, VT 05822
**Phone:** 802/755-6127
**Location:** In the "unspoiled" Northeast Kingdom. Up on a hill on a dead-end road, seven miles from I-91. Very very quiet. Surrounded by cows and woods. Near Craftsbury, Jay Peak, and Burke ski areas. (Dinner restaurants are about half hour away.)
**Hosts:** Richard and Rachel Lafont
**Open:** Year round. Advance reservations strongly recommended during Bread and Puppet Theater performances in August.

You almost feel as if you have discovered Vermont at this B&B.

"After farming here for 34 years, we sold our farm to our son, the sixth generation to keep it going. We moved to this nearby renovated farmhouse and are working for our son. Since 1981 B&B has added to our excitement. We meet so many people from other places. We never lack for conversation. We talk 'sugaring' over pancakes and coffee."

Guests are long remembered. Rachel keeps the pictures she has taken of each one on a calendar.

**In residence:** One daughter, a dental assistant. Mascot is a very independent cat. Sometimes grandchildren, age six and eight, are visiting.
**Restrictions:** No guests' pets. Nonsmokers preferred. No alcoholic beverages, please.

**Bed and bath:** Two upstairs rooms with private outside entrance share a bath. "Rooms are not fancy, but comfortable." A double bed in each. Cot and crib available.
**Breakfast:** Anytime, usually 8 or 8:30. Full country breakfast with cereal or oatmeal, muffins or toast, bacon and eggs or pancakes with Lafont maple syrup and sausage. Served in kitchen with wood stove and cabinets made from old barn boards. Leisurely.
**Plus:** Intermediate-level cross-country skiing on a marked miles-long snowmobile trail on the property. Coffee or hot chocolate after skiing. Pond for experienced swimmers. Dinner sometimes available, only by previous arrangement. Babysitting. TV in the living room. Kitchen privileges. Laundry facilities (extra charge). An opportunity to watch the evening milking.
**Rates:** $20 single, $25 double. $5 cot. Winter rates are $5 higher.

## The Parmenter House

P.O. Box 106, Belmont, VT 05730
**Phone:** 802/259-2009
**Location:** In a small mountain lakeside village that has retained the character of a turn-of-the-century resort village. On a rarely traveled road between Routes 103 and 155; 12 miles from Weston, 17 miles from Rutland, 2 miles to oldest extant cheese factory in Vermont, 15 minutes from Okemo, 40 minutes from Killington, Pico, Stratton, Bromley, and Magic Mountain.
**Hosts:** Lester and Cynthia Firschein
**Open:** Year round, except for part of April or May. Three-night minimum stay on national holiday weekends; two nights on non-holiday weekends in foliage and ski seasons.

The well-traveled hosts (they especially liked East Africa) discovered Belmont while on a motorcycle trip in 1982. A year later they began to share their love of the village, the house, and entertaining with B&B guests.

The house has a fascinating history. In response to guests' inquiries, the Firscheins gladly share background information, sources for wallpapers and antiques, and hints about adding bathrooms to a Greek Revival house without destroying the original layout.

Cynthia's seasonal wildflower arrangements reflect her training in fine arts. The Central American solidarity posters in the kitchen reflect the concerns of both Lester and Cynthia. Lester is a retired anthropology professor and Cynthia, too, did graduate work in anthropology.

With all that under one roof, it is no wonder that guests call a stay here an experience. At least two former guests have become Belmont residents!

**In residence:** "Our zoo: Badger and Harriet, two large dogs, and two house cats, Buffy and Mr Peepers." Usually confined to hosts' quarters but sometimes they "escape."
**Restrictions:** Children should be at least seven. No guests' pets. No smoking, please.
**Foreign languages spoken:** A little French and Spanish.
**Bed and bath:** Five rooms. All private baths, some with shower or tub only. One small room on first floor. Second-floor rooms range from small with double beds to very large with double and single beds. Each room furnished with Victorian antiques.
**Breakfast:** 7:30-9:30. Homemade maple walnut granola, cold cereals, fresh fruits, yogurt, Vermont cheddar cheese, waffles and French toast. Homemade scones/biscuits or local bakery's croissants/rolls. Jams and honey. Served in dining room or on deck.
**Plus:** Beverages (mulled cider in fall) and snacks. Tours of the house. Back roads foliage tours. Time permitting, hiking or cross-country skiing (through woods and/or across lake) with hosts. Use of canoe and rubber rafts (no charge) on lake behind the house. Croquet. Porch. Parlor games. Bicycles for rent. Danish Christmas weekend. Foliage harvest weekend with horse-drawn hayride.
**Rates:** Memorial Day-Labor Day $40-$55 double occupancy. Foliage and ski season $50-$65 with $5 surcharge on foliage season weekends, New Year's, Martin Luther King, and Presidents' weekends. $15 third person. Special rates for groups and midweek stays of three to five nights. MasterCard and VISA accepted.

---

## The American Country Collection Host #006

---

Bennington, VT
**Location:** Near the library and Main Street, in a residential section 5 minutes from Bennington College campus, 10 minutes to Prospect ski area, 30 minutes to Manchester center.

**Reservations:** Available year round through The American Country Collection, page 135.

This impeccably kept Victorian has the feeling of a big old house that has been in a family for a long time. It was the summer home of the hostess's grandparents. Now her own grandchildren come to visit. Hardwood floors, wainscoting, a country kitchen, a knitting basket here, a rocking chair there—a warm atmosphere, freshly decorated with comfortable Victorian charm.

The hostess has lived in the area nearly all her life and has special interests in music, theater, and art. She works in real estate and at the hospital, and enjoys cross-country skiing.

**In residence:** An eight-year-old silver poodle.
**Restrictions:** Children should be at least 14.
**Foreign language spoken:** Some French.
**Bed and bath:** Three second-floor rooms (for two parties) share one guest bath. Two rooms with double beds, one with adjoining sitting room with a single bed and fireplace.
**Breakfast:** 7:30-9:30. Fresh fruit, juice, Irish oatmeal, home-baked fruit breads and muffins, coffee or tea served in the dining room.
**Plus:** Late-afternoon or evening beverage. Thick towels, fancy soaps. Much reading material; books on Victorian Vermont.
**Rates:** $25 single, $40 double.

## Eastwood House

River Street, Bethel, VT 05032
**Phone:** 802/234-9686
**Location:** Just outside the village, 3.2 miles from I-89. On Route 12 with a view of the White River and valley. Half hour north of Killington.
**Hosts:** Christine and Ron Diamond
**Open:** Year round. Two-day minimum stay during foliage weekends.

They looked for a small town, but didn't know they would be the connecting link between two Bethel classmates who had graduated 40 years ago. One was the local postman and the other a Nova Scotia resident who happened to stay at Eastwood House.

Because Ron and Chris had already restored a house in Maryland, they felt they were up to tackling the long-neglected Federal house that they saw in 1983 after a very long search. Chris is responsible for the Williamsburg decor of the brick mansion, a stagecoach stop in the early 19th century. She made all the tab curtains (over 4,000 tabs!) and hand-sewn quilts, and plans to do stenciling on those horsehair walls. Both Diamonds do just about everything. When Ron isn't wearing the hat of innkeeper, he works in a woodworking shop. In Maryland he did administrative work with a labor union. Chris worked in customer service with the National Geographic Society.

The house is furnished with antiques. It's a peaceful place not far from lots of activity including skiing, antiquing, river tubing (rentals four miles away), and Woodstock.

**In residence:** Samantha, an eight-year-old Labrador retriever, "admired by all guests."
**Restrictions:** No guests' pets. Smoking and drinking restricted to the Keeping Room.
**Bed and bath:** Eight rooms, four with fireplaces, share three baths. Crib available.
**Breakfast:** 7-8:30. Quiches, omelets, home-baked breads, pumpkin pancakes, aebelskivers (Danish pancakes), popovers, fruit, tea or coffee, Vermont cheddar cheese, Vermont maple syrup. Served in the Keeping Room at a long harvest table.
**Plus:** Set-ups for BYOB. Formal gardens in progress.
**Rates:** $30-$45 double occupancy depending on room size. $10 for each additional person. MasterCard, VISA, DISCOVER, and AMEX accepted.

From Connecticut: "It feels like a home away from home. Breakfasts are ample and tasty. It's beautifully clean, has unusually comfortable beds and soft, thirsty towels. Best of all is the welcome from Chris and Ron."

*Can't find the community you are going to? Check with a reservation service described at the beginning of this chapter. Through the service, you may be placed (matched) with a welcoming B&B that is near your destination.*

## Beauchamp Place

31 Franklin Street, Route 7, Brandon, VT 05733
**Phone:** 802/247-3905
**Location:** In historic Brandon, 1/4 mile south of village center on U.S. Route 7 south. Walk to shops and restaurants. Near cycling routes; sleigh rides; downhill skiing at Killington, Pico, and Middlebury Ski Bowl; and several cross-country centers.
**Hosts:** Georgia and Roy Beauchamp
**Open:** Year round. Reservations recommended for special Middlebury College weekends. Two-day minimum stay on holiday weekends.

From Texas, from Manhattan, from California and Florida, guests have written letters of praise. "Exquisite . . . the consummate hosts . . . a Victorian gem of lavish comfort . . . a time capsule." In 1985, as Georgia tells it, "Our aim was to recreate an elegant Victorian inn with modern creature comforts. We had been collecting nice antiques for many years, without any thought of operating an inn. But when we were 'merged' out of our London position we decided to share our collections this way. We have had the opportunity to travel a great deal, often B&B, and we were ready to have the world come to us. So here we are."

Roy was chief executive officer of an engineering and construction company in London, where they lived for 15 years. For this house, which is listed on the National Register of Historic Places, he merged his expertise with Georgia's decorating and design skills. The Beauchamps have added yards of wonderful fabrics, authentic wallpapers, custom-made metal ceilings on the third floor, a fireplace in the parlor, and Victorian and Empire furnishings from two continents. Within the first year of operation, these energetic grandparents (of three ranging from preschool to teenage) found that, in addition to contented guests, several potential innkeepers came to them for advice.

**Restrictions:** Not the perfect place for active children. Sorry, no pets and no smoking allowed.
**Bed and bath:** Eight spacious rooms with individual thermostats. Four on second floor share two baths, one with shower and one with "a lovely old tub on legs." Four rooms on third floor share two baths with showers. King-sized (one is canopied), queen-sized, double, and twin beds available. Down pillows and duvets.

**Breakfast:** 8:30-9:00. Served in the dining room at tables for four or eight. Juices, fruit, homemade granola, hot muffins, homemade jams and jellies. Eggs, if desired. Coffees, teas, milk.
**Plus:** Wine, cheese, and snack "hour or so" in the double parlor. Tours of the house. Dinner on special occasions by previous arrangement. Fans in third-floor rooms. Porch rockers. Gardens, garden swing and hammock. Books. Magazines. Daily newspaper. Croquet and other games. Hand-made truffles on pillows of turned-down beds. Flowers in summer, dried arrangements in winter.
**Rates:** Double occupancy. $70-$85 depending on bed size. Off-season and midweek discounts. MasterCard, VISA, and AMEX accepted.

## Northview

Lightning Ridge Road, Calais, VT
Mailing address: RD 2, Plainfield, VT 05667
**Phone:** 802/454-7191
**Location:** Off a rural country road, 8 miles north of the capital city of Montpelier, in a historic and picturesque town. On a hill, surrounded by stone walls and white fences, with meadows and mountain views. Five minutes from swimming, boating, horseback riding.
**Hosts:** Joani and Glenn Yankee
**Open:** Year round. Reservations required.

> "Just what I always pictured New England to be—stenciled walls, tab curtains, maple furniture, dried herbs, theorem paintings, French toast with Vermont maple syrup, freshly picked blueberries in muffins and a friendly host and hostess. . . . I loved the countryside and quiet."

Those words from Dallas, Texas were echoed by others who commented on "new plumbing in a meticulously restored house" (a garrison colonial) or "hours sitting with Glenn, talking about his extensive baseball card collection and library."

A New Mexico family that stayed for ten days took time to borrow the Yankees' big deep boots so that they could tromp around on the quaking bog that is a five-minute walk from the house. Glenn, a school superintendent, and Joani, a teacher who lists windsurfing among her interests, sometimes join visitors in the unusual nature preserve, which has carnivorous plants, orchids, and other rare flowers.

**In residence:** Pal, "a 17-year-old friendly calico cat."
**Restrictions:** Pets must be quiet and well trained. No smoking indoors, please.
**Bed and bath:** Three antique-filled rooms share a full bath. One double-bedded corner room has a canopied rope bed. Another double-bedded corner room boasts a hand-crocheted bedspread. Two twin beds in cozy third room. Cot available.
**Breakfast:** 6-9. In the country kitchen by the pot-bellied stove, in the dining room, or on the patio. Homemade coffee bread, muffins, and jams. Eggs, meats, Dutch babies.
**Plus:** Beverages. Tours of the house and area. Fresh flowers. Mints. Picnic area with table and fireplace. Yard games.
**Rates:** $28.50 single, $33 double. $10 cot. No charge for small children. Special rates for stays that are longer than three nights.

## Green Meadows

Box 1300, Mt. Philo Road, Charlotte, VT 05445
**Phone:** 802/425-3059
**Location:** In a small valley surrounded by meadows and woods. Five miles from Shelburne Museum or Charlotte-Essex ferry. Between Burlington and Middlebury in view of the Green Mountains.
**Host:** Mary Louise Smith
**Open:** Year round.

Having a daughter who decided to go to college in Vermont gave Mary Louise Smith the push to sell her Colorado home. While she was house hunting in the area, she stayed at a B&B and got the idea that it could work out in the big house she was looking for. What she found was an 1864 restored Victorian, just perfect for her 19th-century antique oak furniture. She has repapered ("I love to wallpaper") with small prints. White curtains are in all the windows. Floors are wide board pine, some fir, and even the bathrooms have wooden floors.

"It's a warm, comfortable nonintrusive atmosphere. Most people leave after breakfast and come back after dinner. Guests have come from all over. Just last week I had a call from France!"

Ms. Smith is an elementary school teacher.

**In residence**: Daughter Leslie is in her twenties. Pets—Cleo the cat, Maud the basset and Margaret the Great Dane.
**Restrictions:** No guests' pets. No smoking.
**Bed and bath:** Two small rooms, one with two twin beds, the other with a double bed, share a bath. A large attic bedroom has twin beds; bath is downstairs. Cot and crib available.
**Breakfast:** 7-9. Served in the dining room, which overlooks the Vermont countryside. Homemade breads, fruits, pancakes with Vermont maple syrup. (Breakfast is the best "visiting time" here.)
**Plus:** Tours of the house. Fans in bedrooms.
**Rates:** $25 for one, $30 for two.

## The Hugging Bear Inn

Main Street, Chester, VT 05143
**Phone:** 802/875-2412
**Location:** Across from the Village Green in historic district, 30 miles north of Brattleboro, 30 miles northeast of Manchester, Vt.
**Hosts:** Georgette and Paul Thomas
**Open:** Year round. Reservations required. Two- or three-day minimum stay on holiday weekends or during major holiday weeks.

"We have had guests who have asked for a room with two beds so they could bring their teddys for a visit, and others who never realized how much fun and comfort a teddy bear can be."

Everyone gets hugs ("98 percent accept them") at this unique B&B hosted by a lawyer who spent over 25 years in industry and government, and his wife, a trained personal counselor. Paul has spent "practically a lifetime in community theater"; his breakfast performances, with both hand and almost-life-sized puppets, are fun for both puppeteer and audience.

The Victorian house with wraparound porch, bay windows, and three-story tower has often been called "the prettiest house on the Village Green." The inn, established by the Thomases in 1983, has a mix of antiques and modern furniture. It's a great environment for travelers with or without children.

If you can bear to leave the furry stuffed animals (hundreds in the inn, at least one in every bed, and 2,000 in the shop), Georgette and Paul might suggest a nearby village that has stone buildings built in the 1830s, or a pedestrian suspension bridge that leads to beautiful views, horses, donkeys, and small sheep farms.

**In residence:** Sophie, a loving black Labrador/German shepherd mix.
**Restrictions:** Sorry, no smoking. Pets allowed only by special arrangement.
**Foreign language spoken:** A little Spanish.
**Bed and bath:** Six second-floor rooms with new private baths with shower. Two rooms each have one double bed. Others have two double beds and room for a cot; a double and single bed; twin beds and a sofa bed; and a double and 3/4 bed. Cot and crib available.
**Breakfast:** 8-9:30. Full leisurely breakfast served in the family-style dining room. Juice, eggs, bacon, sausage, French toast, special whole-wheat pancakes with cider, coffee, tea, and milk.
**Plus:** The company of as many teddy bears as you would like for overnight. Complimentary teddy bear soap. Unscheduled puppet shows. Fireplace and library in den. Flannel sheets. Late-afternoon beverage and snacks. Two miles of hiking trails through woods. Will meet guests at local train and bus stops. Babysitting available. Horseshoes, croquet, badminton in large yard. Bikes free of charge.
**Rates:** $60 double. $20 each additional adult. $10 child under 14. $5 crib. $65 on major holidays. Midweek discounts during off-season. MasterCard and VISA accepted.

## Gary-Meadows Dairy Farm

RR 1, Box 11, Craftsbury, VT 05826
**Phone:** 802/586-2536
**Location:** Off the beaten path, 500 feet off Route 14, two miles from Craftsbury Sports Center and picturesque Craftsbury Common, one mile from Craftsbury village.
**Hosts:** Gary and Nioka Houston
**Open:** April if warm. May-October.

This was our very first American B&B. After calling from the village store for directions, we pulled up to the 1884 farmhouse on an unpaved road and were greeted by hundreds of cows and dozens of calves. We wondered what country we were in!

Since that visit, Anne has been born and Nicki has completed graduate work and returned to teaching. She is involved with the local theater group and the Craftsbury Chamber Players. Gary, trained as a mechanical engineer, is on the school committee.

During our stay, we learned about changes in farming. It is a computerized business now. Gary started with 12 Holsteins. Of today's 800, half are milkers. Nicki has changed too. She'll tell you how she "helped" during her first visit with Gary's family: she let the cows out all right, but quickly learned that she had, unknowingly, also released the bull.

This is an active household that is great for traveling families. The Houstons and guests have been known to exchange children for a day trip. And then there's an incredible saga about a New Mexico guest who made the old grandfather's clock work for the first time since its purchase at an auction years ago.

**In residence:** Four children, Meagan, ten; Jody, eight; Jesse, six; Anne, two. "They all love to play host."
**Restrictions:** "Please, no pets. We do not smoke, but smoking is allowed."
**Bed and bath:** One first-floor room (not accessible to handicapped) with double bed and shared bath. Cots and cribs available. Refinished wide pine floorboards, attractively arranged Shaker pieces, and a bed covered with a glorious starburst-pattern quilt made and sold locally. Information shelf includes pamphlets of attractions and newsclippings on how to resist the temptation to sell the farm.
**Breakfast:** Available 6:30-11:30. Full country breakfast served in the country kitchen or on the sun porch. Nicki's favorite time, "my reward for all the housecleaning I do before guests arrive."
**Plus:** Lots of toys, outdoor games, bicycles and entertainment for children. Books, magazines, B&W TV, radio, piano. Late-afternoon or evening beverages. Kitchen privileges. Babysitting (under 18 months and over 3). Gas grille, lawn chairs, sandbox, even the lawn mower if you'd like! Farm tour. Hints for cycling routes. Rental canoes, mountain bikes, and sculling lessons available nearby.
**Rates:** $25 single, $35 double. $5 additional person.

## Craftsbury B&B on Wylie Hill

Craftsbury Common, VT 05827
**Phone:** 802/586-2206
**Location:** Rural and peaceful. One and one-half miles from Craftsbury Common. High on Wylie Hill with views, sunrises and sunsets, "startlingly beautiful moonrise seen through slats of our barn." Near lakes and miles of back roads (good for mountain bikes). Thirty miles from Stowe. One mile from Sterling College.
**Host:** Margaret Ramsdell
**Open:** Year round. Reservations preferred.

Several returnees have commented. "What a find! . . . cozy and spotlessly clean . . . excellent food with a friendly, caring family in a scenic and rustic area of Vermont near a major sports center (Craftsbury). . . . You come away with a good warm feeling."

The 1860s farmhouse pleases Margaret too. "I feel so peacefully in tune with my surroundings. It is a joy to share this with my guests. . . . We had run a summer residential riding camp here. It was just perfect to convert to B&B." Her husband, Bob, is an educator, and their two children are in college.

**In residence:** Michelle, a "mostly Morgan" horse; Dusty, a barn cat who wishes she could live inside; and two golden retrievers, Minden and Willoughby.
**Restrictions:** No guests' pets. No smoking, please.
**Foreign language spoken:** French.
**Bed and bath:** Four rooms on the ground level in a separate wing of house. Two shared guest baths. Three rooms with a double bed, one with a single. Electric heater in each room. Cot and crib available.
**Breakfast:** At the convenience of guests; usually not before 8. Juice, fruit, cinnamon-apple pancakes. Or cinnamon-apple coffee cake and omelets with Vermont cheddar. Vermont maple syrup and Craftsbury honey are staples. Served in dining room (off the country kitchen with wood stove) on table set with hand-thrown pottery, silver, and fresh flowers.
**Plus:** Guest living room with wood stove, no television. Flannel sheets. Dinner can be arranged for groups of six or more. Babysitting can be arranged. Use of barbecue. Use of canoe, no charge. (Half-mile to launching site.) Nordic ski trail through the fields.
**Rates:** $25 for the single room, $40-$50 double rooms. $5-$10 for crib or cot.

## The Quail's Nest

P.O. Box 221, Main Street, Danby, VT 05739
**Phone:** 802/293-5099
**Location:** In a quiet Vermont village, surrounded by the Green Mountains. Between Manchester and Rutland, just off Route 7.
**Hosts:** Anharad and Charles Edson
**Open:** Year round.

Anharad (a Welsh name meaning "country flower") and Chip have worked in the restaurant business and wanted to try their own related activity. Their parents are artists, and Chip has been an art teacher. Anharad was also in real estate in New Jersey. The young couple came to Vermont in 1984 to work on the 1835 house. The outside has a fresh coat of colonial blue paint trimmed with white. For the inside, they chose "original art work and yesteryear pieces and fixtures that we love."

They love Vermont and B&B too—". . . the most fun we have ever had working. Every guest is different and interesting. We encourage people to curl up by the fireplace or to see the waterfalls and explore the woods. If they want excitement, we steer them to the ski areas or the country auctions or the alpine slide. And we often recommend a restaurant where mom and pop do home cooking."

**In residence:** Pumpkin, "our chief entertainer," a golden Lab retriever, and Daisy, the cat and Pumpkin's good friend.
**Restrictions:** Pets sometimes allowed.
**Bed and bath:** Five rooms with two shared baths. One room with three twin beds. Four rooms with double beds. All with handmade country quilts.
**Breakfast:** Usually 8-10. Served family style at large dining-room table. Hosts always join guests for cheese baked eggs, apple muffins, fruit and cereal or apple puff pancakes, grapefruit, banana bread and cereal. Juice, coffee, tea, and milk.
**Plus:** Beverages and home-baked goodies in late afternoon or evening. Deck and two front porches.
**Rates:** $30 single, $35 double. $10 for each additional person. MasterCard and VISA accepted.

## Dovetail Inn

P.O. Box 976, Main Street, Route 30, Dorset, VT 05251
**Phone:** 802/867-5747
**Location:** Six miles north of Manchester on Route 30. Across from the village green in historic district "free of architectural intrusions," according to the National Park Service.
**Hosts:** Jean and Jim Kingston
**Open:** Year round except early December and a brief time in April. Two-night minimum stay required during three-day holiday weekends.

What was once an annex to the Dorset Inn (located across the street) is owned by one of the town listers and his wife. In Connecticut Jim was a marine engineer and Jean a school and church secretary. When they moved here with their teenagers in 1984, they found a village that has the strong sense of community that they hoped for, and a business that allows them to combine their interests and skills. After all the work they have done (ask for pictures to see the "before") with the warm and comfortable country decor, they enjoy meeting travelers and providing a setting where guests can meet each other.

**In residence:** Son Tim works at Bromley Mountain in the winter and a bike shop in the summer. Holly helps out when she is home from college. Daisy, an Irish setter/golden retriever mix, and Spunky, a black and white cat.
**Restrictions:** Children should be at least eight to ten. Younger children are welcome if designated rooms are available.
**Bed and bath:** Eleven rooms, each with private bath, reading chair, and lamp. King, queen, double, or twin beds. Cot and crib available.
**Breakfast:** 8-9:30. Fresh fruit in season. Jean's yeast breads, muffins, or coffee cakes. Plenty of coffee and tea served in front of the fireplace in the cozy Keeping Room in winter and by the pool in the summer. On request, breakfast delivered to room in a basket.
**Plus:** Afternoon tea and sweets served 4-5. Free use of pool (unguarded) and bicycles. Library nook with cushioned window seat. Flowers. Tour of house. Will meet guests at Manchester bus stop. Jim's own suggestions for a hidden upland valley ("spectacular views!") reached by an unpaved road.
**Rates:** $55-$75 double occupancy. $5-$15 cot. No charge for crib. Discounts for long-term stays and winter midweek nonholiday stays. MasterCard and VISA accepted.

## The Little Lodge at Dorset

Box 673, Route 30, Dorset, VT 05251
**Phone:** 802/867-4040
**Location:** On a hillside, one block from the village green, set back from a quiet main road. A pretty pond in front and mountain view beyond. Across the street from one of New England's oldest golf courses and adjacent to hiking and cross-country trails. Close to craft and antique shops and summer theater, 15 minutes to Bromley, 30 minutes to Stratton and Magic Mountain. Six miles to Manchester.
**Hosts:** Allan and Nancy Norris
**Open:** Usually year round. Reservations preferred. Two-day minimum stay in foliage season and busy weekend times. "We think April and May are especially beautiful months here."

Restoration had taken place when the Norrises bought the private home in 1981. The original part, c. 1810-20, was moved here in the 1930s from Hebron, New York. Two subsequent additions resulted in an usual and interesting arrangement of windows, staircases and halls. Among the antiques that add charm to the comfortable lodge is a wonderful corner cupboard that looks like it was custom made for the height of the dining room.

The Norrises had always talked about making a career change when the children graduated from high school, and they did it. In Baltimore, Maryland, Allan was a wholesaler and Nancy had years of active volunteer work and motherhood. Now their grown children have graduated from college. Repeat guests (and there are many, including entire families) comment on the pleasant environment and friendly hosts. Zest runs high in this family; one summer, their daughter, a great muffin baker, had a stint as a salmon packer in Alaska and then cycled home across the country.

**In residence:** A very friendly dog.
**Restrictions:** Sorry, no pets.
**Foreign languages spoken:** Some Spanish and French.
**Bed and bath:** Five rooms, all with private baths and crocheted or quilted bedspreads. Each room has two twin beds that can be made up as a king. Two largest and one small room have both tub and shower. Two smaller rooms have shower only. One of these smaller rooms is on the first floor and has a separate exterior entrance. Cot, crib, and extra bed available.

**Breakfast:** Served 8-9:30. Juice, cereals, toasted homemade breads, muffins and beverage. Both Nancy and Allan cook and serve in the dining room or on the screened porch. Nancy exchanges recipes with guests, and therefore has especially good and unusual ones.
**Plus:** Tea, coffee, and hot chocolate always available. Cheese and crackers in late afternoon. Turned-down beds and mints on your pillow. Refrigerator and (BYOB) wet bar. Dartboard, games, books, and puzzles in room with barn-board walls. Living room with wood stove. Room to lounge and socialize. Terrace and lawn chairs. Barn for bikes and skis. Skating in winter.
**Rates:** $60-$75 for two. $25 extra bed. $20 cot. $15 crib. Discount for extended stays. AMEX accepted, preferable for deposits only.

## Inwood Manor

Lower Waterford Road, East Barnet, VT 05821
**Phone:** 802/633-4047
**Location:** On a plateau—on 20 acres—overlooking the Passumpsic River. Six miles south of St. Johnsbury, off of Route 5.
**Hosts:** Peter Embarrato and Ron Kaczor
**Open:** Year round. Reservations preferred.

Among the tidbits, hints, and suggestions for places "just down the road": the lake where Jacques Cousteau learned to swim, a Rockefeller-restored building, the largest Buddhist meditation center on the east coast, the studio of a nationally recognized glass-blower, and the oldest parsonage in America.

Those all come from two men who have been hosts for nine years. Before they chose this new lifestyle, Peter had studied prelaw and ultimately became a systems analyst in New York City. Ron was a Marist Brother (teaching order) for five years in New Jersey.

The former 1820 stagecoach stop is connected to another structure that was lodging—until 1937—for the workers at the world's largest croquet factory. With all the work Ron and Peter have done (see their albums called "What A Dump" and "At Long Last"), they have plans for more. Each room is different, filled with "early attic, antique finds, and color-coordinated linens. Plenty of plants and fresh flowers. Nothing stuffy."

**In residence:** Mocha and Topaz, Siamese who love people, and Farah, a Persian, who "also craves attention."

**Restrictions:** "We are geared to adult getaways. Our inn is not child proofed." Smoking in designated areas.
**Foreign languages spoken:** Some Spanish and French.
**Bed and bath:** Nine rooms, double bed in each. Two rooms on first floor share one huge bath. Seven second-floor rooms share four baths.
**Breakfast:** 8-9:30. Continental breakfast is included in the rate; full breakfast is available. Juice, almond corn bread, assorted home-baked muffins and fresh fruit, coffee, tea. Leisurely.
**Plus:** Porches and decks. Turned-down beds. Mints. Thick towels. Wood stove and games in living room. Dinner ($17.50) available by arrangement. Will meet guests at airport, train, or bus. Trails for hiking. Pond for swimming, fishing, ice skating. Canoe rentals (they have six). Inn-to-inn canoe program May to October.
**Rates:** $30 single, $45 double. $10 more in fall.

## Blue Wax Farm

Pinkham Road, East Burke, VT 05832
**Phone:** 802/626-5542
**Location:** On 325 acres adjoining Burke Mountain ski area, 2.5 miles from small village and Route 114. Not far from Lyndon State College.
**Hosts:** Kenneth and Ingrid Parr
**Open:** Year round. Advance reservations preferred.

Since the Parrs "retired" in 1970, they have just about completely redone the 1862 farmhouse. They began taking overflow guests from a nearby inn in 1981 and enjoy providing "friendly comfort on a lightly traveled road" to skiers, hikers (lazy and aggressive), cyclists, sightseers, and people who "wind down."

Many items in the house reflect 17 years of overseas living in the Middle East and South America when the hosts were in educational and personnel work for institutions and corporations.

From their newsy update letter sent to guests: "Bumper crop of 150 kinds of apples and plums [from their experimental orchard] this year. . . . Pinkham Road clockwise and counterclockwise is a glorious foliage. . . . Our beavers are back with a new set of dams. . . . Fresh moose tracks seen today within a few hundred feet. . . ."

**In residence:** The Parrs do not smoke, but smoking is allowed.

**Restrictions:** No guests' pets indoors.
**Foreign languages spoken:** Spanish, Finnish, and some French and Arabic.
**Bed and bath:** Three rooms, each with a double bed plus twin bed. Electric heat. Two guest baths. Crib available.
**Breakfast:** Continental. Juice, hot rolls, fruit from harvest in season, beverage. Sit down and enjoy.
**Plus:** Piano, lots of books, open fireplace in large living room. "Ubiquitous TV." Collection of classical and other music for stereo. Outdoor sauna; robes furnished. Maybe Ken's arborist's tour for tree identification. Cross-country ski trails and hiking trails on the land; one skirts the beaver pond. Suggested routes and trails for 1-4 day cycling and hiking trips; safe parking provided.
**Rates:** $13 single, $25 double. No charge for crib.

## The Kiln Guest House

R.R. 1, Box 582, Benedict Road, East Dorset, VT 05253
**Phone:** 802/362-4889
**Location:** Just off Route 7, 4½ miles north of Manchester center, 15 minutes from Bromley Mountain, half hour from Stratton and Magic Mountain.
**Hosts:** Dennis and Catherine Conroy
**Open:** May-March. Advance reservations required.

Through 20 years of vacationing on his property in Vermont, Dennis thought of retiring here. On Long Island he had been supervisor of meter readers for a utility company. After he and Catherine vacationed in Ireland, they knew that they wanted to become B&B hosts.

Two of the four guest rooms in their contemporary house are reached via a spiral staircase that leads to a balcony overlooking the living room. Dennis and friends built the house next to a c. 1840 blast furnace that used to make iron for stoves and frying pans.

I love this guest's letter: ". . . spotless, raising envious feelings in regard to my own home." A New York guest wrote, "After one stay, we quickly made reservations for more skiing weekends . . . delicious and plentiful breakfasts. . . . But most of all, we found the Conroys to be hospitable and helpful with suggestions of restaurants and directions and points of interest."

**In residence:** One cat named Cuffy.
**Restrictions:** Nonsmokers preferred.
**Bed and bath:** Four rooms. On the first floor, one room with two twin beds and a double-bedded room share a bath. Two rooms on the second floor, one with twins that convert to a king-sized bed and the other with a double bed, share a bath. Cot and crib available.
**Breakfast:** 7:30-9:30. Main course will not be repeated within a six-day stay. May be French toast with strawberry sauce and bacon or blueberry pancakes and sausages. Served with orange juice, coffee or tea, and homemade coffee cake in the dining room.
**Plus:** Late-afternoon or evening beverages and snack. Limited use of refrigerator. Babysitting available.
**Rates:** $25 single, $40 double. $10 cot. Discount for senior citizens. No charge for children under ten sharing parents' room.

## Brick House Guests

Box 128, Montgomery Road, East Hardwick, VT 05836
**Phone:** 802/472-5512
**Location:** Among glorious gardens, on a rise above small village, bordering on the Lamoille River. In a rural "unspoiled" area. Half hour to Stowe. Four miles from 30 miles of cross-country skiing through woods and meadows.
**Host:** Judith G. Kane
**Open:** Year round. Reservations preferred.

Most of the five Kane children grew up here in the "old Albee place on the hill" as old-timers still call this 1830 Federal brick house. The Kanes are bent toward "all growing things." Judith's husband is a landscape architect based in New York. She is interested in alternative medicine and holistic health, teaches crafts and painting, and is a published poet and writer. She has a craft and gift shop in Hardwick and runs an herb nursery at the B&B in summer. Over the last eight years, Rachel, a daughter, has specialized in historic and unusual perennial flowers. Her Perennial Pleasures Nursery, located here, was featured in *Horticulture* magazine.

Judith says that her style has certainly been influenced by her English upbringing. Everything is "scrubbed clean and yes, I still starch and iron things."

Perhaps you'll have tea in the gazebo, maybe take a tour of the gardens. Explorer types could be directed to a "hard-to-find-but-worth-the-effort breathtakingly beautiful small lake with an island in the middle and a place to swim," or to the nearby Bread and Puppet Theater's barn with its "thousands of masks and costumes arranged in spectacular tableaux."

Guests wrote: "It seemed different from other B&Bs in a way that I personally value a lot; the B&B business seems to be an organic extension of the family life. . . . A warm and interesting family. . . . Mountains of quilts. . . . The house is furnished with the most amazing collection of antiques, uniques and oddments, all of which somehow fit and complement each other. . . . The decor is the result of intelligence and natural grace."

**In residence:** Daughter Rachel. Mattie, a German short-haired pointer; Winnie, a vocal young cat; and Becky, a black cat, estimated age 24. "My husband, Tom, and I smoke occasionally, never in the company of nonsmokers."
**Restrictions:** Pets must be well behaved.
**Foreign language spoken:** Some French.
**Bed and bath:** Three rooms, one shared guest bath. One large room, queen-size canopied bed with velvet curtains; one with double bed and a single bed; in addition to a single bed in third room, a built-in curtained bed overlooking the garden. Feather beds over mattresses on some beds. Cot available.
**Breakfast:** 7-9. Juice, fresh fruit or fruit salad, bacon and eggs or poached eggs on creamed chipped beef on an English muffin. Variety of freshly baked fruit muffins and homemade jams. In summer, homegrown herb and egg omelets. Served in dining room or more casually at large table in kitchen. Flowers, china and white linen.
**Plus:** Fresh flowers from extensive gardens that have secluded sitting areas. Study with fireplace. Piano. Late-afternoon or evening beverage. Early morning wake-up tea or coffee tray with toast and marmalade, by request. Babysitting could be arranged with advanced notice. Kitchen and laundry privileges.
**Rates:** $25 single, $35 double, $50 triple. MasterCard and VISA accepted.

## October Pumpkin Inn

P.O. Box 226, Route 125E, East Middlebury, VT 05740
**Phone:** 802/388-9525
**Location:** "A quiet apple-pie and screen-door American village setting on a historic stagecoach road in Robert Frost country." Four miles south of Middlebury village; one mile east on Route 125 to the foot of Middlebury Gap.
**Hosts:** Eileen and Charles Roeder
**Open:** Year round.

"We don't want to get so big that we have to hire a staff," the Roeders told us when we stayed at their Stone Mill Farm B&B in Brandon. Their personal touch and complete joy of what they are doing at the moment comes through.

They just love restoring and redoing, so in 1986 they sold the farm (as a private residence to previous guests) and redid this 1856 Greek Revival house. Restoration of "the charm of the old with amenities of the new" is complete with English and colonial antiques acquired during their days as dealers and auctioneers in New Jersey. They both did the stenciling seen throughout the inn.

This couple seems to thrive on new challenges. They are immaculate housekeepers and have had experience managing a historic inn. Eileen has worked in the field of mental retardation. Charles is looking into becoming a foster grandparent. At October Pumpkin they have opened a shop in the barn/carriage house featuring quilts, basketry, stenciled items, and true Vermont foods. They can tell you wonderful tales of the various guests who blend in this friendly atmosphere. Families, too, are comfortable here.

**In residence:** Woodstock, the resident duck. On college vacations, Patrik and Aimee. Some family members smoke.
**Restrictions:** Polite pets only.
**Bed and bath:** Three second-floor rooms. The one with private bath has a canopied double bed. Another room, also stenciled, has an antique cannonball double. Two single wicker beds in third room. Cot available. Handmade quilts by Eileen.
**Breakfast:** At guests' convenience. Continental or full breakfast featuring Charles's cast-iron baked corn sticks and homemade jellies and jams. Served by wood stove in dining room.

**Plus:** Window fans in bedrooms. Air conditioning in public rooms. Cozy parlor with piano and abundant reading material. Reasonably priced robust country dinner with advance request. Carriage house hosts guests' bicycles, skis, canoes, and vintage autos.
**Rates:** $35 single, $45 double with shared bath. $55 private bath. Third person in a room $8. Extended-stay rates available.

---

## Silver Maple Lodge

RR 1, Box 8, South Main Street, Fairlee, VT 05045
**Phone:** 802/333-4326
**Location:** On Main Street, one mile south of town center. Opposite open farmland with views of White Mountains to the east and Green Mountains to the west; 17 miles from Dartmouth College in New Hampshire.
**Hosts:** Gayl and Paul Coppeta
**Open:** April-November. Two-night minimum stay during fall foliage weekends.

Two vacationing couples saw the lodge for sale, "liked the idea and bought it." That was in 1985. Until then, one family had owned it for 60 years, first as a family farmhouse, then as an inn.

Paul is retired from government employment in Massachusetts. Gayl is grandmother to 12. Paul's daughter Sharon is a receptionist in Boston, and her husband Scott works for a financial service organization. Together they have worked on the lodge, furnished it in simple country decor, and welcomed travelers.

Their favorite local suggestions are a waterwheel-powered cider mill that offers free wild apple cider samples and, in Thetford, Gray's Auction Barn, where everything from livestock to furniture is sold on Monday nights.

**In residence:** Sharon and Scott also host on weekends.
**Restrictions:** No guests' pets. Smoking allowed in the cottages.
**Bed and bath:** Nine second-floor rooms (all with mountain views) in the inn; four with sinks, all with shared baths. One room has a king-sized bed, five have double beds, and three have twin beds. Five pine-paneled cottages with private baths. Cot available.
**Breakfast:** 7-9. Juice, fruit, homemade breads and rolls, coffee or tea. Served in the dining room.

**Plus:** Wraparound porch. Late-afternoon or evening coffee. Piano. Games. Horseshoes, croquet, badminton, shuffleboard, and volleyball. Picnic tables among the apple trees. Babysitting can be arranged.
**Rates:** $24-$36 single, $28-$38 double. $4 additional person in a room. MasterCard and VISA accepted.

## Fair Meadows Farm

Box 430, Route 235, Franklin, VT 05457
**Phone:** 802/285-2132
**Location:** In the land of "big sky," minutes from the Canadian border. Three miles west of Franklin, 12 miles from I-89, 60 miles from Montreal.
**Host:** Terry and Phil Pierce
**Open:** Year round.

Fortunately the hills were too much for our planned cycling route! We had a further destination, but my legs decided that we would never make it. So the welcome B&B sign was in the right place at the right time. And it meant we met the Pierces.

Here we were, seemingly in the middle of nowhere, at a farm that had been in the family since 1853. On the hall wall were family pictures that told of the widespread younger generation. The five children, educated at five different colleges, are now in five different states. One has been in the Peace Corps. The youngest has just returned from a year as an exchange student in England.

Dad's sense of humor came through. And so did his perspective; he spoke of the changes he had seen in dairying through the years. Since our visit, Phil has retired from the farm, but his nephew has taken over and it looks like the dairying will continue for some time to come. Terry continues her gardening and cooking and community involvement. When we last spoke, she and Phil were repapering the hall "all the way up the stairs."

Their farmhouse is comfortable and immaculate. Flowers and views are everywhere. Recipes are shared and so are practical hints. "Change your currency at a bank and buy gas before entering Canada."

**Restrictions:** Pets must be very well behaved.
**Foreign language spoken:** French.

**Bed and bath:** Four rooms, each with double bed. One on first floor with private half-bath. One shared full bath. Two cribs.
**Breakfast:** At guests' convenience. A real farm breakfast including homemade muffins and butter. Served in the pine-paneled room off the kitchen and overlooking the meadow.
**Plus:** Large living room. TV. Bicycles can be kept in the barn.
**Rates:** $22 single, $30 for two.

## Cobble House Inn

P.O. Box 49, Childrens Campground Road, Gaysville, VT 05746
**Phone:** 802/234-5458
**Location:** Atop a mountain road, 15 miles from Killington and Pico. Six miles west of Bethel, one half mile off Route 107.
**Hosts:** Beau and Phil Benson
**Open:** Year round. Two-day minimum stay required for foliage and holiday weekends.

> Guests wrote: "I was born and raised in Vermont and when I go to the Cobble House Inn, I feel like I am back home again. It is just so homey and comfortable and peaceful a place to stay. . . . Service is beyond anything I have ever experienced at the best hotel I had ever stayed. I have always felt the best barometer for good food and lodging is consistency. Each time I go back, it is better than the last."

The 1864 Federal-style house, with cupola and huge barn, was a summer residence for its first 100 years. When the Bensons bought it in 1985, they gutted half of it, learning a lot along the way. Each piece of the country furniture has a story.

Beau, a trained chef (who still caters), and Phil, president of a small Washington, D.C. research company, traveled B&B for five years. "We decided that it was a way of life for us, and the country looked very appealing! Among our guests are diehard skiers and others who come to do nothing but relax here."

**In residence:** Three-year-old son Sam. In the pasture, "a little Noah's Ark . . . sheep, goats, a dog."
**Restrictions:** Sorry, no smoking allowed. Guests' pets may sleep outside or in the barn, and if guests bring the food, the Bensons will feed animals while you are gone, but no pets may come into the inn.

**Bed and bath:** Six rooms, all with private baths. Quilts and flannel sheets. Two rooms on first floor each have a double bed, bath with shower, no tub, private outside entrance, and accessibility for the handicapped. Four on second floor, one with queen-sized brass bed and one double with eight-foot-tall headboard. Two rooms each have two twin beds. Rollaway beds and crib available.
**Breakfast:** 7-11. Special hours on request. Pancakes, fresh pumpkin spice muffins, banana muffins, apple and corn fritters, grapefruit with raspberries and chambord, omelets or any style eggs. Seconds, if you'd like. Breakfast in bed, if you'd like.
**Plus:** Two guest parlors. Wine or hot cider late winter afternoons. Morning coffee outside your door, if requested. Option of dinner with advance arrangements. Tour of house. Sometimes, four-wheel-drive tours of the area. Three swimming holes. Miles of hiking trails. Babysitting can be arranged. Use of refrigerator; dryer for skiers. Inner tubes for floating on river that borders the property. Two fishing rods available. "We'll cook and store your catch for you." Two ten-speed bicycles on first-come first-served basis.
**Rates:** $35 per person. Children under four are free. No charge for cribs. $30 for each added person in a room.

## The Hayes House

Grafton, VT 05146
**Phone:** 802/843-2461
**Location:** Adjacent to an 1870 covered bridge. On a side street near the village center. Close to Grafton Village Cheese Company (visitors welcome), Grafton Historical Society Museum, antique shops, country store, printmaking workshop, ski shop, and trail system.
**Host:** Margery Hayes Heindel
**Open:** May through March.

"I was a summer kid from Cambridge, Massachusetts, when this first became 'home.' I fell in love with my town then—and I'm still in love." Today Marge is chairman of the Board of Selectmen, but 20 of the in-between years were filled with 28 moves while she was wife of a naval officer and mother of "two great children."

The house, built in 1803, is "cluttered, clean, and welcoming. It's furnished with many Oriental things that fit in well with old pieces—including me!" Marge doesn't spend too much time on the porch chairs. "I am gardener (flowers and vegetables), and good cook, enjoy arranging flowers, knit, sew, do stitchery, read far too many books—and I'm grateful to my cleaning lady because I hate to vacuum." In addition she is a registered occupational therapist.

Among her memorable guests: A party of three generations including an 89-year-old woman who found her own great-grandmother's tombstone in the hilly village graveyard.

**In residence:** A Chesapeake Bay retriever—Velva—and three cats, Tyl, Grace, and Cal (Coolidge).
**Restrictions:** Dogs are the only guests' pets allowed. Infants and children over four are definitely welcome. (The house is not child-proofed.) Smoking is not allowed in bedrooms.
**Bed and bath:** Four rooms. A double on the first floor with four-poster bed high enough to require the stool provided to climb into it. Working fireplace and private bath. On second floor, one single, one room with twin beds, and one with a double share one full guest bath (plus a half-bath spring through fall).
**Breakfast:** 8-11. Family style in the dining room. Continental with homemade breads, muffins, jellies, and jams. Leisurely.
**Plus:** Fruit and cookies in rooms. Flowers in season. Thick towels. Babbling brook (toe-dabbling allowed) by the house. Porches. Kitchen privileges in winter or for bicyclists without a car. After 2 p.m. on winter afternoons, self-service for homemade soups. Baby-sitting arranged with advance notice. Suggestions for back-road tours.
**Rates:** $25 single, $40 double with shared bath, $50 double with private bath. Child in sleeping bag in parents' room, $5 per bag per night.

## Stronghold Inn

HCR 40, Grafton, VT 05146
**Phone:** 802/843-2203
**Location:** Along the road bordered by a white picket fence, a half-mile from the center of the picture-book town (pop. 600). Near walking trails, antiquing, and a river stocked with brown trout. One mile to 40 km of cross-country trails, 12 miles to Magic Mountain.
**Hosts:** Obe and Ed McMahon

**Open:** Year round. Three-night minimum stay on national holiday weekends. Two-night minimum on winter and other holiday weekends.

Both Ed and Obe have experience working in inns, so in 1980, when they bought this private home with all its extra rooms, B&B seemed like a good way to subsidize the restoration. From the outside, this white clapboard c. 1820 Vermont Cape's 12-over-8 windows, picket fence, red barn (now Ed's antique shop), and stone wall give you the right idea about what's inside: antiques—lots of primitives, quilts, stenciling, wide floorboards, and old hardware.

Many guests consult with the McMahons about antiques. Others visit students in the area schools, ski, or explore the four-season Vermont that the hosts extol.

**In residence:** Meghann, age eight, and Kelly, age six. Ed is a pipe smoker. Two dogs, Casey and Tucker, mixed collie/husky, and Molly, a calico cat.
**Restrictions:** Only well-behaved pets are allowed.
**Bed and bath:** Four rooms. All with private baths, three with shower only. Three first-floor rooms; one with a double and a twin bed, nonworking fireplace, and four windows; another with two twin painted iron beds. Room with a full private bath has a double bed, nonworking fireplace. In second-floor room, double-sized spool bed. Crib and extra mattress available.
**Breakfast:** 8-9:30. Exceptions arranged in advance. Chef's choice of farm-fresh eggs, homemade muffins, bacon, sausage, fruit, pancakes, Vermont syrup, juice, tea, coffee, milk, cocoa. Served in country kitchen with fireplace and beehive oven or in the living room, which overlooks the gardens.
**Plus:** Front porch rockers. Babysitting arranged with advance notice. Suggestions of hiking places and abandoned quarries.
**Rates:** $50-$60 for two. Singles, $10 less per room. Third person, $10 more per room. Special rate for children under 12. All rooms $10 higher mid-September through the end of October. MasterCard and VISA accepted.

*Can't find the community you are going to? Check with a reservation service described at the beginning of this chapter. Through the service, you may be placed (matched) with a welcoming B&B that is near your destination.*

## Capt. Henry Chase House

Hinesburg Road, Guilford, VT
Mailing address: Box 788, RFD 4, West Brattleboro, VT 05301
**Phone:** 802/254-4114
**Location:** Six miles from Brattleboro in an agricultural valley with "breathtaking views." Directions sent to guests.
**Hosts:** Pat and Lorraine Ryan and daughter Laura
**Open:** Year round. Advance reservations preferred.

"The kind of place where few people seem to be in a hurry."

It's a bit of a treasure hunt to find the 188-year old farmhouse, but guests frequently comment on the lovely house and area, friendly people, and those pancakes. Explorers discover an old-fashioned swimming hole, a covered bridge, and a waterfall dam, all part of the Vermont the Ryans came for when they moved here eight years ago.

There's a good deal of mutual appreciation: When a British ambassador and his family stayed here for a week "they felt like family." Before leaving, the children put on a puppet show for the Ryans.

Pat is a telephone company technician; Lorraine is a travel agent. They find time to walk in the hills and fish in the river on the farm and to be active in both the historical society and church activities.

**In residence**: Laura, age 16, "guest relations director." In the barn—Kay, Laura's horse; four cats; two goats; and whatever other creature may find a home in the barn.
**Restrictions:** No guests' pets. No smoking in the bedrooms.
**Bed and bath:** Two air-conditioned rooms. A double bed in each, wide pine floors. One shared guest bath.
**Breakfast:** Vermont style, with pancakes and homemade maple syrup. Served in the dining room or on screened-in patio.
**Plus:** Upstairs den off of the bedrooms. Large family living room with wide floorboards and ten-foot hearth, beehive oven, cauldron that swings. Screened summer room. Kitchen and laundry privileges. Babysitting possibilities. Evening refreshments.
**Rates:** $25 for one, $35 for two. $10 cot. $20 child in a separate room. $5 each additional child.

## Kahagon at Nichols Pond

Nichols Pond, Woodbury
Mailing address: Box, 728, Hardwick, VT 05843
**Phone:** 802/472-6446
**Location:** Rural. Four miles along a dirt road east of Hardwick. Off Route 14 on Nichols Pond, a natural lake. Twenty miles from Stowe, 100 miles to Montreal on scenic back roads.
**Hosts:** Lesley Schlosser and Paul Smith
**Open:** Year round. Reservations only.

"We're out of the way but close to so much. There's beauty, the loons on the lake, and just a few minutes up the trail is Nichols Ledge, 500 feet above the lake with vistas in all directions, even a glimpse of Mount Washington. . . . And, as guests say, we're just 20 minutes from 52 gourmet restaurants and Vermont Symphony concerts. Now that we're opening up 15 miles of cross-country trails, Kahagon will be shared year round."

It's homey and relaxing at the 1870 farmhouse, the only sign of civilization on the road. Once a family farm and later an exclusive boys' camp, Kahagon ("the secret place" in Abenacki, old Indian) became a retreat for families, mostly from mainline Philadelphia, when bought by Lesley's grandfather in 1936. It has been revived during the last five years by two restauranteurs—Lesley, a former Colorado ski instructor, and her fiance, Paul, a former university instructor. The self-contained cabins are still rented to families, but the main house with its birch floors and handmade Birdseye maple staircase is now a B&B. The family tradition of hospitality lives on.

**In residence:** Two horses, two cats, and three well-behaved golden retrievers.
**Restrictions:** Sorry, no guests' pets.
**Bed and bath:** Three second-floor cozy double-bedded rooms share a full bath with the hosts. Cot and crib available.
**Breakfast:** Provided only for B&B guests. 7:30-9:30. Juice, fresh eggs, bacon or ham, homemade muffins or bread, pancakes or French toast, fresh fruit, hot beverages.
**Plus:** Cocktails. Swimming, sailing, fishing, canoeing. Hiking on the 175 acres. Croquet. Horseback riding (no charge to B&B guests). Babysitting. Cabot Creamery (free tours) "just over the hill." Carriage rides (fee charged) in a Meadowbrook cart from Amish country. Wine-tasting, gourmet-cooking, and foliage weekends. Dinner

($8-$12) on request. Kitchen privileges. Will meet guests (fee) at Burlington airport or Montpelier bus or train.
**Rates:** $28-$32 single, $42-$48 double. Ten percent seniors' discount. MasterCard and VISA accepted.

## Camel's Hump Nordic Ski Center

RD 1, Box 99, East Street, Huntington, VT 05462
**Phone:** 802/434-2704
**Location:** Pastoral. At the end of a dirt road, seven miles south of Richmond, I-89. High in the foothills of "Vermont's best loved and most photographed mountain" with spectacular views from alpine meadows. Within 45 minutes of Burlington, Stowe, Middlebury.
**Hosts:** David and Myra Brautigam
**Open:** December-March and May-October. Reservations requested.

Enthusiastic letters recommending Camel's Hump have poured in. For a sample, "In the course of travel through Europe, Canada, Japan, and this country, I cannot recall a more charming weekend than that spent with David and Myra Brautigam. Every facet of our stay was wonderful. . . . Located near Vermont's only undeveloped 4,000-foot peak. . . . Meals are a feast. . . . Although we went for the skiing, we will return for the hospitality."

The young (in their thirties), active couple came here in 1979, six years after Myra's family had built the log cabin. Dave has been a psychiatric aide, a high school history teacher, and ski shop manager. Now he teaches tennis in the summer, sells firewood, and is a graduate student in history. Myra, a life-long resident of Vermont, is a social worker. Both have had a lifetime of outdoor sports participation and have carefully created the Nordic Center to be in tune with their appreciation of their surroundings. Even when there isn't snow, they have been known to host ecstatic winter guests on hikes through trails. "The view would look super in watercolor," wrote one guest who is an artist.

**In residence:** August Brautigam, age two. Two dogs, Arrow, small and black, and Buckwheat, a golden retriever; and Glover, the cat.
**Restrictions:** No guests' pets. No smoking, please.
**Bed and bath:** One guest room until addition is completed. Double bed. Shared bath. (If two couples come together, two guest rooms are available.) Handmade quilts, fresh flowers in summer.

**Breakfast:** 7:30-9. Choice of juices, yogurt, homemade pancakes with local maple syrup, fruit, bacon, coffee cake, homemade muffins, eggs, Vermont butter, jams, English muffins, toast, hot cereal, coffee, tea. Served in living/dining room.
**Plus:** Late-afternoon or evening tea, wine, or sherry if desired. Extensive library. Bluebirds outside. Will meet guests at Burlington airport or bus station ($20). Swimming holes in nearby Huntington River. Ski equipment and snowshoes for rent; ski instruction; 65km ski trails (use fee $6), 35km groomed.
**Rates:** December 1-April 1, $35 single, $50 for two. May 1-November 1, $30 single, $40 for two. Extra person in room, $15.

---

## Pineapple Hospitality Host #VT 617

Hyde Park, VT
**Location:** Just outside the village, on a hill overlooking the Green Mountains. Ten miles north of Stowe, on the edge of the Northeast Kingdom. Near Jay Peak and Craftsbury. Cross country skiing from the door or at many nearby areas.
**Reservations:** Available year round through Pineapple Hospitality, page 214.

This B&B was bought at auction in 1985!

Originally built as a farmhouse around 1800, it has been modified and expanded, has seen use as a schoolhouse, and has been a summer boarding house. Today it offers "Old English hospitality in a New England setting," has wide pine or stenciled floors, and is furnished with antiques.

"I was born in England, am a former health care administrator who lived in Boston and New Jersey before realizing that Vermont is the next best thing to home. I have worked for an auctioneer, forester, and Realtor. Running a B&B allows me to continue to work with people, and to maintain my interest in crafts, phtography, music, gardening (there are four acres of gardens here), the environment and literature. I did not anticipate the degree of pleasure I would get from sharing my home and the area. . . . Some breakfasts have extended through lunch. There have been lots of heartwarming experiences.

"This is an excellent area for skiing, fishing, hiking and hunting. My 'secret discoveries' include swimming holes, hiking paths, back roads and restaurants."

**In residence:** "At the moment, two cats, Tat the Cat and Hobo, the Vagrant. Sable is a dog of dubious heritage but winning smile."
**Restrictions:** No facilities for young children. No guests' pets. Smoking in specified areas and only with the agreement of other guests.
**Foreign language spoken:** French, un petit peu.
**Bed and bath:** Four second-floor rooms share 1½ baths (additional second bath planned). Two rooms with queen-sized beds. One with a double bed. One with two twin beds. Rollaway bed available.
**Breakfast:** 7-9 but flexible. "The kind of breakfast that you rarely have time to cook at home. That's what a holiday is all about!" Bacon, sausage, eggs, tomato, and mushrooms, or whole-wheat apple or banana pancakes, or French toast from homemade bread; juice or fresh fruit, cereal, homemade breads, muffins (and sometimes hot doughnuts). Served in wainscoted dining room at a huge trestle table, in large kitchen, or on patio. Hostess often joins guests for coffee.
**Plus:** Central air conditioning. Beverages. Apres ski hot mulled cider or cocoa and nibbles in winter. Sitting room with books, games, record collection, and a pink piano. Dinner and afternoon tea available with advance notice. Special ski packages in winter. Two porches. Woodland walk. Kitchen or laundry privileges.
**Rates:** $45 single, $50 double. $5 rollaway bed.

## The Jefferson House

P.O. Box 288, Jeffersonville, VT 05464
**Phone:** 802/644-2030
**Location:** On the main street of a village in the Green Mountains, 25 miles east of Burlington, 5 miles north of Smuggler's Notch, 5 miles from the Long Trail, 18 miles (not passable in winter) to Stowe. Near good cycling routes. Within a mile of three covered bridges.
**Hosts:** Pat and Bill MacBride
**Open:** Year round. Reservations preferred.

"When Bill retired from his school superintendent's position, we found this lovely old house that was just right for B&B. It's in an historic village with residences, a church, and stores that have been maintained. Jeffersonville is pretty quiet. Well, I suppose it does get busy on Saturday mornings."

When Bill and Pat bought the 80-year-old Victorian two years ago, they redecorated and updated, retaining the character of the house. The MacBrides were hosts 25 years ago when they lived in Vermont for a year. They have also lived in other parts of the country (and state) when Bill was a teacher and school principal, and Pat, a registered nurse. In addition, for a short time they ran a breakfast restaurant! It's no wonder that artists as well as sports-oriented and foreign travelers are among those who find this comfortable, friendly home just as the MacBrides found it—just right.

**In residence:** Two dogs, Sidney and Savoy, form an enthusiastic welcoming committee. "The greeting of our aging cat, Jack, is somewhat more restrained."
**Restrictions:** Smoking discouraged in the bedrooms, but allowed in sitting room.
**Bed and bath:** Three rooms on the second floor share a full bath. One room has twin beds. Each of the other two has a double bed. Rollaway bed and crib available.
**Breakfast:** At guests' convenience, served in the dining room. Juice, coffee, tea, milk, eggs, French toast, pancakes with maple syrup, bacon, ham, and fruit are always on the menu. Homemade muffins and jams and jellies also appear frequently.
**Plus:** Second-floor deck. Sitting room. Satellite TV in the living room. Ping-pong table in basement. Porch with swing. Barn for bicycles and skis. Fishing in local rivers and lakes. Fine art gallery in the village.
**Rates:** $25 single, $35 double. Tax included. Small additional charge for crib or rollaway cot.

## Eatonhouse

Box 139, Browns Trace, Jericho, VT 05465
**Phone:** 802/899-2354
**Location:** On a quiet main road, in a pastoral setting with mountain views. Three miles off I-89. Twenty minutes from Burlington. Eight miles from IBM in Essex and from Sherman Hollow cross-country ski center; 45 minutes from Shelburne Museum and three major downhill ski areas; 20 minutes from Bolton Valley.
**Hosts:** Sue and Dave Eaton

**Open:** Year round. Eaton family plans vary for Thanksgiving, Christmas, and Easter. Reservations preferred. Two-night minimum stay mid-September–mid-October. Business travelers welcomed for short or long-term stays.

Sue was preparing for a pre-Christmas dinner party when a young couple stayed with them to plan a wedding in the area. Eventually, Sue and Dave went to the wedding as friends *and* hosted the rehearsal dinner!

I have a pile of guests' rave reviews about Eatonhouse. All speak of a "beautiful home with charming hosts." The reproduction saltbox, once on an Old House tour, was designed by one of the Eatons' sons when he was an architecture student. The artwork of another son can be seen throughout the house. Overall, a cozy country feeling prevails with wide board floors, open fireplaces in old brick, and colonial colors.

Sue has just given up her bed and breakfast referral service, and hopes to have time to quilt, garden and be a grandmother. Dave hosts and is an agency manager for an insurance company.

**In residence:** Jacynne (spelling intended for a ten-year-old kitty inadvertantly named Jason).
**Restrictions:** No guests' pets. The Eatons are nonsmokers and request that smoking be limited to specific areas.
**Bed and bath:** Two charming and cozy double-bedded second-floor rooms share a shower bath. Cot and crib available.
**Breakfast:** 7-9. Plenty of juice, homemade muffins, fruit cup, and an entree that may be bacon or sausage with eggs, homemade waffles, frittata, or some exotic casserole. Served in the dining area in front of the fireplace and in view of the Adirondack Mountains.
**Plus:** Study/library with books and TV. Grand piano and pump organ. Laundry facilities. Workbench for waxing skis. Two garage spaces. Tour of house that has details such as square-headed nails and wrought-iron latches and hinges, and a back stairway.
**Rates:** $25 single, $40 double. $7 Children 12 and under in parents' room. $10 other additional person. $5 one-time crib fee.

## Homeplace

RR2, Box 367, Jericho, VT 05465
**Phone:** 802/899-4694
**Location:** Very quiet. "Way off in the woods, down a half-mile-long driveway. Watch out for animals!" One and one-half miles off Route 15, 15 miles from Burlington, 3/4 hour from Stowe and Mt. Mansfield.
**Hosts:** Hans and Mariot Huessy
**Open:** Year round. Reservations appreciated.

An 82-line poem written by a couple from Ohio comments on everything from "appointments fit for bride and groom" to "A flock of sheep with bells and bleat. They seemed to say, 'We're glad to meet.' "

Spring is the season for sugaring and newborn lambs here. When the Huessys built this wonderful modern country home on 100 acres of woodland in 1968, they furnished it with lovely antiques from Mariot's American family and Hans's European family. Presently Hans is "slightly retired" from his teaching position at the University of Vermont Medical School. Mariot, mother to eleven (all grown now), is caretaker of the farm.

**In residence:** In addition to a golden retriever and an Australian shepherd there are three cats, two horses, a donkey, sheep, chickens, pigs, and ducks.
**Restrictions:** No guests' pets. Smoking in the living room only.
**Foreign language spoken:** German.
**Bed and bath:** Four ground-floor rooms with shared bath. All located in a separate wing. One room has two antique twin beds; another has twin beds made by a local craftsperson. The third room has a double bed, twin bed, and a crib. One room with double bed. Crib and cot available.
**Breakfast:** 7-10. "Homegrown" eggs, bacon or sausage, croissants from a local bakery or homemade muffins, orange juice, fresh-ground coffee. Served in dining room or in kitchen by the wood stove.
**Plus:** Fireplaced living room with flagstone floor, Oriental rugs, floor-to-ceiling windows, and bookcases. Patio. Trails for hiking and cross-country skiing. Pond for swimming (at your own risk). With advance notice, can arrange for babysitting.
**Rates:** $30 single, $35 double.

## Milliken's

RFD #2, Box 397, Jericho, VT 05465
**Phone:** 802/899-3993
**Location:** On Route 15, surrounded by ancient maples. Twenty minutes to either Burlington or Mount Mansfield. Accessible to restaurants and happenings.
**Hosts:** Rick and Jean Milliken
**Open:** Year round. Reservations required.

For Rick and Jean, running a B&B is natural extension of their combined experience and interests. Rick has spent ten years working in hotel management. Jean is a professional dancer/choreographer with a penchant for things antique, and a need for space to store trunks of costumes, mirrors, paraphernalia, and brochures she designs. Accordingly, their mansard-roofed Victorian has 17 spacious rooms. Built by a lumber magnate who made his fortune in the California gold rush, it is still stately, with original woodwork and high ceilings. The atmosphere is informal and welcoming.

**In residence:** Bethany, age ten. Patrick, age three, the one who is "peeking" at you on Milliken's brochure. Bailey, the dog, "with soulful eyes and friendly manner."
**Restrictions:** Sorry, no guests' pets. No smoking, please.
**Foreign languages spoken:** "Bare bones" Spanish and French. "When a lovely non-English speaking Japanese lady stayed with us, we had a four-day game of charades and sign language."
**Bed and bath:** Three rooms. Parlor suite on first floor with brass and iron double bed and pull-out sofa has private bath. One second-floor double-bedded room has direct access to bath shared by a double-bedded room across the hall. Cot and crib available.
**Breakfast:** 6:30-10:45. French toast with sausage; or croissant filled with scrambled eggs and fresh fruit or fruit compote; or omelet, muffins, sausage or bacon, and grapefruit. Juice, coffee, tea, cocoa. Served in glass-enclosed porch or in the former butler's pantry. Rick cooks. Jean serves. Both join guests.
**Plus:** Late-afternoon or evening tea, wine, or brandy. Window fans in bedrooms. With advance notice, babysitting arranged. TV. Grand piano.
**Rates:** $30 single, $35 double. Suite $50, $55 double. Tax included. Additional person in room, $6.

From New York: "Filled with charm. We were delighted."

## Mountain Morgans

McClallen Drive, Box 138A, RD 1, Killington, VT 05751
**Phone:** 802/422-3096
**Location:** On Killington Mountain, a little off a main road, near the Killington ski area.
**Hosts:** Jeff and Susan Hiers
**Open:** Year round.

"There's no time to give you directions. Hop in the car and I'll take you to church right now."

The grandmother of six from New Jersey who had never been to Vermont wrote me not only about that offer by Jeff, but about the Hiers as her new extended family. She went to Mountain Morgans for a day, stayed a week, and plans on returning "home" every year. Other laudatory letters from all over the country mention the setting and clean accommodations as well as the hospitality.

The Hiers live in a duplex; the "other half," a fully equipped home, is for B&B guests. Families are welcome and are particularly comfortable in the unusual arrangement.

Because Jeff has been an official tour guide in the area, he can direct guests to museums, historic sites, outdoor activities, and covered bridges. Now he is full time at the farm except for conducting sleigh rides in the winter or carriage rides in the summer. Susan, a registered nurse, helps "share the Vermont we love."

**In residence:** Joanna, 11, and Lisa, 6. Two friendly dogs, Missy and Max, and an assortment of small farm animals.
**Restrictions:** Sorry, no guests' pets.
**Bed and bath:** Three rooms, each with full private bath. Two double-bedded rooms. One with two twin beds. Crib available.
**Breakfast:** Provided by hosts. Prepared by guests in own kitchen. Juice, farm-fresh eggs, English muffins, beverage.
**Plus:** Guest duplex has fully equipped kitchen for 24-hour use by guests. Living room with fireplace and mountain views. Swings and sandpile for children. Lots of room for running. Babysitting possibilities. Possibility of tours of Killington ski area by horseback, horse-drawn carriage, or car. Horses to ride nearby.
**Rates:** $20 single, $32 double. No charge for crib. No charge for children in same room with parents.

## Black River Inn

100 Main Street, Ludlow, VT 05149
**Phone:** 802/228-5585
**Location:** In the center of Ludlow, on the village green, on a bank of the Black River. At the foot of Okemo Mountain ski area, 20 minutes south of Killington.
**Hosts:** Rosemary Krimbel and John Garton
**Open:** Year round except April. Reservations not required but preferred. Two-night minimum weekend stay foliage and ski seasons.

Home of firsts. Built in 1835 by the first doctor in Ludow. The first bath installed in southern Vermont with interior plumbing, c. 1859. Maybe your first opportunity to sleep in a bed that Abraham Lincoln slept in. And now the first B&B for a couple who had been dreaming of it for a long time while she was a finance manager and he a data processing manager.

Four years ago Rosemary and John personally restored this home, which features a staircase of hand-carved oak and a dining room with walnut and maple concentrically crafted floorboards. Most fixtures, including the sinks, are original.

As full-time innkeepers they think they have learned "to be prepared for everything," but they still recall the fall Saturday when an early frost meant that John had to bring in everything from the garden. "That evening everyone helped can. Ten people shucking vegetables in the kitchen and loving it!"

Their favorite suggested activity for the adventurous is Buttermilk Falls, a local swimming hole with slippery granite rocks that is both exciting and challenging.

**In residence:** Ben, age two.
**Restrictions:** Children should be at least 18. No guests' pets.
**Foreign language spoken:** French.
**Bed and bath:** On three floors, eight double-bedded rooms with handblown etched lighting fixtures. Four rooms with private baths; four with semiprivate baths.
**Breakfast:** Anytime after 7. Eat in dining room, on porch, or in your room. Flowers on tray by special request. Popovers, bran muffins, apple puff pancakes, homemade strudels and coffeecakes. Choice of juices and hot beverage.
**Plus:** Late-afternoon or evening tea, wine, or beer. Tour of the house. Thick towels. Down comforters. Dinners ($36 a couple) offered on Saturday nights and during foliage season. Marble fireplace

to curl up by. Will meet guests at Rutland airport or Ludlow bus. Trout fishing on the property.
**Rates:** \$78 per couple. MasterCard, VISA, and AMEX accepted.

## Brookside Meadows

RD #3, Box 2460, Painter Road, Middlebury, VT 05753
**Phone:** 802/388-6429
**Location:** On a meadow with a view to a pond and brook just behind the house, with the Green Mountains behind them; 2½ miles from the center of Middlebury, 3 miles to the campus. Convenient to Shelburne Museum and Fort Ticonderoga.
**Hosts:** Linda and Roger Cole
**Open:** Year round. Two-night reservations preferred. Two-night minimum stay during major college weekends.

"It's a terrific place with wonderful hosts. They know how to do it." I knew the caller from my PTA days, and she wanted me to know that Brookside Meadows belonged in this book.

The Coles enjoy meeting their guests so much that they hope you can come for two nights, just so they can get to know you. They recently added the first-floor guest room in order to double their capacity (from one to two rooms).

Linda has been a teacher and Roger is an administrator at Middlebury College. Their house is designed on the lines of a late-1800s colonial story-and-a-half farm home. Linda worked closely with the architect when it was built in 1979 and is responsible for the attractive decor and the beautiful gardens and flower arrangements. The barn behind the house is an oldie, from 1876, moved just a year ago from 12 miles away.

Whether you want to watch maple sugaring, find a local (incredibly beautiful) swimming hole within view of a covered bridge above a waterfall, spend time in museums, or find a lighted ski area, the hosts—and their friends who might stop in—are prepared with more than directions.

**In residence:** David, age 17, and during college vacations, Josh. Japanese Spaniel dogs named Tori and Tyke. Taci, an aloof cat. Geese, goats, and chickens are in the shed.
**Restrictions:** Prefer children to be at least five. No guests' pets, please. No smoking in bedrooms.

**Bed and bath:** Two rooms, electrically heated, each with a large private bath. One on first floor with handmade queen-sized bed and old wide pine floors. Second-floor room has two twin beds; bath has tub with shower and double sink. Cot available.
**Breakfast:** 7-9 (sometimes 9:30 on weekends). Juice, coffee, cereal and eggs, or pancakes, or French toast with real maple syrup.
**Plus:** Tea, wine, or soft drinks in afternoon/evening. Wood stove in family room. Mints in the room. Tours of the house and property. Will meet local bus. With advance notice, will arrange babysitting. Limited kitchen privileges. Full use of the property—picnic table, grille, patio, lawn chairs. Cross-country wooded trail by beaver dams, and, in early summer, wild strawberries.
**Rates:** $45-$55 single or double occupancy. $10 additional person in room.

---

## Meadowbrook Farm

North Rupert, VT
Mailing address: RR 1, Box 805, Pawlet, VT 05671
**Phone:** 802/325-3410
**Location:** On a main road (state Route 30), four miles from villages of Dorset and Pawlet. Ten miles from Manchester and 30 miles from Rutland. Near Killington, Pico, Bromley, Stratton, Magic, and Okemo ski areas. Beautiful mountain and valley views.
**Hosts:** Hazen and Margot Mathewson
**Open:** Year round. Two-night minimum stay in October.

> From New York: "When we arrived at the end of a hot August afternoon we were greeted by hosts with towels and immediately sent off for a marvelously refreshing swim in the river behind the barn. It was the most surprising and delightful welcome we have ever received."

The property started out as a dairy farm in 1790 and the house was enlarged in 1850. Dairy farming continued until 1975, and part of the time the North Rupert Post Office was located in the house. The Mathewsons came from Connecticut ten years ago, and "after our four sons left, we found ourselves with a wonderful home for B&B. We are in an area great for hiking, cross-country skiing and cycling. The Mettawee River runs though our property and has excellent trout fishing and a very private beach."

Their antiques and Oriental rugs fit perfectly into the rambling farm house and guest cottage (a former chicken coop). Margot is a fabric store owner and Hazen, has a real estate business.

**In residence:** One dog and one cat.
**Foreign language spoken:** Swedish.
**Bed and bath:** Four rooms, each with private full bath. First-floor suite—bedroom with double sofa bed, private sitting room with fireplace. Second floor—bedroom with antique twin beds and private den/library; one single room with antique bed. Cottage with living room with double sofa bed, wood stove, kitchen.
**Breakfast:** Juice and fruit, homemade muffins, tea or coffee. In winter, hot oatmeal with Vermont maple syrup. Served in breakfast room adjoining the country kitchen.
**Plus:** Tour of house, property, old barns. Suggestions for restaurants, interesting attractions, shops, art galleries. Free admission to American Museum of Fly Fishing as guests of hosts. Join hosts in living room or on marble terrace under the awning in evening.
**Rates:** $25 per person. $30 per person in October. Extra person on cot $10.

From Connecticut: "Beyond its expected amenities and genial hospitality . . . magical quality of a 'time machine' which has attracted our repeat visits."

## Sunning Hill

Arch Street, Pittsford, VT 05763
**Phone:** 802/483-9402
**Location:** On a quiet side road in Pittsford, about 7 miles north of Rutland. Pico is about 15 miles away, Killington 20.
**Hosts:** Betty and Lawson Stewart
**Open:** Year round. Reservations preferred; required for holidays and foliage season.

The Stewarts directed us to a trafficless road during that spectacular foliage season. It led up to a nature preserve complete with pond on a hill, a magazine-cover kind of scene. Although they were relative newcomers—from Baltimore—they knew about other Vermont attributes too; in the morning they were on their way to a Vermont Symphony Orchestra board meeting.

Lawson, a former engineer and editor, puts his woodworking talents to use in this 1806 farmhouse. Betty was a teacher and school administrator in Maryland. She has a dream workspace for sewing and needlework projects.

Their interest in getting to know people is what really triggered their hosting in 1981. And they have succeeded. From Boston: "The Stewarts complement our fall ritual (hunting) and have become an important part of it." Several from Canada wrote about their repeat visits. Niffer is not forgotten in letters from New York.

The house, originally the home of the village blacksmith, and later owned by the manufacturer of the Pittsford Chair, is welcoming and lovely, furnished with antiques, reproductions, and art.

**In residence:** Daughter Nancy, a college student, is home occasionally. "Our son, his wife and their children sometimes pop in from their home on the property." Niffer, a loving golden retriever, enjoys people of all ages.
**Restrictions:** No guests' pets. Smoking allowed downstairs.
**Bed and bath:** Two rooms on the second floor share a bath. One room with a double bed, and a larger room with two twin beds. Crib and cot available.
**Breakfast:** Time agreed upon the night before, 6:30-10. Waffles, pancakes, or omelets. Some home-baked breads, always fruits, juices, beverages. Hosts usually join guests for breakfast either by the fireplace in the kitchen or in the gracious dining room.
**Plus:** Beverages upon arrival. Electric blankets. Babysitting can be arranged. Kitchen and laundry privileges upon request. Meadow and knoll for practice cross-country skiing. Good beginner alpine hill in yard for children. Brook has trout for the anglers. Five acres to explore and enjoy. Tour of the house. Will meet guests at Rutland airport or Pittsford or Rutland bus stop.
**Rates:** \$18 for one, \$25-\$28 for two. \$5 crib. \$10 additional bed.

---

## Quechee Bed & Breakfast

P.O. Box 0080, 753 Woodstock Road, Route 4, Quechee, VT 05059
**Phone:** 802/295-1776
**Location:** On 2½ acres with spectacular cliff edge views of the Ottauquechee River. Half-mile west of Quechee Gorge, within walking distance of old Quechee village; 6.5 miles to Woodstock,

30-45 minutes to Killington, Pico, Okemo ski areas; 15 minutes to Dartmouth College in Hanover, NH.
**Hosts:** Susan and Ken Kaduboski
**Open:** Year round. Two-night minimum stay on long weekends, three for Thanksgiving and Dartmouth graduation.

"Prior to this we led a very corporate life. Our initial exposure to B&Bs was in England where we lived for three years. . . . People have been nicer than we could have ever dreamed." The satisfaction is mutual: "Word of mouth is our best advertising."

Ken and Susan were already familiar with the area when they moved in 1985 to this 1795 colonial, once a coach stop. Recent owners had restored it structurally, but the Kaduboskis moved the kitchen and redecorated, furnishing the guests' living room with antiques and contemporary art.

**In residence:** Jessica and Benito, "two wonderful cats who are not allowed into guest areas unless invited." One smoker, Susan. Adult relatives sometimes visit.
**Restrictions:** Children should be at least 13. No guests' pets, please.
**Foreign language spoken:** "Slightly rusty fluent Spanish."
**Bed and bath:** Six rooms with antiques, stenciled curtains. All private full baths. Three first-floor rooms, two with a queen-sized four-poster bed and nonworking fireplace in each, and a third with two twin-sized sleigh beds. Three second-floor rooms with queen-sized beds (two four-posters); two of the rooms have original beamed ceilings. Sorry, no provisions for extra beds in a room.
**Breakfast:** Usually 8:30-9:30. Fresh fruit dish, maybe broiled bananas or grapefruit, fruits in Grand Marnier, baked apple with sour cream and nuts, and a main entree—stuffed French toast, apple-cinnamon pancakes, eggs any style served with homemade muffins, nut bread, or croissants; beverages. Served in dining room.
**Plus:** Cider upon arrival. Fireplaced living room and TV area. Air conditioning in some bedrooms; fans in others. Thick towels. Comforters. Refrigerator space. Lawn chairs. Tour of house. Will meet guests at Lebanon, N.H. airport, White River Junction train, or bus stops.
**Rates:** $85 based on double occupancy. MasterCard, VISA, and AMEX accepted.

## Placidia Farm Bed and Breakfast

RFD 1, Box 275, Randolph, VT 05060
**Phone:** 802/728-9883
**Location:** Six miles out of Randolph, 1½ miles up a dirt road. On 81 quiet acres with mountain views, pond, and brook.
**Host:** Viola Frost
**Open:** Year round. Reservations required.

The hand-hewn log house was a weekend retreat for two when Vi and her husband purchased the hideaway in 1978. Eventually they moved here from Massachusetts.

Vi was a a tax adjuster for the federal government. "Now I am busy with too many interests—cooking, needlecrafts, stained glass work, and some travel too."

Because she knew B&B from her business travels with her husband, she decided to share this idyllic spot with travelers. "It just seems like I have a lot of new friends!" Depending on the season, you might see a farmer harvesting hay. His cows graze in the meadow "and there are lots of birds."

**Restrictions:** No guests' pets. Nonsmokers preferred.
**Foreign language spoken:** A little German.
**Bed and bath:** Large bedroom with double bed and rollaway cot, double sleeper couch in living room of this private apartment. Full bath.
**Breakfast:** Usually at 8. Omelets, German apple pancakes, popovers. Served upstairs on Vi's plant-filled sun porch overlooking a pretty view. She usually joins guests for coffee and conversation.
**Plus:** Living room with TV, hi-fi, and radio. Cookies. Deck. Fans for bedrooms if needed. Kitchen privileges (extra charge). Walks, hiking, make-your-own cross-country ski trails on property.
**Rates:** $45 single, $60 double.

*Can't find the community you are going to? Check with a reservation service described at the beginning of this chapter. Through the service, you may be placed (matched) with a welcoming B&B that is near your destination.*

## The Peeping Cow

Route 106, P.O. Box 47, Reading, VT 05062
**Phone:** 802/484-5036
**Location:** Surrounded by meadows, brook, and forest. In the Vermont dairy farm country where "thirty bovines look in the living room windows at us." About 15 minutes south of Woodstock, 30 minutes from Dartmouth College; 5 minutes from Mount Ascutney, 11 miles from Woodstock.
**Hosts:** Anne (Nancy) and Francis (Frank) Lynch
**Open:** Year round. Reservations required for fall foliage, Christmas, George Washington, and Martin Luther King weekends.

Frank, a consulting engineer, has been an old-car buff since his youth in Scotland. He has owned and rebuilt a J2 MG, a Jaguar XK120, and Royal Enfield, BSA, and Velocette motorcycles. In the 13 years that the Lynches have lived in this c. 1830 farmhouse, he has added house renovating to his experience. Nancy states, "We have pretty much completed the downstairs. We have a 50-year building/renovation plan and are going to be dead in about 20!

"This is a fantastic place for wallowing in peace and quiet. B&B has been a sideline for us for nine years, but we are working at making it full time."

Antique furnishings predominate. In season, fresh flowers are everywhere. Only wood heat is used. Horseback riding is just down the road. "For those who love browsing in old cemeteries, we are surrounded by them. Free sugaring self-guided tours are just across the road from us. Ogden's Grist Mill is a favorite of ours. So is '20 Foot,' our village swimming hole."

**In residence:** Two college-age children might be home. The animals left when children went to college, but you might want to ask about the Black Angus Fiona MacGuiness Stout; Sam, the pig whose name was changed to Samantha; and the horse, Pegasus. (Every one is worth a story.)
**Restrictions:** Children should be at least 16. No guests' pets because of allergies. No smoking indoors.
**Foreign languages spoken:** "Fluent French. So-so Spanish."
**Bed and bath:** One or two or more rooms. First-floor room with two twin beds, private bath, and large sitting room with queen-sized sofa bed. Inquire about addition in progress.

**Breakfast:** Usually 8:30. Continental until addition is completed. Juices, fresh fruits, home-baked goodies, homemade jams and honey. "We think our pure (well and spring) water is what makes the brewed coffee and steeped tea extra great." Served in the dining room furnished with English antiques and oil paintings.
**Plus:** Sherry. No television. Piano, mandolin, ukulele yours to use. Chess. With notice and for a small fee, picnic lunches.
**Rates:** $30 single, $40 double.

## Rich Mound Acres

Rt. #1, Box 24, Williams Hill Road, Richmond, VT 05477
**Phone:** 802/434-2454 after 5 and on weekends.
**Location:** On a pastoral country road with mountain views. Three miles from Richmond village, 20 minutes from Burlington. Half hour to Stowe, Bolton, Mad River Glen.
**Hosts:** Joan and Bruce Hathaway
**Open:** Weekends only, year round, except Thanksgiving through New Year's Day. Reservations required. Two-night minimum stay required during fall foliage weekends and University of Vermont graduation.

Tales of hunting wild boar in Mississippi! The Hathaways enjoyed the storytellers so much that they have a full correspondence going with them. "There is something to learn from each guest," says Joan.

She is a chemical engineer at IBM. Bruce is a welding supervisor and probably spends an equal amount of time avocationally on photography. When they bought this 1830/1890 farmhouse three years ago with B&B in mind, it had been renovated by previous owners who were interior decorators. The young couple has carried out the country look, with antiques, crafts, and "some ad-libbing for an antique look." Returnees will find that the wall decor changes; Bruce has an ongoing rotating photography exhibit throughout the house.

**In residence:** Alphie, a country hound who is mostly beagle, and Comet, a tiger cat.
**Restrictions:** Children should be at least 12. No guests' pets. Smoking only in the kitchen and common room.
**Foreign language spoken:** Some French.

**Bed and bath:** Three second-floor bedrooms. One shared guest bath with two sinks, lighted stall shower and claw-foot tub. Two rooms each have a double bed. One has two twin beds. Individually controlled electric heat in each room.
**Breakfast:** One sitting at a predetermined time, 7-10. Juice, homemade muffins, scrambled eggs with jam, homemade jellies, home-canned fruit or breakfast souffle or pancakes and sausage or French toast with Vermont maple syrup. Served in country kitchen or dining area of the common room.
**Plus:** Scenic views, even from the bathtub. Fireplace and wood stove in common room. Tour of house. Dinners by special arrangement. Two acres of hidden walks and mown grass; eight acres with gardens and pond with waterlilies. Champagne for honeymooners.
**Rates:** $35 single, $40 double.

## Hillcrest Guest House

RD 1, Box 4459, Rutland, VT 05701
**Phone:** 802/775-1670
**Location:** Two miles from the junction of Routes 4 and 7, one-third mile from Route 7. About 20 minutes to Pico and a half hour to Killington ski areas.
**Hosts:** Bob and Peg Dombro
**Open:** Year round. Advance reservations preferred. Two-night minimum stay during foliage season.

"We like to think of B&B as hosting new friends, exchanging ideas, learning abut other home towns, and sharing with guests our love of Vermont."

Their rambling mid-19th-century post-and-beam farmhouse has been their home for 17 years. Country antiques enhance the New England flavor. Herb and vegetable gardens grow on the site of the old dairy barn. Plants thrive inside and out.

Bob has directed a school and rehabilitation agency for exceptional children. Now he is coordinator of an art gallery and a member of the district environmental commission. Peg is active in community theater, and horticulture is her year-round love.

**In residence:** Mary, Peg's mother. Two aging cats, Stanley and Bessie.
**Restrictions:** Sorry, no guests' pets. No smoking.

**Bed and bath:** Three second-floor rooms share one bath. Two rooms each with a double bed. One with a single bed. Crib available.
**Breakfast:** Available 7-9. Vermont-style continental, with homemade muffins, Very Special French Toast served with maple syrup and Peg's original "little fruit things," fresh-brewed coffee. Served on screened porch or in the country dining room.
**Plus:** Usually a beverage in late afternoon or evening. Line-dried sheets when weather permits. Two porches. Wood stove and fireplace in living room. Fresh flowers. Down comforters. Packed lunches can be arranged for bikers, hikers, and skiers. Dinner on special request for guests only.
**Rates:** $25 single, $35 double. $10 for crib.

From Massachusetts: "Friends have never welcomed us with more warmth or more generous hospitality."

## Montvert Park

8 Porter Street, Route 4 East, Rutland, VT 05701
**Phone:** 802/775-4004
**Location:** In a residential area, 300 feet from Route 4 East. 8 miles from Pico, 16 miles from Killington and two top-rated cross-country ski areas. Three miles from the world's largest marble exhibit and Vermont's own owner-occupied 17th-century castle. One mile from Vermont State Fair.
**Hosts:** Ethan and Dot Geraw
**Open:** Year round except April.

"We Are Going To Take You Two Home With Us" is one of the chapter titles of *Hello, Come On In,* the book Dot is writing. Since the Geraws answered the call for more area lodging in 1981, they have hosted bicyclists, members of ski teams, antique dealers, salespeople, buyers of log or vintage homes—and skiers who, when unable to go to the mountain because of weather or injuries, have unwound here. One father admitted that his afternoon nap was the first in 12 years. Many former guests drop by for a visit when passing through. The grandparents of six have an ever-expanding extended family.

"Soup Not Out Of A Can!" is another chapter of that book. Even though the kitchen table (where frequently they hear "Olympics, here I come") seems to be the focal point of the house, the yard is the place where they both do rug braiding and Dot quilts. The Christmas tree remains up "as long as possible." For about four weeks, guests are invited to take an ornament: calico and stenciled items made by the Geraws themselves.

Before retiring, Ethan was an Ivy League umpire for many years, and supervisor of Vermont Liquor Control. Recently he regained his Vermont State Straight Pool championship. He resurfaces and restores new and antique billiard tables. Dot was an executive secretary. They *are* native Vermonters, have lived in Rutland for over 40 years and in this 85-year-old house since 1951. That railing in the kitchen came from a church and was found in a pig sty. Ethan cut and set all the bricks in the kitchen. Many of the furnishings are family pieces and have histories. Comfort and utility are bywords.

**Restrictions:** Children should be at least seven or eight. Sorry, no guests' pets, no smoking, no sleeping bags.
**Bed and bath:** Two rooms share a full bath. One room with two twin brass beds, the other with an antique cherry double bed and exposed brick chimney wall. Both have cross-ventilation; air conditioners have been removed at guests' request.
**Breakfast:** Time determined the evening before. Fresh garden herbs used. Juices, fruitcup, homemade breads and jams. New menu each day. Bacon, sausage, or ham from area smoke-house. Puffed omelet with cheese, mushrooms is Ethan's specialty. Maybe homemade English or fruit muffins, whole-wheat or strawberry-puff pancakes. If 14-year-old (youngest) grandchild is around, he "makes a mean scrambled egg." Served at round oak kitchen table set with crystal, silver, tablecloth, and flowers. Hosts used to eat with guests. "We gained too much weight. Now we settle for coffee."
**Plus:** Late-afternoon or evening beverages. Air conditioning. "Homemade minestrone or corn chowder goes well after a day on the slopes." Goose-down pillows. Tour of nearby farm to observe the wood-fired sugar house where the maple syrup served here is made. Warm storage space for ski equipment. Their shared double living room downstairs. Wurlitzer spinet piano. Private upstairs den with TV. Album with information about their sources of jam, maple syrup, honey, and meats. Wooded cool yard with plenty of fall leaves.
**Rates:** $35 per room.

# Shrewsbury

About a mile and a half from the farm where a 700-pound bull moose courted Jessica the Hereford (and the national press) are two B&Bs that are across the road from one another. A landmark with a longer history is *up* the road at the top of the hill: W.P. Pierce, one of the most authentic (1918) country stores in the country. Going *down* the road are views that are so spectacular that I applied my bicycle brakes to savor them all.

## Buckmaster Inn

Box 118, Lincoln Hill Road, RD # 1, Shrewsbury, VT 05738
**Phone:** 802/492-3485
**Location:** About 20 minutes to Killington and Okemo Mountains. On a paved country road in the Green Mountains. Two miles north of Cuttingsville.
**Hosts:** Grace and Sam Husselman
**Open:** Year round. Reservations preferred. Minimum two-night stay on weekends.

"We made a dream come true when we retired and opened here in 1984." In New Jersey Grace was a teacher and a director of a public library. Sam was an engineer. Their "gorgeous and functional" ten-room house, originally a coach stop and known as Buckmaster Tavern in the early 1800s, has a grand staircase and wide floorboards. Antiques are everywhere, yet Grace and Sam still "hunt." To interested guests, they offer the name of one auctioneer whom they think has down-to-earth prices.

Sam enjoys his horses, golf, chess, and fishing, "anything outdoors." It takes him about a day to mow the rolling hills with a tractor. In winter, he appreciates those grounds for cross-country skiing. Grace enjoys knitting Icelandic sweaters as well as other handwork; many of her framed crewel pieces are throughout the house.

**In residence:** Two horses, Razalla and Marty. Grandchildren may visit during ski weekends and summer vacation.

**Restrictions:** Children should be at least four. No guests' pets. Smoking not encouraged; restricted to first floor.
**Foreign language spoken:** Dutch.
**Bed and bath:** Four rooms, one with private bath. Three second-floor rooms share a bath. Full-sized antique four-poster in one room with fireplace. Two twin beds in another large room. Third room has queen-sized bed. On the third floor, a huge beamed-ceiling hideaway, a king-sized bed, private bath with shower. Cot available.
**Breakfast:** 7:30-9:00. If later, self-service continental. Homemade Vermont jams, jellies, sweet breads and buns, and/or Vermont cheddar cheese and egg casserole, hot beverages. Served in the country kitchen with wood stove, in dining room, or in porch.
**Plus:** Tea and cookies upon arrival. A good library. With advance notice, will bake a birthday cake. "Wine, cheese and crackers, and wedding bells, if we know honeymooners are arriving." Use of entire house, TV, library, and fireplace. In summer, outdoor grilles, picnic tables and umbrellas, and screened-in porches. Croquet. In winter, use of toboggan on property. Babysitting available.
**Rates:** \$30-\$40 shared bath, \$45 for private bath. \$5 off regular room rate for singles. \$15 cot.

> "Gracious hosts . . . immaculate home. . . . Our daughter and her husband are skiers and because of our pleasant stay at the inn, they, too, are going to stay with Sam and Grace the next time they visit in the area."

## Maple Crest Farm

Shrewsbury, VT
Mailing address: Box 120, Cuttingsville, VT 05738
**Phone:** 802/492-3367
**Location:** High in the Green Mountains, ten miles south of downtown Rutland and ten miles north of Ludlow. A wonderful setting on a quiet road. Near Killington and Okemo ski areas.
**Hosts:** Donna and Bill Smith
**Open:** Year round. Two-night minimum stay required.

Guests—including many artists and photographers—comment about "true Vermont hospitality" or "a step into the past" where dairy farming and sugar making are carried on by a fifth generation. Except for the first 20 years, when it was run as a tavern, this 27-room landmark, built in 1808, has been a private home with each generation having guests on a small scale. Robert Frost and past governors slept here.

Donna met Bill when she was working at a nearby inn. In 1969, soon after they married, she started B&B at Maple Crest as a real home away from home. "This is the way B&B started. If I have to be commercial, I don't want to stay in B&B." Donna's interests go beyond the farm. She serves as town treasurer and is a bank director.

Guests appreciate the antiques and personal treasures. One from Bainbridge Island, Washington, who hadn't been in Vermont for 20 years, wrote that his stay here was the most memorable part of his trip. "We were even lucky enough to be there the day Fred was being shoed by the blacksmith."

**In residence:** Son Russ, 21, and KC, a Labrador retriever. About 105 cows and a large part-Clydesdale horse named Fred.
**Restrictions:** No guests' pets.
**Bed and bath:** Five large rooms, some with wood stoves. One room on first floor with half-bath. Four rooms on second floor share a full bath. Each room has a double and a single bed. Two apartments—each sleeps five—can be B&B or efficiencies. Cot and crib available.
**Breakfast:** Served 8-9:30 in the kitchen or dining room. Full country meal with bacon and eggs, pancakes with maple syrup made here on the farm, homemade muffins and jams.
**Plus:** Seasonal flowers. Late-afternoon or evening beverage. Tour of farm and maple-sugaring operation. Cross-country skiing and hiking on the property.
**Rates:** \$18 single, \$35 double, \$40 triple. \$5 cot or crib. One night's deposit required.

> From Rhode Island: "It was wonderful. I had to arrive late at night and leave early in the morning, yet was met with great warmth. In that short time I knew it was a place that I wanted to return to with my family!"

## Watercourse Way

Box 101, Route 132, South Strafford, VT 05070
**Phone:** 802/765-4314
**Location:** On a country road with streams, wildflowers, and horse farms. On the Ompompanoosuc River, three miles south of the Strafford Meeting House and Old City Falls. Twelve miles north of Norwich, Vt. and Hanover, N.H.
**Hosts:** Lincoln Alden and Anna Dewey Alden
**Open:** Year round. Reservations required.

> Guests said, "It's just a wonderful and comfortable place that makes you feel very much at home. Not fancy. . . . You feel as if you are visiting with real Vermonters, even though they are newcomers."

According to Lincoln, "Guests come here to escape the city pace and to reacquaint themselves with nature and the country life . . . in an undisturbed valley in the heart of Vermont."

No restoration was needed when Anna and Lincoln came here in 1984. So far, two people have stopped by to tell them stories of the "luxurious" farmhouse built by the Strafford-based (until 1950) Vermont Copper Co. Lincoln is a health care worker and carpenter, Anna a music teacher. They delight in sharing directions to waterfalls, "the mysterious copper field, and the amazing view on the hill up behind us." They have become well versed in activities and attractions, traditional and unique.

**In residence:** Two outdoor cats, Ginger and Crystal. Three sheep; Barney "bahs" at every arriving guest but is quiet through the night. Susie, a small friendly dalmatian, stays in hosts' quarters.
**Restrictions:** Pets allowed only with advance notification. Smoking in common room only.
**Bed and bath:** Three rooms on the second floor in a wing set apart from the hosts' quarters. One half and one full bath shared. One room with double bed, twin, and trundle bed, rocking chair and writing desk. Two other rooms each with a double bed. All mattresses are new; some are futons, others foam. Original wide floorboards, country wallpaper, quilts, and herbal wreaths.
**Breakfast:** 8-9, unless otherwise arranged. Fresh-ground gourmet coffee, tea—herbal or regular, orange juice, fruit in season, homebaked muffins or eggs with toast or French toast or pancakes with Vermont maple syrup. Served by the flagstone fireplace in the common room. Anna and Lincoln usually join guests for coffee.

**Plus:** In season, fresh herbal teas from the garden. Seven acres of woods, gardens, pasture to roam. Library. Piano. Babysitting sometimes available. Picnic table, hammock, and chairs down by the river. Swimming hole. Lounging chairs in the perennial rock garden that overlooks the tree farm.
**Rates:** \$20 single, \$40 double, \$50 triple.

---

## Guest House Christel Horman

Mountain Road, RR 1, Box 1635, Stowe, VT 05672
**Phone:** 802/253-4846
**Location:** On Mountain Road (Route 108), 1½ miles from Mount Mansfield, 5¼ miles from Stowe village, 45 minutes from Burlington.
**Hosts:** Christel and Jim Horman
**Open:** Thanksgiving-April, June-October.

Much of the old woodwork in this 1980 chalet-style house is from another lodge that was dismantled. Many of the decorative accessories, such as the kangaroo skin and the hand-painted ceramic plaques, are from "home."

Jim was an auto mechanic and ski instructor in Australia. Christel was a secretary in West Germany. They met in Stowe, where they have lived for two decades. Jim works for the Mt. Mansfield Company. Christel is here full time.

In 1980, after they had the shell of their own guest house built, they did all the finishing work and decorating themselves. The Hormans made corner benches, painted a mural of children sitting on a fence, constructed all the headboards, painted flowers on them, and did the stenciling. Now Christel and Jim have the satisfaction of many a good conversation by the fire.

**In residence:** Neil, age 12.
**Restrictions:** Sorry, no guests' pets.
**Foreign languages spoken:** German and a little Swedish.
**Bed and bath:** Eight rooms, each with two double beds and private full bath. Wall-to-wall carpeting and individual thermostats.
**Breakfast:** 8-10. Full breakfast, often with apple pancakes, served by living room hearth.

**Plus:** Living room with hearthstone fireplace. Books, magazines, color TV. Cross-country skiing from the door. Small outdoor swimming pool. Trout fishing in brook behind the house. Babysitting possibilities. Coffee and tea always available. Nearby indoor and outdoor tennis.
**Rates:** Per person. Double occupancy. Summer $24-$30. Winter $29-$40. Ski week (five nights, Sunday-Thursday) $27. Cot in same room $22. Crib $6 (no food included). MasterCard and VISA accepted.

## The Inn at Sunderland

Historic Route 7A, Sunderland
Mailing address: RR 2 Box 2440, Arlington, VT 05250
**Phone:** 802/362-4213
**Location:** At the foot of Mount Equinox, midway between the villages of Manchester and Arlington. About 20 minutes to Stratton, Bromley, and Magic Mountain.
**Hosts:** Tom and Peggy Wall
**Open:** Year round. Reservations preferred.

"Almost everyone says we are living their fantasy. The neat thing is we *are* living our own fantasy and loving it! We started talking about it when we were married eight years ago. We had planned to do B&B when we retired but decided to jump in now.

"We have furnished in 'country comfortable' solid pieces. We love to share our 'secret' antique sources with guests. The inn, built in 1840, has all the original glass and (mostly chestnut) woodwork. . . . And finally, there is my 'collection of pigs' everywhere, each one with a story." Fans of the inn appreciate the attention to detail and guests' needs.

In Washington, D.C., Peggy was community development director and Tom was a Federal Home Loan Bank Board attorney. In his current Manchester-based private practice, he has represented several people in their purchase of an inn.

**In residence:** Midnite, a part-Persian black cat who greets everyone. "There is a large horse barn across the yard which is home to our three goats—Nanny, Willie and Smurf, and is usually home to some horses. Current residents include Alexander and Abercrombie, the carriage horses for the Village Carriage Company."

**Restrictions:** No guests' pets, please.
**Foreign language spoken:** Very little French.
**Bed and bath:** Ten rooms, two with shared baths and eight with private baths. Fireplaces in four rooms. Four rooms with queen-sized beds. Five have double beds. One has two twin beds. Two rooms have porch with a wonderful view of the Green Mountains. All furnished with country antiques. Cots and crib available.
**Breakfast:** 8:30-9:30. Choice of juice, fresh fruit, and main dish such as Sunderland sausage bake and fresh-baked sweet roll, ham and eggs with spiced applesauce and blueberry muffins, or thick-sliced French toast. As long as guests appear before 9:30 they can linger over breakfast as long as they like.
**Plus:** Reduced Stratton ski-lift tickets. Late-afternoon seasonal beverage, crackers, and house blend of herb cheese. Thick towels and fresh flowers in rooms. Tour of the house and barn. Ceiling fans in most bedrooms. Seven acres stretching to the Battenkill River, one of the best trout streams in America. Guest privileges for golf and tennis at Manchester Country Club (fee charged).
**Rates:** $65-$85 double occupancy; additional surcharge for foliage and holidays. Singles, $5 less. $15 cots. $5 crib. Lower rates available winter midweek. MasterCard, VISA, and AMEX accepted.

## Emersons' Guest House

82 Main Street, Vergennes, VT 05491
**Phone:** 802/877-3293
**Location:** On the wide main street of this Champlain Valley city of 2,300. Skiing 45 minutes away at Sugarbush and Mad River Glen. Shelburne Museum and Morgan horse farm just a short ride away.
**Hosts:** John and Pat Emerson
**Open:** Year round.

At "How To" B&B workshops, I am sometimes asked the secret to convincing husbands that they should accept "strangers" as paying guests. Emersons' Guest House is the source of my "kick under the table" answer. John, a high-school math teacher, was one of those who wasn't too keen on the B&B idea. It didn't take long before Pat found herself kicking him under the breakfast table because it really was time to stop the (interesting) conversation and get on with the day. Indeed, we did have a fascinating breakfast discussion with two other guests, itinerant organ experts who were revitalizing a local church organ.

The spacious 1850 home is comfortable and impeccably clean. Pat has refinished all the pine floors, papered and painted all the rooms. "As my parents were in the restaurant and hotel business for about 40 years, the work of B&B 'seems like nothing.' Our lives have been enriched through guests from all over the world."

**In residence:** Son Peter, age 14. Laura and Lisa may be around during college vacations. Blackie, a 14-year-old black Lab, "very quiet and lazy, loves people but stays within a designated area."
**Restrictions:** No guests' pets. No smoking in the bedrooms.
**Bed and bath:** Four second-floor rooms with two shared guest baths. Three large doubles, one with two single four-poster beds, one with a double bed and nonworking fireplace, and one with a double bed. A cozy smaller room has a double bed. Rollaway beds available.
**Breakfast:** Usually 7:30-8:30. Bottomless cup of coffee, tea, or milk, orange juice, hot homemade muffins, eggs, homemade toast, jams and jellies from the Emerson's own berries. Hosts usually join guests in the large, homey country kitchen.
**Plus:** Window fans in bedrooms. Tour of house. Lawns. Porches. Babysitting can be arranged. Community pool, tennis courts, public playground nearby.
**Rates:** $20-$30 single, $25-$35 double. $10 for rollaway bed. Off-season rates October 20-May 1.

## Strong House Inn

RD #1, Box 9, Vergennes, VT 05491
**Phone:** 802/877-3337
**Location:** In the Champlain Valley, with superb views of the Green Mountains and the Adirondack Range. On Rte 22A, 3/4 mile south of the stoplight located in the center of town. Twenty-two miles from Burlington.
**Hosts:** Laura and Liam Murphy
**Open:** Year round. Two-night minimum stay required September 15-October 15.

For their third restoration, the Murphys chose this Federal-style 150-year-old house that is on the National Register. A 19th-century portrait of Samuel Paddock Strong hangs over a marble fireplace. Furnishings include antiques, handcrafts—and whimsical items such as a three-quarter-size wooden cow beneath the staircase and a neon sculpture in the dining room.

Liam, born in Ireland and raised in a B&B in Wales, met Laura in Washington, D.C. where he was a lawyer and she a management consultant. They moved to Vermont where he practices law and she runs this "comfortably elegant B&B."

**Restrictions:** Pets must stay outdoors or in the garage. Smoking in designated areas only.
**Foreign language spoken:** "We can understand basic needs in French."
**Bed and bath:** Seven rooms, on three floors. Four rooms with private bath. One on first floor has two double four-poster beds and private bath. Five rooms on second floor include master bedroom with double sleigh bed, working fireplace, and private half-bath, and three rooms with a double and a single bed. Varied antique furnishings in oak, mahogany, maple, irons, and brass.
**Breakfast:** 8-9:30. Apricot/walnut bread, poppyseed muffins, French bread or raisin French toast, apple, banana or walnut pancakes, "make your own fruit salad sundaes." Locally grown products used. Served in dining room or in courtyard.
**Plus:** Beverages. Piano (marbleized) in living room. Tour of house. Fans (rarely needed) in all rooms. Dinner ($15 per person) by advance reservation only. Will meet bus in Vergennes. Locked garage for bicycles. Courtyard. Many suggestions for good bicycle routes.
**Rates:** $40-$45 double occupancy with shared bath. $55 with private half or full bath. $5 additional bed. $5 additional person. $5 less for singles. MasterCard, VISA, and AMEX accepted.

## Knoll Farm Country Inn

Bragg Hill Road, RR Box 179, Waitsfield, VT 05673
**Phone:** 802/496-3939
**Location:** Off the beaten track, on 150 acres, a half-mile up a hill away from Route 100. Views of rolling farmlands, mountains, and the Mad River Valley below as well as Sugarbush and Mad River Glen ski areas.
**Host:** Ann Day Heinzerling
**Open:** May 1-November 1. Reservations strongly recommended.

B&B travelers have been coming here since 1957, but many stay through the day and make it a real farm vacation.

Ann is an Audubon Society director, a naturalist guide, a member of the Poetry Society of Vermont, and a free-lance writer and photographer. Originally it was the ski business that brought her and her first husband, Frank Day, to Vermont from Massachusetts. In 1957 they bought the fixed-up 19th-century farmhouse that has had guests and been a working farm ever since. After Frank's untimely death in 1970 Ann continued the inn with the help of her two grown children. She can direct you to a hidden swimming hole, a beaver pond, a mountain trail, or a special view.

Maple floors, turn-of-the-century and older antiques, and braided rugs enhance the authentic farmhouse feeling. With 12 guests at most, camaraderie reigns. And so does rejuvenation. Returnees are many; summer reservations, in particular, can be hard to come by.

**In residence:** Grandchildren Megan, age 14, and Haven, age 10, visit during the summer. Three dogs, five cats, and all the farm animals—horses, Scottish Highland cattle and calves, a pig, and Araucana chickens that lay edible blue and green eggs.
**Restrictions:** Children should be at least six. No smoking indoors.
**Foreign languages spoken:** A little French and Spanish.
**Bed and bath:** Five second-floor rooms share three full baths. Two downstairs baths. Two rooms with a double and a single bed, one with two twin beds, two with two twins and a double. One (actually two rooms) is a good family room and has a porch. Cots available.
**Breakfast:** Served family style at 8. Cooked cereals and Knoll Farm's own bacon, eggs, sausage, and ham. French toast, maybe cornbread with apples. Blueberry pancakes on Sunday. The farm's own food. In dining room or cozy sun room.
**Plus:** Tea or mulled cider in fall, lemonade in summer. Pantry privileges. Option of dinner is very popular. So is horseback riding for beginners and experts alike. Guests can help with care of horses. Buggy rides available. Extensive library, puzzles, ping-pong, use of typewriter, piano, antique pump organ. Pond for rowing (boat available) and swimming. Croquet, horseshoes, badminton. Huge lawn. Acres of pasture. Hiking. Tour of farm; lots of opportunities to help with chores. If needed, transportation to and from shopping, bus, train, or airport.
**Rates:** $34 single, $28 per person double occupancy. Family and weekly rates available. Dinner $10 per person.

## Lareau Farm Country Inn

Box 563, Route 100, Waitsfield, VT 05673
**Phone:** 802/496-4949
**Location:** In a large open meadow, on Route 100, one mile south of Waitsfield; 45 minutes to Sherburne Museum and Lake Champlain.
**Hosts:** Susan and Dan Easley
**Open:** Year round. Reservations suggested. Two-day minimum stay on holidays.

Waitsfield had been the vacation town for a bank training director and her science teacher husband when they decided to leave the jobs they had held for 18 years in Pittsburgh. It just so happened that the Lareau Farm, in the same family for 40 years and only recently a six-room inn, was for sale. Susan and Dan had already restored three houses. Here, in addition to redecorating, they added four new rooms with private baths and built an apartment for themselves in the barn, never missing a guest day.

"This area has activities in all seasons. . . . Our favorite hikes and skis are through what we call 'the enchanted forest,' to the rock precipice high over the farm, and to the tiny cemetery of the first owners, the family of the first doctor in town."

**In residence:** Teenage children may be at home. Three dogs—Fannie, a weimaraner, Fred, a Lab mix, and Daisy, a beagle mix.
**Restrictions:** Parents must monitor their children closely. Prefer not to have guests' pets. No smoking in bedrooms.
**Bed and bath:** Ten rooms. Four with private baths. All rooms have double beds, one room has an additional twin bed, and one room also has two twin beds. Six rooms share two hall baths. All rooms have antique furnishings; some have wide plank floors and stenciled walls. Susan made the hand-tied quilts. Rollaway and crib available.
**Breakfast:** Generally 8-9. Fresh fruits, baked goods such as pumpkin muffins from Easleys' pumpkins, egg souffles, raspberry pancakes or fabulous French toast. Served family style in the dining room at large oak tables.
**Plus:** Afternoon hors d'oeuvres in the winter. Tour of house. Dinner ($15-$18) offered Saturdays or by special arrangement. Swimming in the "crystal clear Mad River," which borders the property. Volleyball, hiking, cross-country skiing, canoeing, and fishing on premises. Soaring, horseback riding, and antiquing nearby.

**Rates:** Winter, fall $35/$40 per person double occupancy shared/private bath. Spring, summer and late fall $30/$35 per person double occupancy shared/private bath. Singles add $15. Discount on five-night (Sunday-Thursday) stays. MasterCard or VISA accepted; cash or personal checks preferred.

From Massachusetts: "It is like a home away from home where one can enjoy the relaxing atmosphere of a country inn . . . delicious gourmet breakfasts, reasonable prices, and a good location for skiing. . . ."

## The Inn at Beaver Pond Farm

RD Box 306, Golf Course Road, Warren, Vermont 05674
**Phone:** 802/583-2861
**Location:** On a quiet dirt road, minutes from restaurants and shops of the Mad River Valley. One mile from the downhill ski runs of Sugarbush. Adjacent to cross-country trails of Sugarbush Valley; 200 yards from the first tee of Club Sugarbush Golf Course (open to the public) designed by Robert Trent Jones.
**Hosts:** Bob and Betty Hansen
**Open:** Year round except May. Reservations required. Two-day minimum stay during fall and winter.

From New York: "A real find . . . spent our honeymoon there and have been back in all seasons. Betty and Bob have the gift of being able to offer warm hospitality as well as privacy to their guests. . . . We have been made to feel like very treasured friends. . . . The inn itself is lovely. Betty has not missed a trick in the decorating—down to hand-painted doorknobs . . . always immaculate, but never sterile. . . . Betty is an incredible cook—energetic and creative. . . . The best part, however, is at the end of a 'long hard day of skiing' or whatever—coming in to the smell of home-baked chocolate-chip cookies and hot mulled cider (in the winter) and shortbreads and iced tea (in the summer). It really feels better than home!"

What many call "the best of the best" has a story: "Our 1860 farmhouse was originally a dairy farm, but most recently a sheep farm. When we purchased it in 1977 it had been vacant and boarded up for years. We slowly restored it to a comfortable home with the antiques that we have acquired over the years."

In New Jersey, Betty was a caterer until deciding, in 1983, to share the Vermont home with B&B guests. Bob, a banker for 27 years, became a full-time innkeeper in 1986. They ski, play golf, fish, travel, and enjoy classical music. They can tell you about polo fields, an airport that offers soaring, the Long Trail, or a hamlet with "a jewel of a museum."

**In residence:** Jesse, a yellow Labrador retriever, and Jasper, a gray cat "who somehow found his way to our barn."
**Restrictions:** Children should be at least seven. No guests' pets.
**Foreign language spoken:** French. (Betty attended the Sorbonne.)
**Bed and bath:** Five rooms. Three with queen-sized beds, two with two twin beds in each. All baths, three private and one shared by two rooms, are large, full, and tiled. Antiques, down comforters, carpeting—and mountain views. Cot available.
**Breakfast:** 7:30-10. Juice, fresh fruit, homemade Danish pastries, a choice of eggs or French toast or "special" pancakes, breakfast meats, and locally roasted coffee. Served by Bob on antique china with sterling silver in the dining room or on large deck.
**Plus:** Afternoon beverages. Setups and hors d'oeuvres in the evening. Tour of house. Prix-fixe dinners Saturdays, some Tuesday and Thursday nights. Thick towels. Suggested bicycle routes (15-70 miles) and the best local trout fishing streams. Will meet guests (fee charged) at Burlington airport, Waterbury train or bus. Inquire about Thanksgiving and Christmas dinner arrangements.
**Rates:** Per person. Double occupancy. $37 shared bath, $40 private bath. June through September, about 10 percent less per person. Five-day midweek stays, 10 percent discount. MasterCard and VISA accepted.

---

## South Hollow Farm

RR 1, Box 287, Warren, VT 05674
**Phone:** 802/496-5627
**Location:** Near the small village, up a township-maintained dirt lane to a secluded setting with mountain views. Adjacent to land deeded to the National Forest to be "wilderness forever." Less than three miles from Sugarbush Valley ski area and less than two miles from Route 100.
**Hosts:** Pat and Bob Dockendorf
**Open:** Year round. Reservations required.

Exposed beams, random-width floors, handmade quilts, family antiques. It all adds up to a relaxed, homey ambiance in the 1837 Vermont farmhouse that Bob and Pat "retired" to in 1981. In Baltimore, Bob had been an administrator at a rehabilitation center and Pat was a mental health counselor and professor of health and physical education. For two years they ran a restaurant and deli in the Warren area. Now they are in real estate.

Some guests make it a point to gather their own breakfast eggs (right here) or to pick, in season, red raspberries, elderberries, and blackberries.

**In residence:** Adult children drop in occasionally. Garfunkle, an 18-year-old Siamese cat and PowPow, a very friendly 4-year-old golden retriever.
**Restrictions:** Children should be at least six. No guests' pets, please. No smoking.
**Bed and bath:** Three rooms, one with private bath. The first-floor room has two twin beds and an full bath. Upstairs a large room with double bed and antique "hired hand" bed share a full bath with a small room with double bed. Cot available.
**Breakfast:** 7-10. Fresh fruit or Bob's great fresh fruit salad, bacon or sausage, omelets, French toast, pancakes and eggs, homemade breads and jam. Served in the dining room, which has exposed beams, pewter chandelier, trestle table, and hutch. More than one couple has written that it was "the best they have ever eaten."
**Plus:** Late-afternoon or evening beverages. Tours of the house and farm. Electric blankets. Babysitting can be arranged. Kitchen and laundry privileges. Trout fishing or wading in the pond. Patio with a view. Horseshoes and badminton. Hiking trails.
**Rates:** April–mid-June and November–mid-December $30 single shared or private bath, $40 double with private bath, $35 with shared bath. Mid-June–mid September $5 more. Mid-September–October $37.50 single, $50 double with private bath, $45 with shared bath. Mid-December–March $40 single, $50 double with private bath, $45 double with shared bath. Ten percent discount for seniors (62+). MasterCard and VISA accepted.

From Massachusetts: "There's something about them that is serene. . . . And they have a great sense of humor . . . a quality, friendly and delicious B&B. . . . We also walked around their grounds and made use of their patio. Played with their dog. We had a ball!"

## Blush Hill House

RD 1, Box 1266, Waterbury, VT 05676
**Phone:** 802/244-7529
**Location:** At the top of a hill, across from a nine-hole golf course. Five minutes from I-89. Within 20 minutes of Stowe, Sugarbush, and Bolton Valley ski areas.
**Hosts:** Bobbi and Thomas O'Connor
**Open:** Year round.

From New Jersey: "After staying in a number of B&Bs on our honeymoon, we found Blush Hill to be most enchanting. . . . The charm of the house as well as the magnificent countryside and the gracious hospitality convinced us to spend an extra day."

The O'Connors, longtime residents of Vermont, were "looking for the perfect place when we found this former stagecoach stop with four fireplaces and wide board floors." Exposed beams and a large double fireplace are features in the kitchen of the brick Cape that was the very first house on the hill in 1815. It is decorated with warm colors, country prints and "a collection gathered from years of auction-going."

Tom has been with IBM for over two decades. Before the O'Connors moved here in 1986, Bobbie had a hair and tanning salon in Burlington.

**Restrictions:** Children should be at least ten. No guests' pets. No smoking in bedrooms.
**Bed and bath:** Six rooms, two with private full baths. Two shared full baths. The first-floor room has a double bed, working fireplace, private bath. Upstairs rooms have a double or two twin-sized beds.
**Breakfast:** 8-9:30. Fresh fruit, homemade muffins, cheese, juice, and coffee served in the large country kitchen overlooking mountains (and bluebirds).
**Plus:** Beverages. Bedroom window fans. Golf and ski weekends in season. Wide porch with rockers facing golf course. Deck. Canoe (for rent) for use in lake at end of the road.
**Rates:** $45-$55, double occupancy, depending upon room size and season. $10 cot. Package rates for ski and golf weekends. MasterCard and VISA accepted.

## Weathervane Lodge

Dorr Fitch Rd., Box 57, West Dover, VT 05356
**Phone:** 802/464-5426
**Location:** One mile off Route 100, up a hill, in peaceful countryside with a panoramic view of mountains and valleys. Within minutes of Haystack, Mount Snow, Carinthia, and Maple Valley ski areas. Near the Marlboro Festival and golf, tennis, lake swimming, horseback riding, hiking, and museums.
**Host:** Ernie Chabot
**Open:** Year round. Advance reservations required in foliage and ski seasons. Two-night minimum stay on weekends during ski season.

"Returnees ask which room is available, and they know just where to settle in—'at home.' That's the way my wife and I intended it to be. This is very much a family place; sometimes we have three generations at one time. Because of my work in precious metals, I have traveled all over the world, and we seem to have a very international clientele.

"In the winter we start making our ice fountain; it grows to about 30 feet high and almost that wide and lasts until Memorial Day. Kids climb on it. We put colored lights on it from below. The snowshoes and toboggans get a lot of use. In the summer Weathervane is equally beautiful with the landscaping and flowers.

"I built this Tyrolean style place as my second home 20 years ago, and if you want, I can tell you how many nails there are, how I laughed, and how I cried. We have heating systems, but the four fireplaces—for atmosphere—burn ten cords of wood a year.

"This place is loaded with antiques and charm. And there are ice boxes all over the place so you can put your stuff in there for the next day's trip. During the week I now have a staff to welcome you. New England is my current sales territory for fine silver, china and crystal, so I'm here Thursday through Sunday. . . . There have been lots of changes in tourism, but the homey, comfortable place is what works for us and our guests."

**In residence:** Cats, Spooky and Pumpkin.
**Restrictions:** No guests' pets.
**Bed and bath:** Ten rooms and a suite. Most rooms have shared baths. Suite has a room with double bed, living room with sleep sofa (double), and private bath. Another room has two doubles, a sleep sofa that makes up into a double, and a private bath. Others

have two twins, double, set of twin bunks, double and a bunk, double and single, or four singles. Cot and crib available.
**Breakfast:** 7:30-9:30. All sorts of choices, maybe pancakes, French toast, eggs poached in pure Vermont maple syrup. It's a full meal served at two antique tables in beamed and fireplaced dining room with plants, 30-gallon fish tank, antique clocks, atmosphere.
**Plus:** Late-afternoon or evening beverages. Lounge with fieldstone fireplace and setup bar. Dinner ($9) offered in ski season, during holiday weeks, and on Saturdays. Trails, open field, and old town roads for cross-country skiing. Free snowshoes, sleds, toboggans.
**Rates:** Vary according to room and season. Winter weekdays are lower than weekends and holiday weeks. Based on double occupancy. Winter rates with bunk facilities and shared bath $21-$29 per person. Suite with private bath $30-$36 per person. About $3 lower other seasons. Singles add $10.

## Rodgers' Dairy Farm Vacation

RFD 3, Box 57, West Glover, VT 05875
**Phone:** 802/525-6677
**Location:** Quiet. About eight miles from town (pop. 600), up a paved hilly road to scenic views and a turn onto a dirt road to the farm. Closest neighbor one mile away. Thirty-five miles to Canadian border; 30 miles to Stowe.
**Hosts:** Jim and Nancy Rodgers
**Open:** June 1-December 1. Reservations required.

Nancy grew up as the youngest child on a farm that hired help; then in high school she met Jim and eventually became a farmer's wife. Her mother-in-law's Scottish ancestors built this house in 1834. Jim's parents set up the farm vacation program, offering three meals a day because the nearest restaurant is about 12 miles away. When Nancy and Jim moved here five years ago, they continued the farm vacation idea, but now they offer B&B too.

You don't have to have children to enjoy the farm, but some grandparents have been known to return with grandchildren in tow. Nancy has rarely heard a visiting child ask for something to do or if they could watch TV. There are ponies to ride. You can watch the cows being milked and maybe try to do it yourself. Kids gather their own eggs. "They're out there waiting for them to drop." You are welcome to give a hand with haying. Help feed the animals. Take a day trip or just stay here all day. It's a real working farm that is truly family run.

If you come in the fall, Nancy will gladly show you how she shapes her gravevine wreaths. "I love to make things and have each room look different." When we last spoke, she had just made some new balloon shades. The patchwork quilts are also her creations.

**In residence:** Sons Craig, 9, and Chris, 17. Barn pets—three beagles, a border collie, several cats, horses, cows, hens, goats, and a rabbit.
**Restrictions:** No guests' pets.
**Foreign language spoken:** French.
**Bed and bath:** Five large rooms. Two with two twin beds, one with double bed, another with double bed and a crib, and another with double bed and sleep sofa. Shared bath with shower upstairs and bath with tub-shower downstairs. Cot and crib available.
**Breakfast:** At 8:30. Different menu each day. Could be pancakes and sausage, or scrambled eggs, bacon, blueberry muffins, and toast, or fried eggs, home fries, ham, and sour cream coffee cake. Nancy and Jim always join guests for breakfast.
**Plus:** Ping-pong table, games, magazines, TV, video games. Lawn chairs, picnic table, swing set, sand box, badminton, and horseshoes. Option of dinner ($7.50).
**Rates:** $25 per adult, $12.50 under age 12, $5 for babies (for whom guests provide food). Full-day and weekly rates available.

## The Darling Family Inn

Route 100, Weston, VT 05161
**Phone:** 802/824-3223
**Location:** Half-mile north of village with panoramic view of surrounding mountains and farmland. Near Bromley, Stratton, Okemo, and Magic Mountain (all have snow making), summer theater, antiques and crafts, and art exhibits. Three miles from Weston Priory.
**Hosts:** Chapin and Joan Darling
**Open:** Year round. Two-night minimum stay required on weekends.

"The kids grew up. We were ready for a change from corporate life, and wanted to work together at something."

And they are enjoying their new occupation, which involves interaction with each guest and much restoration. They do everything (with taste and charm) themselves in the 150-year-old farmhouse that provides a wonderful backdrop for their early American and English antiques. Joan paints on wood and tin items. The coffee table was once a wash bench. There are many comments on the thimbles painted with minute New England scenes that have a discernible twigs on the trees. Chapin makes miniature and sophisticated wood items. Joan's childhood teddy bear has a place of honor in an antique child's wagon.

The farmhouse was a private home until 1957, a guesthouse until the Darlings made it an inn in 1980. How's it going? "One out of every five guests leaves here dreaming of becoming innkeepers."

**In residence:** Sam, the dog; Cinder, the cat. Any or all of the four grown Darling children might be visiting, including son Jeff, who is a blacksmith and has crafted much of the inn's hardware in his forge out in the barn.
**Restrictions:** Children should be at least eight. Sorry, no guests' pets. Smoking is allowed.
**Bed and bath:** Five rooms, two with private baths. One large first-floor double-bedded room, with private full bath across hall. On second floor, one large room has a canopied four-poster double bed, adjoining private full bath. Another large room has two twin beds and a sink and shares a full bath with two smaller but cozy double-bedded rooms (with sinks).
**Breakfast:** 8-10. Juices (freshly squeezed orange juice), bacon, ham and sausage or eggs, omelets, home fries, or maybe French toast or pancakes (blueberry, raspberry, and blackberry in season) and beverage. Cloth napkins. Chapin cooks. Joan serves by candlelight.
**Plus:** Late-afternoon or evening beverages. Living room with wood stove. Chapin's guitar accompaniment for impromptu sing-alongs. Swimming pool. In season, hayrides and sleigh rides nearby (fee charged). Four-course candlelit dinners (extra charge) available with advance notice.
**Rates:** \$50-\$70 per room depending on size and location. Special rates for a stay of five or more nights.

Guests wrote: "A place to return to, to enjoy, to savor. . . . We left relaxed and refreshed."

## Partridge Hill Bed & Breakfast

P.O. Box 52, 102 Partridge Hill, Williston, VT 05495-0052
**Phone:** 802/878-4741
**Location:** Up a dirt road to 900 feet above sea level for a panorama of Vermont's Green Mountains. Eight miles east of Burlington, 30 minutes from Shelburne Museum, 1.2 miles from Route 2 in Williston village.
**Hosts:** Sally and Roger Bryant
**Open:** Year round.

"The view." After 20 years of living up here, the Bryants still marvel at it. When Roger became athletic director (he still is) at the University of Vermont in 1965, they built a contemporary chalet. After raising four children, they decided to stay, to enjoy that sun that pours in from the east through those big glass windows. Their pleasure in maintaining the grounds led them at one point to consider raising geranium specialty plants. They decided on B&B instead.

**Restrictions:** No smoking. Sorry, no guests' pets.
**Bed and bath:** Private entrance to guests' level. Off of guests' common room is one room with a queen-sized bed and a room with twins and vanity and sink. Adjacent full bath is shared.
**Breakfast:** Usually at 8. Freshly squeezed orange juice, if possible, and fresh fruit. French toast made with homemade bread, their own maple syrup, or bacon-ham-sausage, pancakes, cereals, eggs. Served in dining room by the fireplace or on the deck overlooking the view. "Guests usually have plans set and are on their way by 10."
**Plus:** Common room with fireplace and TV. Late-afternoon or evening beverages and homemade cookies. Fresh flowers. Electric blankets. Will meet guests at Burlington airport or bus or Essex Junction train, and take to rental car.
**Rates:** $25 per person. $5 children under 12.

Guests wrote: "The essence of a B&B, with marvelous hosts and immaculate accommodations, near the University of Vermont and only 35 minutes from the Stowe ski area. One is truly treated like family with a gourmet breakfast fit for kings."

## Darcroft's Schoolhouse

Route 100, Wilmington, VT 05363
**Phone:** 802/464-2631
**Location:** In Mount Snow area on main (two-lane) scenic road. Four miles north of town and shops. Within walking distance of restaurants, tennis, golf, cross-country skiing, free pool. Short distance to Mount Snow and Haystack ski areas.
**Host:** Doris Meadowcroft
**Open:** Year round. Availability limited December-March.

When the schoolhouse was built in 1837 it was the whole school district. In the late 1800s the town of Wilmington made it part of their school system. Along the way a second floor was added; and in 1979 Doris made it her home. She now operates a very small kennel on the premises and raises and shows keeshond, Belgian Tervuren, and Shih Tzu.

Doris looks forward to the evenings in front of fireplace with guests in her living room/lounge that was once a classroom. It's a relaxing time when she often helps to plan routes or activities. She is familiar with the flea market scene and is quite knowledegable about dolls, spinning wheels, and fireplace utensils.

**In residence:** Belle and Bakky, keeshond dogs, and cats Mister and Sassy. (Not allowed on the second floor. All are a big hit with children.)
**Restrictions:** No guests' pets in the schoolhouse. Kennel facilities can be provided right here.
**Bed and bath:** Three rooms, plus a loft area (no privacy) for children. First floor has a double room with private bath and shower. Two double-bedded rooms and open area with three single beds on the second floor share a bath with shower. Crib available.
**Breakfast:** Continental with pastry and/or muffins and homemade jam or jelly. Various seating arrangements possible, including an old ice cream booth. Very casual, even help-yourself.
**Plus:** Kitchen privileges available for evening meals.
**Rates:** Spring $20 single, $28 double; summer $24, $30; fall $38, $50; winter $42, $60. $15 per person for the loft (spring and summer only). MasterCard and VISA accepted.

## The Charleston House

21 Pleasant Street, Woodstock, VT 05091
**Phone:** 802/457-3843
**Location:** In the historic district. A three-minute walk from the Village Green.
**Hosts:** Laird and Betsy Bradley
**Open:** Year round except part of December and part of April. Reservations required. Two-night minimum stay required on weekends and during the fall foliage season.

"What was the house like when you bought it?" guests ask the Bradleys. The 1835 Greek Revival brick townhouse, listed on the National Register of Historic Places, has been totally renovated. "It was a frustrating, exhilarating experience. . . . We are also responsible for decor and furnishings (period antiques and reproductions with art and Oriental rugs in all rooms). We have passed along names and advice on resources. This has been an especially rewarding part of the whole thing."

They moved to the area in 1977. Laird had been a chef and Betsy an interior designer, and "we have both had experience in the inn business. When we were looking for a business of our own, we found that the building and all the other pieces fit together." They opened in the winter of 1985. Laird is a real estate salesman. They golf and ski—and know back roads of classic Vermont that can be enjoyed on the bicycles they lend (without charge) to guests.

**In residence:** One small cat named "Kitty."
**Restrictions:** Children should be at least six. No accommodations for pets. No cigars, please.
**Foreign language spoken:** Laird speaks Spanish.
**Bed and bath:** Seven rooms, three on first floor. All with private bath. One room with (inherited) double sleigh bed. Five rooms with two queen-sized four-poster beds in each. One room with two twin-sized four-poster beds. Rollaway bed available for one room.
**Breakfast:** Depending on the season, served for a 1½ hour period between 7:30 and 10. Eggs any style, omelet with a variety of stuffings, and either French toast (Grand Marnier or topped with raspberry sauce and sweetened sour cream) or pancakes (apple cinnamon or blueberry). Sometimes cheese grits. Plus juice, fresh fruit, meat, homemade bread. Hosts usually visit with guests during breakfast. Served in crystal-chandeliered dining room with

china, crystal, and cloth napkins. By request, continental in your room.
**Plus:** Air conditioning in living room, dining room, and three bedrooms. Window fans in four bedrooms. Fireplace in living room. Fine linens, comforters. Late-afternoon or evening snacks such as pate, cheese, and crackers. Fresh flowers, fruit, and chocolate in rooms. Homemade hand-dipped chocolate meringues beside beds. Tours of the house. Occasionally offer dinner in fall foliage season ($18-$25 per person for four-course meal). Will meet guests at West Lebanon, N.H. airport. Ice. Some kitchen privileges.
**Rates:** $75-$90 double occupancy. $4 less for single. $15 rollaway (available only in cable TV room). MasterCard and VISA accepted.

---

## Jackson House at Woodstock

Route 4, Woodstock, VT 05091
**Phone:** 802/457-2065
**Location:** One and a half miles west of Woodstock village. On three acres with a brook, a pond, mountain views to the north and south.
**Hosts:** Bruce McIlveen and Jack Foster
**Open:** Year round except November 1-December 15 and April 1-May 15. Reservations suggested. Two-day minimum stay on weekends July 4 through March.

A banker from San Francisco joined a director of marketing from New York to realize their "dedication to the very best" in restoring this 1890 house. It was originally built by a sawmill owner who wanted "the finest house in Woodstock." Today it is a landmark.

Through two years of traveling, Jack and Bruce became interested in owning an inn that would attract travelers who appreciate "fine things like Chinese porcelains and rugs, French cut crystal and the polished cherry staircase."

**In residence:** A cat named Chester.
**Restrictions:** "Because the Inn is furnished with antiques and fragile accessories, we cannot accommodate children under ten." No guests' pets and no smoking, please.
**Bed and bath:** Nine rooms on two floors, seven with private baths, two share a bath. One double or two twin-sized beds in each room. Every room is decorated in a different period or style, including

French Empire, Victorian, brass and bamboo, and New England country.
**Breakfast:** "Memorable." 7:30-9:30. Omelets, walnut-spice pancakes, cheese blintzes, French toast Santa Fe or eggs Grisanti, homemade muffins, croissants. Something different every day served family style in Queen Anne dining room.
**Plus:** Wine and champagne hour (included in rate) with hors d'oeuvres (e.g. pate or caviar Romanoff). Ceiling fans in bedrooms. Parlor, library, and dining room with period antiques. Tours of the house. Godiva chocolates on the pillow. Pond for swimming, fishing, and skating. Video library. Walking trail. French touring bikes.
**Rates:** Per room. $85 with private bath; $65 with shared bath. MasterCard or VISA accepted.

## Riverside Guest House

61 River Street, Woodstock, VT 05091
**Phone:** 802/457-3896
**Location:** On Route 4, a five-minute walk to the village center. Hiking trail up Mount Tom is just around the corner.
**Hosts:** Carol and Harold Fisher
**Open:** Year round except April. Minimum stay of two nights on three-day weekends, holiday weeks, and during foliage season.

"During one foliage season we rented our efficiency unit to tourists and found that we really enjoyed meeting new people. I was working as a secretary for Harold's plumbing and heating business . . . when we decided to change vocations. Harold still does some plumbing, working by himself. Here he installed pedestal sinks in all the bathrooms, but the whirlpool is the big hit."

The 100-year-old Cape with renovated attached barn is done in Shaker and country style, simple with lots of colonial blue and gray accents. Friends played a big part in this B&B. One made all the bedroom furniture; another wove some rugs. Another made the six copper lanterns on posts that line the side road. Now the network of friends is even bigger. The family has invitations to stay in Alaska, England, Central America, or many states if "they are ever in the area."

In addition to cross-country and downhill skiing, all four Fishers participate in triathlons. If you jog, they might join you.

**In residence:** Teenage sons, Todd and Jeremy.
**Restrictions:** No guests' pets, please.
**Bed and bath:** Six rooms with private full baths and one efficiency unit with fully equipped kitchen. One double-bedded room on the first floor is accessible to the handicapped. All rooms are large enough to accommodate two twin beds or a double bed plus a rollaway or crib. One room can accommodate two rollaways. Upstairs rooms are in back and quieter.
**Breakfast:** 8-10. Continental buffet with Carol's streusel coffee cake, sticky buns, or cinnamon rolls, bagels or muffins (Carol loves to bake), with jellies, jams, and cream cheese. Juice and beverages.
**Plus:** Whirlpool on sign-up basis. Thick towels. Two rooms with air conditioners, one with ceiling fans. Living room with cable TV, VCR, games and puzzles. Will meet guests at Lebanon Regional airport or White River Junction train or bus. Hot water for beverages and snacks in winter. Bowl of fruit in summer. Babysitting. Laundry privileges.
**Rates:** $50-$60 double. $45 single. $10 rollaway. No charge for crib. MasterCard and VISA accepted.

*Can't find the community you are going to? Check with a reservation service described at the beginning of this chapter. Through the service, you may be placed (matched) with a welcoming B&B that is near your destination.*

# MASSACHUSETTS

1. Cape Cod, 217
2. Martha's Vineyard, 218
3. Nantucket, 218
4. Southeastern Massachusetts
5. Boston
6. North Shore
7. Central Massachusetts
8. Pioneer Valley
9. Berkshires

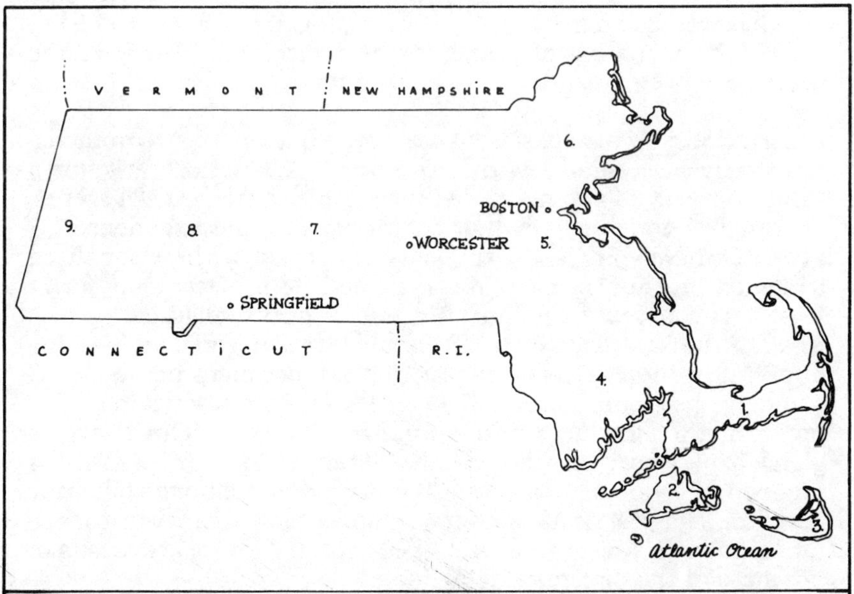


*The numbers on this map indicate the locations for which there are detailed maps in this chapter.*

# Massachusetts Reservation Services

## Pineapple Hospitality, Inc.

47 North Second Street, Suite 3A, New Bedford, MA 02744
**Phone:** 617/990-1696. Monday-Friday 9-5. Usually live. Answering machine at other times.
**Listings:** 100+. Located throughout all six New England states; about half are in Massachusetts. They are in big and small cities and towns, villages and farmlands—and even on a boat (summer only). Mostly hosted private residences, some inns and a few unhosted apartments. Short-term (one month +) housing available in some hosted and unhosted homes. Directory ($4.95), a booklet with descriptions, rates, some sketches.

Since taking over one of the oldest Massachusetts-based reservation services in 1986, Judy Mulford, a historic preservationist who has worked on many revitalization programs, has continued to stress "the matching of guests to the right hosts." Many of the hosts have been with the service since its beginnings in 1981.

**Reservations:** Two weeks' advance notice preferred. Accommodations may be available with less notice. A few hosts ask for a minimum stay of two nights. Also available through travel agents. Two weeks' notice required for "Our New England Experience."
**Plus:** "Our New England Experience," a packet with personalized itinerary, brochures, maps, routings, and B&B placements for at least four consecutive nights. Two weeks' notice required.
**Rates:** $31-$60 single, $35-$110 double. Rates negotiable if staying a month or more. Deposit required is $10 per night per room. $3 surcharge per room for one night or last-minute reservations. $12 processing fee (includes postage and handling) for "Our New England Experience." In case of cancellation, a $10 per room fee is retained for a one night's stay, $20 for two or more nights (plus any handling charges). Inns and some homes have their own cancellation policies. MasterCard and VISA accepted for basic deposits or purchase of the directory.

Other Massachusetts-based services concentrate on one area but a few have hosts in neighboring regions. Those services, going from east to west, are:

**Cape Cod**
Bed & Breakfast Cape Cod. Please see page 219.
B&B House Guests, Cape Cod. Please see page 219.
Orleans Bed & Breakfast Associates. Please see page 220.

**Southeastern Massachusetts**
Be Our Guest, Bed & Breakfast, Ltd. Please see page 286.
Christian Hospitality Bed & Breakfast of New England. Please see page 287.

**Metropolitan Boston**
Bed & Breakfast Agency of Boston, Inc. Please see page 300.
Bed and Breakfast Associates Bay Colony, Ltd. Please see page 301.
Bed and Breakfast, Brookline/Boston. Please see page 302.
Boston Bed and Breakfast, Inc. Please see page 302.
Greater Boston Hospitality. Please see page 303.
Bed and Breakfast in Minuteman Country. Please see page 304.
Host Homes of Boston. Please see page 304.
University Bed & Breakfast, Ltd. Please see page 305.

**North Shore**
Bed & Breakfast Marblehead and North Shore. Please see page 321.

**Central Massachusetts**
Folkstone Bed & Breakfast. Please see page 336.
Greater Springfield Bed and Breakfast. Please see page 347.

**Berkshires**
Berkshire Bed & Breakfast Homes. Please see page 346.

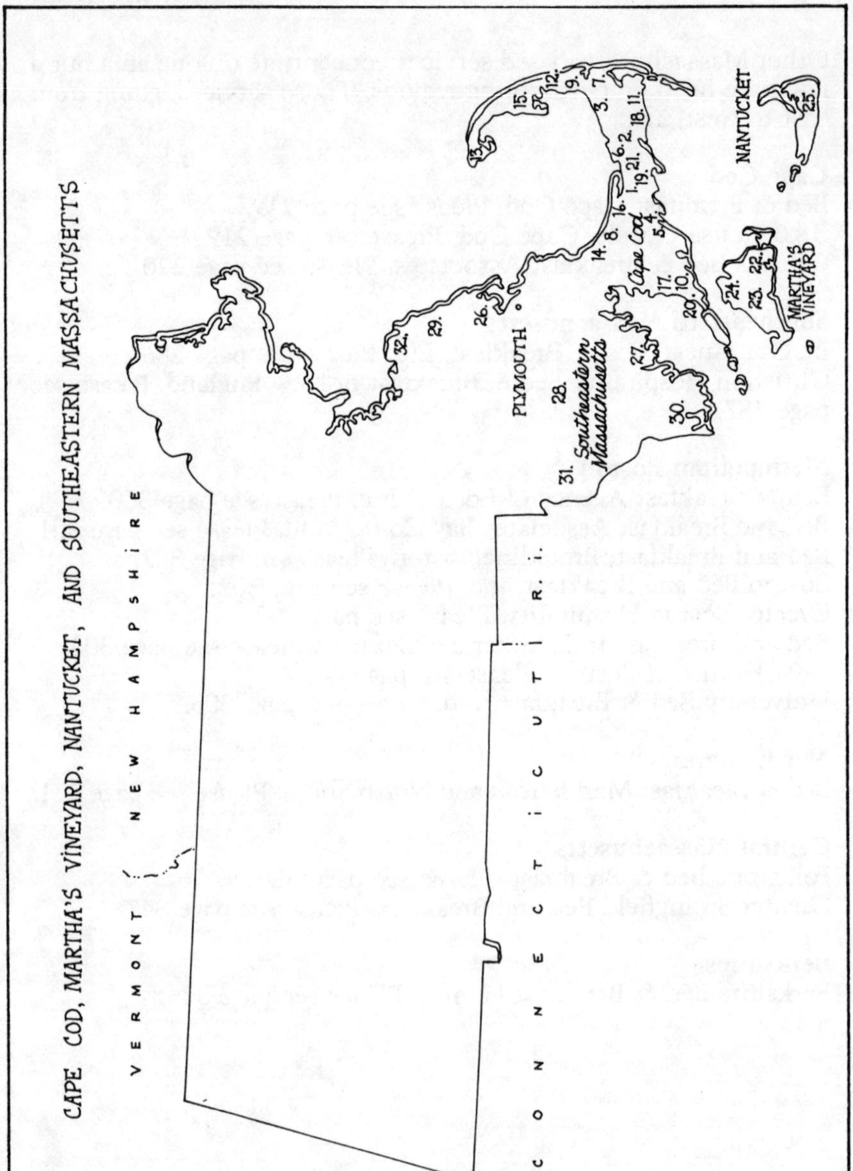


*The numbers on this map indicate the locations of B&Bs described in detail in this chapter.*

# CAPE COD, MARTHA'S VINEYARD, NANTUCKET, AND SOUTHEASTERN MASSACHUSETTS

# Cape Cod Reservation Services

## Bed & Breakfast Cape Cod

P.O. Box 341, West Hyannisport, MA 02672
**Phone:** 617/775-2772. Year round except for some time in January or February. Best time to call is 8:30-5. Mail requests answered by return mail.
**Listings:** 55. Mostly on Cape Cod and the islands, but a few are in metropolitan Boston. Some inns, but most are hosted private residences. Apartment or studio available for weekly rental only.

Joyce and Clark Diehl, experienced B&B hosts who know the Cape well, feature 150- to 300-year old private homes that have one or two rooms for guests. Many accommodations include private baths and fireplaces. Each location is inspected before it is listed and once each year thereafter. The Diehls strive to provide the traveling public with a service that "assures guests of getting what they expect and expecting what they get. We match needs and available locations as completely as we can."

**Reservations:** Advance reservations of two or more weeks is strongly suggested. Two-night minimum stay in season (summer and fall) and on weekends. Also available through travel agents.
**Rates:** $36-$45 single, $40-$105 double. Weekly rates available at some locations. $5 surcharge for one-night stay. Deposit of 25 percent of the daily room rate plus a $5 one-time booking charge. If cancellation is received at least one week before scheduled arrival, deposit will be refunded with the exception of a $5 service charge. MasterCard, VISA, and AMEX accepted for deposit only.

## B & B House Guests, Cape Cod

Box AR, Dennis, MA 02638
**Phone:** 617/398-0787. April 1-October 31, Monday through Saturday, 10-7.

**Listings:** 80. Some inns, mostly hosted private residences. All over the Cape; some on Martha's Vineyard and Nantucket. Directory ($3) is a booklet including descriptions and rates.

Ellie Coyle Greenberg became, in 1984, the second owner of the Cape's original bed and breakfast reservation service. She enjoys the opportunity to talk to guests, matching them according to their interests, if possible, as well as to their specifications for accommodations. Many of her hosts have had several years' experience.

**Reservations:** Two-day minimum stay required in July and August. Midweek one night possible.
**Rates:** $32-$48 single, $44-$100 double. Weekly rates available. Some homes charge $10 surcharge for one night. Twenty-five percent deposit required. With two weeks' notice of cancellation, the deposit, less a $10 service fee, is refunded. MasterCard and VISA accepted.

## Orleans Bed & Breakfast Associates

P.O. Box 1312, Orleans, MA 02653
**Phone:** 617/255-3824. Live year round 8-8. Answering machine at other times. Office closed December 21-January 3.
**Listings:** 60. Hosted private residences plus two inns located in the area known as the Outer or Lower Cape, "on the elbow that juts out to sea," in Harwich, Chatham, Brewster, Orleans, Eastham, Wellfleet, and Truro. Directory ($1) describes each B&B.

Mary Chapman is more than a reservation service owner. She hosts in her own home, knows her hosts, and is active in her community. She has established an organization so that the hosts in her service are a community in themselves, meeting regularly to help new hosts, to give support and suggestions, and even to take tours of each other's homes. It's a complete sharing system. Rare and refreshing.

**Reservations:** Two weeks' advance notice preferred. Last-minute reservations accepted if arrangements can be made. Two-night minimum stay required. A few hosts will take one-night reservations prior to Memorial Day and after Columbus Day.

**Rates:** $40-$80 for single or double occupancy. Full price of two nights' stay required as deposit. $10 surcharge for one night. Reservation deposits will be refunded, less a $20 service charge, with notification seven days prior to arrival. No refund with less than seven days' notice. MasterCard, VISA, and AMEX accepted for deposit only.

Other services with B&Bs on Cape Cod:

Be Our Guest, Bed & Breakfast, Ltd., page 286.
Bed & Breakfast Agency, page 300.
Bed and Breakfast Associates Bay Colony Ltd., page 301.
Pineapple Hospitality, page 214.

## Cape Cod B&Bs

Many Cape Cod hosts report that guests come to see all of Cape Cod in a weekend. "Please remind them in your book that Cape Cod is 90 miles long."

The following B&Bs are in alphabetical order according to the towns and villages where they are located. B&Bs on the islands of Martha's Vineyard and Nantucket are on pages 274 and 281.

### Ashley Manor

Box 856, 3660 Main Street, Barnstable, MA 02630
**Phone:** 617/362-8044
**Location:** In historic district on Route 6A, with long sweeping driveway behind high hedges, on two acres.
**Hosts:** Alan and Maggi Tyson
**Open:** Year round. Reservations preferred.

The hunt took two years—through New England and Pennsylvania. On Long Island Alan was a school district administrator, and Maggi, a nursery school teacher, but they wanted to become "landscaper, handyman, and official greeters—tour guides, sharers, and chefs—the ultimate innkeepers."

The "perfect place" was a private home built in 1699. It was in the same family for its first 200 years and was fully restored in 1964. When the Tysons bought it, complete with gazebo in 1985, it still retained its wide board floors, seven fireplaces, and Cape Cod blown glass windows. The stairway is still a steep one. The secret passageway that now connects two suites was probably used as a hiding place for Tories during the Revolutionary War.

Maggi's buoyancy comes through. "All those pine and oak pieces that I collected and refinished, and often stored in the basement, now have a home. Yet, we have discovered some great hidden antique sources that we share with our guests. . . . As for this wonderful historic mansion, we agree with the guest who said that once you pull in behind the hedges, you feel like you have left the rest of the world behind."

**In residence:** Two children, Jennifer, 12, and Brian, 5.
**Restrictions:** "The Inn does not meet the needs of children or pets. Cigarette smoking is permitted in designated areas. No cigars or pipes, please."
**Bed and bath:** Three suites, two guest rooms, and one garden studio, all with private baths. The first-floor suite has a queen-sized four-poster bed. Second-floor accommodations have king, queen- or double-sized beds. Some with fireplaces. Garden studio, 100 feet from mansion, has queen-sized bed, bath with shower only, freestanding fireplace, efficiency kitchen, country decor. Cot available.
**Breakfast:** 8:30-10. Served in the dining room or on the brick terrace. Fresh fruit, homemade bread, rolls, strawberry butter, coffee cakes or crumb cake, waffles, French toast, bacon, sausage, coffee and tea.
**Plus:** Forty-foot brick terrace with tables and umbrellas facing two acres of manicured lawns and age-old plantings—beautiful boxwood and apple, cherry, and pear trees. Use of three-speed bicycles. Croquet. Living room, library, and dining room, all with fireplaces and braided rugs. Tour of house. Current magazines. Antiques news publications. Will meet guests at Barnstable municipal airport, Hyannis railroad station or bus.
**Rates:** $70-$80 rooms, $85-$95 suites. MasterCard, VISA, and AMEX accepted.

## Bed & Breakfast Cape Cod Host #27

Barnstable, MA
**Location:** On a country lane, just steps from Barnstable village, shops, restaurants; within walking distance of Barnstable Harbor.
**Reservations:** Available May 1-October 31 through Bed & Breakfast Cape Cod, page 219. Minimum stay of two days preferred.

"Our daughter and son-in-law started their B&B in 1982, so when we were ready to retire and move from the Boston area, they helped us start. We restored the place ourselves, decorating with soft colors and a bent towards Victorian. Our guests seem to come for the ocean, antiques and seafood. They have helped make this a very rewarding experience by being just ordinary folks from many different areas, diverse occupations and talents. They share their discoveries with us and with other guests."

Their 1852 Victorian now has beautiful wallcoverings, period furnishings, and a warm and inviting common room and dining room.

**Restrictions:** Children should be at least 12. No guests' pets.
**Foreign language spoken:** Some German.
**Bed and bath:** Four rooms. On second floor, one with two twin beds, bath with shower; one with double bed, full bath; one with double bed, bath with shower. Third floor room has king-sized bed, bath with shower. Cot available.
**Breakfast:** Usually 8-10. Orange juice, croissants, homemade bread, jellies and jams, muffins, coffee cake, seasonal fruits, coffee or tea. Served in dining room.
**Plus:** Tea on arrival. Wine in late evening. Wraparound porch. Third-floor bedroom has air conditioning; fans in other bedrooms.
**Rates:** $55 double occupancy. $40 off-season. $10 cot.

Guests wrote: "Immaculate. At least three homemade goodies at breakfast! Hostess made our stay special."

## Beechwood Inn

2839 Main Street, Route 6A, Barnstable, MA 02630
**Phone:** 617/362-6618
**Location:** On Old King's Highway, in the village historic district. Close to restaurants, galleries, and shops.
**Hosts:** Myles and Sandra Corey
**Open:** Year round. Two-day minimum stay preferred holidays and weekends.

"A dream—for us and our guests. We purchased this beautiful romantic hideaway with views of Cape Cod Bay from the young couple that painstakingly restored it. The tall beech trees stand as permanent monuments to a pre-Lincoln era."

The Coreys took over in 1986, coming from Boston, where Myles was an artist and theater instructor and Sandy a marketing executive. From lighting fixtures to antique furnishings to hand-cut exterior shingles painted yellow, gold, and jade green, this Victorian is a wonderful example of fanciful Queen Anne style.

**In residence:** Daughter Alyssa, age 14.
**Restrictions:** Children should be at least 16. No guests' pets. Smoking not permitted in the dining room.
**Foreign language spoken:** French.
**Bed and bath:** Six rooms, each with private bath. One first-floor room with an antique queen-sized canopied four-poster bed, French doors to veranda; another with brass double bed, marble fireplace. Two double-bedded second-floor rooms, colored glass windows. The Gallery, also on second floor, has king-sized bed and is decorated with works of art by Myles and other local artists. A double bed is in third-floor bed-sitting room that has panoramic view of bay.
**Breakfast:** 8-9:30. In dining room at candlelit tables for two. A leisurely breakfast of fresh juice and fruits, home-baked breads and muffins, eggs, French toast, and breakfast meats.
**Plus:** Late-afternoon tea with scones or Beechwood torte. Flowers, candy, Perrier on ice, lace-trimmed sheets and pillow cases in guest rooms. Veranda with rockers. Tour of house. Special Valentine's Day weekends. Extensive library. Chess. Croquet, badminton, shaded grounds with picnic tables. Will meet guests at Barnstable airport or Hyannis bus.

**Rates:** May 1-November $85-$105 double occupancy. Extra bed $10. Off-season $65-$85 double occupancy. MasterCard, VISA, and AMEX accepted.

From New York: "Sandra and Myles have created a very inviting, warm and comfortable atmosphere. Theirs is a world of enjoying people and generously sharing their lovingly cared-for home with guests. Never have we found any breakfast equal to those at Beechwood."

## Charles Hinckley House

Route 6A (Old King's Highway) and Scudder Lane, Barnstable
Mailing address: P.O. Box 723, Barnstable, MA 02630
**Phone:** 617/362-9924
**Location:** High on a hill, a short distance from Exit 6 off Route 6. A five-minute walk down a lane to Cape Cod Bay.
**Hosts:** Les and Miya Patrick
**Open:** Year round. Reservations recommended. Two-night minimum stay on weekends. Three-night minimum on holidays.

From Kentucky: ". . . charming and filled with much rich history, but Les and Miya make it come alive with their own unique talents. They're quite a team!"

"The team" consists of a caterer/landscape gardener married to a contractor/renovator/designer. Together they have had almost a decade of involvement in B&B, beginning when they restored an inn. When they decided to open their own in 1983, they found this house, built by shipwright Charles Hinckley in 1809. It hadn't been lived in for five years, and before that the residents in their nineties had been here for 43 years.

Now it's picture perfect from the outside as well as in, so much so that it has been featured in several publications, including *Country Living Magazine.* Outside the twin-chimneyed hip-roof Federal colonial is a hip-high wildflower garden that makes this "the most photographed inn on the Cape." What was the summer kitchen is now a guest room with private entrance and a skylight. Floor boards are a golden pine. Country furniture is painted or refinished. Enormous flower arrangements—gladioli, cosmos, lilies, or daisies—are replenished daily in season. Oriental scatter rugs, paint colors (often mixed by the Patricks themselves), and fabrics all say "country" in the warmest sense.

**In residence:** Morgan, a quiet, refined, Great Dane, and Miles, a mild-mannered and laid-back golden retriever.
**Restrictions:** Children should be at least 12. Sorry, no guests' pets. No smoking.
**Bed and bath:** Four rooms, each with private bath and a fireplace. One room has a double four-poster bed and a large bath with tub only. Another has a queen-sized four-poster, a sitting area, and a bath with shower only. The old summer kitchen room has a skylight, queen-sized brass bed, and bath with shower only. Library room has a queen-sized four-poster, generous sitting area, and bath with shower only.
**Breakfast:** 9-9:30. Coffee, tea, or espresso; fresh orange juice; variety of homemade pastries; fresh fruit plate garnished with flowers; crepes, omelets or French toast. In dining room by the fireplace.
**Plus:** A tour of house, but yes! Oversize towels. Chocolates. Fresh fruit. Beverages. Cracking fires in bedrooms on cool nights. Maybe homemade cookies. Lots of surprises as a result of personalized attention; let them know if you're celebrating an event. Use of ten-speed bicycles. Will meet guests at the airport.
**Rates:** Double occupancy. $85 double-bedded room. Others, $105-$115.

## The Polsons'

110 Salt Rock Road, Barnstable, MA 02630
**Phone:** 617/362-6556
**Location:** On a quiet residential street surrounded by trees. Within walking distance of the village and beach.
**Hosts:** Barbara and Dick Polson
**Open:** Year round. Reservations required.

"We moved into this brand new large Cape style house 15 years ago. From our own travels in the British Isles and from talking with friends who host, we were encouraged to try hosting in 1983. Since then we have had just two types of guests—the good ones and the better ones. We haven't had any that we wouldn't want back."

Sprinkled among the traditional furnishings, there are some family treasures. Barbara's own spool maple crib is used for "wee ones." It was also used for her brother and sister, the Polson's son, and two nephews. The century-old rolltop desk was Dick's grandfather's first-bought furniture on his arrival from Sweden.

Barbara is in retailing and insurance is Dick's field.

**Restrictions:** No guests' pets. Smoking in guest rooms only.
**Bed and bath:** Two large bedrooms share one full bath. One room with double bed and headboard bookcase, the other with two twin beds that convert into a king-sized bed. Each room has an easy chair, reading lamps, large closet. Guests have own locked entrance. Cot and crib available.
**Breakfast:** 7-8:30. Eggs Benedict, egg souffle, or French toast and muffins, muffins, muffins. Guests set the pace. As often as possible, both hosts join guests in the dining room, which overlooks the sun deck and woods. High chair available.
**Plus:** Plenty of extra pillows ("something we always look for when traveling.") Candies and fresh fruit. Sometimes hosts drive guests to Kennedy compound or to other nearby places. Will meet weekend guests at airport, train, or bus. Bedroom window fans. Chairs on the spacious front lawn (Dick's pride and joy). Private rear sun deck.
**Rates:** $45 double occupancy. $10 cot or crib.

## The Thomas Huckins House

2701 Main Street, Route 6A, Barnstable, MA 02630
**Phone:** 617/362-6379
**Location:** In the historic district. Fifteen minutes from the Cape Cod Canal. A short walk from a salt-water inlet overlooking the ten miles of dunes of Sandy Neck Beach. Five minutes from the departure area for whale watches.
**Hosts:** Burt and Eleanor Eddy
**Open:** Year round. Reservations required. Two-night minimum stay required on weekends from May through October.

"*Early American Life* recently featured the hardware of this house that the Huckins Family occupied from 1705 to 1956. The last Huckins ran it as a guesthouse. When we bought it in 1979, we took it apart (structurally) and put it back together again. The 18th-century features are what make it so unusual: hinges, latches (no doorknobs), paneling, flooring, three cooking fireplaces—one with beehive oven, and nine-over-nine window panes."

The Eddys lived in Maine and on Cape Cod and traveled as far west as Michigan and south as Washington, D.C. with their antiques business. In 1984, their children grown, Burt and Eleanor found themselves living in a large house in a tourist area, a bit weary of travel. Now travelers come to them—for research in a genealogy library "just down the street," for antique auctions, for sightseeing, or just for a getaway.

All furnishings are either antique or colonial reproductions. When time permits, Burt makes Windsor chairs and other reproductions for sale—and he carves birds.

**In residence:** A collie named Barney. O'Malley, an Irish setter, is a temporary resident while son is abroad. Two outside cats. "All pets do not enter the guest areas and are not a problem unless a guest has severe allergies."
**Restrictions:** Children should be at least six. No guests' pets, please.
**Bed and bath:** Three large rooms, each with modern private bath. First-floor room has canopied double bed, full bath, working fireplace. Double second-floor room with 18th-century paneling has its own staircase and a sitting area, cedar closet, and bath with oversized shower with seat. Second-floor suite includes a parlor with working fireplace, double hide-a-bed, separate bedroom with antique double bed, shower bath. Cot available.
**Breakfast:** 8-10. Fresh fruit, juice, bacon, sausage, eggs any style, French toast with New England maple syrup or banana pancakes, Cape Cod cranberry muffins, maybe Swedish coffee cake. Served in the keeping room, opposite a ten-foot walk-in fireplace.
**Plus:** Tours of the house. Parlor with fireplace and TV. Portable telephone. Patio. Croquet. Fresh flowers from "old-fashioned" perennial garden. (Many guests leave with cuttings.)
**Rates:** May-October $75 double occupancy for rooms, $95 for the suite. November-April $55 and $65. MasterCard and VISA accepted.

A guest wrote: "Not only is the house charming, but so are the proprietors!"

## The Old Cape House

108 Old Main Street, Bass River, MA 02664
**Phone:** 617/398-1068
**Location:** On historic street in an old village named after the river dividing Yarmouth from Dennis. Four miles from Hyannis.
**Hosts:** George and Linda Arthur
**Open:** Mid-May through October. Reservations preferred. Two-night minimum stay July, August, and holiday weekends.

After years as an executive in electronics in this country and Europe, George decided with his wife Linda (an executive secretary in England, Belgium, and Italy) that corporate reorganization time was a good time to reorganize their lives. Since living here, the Arthurs have brought the 1815 Greek Revival home "back to life" with extensive painting and papering, and they exposed the old beehive oven in the dining room. Linda's hooked rugs on the pine floors of the beamed-ceilinged guest rooms complete the Laura Ashley country look. In the wintertime, George does taxes; Linda makes teddy bears, and calico and gingham cats for sale.

Among those who have come for a real B&B experience is "a 92-year-old lady who climbed our steep stairs and drove herself all over the Cape. She entertained the breakfast table with her recollections of the 1920s. We also had a South African family and another from New Zealand who shared some interesting views of their lives."

**In residence:** A playful gray cat, Dusty. Teenaged grandchildren occasionally house-sit in the evenings.
**Restrictions:** Children should be at least 12. No guests' pets. No smoking, please.
**Foreign languages spoken:** French, Italian, and some German.
**Bed and bath:** Six rooms, each named after a London street. The two with private baths are suites. The first-floor suite has a private entrance, fireplace, and kitchen unit and overlooks the garden. On second floor—the other suite with queen-sized bed; two shared hall baths for two rooms with double beds, one room with two twin beds, and one with a single bed.
**Breakfast:** 7:30-9:30. Home-baked muffins (maybe chocolate chip), sour cream coffee cake, breads, cereals, seasonal fruits (strawberries and cream during Wimbledon week), juice, tea and coffee. Hosts join guests for breakfast in the dining room or on the porch. "In rainy weather breakfast can take up to four hours!"

**Plus:** Fresh flowers. Large living room with music, plenty of games, a library, and TV. Porch overlooking the garden. Barbecue and picnic table. Tour of the house. Extensive menu book.
**Rates:** June 15-September 15, $28 single, $40-$45 double with shared bath, $50-$60 with private bath. Weekly and off-season rates available.

---

## The Brewster Farmhouse Inn

716 Main Street, Brewster, MA 02631
**Phone:** 617/896-3426
**Location:** On scenic 6A, across from the Drummer Boy Museum's windmill and field. Two miles from Route 134. Fifteen-minute walk to bay beach. Near Cape Cod Rail Trail and Dennis Playhouse.
**Host:** Barbara Thomason
**Open:** May-October. Two-night minimum stay required during peak summer season.

From the front it looks like an attractive farmhouse, white with green shutters. The surprise comes as you step through the main entrance to find a dramatic tall angle-ceilinged room with Mexican tile floor and sliding doors that lead out to a huge deck and a pool and hot tub, surrounded by a big lawn, many flowers, and an old apple orchard.

The previous owners had made the major architectural changes for an inn, but before opening, they sold it to Barbara. Guests frequently comment on what she calls "unsuspected luxury." Every room has the stamp of her flair—color, antiques, plants, and interesting accents. Her collection of quilts can be seen in the guest rooms. As an example of combining old and new, the house was on a Brewster Historical Society's annual house tour.

In Connecticut Barbara raised three children (now grown) and was an alcoholism counselor. Here she runs the B&B, tends her vegetable and flower gardens, and plays tennis.

**In residence:** Clyde, a friendly schnauzer terrier, and Mike, a golden retriever. Yoda and Molly, two friendly cats.
**Restrictions:** Children should be at least 12. No guests' pets. Smoking allowed in the gathering room and den.
**Foreign language spoken:** Some French.

**Bed and bath:** Four rooms. The two with private baths are in the back of house. Large first-floor room has queen-sized wicker bed, private full bath, sitting area, and private deck. On second floor—one room with queen-sized bed, sitting area, and private bath with shower. Two rooms, one with a queen-sized bed, the other with a double, share a bath with shower.
**Breakfast:** 8-9. Hearty continental buffet, in the gathering room or on the outdoor deck. Juices, herbal and regular teas, coffee, fresh fruits, cereals, homemade bread or muffins, jams and honey.
**Plus:** Behind the stockade fence in back—the pool and hot tub, umbrella tables, and quiet. Tour of the house. Fireplace, books, television, and stereo in den. Stereo in private baths. Thick towels. Hair dryer. Extra "forgotten items" such as aspirin, toothpaste, shampoo. Turn-down service. Mints on pillows. Fresh flowers. Champagne for honeymooners.
**Rates:** May 31-October 12, $65 double occupancy with shared bath, $80-$90 with private bath. MasterCard and VISA accepted.

From Connecticut: "The spacious sunlit house and rooms, the wonderful grounds and pool where we sometimes spent our whole day, and Barbara's warmth all make this a little bit of heaven."

## The Captain Freeman Inn

15 Breakwater Road, RR 4, Brewster, MA 02631
**Phone:** 617/896-7481
**Location:** In Brewster center, next door to Brewster General Store and First Parish Church. The "egg" (town green) is the front yard. Five minutes to bay beach.
**Hosts:** John and Barbara Mulkey
**Open:** Year round. Reservations suggested June through October. Two-night minimum stay on July and August weekends and on Memorial and Labor Day weekends.

Peace and quiet. A stroll on the beach. A small town with a pretty main street. The General Store with half a dozen Cape papers and *The New York Times*. A nearby 20-mile-long bicycle path. "And perfect plastering." It's the life the Mulkeys chose when they left their Washington positions as U.S. Senate staffers in 1983. Earlier, both were school teachers in Phoenix, Arizona.

When asked about innkeeping—and most people do ask—John is likely to tell you that "it *is* an interesting experience. You never know what will come from the breakfast conversation." For those who wish to delve into the practical nitty gritty, the Mulkeys sometimes cosponsor (with another B&B) an "Innkeepers & Dreamers" program.

Captain Freeman had the house built in 1860 with ornate plaster moldings imported from Italy, hall floors laid in a herringbone pattern, nine-over-nine windows, and a staircase with a carved banister. Today, a picture of Freeman's ship is in the entry hall. There's a warm, friendly feeling here.

**In residence:** Nikka, a calico cat, Fenix, an orange tabby cat, and a cocker spaniel named Toby.
**Restrictions:** Children should be at least 12. No pets please.
**Bed and bath:** Ten rooms on three floors (two on first floor). Seven have private baths. Three third-floor rooms share one hall bath. Rooms have a queen-sized bed, one or two double beds, or a double and a twin. Some four-posters. Rooms with canopied beds also have a trundle bed.
**Breakfast:** 8-9:30. Homemade muffins (almond chocolate chip, zucchini nut, pineapple coconut, cranberry), fresh fruit, juice, coffee, tea. Served in the parlor or on the porch overlooking the pool.
**Plus:** Late-afternoon wine or cider. Swimming pool. Porch. Three- and ten-speed bicycles. Tour of house. Bedroom window fans.
**Rates (per room):** July 1-Labor Day $40 shared bath, $54-$58 private bath. May, June, September, and October $35 shared bath, $47-$51 private bath. January-April, November, and December $30 shared bath, $38-$42 private. $15 additional person in a room. MasterCard, VISA, and AMEX accepted.

## Copper Beech Inn

497 Main Street, Centerville, MA 02632
**Phone:** 617/771-5488
**Location:** On the tree-shaded historic street. Bordered on one side by the Howard Marston estate built in 1881 with a 67-acre park designed by Frederick Law Olmstead. A half-mile to warm-water Craigville Beach. Six miles west of Hyannis.
**Hosts:** Joyce and Clark Diehl

**Open:** Year round. Reservations required. Two-night minimum stay from Memorial Day weekend through October.

In 1985, after 30 years of coming to the Cape "vacationing and visiting virtually all areas," Clark, a former field executive for a major corporation, and Joyce searched for a place that could be a B&B recognized for its comfort, congeniality, and location.

The original graceful stairway and wrought-iron latches are part of the charm of their house, built by Captain Hillman Crosby in 1830 for his bride. (To this day Crosby is a well-known area name.) The Diehls have carefully restored this ¾-Cape-style house with their own hard work and the help of a contractor who has been a caretaker here for 25 years. Even with the addition of many baths, the character of the old has been retained in this traditionally furnished inn.

With the acquisition in 1985 of Bed & Breakfast Cape Cod, a reservation service described on page 219, the Diehls have even more contact with B&B travelers—as well as with other hosts who appreciate Cape Cod.

**In residence:** Two who smoke.
**Restrictions:** Children over 12 welcome. No pets, please.
**Bed and bath:** Three rooms. All private baths. Two rooms on first floor, a double bed in each. One with four-poster; the other with pegged floors, quilt made by the hosts' artist daughter. Second-floor room has a king-sized bed, 19th-century decor.
**Breakfast:** 8-10. Fresh fruit, pastries, and house specialties including berry bowl with whipped cream, pancakes, eggs, and breakfast meats. Served family style in the dining room or in the kitchen by the 100-year-old cookstove.
**Plus:** Refreshments in late afternoon or evening in family living room or parlor. Bicycles. Beach mats. Outdoor heated shower. Tour of house, if you'd like. Lounge chairs in yard overlooking pond. Porch. Will meet guests at Hyannis airport, bus, or train.
**Rates:** Memorial Day-October $65 double occupancy. Off-season $60. AMEX accepted.

*Can't find the community you are going to? Check with a reservation service described at the beginning of this chapter. Through the service, you may be placed (matched) with a welcoming B&B that is near your destination.*

## The Allen's

P.O. Box 222, 60 Nickerson Lane, Cotuit, MA 02635
**Phone:** 617/428-5702
**Location:** In a quiet village within one mile of three beaches. Ten miles south of Sandwich, east of Falmouth, west of Hyannis.
**Hosts:** Jim and Ellen Allen
**Open:** Year round. Reservations suggested.

What had been a summer home for 25 years has been redecorated and restored as a year-round residence by this warm couple, grandparents of five. There's no sign, but this "low-key" B&B has become a welcome addition to the town, especially for wedding guests and overflow guests of residents. Families—three generations sometimes—find this a "just right" place, and use it as a base for trips to Provincetown, Martha's Vineyard, and Nantucket.

"Here in Cotuit we have a playground nearby, tennis courts, a lifeguarded beach, and one of the top teams in the Cape Baseball League. (Big League scouts come to all the games.) We give tours of the town—beaches, homes of famous people, the oyster company."

The house, a big old Victorian with a large porch, was built around 1900.

**Restrictions:** Children and pets should be well behaved. Nonsmokers preferred, but smokers are tolerated.
**Bed and bath:** Three rooms. The one with a private full bath has a double bed plus a trundle bed big enough for two little ones. A single with shared bath. Also a room with two twin beds and private half-bath. Cot and crib available.
**Breakfast:** A full country meal served with fresh fruit, blueberry muffins, and one of many specialties—maybe waffles or ham and egg on English muffins.
**Plus:** Bikes and beach towels. TV in all rooms. Boat launch, tennis courts, harbor, golf course within walking distance.
**Rates:** $25 single, $50 double. $5 crib. $10 cot. Seventh night free.

## The Four Chimneys Inn

Route 6A, 946 Main Street, Dennis, MA 02638
**Phone:** 617/385-6317
**Location:** Mid-Cape. In a quiet residential area. Directly across the street from Scargo Lake. Within walking distance of a bayside beach, Dennis village, the Cape Cod Playhouse and Cinema, fine restaurants and antique shops.
**Hosts:** Christina Jervant and Diane Robinson
**Open:** Mid-February through December 31. Reservations recommended June through October.

> From Massachusetts: "A renaissance lady indeed. . . . It is an uncommonly real and welcoming threshold to cross over."

Perhaps it was their professional experience that gave them the courage just to "do what needs to be done." Chris, a banker, and Diane, a hospital administrator, bought location and charm potential. With pure naivete, they made an early purchase of a small package of plaster patch. Today they have pictures that tell the story of 180 pounds of joint compound, a New Hampshire antique dealer who took them under his wing, and friends who offered physical and emotional support.

Within one season they had memories of guests from a groom's family who used the house to prepare wildflower arrangements for the rehearsal dinner and of a honeymoon couple who helped tape 44 windows for an oncoming hurricane, and then stayed for six days after in spite of the absence of hot water and electricity.

This 15-room 1881 Victorian home—with its 8-foot windows and 11-foot ceilings—had been built as a summer home, but was a bakery in the 1970s. Now, Victorian, country, and Scandinavian touches can be seen throughout. It's eclectic and cozy, light and cheerful.

A CBS executive wrote, "The great luck we experienced in finding a vacancy made the weekend for us."

**In residence:** One host who smokes.
**Restrictions:** Sorry, the inn is not suitable for children under the age of ten or pets.
**Foreign language spoken:** Swedish.

**Bed and bath:** Nine rooms—some big, some small—on three floors. Seven have private baths. One room with two twin beds, one with a queen-sized bed and a twin bed, six with a double bed in each, one single. One room is wheelchair accessible. Some full baths, some with tubs and separate shower. Features include fireplaces, a skylight, lake view, view of highest point on Cape Cod.
**Breakfast:** Generally 8-10. Juice, coffee, tea are buffet style. Muffins/breads baked and served by the innkeepers. At the large dining room table or on the summer porch or, if you wish, in your room. Can be quick or a morning-long event.
**Plus:** Fireplaced living room. Library. TV, VCR, and stereo. Fans for third-floor rooms. Library. Porch. Expansive front lawn. Inquire about mystery weekends. Will meet guests at airport or bus. Use of refrigerator. Kitchen can be rented for special events. Monthly antique auction held one mile away. Bicycle trails, golf courses, and tennis courts within two miles.
**Rates:** July-Labor Day $40-$50 per room with semiprivate bath, $60 double with private bath. September-June $30-$40 single or double with semiprivate bath, $50 with private bath. Additional person in same room, $10 per night. MasterCard and VISA accepted.

## Isaiah B. Hall House

152 Whig Street, Dennis, MA 02638
**Phone:** 617/385-9928
**Location:** In a quiet year-round residential area on the historic bay side. A half-mile from the beach and one-third mile from the village and Route 6A. About 15 minutes from Hyannis.
**Hosts:** Marie and Dick Brophy
**Open:** Year round. Reservations required; drop-ins accepted if room available. Two-day minimum July, August, and on holidays.

"Charming . . . homey . . . warm atmosphere . . . relaxed . . . clean . . . casual . . . great innkeepers . . . centrally located." In about 15 different ways, guests salute this B&B.

Some actors from the Cape Playhouse stay here. Lots of vacationers come too—to the 1857 Greek Revival farmhouse originally built by Isaiah Baker Hall, a cooper and binder. As Marie tells it, "The house is in front of what is believed to be the first cultivated cranberry bog on Cape Cod. . . . Isaiah, using typical Yankee ingenuity, patented the first barrel for transport of cranberries."

For about 25 years, Dorothy Gripp, a famous artist and craftsperson, had the property as an inn and restaurant. Examples of her artwork can be seen in museums all over the country and in the kitchen and dining room here. Since the Brophys took over three years ago, they have made major changes, still "retaining the feel of another era." Guest rooms have quilts and antique rockers. The charming rooms in the renovated barn feature fresh Cape Cod curtains and wicker.

Marie has had experience as a school counselor and more recently in high tech. Dick is a personnel manager in the high-tech industry.

**In residence:** Niece Susan is a summer resident. "Clyde is our 11-year-old black cat who minds his own business."
**Restrictions:** Children over six welcome on first floor. No guests' pets. No smoking in the dining room.
**Foreign language spoken:** Susan speaks French.
**Bed and bath:** Ten rooms; nine with private baths, some with fireplaces. Five rooms (one on first floor) in main house and five (one on first floor) in attached barn/carriage house. A double bed in most rooms. Some have a double and a single bed. Four carriage-house rooms have a balcony. Extra bed available.
**Breakfast:** 8:30-10. Fruit, cereal, English muffins, homemade breads and muffins, butter, jams, jellies, raisins. Juice, coffees, teas. Served from a 19th-century buffet in the antique-filled dining room.
**Plus:** Guests' parlor with Victorian coal stove. Great Room for guests in the converted barn. Table games. TV. Large back yard with badminton/volleyball and croquet. Lawn chairs. Front porch rockers. Afternoon or evening tea. Tour of the house. Use of refrigerator. Inquire about mystery weekends.
**Rates:** June 15-Labor Day $35-$45 single, $40 double with shared bath, $50-$60 double with private bath. Off-season $25-$40 single, $35 double with shared bath, $40-$56 double with private bath. $10 each extra person. MasterCard, VISA, and AMEX accepted.

## The Whig

94 Whig Street, Dennis, MA 02638
**Phone:** 617/385-2614
**Location:** A ten-minute walk to the beach and Cape Playhouse. Off Route 6A, in a residential area, one street away from Dennis village.

**Host:** Lois Hirshberg
**Open:** June-September. Reservations required.

From Ohio: "When I stayed there for four nights, I really wanted to stay the whole summer. I love quiet, simplicity, and a sense of place."

When three generations of one family stayed with Lois for a week, the young boys wouldn't leave until Lois promised to visit them at their home in Switzerland.

Contented guests are interested to learn that Lois started B&B as a way to support her studio. She is a potter and expressive therapist. "I didn't realize how much I would enjoy B&B. . . . It offers a marvelous balance to my life."

During winters, she has her studio in Cambridge, Massachusetts. However, her master's degree is in Community Mental Health and her work experience includes five years as an adolescent therapist. During those professional years she took a course in pottery, and it wasn't long before she focused on raku, a ceramic process developed in Japan centuries ago. Lois's summer studio and gallery are here on the premises.

Originally built by a shipping exporter over 200 years ago, her farmhouse is furnished with early American pieces, Japanese touches, and Lois's pottery and sculpture.

**In residence:** "Afficomen is an extremely friendly dog. She is especially good with young people."
**Restrictions:** No guests' pets. Smoking only on outside porches.
**Foreign language spoken:** A little Hebrew.
**Bed and bath:** Three rooms on two floors. The one with a private bath is on the first floor, has a double bed and a twin-sized sofa sleeper, is furnished with antiques. The floor is purple. Two rooms, one with a double bed and a blue floor and one with two twin beds and a brown floor share a bath with shower, no tub. Linens are coordinated to the color of each room's floor. Cot and crib available.
**Breakfast:** 8:30-10. Granola and dry cereals, fruit muffins, bagels or fruit breads, herbal teas, black teas, coffees. Sometimes, whole-wheat banana pancakes or French toast. Served in dining room or on adjoining porch. Fresh flowers from the garden on table.
**Plus:** An acre of flower and vegetable gardens. Two porches overlooking lawns. Bedroom window fans. For a small fee will meet guests at the airport, train, or bus.
**Rates:** $50 double with shared bath, $60 with private bath. Cot, crib or sleep sofa $10 per night.

## The Parsonage

P.O. Box 1016, 202 Main Street, East Orleans, MA 02643
**Phone:** 617/255-8217
**Location:** In the village, opposite farm stand, on the road to Nauset Beach (Atlantic Ocean). Within walking distance of fine restaurants and shops. Two miles from Route 6.
**Hosts:** Chris and Lloyd Shand
**Open:** Year round. Reservations required. Two-night minimum on holiday weekends.

From Missouri: "An outstanding example of the best of bed and breakfasts." From Ohio: "I had planned on spending one night and ended up spending three in the quiet, unspoiled atmosphere." From New York: "They knew it was our honeymoon. We were welcomed with champagne. The Parsonage was perfect."

All the Shands' creative talents have had a chance to shine in the private home they bought four years ago. It was a parsonage for about 40 years in the 1800s. The Loft Room was a cobbler's shop at the turn of the century. With all the changes, including heating, plumbing, and added staircases, little of the 1770 part of the house has been remodeled. "We've been careful not to let the decorating show." All the touches are appreciated by the community and an even wider audience: The Parsonage was on a 1985 House Tour.

Whether you want to study menus of local restaurants at breakfast, "do all of Cape Cod in two days" (impossible), or find "a real B&B experience," Chris and Lloyd seem to be naturals at providing the opportunity for any and all. Chris was an office manager in Washington, D.C. and New York City. Lloyd worked with a large chemical company and as a lobbyist in Washington. In his retirement years, he combines B&B with his love for sailing and golf.

**Restrictions:** No guests' pets.
**Bed and bath:** Six "Old Cape Cod" rooms, two with private baths. Bed sizes include queen size, double, one room with a double and a single. Features vary according to room: Private entrance, skylit bath, some wide-plank painted floors, eaves, and "wavy old glass." Victorian decor in one room. A first-floor room has queen-sized bed, sitting area, cable TV, kitchenette, and private bath with shower.

**Breakfast:** 8-9:30. Continental breakfast with homemade muffins or bread and jam. Served in a pretty basket, in your room, in the sitting and dining areas, or, weather permitting, on the patio.
**Plus:** Air conditioning in two bedrooms; window fans in others. Fresh flowers. Fresh fruit in common areas. Tour of the house. Guest refrigerator. Large brick courtyard with tables and chairs available all day. Chairs on grounds. Bicycle storage in the barn.
**Rates:** $45 double shared bath, $50-$60 double with private bath. $5 less for singles. $10 for additional person. November-April, $10 less per room. Efficiency available for B&B September-June. MasterCard and VISA accepted.

## The Red Geranium

East Orleans, MA
**Location:** On a rural main street in a residential neighborhood. One and one-half miles to Nauset Beach, two miles to bayside beach. Within walking distance of shops and fine dining.
**Reservations:** Available January-October through Orleans Bed & Breakfast Associates, page 220. Two-night minimum stay required.

There's a strong sense of old-fashioned caring in this charming and impeccable English-style Cape furnished with many family heirlooms and original oil paintings. It's warm and sunny and friendly.

Before the hosts settled here almost a decade ago, they had vacationed in the area since the 1940s. Their before-and-after album shows their addition of wainscoting, tongue-and-groove paneling, painting and papering. "We love our home and feel fortunate to be able to work here. My husband restores antiques for many clients and I am a painter. I always wanted a small inn. This has been the perfect solution."

Beyond the leisurely breakfast time, guests are welcome to use the yard, which has a reflecting pond, picnic table, and lawn chairs.

**In residence:** Hostess's mother. A cocker spaniel who is not allowed to visit guests unless they express a desire.
**Restrictions:** Children should be at least 12. Sorry, no guests' pets. No smoking.

**Bed and bath:** Two second-floor rooms share a full bath. One room has twin beds, another has a double bed. Quilts and stenciling done by the hostess.
**Breakfast:** 7:30-9:30. Fruit compote, juice, cereal, toast, jams, jellies, honey, freshly brewed coffee, homemade New England muffins and Old World sweet or yeast breads. French omelets on request.
**Plus:** Air conditioner/fan and TV in each bedroom. Antique freshly ironed linens. Flowers. Freshly brewed iced tea. Sherry. Lots of thick towels. Guest sitting room with games, puzzles, glasses, and a cooler. Private guest entrance. Tour of house.
**Rates:** $48 per room.

## Wingscorton Farm Inn

11 Wing Boulevard, East Sandwich, MA 02537
**Phone:** 617/888-0534
**Location:** "On 7½ acres of unspoiled land." Just off Route 6A, across from the Great Marsh and Bird Sanctuary. Five miles from historic Sandwich village. Five-minute walk down a lane to private beach on Cape Cod bay. Minutes to antiquing, restaurants, museums.
**Hosts:** Sheila Weyers and Dick Loring
**Open:** Year round. Reservations required.

"Even on the fourth of July, you can be here and not know anyone else is on the Cape. This lifestyle is, for me, a switch from aquaculture (breeding and raising clams) to agriculture. In 1980 I bought this large 1758 farmhouse that had been in the Wing family for six generations, until 100 years ago. Behind the den fireplace is a passage where slaves were hidden in the days of the Underground Railway. . . . Today there are 51 (the number keeps changing) little piglets running around. And there are chickens, cows, horses, sheep. We are a real working farm." Dick goes on to explain that it took three years to clear the fields and redo the barn.

Restoration of the property, with the aid of a meticulous Cape craftsman, has resulted in a gracious home. Sheila has had experience with resorts in California and Vermont, and observes that once guests drive up the long driveway and see the grounds, manicured lawns, gardens, and animals, they begin to unwind.

**In residence:** One host smokes. The four dogs, Woody, Walter, Randy, and Lady are all well behaved and people loving.
**Restrictions:** Pets should be well trained; children manageable!
**Bed and bath:** Three main house rooms, each with a double bed and private bath; two have adjoining singles only available as suites. Cottage has two bedrooms with two twins/king in each room plus a convertible double sofa in living room. Carriage house has one queen-sized bed and one queen-sized convertible couch. Features vary and include a canopied bed, four-poster, sitting rooms, one room with balcony, one with a Jacuzzi tub. Carriage house suite has fireplaced living room and kitchen, sunning deck. Cots and crib available.
**Breakfast:** 9-10, five-course farm meal; 10-10:30, continental. Fruit, fresh eggs and breakfast meats, bread pudding, cold or hot cereal, homemade jams and jellies, home baked breads and cakes, coffee, tea. Served in charming fireplaced dining room.
**Plus:** Beverages. Tours of the house and farm. Gather your own eggs. Maybe observe a delivery in the barn. Fresh flowers in rooms. Thick towels. Paneled library with fireplace flanked by wing chairs. Bedroom window fans. Dinner (extra charge) by advance arrangement. Will meet guests at Hyannis airport or bus station. Bicycles loaned free to guests. Croquet. TV and VCR.
**Rates:** $75 single, $95 double. Carriage House $125 for two and $175 for four. $4 for crib or cot. $30 additional person in room. MasterCard, VISA accepted.

> From California: "A wonderful environment. Being there was fun and relaxing for all of us. . . . Breakfasts were outstandingly delicious. . . . Our three-year-old daughter was enthralled with the dogs, sheep, chickens, goats. . . . Walter, an adorable terrier, was her favorite."

## The Over Look Inn

P.O. Box 771, County Road, Eastham, MA 02642
**Phone:** 617/255-1886
**Location:** Directly across from the entrance to main Cape Cod National Seashore visitors' area. Bike paths are right here (rental bikes nearby). Three miles from Orleans and fine restaurants.
**Hosts:** Nan and Ian Aitchison
**Open:** Year round. Reservations required.

From Florida: "They care about each other, about you, about how the Inn looks and feels and you leave there knowing you've experienced something special."

For twenty years the Scottish ("our accents give us away") couple had a summer home in the area, so when the time came to think about living here year round, Nan, director of development at a girls' school in Toronto, and Ian, a chartered surveyor, bought this Queen Anne Victorian house that had been a lodging establishment for about 60 years and recruited their two college-age sons, both artists, for the restoration. The house was brightened with bold color. Then came brass beds, down comforters, antiques, reproductions, some Eskimo art, and the sharing of Ian's collection of Churchill's works. The robes provided in each bedroom still cause much favorable comment; they also made for a most unusual scene during the first (1985) Over Look season when the fire alarm malfunctioned, resulting in a porch filled with 12 guests—all identically dressed in white terry cloth.

Ordinarily, the peace here is what appeals to hosts and guests alike. Nan and Ian have lots of suggestions of nearby activities and day trip possibilities, but their own inclination is to savor the accessible open space in all its natural beauty.

**Restrictions:** "The Inn does not meet the needs of children under twelve." No pets. Smoking in the library only.
**Bed and bath:** Six rooms. All with private baths; all with showers, three with claw-foot tubs and pedestal sinks. Four rooms on the second floor and two on the third. Four rooms with queen-sized beds, one with a double, and one with two twin beds. Views of garden, the barn, and in the distance, Salt Pond inlet to the Atlantic.
**Breakfast:** 8-10. Scottish fare made from grandmother's recipes that might include kedgeree, made of finnan haddie, rice, onions, chopped eggs and raisins sauteed in butter and served with a dab of mango chutney. At small tables in the dining room.
**Plus:** Tea and hot scones at 4. Bedroom ceiling fans. Parlor painted deep pink, with velvet sofa, Japanese art, and Victorian prints. Library with green walls, tufted leather sofa, and Victorian card table. Tour of house. Occasional dinners on holiday weekends. Will meet guests at airport, train, or bus.
**Rates:** July-September $80 per room. Off-season $70. MasterCard, VISA, AMEX, and Diners' Club accepted.

## Capt. Tom Lawrence House

75 Locust Street, Falmouth, MA 02540
**Phone:** 617/540-1445, 548-9178
**Location:** In historic district, 100 feet back from road that leads to Woods Hole. A three-minute walk to shops on Main Street. Within walking distance of wildlife sanctuary, birdwatchers' paradise. Half-mile to beach with warm-water swimming. Four miles to island ferries.
**Host:** Barbara Sabo-Feller
**Open:** Year round except December and January. Reservations preferred. Two-night minimum stay July and August weekends.

> From Massachusetts: "The bright, sunlit interior is a reflection of the gracious hospitality. We felt at home in surroundings which blend the history of the house with continental living. . . . Everything is fresh and clean. . . . Breakfast is the highlight of the stay. . . . Adjacent to one of the best kept secrets (bike path) in New England."

Other guests have written about attention to detail. Among those details is the decor, all Barbara's ideas that have been implemented since she bought the 1861 sea captain's house that had become a guesthouse in 1978. She made decisions about wallpapers, colors, and the arrangement of hand-carved antique furniture from Germany and the Steinway baby grand piano.

Barbara moved to New England from Europe ten years ago. After years of thinking about B&B while she was an office manager in Boston, she opened here in 1985. Memorable guests include a marine biologist on his way to Jacques Cousteau's boat in Woods Hole and a backpacking professor from China who called from a local phone booth looking for lodging.

**In residence:** Barbara's mother. Daughter Jacqueline helps out during college vacations.
**Restrictions:** Children should be at least 12. No guests' pets.
**Foreign language spoken:** German.
**Bed and bath:** Six rooms with French country flavor. Two large first-floor rooms each have a king-sized bed and private bath. A queen-sized bed in each of four second-floor rooms; two shared baths. Cot available.
**Breakfast:** 8-10. Full gourmet breakfast served in the common room. Fresh fruit, an egg dish, homemade bread and pancakes made from freshly ground organic grain.

**Plus:** Tea in late afternoon or evening. Tour of the house. Will meet guests at airport or bus. Courtesy transportation to Woods Hole ferries for reservations of two nights or more. Porch and large yard.
**Rates:** Double occupancy. $42-$55 shared bath, $52-$69 private bath. June 15-September 15 $55 shared bath; $69 private bath; $40 single, shared bath; $15 additional person. Lower rates in fall, winter, and spring. MasterCard and VISA accepted.

## The Inn at One Main Street

One Main Street, Falmouth, MA 02540
**Phone:** 617/540-7469
**Location:** In a historic district, surrounded by old New England homes. At the west end of Main Street, where the road to Woods Hole begins. Just 300 feet from the Village Green. Walking distance to ferry shuttle, beaches, dining, shopping.
**Hosts:** Karen and Alan Cassidy
**Open:** Year round. Reservations recommended. Two-day minimum stay required on weekends, June-October.

"Thirty-seven countries and 46 states." That's the representative guest tally from three years of running the Sjöholm B&B in West Falmouth until they sold it in 1985. Then Alan and Karen talked of sailing around the world, but opted for the challenge of opening this inn instead. Currently, most of their sailing is fairly local, on a 38-foot sloop that is also used for charters.

Alan, formerly in architectural engineering, met Karen in Sandwich. Eventually these two potential innkeepers were married and, at their first inn, found that it was a relaxed homey ambiance that counted. Their guests flooded me with letters about the friendliness as well as the respect for privacy.

Now as "professionals" they conclude, "Every time the pressure of being 'on stage' seven days a week starts to get to either of us, a new guest with a fresh smile and a new outlook jolts us back to the reality that we really love our work."

The Inn at One Main Street was built in 1892 for the Swifts, founders of a renowned Cape Cod butcher shop. It was a guest house when the Cassidys took it over. As always, expanding, upgrading, and redecorating are constant.

Karen is no longer a special needs classroom teacher; she frequently gives workshops throughout New England on alcohol and substance abuse.

**In residence:** One host who smokes "talks of stopping. Time will tell if she does."
**Restrictions:** Children should be at least ten. No guests' pets. Smoking permitted except in the living room during breakfast.
**Foreign language spoken:** French (by Alan).
**Bed and bath:** Eight. Six rooms have private baths, each with shower, no tub. One shared bath for the other two rooms. One room has a queen-sized bed and a twin bed, one an antique double bed and a twin bed. Several rooms with double beds, two with two twin beds. Cots available. Furnished comfortably with traditional furniture.
**Breakfast:** 8-10:30. Those leaving before 7:30, perhaps to catch the ferry, receive a "doggy or boat bag" breakfast. Alan and Karen join guests for an expanded continental buffet in the living room. A cheese plate with five kinds of cheese, Danish, Portuguese bread, toasted bran or corn muffins, juices, tea, coffee, fresh fruits, bagels, and Karen's home-baked breads.
**Plus:** Directions from these romantics for a six-minute walk through woods to an elevated rock outcrop with adjoining warm-water beach. Ferry tickets sold here. Living room/sitting room with fireplace. Large yard. Veranda with rocking chairs. Book collection. Will meet guests at train or bus.
**Rates:** In season $53 double occupancy with shared bath, $68 private bath. Off-season $43 shared bath, $53 private bath. $10 less for singles. $9 extra person in a room. Senior citizen discounts (except June-October weekends). $10 surcharge for one-night weekend stays that can be arranged. MasterCard and VISA accepted to hold reservations.

## Mostly Hall

27 Main Street, Falmouth, MA 02540
**Phone:** 617/548-3786
**Location:** In the historic district across from the village green on Route 28. Set back from the road on over an acre of lawn, trees, and shrubs. One mile to town beaches. Around the corner from the bike path to Woods Hole. Two blocks to the bus and train stations.

**Hosts:** Caroline and Jim Lloyd
**Open:** Year round. Reservations strongly suggested. Two-night minimum stay from June through October.

Of the 14 who completed the innkeeping course, only the Lloyds followed through. What they bought in 1986 was a very personalized well-run B&B named decades ago by an owner's youngster when he first saw the inside of the new family home.

It has been a B&B since 1980, but the four-storied Mississippi-style residence was originally built as a wedding present by a sea captain for his bride in 1849. They say it was the only way the New Orleans belle would come to Falmouth.

Jim and Caroline became seasoned innkeepers very quickly. Within a few weeks of ownership, they shared the joy of a couple who became engaged in the gazebo on the back lawn. They accepted beignet cooking instructions from a New Orleans guest who knew they were trying to bring some historical link to the menu. They offered a glass of sherry to London guests who arrived at the same moment as the piano movers. They heard a question that could be considered the highest compliment to innkeepers who make guests feel so much at home: "Is this all you do for a living?"

"It is even more enjoyable than we expected," Caroline says. She had worked as a department store buyer, and planning director; Jim was a computer corporate executive. Both felt ready for a people-oriented business—in a place where there would be a sense of community, not too far from Boston.

Some walls are fabric covered. Some beds are Victorian, some are four-posters. Oriental rugs, antiques and traditional furnishings, paintings and prints please the eye in the 13½-foot ceilinged rooms.

**In residence:** A 12-year-old Samoyed named Yuki, not allowed in guests' areas.
**Restrictions:** Children should be at least 16. No guests' pets. Nonsmokers preferred.
**Foreign language spoken:** Some German.
**Bed and bath:** Seven rooms. Five with private baths including one twin, one double, one queen and two king. The cupola room shares a bath with one double. All rooms are spacious except for the popular cupola, which has ten windows, two iron beds, hardly any space or closets, but a wonderful view of the village green in the winter. Cot available.

**Breakfast:** At 9. Juices, fresh fruits, home-baked sweet breads and muffins, and an entree that might be eggs Benedict, souffles, stuffed French toast, or ham and mushroom gratinee. If you're a vegetarian or have a kosher diet, just mention that ahead of time. Served on the porch or in lovely living room with French stove.
**Plus:** Sherry, iced tea or lemonade. Tour of house. Ceiling fans in the common areas. Library/game area. Piano. Wraparound covered porch on all four sides. Gazebo with swing. Croquet. Badminton. Complimentary bicycles. Will meet guests at the train and bus stops in Falmouth and at the ferry in Woods Hole.
**Rates:** June-October $85-$95 double with private bath, $60-$75 with shared bath. Off-season rates are 20 percent less.

From Missouri: "Mostly (H)all one could wish for."

## Palmer House Inn

81 Palmer Avenue, Falmouth, MA 02540
**Phone:** 617/548-1230
**Location:** In the historic district, two blocks from Falmouth village, walking distance to restaurants and shops. Two and a half blocks from bus and train stations; 1½ miles from the beach.
**Hosts:** Phyllis Niemi and Bud Peacock
**Open:** Year round. Reservations preferred.

"Restoring this house was an opportunity to use our interests in decorating and entertaining to begin a business. . . . The house is comfortable, yet interesting. There are things to look at and enjoy everywhere, a type of artistic clutter very appropriate for an old Victorian house. There are baskets of magazines, flowers in the parlor, new wallpapers, refinished floors. I make wreaths from old doilies, use old photos in unusual ways."

Phyllis was a nurse for 15 years, and Bud worked in the computer field. Now they answer questions about "the best" beaches, restaurants, antique shops, and the source of the inn's furnishings. Honeymooners return on their anniversaries. Family reunions are held here. Former guests stop in when passing through town.

**In residence:** Bud smokes. Bonnie, Joy, and Lana Peacock, ages 8-13.
**Restrictions:** Children over 14 welcome. Sorry, no pets.

**Bed and bath:** Eight rooms, each with private bath. Two rooms have two twin beds. A double bed in other rooms. All furnished with antiques and each different, e.g. Grandpa's Room is olive green and white with a large sleigh bed. Grandma's Room has pink and lace and frilly curtains.
**Breakfast:** 8:30 and 9:45. Fresh fruit cup or seasonal fruits; specialties such as pain perdu (custard-soaked French toast), Finnish oven pancakes with strawberry soup, cheese blintz and blueberry puree, bacon and mushroom quiche. "You may stay a week without a repeat." Also sticky buns, croissants, cranberry coffee cake, and many extras. Served in the bay windowed dining room at tables set with pink and white linen, cloth napkins, and china.
**Plus:** Late-afternoon and evening beverages. Coffee and tea usually available throughout the day. Turned-down beds. Mints on pillow. Tour of house. Occasional lobster dinners ("as well as needed instruction on how to eat them"). Rockers and gliders on shaded front porch. Back yard with lawn furnishings and hammock. Living room with fireplace, gramophone, and Victorian furnishings. Backgammon and chess. Bedroom window fans.
**Rates:** Per room. Summer \$81-\$87; early spring \$54, late spring and fall \$65, winter \$43. Singles rates, midweek, weekly, honeymoon, and holiday package rates available. MasterCard and VISA accepted.

## The Village Green Inn

40 West Main Street, Falmouth, MA 02540
**Phone:** 617/548-5621
**Location:** On the village green, surrounded by homes and churches dating to early 1700s. Post office, banks, shops, restaurants begin at the opposite end of the green in downtown Falmouth. One-quarter mile from bus station. Walk to ferry shuttle. Bike to beaches or Woods Hole on bike path.
**Hosts:** Linda and Don Long
**Open:** Year round. Reservations recommended. Two-night minimum stay required on summer and holiday weekends.

Changes, changes. It was originally a Federal-style family home in 1750. Another family in the late 1800s made it Victorian. Two more families occupied it before restoration was done by the 1982-1985 owners. Don and Linda, former East Falmouth residents, bought it in 1985 and are still changing it. Linda dreams up the projects and decorating ideas and "handy Don does everything around here."

Don retired in 1986 from teaching physical education. Linda still teaches second grade. For the inn's opening, they have focused on color coordination, comfort, plants, and now Victoriana.

**In residence:** Karen, age 20, is home from college in summer.
**Restrictions:** Sorry, the inn is not appropriate for children. No guests' pets. Smoking limited to porches.
**Bed and bath:** Four large rooms, two with private baths. The first-floor room with double bed, full bath, fireplace, and stained glass window overlooks the green. On the second floor is a suite with queen-sized bed, sitting area, and private bath. Two other second-floor rooms, one with double bed and a fireplace and the other with two twin beds and a fireplace, share a large full bath. Cot available.
**Breakfast:** 8-9:30. Fresh fruit bowl, fruit juices, granola-type dry cereals, homemade muffins and breads, coffee and assorted teas. Served in the dining room or on the large front porch. The Longs usually join you for coffee and conversation.
**Plus:** Afternoon lemonade, iced tea, and cookies on the wicker-furnished porch. Plenty of magazines and books in rooms. Games. Puzzles. After-dinner mints. Extra pillows. Free beach parking stickers. Croquet. Will meet guests at bus station.
**Rates:** June 15-October 15/October 16-June 14 $60/$50 twin or double with semiprivate bath, $70/$60 double with private bath, $80/$70 queen suite with private bath. Deduct $10 for singles. Add $10 for a cot.

From Pennsylvania: "Quaint. Well appointed. Friendly hosts. I have . . . stayed in many B&B inns. The Village Green is certainly to be added to the list of 'the bests.' I loved it!"

## The Inn on Bank Street

88 Bank Street, Harwichport, MA 02646
**Phone:** 617/432-3206
**Location:** In a residential area in center of town. Five-minute walk to ocean. Near restaurants, galleries, shops. Ten miles from ferry to Martha's Vineyard and Nantucket.
**Hosts:** Janet and Arky Silverio

**Open:** April-November. Reservations required. Two-night minimum stay on holidays and throughout the summer.

"We knew we wanted to retire on Cape Cod, so we started (in 1983) to look for just a little house near the beach. After many months and many houses, we saw this 45-year-old Cape that is too big for two people. Its location and layout were ideal for a B&B, so we said, 'Why not retire early and move to the Cape now?' After three years we can honestly say that this house and lifestyle give us great satisfaction and pleasure."

They came from Connecticut, where Janet was a teacher. Arky was an executive in industry. Here they appreciate their proximity to a bicycle trail and opportunities to sight the great blue heron in winter and black bellied plover during the fall migration. In 1985 they received a plaque recognizing their part for enhancing the neighborhood; wild and cultivated flowers, including roses, are on the grounds.

**In residence:** Daughter, Carol, during college vacations.
**Restrictions:** Minimum age for children is usually about seven. No guests' pets, please.
**Foreign languages spoken:** Italian, Spanish.
**Bed and bath:** Six first-floor rooms. Four have private baths with showers and private entrances from the outside. Two large rooms with wide pine floors in the main house share a full bath. Double or twin beds available. Extra bed can be added in some rooms.
**Breakfast:** 8-9:30, earlier for guests catching the ferry. Juice, granola, oatmeal, coffee, tea, homemade bread, or maybe mile-high corn muffins or coffee cake and fresh fruit. "We are health food nuts and serve raisins, whole wheat breads." Served on enclosed sun porch, or in patio or garden.
**Plus:** Living room and library with TV, fireplace, piano, books, magazines, and games. Outdoor tables and chairs, grille, hot and cold shower. Late-afternoon or evening beverage. Flowers and champagne for special occasions. Will meet guests at Hyannis airport or bus. Babysitting probably available. Theater passes.
**Rates (per room):** In season $55 double occupancy. Fall and spring $50. Single $5 less. $12 cot. MasterCard and VISA accepted.

From New York: "Location is ideal. Great beach within walking distance. Wonderful restaurant nearby, gourmet cooking and inexpensive. Inn was spotless. Fresh fruit and granola and herb tea if you want for breakfast. Warm, helpful hosts."

## The Penny House

Route 6, Box 238, North Eastham, MA 02651
**Phone:** 617/255-6632
**Location:** On 1½ acres of lawn. In the Cape Cod National Seashore area, midway between Hyannis and Provincetown.
**Hosts:** Barbara and Paul Landry
**Open:** Year round. Reservations preferred. Minimum stay of two nights on holiday weekends.

Some guests compose poems about the hosts. Letters to me refer to "warm people full of great advice on local attractions" or "thoughtful touches, charming rooms and great breakfast."

Barbara and Paul find that their B&B is just what many travelers hope to find in this area of natural beauty. They came here in 1985 from Rhode Island, where Paul was a quality assurance manager and Barbara a hair stylist and manager of a salon. For 20 years they had been collecting country antiques, and Barbara's real love is folk art, so when they located this captain's house with bow roof—a reflection of the shipbuilding techniques of 1751—they knew immediately that the decor would include Barbara's painting and stenciling. For their sign they use the traditional pineapple, a symbol of hospitality.

Paul has become a Realtor, and Barbara is a full-time innkeeper "with a feeling of living the dream we searched for."

They know all about the extensive—and free—programs at the Cape Cod National Seashore, the bicycle paths, and whale watching trips, but one sure "must" in their opinion is sunset time at First Encounter Beach.

**In residence:** Teenagers Mark and Shawn. Ziggy, an adorable Yorkshire terrier, is not allowed in the guest area but can be seen romping around in the yard.
**Restrictions:** Sorry, adults only. Maximum of two guests per room. No pets, please.
**Foreign language spoken:** French.
**Bed and bath:** A total of 11 rooms in original house and in recent addition. Five full and one half shared baths. One queen-sized bed. One canopied bed. Eight rooms with double beds and one with two twin beds. Two of first-floor rooms have cathedral ceilings. Cozy upstairs rooms have bow-roof ceilings.

**Breakfast:** 8-10:30. Off-season—fresh fruit, homemade breads, muffins or puff pastry, cereal, and beverages. In season, an entree such as quiche or French toast is added. Eat at the large oak table or in the sun room at small ice-cream parlor tables.
**Plus:** Coffee or tea in the Public Room. Books, games, cards, magazines in common room. Fireplaced living room. Wine and candy in room. Tour of house. Bedroom window or ceiling fans. Ice in guest refrigerator. Outdoor furniture. Lawn games. Parking.
**Rates:** In season $55 second-floor rooms, double occupancy, $60 main-floor rooms, double occupancy. Less during off-season. MasterCard and VISA accepted.

## Bradford Gardens Inn

178 Bradford Street, Provincetown, MA 02657
**Phone:** 617/487-1616
**Location:** Within a mile of just about everything in Provincetown. Five blocks from the center of town in a beautiful garden setting. Two miles from the Provincetown airport.
**Host:** Susan Culligan
**Open:** April-October. Reservations suggested.

If you're going to make your mark on a well-established B&B, one that you buy fully furnished with wonderful antiques, let it be the breakfast! That's just what Susan did a year ago, when she took over from an owner who had had the inn for 15 years. Originally, it was built in 1820 as a private home.

"I had no intention of going into the inn business, but while I was looking for a new abode . . . a realtor insisted on showing me this place. It felt so warm and good and right when we came in. I have retained the old look, bought all new beds, have done some work on the baths, and found that I can be a very fussy housekeeper. With my experience in retailing (in Ottawa for eight years) and real estate (another eight years), I am used to dealing with the public and know the importance of personable help. I find that many of our morning conversations are about travel, business, and politics, too."

**Restrictions:** Children welcome during off-season. No guests' pets. Smoking in rooms only.
**Foreign language spoken:** French.

**Bed and bath:** Eight rooms. All private baths. One or two doubles or queen-sized beds available in each room. Six rooms with working fireplaces. One with original Franklin stove. Three garden-view first-floor rooms, two with private entrances. Each room decorated differently. Crib available. The four cottages are also B&B.
**Breakfast:** 9-10:30. Specialties include cinnamon pancakes with blueberry maple syrup, broccoli cheese omelets, French-Swiss melt, Portuguese flippers, and shirred eggs with tarragon Mornay sauce. Served in antique-filled morning room with central fireplace or in the orchard.
**Plus:** Color TV in rooms. Original artwork. Gardens with flowering fruit trees, rose bushes, and Japanese cherry. Outdoor barbecue. Ice and buckets provided.
**Rates:** Late June-early September, $79-$94 double occupancy. Cottages $105-$140. Off-season $69-$79. Cottages $85-$110. MasterCard, VISA, and AMEX accepted.

## Bed & Breakfast Cape Cod Host #43

Sandwich, MA
**Location:** In tree-shaded village, a historic district, less than a mile from beach. Within walking distance of all major sightseeing attractions.
**Reservations:** Available year round through Bed & Breakfast Cape Cod, page 219.

Guests wrote: "Perfect hosts. A warm, inviting home. We stayed in B&Bs from Virginia to Massachusetts and this was one of our favorites. The pool was very nice. And we liked our rooms so much, we hated to leave in the mornings!"

The feeling is mutual. The hosts, former Hilton Hotel staffers, say that "B&B is a gratifying, exhilarating experience—very special." They share the comfort and charm of their five-year restoration project, an 1829 Victorian creatively decorated with antique quilts and country furniture. Some guests leave inspired to carry out their own projects. Many return to enjoy the ambiance and hospitality.

The host, a retired Air Force pilot, now works part time for the post office. He and his wife have chosen the perfect location for their interests of golfing, swimming, travel, and people.

**In residence:** One host who smokes.
**Restrictions:** Children seven and over welcome. No guests' pets.
**Foreign language spoken:** A bit of Spanish.
**Bed and bath:** Four second-floor rooms share one bath. A room with canopied queen-sized bed adjoins one with double bed, wicker furnishings. One room with two twin mahogany pineapple beds; one single iron bed in room with child's decor. Cot and crib available.
**Breakfast:** 8-10. Fresh fruit (homegrown strawberries in season), homemade muffins, croissants, cold cereals. Usually served in dining room or poolside on the patio.
**Plus:** Sherry, cheese and crackers. Beverages. TV and game table in living room. Fresh flowers. Bedroom fans. Tour of house. Patio and in-ground swimming pool. Will meet at Sandwich train.
**Rates:** $35 single, $40-$45 double. $5 crib, $5 cot. $5 surcharge for one-night stay.

## Captain Ezra Nye House

152 Main Street, Sandwich, MA 02563
**Phone:** 617/888-6142
**Location:** In the center of town, about five miles from Sagamore Bridge. Within walking distance of museums, shops, historic homes.
**Hosts:** Harry and Elaine Dickson
**Open:** Year round except January.

Harry and Elaine came here on their honeymoon two years ago, so when Harry retired from 10 years as an engineer with GTE (preceded by 25 in the Air Force), they started to search for a B&B site. "This 1829 sea captain's house on a main street in a small town, near the ocean and surrounded by greenery, gives the feeling of a private home. After our world-wide travels, it is just what we were looking for. There's so much to do right here, that you can leave your car for a few days and just walk."

That was in the spring of 1986. They have furnished with four-posters, a sleigh bed, a pineapple bed. Some of Harry's family pieces from Concord, Massachusetts, as well as Elaine's New Mexico paintings, have found a home here too.

If you take a tour of the house, you'll see the first owner's name chalked under a roof beam, and the name and date of a subsequent owner etched by diamond on a window pane. Those fresh bouquets are brought in every day (in warm months) by a local woman who uses her own perennial gardens for arrangements—both at The Ezra Nye House and at the Sandwich Glass Museum. "We are surprised each day with the variety and colors—sometimes foxglove, monk's hood, coreopsis, hosta, veronica, trillium—almost a garden catalogue come to life."

**Restrictions:** Children should be at least ten.
**Bed and bath:** Six rooms. Four with private baths; some with shower or tub only. One room with twin beds, two with double beds, one with a canopied double bed. The two rooms that share a (full) bath are a cozy room with double bed and a sunny back room with twin ¾ beds.
**Breakfast:** 8-10. Continental with a homemade specialty that might be blueberry or cranberry nut muffins or Indian bread pudding. Served in the dining room.
**Plus:** Living room with piano and fireplace. Games, books and TV with VCR in the parlor. Often, sherry about 6.
**Rates:** June-October $40-$50 with shared bath, $60 with private bath. Off-season $35-$45 with shared bath, $55 with private bath.

## Ocean Front

273 Phillips Street, Sandwich
Mailing address: Box 346, Sagamore Beach, MA 02562
**Phone:** 617/888-4798
**Location:** On Cape Cod Bay with private beach, two miles from Sagamore Bridge rotary. Within walking distance of path along the Cape Cod Canal.
**Host:** Mary Blanchard
**Open:** April 15-October 31. Reservations required.

"Well, Mary, what are you going to do with your big beautiful home?" my friends asked. "And that's how I got the idea of B&B."

Mary used to have a restaurant in a small town outside of Boston. She bought this Cape Cod weathered shingled house in 1975 and over a ten-year period did extensive remodeling to take advantage of the views. Furnishings, including much wicker furniture, add to the summery feeling. For a fun year-round accent, there is a Christmas tree with satin decorations in the living room.

Ocean Front is acclaimed in at least a dozen ecstatic letters from all over the country. Excerpts from one: "The panoramic view is spectacular—open Atlantic ocean, ocean liners and many ships and sailboats can be seen entering and leaving the Cape Cod Canal—and to the right, sand dunes of Sandy Neck Beach, to the left the White Cliffs of Plymouth. . . . Low tide is a special treat with its huge sandbars for walking. In the morning, beautifully set table, delicious home-baked goods. . . . Immaculately maintained. . . . Mary Blanchard is warm, kind, and compassionate. . . . Our cup runneth over."

**In residence:** Occasionally some grandchildren may be visiting.
**Restrictions:** No guests' pets. No smoking.
**Foreign language spoken:** Italian.
**Bed and bath:** Three rooms. The one with private bath encompasses an entire floor; it has a double and two twin beds, and sliding glass doors that lead onto a large oceanfront balcony. The two lower-level rooms, one with a king-sized bed, the other with a double bed, share bath with shower. Cots available.
**Breakfast:** 8-10. Juice, fresh fruit, muffins, toast and cinnamon bread, coffee. Served in dining room overlooking the ocean.
**Plus:** Late-afternoon or evening beverage. Living room with wood stove, TV, organ. Private sandy beach. Babysitting. Use of refrigerator. Huge decks. Outdoor furniture.
**Rates:** April 15-October 31 $45-$55 double with shared bath. $75 oceanfront double with private bath.

## The Quince Tree

164 Main Street, Sandwich, MA 02563
**Phone:** 617/888-1371
**Location:** In the center of historic Sandwich, within walking distance of museums, restaurants, shops, and public tennis courts. A short ride to beach and bike trails.
**Hosts:** Kathy and Steve Catania
**Open:** May 15-October 31, weekends mid-February–May, November, December. Reservations preferred. Two-night minimum stay on holiday weekends.

In this family, hospitality is just part of growing up. It was off-season when I called the first time, and Bethany handled me nicely, thank you. Later, I learned that Kathy had been training director for dining room personnel in a family-owned business that includes four restaurants and the historic Daniel Webster Inn. Steve is now innkeeper and general manager at the Daniel Webster in Sandwich.

In 1985 the Catanias bought this 1825 home with the intention of having "just a family home." Then the two older children decided it was time to move on (out), so Kathy became innkeeper at home. The first guests arrived two weeks after moving day, but lots of effort, paint, paper, and a sign soon followed. Antiques and reproductions of period furniture are throughout the house, which still has several original Sandwich glass door knobs.

**In residence:** Bethany, age nine, and Michael, age five. Leia, a low-keyed, nonshedding Maltese not allowed in guest areas.
**Restrictions:** Children should be at least 12. No pets. No smoking.
**Bed and bath:** Three second-floor rooms, one with private bath. Front corner room has queen-sized four-poster, private bath with shower. Another front corner room has queen-sized canopied bed and private half-bath, shares tub and shower with third room, which has brass double bed.
**Breakfast:** 8:30-9:30, earlier on request. Apple, orange cranberry juice, fresh fruits, homemade breads and muffins, quince sauce or jelly made with quince from three trees in yard, grape jelly made from grapes of arbor on property. Herbal teas, special blend freshly brewed coffee. By candlelight in the dining room.
**Plus:** Front parlor with baby grand piano. Terry robes provided in each room. Toiletries you may have forgotten. Afternoon/evening beverages. Tour of the house. Fans available.
**Rates:** May 15-October 31 $45-$65 double occupancy. November 1-May 14 $40-$50. $5 less for singles. Cash, personal or travelers' checks are preferred; MasterCard and VISA accepted.

From California: "The Quince Tree was clearly the highlight of our trip. . . . When we returned from dinner, the fire was roaring in the library. . . . Breakfast was delightful . . . packed leftovers for us to snack later. . . . Even though we felt like we were leaving old friends, we knew that we were leaving new friends."

## Six Water Street

P.O. Box 1295, 6 Water Street, Sandwich, MA 02563
**Phone:** 617/888-6808
**Location:** On Shawme Pond in the center of village. Next door to Thornton Burgess Museum. Within minutes' walk to several museums, shops, and restaurants. One mile to Heritage Plantation.
**Hosts:** Linda and Mike Levitt
**Open:** Year round. Reservations preferred.

"We try to include the touches we appreciate when we travel. Coffee and tea are always available. Plenty of extra blankets and pillows. Turned-down beds, spring water at bedside, tons of thirsty towels."

Several families have owned the house since it was built in 1845, but it has been a B&B only since 1985, when the Levitts finished their four months of basement-to-roof redoing. A photograph album holds a record of the before, during and after. Guest areas are carpeted. Pastel shades combined with white trim give a warm and airy feeling to the house set on a storybook pond complete with swans and operating grist mill.

Mike, a former television news reporter in Boston, is now freelancing. Retailing was Linda's professional world before she started her line of stuffed animals. One of her sheep-with-hat is likely to be on your bed, and most guests visit her in-house studio to see the other versions in progress.

**In residence:** Bonnie, a rabbit, receives guests in Linda's workroom.
**Restrictions:** Children should be at least 15. Sorry, no guests' pets. No smoking.
**Bed and bath:** Two second-floor rooms. One with queen-sized brass and white iron bed, skylights; French doors lead to private bath with antique claw-foot tub. Second room with queen-sized sleigh bed has private bath with shower.
**Breakfast:** At 9. Specialties include grapefruit topped with kiwi, stewed apples and cinnamon, johnnycake, peach muffins. Seasonal fruits, juices, homemade baked goods, coffee. Served by candlelight at small tables. Or, if you prefer, Linda will pack your breakfast in a wicker basket to enjoy by the pond—or even at the beach.
**Plus:** Sherry in each room. Upstairs sitting room. Will meet guests at train depot. Bedroom ceiling fans. Two rowboats "for a soul-soothing cruise." Lawn chairs under willows by the pond.

**Rates:** June 1-October 31 $85-$90. November 1-May 31 $60-$65. $5 less for singles.

## Bed & Breakfast in Truro

Castle Road, Box 431, Truro, MA 02666
**Phone:** 617/349-6610
**Location:** On a winding picturesque Cape road. Between ocean and bay, next door to the Truro Castle Hill Center for the Arts, in a quiet, rather sparsely settled residential area.
**Host:** Tonie Strauss
**Open:** Spring to October. Reservations required. Two-day minimum stay.

Tonie's flair means that the house is comfortable and she welcomes you graciously, but there's nothing formal about the 200-year-old captain's house set among lilac bushes, apple trees, and rolling lawns. Tonie is an abstract colorist who paints in oil. She is happy to show you her studio as well as tell you the history of the house.

"Most guests are seeking a quiet time. They come here because Truro leaves the hectic pace and fast food concessions behind. They usually leave by 10, enjoy the Cape, come back to get ready for dinner, and retire early."

**In residence:** Tonie smokes. She breeds wirehaired dachshunds and has two champion females (mother and daughter), Lucy and Steffi, and a toy Pekinese named Lolly.
**Restrictions:** Sorry, no children or pets. No food in rooms.
**Foreign languages spoken:** French and German.
**Bed and bath:** Two rooms share one guest bath. Private guest entrance and up a captain's staircase to one room with twin beds and another with a double bed. Furnished eclectically with antiques and "Cape decor."
**Breakfast:** 8-10. Fresh fruit and juices, croissants or muffins, a specialty such as fruit soup, yogurts, cheese, coffee. Served in a stylish European manner—"no plastic ever"—on the covered porch or indoors at a wonderful big table.
**Plus:** Fans in bedrooms. Comforters. Duvets. Flowers. "Mints, of course." Hammock under apple trees. Landscaped grounds.
**Rates:** $55 double occupancy.

From Massachusetts: "We were thoroughly refreshed by the setting, the tasteful furnishings in this interesting old home, the comfortable bed, and the flowers and candy that reminded us of our European travels. The delicious breakfast was beautifully served. But, above all, it was Mrs. Strauss's hospitality that made the visit memorable."

## Parker House

Route 6A, Box 114, Truro, MA 02666
**Phone:** 617/349-3358
**Location:** In the center of this tiny beautiful town, not far from Provincetown and the beautiful beaches of the Cape Cod National Seashore.
**Host:** Jane Parker
**Open:** Year round "unless host is lucky enough to be on vacation." Reservations required. Two-night minimum stay on summer weekends.

After a career of story-department work in film and television in New York and California, Jane returned in 1980 to restore the lovely old Cape residence where she had spent her childhood summers and a number of winters. The house, which has been in the family since 1920, has wide painted floorboards and family antiques—and a hostess who rounds out the feeling that many vacationers are looking for. "Housekeeping counts, but I make time for my real love, the daily sojourn to the beach." She loves this wonderful place and the casual lifestyle and is delighted to find that B&B travelers do too. Her new career is with the local Council on Aging.

**In residence:** One cat, Sadie, "a sort of Burmese."
**Restrictions:** Sorry, no children, because of noise factor in an old house. No guests' pets.
**Bed and bath:** Three rooms; two with double beds and one with two three-quarter beds. Extra mattresses available. Two shared guest baths.
**Breakfast:** 8-9:30 (more or less) in the dining room. Fruit, a variety of breads, jams, jellies, cold cereals.
**Plus:** Parlor with color TV, screened porch, grounds, lawn chairs.
**Rates:** All include tax. $44 single, $50 double. $10 less in winter. $10 for extra mattress.

## Bed & Breakfast Cape Cod Host #3

West Barnstable, MA
**Location:** Overlooking a marsh and Cape Cod Bay. Not far from the mid-Cape highway, close to "most everything," on a dead-end street where all seems peaceful.
**Reservations:** Available through Bed & Breakfast Cape Cod, page 219.

The host's relatives have been on the Cape for several generations, but this couple summered here for two decades before building this marvelous contemporary house about ten years ago. They enjoy sharing their high vantage point and deck with its spectacular bay view as well as the history of family heirlooms.

The hostess is a folk artist who specializes in painted country objects. Her husband, a sailor, is in the insurance business. They are well prepared with touring and restaurant hints.

**In residence:** One 15-year-old dog.
**Restrictions:** Children should be in their teens. Sorry, no guests' pets.
**Bed and bath:** Two rooms each with two twin beds share a full bath.
**Breakfast:** Juice, fruit, homemade rolls, and jams and jellies. Eggs, cereals, and specialities too.
**Plus:** Guest refrigerator. TV in guest sitting room. Hosts' parlor. Private guest entrance through sliding glass door on terrace.
**Rates:** $40 single, $50 double. $25 third person in same family in separate room. $325 per week for two. $5 surcharge for one-night stay.

Guests wrote: "We were completely taken with the hosts and their beautiful home."

## Honeysuckle Hill

591 Main Street, West Barnstable, MA 02668
**Phone:** 617/362-8418
**Location:** On historic Old King's Highway, within walking distance (by sheep, cranberry bogs, and salt marshes) of village center. Five-minute drive to Sandy Neck Beach.

**Hosts:** Barbara and Bob Rosenthal
**Open:** Year round. Reservations advisable. Two-night minimum stay on weekends.

> From Pennsylvania: "The Victorian decor was charming; our hosts knowledgeable about the Cape. The breakfasts were memorable; during the four days no menu was repeated. . . . served in whimsical china collected over a lifetime. There was tea on the days when we were not too busy exploring the area. There was a thermos of ice cold water and glasses on a bedside table; cuddly terry bathrobes for each of us on the bathroom door. We felt truly coddled!"

Pampering is intentional at Honeysuckle Hill. Bob, "too young to just do nothing" after being a business executive (and hockey referee) in St. Louis, and Barbara, an art teacher and miniaturist who has also been in real estate, took over this young B&B in 1986. The weather-shingled Victorian farmhouse is "at least 125 years old." The inside was restored by former owners, a well-known Cape family of weavers.

**In residence:** Two dogs: "Fred, a Lhasa apso, manages the inn, checks out the guests and is everyone's friend. Annie strikes glamour poses and hopes you won't ask about her pedigree (none)."
**Foreign languages spoken:** A little French and Italian.
**Bed and bath:** Three rooms, each with a private bath. A queen-sized bed in each of two first-floor rooms. The very private second-floor room has a king-sized bed. Features include a working fireplace, parlor stove, or feather bed. Cots and crib available.
**Breakfast:** 7-10 full, 10-12 continental. Fruit mixtures, hot breads and muffins, "river rafting souffles" (recipe from their Salmon River rafting trip). Also Scotch eggs, blueberry pancakes, French toast. Served on the porch or by dining room window bird feeder.
**Plus:** Late-afternoon tea, homemade cakes, cookies, or scones. Fresh flowers. Bedroom fans. Needle, thread, missing button too. Ten-speed bicycles and car bike rack. Beach towels, chairs, umbrellas, pails. Binoculars and bird books. Miniature and bird-watching weekends. Will meet guests at Hyannis airport, West Barnstable train, or bus stop. Up-to-date events' notices.
**Rates:** Summer and early fall, $80 and $95 double occupancy. $10 third person in a room. Off-season $60 and $75. MasterCard, VISA, and AMEX accepted.

## The Elms

495 W. Falmouth Highway, West Falmouth, MA 02574
**Phone:** 617-540-7232
**Location:** On shore route (28A), within walking distance of Chapoquoit Beach. Half hour from departure point (Barnstable harbor) of whale watch trips. Ten minutes to Woods Hole and four public golf courses.
**Hosts:** Elizabeth and Joseph Mazzucchelli
**Open:** Year round. Reservations required. Two-night minimum stay on weekends, June through October. Three-night minimum stay on long holiday weekends.

Betty was literally born into the business. Her mother had an B&B in Ireland. Still, it was a recent trip to Europe that spurred the Mazzucchellis on to starting their own in this country. Perhaps it is no coincidence that many Europeans find their way to The Elms. Those who have written to me rave about how much at home they felt, about the food and the food and the food. They appreciated local suggestions as well as directions to a secluded nature walk that leads to a breathtaking view of the ocean.

Betty, formerly a nurse in Boston, and Joe, an insurance administrator, can fill you in on the history of the house built in 1739 and added on to in 1850. "It has nooks, unexpected closets, and an alcove that only an old-house sleuth could explain." A large fireplace with crane is in the huge living room.

**In residence:** Annie, a Lhasa apso.
**Restrictions:** Children over 14 welcome. No guests' pets.
**Bed and bath:** Nine rooms, seven with private baths. Two first-floor rooms, one with twin beds and one with a double. Five rooms on the second floor have private baths, two share a full bath. Some double four-posters, twin brass beds, one canopied bed, two queen; all are antiques.
**Breakfast:** A gourmet meal, 8-9:15. Fresh fruits and juice. Eggs Benedict or bananas Foster served on French toast, or crepes, homemade codfish cakes. Irish bread, blueberry and cranberry muffins. Formal setting in plant-filled solarium that overlooks deck.
**Plus:** Late-afternoon/evening sherry. Living room with TV. Deck and lawn furniture. Ironed percale eyelet-trimmed sheets. Will meet guests at the Falmouth bus. Bicycles on a first-come basis. Winter "Stressless Weekends" with gourmet dinners.

**Rates:** Double occupancy. June 15-Columbus Day $65 with shared bath, $75 private bath. Off-season $50 shared bath, $60 private bath.

---

## Sjöholm Bed & Breakfast Inn

17 Chase Road, West Falmouth, MA 02574
**Phone:** 617/540-5706
**Location:** In a quiet country area, on 2½ acres, one mile to a beautiful beach. Minutes to Falmouth and Woods Hole.
**Host:** Barbara Eck Menning
**Open:** Year round except for several weeks in winter. Reservations recommended.

"The quiet is one of the things people remark about most. We go to sleep hearing the crickets and wake up hearing the birds. . . . Some come all scheduled with things they have to do while on vacation, others just let each day unfold. Many just sleep until noon or read on the porch. This is a good place to relax.

"I bought Sjöholm in 1985 and moved here from the Boston area. Originally I am from Wisconsin, but I have lived in New England half my life. With my background as a nurse and counselor, I love conversations and never tire of guests' stories. The timing was just right for my family and me, and the name of this inn was appealing because I am Swedish on my father's side. So here we are. . . . With our range of accommodations, we are set up for honeymooners and families too."

**In residence:** Jonathan, 14, and Rebecca, 13. Tinker, a nine-year-old black cat who accommodates cat lovers by sleeping on the bed. The official welcomer is Amber, a female golden retriever.
**Restrictions:** Children should be at least five. No guests' pets. Smoking discouraged but allowed in designated rooms and on porch and grounds.
**Bed and bath:** Fifteen rooms mid-May through mid-October, ten rooms rest of year. Bed sizes vary from a single twin to queen size. Some rooms sleep three or four. Private baths in four ground-floor rooms of carriage house and one upstairs in the inn. Five upstairs rooms in the inn share three baths with showers. The five summer "economy" unheated (space heaters available) rooms (one is a four-person room) share two baths.

**Breakfast:** Full all-you-can-eat buffet includes lots of fruit (strawberries and blueberries from the garden), homemade quick breads, donuts and muffins, eggs and sausage, quiches, homemade jams. Homemade granola and three varieties of bran. Swedish dishes include rosettes, a deep-fried sugared pastry.
**Plus:** Outdoor hot/cold shower, also available as a refresher for beachgoers later on the day of checkout. Line-dried linens in good weather. Big screened porch with extensive library and games. Living room with TV, stereo, books, and magazines. Picnic tables and lawn chairs. Large grass lot for spontaneous ball games. Outdoor clotheslines. Use of refrigerators. Beach permits ($2 day).
**Rates:** Mid-June–mid-September, $30-$40 single, $45 double economy, $55 double with shared bath, $65 double with private bath. November–mid-April $30 single, $40 double with shared bath, $50 double with private bath. Fall and spring $30-$35 single, $50 double with shared bath, $60 double with private bath. $10 extra person in room. Ten percent discount for stays over five nights.

## Lion's Head Inn

P.O. Box 444, 186 Belmont Road, West Harwich, MA 02671
**Phone:** 617/432-7766
**Location:** On a tree-lined street in a residential neighborhood, half-mile from beach on Nantucket Sound. Surrounded by greenery that offers sanctuary to birds, rabbits, and raccoons. Five minutes to Dennisport. Close to biking, golf, shops, and restaurants. One mile to bike trail.
**Hosts:** Laurie and Djordje (George) Soc
**Open:** Year round. Reservations required. Two-night minimum stay on weekends June through August.

"We fondly remember a couple who spent much time rewriting Greek mythology to fit the taste of today's teenagers for national public radio, a free-lance writer who wrote and illustrated an article on our inn, and all the lovely couples, young and old, who have shown us how great marriage can be regardless of what we read and see in the media."

Yes, innkeeping suits Laurie and Djordje just fine. And according to the many thank-you notes, it pleases guests who come for the breakfast, swimming, the Cape—and the Socs.

Until four years ago, Laurie taught social policy and Djordje clinical work at Bryn Mawr College in Pennsylvania. When they found the inn that would be the focus of their career change, they did extensive work, including papering and painting, to bring back the ambiance of seafaring days. Since being built as a captain's home about 180 years ago, it has been expanded several times. At one point it was a parsonage. Furnishings are antique or traditional and include a collection of pewter. Pine floors add to the warmth.

Laurie makes jewelry and refinishes furniture. Djordje writes and paints. Their favorite Cape places include a preservation area and the Race Point Lighthouse at sunset time.

**In residence:** Both innkeepers smoke; they supply many air filters for the comfort of nonsmokers.
**Restrictions:** Children should be at least 12. No guests' pets.
**Foreign languages spoken:** French, Italian, Serbocroatian.
**Bed and bath:** Five rooms, two with private bath. First-floor two-room suite is accessible to handicapped. At the top of steep (captain's) stairs are three other rooms. The one with a private bath has double bed, a twin bed, and a sitting area. A room with double bed and a room with two twin beds share a bath.
**Breakfast:** 8:30-9:30 (other times with advance notice). Favorites are omelets made with lobster, eggs Benedict, and quiches. Accompanied by meats or fish. Juice, fruit, coffee or tea, homemade muffins and breads. Regardless of the length of a guest's stay, no part of menu ever repeated! Served in the dining room.
**Plus:** Sherry hour, 5-6, by the hearth. Living room with games. Library. Fresh flowers. Chocolates at bedtime. Wine in rooms for returning guests. Bedroom ceiling fans. Wraparound porch, partially screened. Croquet. Orchard with benches. Private woods. Will meet guests at Hyannis airport, bus, or train. Custom-designed self-guided tours of the Cape. Dinner offered to guests only ($15 per person) by prior arrangement.
**Rates:** Singles, $33 shared bath, $43 private bath. Doubles, $38 shared bath, $48 private bath. $10 additional person. Add $2 per room, per night in June, July, and August. Discounts for extended stays September-May.

*Can't find the community you are going to? Check with a reservation service described at the beginning of this chapter. Through the service, you may be placed (matched) with a welcoming B&B that is near your destination.*

## Sunny Pines B&B Inn

77 Main Street, West Harwich, MA 02671
**Phone:** 617/432-9628
**Location:** A 15-minute walk to warm-water beaches of Nantucket Sound. Near Dennisport, theater, and restaurants.
**Hosts:** Jack and Eileen Connell
**Open:** Year round. Reservations preferred. Two-night minimum stay in July and August and during holiday weekends.

From Connecticut: "Warm and gracious hosts. Jack does most of the cooking, which includes enormous breakfasts served in a pleasant dining room with crystal glasses, fancy dishes and cloth napkins. . . . At cocktail time one can hear many an interesting tale from Jack about his lengthy career on the sea and his years at the Oceanographic Institute at Woods Hole. . . . The house is an old Victorian, furnished with many antiques that Eileen purchases 'every Saturday night' at auctions. . . . Cozy bedrooms. . . ."

From Virginia: "Spotlessly clean and one of the most delightful B&Bs we have ever stayed at."

Eileen's aunt has a B&B in Ireland's County Kerry, so the Irish hospitality here is well founded. When Jack and Eileen share some of their adventures of running Sunny Pines, they find that the ghost stories cause the most excitement and fun! There's a wide age appeal to their style of hosting. "The most endearing are the folks who treat us like mom and dad, making it a point to tell us where they're going and when they'll be home. They can be any age."

Once a guesthouse for the young women working at the famed Belmont Hotel, the Victorian house, built around 1900, is furnished with period furniture meant for comfort. Before becoming an innkeeper, Eileen was a psychiatric nurse. The latest theme idea at the inn is a "Pamper Yourself" weekend offered October through May, a time when the Cape is still active, but not crowded.

**In residence:** "Our four grown children, all in their twenties, live nearby and visit almost daily." One smoker, Eileen.
**Restrictions:** Children should be at least 12. Lap pet or seeing-eye dogs allowed.
**Bed and bath:** Six and a half rooms. Two private baths. First floor has twin or king-bedded room with private entrance, sitting room, and private bath. On the second floor are five rooms of varying size

with twin beds, double, or queen, that share two baths. One room with twin beds can accommodate three or four people.
**Breakfast:** 8-10. Homemade Irish soda bread and muffins, seafood or vegetable and cheese omelets, Belgian waffles, or silver-dollar buttermilk pancakes served with fresh fruit and a dollop of "tipsey," mixed grilled meats. Juices, tea, coffee. In summer, bowl of fresh fruit and homemade yogurt and granola. In winter, Irish oatmeal with cranberry-raisin conserve and heavy cream. By candlelight.
**Plus:** Beverages and snacks. Use of refrigerator. Two large living rooms. Wraparound porch with wicker and a glider. Swimming pool. Bedroom fans. Two acres of lawn. Will meet Hyannis bus.
**Rates:** $25 per person double occupancy. $35 single. Terms negotiable for families or stay of a week or more. "Pamper Yourself" weekends, two-night minimum, 10 percent discount.

## Tern Inn

91 Chase Street, West Harwich, MA 02671
**Phone:** 617/432-3714
**Location:** In a residential area on two acres of pine and oak trees. A ten-minute walk to Nantucket Sound beach. "Maximum thirty miles from everything."
**Hosts:** Bill and Jane Myers
**Open:** April 1-November 30. Reservations essential. Two-night minimum stay.

For six years now Bill and Jane have been living their dream of being on the Cape with an old home as a backdrop for their antiques. Bill, an early retiree from the food-service profession, and his wife have five grown children, now settled from California to western New York.

The shingled and shuttered main house of the property (there are also eight cottages) was built as a summer home about two hundred years ago. Through the years it has expanded to about four times its original size, and for the last 20 it has been a guesthouse. For the Myerses, antique collecting is ongoing, and so is renovation and woodworking. Bill has made some of the traditionally styled furniture.

"B&B brings the world to our doorstep. We seem to find things in common with all our guests, treat them like family, and sincerely enjoy them."

Bill and Jane "go the extra mile" for the suggestion list. You'll be given printed directions to their own favorite spots along with a packet of Cape Cod highlights.

**In residence:** Kizzy, an elegant setter.
**Restrictions:** No pets. Generally, children welcome.
**Bed and bath:** Five rooms, three with private bath. First-floor suite with full bath has two bedrooms—one with queen-sized bed, two twin beds in the other. Upstairs, a room with canopied four-poster double bed and a twin bed, another with Jenny Lind twin beds, a double bed (ladder back) in third. Cots and cribs available.
**Breakfast:** Fresh fruit, muffins, maybe egg crisps, quiche, or waffles, nonstop coffee and tea. In dining room with everyone seated at one long, elegantly set table.
**Plus:** Late-afternoon or evening beverages. Patio. Barbecue. Publick Room with books, games, and TV. Large living room with fireplace.
**Rates:** $55 double with private bath, $65 triple with private bath. $85 first-floor suite (sleeps four). April 1-June 15 and September 15-November 30, $5 less. $10 cot.

## The Manor House

57 Maine Avenue, West Yarmouth, MA 02673
**Phone:** 617/771-9211
**Location:** In a residential neighborhood, overlooking Lewis Bay on the Cape's south shore. Minutes to Hyannis, golf, tennis, restaurants, and antique shops.
**Host:** Sherry Braun
**Open:** Mid-May through Columbus Day. Reservations recommended.

> From Pennsylvania: "It's a jewel . . . Sherry Braun made our stay one of the most pleasurable vacations we have ever had . . . makes each guest feel like a personal friend visiting on holiday."
>
> From New York: "The rooms are bright, clean and decorated in a colonial style with brass lamps, comfy chairs and handmade quilts."

Sherry's B&B used to be an annex for a summer resort called The Englewood Hotel. When she bought it in 1983, as she says, "I painted and papered my heart out!" Although this is a first for her, she has had experience with travelers; her parents own a motel in

Vermont. This is the kind of place where first-time B&B guests quickly blend in with the experienced, particularly at breakfast. Some guests come primarily for the beach and then there are others who intend to see the Cape—"all of it."

Sherry is still a full-time science teacher for grades 7 and 8 in Barnstable. The Manor House reflects her interest in antiques, sewing, crafts, and furniture refinishing. For outdoor activity, she finds time to run—and, in the winter, ski.

**Restrictions:** Children should be school age. No guests' pets.
**Bed and bath:** Six large rooms. All private baths. The two rooms on the first floor each have a double bed and a bath with shower only. Those on the second floor have either double or twin beds; all baths have claw-foot tubs with showers. Cot available.
**Breakfast:** 8-10. Homemade muffins, breads, coffee cakes, jams. Juices, coffee, and tea. "Guests *never* get the same thing twice during their stay." Buffet style in sitting room.
**Plus:** Fireplaced sitting room. Window fans, if needed, for downstairs rooms. Yard with lounge chairs.
**Rates:** Mid-May through mid-June and mid-September–mid-October, $38-$45 for two. Mid-June–mid-September and all holiday weekends, $50-$56. $3 less for single. $7 for third person in room.

## The Marlborough

320 Woods Hole Road, Woods Hole, MA 02543
**Phone:** 617/548-6218
**Location:** In a residential section, on a main road, on a secluded wooded half acre ("a little Brigadoon"). One mile from the center of town and from a private beach with parking. Two and one-half miles to Falmouth. One mile to bus terminal for New York or Boston.
**Host:** Patricia Morris
**Open:** Year round. Reservations strongly suggested.

Patricia's full Cape reproduction is decorated in Laura Ashley style, with sheets and comforters that match walls, and color-coordinated carpeting and tissues too. Furnishings include antiques, collectibles, and some handmade spreads. And yes, guests—including honeymooners—are often inspired to duplicate her decorating ideas—and to start an inn. Patricia's own story is possibly a B&B classic.

"In California I was a teacher and an architectural and interior designer. After staying in many B&Bs, I began dreaming about how I could stay 'home' and still earn my living. In May 1980 I came east to see my older daughter graduate from college, after which I decided to come to the Cape for a rest. A certain guesthouse kept beckoning to me. I spent the next few days there and each morning that I awoke I felt so positive—the bright sunlight pouring in my windows, the new green leaves on the maples. I began prowling the rooms (I was the only guest) planning how I could make them look. . . . As I was warming up my rented car to leave, the owner tapped on my window and said, 'Did you know this place is for sale, Mrs. Morris?' There was no sign posted. I had not told him of my interest in buying a B&B. I made an offer, he accepted, and two days later I owned the Marlborough. On June 30 I became an innkeeper with a full house of guests. What a shock, but what an adventure. I have loved every moment (well, almost) of it since."

Although Patricia will never pass as a native, her enthusiasm for all the Cape has to offer rates with the best of them.

**In residence:** A cat named Dr. ("he's intelligent") Nigel Culpepper TPC ("The Perfect Cat").
**Restrictions:** Pets rarely allowed.
**Foreign languages spoken:** "Je parle francais un petit peu, but often have staff members who are fluent in German and Spanish."
**Bed and bath:** Six rooms, four with private baths, some adjoining, some down the hall. Five with double beds. One with a twin trundle bed in addition. Sixth is a large studio family basement apartment that can sleep two to six people. Beds include antique iron and brass and four posters. Room sizes vary from large to cozy gabled. Two rooms are on the first floor.
**Breakfast:** Early buffet, 6-8:30, includes juice, fresh fruit, cereal, eggs, hot breads, perhaps scones or fruit loaves, small quiches occasionally. 9 and 10 a.m. seatings are treated to dishes from a repertoire of 37 entrees "as the spirit moves the chef." Maybe hot fruit soup, topped with a dollop of creme fraiche and garnished with a cinnamon stick; omelet could be caviar and sour cream, apple, walnut and brie, or Veronique (grapes with champagne sauce), or Oscar (ham slices poached in beer, sauteed in butter); cranberry coffee cake. Breakfast in bed, outside in garden, or in the parlor at table set with lovely linens, china, and fresh flowers.

**Plus:** Pool, available 9-6 for all ages; 3-5 p.m. adults only. Air conditioning in four guest rooms. Midafternoon wine and cheese. Croquet, hammock, rope swing, picnic facilities. English paddle-tennis court. Fireplace in the living room. Formal herb and flower garden. A proper English tea, 2-6 p.m. (elaborate menu) in winter by the fire. Gift packets or recipes sold in antiques shop on the premise.
**Rates:** Singles $55-$75 private bath, $55-$60 semiprivate. Doubles $65-$85 private bath, $65-$70 semiprivate. Less November 1-April 1, April and May weekdays. $12.50 trundle twin. $10 cot. $7.50 portacrib.

## Liberty Hill Inn

77 Main Street, Yarmouthport, MA 02675
**Phone:** 617/362-3976
**Location:** Along "Captain's Mile" with its more than 40 captains' houses on Route 6A. Within walking distance of fine restaurants and antiques and crafts shops. Minutes to beaches.
**Hosts:** Art and Joanne Devine
**Open:** Year round. Reservations preferred.

"It's a house full of life! One day a concert pianist gives an impromptu recital in our living room and the next day a famous model from France is here. People come from all over the world, from places we have never seen. It's great to work at home, to see your kids growing up, and to have such an extended family."

A corporate job in the health care field kept Art on the road before he changed careers and the Devines moved from the north shore of Massachusetts. Here he is a full-time enthusiastic innkeeper; Joanne is a dental hygienist three days a week. In 1985 they bought this B&B, which had been renovated and licensed by the previous owners. Most of their furnishings fit into the period of this 1825 Greek Revival house with its ten-foot ceilings and floor-to-ceiling windows.

According to guests, what was once the home of a sea captain is now the home of "fabulous" or "delicious" or "unbelievably good" breakfasts and warm hospitality.

**In residence:** Three "staff members," Kerri, 13; Matthew, 11; and Eileen, 8. A cat, Smokey. "Larry Bird" is a green parakeet.

**Restrictions:** Children should be at least 12. No guests' pets. Designated guest rooms for smokers; no smoking in other areas.
**Bed and bath:** Five second-floor rooms. Of the three with private baths, two rooms have queen-sized beds, one a double pineapple post bed. Two other double-bedded rooms share a skylit full bath. All rooms have antique quilts (for sale!). Twin-sized cot available.
**Breakfast:** Two sittings, at 8 and 9. Option of breakfast in bed. Juice, coffee or tea, fresh fruit cup, Joanne's fresh-baked breads and muffins. Soft-boiled eggs and bacon, herbed mushroom quiche and ham, or house specialty of Portuguese French toast and sausages. Served in the dining room or on the wraparound porch.
**Plus:** Iced tea or juice in summer afternoons. Piano and guitar in parlor. Mints on the pillow. Bedroom window fans. Cross ventilation. Refrigerator available. Plenty of rockers on that big porch.
**Rates:** May 15-October 15 $60 double with shared bath, $75-$85 queen/double with private bath. Off-season $45 double, shared bath; $50-$70 queen/double, private bath. $20 rollaway bed. MasterCard, VISA, and AMEX accepted.

## Martha's Vineyard Reservation Services

The following reservation services represent B&Bs on Martha's Vineyard:

Bed & Breakfast Cape Cod, page 219.
B&B House Guests, Cape Cod, page 219.
Bed & Breakfast Agency of Boston, Inc., page 300.
Pineapple Hospitality, page 214.

# Martha's Vineyard B&Bs

## The Arbor

222 Upper Main Street, P.O. Box 1628, Edgartown, MA 02539
**Phone:** 617/627-8137
**Location:** Six-minute walk into town, ten minutes to harbor. On the bicycle path. Shuttle bus to downtown Edgarton, South Beach, Oak Bluffs, Vineyard Haven (in season) stops at front door.
**Host:** Peggy Hall
**Open:** May-October. Reservations recommended. Two-day minimum stay in June, September, and October, three days in July and August.

The weathered shingled house was moved from the adjoining island of Chappaquiddick in 1910 and added on to through the years. Since Peggy took it over eight years ago, she has been in a position to share her love affair with the island and its hideaways, but not before she designed some changes. "And everything came out just as I had pictured it. When English guests say it looks like an English country cottage, I feel I succeeded."

It's all because she played an experimental game that asked what you wanted to be doing in ten years. Why wait? she thought. "The children were grown, so the time was right. After training real estate brokers for 20 years, I can say that work has never been so much fun. . . . Recently two high powered advertising people from New York spent two weeks here. When they arrived, they walked and talked as though they were in a contest to finish first. By the time they left, they were strolling casually. I told them they would probably be picked up for loitering when they returned to Manhattan. . . . We get a great mix of people—young, retirees, singles, couples, lots of Europeans."

**In residence:** One who smokes.
**Restrictions:** Children should be at least 12. No guests' pets, please.
**Bed and bath:** Ten rooms, eight with private baths. Five rooms have queen-sized beds. Two rooms each with a pair of twin beds. One cozy single room. Two rooms with double beds share a bath. Designer linens. Comforters. Vintage furniture.

**Breakfast:** 8-10. Juice, homemade corn and other breads or muffins, tea or coffee. Buffet style with linens, cloth napkins, silver service. Eat in dining room, outside at umbrella tables, or on the deck.
**Plus:** Outside enclosed hot/cold shower. Hammock for two. Fans (rarely needed). Set-ups 5-7 p.m. Bicycle rack.
**Rates:** Mid-June–mid-September $65-$85 double occupancy, single $65. Off-season $45-$65, single $45. MasterCard and VISA.

## Phil and Ilse Fleischman

Box 1176, off Planting Field Way, Edgartown, MA 02539
**Phone:** 617/627-5411 or 693-1111
**Location:** In a secluded setting, on a sandy pine-treed road, just a ten-minute walk to Main Street.
**Hosts:** Phil and Ilse Fleischman
**Open:** Year round.

> From Massachusetts: "... Extraordinarily delightful place to visit. The Fleischmans are friendly and extended their warmth to our year-old daughter. The suite we enjoyed has a cozy reading nook and an expansive sun deck. ... There are plenty of restaurants in Edgartown. My cooking is better. I cooked our best meal in the kitchenette, using fish caught that day and bought in Menemsha. We are looking forward to a longer visit this year."

The Fleischmans designed and built their German country-style house themselves 15 years ago. It's built in post-and-beam style and has many European details.

Phil is an architect now, but he has been a yacht captain and boat builder. Ilse was a kindergarten teacher in her native Germany, and also in Greece; here she is a travel agent and an exuberant hostess.

**In residence:** Mietze, a large (13 pounds) and friendly cat.
**Restrictions:** No guests' pets.
**Foreign language spoken:** German.
**Bed and bath:** Two rooms, one on the first floor with queen-sized bed, bath with tub and shower, and small patio. Second-floor room has double bed, bath with shower only, a large, very private sun deck, "very romantic setting."
**Breakfast:** Continental provided at guests' convenience.

**Plus:** Horseshoes, bocci. Use of hibachi.
**Rates:** Mid-June–mid-September $75. Off-season $50.

## The Bayberry

Old Courthouse Road, North Tisbury, MA 02568
Mailing address: RFD #1, Box 546, Vineyard Haven, MA 02568
**Phone:** 617/693-1984
**Location:** Five miles from ferry landing. Down a country lane where there are birds, woods, meadows, horses. Ten minutes to beaches.
**Host:** Rosalie Powell
**Open:** Year round. Reservations recommended. Two-day minimum on weekends in summer.

From Massachusetts: "The Bayberry needs your attention! Rosalie Powell, a native who can boast of her great-grandfather, Mr. Thomas Mayhew, founder of the Vineyard and Nantucket, and her friend, Phyllis, extend themselves to their guests in every way possible—from the quaint open-aired rooms, to fresh flowers bursting everywhere, to passes to wonderful beaches and tennis courts, to providing sherry and mints upon our return to our room . . . but most importantly, they make you feel welcomed and appreciated!"

Upon early retirement from her position as a home economist for the University of Massachusetts extension service, Rosalie decided to turn her shingled Cape Cod home into a B&B. For cohostess, she called upon Phyllis, a home economist colleague. Although the rambling B&B looks old, it was built 20 years ago on land settled by Rosalie's family in 1642. Some of the furnishings are heirlooms; many are antiques. Caned chairs, a beamed ceiling with hanging baskets, early kitchen tools, pottery, hooked rugs (Rosalie teaches the craft), and lacy pillows (made by Rosalie)—all contribute to the ambiance. It's a place filled with joie de vivre, where you can join in or choose to be by yourself. If you're really looking for solitude, follow the hints for beaches with shells and fossils.

**Restrictions:** Children should be at least 12. No guests' pets. Smoking only in the common room.
**Foreign language spoken:** French, "but not fluently."

**Bed and bath:** Five rooms, one with private bath. Two rooms on first floor, one with canopied double bed, garden view; the other has twin beds, highboy, rolltop desk. On second floor, king-sized bed, space for cot, semiprivate bath; another room overlooking the gardens with a double bed and patchwork quilt. The room with private bath has king-sized bed, wicker furniture, view of the meadows.
**Breakfast:** 8:30, unless requested earlier. Eggs Benedict, omelets, souffles, quiches, blueberry waffles, popovers, aebleskivers (Danish pancakes), fresh fruits, homemade jams, honey and muffins. Served with immaculate linens at fireside tables overlooking gardens. Rosalie and Phyllis join you for coffee.
**Plus:** Afternoon tea, wine, and hors d'oeuvres. Coffeepot on for early risers. Occasional seafood chowder or barbecues. Champagne for honeymooners. Grand piano. Tour of the house. Will meet guests at the airport or ferry. Croquet. Library of books on antiques. Hammock under trees. Woods with paths. Gardens.
**Rates:** June-mid–September $70-$80 double occupancy with shared bath, $95 private bath. Off-season, reduced rates. MasterCard and VISA accepted.

## Captain Dexter House

P.O. Box 2457, 100 Main Street, Vineyard Haven, MA 02568
**Phone:** 617/693-6564
**Location:** One block from the Vineyard Haven ferry dock.
**Hosts:** Lara and Beyer Parker
**Open:** Year round. Reservations recommended. Two-night minimum stay in summer and all weekends in fall and spring.

"Over the years we have restored and lived in three old houses. Doing it for the enjoyment of others as well appealed to us. Plus, we like people!" About the time their youngest (seventh) child went off to college, the Parkers were ready for a change from the New York corporate lifestyle. "After four years on this beautiful island, we can say that innkeeping is very much a full-time job, but very fulfilling."

Lara is a consultant on 18th-century house restoration and decorating, and she put her knowledge to work in this 1843 captain's house. The entire house is furnished with fine antiques. Downstairs there are Oriental rugs, oil portraits of ancestors, and many Sheraton and Chippendale pieces. The owners were pleased when, in 1985, the Island Historical Society asked them to be the first inn included in the annual historic house tour.

**Restrictions:** Children should be at least 12. No guests' pets. No smoking in common rooms.
**Bed and bath:** Eight rooms, each with private bath. A canopied queen-sized four-poster and fireplace in two rooms. The suite has a queen canopied bed and a living room with queen-sized sleep sofa. Other rooms have a king, a double, or twin beds. Cot available.
**Breakfast:** 8:30-9:30. Continental breakfast served in the elegant dining room. Homemade croissants, hot breads, coffee cakes. Freshly squeezed orange juice, coffee, teas.
**Plus:** Fireplace in guest living room. Fresh flowers (in season) in the bedrooms. Sherry in rooms in fall and winter. Bedroom ceiling fans. Thick towels. Tour of house. Guest refrigerator. Locked garage for bicycles. Garden with tables and chairs. Off-street parking.
**Rates:** June 6-September 6 $80-$110 double occupancy. Interim season $65-$85. Off-season (October 26-May 8) $50-$85. $15 additional person in a room. MasterCard and VISA accepted.

From Washington, D.C.: "Extraordinary furnishings and hosts. I went back just to visit with the Parkers."

## Thorncroft Inn

P.O. Box 1022, 278 Main Street, Vineyard Haven, MA 02568
**Phone:** 617/693-3333
**Location:** On 3½ acres with big old trees in a residential neighborhood. A half-mile beyond the edge of the village. One mile from ferry landing.
**Hosts:** Karl and Lynn Buder
**Open:** Year round. Two-night minimum on weekends May-October.

"It's the type of place where we find ourselves falling in love all over again." Since that comment from a guest about Haven Guest House (the earlier name before the Buders discovered the original name of Thorncroft) appeared in my first B&B book, many have written about "a place to relax when I needed to get away from it all." Honeymooners add that everything is complemented by the friendly hosts "who share their knowledge of the wonders of Martha's Vineyard and career transitions too." Karl always is able to come up with hidden spots, even an ocean beach and freshwater pond "that I have never seen up to capacity."

Peace is just what the Buders intended to offer (mostly for couples) when they bought the house that had been built in 1918 for the son of an industrialist. Karl, a marathon runner, put his master's degree in public administration in one pocket and his title as probation officer in another, and became a carpenter for a winter. Together with his father, he supervised and was involved in installation of new baths, designing, and redecorating. Lynn, commuting on weekends from her executive position in Connecticut, selected turn-of-the-century lamps, claw-foot tubs, brass fixtures, chestnut headboards, some brass beds. Each room is different, with furnishings from colonial as well as early and late Victorian periods. Improvements to the inn and grounds continue.

The Buders have made changes in their personal lives too; they are thankful that innkeeping, now with the help of an assistant, allows them to spend time with their two younger innkeepers-in-residence.

**Restrictions:** Two guest rooms, both with separate entrances, are designated for smokers; smoking is not allowed elsewhere. Children over 12 are welcome. No guests' pets.
**Foreign language spoken:** French.
**Bed and bath:** Ten rooms, each with private bath. Bed sizes include queen, some doubles, one set of twins. Some rooms have balconies or private entrances.
**Breakfast:** Full. Buttermilk pancakes and bacon, house blueberry honey or strawberry honey sauces, almond French toast, quiche, croissant sandwiches, baked goods or granola. Served in dining room.
**Plus:** Wicker sun room with color TV. Screened porch. Victorian reading parlor. Yard with lawn furniture. Extra bath for post-check-out refresher.
**Rates:** Mid-June–September 1, $90-$120 double occupancy. Interim season $70-$95. Off-season (October 31-May 8) $55-$75. MasterCard, VISA, and AMEX accepted.

## Nantucket Reservation Services

The following reservation services represent B&Bs on Nantucket:

Bed & Breakfast Cape Cod, page 219.
B&B House Guests, Cape Cod, page 219.
Bed and Breakfast, Brookline/Boston, page 302.
Pineapple Hospitality, page 214.

Nantucket's unique characteristics have always been appreciated by its residents. Since others have discovered the island, it has become increasingly popular. Reservations in season are strongly recommended. Prices vary and tend to be expensive. Since real-estate values have skyrocketed, bed and breakfast places with less expensive rates may be those that have been in business for a while.

Baked goods are allowed to be served at B&Bs, but the town fathers have ruled that a full cooked breakfast is not. Many restaurants, just a short walk away, are open for the morning meal.

At most Nantucket B&Bs, tipping is an accepted practice.

The Steamship Authority (phone 617/540-2022) services the island from Hyannis and Woods Hole. Hy-Line (phone 617/775-7185) sails from Hyannis spring through fall. Bicycles (extra charge) are allowed. B&B guests are likely to find little need for a car. Advance reservations for autos (carried by the Steamship Authority only) are essential and are often made months before the summer season.

## Nantucket B&Bs

### The Century House

10 Cliff Road, Nantucket, MA 02554
**Phone:** 617/228-0530
**Location:** Five-minute walk from steamship landing. In quiet section of the historic district, at the top of the hill, surrounded by sea captains' mansions.

**Nantucket**

**Hosts:** Gerry and Jean Heron-Connick
**Open:** Year round. Advance reservations recommended June-September, when there is a three-night minimum stay. When possible, shorter stays may be accommodated.

"It's blowing down here on this gorgeous April day! Today our guests took a tour of the museum, went shopping, and came back for tea. Tonight we're going to a town meeting, tomorrow to an artist's studio. . . . In December we took a seminar group on a spontaneous jeep sleigh ride to Great Point, driving in the snow along the seashore."

Exuberance—for Nantucket, for the inn, for life! The bride ("we're late bloomers") finds that the inn has special appeal for people with stressful careers. "They just enjoy the beauty and tranquility of the island, sit by the fire with a book, read *The New York Times* on Sunday."

Jean understands her happy guests. She spent 20 years as a traveling computer industry executive. Gerry commutes by plane on weekends from his high-tech job to his role as host.

For an idea of the changes they have made, take a look at the before-and-after book, "but it doesn't show the ceiling that fell in two hours before our first guests arrived in 1984." A National Interior Decorator with Laura Ashley assisted with the new decor of Nantucket's oldest continuous guesthouse.

Jean is still researching the history of the house, which was built in 1833. Its first paying guests came in 1870. An 82-year-old island resident is filling in with oral history.

**Restrictions:** Children should be at least nine. (Families with younger children accommodated in a separate cottage on the property.) No guests' pets, please.
**Foreign languages spoken:** Varies according to staff. At the moment—Chinese, Japanese, Russian, French, German.
**Bed and bath:** Ten in season, eight off-season. All but two rooms have private baths. The two with shared bath have sinks in the rooms "and the best harbor views." Beds include canopied or four-poster and many are draped. Six rooms have fireplaces. Some rooms have separate entrances; two have direct access to their own section of the veranda. Cot and crib available.
**Breakfast:** 8-10. Bach music indicates it's time for fresh fruit, juice, muffins, coffee cakes, granola and cereals, hot beverages. Served in the pine kitchen or on the veranda.

**Plus:** Setups and afternoon or evening wine or soda. Afternoon tea. Use of refrigerator. Rocking chairs on huge wraparound veranda overlooking garden. Mints. Fresh flowers. Thick towels. Special occasions celebrated. Off-season innkeeping seminars and special group arrangements/retreats.
**Rates:** June 15-September 15 and holidays $50-$60 single with private bath, $60-$80 double with semiprivate bath, $80-$100 private bath. Off-season $40 single, private bath; $50-$60 double, semiprivate bath; $60-$80 double, private bath. Group rates. MasterCard, VISA, and AMEX accepted.

## Cliff Lodge

P.O. Box 2452, 9 Cliff Road, Nantucket, MA 02554
**Phone:** 617/228-9480
**Location:** Five blocks from village center and ferry dock on the first part of Cliff Road. Set on a hill overlooking town and harbor. Residential area with many large homes dating back to whaling times.
**Hosts:** Mary Coughlin
**Open:** Year round.

After the owner (of 30 years) sold Cliff Lodge in 1986, Mary supervised the renovations of the 1771 captain's house that has been a well-cared-for guest house since the 1880s. The very day that Mary's first guests arrived, so did *Family Circle* magazine! This timely visit followed many weeks of work, so now "just having B&B guests seems easy, as well as interesting and fun." The decor is all new. Mary spatter-painted the floors and put dhurries and rag rugs on them. Laura Ashley wallpapers, white eyelet dust ruffles, pillow shams, and duvet covers give the guest rooms a light, cheerful feeling.

Now the Cliff Lodge style of hosting is somewhat unique on the island. In extending the home-away-from home feeling, the hosts invite you to utilize the pantry and refrigerator and dine on the patio. Because Mary has had experience working at other guest houses and managing Nantucket apartments, she could see the need and has filled it. "It's less expensive and more personal and something many people enjoy."

Perry, a carpenter in summer, scallops during winter. Yes, there's special treatment given to guests who wish to purchase fresh lobsters packed in seaweed and ice shortly before departure.

**In residence:** Husband, Perry Patton. Max, a gentle and playful rottweiler.
**Restrictions:** Pets not usually allowed. Check first.
**Bed and bath:** Eleven rooms on three floors, each with adjoining private bath. Twin, double, queen, king-sized beds. Some rooms have cross-ventilation and views of harbor. Cots available.
**Breakfast:** 7:30-10:30. Whole bran and berry muffins, breads, scones, cereals and fresh fruit. Served buffet style in tea room.
**Plus:** Late-afternoon/evening snacks. Color/cable TV, fresh flowers. Outside shower. Beach towels. Two patios; one with morning sun, one for early-evening drinks. Large lawn. Widow's walk with panoramic view of harbor is accessible to guests. Window fans in some bedrooms. List of potential babysitters. Laundry facilities (small fee). Garden party with music and barbecue on some weekends. Wine for honeymooners. Six common rooms, some with 17th-century antiques. Games. Croquet. Parking lot.
**Rates:** June 15-September 15 $80 (smaller room with double bed) to $105 (large room with king-sized bed). Off-season $60-$90.

## Four Chimneys

38 Orange Street, Nantucket, MA 02554
**Phone:** 617/228-1912
**Location:** In historic district on street where 125 sea captains built their mansions. A short walk from cobblestoned Main Street.
**Host:** Betty York
**Open:** April-October. Christmas Stroll Weekend in December. Reservations required. Three-night minimum stay for most periods.

Gracious style has always been a hallmark of this house. It was a captain's mansion for about 20 years before being purchased in 1856 by Freeman Adams, who advertised, "no pains will be spared to ensure the comforts of its patrons." Betty carried on that tradition when she restored the largest and highest captain's house on the island and furnished it with period antiques, Oriental and exquisite Chinese rugs, and porcelains. Still, it is her approach to B&B that makes you feel like a guest in her lovely home. If all this makes Four Chimneys sound like a good place for a wedding, Betty will tell you that several have taken place here.

Among the antiques is a Pennsylvania cupboard used for guest glasses and drink supplies. It has not gone unnoticed; Haggerty Furniture Co., Cohasset Colonials is marketing a kit for reproductions of this unusual piece. Many guests inquire about sources for fine antiques, and Betty has some ready answers.

When did Betty begin in B&B? Officially 1981, but before that she was used to lots of company at her Massachusetts beach house. Her previous careers were good orientation, too. She has been an interior designer, sold real estate, and taught school.

**In residence:** Adult daughter and son, Anne and Tony.
**Restrictions:** Children should be at least 16. No guests' pets.
**Bed and bath:** Ten rooms, all with canopied double or queen-sized beds, on three floors. All with private baths. Second-floor rooms have 12-foot ceilings; some have interior shutters, oil paintings, Oriental rugs; one with private porch. Third floor includes a suite with sitting room and views of harbor. Each of the five original "Master Rooms" has its original fireplace (not to be lit.)
**Breakfast:** 8-9:30. Delivered to your room, the porch, or the drawing room on a tray with linen, china, and silver pot. Juice, muffins or croissants, coffee or tea.
**Plus:** Late-afternoon beverages, cheese and crackers, caviar pie sometimes. Tours of the house. Extra pillows. Good reading lights. Handmade quilts. Double drawing room with twin fireplaces. Piano. Television. Large porch with wicker. Refrigerator, ice machine. Third-floor deck with views to harbor. Bike rack. Garden.
**Rates:** $90-$145. Major credit cards accepted.

## Phillips House

54 Fair Street, Nantucket, MA 02554
**Phone:** 617/228-9217
**Location:** A six-minute walk to Main Street.
**Host:** Mary Phillips
**Open:** Year round. Reservations strongly recommended for summer months.

"Restored by many over the last 200 years, it's a former whaler's house with comfortable antiques." Mrs. Phillips had spent many summers on Nantucket before she decided to work for herself in her pure Quaker-style home. As a year-round resident she loves the fog and mist of the "Grey Lady's" winters and finds the fall "perhaps the most beautiful of all seasons here." In the quieter times she makes baskets. Then guests cycle, walk the beaches, "do the island in about two days," and enjoy the peace in general.

In season, she finds that visitors come for two or three weeks at a time. Sometimes I wonder if they aren't coming just to be at Phillips House again. "No, I don't have wall-to-wall carpeting or a pool, but I do have a bike rack!" In addition she specializes in hints about hidden and empty beaches and unusual restaurants that "stretch your holiday budget."

**Restrictions:** Sorry, no guests' pets.
**Bed and bath:** Four rooms. One with twin beds. Three with double beds; one has a private bath. Two shared baths for three other rooms.
**Breakfast:** Served mid-June through mid-October. Continental with homemade blueberry or cranberry muffins.
**Plus:** VCR available.
**Rates:** $50 small twin or small double room, $60 large double. $70 large double with private bath. Lower rates October 15-May 15. $10 for a third person, crib, or "floor bed."

## Southeastern Massachusetts Reservation Services

## Be Our Guest, Bed & Breakfast, Ltd.

P.O. Box 1333, Plymouth, MA 02360
**Phone:** 617/837-9867. Monday-Saturday 10-9, 10-1 Sunday.
**Listings:** 18 and growing. Located in Plymouth area including other nearby seacoast towns—Kingston, Marshfield, Duxbury, and Scituate. Also in Bourne (Cape Cod) and Canton, with plans for expanding to Quincy. All hosted private residences. Directory $1.

Two couples, Diane and David Gillis and Mary and Jaime Gill, have all had jobs working with the public. When they select hosts for Be Our Guest, they stress cleanliness, congeniality, and knowledge of the area, with an eye to the type of atmosphere they themselves would enjoy staying in.

**Reservations:** Last-minute calls accommodated, if space available. Also available through travel agents.
**Plus:** Short-term (one week) hosted housing available. All hosts have tourist brochures and restaurant menus. Some hosts provide tours of area. One provides dinners (extra charge) upon request.
**Rates:** $32-$45 single, $40-$65 double. $7 for children in adults' room. Weekly rates available upon request. $25 deposit required. $10 service charge for cancellations; if less than seven days' notice, $25 deposit is also retained; if less than 24 hours' notice, rate for one night is charged. MasterCard, VISA, and AMEX accepted.

## Christian Hospitality Bed & Breakfast of New England

636 Union Street, Duxbury, MA 02332
**Phone:** 617/834-8528. Monday through Saturday, 9-9.
**Listings:** 40, with some in each New England state. Most are private residences; a few are inns. In Massachusetts, hosts are in southeast in Duxbury, Plymouth, Sandwich, Barnstable, Woods Hole; north in Swampscott; west in Gardner.

Ann Kopke says, "Our travelers are placed in Christian homes of all denominations. Some of our hosts have been on our roster for four years. They all have the gift of hospitality."

**Reservations:** Minimum of two weeks' advance notice preferred. Last-minute requests can usually be accommodated.
**Rates:** $25-$35 single, $35-$55 double. Some family and weekly rates available. Deposit is $5 plus 20 percent of the booking. Deposit, less $5, is returned if cancellation is received with more than 72 hours' notice; with less than 72-hours' notice, no refund is made.

## Bed and Breakfast Associates Bay Colony

This service has hosts in Braintree, Hingham, Kingston, Plymouth, and Scituate. Please see page 301.

## Pineapple Hospitality

This service has hosts in Assonet, North and South Dartmouth, Fall River, Fairhaven, Freetown, Lakeville, Marion, Mattapoisett, New Bedford, Plymouth, Rehoboth, Westport. Please see page 214.

# Southeastern Massachusetts B&Bs

## Christian Hospitality Host #200

Duxbury, MA
**Location:** On a quiet road with fields full of wildflowers. Thirty miles southeast of Boston, 10 miles north of Plymouth, 25 miles from Cape Cod, an hour from Newport. Four miles from seven-mile-long beach.
**Reservations:** Available year round through Christian Hospitality Bed & Breakfast of New England, page 287.

The original saltbox, almost 300 years old, has seen several additions and changes since its early days as a sheep farm. "We have a mixture of antiques and 'grandma's attic.' It's warm and inviting. Color is important to me." The dining room has fireplace, wide board pine floor, and spinning wheel.

The hosts have lived here for 30 years, been B&B hosting for four. They enjoy sharing their knowledge of this historic area, often suggesting scenic routes, including a long street with the greatest number of unaltered Federal houses in the country. "We also enjoy sharing our Faith with guests by showing a Christian home."

The host, retired from employment with a paper company, is now in real estate. The hostess is an artist and teen counselor.

**In residence:** Two cats: Tina, age 18, "owns the house," and Trina.
**Restrictions:** Children should be at least five. No guests' pets. No smoking in the bedrooms.
**Bed and bath:** Two second-floor rooms share a full bath. One sitting room/bedroom combination with antique twin beds, color TV. The other room has a double four-poster bed, antique dolls, and TV. Cot available.
**Breakfast:** 8-9:30. Menu changes daily. Maybe scrambled eggs (host's specialty), pancakes or French toast, cranberry or blueberry muffins, juice, coffee or tea. Hosts join guests in the dining room or in eating area overlooking patio.
**Plus:** Late-afternoon or evening beverages. Tour of house and town. Bedroom window fans. Seating on flower-filled patio.
**Rates:** $30 single, $40-$45 double. $5 cot.

## Edgewater

2 Oxford Street, Fairhaven, MA 02719
**Phone:** 617/997-5512
**Location:** On the water, facing New Bedford harbor. Five minutes from I-95, in a quiet residential neighborhood.
**Host:** Kathy Reed
**Open:** Year round. Reservations required.

The idea of living in a historic home had always appealed to Kathy, a reading/language coordinator in an area school system. Since she moved here in 1983, some redecorating has been done. It was originally built in the 1760s by Elnathan Eldridge as his store and home when he was involved in shipbuilding and the East Indies trade. The colonial part of the large house reflects that era with some stenciling and simple furnishings. The Victorian part is more formal, and the sunken living room with big windows is rather contemporary in feeling. Guests comment on the quiet, privacy, and hospitality. Fairhaven is a town of architectural gems. The high school has Tiffany windows, Italian marble floors, and intricately carved plaster ceilings. The town hall was dedicated by Mark Twain; its auditorium has been used as a summer theater. Just across the bridge, within walking distance if you are energetic, is New Bedford, the largest fishing port on the east coast, with its

Whaling Museum, cobblestone streets, and manageable historic trail.

**In residence:** Son Sean, age 18. Buffy is a lovable small, blond, long-haired dog, age 10, "but still thinks she's a puppy."
**Restrictions:** Children should be at least six. Sorry, no pets.
**Bed and bath:** Five large rooms, some with fireplace and/or water views. All with private baths. Three rooms with double beds. Two suites, each with sitting room and two twin beds in bedroom; one of the suites has private entrance, living room with fireplace, bay window, Pullman kitchen. Cot available.
**Breakfast:** 8-9:30 summer; rest of the year 7-8:30 weekdays, 8-9:30 weekends. Homemade muffins, toasted Portuguese sweet bread, coffee, tea, juice, jams, butter shaped as flowers or swans. Served in the formal dining room, which overlooks the harbor.
**Plus:** Spacious lawns bordering water. Upper deck for sunbathing or watching the sunset.
**Rates:** \$30-\$60 single, \$40-\$70 double. Each extra person \$10.

## Pistachio Cove

229 County Road, Lakeville
Mailing address: Box 456, East Freetown, MA 02717
**Phone:** 617/763-2383
**Location:** At the end of a winding pine-lined drive, fronting on a scenic lake which offers swimming, boating, and fishing. On a picturesque country road, one mile south of Route 140.
**Host:** Dana Lapolla
**Open:** Year round.

Where do I start to describe this B&B—on the outside, with the lakeside setting and the woods filled with lady's slippers, lily of the valley, mountain laurel; and lowbush blueberries or on the inside, with its furnishings and facilities ("we are sybarites and love comfort"); or with the effervescent hosts? "We started as house exchangers, but bed and breakfast has taken care of our itchy feet to travel. We're hooked. "We love meeting people from many different cultures, have boundless energy, a great staff and enjoy having a party seven days a week in our own home."

Joseph is an electrical contractor and, according to Dana, "a flower freak." Dana, designer and decorator of the house, is a business consultant. Built in 1974 as their second home, the 12-room house with pistachio green shutters and much glass became their permanent residence in 1979 and a B&B in 1981. It is fully carpeted and soundproofed. Furnishings are upholstered in velvets, silks, and deep piles. Walls are covered in silk moire. Color is important in the decor, even with the plants—Christmas cacti, gardenias, jasmines, impatiens, and dozens of African violets.

Guests find a banner with their name on the door proclaiming their welcome. Some come for "pure escape." Others tear themselves away from the morning repast for day trips to Boston, New Bedford, Plymouth, or Newport.

**In residence:** Husband, Joseph.
**Restrictions:** No pets in the house. "We have a private kennel for guests to use."
**Foreign language spoken:** French.
**Bed and bath:** Four rooms. One, "Shalom," with private bath, has a king-sized bed and faces the lake. Three other rooms share two baths. "Luv" has a double and a single bed—and a refrigerator. "Joy," a single perfect for youngster. "Serenity" is a tiny room with double bed, lace curtains, oodles of pillows. All rooms have color TV, radio, intercom, phone, fan, electric blanket, extra pillows, and "most importantly, blackout shades for late sleepers." Backrests and bed-tables or trays for late-night reading or snacking.
**Breakfast:** A gourmet brunch. Fresh fruit, blueberry or apple streusel, coffee cake, ham or maple-seasoned sausage, eggs a million different ways, maybe quiche with homegrown herbs and Wisconsin cheese. Kosher and other special diets catered to.
**Plus:** Beverages. Use of the 28-foot living room with fireplace; dining room, solarium. Rowboat, picnic tables, dock. Possibly skating, ice boating, and ice fishing in winter.
**Rates:** $55 king with private bath, $45-$50 double, $40 single. $10 for additional person in a room.

*Can't find the community you are going to? Check with a reservation service described at the beginning of this chapter. Through the service, you may be placed (matched) with a welcoming B&B that is near your destination.*

## Be Our Guest Bed & Breakfast Host #301

Marshfield, MA
**Location:** On a quiet scenic road, less than a mile to marina and five-mile-long beach. Twenty minutes to Plymouth and 40 minutes to Boston.
**Reservations:** Available year round through Be Our Guest, Bed & Breakfast, Ltd., page 286.

The gracious 200-year-old white Federal colonial has brick sides, clapboard front and back, and mature plantings. Inside there are original moldings, wide pine floors, six working fireplaces, Oriental rugs, and antique furnishings.

Within their first year of residence, the hosts, a chemist and a former marketing representative, experienced an unforgettable holiday weekend. When, in the middle of the night, the hostess went into labor, they left B&B guests sleeping and went to the hospital. The baby came quickly and the new father rushed home to serve breakfast.

Less eventful visits have followed, with plenty of suggestions for fine dining and for sights on land or sea, in the city or in the country, in this in-between and historic location.

**In residence:** One-year-old son. One well-behaved cat that likes people. Four outdoor pets—ducks Sally and Fred, and geese named Hans and Ollie.
**Restrictions:** Guests' pets allowed only if they stay outside or in the barn. No smoking in bedrooms.
**Bed and bath:** Three rooms. First-floor room has queen-sized bed, private full bath, white wicker furnishings. Two second-floor fireplaced rooms share a full bath. One has antique double brass bed and stenciling; other has two twin maple high-post beds.
**Breakfast:** Between 8:30 and 9:30. Orange juice in champagne flutes, coffee, tea, homemade breads, fruit, eggs or pancakes, sausage or bacon. Served in dining room with fireplace.
**Plus:** Welcoming beverage. Fresh flowers in rooms. Candies on pillow. Complimentary wine for special occasions. Solarium for evening cocktails. Outside deck. Tour of the house.
**Rates:** $35 single, $45 double.

## Pineapple Hospitality Host MA #123

New Bedford, MA
**Location:** In historic district of downtown. On a lamp-lined residential street within a five-minute walk of Whaling Museum, restaurants, and most attractions. Three blocks to bus terminal and tourist trolley.
**Reservations:** Available year round through Pineapple Hospitality, page 214.

Writers for *Early American Life*, *The Boston Globe*, and *Yankee Magazine*, among others, have appreciated the hospitality of the hosts, who have had more than a decade of involvement with the New Bedford Historical Society, a group that has contributed much to the renaissance of my home town. Thirteen years ago, the hosts were among the very first young New Bedford couples to buy and restore a center city location where you can (always could!) walk cobblestoned streets, take a walking tour past whaling captains' houses, visit museums, and see the largest fishing fleet on the east coast. It's a city that has been rediscovered in the 1980s.

In addition to sharing restoration expertise, the hosts have a turn-of-the-century formal photograph album showing the interior of the 1857 Greek Revival house originally built for a descendant of a *Mayflower* passenger. Guests here also enjoy the antiques, collectibles—and ethnic cooking.

**In residence:** An 11-year-old daughter. Hosts smoke but are willing to refrain. Hamlet, "an adorable taffy colored cocker spaniel with limited indoor privileges." Leroy and Caitlin are independent outdoor cats.
**Restrictions:** Sorry, no guests' pets. Smoking allowed with respect to others.
**Foreign languages spoken:** Portuguese and French.
**Bed and bath:** Three second-floor rooms, one with fireplace; a double bed in each room. Two full (private or semiprivate) guest baths. Extra bed, wicker bassinet and full crib available.
**Breakfast:** Hours arranged. Fruit or melon, juice, warm breakfast pastries, coffee or tea served in the formal dining room. Cereal for children. Hosts usually join guests.
**Plus:** Outdoor patio. Enclosed tree-lined yard with swing set for children. Television on sun porch. Window fans. Phone jacks in each bedroom. Beverages. Tour of the house. On-street parking.

**Rates:** $35 single, $43 double. $5 crib. $10 child/$15 adult for extra twin bed in a room.

## Gilberts' Bed & Breakfast

30 Spring Street, Rehoboth, MA 02769
**Phone:** 617/252-6416
**Location:** On a 70-acre tree farm in a rural town, 35 minutes from Great Woods Center for the Performing Arts, 20 minutes from Providence and from the shopping outlets in Fall River.
**Hosts:** Jeanne and Pete Gilbert
**Open:** Year round. Advance reservations, even last-minute ones, required. (Please do not arrive at door unannounced.)

> From an administrator of Historic Properties Commission in North Carolina: "The 1830 farmhouse is exceptionally well cared for, and its tasteful and appropriate decorations and furnishings combine to create a cozy and comfortable atmosphere. . . . I have stayed in other B&Bs in this country, England and Continental Europe, but I have never stayed in one that I liked better than the Gilberts'."

Other letters have come from parents visiting students at nearby colleges, from traveling families, from a businessperson who calls it "a real find." Those who are just here overnight often wish they could stay to enjoy all that the Gilberts have to offer—far beyond the basics of B&B.

After a trip to a Vermont farm early in the Gilberts' marriage, Jeanne knew that she would like to host in her in-laws' 13-room farmhouse some day, and in 1984 her dream became reality. She's also been a local newspaper reporter and photographer for nine years, and enjoys horseback riding. Pete takes care of the tree farm, is a pipe organ repairman, and plays bluegrass music on banjo and bass. Through B&B, the whole family has learned about ostrich eggs in Australia, the study of zebra in Africa, and earthquakes in California.

**In residence:** Other staff members—teenagers David and Amy and John, nine. Inside, in cages, Christopher, the rabbit; guinea pigs named Runt Rabbit and Ground Hog. Outside, four registered Shetland ponies, three horses, roosters, and several hens.
**Restrictions:** Children should be at least two. No guests' pets. No smoking indoors.

**Bed and bath:** Three second-floor rooms with shared new full bath. Two rooms have a double bed, one with two twin beds. Furnished with family heirlooms, country antiques, comforters, books. On the pine floors are braided and rag rugs. Cot and crib available.
**Breakfast:** Flexible hours. Varied menu of eggs, bacon, pancakes, sausage, Jeanne's brother's Vermont maple syrup, homemade muffins, fresh fruit, juice, coffee or tea. Served in country kitchen.
**Plus:** Beverages upon arrival. In-ground pool. Guest sitting room that also serves as storage area for saddles and bridles. Evening popcorn. Wood stove in music room. Mints by the bed. Fresh wildflowers in rooms. Fans. Babysitting. Piano, 90-year-old reed organ, pipe organ. Hiking and bridle paths. Pony cart for tour of area. Trails for cross-country skiing. Tour of the house and farm. Cabin (12 feet square) in the woods behind the house is a great site for cookouts, campfires, and listening to the great horned owl. Limited kitchen privileges.
**Rates:** $32 single, $40 double. $10 for an additional person in a room except $5 for children under 12. Two horse stalls for rent ($10 each includes shavings and water).

## Perryville Inn

157 Perryville Road, Rehoboth, MA 02769
**Phone:** 617/252-9239
**Location:** Quiet country setting. Seven miles east of Providence, within an hour of Boston, Plymouth, and Newport. Twenty minutes from Great Woods Center for the Performing Arts. Across the street from public 18-hole golf course. Near antique shops.
**Hosts:** Betsy and Tom Charnecki
**Open:** Year round except a short time in February. Reservations not required but please call first. Minimum two-night stay on holiday weekends.

Antique armoires; brass, oak, and canopied beds; quilts made by a 94-year-old neighbor; comfortable and immaculate country charm. With only the light from candles, all this took on a special glow just four months after the inn opened, when a hurricane struck and left the area without electricity. For water, the resourceful innkeepers used the brook.

The Charneckis are quite flexible. Tom (a Rehoboth native) was a bank president in Colorado and Betsy was a nurse when they thought about a career change. What they took on was a challenge! When they welcome you into the fresh crisp inn, you can hardly imagine the abandoned farmhouse they bought in 1984. Their story goes beyond paint and paper to steel support beams, new heating, wiring, and plumbing. The house has an unusual combination of architectural styles. The two top floors, built in the 1820s, were raised in 1897 to make room for a new Victorian first floor. The third floor, reached by a private staircase, was used for hired hands. "Still is," says Betsy, referring to the family's quarters.

When they are not greeting guests from all over the world, Tom finds time to sail on his 22-foot sloop. Betsy has completed three marathons. As a family, they have done considerable camping.

**In residence:** Sara, 13; Tim, 11; and Tina, 6. Horsefeathers and Junior are their two cats.
**Restrictions:** No guests' pets. Smoking in designated areas.
**Bed and bath:** Five rooms on two floors. Some rooms have private or semiprivate baths. Queen, double, and twin-sized beds. One room has both a queen and a double bed. Cot and crib available.
**Breakfast:** Freshly squeezed orange juice, seasonal fruit, croissants, homemade bread, muffins, or sticky buns. Served in dining room or, weather permitting, on screened porch.
**Plus:** First-floor sitting and dining rooms. Second-floor sitting/game room. Four and a half acres of wooded grounds with trout stream (fishing allowed). Access to additional 30 acres with ponds and old mill site. Tandem bicycle. Within minutes, clambakes, hay and sleigh rides on the beautiful rural roads, and even champagne (after landing) hot-air balloon rides, all by arrangement. Babysitting sometimes available. Limited kitchen privileges.
**Rates:** \$40-\$65 semiprivate bath, \$55-\$75 private bath, double occupancy. \$10 extra person in room. MasterCard, VISA, and AMEX.

## Be Our Guest Bed & Breakfast Host #602

Scituate, MA
**Location:** In a residential neighborhood, five minutes to Scituate Harbor. Twenty minutes to Plymouth, 45 to Boston, 55 to Cape Cod.

**Reservations:** Available year round through Be Our Guest, Bed & Breakfast, Ltd., page 286.

Original carriage sliders are in the bedrooms of this former 1743 carriage house. Elsewhere, beams can be seen. First converted to a residence and restored in the early 1900s, it was redone again in 1979.

The hosts, a young couple, find that most guests are tourists who love the seacoast, antiquing, and fine dining. Many international travelers have expressed appreciation for the personalized hospitality here. The hostess, employed with a health insurance agency, and her husband have decorated with a country theme, using antiques and collectibles gathered from auctions and area sales.

**In residence:** Sam the Samoyed, who lives outdoors in doghouse.
**Restrictions:** No guests' pets. Smoking in designated areas.
**Bed and bath:** Three second-floor rooms share a full bath. One room with pineapple double bed, one with maple double, and one room with two twin beds. Extra beds available.
**Breakfast:** Usually 8-9. Fruit, cereal, scrambled eggs and bacon or pancakes and sausage, English muffins, jellies and jams, perhaps a pumpkin roll with cream cheese, beverages. Served on china at a Queen Anne table in the fireplaced dining room or in a screened porch overlooking horses and 100-year-old blue spruce trees.
**Plus:** Late-afternoon or evening beverages and snack. Tour of house. Window fans. Guest refrigerator. Screened porch. VCR with films for children and adults. Fresh flowers. Chocolates on pillow.
**Rates:** $36 single, $45 double. Cot is $20 for adult, $7 for child over 11 and $4 under 11.

*Can't find the community you are going to? Check with a reservation service described at the beginning of this chapter. Through the service, you may be placed (matched) with a welcoming B&B that is near your destination.*

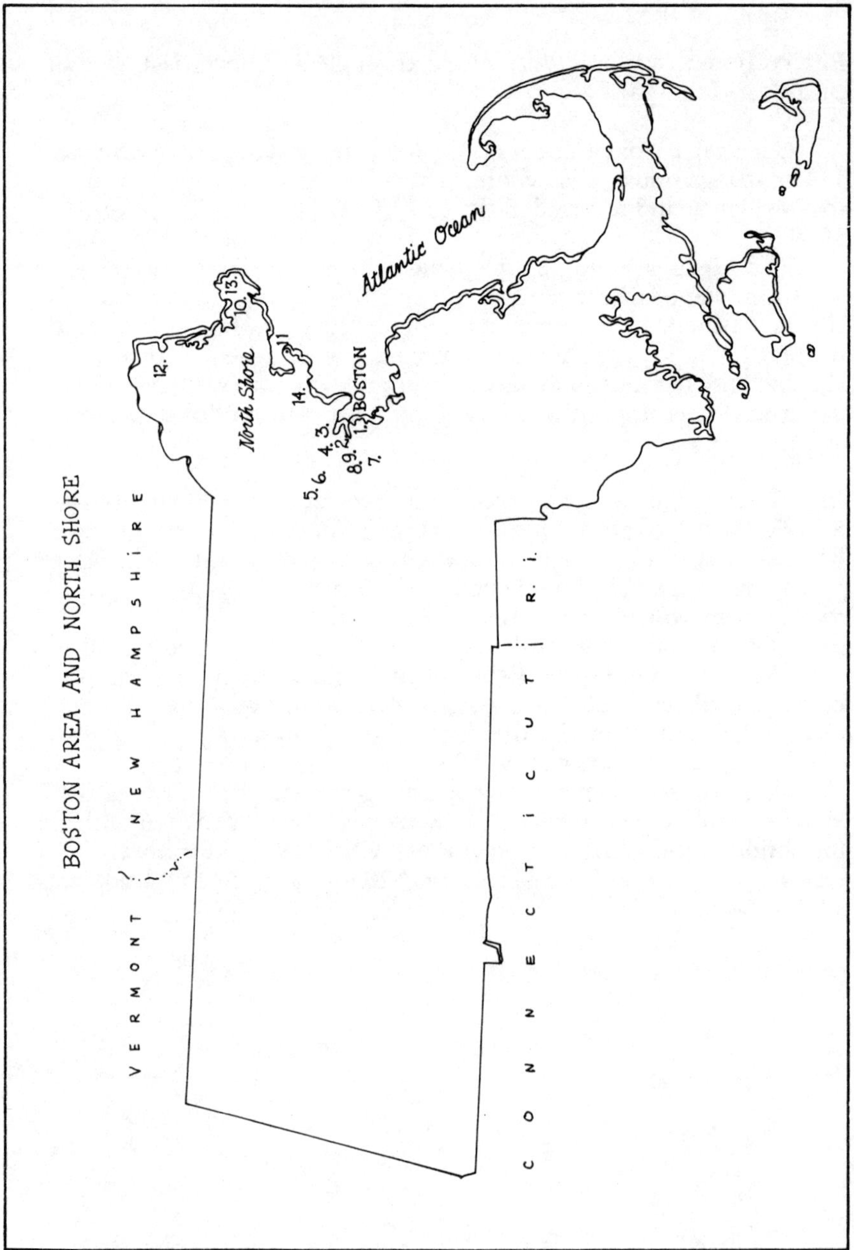


*The numbers on this map indicate the locations of B&Bs described in detail in this chapter.*

# BOSTON AREA; NORTH SHORE



**KEY**

Recipes shared, often for house specialties.

Inquiries welcomed about restoration and/or decorating. Symbol indicates that host is willing to share experiences with guests. Tips range from a before-and-after album to rebuilding advice, from furniture refinishing to curtain making. Expertise of hosts ranges from learn-by-doing to professional.

How-To B&B workshop, seminar or apprentice program offered.

# Boston Area Reservation Services

Bed and breakfast is very popular in Boston, with only a handful of residents accepting direct reservations, but more than 500 homeowners represented by a dozen reservation services. The differences among services? Sometimes slight. All the suggestions about reservation services in general, pages 469–71, hold here. A call to one might give the best sense of attitude.

For many, the convenience of being in the city is primary. However, the Greater Boston area is compact; several hosts in "outlying" areas are actually closer to downtown Boston than many who live in the city. If you have time to commute, many of these B&Bs are less expensive than in-town locations. The public transportation system, relatively simple and color coded, has convenient routes. Its schedules are not as dependable as those Europeans are used to, but the "T" is recommended. Traffic and parking in the city can be time-consuming hassles.

## Bed & Breakfast Agency of Boston, Inc.

47 Commercial Wharf, Boston, MA 02110
**Phone:** 617/720-3540. 8 a.m.-9 p.m. daily.
**Listings:** 38. Located mostly in Boston in the waterfront, Back Bay, Beacon Hill, and Faneuil Hall neighborhoods of the city. Also represented: Brookline and Newton to the west; Cambridge, Gloucester, Wenham, and Newburyport to the north; Chatham, Falmouth, and Truro on Cape Cod; and Martha's Vineyard. All private residences; many hosted but some unhosted available.

Before Ferne Mintz started her service, she was a host for several years. She feels that "everyone should at least try B&B once as a traveler. And it brings the world to hosts."

**Reservations:** Also available through travel agents.
**Plus:** Car rentals and tours arranged. Short-term (two weeks to six months) hosted and unhosted housing available.

**Rates:** $50-$70 single, $60-$80 double; 10 percent discount after two weeks. One-night surcharge $10. Deposit of 30 percent required, nonrefundable unless cancellation is made five days in advance; then 35 percent of deposit is retained as a processing fee. MasterCard and VISA accepted.

## Bed and Breakfast Associates Bay Colony, Ltd.

P.O. Box 166, Boston, MA 02157
**Phone:** 617/449-5302. Live 10-12, 1-5 Monday-Friday. Answering machine at other times. Closed Christmas-New Year's.
**Listings:** 90-100. Located primarily in Greater Boston area in 35 communities including downtown Boston, as far west as Framingham, north to Gloucester, and south to Brewster on Cape Cod. Mostly hosted private residences. Directory ($2) is a detailed booklet including descriptions and rates.

Arline Kardasis and Marilyn Mitchell focus on minute details that even the experienced traveler may not think of. Hosts, many of whom have been with Bay Colony since it started in 1981, often speak of the professional, personal, and efficient service that the agency performs. Frequently, Marilyn and Arline find that callers are first-time B&B travelers. "Once placed with one of our Boston homes, they realize that B&B offers as much convenience as a major hotel, plus a great deal more in terms of hospitality and extra attention. Subsequently bed and breakfast is a preference, not just an experience."

**Reservations:** Advance notice of a week or two preferred. Two-day minimum (except on short notice) in the city. Available through travel agents but service prefers direct contact with guests.
**Plus:** For extended stays, there are also suites, apartments, and house-sharing opportunities.
**Rates:** $35-$55 single, $45-$75 double. A few higher. Family rates. Some homes offer the seventh night free. $10 surcharge for one-night stay. Thirty percent of total is required as a deposit. For notice of cancellation received five days before arrival, deposit refunded minus $20 processing fee. MasterCard, VISA, and AMEX accepted.

## Bed and Breakfast, Brookline/Boston

Box 732, Brookline, MA 02146
**Phone:** 617/227-2292. Monday-Friday, 10-4.
**Listings:** 60. Located primarily in Boston, Brookline, and Cambridge convenient to public transportation. Mostly hosted private residences; one inn and a few apartments. A few are on the north and south shores, Cape Cod, and Nantucket.

Anne Diamond, a mother of seven and grandmother of eight, was a summer B&B host on the island of Nantucket. After coming to Boston to work for the service, she became the owner. Her roster includes hosts who have two or three years' affiliation with Brookline/Boston. "Putting together the best possible package of guest and host is the most meaningful part to me. In selecting hosts, of course cleanliness and comfort counts. And I know that a host who smiles a lot is a gem. We also feature full breakfasts."

**Reservations:** Two-day minimum stay required except in winter. Last-minute reservations made if host is available and credit card used for deposit. Occasionally available through travel agents. Hosted short-term (one to four weeks) housing also available.
**Rates:** $40-$45 single, $50-$65 double. Biweekly and monthly discounts available. One-night surcharge of $5 (possible only in the winter). Twenty-five percent of total required as deposit. $10 service charge for cancellations up to 72 hours before reservations; after that, deposit is retained. MasterCard and VISA accepted.

## Boston Bed and Breakfast, Inc.

16 Ballard Street, Newton, MA 02159
**Phone:** 617/332-4199. Office hours are Monday-Friday, 9-5.
**Listings:** Most are in Boston, but many are in Cambridge, Brookline, and Newton.

Liz Moncreiff and Cynthia Spinner offer accommodations for a specialized audience rather than for the general traveling public. Organized in 1980 at the request of the Continuing Education Department of the Harvard Medical School, their agency takes advance reservations (only) from professionals attending courses, conferences, and seminars. They offer mostly hosted residences that are within walking distance of major hotels or a maximum of 20 minutes by public transportation to Boston and Cambridge.

**Reservations:** Two-day minimum stay at all times. As much advance notice as possible appreciated.
**Plus:** Some unhosted residences are available.
**Rates:** $45 single, $60 double. Total amount is due as deposit. If stay is longer than 20 nights, billing is done weekly. If reservations are cancelled more than 48 hours before scheduled arrival time, a $15 processing fee is charged and the remainder of deposit returned. If cancellation is made within 48 hours of arrival, one night's deposit is retained. MasterCard, VISA, and AMEX accepted.

## Greater Boston Hospitality

P.O. Box 1142, Brookline, MA 02146
**Phone:** 617/277-5430. Monday through Friday, 8-5, Saturday 8:30-1.
**Listings:** 80. Located mostly in eleven Boston area communities, but a few are on the north shore in Marblehead and Gloucester. Mostly hosted private residences. A few inns and unhosted private residences. Directory (free with SASE) describes homes and rates.

Lauren Simonelli offers a broad range of homes but tries to select hosts who are close to major hospitals, schools, and tourist attractions. "Amenities differ. Most hosts are native Bostonians; all are congenial hosts who make that extra effort for the comfort and convenience of guests."

**Reservations:** Two nights' advance notice generally required for reservations. Two-night minimum stay. Also available through travel agents.
**Plus:** Walking tours of historic Boston. Dining in exclusive private city clubs may also be arranged with advance notice. Hosted and unhosted housing for stays up to several months.
**Rates:** $35-$75 single, $40-$89 double. Some family rates. Seventh night is free. Deposit depends on length of stay. $15 one-night surcharge for some hosts. If cancellations are made ten days prior to booking, all money, less a $10 processing fee, is refunded. Credit cards accepted only at some inns.

## Bed & Breakfast in Minuteman Country

8 Carriage Drive, Lexington, MA 02173
**Phone:** 617/861-7063. Live answering service 9-6 daily. Calls returned the same day.
**Listings:** 40 hosted private residences. Located mostly in Lexington, Concord, and Bedford; a few in Arlington, Cambridge, Needham, Newton, Waltham, and Sudbury.

Sally Elkind and Judy Palmer accommodate tourists visiting the historic Concord/Lexington area, people visiting area universities, and business travelers who work along Route 95/128. In addition, the agency works with high-technology companies that need short- and long-term housing for business consultants and visiting executives.

**Reservations:** Prefer one to two weeks' advance notice. Also available through travel agents.
**Plus:** Special assistance provided for guests relocating in the area. Short-term (up to six months) hosted housing available.
**Rates:** \$35-\$50 single, \$40-\$55 double. Family rates available. Deposit is equivalent to one night's lodging. Service charge of \$10 for same-day reservations. For cancellations, deposit, less \$10, refunded with 48 hours' notice; thereafter, deposit is forfeited.

## Host Homes of Boston

P.O. Box 117, Newton, MA 02168
**Phone:** 617/244-1308. TELEX: 136575. Live most of the time. Answering machine on Saturday afternoons, Sundays, and holidays. All calls are returned promptly. Closed December 23-January 2.
**Listings:** 45 and growing. Located in eleven metropolitan Boston communities, plus some on Cape Cod and on the north shore in Marblehead. Mostly private residences. One inn. Fewer accommodations available November-March.

Marcia Whittington has carefully selected hosts who live in city brownstones or in close-to-Boston Victorians and colonials near the public transportation system. Some country homes have pools and are within a half hour's drive of downtown Boston. The others are called B&Bs By The Sea. She has developed her business over a five-year period, giving personalized attention to both hosts and guests. It's a spirit and style that is appreciated by visitors from all over the world.

**Reservations:** With few exceptions, three days' advance notice required. Two-day minimum stay.
**Plus:** Occasional short-term housing (more than a week) available in hosted homes.
**Rates:** $37-$55 single, $47-$65 double. A few host homes offer weekly rates during the winter months. Cost of first night's lodging is required as deposit; balance due 72 hours before arrival. (For those staying short term, half of the total cost is required as a deposit.) $10 surcharge for one night. With 72-hour advance notice of cancellation, all monies, less a $15 cancellation fee, are refunded. MasterCard, VISA, and AMEX accepted.

## University Bed & Breakfast, Ltd.

12 Churchill Street, Brookline, MA 02146
**Phone:** 617/738-1424
**Listings:** About 30 hosted private residences. All are located in and around Boston. Most have private baths. Some have air conditioning. Most offer the ambiance of the countryside and convenience to the city, and are accessible to public transportation or are within walking distance of universities and other meeting places.

Ruth Shapiro and Sarah Yules accommodate visiting professionals, accompanying spouses, and/or traveling companions who come to the Boston area primarily for academic reasons.

**Plus:** Short-term housing (two weeks or more) also available.
**Rates:** $40-$50 single, $55-$65 double. $10 surcharge for one night. Some weekly rates available. $10 service charge for cancellation. Prepayment required. MasterCard and VISA accepted.

## Boston Area B&Bs

### Bed and Breakfast Associates Bay Colony Host #M240

Boston, MA
**Location:** In Boston's Back Bay. Five minutes' walk to Prudential Center, Symphony Hall, Copley Place; to direct bus to Harvard Square; subway to anywhere. Within walking distance of Fenway Park and downtown Boston.
**Reservations:** Available year round through Bed & Breakfast Associates Bay Colony, Ltd., page 301. A two-night minimum stay is usually required.

"We were nagged by a friend and fellow host to try it. She was right. We love B&B. Many guests come for conferences or business but the tourists find that this city is a feast."

"Our Victorian brick bowfront town house, built in 1881, has always been a private home. The decor is Victorian with furnishings that are everything from middle mother-in-law to 18th-century antiques. Everything seems to fit quite nicely. It is us."

The host is a retired insurance company executive who has developed a consulting business that combines financial planning and career counseling. His wife co-owns and directs a girl's summer camp in New Hampshire. Both enjoy cooking and foods and are active in college alumni activities. Their enthusiasm for the city and B&B was certainly evident when we were all on a two-hour radio talk show together.

**In residence:** A B&B assistant, an art student. Smitty is "our 12-year-old city kitty who goes to New Hampshire in the summer."
**Restrictions:** Younger children should be under close parental supervision. Sorry, no guests' pets. No smoking.
**Foreign language spoken:** Very little French.
**Bed and bath:** Two second-floor rooms share a bath with tub, no shower. One very large room with a double and a twin-sized bed. The other with two twin pineapple beds. Both rooms have good closet space, TV, clock radio. Extra bed available. Plus a double

(Murphy) bed in studio apartment with private entrance, private bath with shower.
**Breakfast:** At 8 weekdays (earlier if necessary), 8:30-9 on weekends. Host's special home-baked beans, home fries, homemade salsa, omelets or sometimes coddled eggs or French toast with fresh-ground nutmeg and hot maple syrup. On a hot day perhaps breakfast salad with sprouts along with a poached egg on toast. Hosts usually join guests at formally set table in the dining room.
**Plus:** Late-afternoon or evening cocktails. Sherry in each room. Bedroom window fans. Garage parking available at $10 per day; in yard $8. Cable TV in living room. Tour of the house. By prior arrangement can accommodate (extra charge) six to eight people for small meetings.
**Rates:** Shared bath, $40-$45 single, $50-$55 double. Cot $10. Suite $65.

## The Little Stone House

P.O. Box 448, Town Hill, Boston, MA 02129
**Phone:** 617/242-1799
**Location:** A total surprise and delight near the Tobin Bridge (and Logan Airport), atop tiny Town Hill, in the National Historic District, on the Freedom Trail and steps from the USS *Constitution* and Bunker Hill. A 15-minute walk or 5-minute bus ride to Quincy Marketplace, Filene's Basement, and downtown Boston.
**Host:** Maria Paul-Welling
**Open:** Year round. Advance reservations necessary.

One of a kind. Not only is this one of the few remaining stone houses in Boston, but it is probably the only B&B like it in the country. This "little gem," built in 1799—with a kitchen added just 80 years ago—is surrounded by new condominiums in old brick buildings, one of them a schoolhouse. In back of the Little Stone House is a real neighborhood park. The street pattern here was actually laid out in England before Governor Winthrop came to America.

The transformation of the house has taken five years. Four fireplaces were "discovered." The kitchen, planned by centimeters, is a handcrafted room designed and built by son Mark, a wooden-boat builder and foreman of the shipwright crew which built the *Spirit of Massachusetts,* the tall ship of Massachusetts in 1984.

Maria grew up in Boston and taught art in both North and South America before returning to live on Beacon Hill. Beyond historic preservation (and community involvement), she specializes in traditional folk art; some examples in the house are combing on woodwork, the treillage with morning glories in the smaller guest room, reverse painting or spatter work on frames, stenciled trompe d'oeil carpet on the staircase.

Her delight in sharing is extended when guests ask for suggestions of cafes, art galleries, museums, and ethnic neighborhoods.

**Restrictions:** No pets. No smoking, please.
**Bed and bath:** Two rooms. A large second-floor room with four-poster double bed, fireplace, and private full bath; overlooks a park. Second room, a single with Victorian brass bed and fireplace, is available only as a suite for someone in the same party.
**Breakfast:** Until 11. Continental with home-baked breads and pastries, fresh fruits and juices. Served in your room, the dining room, or the kitchen, or on the roof deck.
**Plus:** Air-conditioned bedrooms. Late-afternoon or evening beverages. Window boxes filled with geraniums in summer, evergreens and holly in the winter. Package weekends arranged for special events or major shows in Boston. On-street parking in the cul-de-sac. Color TV. Iron. Hair dryer. Sunning on the roof deck. Harbor park nearby for jog or stroll. Fenced patio (for bicycles).
**Rates:** $60 double with private bath, $90 suite of double and single room with shared bath. MasterCard and VISA accepted.

## Pineapple Hospitality Host #MA 153

Boston, MA
**Location:** In historic district, one block from the Freedom Trail. A 10-minute walk to USS *Constitution*, 15-minute walk or 10-minute bus ride to Faneuil Hall Marketplace.
**Reservations:** Available year round through Pineapple Hospitality, page 214.

"We moved to Charlestown after living in the suburbs for 16 years. There are several differences. Here many of our neighbors are seventh-generation residents (whom guests sometimes meet). I still have a garden but it is actually more private. Now I walk to work in

Boston. And, as it has turned out, we are in a place that is perfect (and has a perfect arrangement) for B&B."

A marathon runner cheered at the finish line by the hosts, Europeans who gravitate to the attractive courtyard, and an intern-to-be at a nearby hospital are among the hundreds who have been guests here within the last few years.

The hostess first came to America as an exchange student from Ireland in 1956. Her permanent return to the United States was in 1965. Shortly after that she met her husband, an engineer who was born of Polish parents in India and brought up in Afghanistan. Their lovely home is a restored 1846 brick town house. From the deck on the roof there is a wonderful view of the North End and Boston Harbor.

**In residence:** No one who smokes, but smoking is allowed.
**Restrictions:** No guests' pets allowed. And it's not an ideal place for small children.
**Foreign languages spoken:** French, Polish, and Turkish.
**Bed and bath:** Second floor has a room with a double bed, adjoining sitting room and private bath. Another bedroom with double bed and shared bath is on the third floor. Rollaway available.
**Breakfast:** At guests' convenience weekdays; self-service after 8. Continental with freshly squeezed orange juice and homemade cake, croissants, or Irish bread. Weekends, you may have orange yogurt pancakes with strawberries in season.
**Plus:** Use of deck and garden courtyard. Storage for bicycles. Parking on the street.
**Rates:** $39-$48 single, $43-$52 double. Rollaway $10.

## Bed and Breakfast Associates Bay Colony Host #M312

Boston, MA
**Location:** On a tree-shaded street four blocks from Copley Place in the South End, bordering Back Bay. In a historic district of Victorian row houses. Seven-minute walk to Copley subway station for connections to everywhere. Within walking distance of Prudential Center, Swan Boats, theaters.
**Reservations:** Available year round through Bed and Breakfast Associates Bay Colony, Ltd., page 301.

"We are both psychotherapists specializing in marriage and family problems. Guests need not worry; it's only by appointment!"

They and their guests consider the location of their home, near everything, very special. In addition, guests enjoy the hosts themselves and their handsomely restored 1872 four-story brick town house.

"We have lived here for 18 years. Rehabbing began in the 1960s. Now we live in what they now call an 'upscale' neighborhood. Boston is a walkable, affordable city with historical sites, museums, universities, the harbor and terrific shopping. We can suggest lots of good inexpensive restaurants too."

**In residence:** Both hosts smoke.
**Restrictions:** "As our house is small, very active children might find it confining."
**Foreign languages spoken:** Minimal French, German.
**Bed and bath:** Two rooms. Third-floor room has double bed, private full bath. Second-floor room has double bed, shares tub bath with hosts. Cot available.
**Breakfast:** Until 10:30. Juice, coffee, tea, milk, cereal, English muffins, blueberry muffins ("our most popular request"), coffee cake, toast. When hosts are available, bacon and eggs. Host is on a gluten-free diet so rice bread usually available. Served in a ground-floor kitchen/dining room with exposed brick walls. Hosts frequently join guests.
**Plus:** Central air conditioning. Plenty of mysteries, fiction, poetry, psych books. Hospitality tray in each room with teakettle and cookies. Parking at nearby public garage is $12 for 24 hours. "On-street parking impossible. Vastly better for guests to take subway or walk. Boston is a small town. Driving is unique and awful."
**Rates:** $45/$55 single/double with private bath. $45/$50 single/double with shared bath. Cot is $10 per night. $90 family rate for two rooms. $10 surcharge for one-night stay.

## The Terrace Townehouse

60 Chandler Street, Boston, MA 02116
**Phone:** 617/350-6520
**Location:** In a row of South End Victorian houses. Two blocks from Copley Place, home of Neiman Marcus. Half-block from Amtrak/subway station. The ethnically diverse neighborhood is changing

and currently includes long-time residents, families, young professionals, and two U.S. congressmen.
**Hosts:** Gloria and Bob Belknap
**Open:** Year round. Reservations required.

"It's 1870 and there's a full staff in this wonderful townhouse." In order to create that impression, Gloria arranges fresh flowers in every room and prepares a breakfast that is a delight to the eye as well as the palate.

The Belknaps, native Californians, searched for five years for a neighborhood B&B location in a cosmopolitan city. When one of their daughters came to Boston to go to college, they discovered their new home. Before Bob moved his consulting engineering business east, Gloria painted and plastered, designed, selected fabrics, went to auctions, got to know antique dealers, and "just about everyone within a three-block radius."

Early on, she gave herself a crash course on the history of Boston, and tested the accessibility of the B&B, by walking to historical sites, Faneuil Hall Marketplace, theaters, and museums.

In California, Gloria was a successful caterer. Now she is surrounded by marble mantels, an antique Waterford chandelier, a mirrored armoire, shuttered windows. She sweeps the steps, sidewalk, "street too," and grows flowers in all the window boxes. The rooms are filled with appreciative guests—executives, parents of college students, tourists, honeymooners. "It's amazing how many give you a hug or kiss when they leave; the ultimate compliment comes when they say, 'Thank you for having us.' "

**In residence:** Two cats "who occasionally fall in love with one of our guests."
**Restrictions:** Children sometimes allowed. No guests' pets. Smoking in limited areas. No parking available. (Three parking lots within a two-block radius; 24-hour rates $12-$17.)
**Foreign languages spoken:** Some Spanish and French.
**Bed and bath:** Four rooms on first two floors. Two with private bath. Beds are queen (canopied) or king-sized. Cot available.
**Breakfast:** 7:30-9. "If you stay two weeks, menu never repeated. Everything made from scratch." Freshly squeezed orange juice, crepes or omelets, homemade bakery, freshly ground coffee. Served in your room.
**Plus:** Afternoon tea. Air conditioning in bedrooms. Down pillows. Down quilts in winter. Turned-down beds. Orange juice and coffee at your door before breakfast. Common room available until 7 p.m. has a wall of books. Phone in each room.

**Rates:** $75 or $85 double with shared bath, $80 or $95 double with private bath.

## The Carriage House

Brookline, MA
**Location:** Serene private setting. A 7-minute walk to a 15-minute trolley ride into downtown Boston. On a quiet tree-lined cul-de-sac among gracious older homes.
**Reservations:** Available year round through Greater Boston Hospitality, page 303. Two-night minimum stay.

A Georgian carriage house, formerly part of a larger estate, has been redesigned over the last 15 years to accommodate B&B guests on a separate level. It is furnished with period pieces, some antiques, and has been called "a five-star accommodation."

The host is in real estate and his wife has worked in academia. "We are native Bostonians, members of the Museum of Fine Arts and many associations, and know the city well. Often we suggest excellent restaurants that do not have long lines." Among the guests they have met since 1982 are travelers from China, Australia, San Francisco, and Maine. "Hosting is far more enjoyable than we had ever imagined."

**In residence:** A pipe smoker.
**Restrictions:** Sorry, no children. No guests' pets. Light smoking allowed in restricted areas.
**Bed and bath:** Two first-floor rooms share a guest bath with shower. One room with a queen-sized bed. One with two twin beds. Both have plenty of closet space and glass doors that lead to a spacious landscaped patio.
**Breakfast:** 7:30-10. Continental weekdays. Full on weekends. Juice, homemade muffins, fresh fruit, assorted cereals, eggs, maybe poached pears or Dutch pancakes, tea and coffee. Served in formal dining room or on patio. Hosts sometimes join guests.
**Plus:** Parking. Fresh flowers throughout house. Color TV in each guest room. Guest den. Piano. Evening soft drinks. Mints.
**Rates:** $50 single, $55 double. $15 one-night surcharge.

## A Cambridge House

2218 Massachusetts Avenue, Cambridge, MA 02140
**Phone:** 617/491-6300
**Location:** On a main street with a smorgasbord of residences and businesses. Bus stop at front door for service to Harvard Square. Five-minute walk to subway stop that is one stop from Harvard Square and from there, an eight-minute subway ride to downtown Boston.
**Hosts:** Ellen Riley and Tony Femmino
**Open:** Year round. Reservations required. Maximum stay of 13 days.

"They have an opening for Thursday. You just have to experience this place!" The ultimate compliment came from a Minnesota guest.

It has been instant success for the two Realtors who found this Hartwell and Richardson–designed house built in 1892 and on the National Register of Historic Places. This is the fourth house done by one particular designer whom Ellen and Tony have worked with over a 30-year period. The living room has a definite Chinese motif. Flowered fabrics abound—on windows, in entryways, on the upholstered dining room walls. There are tall Chinese vases on pedestals, Oriental rugs, and antique furnishings (some original to the house). Of the six fireplaces in the house, the tall intricately carved one in the den is the most outstanding.

Previously, Tony was an investment property broker and Ellen was membership director of the Boston Chamber of Commerce. Ellen is here most of the time to answer questions and give recommendations—and to enjoy her diverse and interesting guests from all over the world.

**In residence:** Some house assistants.
**Restrictions:** Children should be at least six. No guests' pets. Smoking allowed in the Carriage House.
**Foreign language spoken:** Italian.
**Bed and bath:** Eight rooms, each with a vanity and sink, in the main house and the converted carriage house. Shared baths; at least one for two or three rooms, with additional shared bathrooms "all over the house" sometimes available. Bed sizes include king, queen, two twin beds, and a room with two double beds. Fireplace in one room. Cable color TV with remote control in each room.

**Breakfast:** 8-9 weekdays, 9-10 weekends. Specialties include asparagus and eggs, Italian fried dough, eggs Benedict, pepper and egg omelet, maybe orange pancakes, fresh Italian bread, muffins and croissants. Freshly squeezed orange juice and fresh fruit. Served in the formal dining room. "Lately guests have been socializing so much it takes hours. . . ."
**Plus:** Most rooms are air conditioned. Classical music always playing. Afternoon or evening wine and cheese. Sherry, coffee, and tea always available. Theme weekends; one possibly inspired by mystery book store across the street. Exercise room. Parking.
**Rates:** May-December $64 single, $71 double. Off-season $45 single, $55 double. Each additional person $15. MasterCard, VISA, and AMEX accepted.

From Kentucky: "Too difficult to describe, but gorgeous. Our room was very quiet."

## The Pleasant Pheasant

Chestnut Hill, MA
**Location:** On two secluded acres in a residential neighborhood five miles from downtown Boston. Fifteen-minute walk to 20-minute trolley ride into city. Two miles (or ten-minute walk to the ten-minute bus ride) to hospital area of Children's, Brigham and Women's, Deaconess, New England Baptist, Beth Israel Hospitals.
**Reservations:** Available year round through Host Homes of Boston, page 304. Two-night stay preferred.

"We had one businessman who came here many times and then finally returned with his family. This week we've had carless visitors who, tirelessly, are taking in all of metropolitan Boston every single day. The house is so big that all the coming and going is just fine. Everyone has space. People who come here like kids. Our children might greet guests and offer to carry luggage and they sometimes bring out a map to locate your home area."

The lovely colonial home was originally built in 1940 as part of a large estate. "There are still a couple of pheasants that run about." Antiques enhance the gracious living and dining rooms. The hostess was in publishing and the host is in banking. They have lived in the Boston area for over 25 years and enjoy helping visitors plan their day.

**In residence:** Four children, infant to age eight. One host smokes.
**Restrictions:** No guests' pets. Arrival time the first night should be no later than 9. Maximum stay is two weeks.
**Foreign languages spoken:** Some French and Spanish.
**Bed and bath:** Two rooms. Second-floor room has a double and a single bed, a private bath, and a TV. On the ground floor, a room with queen-sized fold-out couch, library decor, wood stove, private half-bath and access to a bath with shower two flights up. Mats and sleeping bags provided for extra children. Crib available.
**Breakfast:** Available 6-noon, continental self-service or cooked and served if within the usual kitchen time of hostess. Cereal, fruit, homemade bread, jam, muffins or croissants, coffee. Could include eggs, pancakes, popovers, sausage, ham, or bacon and eggs. In dining room or on the deck.
**Plus:** Beverage or snack on arrival. Bedroom window fans. Wraparound deck. Babysitting available. Laundry facilities. Parking. Living room. Large deck with tree house atmosphere. For children, a complete line of equipment—scooters, high chairs, playpens, playroom, bicycles and outdoor equipment plus games, puzzles, building toys. Two bicycles. Great area for walking (map provided).
**Rates:** $48 double with half-bath, $53 double with private bath. $10 less for singles. Add $10 for each extra person in room. No charge for infants until they walk.

## B&Bs Just A Little West

## Bed & Breakfast in Minuteman Country Host #12

Bedford, MA
**Location:** On a quiet country road, five miles from Concord or Lexington. One mile from Route 3, four miles from Route 128/95. A ten-minute ride to bus stops, twenty minutes to parking garage at subway stop to Boston.
**Reservations:** Available year round through Bed and Breakfast in Minuteman Country, page 304.

"One businessman who was relocating from Washington subsequently sent his boss to stay with us. We're in a good location for day trips to the north as far as the coastal towns of Rockport and Gloucester and south as far as Plymouth. Locally, everyone visits the Old North Bridge where they fired 'the shot that was heard round the world.' . . . The enthusiasm of visitors has even prompted us to see some places for our first time."

Both hostesses are editors in textbook publishing. Their architect-designed "modified Cape Ann colonial" is on two acres that include a charming rose garden and wildflowers. The house is eclectically and comfortably furnished.

**In residence:** One of the hostesses smokes. Emma and Maude are two affectionate springer spaniels, "who love to play ball and are very hospitable."
**Restrictions:** Sorry, no guests' pets.
**Bed and bath:** Three second-floor rooms, one with private bath. Two rooms with double beds share a bath with tub, no shower. Room with two twin beds is pine-paneled, has air conditioning, individual heat control, stereo, private bath with shower, no tub. Cot available.
**Breakfast:** Coffee is available anytime after 5:30 a.m. Guests select and prepare their own breakfasts from bacon, eggs, juice, pastries, fruit, omelet fixings, muffins, and cereal.
**Plus:** Game room with pool table. Living room with piano. Large-screen TV. Library.
**Rates:** $45 single, $50 double. Cot $20 adult, $10 child.

## Red Apple Inn

Lexington, MA
**Location:** One mile from the center of town, in a magnificent woodland setting, surrounded by trees and perennial gardens.
**Reservations:** Available year round through Bed & Breakfast in Minuteman Country, page 304.

Charming. Picture perfect. It's a gambrel colonial house that has been 35 years in the making and remaking. The builders, the hosts, researched everything carefully at Old Sturbridge Village.

The appreciation for the late 1700s/early 1800s style can be seen in what has been built, refinished, and collected. Braided rugs, curtains and crewel work, quilts, cabinets and furniture, even a carved wood Noah's Ark have been done true to the period. Since the hostess has retired from being a nursery-school teacher and director of the Red Cross, she's taken tin-painting and watercolor lessons. Within the last few years, her husband, a teacher, added a greenhouse, converted the garage to a bedroom, and has built a new double garage to look like a barn. His displayed photographs are reminders of their own travels.

Beyond living history right here, B&B travelers explore Lexington and Concord, and, inspired by their stay here, they seek craft shops and craft supply places. With the assistance of the hosts and their maps and knowledge, day trips are launched complete with parking and age-appeal hints.

**In residence:** A black Persian cat named Carissa.
**Restrictions:** Sorry, no guests' pets. No smoking or alcoholic beverages.
**Bed and bath:** Two second-floor rooms share a bath. One room has twin beds, the other a double. Cot and crib available.
**Breakfast:** 7-9. Fruit medley, home-baked muffins, scones, oven pancakes, homemade yogurt, bacon and eggs, brewed coffee or breakfast tea. Hosts usually join guests for breakfast in the colonial summer kitchen with brick floor and wood stove.
**Plus:** Tea or cider in the evening. Bedroom ceiling fans. Yard. Patio. Kitchen privileges available at extra charge for long term guests.
**Rates:** $45 single, $50 double. $10 crib. Cot $20 adult, $10 child.

## Brocks' Bed & Breakfast

60 Stevens Road, Needham, MA 02192
**Phone:** 617/444-6573
**Location:** In a quiet residential neighborhood, ½ mile from Route 128, two miles from the MA Turnpike (I-90), and nine miles from downtown Boston.
**Host:** Anne Brock
**Open:** Year round. Reservations preferred.

"I started with the colleges in the area in 1984. B&B is great for guests and for us too. Just last night we had a couple from New Jersey who picked up non-English speaking relatives from Germany at Logan Airport and they came here bag and baggage. We all had a wonderful time."

The house, the first by Royal Barry Wills, was built in 1922 when Royal was an architecture student at M.I.T. It was built Cape style, with nooks and crannies, lots of built-ins, and high ceilings. The flagstone walk, landscaping, and Williamsburg decor have all been done by the Brocks, second owners of the house as of 18 years ago. Guests have full use of the house and much privacy; the hosts have their own quarters on the lower level.

Before retirement, Anne was a nurse and Frank a plastics engineer. They are happy to make suggestions for places in and out of Boston. One of their favorites is a great treasure just four miles away, on the Wellesley College campus: 17 greenhouses with ferns, cacti, orange trees, banana plants, orchids . . . open every day of the year, and free.

**In residence:** Husband, Frank. Mike, an affectionate gray and white cat who sleeps a lot on outside porch.
**Restrictions:** Sorry, no children, no pets, no smoking.
**Bed and bath:** Three rooms. One on first floor with double four-poster. Two on second floor, one with two twin beds, other with queen-sized bed. All rooms have cross ventilation, large closets, full-length mirrors, magazines and television.
**Breakfast:** 6-9. Juices, seasonal fruits, hot and cold cereals, homemade muffins, bacon, sausage, 24-hour French toast (marinated in eggs, cream, orange juice, vanilla, and sugar) or Brocks' crepes, hot beverages. Served in the dining room.
**Plus:** Tea and coffee always available. With prior arrangements will meet at Riverside bus depot/subway stop. Sun deck in rear of house. Good neighborhood for walking and jogging.
**Rates:** $40 single, $45 double.

## Red Door Colonial

Newton, MA
**Location:** Quiet residential road, 5-minute walk to 25-minute trolley ride to Boston.

**Reservations:** Available year round through Host Homes of Boston, page 304. Two-night minimum stay preferred.

"B&B really is a way of life, a way of sharing. As a guest recently remarked, 'This is all so civilized.' My family is grown and I still love my cozy center-entrance brick colonial, built for the previous owner 60 years ago with moldings and bathroom fixtures and checkered tile kitchen floor that are stylish once again. Because of the convenient location, between Route 128 and Boston, we have had thc opportunity to get to play tennis with New Zealanders, to meet tourists, businesspeople, and parents of college students. We've had honeymooners and 50th wedding anniversary celebrants."

The home of the former actress and singer is filled with books and music. Her co-host, a Parisien, is an engineer, designer, and entrepreneur.

**In residence:** A hostess who smokes occasionally.
**Restrictions:** Children should be at least ten. No guests' pets. Smoking allowed on first floor only.
**Foreign language spoken:** French.
**Bed and bath:** Two second-floor rooms, one with a brass double bed, TV, and half-bath; the other with twin beds. Shared guest bath has tub and shower.
**Breakfast:** 8-8:30 weekdays, 8:30-9:30 weekends, self-serve at other times. Weekdays—juice, breads, cereal, fruits, yogurt, bagels, cream cheese. Weekends, French omelet with herbs and fruit breads or muffins, freshly ground coffee, tea. Served at a table set with linens and fresh flowers.
**Plus:** Beverages. Bedroom fans. Living room. Screened porch, back patio. Parking. Will meet guests at local transportation points.
**Rates:** $38-$41 single, $48 double.

## Sage and Thyme

P.O. Box 91, Newtonville, MA 02160
**Phone:** 617/332-0695
**Location:** On a hill in a lovely residential neighborhood. One and one-half miles from the I-90, Mass. Turnpike. Five miles from downtown Boston. Within walking distance of restaurants and the

Newton campus of Boston College. Close to Interface in Watertown and "Heartbreak Hill" of the Boston Marathon.
**Hosts:** Edgar and Hertha Klugman
**Open:** Year round. Two-day minimum stay preferred. Reservations required but will accommodate last-minute guests if possible.

> From Connecticut: "I am writing as someone who has done what feels like a lifetime of traveling over the past year, during which time I have stayed in bed and breakfasts in Massachusetts, Maine, Florida, North Carolina, New York and Pennsylvania. One place has really come to feel like a home away from home. . . . It has high standards: spic and span rooms with fresh flowers and a delicious varied breakfast beautifully presented. The house is very peaceful. . . . The hosts seem by some white magic to draw into their home the most friendly and cheerful of travelers from all over the world."

The host is a college professor at Wheelock College in Boston and his wife has taught on the college level as well. The Klugmans' B&B travels in Canada and this country inspired them to extend their usual style of hosting to B&B guests. Perhaps that is the reason that they have been known to drive travelers to job interviews, give advice on housing, or design day trips for entire families.

The eclectic decor of their comfortably furnished center-entrance colonial reflects some of their own travel and living in other countries. Their activities reflect their concern for our total environment.

**In residence:** Pookie and Glow, two orange cats, both friendly with contrasting personalities.
**Restrictions:** Nonsmokers preferred. No guests' pets.
**Foreign languages spoken:** German, some French, Spanish, Persian.
**Bed and bath:** First-floor room with two twin beds, adjacent half-bath, overlooking yard and garden. Second-floor room with double bed, sofa, full guest bath (shared if both guest rooms occupied). Extra mattress available.
**Breakfast:** Usually 7-9. Juice, fresh fruit cup, croissants, fresh bread or rolls or toast, eggs any style, bacon, sausage or ham, hot beverage. Can be quick or leisurely.
**Plus:** Evening beverages. Bedroom fans. Possibility of air conditioning in double-bedded room. Screened porch. Yard. Will meet Newton trolley or bus. Babysitting may be possible. Tanzer 26-foot sailboat available for charter during season. Off-street parking.

**Rates:** $39 single, $49 double. $10 for third person in double room. No charge for children under six. $5 surcharge for one-night stay.

# North Shore Reservation Services

## Bed & Breakfast Marblehead and North Shore

54 Amherst Road, Beverly, MA 01915
**Phone:** 617/921-1336. Daily (best 7-10 a.m., 5-10 p.m.).
**Listings:** 68 hosted private residences located close to the ocean or in historic areas of Beverly, Danvers, Hamilton, Lynn, Manchester, Marblehead, Newburyport, Peabody, Rockport, Salem, Swampscott, Topsfield, West Boxford. More than half are historic homes and/or antique furnished. Some are estates; some are cozy. Enticing sampler, free (with SASE).

Helena Champion's hosts enjoy entertaining in their lovely homes. To her service and its rapid development Helena brings university degrees in food chemistry and business. She is a skilled interviewer who lives and works in a beautiful area that offers many cultural and recreational opportunities.

**Reservations:** Two-three weeks' advance notice preferred. A few hosts require two-day minimum stay on weekends. Also available through travel agents.
**Plus:** Discount coupons to historical attractions. Short-term housing (one week and much longer) available in hosted homes. Arrangements made for B&B stays throughout the country.
**Rates:** $36-$75 single, $42-$90 double. Family, senior citizen, and weekly rates available. Deposit of $20 per room per night required. With at least two weeks' cancellation notice, deposit returned minus a $10 service charge; less than two weeks, no refund. For reservations made outside of service area, $15 surcharge. MasterCard and VISA accepted.

Other services with B&Bs on the North Shore:

Bed and Breakfast Associates Bay Colony, Ltd., page 301.
Greater Boston Hospitality, page 303.
Host Homes of Boston, page 304.
Pineapple Hospitality, page 214.

## North Shore B&Bs

### Greater Boston Hospitality Host #111

Gloucester, MA
**Location:** On an intercoastal waterway in a quiet residential neighborhood, 30 miles north of Boston. Ten minutes to local bus service, which connects to one-hour train ride to Boston. Close to ocean beach and Rocky Neck artists' galleries.
**Reservations:** Available May-October 15 through Greater Boston Hospitality, page 303.

A favorite with honeymooners. Sunsets. Lovely gardens. A deck overlooking river with many sailboats. Steps leading to a private beach. Hosts who do B&B as a natural extension of their love for entertaining.

Early in the history of the Victorian, built in 1898 as a summer home, it became a guesthouse. For the last four years it has been the private residence of the host, a former corporate executive, and his wife. Both are real estate developers and natives of the area. They have completely redone the first floor and retained the 19th-century flavor on the second.

**In residence:** One who smokes.
**Restrictions:** Children should be at least 12. Sorry, no guests' pets.
**Foreign language spoken:** Spanish.
**Bed and bath:** Two second-floor rooms share one full bath. One room with a queen-sized bed, one with two twin beds; both with ocean views. Cot available.

**Breakfast:** Hour is flexible. Meal is leisurely. Fresh fruit or juice, muffins, Danish, or croissants, coffee or tea. Served in large breakfast room, or on the terrace, or 100-foot deck.
**Plus:** Umbrella table on grounds. Fresh flowers in rooms. By prior arrangement, will meet guests at the Gloucester train station. Beach and patio for guests' use.
**Rates:** \$45-\$55 single, \$50-\$60 double. \$10 cot. \$15 one-night surcharge.

---

## Williams Guest House

136 Bass Avenue, Gloucester, MA 01930
**Phone:** 617/283-4931
**Location:** On Good Harbor Beach, on a scenic drive 1½ miles from Gloucester center, five miles from Rockport. View of beach, salt marshes, or the ocean from every window. Thirty miles from Boston.
**Host:** Betty Williams
**Open:** May-October.

Betty agrees with her guests that she is lucky to live in this big old house by the ocean. It was just what was needed for five growing children, but in 1968, when the youngest left for college, she started renting rooms. And for 18 years it has been a bed and breakfast arrangement. Any memorable experiences? "I could write a book." Now that her husband is retired, he gives a hand too.

Hints? Maybe plan on more time! Because there is so much to see and do in the area, including the neighboring communities of Salem, Marblehead, and Newburyport, guests frequently comment that their planned one-night stay isn't sufficient.

**Restrictions:** Please, no pets.
**Foreign languages spoken:** None really, "but I have loads of fun using my high school French and trying to understand my French Canadian guests."
**Bed and bath:** Four rooms. Private baths for a room with a queen-sized bed and a single bed and for another room with two twin beds. One room with a double bed and one with two twin beds share a bath. Cot available.
**Breakfast:** 7:30-9:30. Continental, including home-baked muffins.
**Plus:** Picnic table and grille overlooking the beach.

**Rates:** Late June-Labor Day, $38 double occupancy with shared bath, $45 private bath. Off-season $5 less.

## Spray Cliff on the Ocean

25 Spray Avenue, Marblehead, MA 01945
Mailing address: c/o Salem Inn, 7 Summer Street, Salem, MA 01970.
**Phone:** 617/741-0680
**Location:** Fifteen miles north of Boston, steps away from sandy Preston Beach. High atop a 20-foot seawall "with views that extend forever." In a residential neighborhood, 2½ miles outside of town.
**Hosts:** Diane and Dick Pabich
**Open:** Year round. Reservations strongly suggested along with estimated arrival time, please, so someone will be available to greet you.

"Everyone in town knows of The Spray Cliff Inn. It was the scene of many fashionable weddings and graduation parties. The 18-room Tudor mansion, built in 1919 as a summer home, became an inn in 1940. When we bought it ten years ago, it was a rooming house and in shambles. After we repaired it for our own home, Dick, a software manager for Raytheon for 18 years, and I, a real estate developer, opened our 23-room inn in nearby Salem. That was four years ago. As our children went off to college, opening our own waterside home as a B&B was a natural extension of our inn activity. . . . City people come for an escape. Landlocked people from other parts of the country never want to leave the patio!"

**In residence:** Three college-aged children during vacations. Or you might meet Diane's sister, Jean, and some of her teenagers, who also live nearby. Daffodill is a chocolate Labrador retriever.
**Restrictions:** No children. No guests' pets.
**Bed and bath:** Five spacious rooms, three with ocean views. All private baths. One first-floor street-side room with two double beds, bath with shower only, working fireplace. Of the other four rooms, two are on second floor, two on third. One has a full bath; others, shower only. Three have king-sized beds and ocean views. One on street side has queen-sized bed. All rooms are furnished with antiques, wicker, flowered chintz curtains.

**Breakfast:** 8-10. Continental, buffet style in the oceanfront breakfast room. Variety of pastries, fresh fruit, juice, coffee and tea.
**Plus:** Two-minute walk to sandy beach. Brick patio with that mesmerizing view. Refrigerator and toaster available. Fireplace in breakfast/sitting room. Gardens. Fruit bowl. Aperitifs.
**Rates:** $75 per room. Major credit cards accepted.

## Ten Mugford Street

10 Mugford Street, Marblehead, MA 01945
**Phone:** 617/639-0343
**Location:** In historic Old Town section, one block from town landing on harbor. Eighteen miles north of Boston. On a bus line from Boston (30 minutes). Near antique shops, historic sites, restaurants—everything.
**Hosts:** Liz and Mike Mentuck
**Open:** Year round. Reservations required. Summer fills very early.

"We bought the perfect house for B&B." That may sum things up. Right in the heart of a four-square-mile charming town that needed lodging facilities. The "19th-century beauty" was a home for elderly women, originally donated to the Marblehead Female Humane Society by a local family.

The perfect hosts. They are lifelong residents of Marblehead. Their four children are all grown. They sold their home of 23 years and moved to the B&B—after gaining zoning permit, renovating bathrooms, sanding and finishing all floors, painting and papering, restoring four fireplaces, and stripping and staining exterior and fence. Mike owns tour boats and a marina, and sells floats and docks.

Books and antiques are in each room. Tourists come, but so do businessmen and overflow guests of other Marblehead residents. Three-day sailing courses bring more people. Returnees feel so much at home that sometimes they greet other guests and show them around.

**Restrictions:** Children should be at least five. No guests' pets.
**Bed and bath:** Five guest rooms with three shared baths. Four rooms have double beds and one has twins. Guests have a private entrance. Cot available.

**Breakfast:** 7:30-10:30. Juice, fruit and yogurt, muffins, toast and breads, tea and coffee. Beautifully served with china and silver in the cozy antique dining room.
**Plus:** Night parking. Make-yourself tea or coffee. Yard and garden.
**Rates:** $45 single, $50 double, $75 family of four (two bedrooms and a bath). Special rates for groups, e.g. wedding guests or family reunions, that book entire B&B.

## Tide Crest B&B

Spray Avenue, Marblehead, MA 01945
**Phone:** 617/631-4515
**Location:** On the ocean. Within two miles of Old Town section of Marblehead. Just off Route 129 (Atlantic Avenue). Forty-five minutes from Boston.
**Hosts:** Anne and Doug Nagan
**Open:** April 15-November 15. Reservations suggested.

"Just always wanted to run an inn." And that's just what the Nagans have done for the last two years—since moving into this white stucco with blue trim Mediterranean-style house. It has a portico, high hedges, and windows, windows, windows. The turn-of-the-century minimansion has its own beach and is just a short walk from the popular Preston Beach. Most guests inquire about the effect of ocean storms on the house. At this point the Nagans feel like experts in the restoration of seawalls!

Both Anne and Doug sail. Real estate, writing, and computer management are their professional interests. Their recommended walking tour of Old Town is a wonderful one, with hidden lanes, interesting doorways, and delightful old-fashioned gardens.

**In residence:** Son and daughter at home during college vacations. Year round, Doolittle, an energetic and friendly English sheep dog.
**Restrictions:** Children should be at least six. No guests' pets, please. No smoking in the guest rooms.
**Bed and bath:** Three ocean-view rooms share two baths. Two rooms have twin beds, one a double. Two rooms have fireplaces. With advance notice, a two-bedroom suite can be arranged.
**Breakfast:** 8-10. Juice, croissants or muffins, coffee. Served on the 85-foot sun porch overlooking the ocean. "Lingering is encouraged."

**Plus:** Lovely views of sunrise, sunset, or lobstermen pulling their traps. Tour of the house.
**Rates:** $60 per room.

## The Windsor House

38 Federal Street, Newburyport, MA 01950
**Phone:** 617/462-3778
**Location:** Within walking distance of the harbor and shops. A five-minute drive to the ocean and Parker River Wildlife Refuge.
**Hosts:** Judith Crumb and Jim Lawbaugh
**Open:** Year round. Two-day minimum on weekends and holidays.

Warmth, hospitality, and charm are epitomized here by Judith and Jim, innkeepers who offer that special blend that invites returning guests.

Judith was director of career counseling at the Museum of Fine Arts in Boston at the time she converted the 16-room-mansion into a bed and breakfast inn with each room distinctively different. The three-story brick building, across from Newburyport's Old South Church, was completed in time for the 1786 wedding of Aaron Pardee and Jane, his new bride. The house was built by ship carpenters and has an exquisite combination of colonial, Georgian, and Federal styles of architecture. The huge country kitchen in the former chandlery shipping and receiving room has a high beamed ceiling and a welcoming oak table "where we spend a great deal of time talking and sharing and often laughing."

Guests leave the tastefully decorated Federal mansion with memories of a roaring fire, lively conversation, and often a bear hug too.

**In residence:** Jim's teenage sons Paul and Richard. Two cats, Sir Thomas More and Lord Merlin, and Lilabet's Silver Jubilee, "our toy guard poodle." Jim smokes but is trying to quit.
**Restrictions:** Pets should be well trained. All children welcome.
**Foreign languages spoken:** A little French, less German.
**Bed and bath:** Six large rooms, each with a name and a story behind it. Three with private baths. One shared bath for other three rooms. Some rooms have Sheraton four-posters or sleigh beds, single as as well as double. Window seats and Federal shutters in three rooms. One bedroom has Indian shutters with "gun slits." A first-floor

room with private street entrance and private bath is particularly good for older people and for those traveling with children or pets. Three trundle beds and a crib available.
**Breakfast:** Watch preparations and chat with Judith and Jim. Served 8-9:30, earlier by arrangement. Fruit, fresh breads and muffins, eggs cooked with homegrown herbs, homemade sausage, coffee.
**Plus:** Tour of mansion. The Commons (formal living room), courtyard, and small patio. Alarm clocks, window fans, books and reading materials, candy in all bedrooms. Dinner by advance reservation. Some really good suggestions and directions for hiking and birding places, walking tours for architecture, and back roads for cycling and driving. Inquire about theme weekends.
**Rates:** $72 single with shared bath, $79 single with private bath, $79 double with shared bath, $85 double with private bath. $20 trundle bed. $20 third person in first- and second-floor suites. Tax and service charge included. No charge for crib. Special rates for clergy or guests traveling on business. MasterCard and VISA accepted.

## Inn on Cove Hill

37 Mt. Pleasant Street, Rockport, MA 01966
**Phone:** 617/546-2701
**Location:** One block from village, harbor, and shops. Bus servicing Cape Ann goes by the inn. One mile to train to Boston.
**Hosts:** Marjorie and John Pratt
**Open:** April-October. Reservations strongly recommended in summer and fall. Two-night minimum stay on weekends from Memorial Day through October.

Nine years ago John, a civil engineer specializing in soils and foundations, and Marjorie, a registered nurse in public health and home care, took a trip around the world. They stayed in many homey, clean B&Bs (and also hiked in the Himalayas, Switzerland and the Pacific Northwest). John had an aunt who was once an innkeeper, and the idea of "being together, sharing a business in a lovely location" had strong appeal.

Since 1978 the Pratts have been restoring the classic square, three-story, 200-year-old Federal-style home with its welcoming picket fence, granite walk, and attractive doorway. Inside, the architectural details include pumpkin pine floorboards, H and L hinges, dentil molding, and a spiral staircase with 13 steps symbolizing the original 13 colonies. Furnishings are some fine Pratt family antiques, some reproductions, and original paintings, including one done in 1881 of an ancestor's clipper ship.

The Pratts always tell honeymooners that this is where they spent their own honeymoon, eight years before they bought the inn. What they offer all guests is a friendly atmosphere and the option of privacy. As one guest wrote, "I came to the sea for peace and escape and found it at your inn."

**In residence:** "Little innkeeper" Michelle, age four, who loves to greet guests.
**Restrictions:** Children should be at least ten. No guests' pets.
**Bed and bath:** Eleven rooms, nine with private bath. Two first-floor rooms, one with private entrance. Four rooms on second floor. Via a steep narrow stairway or outside metal circular staircase to five rooms on the third floor. Bed arrangements vary. Some rooms with queen-sized bed (some canopied), queen and trundle, a double bed, a double and a twin; some are four-posters or cannonball.
**Breakfast:** 8-10. Served in the daisy garden, in the living room, or on individual trays in guest rooms. Continental breakfast with one of seven varieties of muffins.
**Plus:** Fresh flowers in rooms. Tour of house, complete with legend of how the mansion was built with pirates' gold. Will meet train. Bedroom fans. Third-floor porch with view of harbor and ocean. Hot spiced cider in fall. Blackboard with events of interest. Suggestion for ocean walk "that never gets crowded." Parking.
**Rates:** Double occupancy. April–mid-May $30 with shared bath, $45-$52 private bath. Mid-May–October $34 shared bath, $52-$70 private bath. Rates vary depending on room and bed sizes.

From Maryland: ". . . a superb host and hostess team . . . with a deep appreciation of truly fine things, and this is reflected in their continuing enthusiasm of redecorating one of their guest rooms each year . . . everything is immaculately cared for, and the people who help in the operation are just as friendly and considerate as the owners. . . . We are also real fans of those huge, delicious, hot muffins and good coffee."

## Seacrest Manor

131 Marmion Way, Rockport, MA 01966
**Phone:** 617/546-2211
**Location:** About 300 yards from the ocean and spectacular miles-long rocky coastline. On a hill, on two acres of garden and woodland, in a residential area one mile from the center of Rockport.
**Hosts:** Leighton T. Saville and Dwight B. MacCormack Jr.
**Open:** Year round except Christmas Eve–Mid-February. Reservations required. Three-day minimum stay on holidays. Two-day minimum stay on weekends from April through November.

"It really is a wonderful place. You ought to consider it for the next edition of the book."

Here it is, highly recommended by that radio interviewer who had just returned from her honeymoon, by guests who return to Rockport just to be at Seacrest, and by many others who wrote about a B&B that "deserves top rating."

The part-Georgian, part-Federal house, built in 1911, was, for many years the summer home of Arthur Park of Boston's Durgin-Park restaurant family. Since becoming an inn in the early 1940s, it has gained a wing and a large second-story deck with a magnificent view of the ocean. In 1973, the two current hosts took it over. Dwight, an ordained Congregational minister, was on the faculty of three area colleges and was looking for an alternative career. Leighton's family home is three doors away, and he was planning for early retirement from his executive position at NBC. (After 27 years' association, he did retire in 1985.)

Furnishings are a mixture of contemporary and antique, with many paintings (some are on consignment) acknowledging Rockport's role as a leading art colony. Leather chairs and dark walls accented with white trim are the fashion here.

Leighton and Dwight host in an English style intended as "concierge-type guest assistance." Hence the attention to turned-down beds, tea at four, shined gentlemen's shoes (when left outside door at night), and peace and quiet in a beautiful setting.

**In residence:** A seven year old black Lab mixture named Tansy "who is friendly and quiet and has been known to greet guests with a paw-shake."
**Restrictions:** Children should be at least 16. No guests' pets. No smoking in the breakfast room. Maximum of two people per room.

**Foreign language spoken:** Some French.
**Bed and bath:** Eight rooms, all carpeted. Six rooms with private bath and a two-room suite with shared bath. Two rooms on the first floor, all others on the second. Queen-sized beds or twins that can convert to a king.
**Breakfast:** 7:30-9:30. Fresh fruit cup, fresh orange juice and other juices, spiced Irish oatmeal with chopped dates, dry cereals, bacon and eggs, toast and sometimes muffins, coffee, English tea, chocolate, and a different specialty each day—peach or blueberry or apple pancakes, French toast, corn fritters, banana buckwheat cakes. All prepared and served "by Lillian Baker, a local lady who has been with us for all 15 years." A leisurely meal served in dining room overlooking gardens at tables set with fine china and linens.
**Plus:** Tea at 4 p.m. Library and huge living room well stocked with books and magazines including English publications. Fans in bedrooms. Rain hats. Mints on pillow with quote from Shakespeare. Deck and gardens. Hammock. Complimentary newspapers Monday-Saturday. Beach towels. Tour of the house. Will meet train. Bicycles ($3.50 for half-day). Suggestions for museums, galleries, and an internationally recognized magic show too.
**Rates:** April 1-November 30 $60-$80 for two. $4 less for singles. Less off-season.

## Christian Hospitality Host #100

Swampscott, MA
**Location:** Residential area in a seacoast town ten miles north of Boston. Views of ocean and Boston skyline. Bus to Boston stops near the front door. Five-minute walk to 25 minute train ride to Boston. Half-mile to Lynn Woods.
**Reservations:** Available year round through Christian Hospitality Bed & Breakfast of New England, page 287. Advance reservations required.

The weathered-shingled early-1900s house has been restored by the hosts, an artist who "dabbles in all media" and a teacher. They have added stenciling, stained glass, and a wood stove, with a country decor using light and warm colors, many quilts and paintings.

**Swampscott**

"We feel fortunate to live in an ideal location where you can walk the beach or go birdwatching early in the morning. We're near fine restaurants and shopping. Sharing is part of B&B. We share our expertise in remodeling and redecorating. We share the feeling of home with a Christian atmosphere."

**Restrictions:** Children should be at least six. No guests' pets. No smoking.
**Bed and bath:** Four second floor rooms share two baths. One room, air-conditioned, has a queen sized bed. Two rooms, each with double bed and ocean views. One room with single bed.
**Breakfast:** 8-10. (Coffee is ready at 7.) Muffins, coffee, juice, fresh fruit and cereal. In the country kitchen, on front porch overlooking the ocean or in the living room.
**Plus:** TV, ceiling fans, and refrigerator in each room. Living room. Porch swing. Gas grill in yard.
**Rates:** $35 single, $45 double. $6 cot.

*Can't find the community you are going to? Check with a reservation service described at the beginning of this chapter. Through the service, you may be placed (matched) with a welcoming B&B that is near your destination.*

## KEY

Recipes shared, often for house specialties.

Inquiries welcomed about restoration and/or decorating. Symbol indicates that host is willing to share experiences with guests. Tips range from a before-and-after album to rebuilding advice, from furniture refinishing to curtain making. Expertise of hosts ranges from learn-by-doing to professional.

How-To B&B workshop, seminar or apprentice program offered.

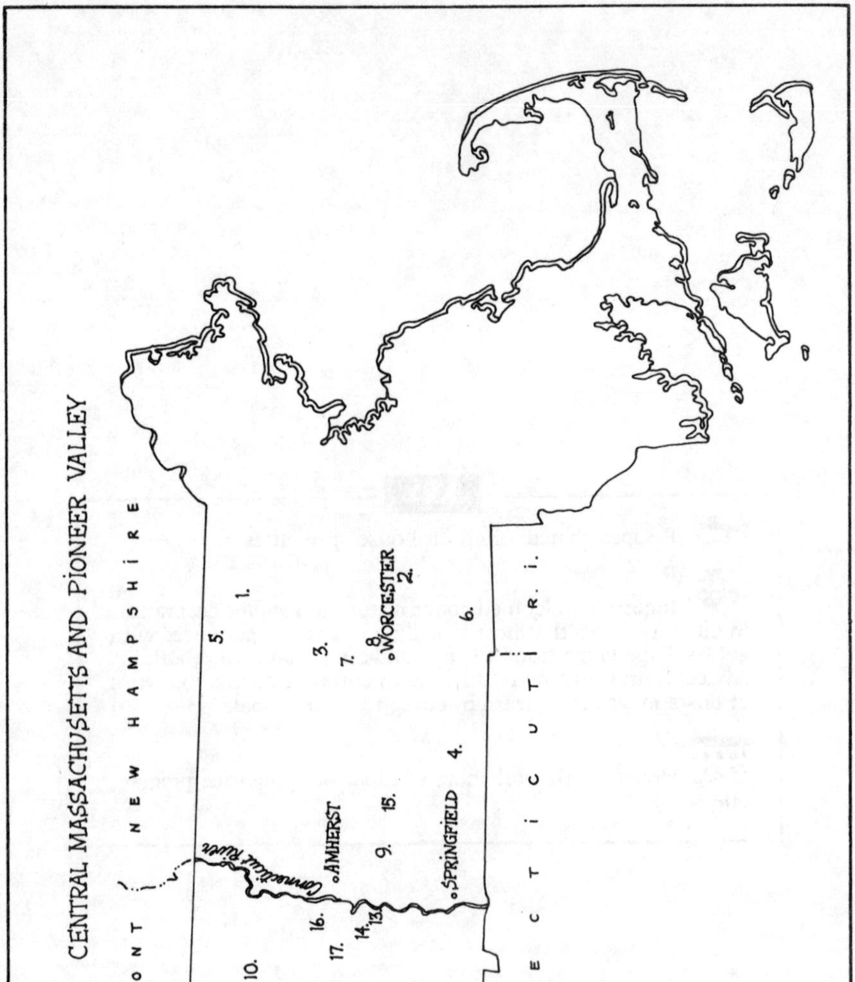


*The numbers on this map indicate the locations of B&Bs described in detail in this chapter.*

# CENTRAL MASSACHUSETTS AND PIONEER VALLEY

# Central Massachusetts Reservation Services

## Folkstone Bed & Breakfast

P.O. Box 931, Station A, Boylston, MA 01505-0931
**Phone:** 617/869-2687. Monday through Friday, 8-1. Closed March 15-31 and December 20-January 4.
**Listings:** 13. Most hosts are within a 15-minute drive to Worcester. Auburn, Ashburnham, Grafton, Holden, Hopkinton, Paxton, Southborough, Sterling, Webster, Westborough, and West Boylston. One is a small inn; the rest, hosted private residences. Directory ($1) includes descriptions and rates.

Margot French, a B&B hostess for many years, saw the need for an agency that would focus on a cultural and recreational area that is thriving. Because her listings are relatively few, she offers a highly personalized (and dedicated) service for both hosts and guests.

**Reservations:** Most hosts appreciate at least 24 hours' notice. Some long-term housing available; host on premises.
**Plus:** Walking and/or motor tours of the area. Limousine service can also be arranged. Brochures of local attractions.
**Rates:** $30-$65 single or double. Some family or monthly rates available. $3 surcharge for a stay of one night. Cost of first night's lodging is required as a deposit. Deposits (less $7 service fee) are refundable if cancellation is made 48 hours in advance. Half the deposit is refunded if cancellation is made 24 hours in advance.

# Central Massachusetts B&Bs

## Greenview

P.O. Box 422, Groton, MA 01450
**Phone:** 617/448-5861
**Location:** Just off Route 119 amidst country views in a town noted for its architecture, schools, and picture-book New England setting. About an hour's drive northwest from Boston.
**Hosts:** Ruth and Norm Johnson
**Open:** April 15-December 15. Reservations required.

"Fifteen years in this house, thirty years in this town, four years doing B&B, and many memorable guests including the 1984 gold medal Olympic equestrian team!"

The hosts, parents of four grown children, experienced B&B in England, Scotland, and Wales. Then they tried it in Vermont before deciding that it was the thing for them to do in their own home.

They have been in the restaurant business, and for quite a while Norm has been a general contractor/builder. Their beautifully landscaped contemporary Cape is close to the Groton School and Lawrence Academy, and within 30 minutes of two national historic parks, Minute Man (in Lexington and Concord) and Lowell.

The feeling of congeniality here is mutual. One guest, an 85-year-old world traveler, commented, "Your home is a castle of perfect comfort."

**In residence:** Izzy, a male tricolored cat "who adopted us four years ago. He usually greets guests at breakfast."
**Restrictions:** Children should be at least 12. No guests' pets.
**Bed and bath:** Three rooms. One with twin beds and one with a double bed share a bath upstairs. A small room downstairs has a single bed suitable for a child.
**Breakfast:** 8. Orange or tomato juice, cold cereal, cheese omelets, English muffins, milk, coffee or tea. Served in the greenhouse area of the dining room or on the porch overlooking the pool.

**Plus:** Late-afternoon or evening beverage (5-6 is usually hospitality hour). Air conditioning throughout the house. In-ground swimming pool during summer. Possibility of dinner occasionally. ("I enjoy cooking.")
**Rates:** $25 single, $40 double.

## Folkstone Bed & Breakfast Host #748

Hopkinton, MA
**Location:** At the starting line of the famous Boston Marathon. Less than two miles from Route I-495, less than five miles from I-90.
**Reservations:** Available year round through Folkstone Bed & Breakfast, page 336.

"In season, the heated lit pool is a welcome sight. Just about all our guests take a swim as soon as they arrive. We're not far from state parks and lakes, and in the winter, there's good cross-country skiing here, but our central location seems to attract guests who day trip. We are within a half hour to Boston, Worcester, Old Sturbridge Village. Some guests explore parts of Cape Cod. We really enjoy sharing our lovely home."

Inspired by their own good experiences at B&Bs, a nurse practitioner and a consultant pharmacist, both lifetime residents of the area, began hosting here in 1985. Their home was built for Judge Riley during the "Gatsby" era, with entertaining in mind. It is light and airy and comfortable with antiques, traditional furnishings, and wonderful original oak woodwork throughout.

**In residence:** Two grown children, college students. A friendly Labrador retriever will welcome guests but is restricted from the living areas of the house.
**Restrictions:** No guests' pets. Smoking in limited areas. Maximum of three people in a room.
**Bed and bath:** Two large second-floor rooms, each with a double bed, share a full bath. Cot and crib available.
**Breakfast:** Hours arranged. Full breakfast, possibly with Finnish pancakes, on weekends; continental on weekdays. Hot and cold cereals and fresh fruits (seasonal grown here) always available. Rhubarb bread and fresh berries are specialties. In dining room with antique furnishings, heirloom silver service, and flowers.

**Plus:** Bedroom ceiling fans. Beverages and snacks. Stationary bike and rowing machine on glass-enclosed porch. Fireplaced living room. Grounds.
**Rates:** $45 single, $55 double. Cot or crib $10 extra. $3 surcharge for one-night stay.

## Folkstone Bed & Breakfast Host #564

Sterling, MA
**Location:** At an apple orchard, on top of hill. Two miles south of Routes 2 and I-190. Seven miles to Wachusett ski area (snowmaking). Ten minutes west of Worcester; 20 minutes to winery tours.
**Reservations:** Available year round except in July through Folkstone Bed & Breakfast, page 336.

There's more than one apple for the teacher—and guests—here at this unusual B&B. The site with acres of spring blossoms becomes a pretty busy place in fall with a "pick your own pumpkins, dig your own mums and eat an apple" arrangement for the public. Glorious country at its best.

Both hosts were employed in Europe when they met in 1960. They returned to what had been the host's family homestead since 1926, brought up their children here, and in 1985, rebuilt the 1720 home with its ell, old Indian shutters, and hand-blown glass in the common room. The original front door is in the kitchen. There are old chestnut beams, some wide pine floors, barn board for walls in one bath, a new solarium and many collectibles.

**In residence:** Two college-age children on school vacations. Three pets, Gingle Bells, a 17-year-old black poodle; Spike, a tan tabby with thumbs; Bridgette, a large Belgian sheepdog.
**Restrictions:** Parents must be responsible for the care and behavior of their children. No smoking. Alcoholic beverages not encouraged.
**Bed and bath:** Two second-floor rooms and private baths. One room with double bed, bath with shower. The other, formerly the town's ballroom (in the 1800s), has a double bed and a trundle; private bath with tub only. Cot and playpen available.
**Breakfast:** 7-9. An English breakfast with southern country food. Homemade biscuits, fried apples, whipped butter, omelets, porridge and seasonal fruit, coffee, tea, apple bars, homemade jellies.

Served in tea room or in solarium, which overlooks the lawns and selling sheds. Leisurely on weekends; quicker during the week.
**Plus:** Late-afternoon tea and goodies. Tour of house and working farm. Bedroom ceiling fans. Common room. Library. Lawns.
**Rates:** $50 double occupancy. Third person in room, $10. $3 surcharge for one-night stay.

## Commonwealth Inn

11 Summit Avenue, Sturbridge, MA 01518
Mailing address: P.O. Box 251, Fiskdale, MA 01518
**Phone:** 617/347-7603
**Location:** Residential neighborhood one mile west of Old Sturbridge Village. On a knoll near Quinabaug River and the base of Stallion Hill.
**Host:** Kevin MacConnell
**Open:** Year round. Reservations recommended.

"I am a real estate broker who fell in love, at age 24, with a Queen Anne Victorian house and bought it! . . . There's an easygoing and relaxed atmosphere here. We have some antiques, Oriental rugs, chandeliers, a real country feeling. A lady friend, Cheryl Farraher, is responsible for the 'Victorian' decor and unique room decor. A piano (I don't play but some guests enjoy it) is in the parlor and we have just added a Victrola to the dining room. I bring enthusiasm to a new adventure, and this B&B continues to be just that. I am active with local politics, and am on the board of directors at the community arts center. Sailing, scuba diving and rafting are among my favorite sports."

Since his big purchase four years ago, Kevin has become the handyman he never thought he was. He has learned by doing, by reading, and by accepting advice (sometimes from guests). He is innkeeper during the warm months. In the winter he has more time for antiquing, more restoration, and his real estate business.

The house built for a single family in 1880 became an inn during the Prohibition era, then a rooming house until 1983.

**In residence:** Bear, a friendly all-black Persian cat.
**Restrictions:** Sorry, no pets. There are kennels nearby.

**Bed and bath:** Five second-floor carpeted rooms. The one with private bath has a double bed. Two rooms each with a double bed share one bath. One room with two double beds and another with queen-sized bed (and wood stove) share a bath. Cot available.
**Breakfast:** Cooked breakfast 8-9; continental anytime. Eggs, bacon, muffins, fresh fruit, cold cereals, and beverages. Served at small tables in dining room. Option of breakfast in bed for birthdays, honeymoons, anniversaries.
**Plus:** Beverages. Color TV in each guest room. Three rooms with window fans; air conditioners in two. Fireplaces. Swing on wraparound porch. Complimentary ice and use of small refrigerators. Champagne for special occasions. Walking distance to fishing, swimming, antiquing, restaurants, and museums. Directions to a great place for picnics, hikes, and exploring caves.
**Rates:** Double occupancy. $35-$45 with shared bath, $55 private bath. $5 extra person in room. $5 cot. Winter packages include free admission to Sturbridge Village or free cross-country ski tickets.

## Wood Farm

40 Worcester Road, Townsend, MA 01469
**Phone:** 617/597-5019
**Location:** On a main road, on a corner 15-acre lot on the bank of the Squannacock River. A half-mile from the town center. Near Harvard Shaker Village, 15 miles from summer theaters, 20 miles from Mount Monadnock in New Hampshire, 10 from Mount Watatic in Ashby. Within a half hour's drive of Nashoba Valley and Mount Wachusett ski areas in Massachusetts and Crotched Mountain in New Hampshire.
**Hosts:** Debra Jones and James Mayrand
**Open:** Year round. Reservations required.

Although the 50 sheep may steal the show here, the residents of this historic home are kind of fun too. Debra and Jim, both electrical engineers and natives of the area, bought the center-chimney Cape-with-an-ell in 1983 with the idea of hosting. They were married by the hearth of what had been the Wood family home until 1964. This was the first house in town, built around 1716.

Extensive restoration efforts have included the refinishing of all those wide-board pine floors. Debra has made curtains and stenciled canvas rugs. In her weaving room she uses wool from her own sheep. Those sheep! "Each one has its own name and personality. Kids are welcome to hold them." Lambing season is April and May. Shearing takes place on Memorial Day weekend with the assistance of Debra's uncle, who lives nearby.

Wood Farm has four fireplaces, two wood stoves, and a relaxing atmosphere. The hosts are active bicycle racers, cross-country skiers, and runners. Craft and antique centers are close by.

**In residence:** Hawkins, "a stately Lab" always bedecked in a red bandanna, and Beannie a cute, cuddly, and confused cockapoo.
**Restrictions:** Children are welcome if supervised by parents. No guests' pets. No smoking.
**Foreign languages spoken:** A little French and Spanish.
**Bed and bath:** Four second-floor rooms in a guest ell with guest sitting room. One has queen-sized bed. Two have doubles. Another has a double and two twin beds. Two shared guest baths.
**Breakfast:** 6-8 weekdays, 7-9 weekends. Could be apple/walnut quiche, smoked slab bacon and fresh bread, fresh fruit and eggs Benedict or an herb souffle, sausage and croissant. Served in keeping room by eight-foot open hearth, or in the dining room or, in summer, on the patio beside the river.
**Plus:** A welcoming beverage. Use of a guest living room or join the hosts in theirs. Bedroom fans. Use of library, weight-training room (for adults). Pond for swimming and skating. Tour of house and 250-year-old barn. Theme weekends with dinner in 1800s style. Spring fast-water canoeing. (Bring your own canoe.)
**Rates:** $25 single, $35 double. $10 extra twin bed.

---

## Capron House

2 Capron Street, Uxbridge, MA 01569
**Phone:** 617/278-2214
**Location:** In historic district, one-quarter mile east of town center, bordered by the Mumford River. One quarter mile from Blackstone Valley Heritage Park. Forty minutes east of Sturbridge, half hour to Worcester and Providence. Near factory outlets.
**Hosts:** Ken and Mary Taft
**Open:** Year round. Reservations required.

> From Buffalo, New York: "A wonderful experience. . . . The rooms are a visual delight with lace curtains, quilts, plump pillows, carved furniture and inviting upholstered chairs. . . . In the early evening we enjoyed drinks on the side porch with the Tafts while our children explored the barn and the grounds. . . . The varied breakfasts were inviting, served with regard to eye appeal as well as taste."

It all started four years ago when an area inn called the Tafts, 20-year residents and parents of seven grown children, to see if they would take overflow guests. Since then, the kids were cajoled into cleaning out the closets and Mary's decorating business was, for a time, focused on redoing some of her own rooms, combining old—wicker furniture and an antique bedspread, for instance—with new, such as balloon curtains.

Although most guests come for the yarn business (you can take tours of the factory) in Uxbridge or the universities and recreation possibilities in the area, Ken and Mary frequently answer many questions about their house, which was built with ornate gaslit ceiling fixtures for Charles Capron, a mill owner who had his own gas manufacturing room. He is also the one who introduced electricity and the telephone to Uxbridge. When the Tafts came here 20 years ago, they used chestnut doors and drawers from the butler's pantry to create a light contemporary kitchen and family space. The house is on the National Register of Historic Places and is described as Uxbridge's finest example of Victorian Gothic residential architecture.

**Restrictions:** No guests' pets. Smoking allowed in common room on first floor.
**Bed and bath:** Four rooms, three with private baths. Two rooms with two twin beds in each. One with queen-sized four-poster. One with double-sized antique sleigh bed and marble sink. Futon available. Mary's antique pillow cases used in each room.
**Breakfast:** 7-9:30, on porch or in one of two dining rooms. Cranberry pancakes, apple crepes with creme fraiche, bismarcks with fruit and creme fraiche. Hosts often join you for coffee.
**Plus:** Late-afternoon/evening wine. Porches with gliders, rockers, and wicker chairs. Tour of the house. Window or ceiling fans in bedrooms. Terrace adjacent to barn. Croquet and ping-pong.
**Rates:** $40 single, $55-$60 double. Discount for families and extended stays.

From Pennsylvania: "Whether it was friendly conversation, restaurant advice, reservations for racquetball, or a game of bridge, Mary and Ken were delightful and knowledgeable. . . . Great hosts!"

## The Rose Cottage

24 Worcester Street, Route 12, West Boylston, MA 01583
**Phone:** 617/835-4034
**Location:** Ten minutes from Worcester, 45 minutes west of Boston in a country setting at the junction of Routes 12 and 140. Across from Wachusett Reservoir. Fifteen minutes to Mount Wachusett ski area (snowmaking). Near a famous chili-dog stand.
**Hosts:** Michael and Loretta Kittredge
**Open:** Year round. Reservations required.

"We have 74 diaries from the second owner who was also the town clerk. As fifth owners of the house, we are the second ones to use the barn as an antique shop. . . . I was born and raised in West Boylston and Mike, an engineer, moved here when we married 30 years ago. We had stayed in B&Bs, and when this house was for sale in 1984, everything just came together."

It's one of those classic Gothic revival cottages, painted yellow, with a gabled roof, lots of gingerbread and finials, tall windows, and black shutters. You approach it via a horseshoe driveway bordered with lawns and mature landscaping. Inside, the house built in 1850 has white marble fireplaces, gaslight (electrified) hanging lamps, and even pale lavender glass doorknobs. Victorian furnishings—"the comfortable kind"—are on the first floor. Rag and braided rugs are part of the country theme on the second. One of the bedrooms has a stained-glass window from a church and art deco furnishings.

Because the Kittredges found that their personalized style has such great appeal for business people, they converted the former music room at the end of the first floor into a perfect room for small meetings. More than one guest has stayed here specifically to find out "how it's done" before opening their own B&B.

**Restrictions:** Children should be in their teens. No guests' pets. No smoking in the bedrooms.

**Bed and bath:** Five rooms, all furnished with antiques. The one with private bath is on first floor, has iron and brass double bed. Three doubles and one room with twin beds on the second floor with two shared baths.
**Breakfast:** At guests' convenience—in time for Loretta to open the antique barn at 11. Anything from waffles with maple syrup to a souffle to scrambled ham and eggs to sausage and Italian toast. Juices, coffee, teas, seasonal fruit. Served in dining room.
**Plus:** Late-afternoon/evening beverages. Candy. Fresh flowers. Thick towels. Extra pillows. Toiletries you may have forgotten. Tour of the house. Three porches with benches and chairs. Large yard.
**Rates:** $65 for first-floor room with private bath. $60 per room, shared baths.

## Heywood House

207 West Main Street, Westborough, MA 01581
**Phone:** 617/366-2161 or 366-7440
**Location:** Minutes from I-90 and Routes 495, 20, and 9, all near high-technology headquarters. On a curve of what is now a main suburban road, 1½ miles from the center of town. Three miles from the Willard House and Clock Museum, 20 minutes to Worcester, 30 minutes west to Sturbridge Village and east to the Wayside Inn.
**Hosts:** Doug and Mary Heywood
**Open:** Year round. Reservations required. Two-night minimum stay during July and August weekends.

"During the spring and summer the birds sing in symphony. If you don't like this kind of music, avoid these seasons. Try our fall instead; foliage at its best without even driving."

Doug, a travel consultant, admits to being a frustrated innkeeper. His family came to town in the mid-1800s and settled in this center-hall colonial farmhouse that had been built around 1729. Gnarled trees are vestiges of the orchard that once was. Inside the house there are some exposed beams and rounded corner walls.

When Mary, a Wisconsin native and occupational therapist, and Doug moved into the homestead as newlyweds a couple of years ago, it was with the specific intention of having a B&B. They redid the whole house themselves, "making it fresh and crisp, but keeping the old flavor." Each guest room is decorated in a different color scheme. In the upstairs hall is the heirloom rocking horse enjoyed by three generations.

Heywood House has been discovered by many travelers, including honeymooners, and has been booked for family reunions and wedding parties. My husband and I are among the cyclists who have pedaled the marvelous area byways bordered with historic homes.

**In residence:** Helcha, their golden retriever, "looks forward to meeting all who wish her greeting."
**Restrictions:** Children should be at least ten. Smoking only in the first-floor sitting room.
**Bed and bath:** Four second-floor carpeted rooms. A private full bath for one double-bedded room; a private bath with shower for another with double bed. A room with twin beds and a room with a double bed share one bath.
**Breakfast:** 7-8:30 weekdays, 8-9:30 weekends and holidays, exceptions arranged. Juices, homemade muffins and breads, cereals, and beverage served in dining room overlooking the back yard and woods.
**Plus:** A welcoming beverage. Fireplaced living room with piano and a good supply of books, magazines, games, and puzzles. Badminton, croquet, horseshoes. Bring your own grille for cookouts. "We specialize in fiery sunsets." Trails for walks and cross-country skiing.
**Rates:** $25 single with shared bath, $30 with private bath. $35 double with shared bath, $40 with private bath. Cots $10 extra. Weekly rates available.

## Pioneer Valley Reservation Services

## Berkshire Bed & Breakfast Homes

This service represents 16 hosts who live in Greater Springfield, Amherst, Ashfield, Belchertown, Buckland, Northampton, South Hadley, West Cummington, Westhampton, Whately, Williamsburg, and Worthington. Please see page 364.

## Greater Springfield Bed and Breakfast

25 Bellevue Avenue, Springfield, MA 01108
**Phone:** 413/739-7400. Monday through Friday 2-6; answering machine at other times.
**Listings:** 10 hosted private residences all in the Springfield area. Up to 12 people in a group can be accommodated in one neighborhood. Six homes are in the historic district (1896-1915). Several are on public bus line to downtown.

Linda McCarthy's extensive travels have shown her the importance of the role of B&B hosts "in making a trip memorable, not just remembered."

**Reservations:** Two days' advance notice required.
**Rates:** \$32-\$38 single, \$42-\$48 double. Family and weekly rates available. \$10 surcharge for one-night stay. Deposit equal to half the total stay required. Cancellations received at least two weeks before expected stay receive refund minus \$10 service charge; within two weeks, refund made only if accommodation can be rebooked for that date. Exception: No deposits returned during peak periods such as the ACC Crafts Fair or the Democratic Convention.

## Pineapple Hospitality

This service has hosts in Bernardston and Wilbraham. Please see page 214.

# Pioneer Valley B&Bs

## MacFadyen's

P.O. Box 301, 38 Park Street, Belchertown, MA 01007
**Phone:** 413/323-7694
**Location:** Faces a small-town New England common. Bordered by an old graveyard. Twenty minutes to the University of Massachusetts, Amherst, Hampshire, Smith and Mount Holyoke Colleges. Minutes to Quabbin Reservoir, Old Deerfield, Mount Tom ski area. Twenty-five miles to Old Sturbridge Village.
**Hosts:** Ann and Don MacFadyen
**Open:** Year round. Reservations required.

Not only have the MacFadyens restored the entire house, but, knowing it was built in 1839, they have researched its history to the point of defining the original boundaries. When they bought the Victorian 15 years ago, its most recent use was as a parsonage. The porch may have been added about the turn of the century. Octogenarian Aubrey LaPolice has told them that he used to groom horses in a large barn (razed in the sixties) at the rear of the property.

Now it is "comfortable and gracious, but not pretentious." The decor is eclectic and clutterless. Both hosts love to cook and have designed and built an interesting island kitchen with open shelves. Ann works at a craft gallery and Don works in sales.

**In residence:** Sophie, a five-year-old bearded collie, "a special member of the family."
**Restrictions:** Children should be at least ten. No guests' pets. Smoking restricted to common rooms.
**Bed and bath:** Three rooms. One private half-bath for first-floor room with double bed. Second floor has study/bedroom with double sleep sofa and a single room. One remodeled bath with clawfoot tub shared by guests and hosts.
**Breakfast:** Usually 8-9. Continental breakfast (croissants or homemade muffins) in dining room with "a definite colonial flavor."
**Plus:** Late-afternoon or evening beverages. Tour of house. Thick towels. Fresh garden flowers. Bedroom window fans.
**Rates:** $30 single, $35 double.

## Amarcord/1797 House

Box 23, Charlemont Road, Buckland, MA 01338
**Phone:** 413/625-2697 days; 625-2975 evenings and weekends.
**Location:** Rural. West of Greenfield, 5 miles from nearest village; 17 miles from historic Deerfield. About 30 minutes' drive to University of Massachusetts, Smith College, Williams College, Deerfield Academy, Stoneleigh-Burham, Eaglebrook, Amherst. Minutes to Bridge of Flowers at Shelburne Falls; Berkshire East and Cummington Farms ski areas.
**Host:** Janet Turley
**Open:** Year round except November and December. Reservations usually required. Two-night minimum stay preferred in May, August, October.

"Each guest is so different and wonderful," Janet says. "Many come for academic related reasons, but return because they love the area. And we're becoming known as a romantic getaway spot!"

Janet, a kindergarten teacher, comes home from school to her large two-story 1797 colonial. Mary Lyon, the founder of Mount Holyoke College, used the house for the Winter School for Young Ladies in 1829-1830. Today the neighborhood is one of 18th- and early-19th-century homes together with a traditional white New England church, and some properties with horses and sheep.

Since Janet moved (with her teenagers) into the house seven years ago, she has designed two new baths and an addition. Earlier, she had experience redoing an abandoned seven-bedroom house that was without any bathroom, heat, electricity, or kitchen. As a result of all she has learned, she now consults within a 150-mile radius for remodeling and decorating—and B&B.

In her home there's a feeling that just makes it all come together. As some guests say, she makes you feel "warm, welcome and very full."

**In residence:** Janet's mother, who has her own apartment in the house, is a big hit with guests. (So are her handstitched items.)
**Restrictions:** No pets or children. Smoking in designated areas.
**Bed and bath:** Two second-floor rooms, each with private full bath. One room has a brass double bed, the other has a ¾ bed and a twin-sized bed. Down quilts on all beds.
**Breakfast:** Served in the 18th-century dining room with fireplace or on large screened porch. Janet usually joins guests for coffee after their breakfast of juice, fresh fruit, beverage and scrambled eggs,

sausage, potatoes and biscuits or French toast with local syrup and bacon.

**Plus:** Beverages. Tour of house. Sometimes a guided tour of area. Lots of suggestions (including auctions). Bedroom window fans. Big screened porch with wicker furniture, plants, overlooking old cemetery and abandoned orchard.

**Rates:** $45 single, $55 double.

## Forest Way Farm

Route 8A, Charlemont, MA 01339

**Phone:** 413/337-8321

**Location:** Where the Texas flag is flying, north of the Mohawk Trail. Five miles north of Route 2 in Charlemont, 13 miles from Stump Sprout cross-country ski center, 6 from Berkshire East downhill.

**Hosts:** Jimmie and Paul Snyder

**Open:** Year round. Reservations requested.

"When I saw a picture of this place, I just knew it was where we ought to be. Then when I first came in, I knew it was it. How unusual to have an old house that's light and airy! Everyone loves the dining room with its huge fireplace, wide floor boards and the chair rail. The living room was once a woodshed and it has 18-inch-thick walls, barn beams and a fireplace. This town has all sorts of good things and good people. Such spirit here! We always had a house full of people in Dallas, so it was natural to think about doing B&B when we came in 1985."

Year-round and seasonal residents book stays for their friends and relatives here. Some guests come specifically for one of the town's well-known craftspeople, a glassblower whose work is on display in the Smithsonian.

Paul, now retired, has been an engineer in Pennsylvania and Texas, and for a time had a tool and die shop in New Jersey. Ten years ago he married his cousin's widow, Jimmie, a Texan "who has a special talent for enjoying people and cooking Southern dishes."

**In residence:** Daughter Yolanda Campbell and grandson Jason Campbell, age 13. Tiffany, the cat, and Appolo, the dog. Jimmie and Paul smoke.

**Restrictions:** No guests' pets. Smoking on the first floor only.

**Bed and bath:** Five rooms, two shared baths. One room with king-sized bed, one with queen, two with double beds, and one with twins.
**Breakfast:** 7-11. Buffet served in the dining room. Juices, endless coffee, and coffee cakes, grits, marvelous scrambled eggs with "hell on the red" piquante sauce. Portuguese and other home-baked breads, homemade conserves and jams from rhubarb and berries from the "fields out back."
**Plus:** Above-ground pool. Lawn games. Trails through woods on property. Laundry facilities.
**Rates:** $35 single, $40 double. $5 additional person in room.

## Cumworth Farm

Rt. 112, Box 110, Cummington, MA 01026
**Phone:** 413/634-5529
**Location:** On a scenic rural road with mountain views; 3.4 miles from town center. Hiking trails nearby. Forty-five minutes to Tanglewood or Williamstown. Near Hickory Hill and Cummington Farm for cross-country skiing and Berkshire Snow Basin (downhill).
**Hosts:** Ed and Mary McColgan
**Open:** Year round. Reservations preferred.

As a youngster Ed worked on potato, dairy, and tobacco farms. He grew up to have a series of careers—as college history professor, director of the Bicentennial celebration for the state of Massachusetts, state legislator, and executive with the Department of Public Health. Ed and Mary, parents of seven grown children, have both been Northampton city councilors. Seven years ago they bought this 200-year-old farmhouse and acquired a workhorse, chickens, pigs, ducks, and a big vegetable garden plot. Mary still works as a congregate housing coordinator, but as a full-time farmer Ed always has a new thing going. The sugarhouse has produced as much as 800 gallons, after using 22 cords of wood to boil the sap collected from 4,000 taps. The wool from the sheep is woven into blankets sold at farmers' markets. The new barn roof went on in one weekend, thanks to friends and a big barbecue.

Visiting parents of summer campers, Tanglewood concertgoers, hikers, balloonfest people, and skiers usually come with a planned day; but there are many spontaneous possibilities for B&B guests here. As Ed says, "Some people choose to be by themselves.

Others join in herding the sheep in the morning. Some parents have returned with their children to give the kids an opportunity to sleep in a real barn. In the spring they watch the baby lambs and the activity in the sugarhouse. One couple helped sort and grade carrots and ended up buying ducks to bring home!"

**In residence:** Two border collies, Nell and Jill. Various barn cats and over 100 sheep.
**Restrictions:** Pets are not allowed in the house. No smoking in bedrooms.
**Bed and bath:** Five rooms. First-floor room has two twin beds and a full bath. Four second-floor rooms include two with double beds that share a bath with tub. One room with two twin beds and one with a double bed share a full bath with hosts. Cot available.
**Breakfast:** Continental breakfast served around the claw-footed oval oak table in the beamed kitchen with restaurant stove and dozens of hanging baskets. $2 charge for a full breakfast.
**Plus:** Late-afternoon or evening beverage. Living room with antique stove in fireplace. Patio with lounge chairs. Tour of the sugarhouse in March and early April.
**Rates:** $30 single, $35 double. $10 one-time charge for a cot.

## The Beeches

Hampton Terrace, Northampton, MA 01060
**Phone:** 413/586-9288
**Location:** Overlooking the valley and hills. On 16 acres one-quarter mile from downtown Northampton and Smith College.
**Hosts:** Daisy Mathias and Bob Nelson
**Open:** Year round. Two-night minimum stay for graduation times and foliage season. Reservations required.

Not only did the president sleep here, this was his home!

Daisy and Bob were living in Virginia when they decided, in 1983, to move to New England—to a place that would be big enough for B&B guests. What they located was one of Calvin Coolidge's homes, a secluded estate that he retired to after the presidency. It is a gracious 16-room shingled Tudor with a wonderful library, furnished with antiques from both hosts' families. B&B hospitality is offered in elegant space that allows for privacy. Families, too, are welcome.

Bob, originally from Kansas, is involved in real estate and owns a gallery and craft shop. Daisy lived in the Boston area for ten years and is a speech and language pathologist. Anne, their daughter, was born in Northampton.

**In residence:** Anne, age three. Sugar Plum, their friendly 14-year-old cat.
**Restrictions:** No guests' pets. No smoking, please.
**Bed and bath:** Three second-floor rooms. Calvin Coolidge's former room has double bed, private bath, working fireplace, air conditioning, and screened porch. A room with double bed, working fireplace, and screened porch shares a bath with room that has two twin beds. Portacrib available.
**Breakfast:** Freshly squeezed orange juice, fresh fruits, and a specialty such as blueberry muffins, apple crepes, herb omelets, eggs Benedict, waffles with maple syrup from Daisy's sister's farm in Vermont. Served in dining room, on terrace, or on porch.
**Plus:** Fireplace in living room and another in full library. Sun porch.
**Rates:** $60 private bath, $50 shared bath. No charge for portacrib. Ten percent less for stay of four nights or more.

Guests wrote: "The warm gracious hosts, outstanding accommodations, and stupendous house place The Beeches as one of our favorite places."

## The Knoll

230 North Main Street, Florence, MA 01060
**Phone:** 413/584-8164
**Location:** Set far back from the road on a knoll overlooking 17 acres of farmland and forest. Three miles from Smith College, 9 from Amherst, 15 from Mt. Holyoke, 12 from Deerfield. Five-minute walk to beautiful public park.
**Hosts:** Lee and Ed Lesko
**Open:** Year round. Reservations preferred.

We overlapped with the Lesko's first B&B guests. The other couple had come from Princeton to look for a house, and they had just succeeded. It was spring and the two-story high Michigan redbud blossoms peeking in our room were magnificent. A third grandchild was expected any day. For the evening activity, we had our choice of contra dancing or a Rudolph Serkin concert.

Time has brought a few changes. The fourth grandchild is now three years old. Ed is semiretired from his window and door sales. Many more B&B guests have discovered the Leskos, Ed a native of Northampton and Lee originally from Biloxi, Mississippi. Although most of their trips on their 40-foot ketch are on Long Island and Block Island Sounds, they once took a seven-month trip down the intercoastal waterway to Florida, across the Gulf of Mexico to Mississippi, back to Florida, and then to the Bahamas.

Their spacious 12-room English Tudor is furnished with many Oriental rugs. In the corner of their large living room is a striking (in every sense of the word) seven-foot-high grandfather's clock made in Germany around 1900. Traditional furnishings are in the guests' rooms. Housekeeping is impeccable.

**In residence:** One German shepherd.
**Restrictions:** Children should be at least 12. No guests' pets. "Absolutely no smoking!"
**Bed and bath:** Three second-floor bedrooms. One with twin beds, the others with double beds. These rooms share two baths (tubs only, no showers). One huge tub still has the fixtures installed when house was built in 1911. Cot available.
**Breakfast:** At guests' convenience, until 9. Lee will usually join you for coffee after you have had your cereal, fresh fruit, their homegrown raspberries, strawberries, fresh farm eggs any style, bacon, toast, muffins or coffee cake, homemade jam. Served in the kitchen or dining room.
**Plus:** Large screened porch. Tour of the house and grounds, if you'd like. Paths for jogging or walking. Walk to Look Park for its beautifully landscaped grounds, plenty of running and roaming space, playground, picnic area, tennis courts, and pool.
**Rates:** $30 single, $40 double.

*Can't find the community you are going to? Check with a reservation service described at the beginning of this chapter. Through the service, you may be placed (matched) with a welcoming B&B that is near your destination.*

## The Wildwood Inn

121 Church Street, Ware, MA 01082
**Phone:** 413/967-7798
**Location:** On a quiet street. Midway between Old Sturbridge Village and historic Deerfield. Half hour southeast of Amherst. Ten minutes from Quabbin Reservoir, "a magnificent cross between the English lake country and mini-fjords."
**Hosts:** Margaret and Geoffrey Lobenstine
**Open:** Daily May through October. Weekends and holidays November-April. Reservations recommended. Three-day minimum stay on holiday weekends. Closed Thanksgiving and Christmas time.

> From California: "The caring, the conversations, the combination of history, nature, and concern for the world—all centered in a classic New England setting."

A stay here has inspired some to write songs and poems. Some return for their weddings—and some have been known to name their children after the hosts.

All this is because the Lobenstines stumbled on Ware when they took a wrong turn during a New England trip nine years ago. The family's move from Berkeley, California (the twin daughters are now in college) fulfilled Margaret's dream of living in a big house with wraparound porch. Furnished with primitive antiques, the Victorian is set on two acres that lead back to the river through woods with old stone walls. Wildwood not only introduced B&B to the town fathers; Margaret designed—and still conducts—what may have been the first B&B apprentice program in the country. (No charge other than room costs. Six days. Hands on.)

Geoff is a social worker in Holyoke. Margaret has taught and worked in the post office; and she has long been involved in the peace movement as well as community, political, and women's issues.

**Restrictions:** Children should be at least six. No guests' pets allowed but there is a kennel in town. No smoking indoors.
**Bed and bath:** Five second-floor rooms. Of the three shared baths, one has only tub and shower. Three doubles with heirloom quilts. Twin-bedded room has a four-window bay. Queen-bedded room has four-poster bed and air conditioner.

**Breakfast** (none served on Monday or Friday): "One of the magic times of the inn." Continental with homemade bread (maybe popovers) and peach butter. "Country yummies" such as chipmunk pie or maple cheese squares $1 extra. Innkeeper sets time, usually around 9, to meet needs of the majority of guests.
**Plus:** Parlor with carpenter's chest full of games, wooden music box. Porch hammock and swing. Free loan of canoe. Swimming in brook-fed swim hole in lush setting. In winter, kerosene lamps, candles, and fireplace here; bald-eagle sighting at the reservoir.
**Rates:** Vary according to room, season, area events. $31-$49 double-bedded rooms, $39-$49 twin-bedded rooms, $46-$54 queen-bedded room. Credit cards only for holding last-minute reservations.

From Massachusetts: "Wildwood should be bottled! We did *so* much while we were there, but we left feeling rested and spoiled rotten."

## Sunnyside Farm

11 River Road, Whately, MA
Mailing address: Box 486, South Deerfield, MA 01373
**Phone:** 617-665-3113
**Location:** In a farming community, next door to Nourse Strawberry Farms. Five miles south of Deerfield, 15 minutes from Northampton and Amherst, near many colleges and private schools.
**Hosts:** Mary Lou and Dick Green
**Open:** Year round. Reservations required.

From New York City: "It's very peaceful, pretty and comfortable. The children loved the sense of freedom that they lack living in the city. The breakfasts are wonderful too, but our favorite thing about Sunnyside is the hospitality of Mary Lou and Dick Green."

From Illinois: "We had such a marvelous time, we've reserved space for next year's graduation weekend."

Mary Lou says, "This 14-room home was owned by my grandparents and has been handed down through the years. This is one of the reasons I want to stay here and hand it down to our children and grandchildren. I spent summers here as a child and have wonderful memories. . . . We have been living here since 1972 when we moved up from Northampton with our four children (now all grown). Although the house, part of a working farm until the 1950s, is basically the same as when my grandparents remodeled it in 1920, we have done much redecorating.

"My husband, a former comptroller at Amherst College, visits with guests in the evening when I am working as head nurse in the emergency department of Northampton's Cooley Dickinson Hospital. Breakfasts are a fun time for me. In season, guests not only wake up to the aroma from one of the largest strawberry (and raspberry) farms in the northeast, but some join me in picking before breakfast."

If you've never had grandparents who lived in a big yellow farmhouse with a red barn complete with big letters that spell out its name, here's the place. Bring your bicycle! The road is flat, very rural, very much old New England.

**In residence:** One dog, Shamus, according to a California guest, "a golden eyed long haired beauty. Look out though, one toss of his stick and you're hooked."
**Restrictions:** No guests' pets, please. Smoking on first floor only.
**Bed and bath:** Three rooms, two shared baths. Two large rooms with twin beds. One room with a double bed. One bath has shower only; one with shower and large old-fashioned tub. Cot available. Cross-ventilation in all rooms. Color-coordinated linens.
**Breakfast:** Sometime after 7. Seasonal fruits, homemade muffins and jams, eggs, bacon or sausage, or a wonderful cheese strata. Please indicate special diets in advance. Served in country kitchen or dining room.
**Plus:** Window fans, if ever necessary. Babysitting.
**Rates:** $30 single, $45-$50 double. $15 cot. Special family rates.

## Twin Maples

106 South Street, Williamsburg, MA 01096
**Phone:** 413/268-7925
**Location:** Two miles from village. Seven miles from Northampton. Nine miles from the I-91 interchange and 25 miles to Springfield. Near Berkshire Snow Basin in Cummington.
**Hosts:** Eleanor and Martin Hebert
**Open:** Year round.

What started out to be a sometime-maybe activity has almost become the headquarters—or at least a model—of B&B in the area. For many years, Eleanor was a librarian in town. Now she not only hosts but is very involved with the expanded regional B&B scene in the Hampshire Hills as well as the Berkshires.

When we stayed at Twin Maples, everything from the linens to the fresh violets in ribboned vase in the bedroom was color coordinated, or as subsequent visitors say, "just perfect." Martin, an engineer, shares the role of host. Since the Heberts arrived in 1962, they have restored the wonderful old farmhouse, now about 200 years old. There are exposed beams in the ceiling of the dining room; the kitchen has a large fireplace with Dutch oven; the antique and reproduction furniture is colonial in style.

**In residence:** One college-age daughter. A miniature sheltie, Toby.
**Restrictions:** No smoking and no guests' pets, please.
**Bed and bath:** Three rooms in a guest wing share a full updated bath. One large room with restored iron and brass double bed, nonworking fireplace, wicker furniture, view of fields and garden. Another large room with twin iron and brass beds, non-working fireplace, view of fields, stone walls, garden and, in the distance, Mount Sugarloaf. Third room has restored double brass bed, antique pine furnishings, mountain view. Cot and crib available.
**Breakfast:** 7:30-9 on weekdays, until 10 on weekends. Juice, melon balls in orange juice/fresh fruit in season; buttermilk pancakes (with or without blueberries), sausage, homemade sweet breads, coffee, tea, homemade maple syrup. Table set with flowers, linens, handcrafted pottery, in dining room or screened porch.
**Plus:** Flannel sheets and electric blankets in winter. Guests' sitting room with TV and games. Wood stove in huge country kitchen. Screened-in porch. Picnic table. Children's swing set. Bedroom fans.
**Rates:** $30 single, $40 double. $10 cot (child only) or crib. Ten percent discount for stays of ten days or more. Winter weekends (two-night minimum, double occupancy, two full breakfasts and Saturday dinner) $110.

From New York City: "Like the candy on the pillow . . . 'mint'!"

## Windfields Farm

Windsor Bush Road, Windsor
Mailing address: RR1, Box 170, Cummington, MA 01026
**Phone:** 413/684-3786
**Location:** On a dirt road two miles uphill from the village of West Cummington off Route 9. Twenty miles west to Pittsfield, 25 miles east to Northampton.
**Hosts:** Carolyn and Arnold Westwood
**Open:** May through February. Reservations required. Minimum stay of two nights on some winter weekends.

Just thinking about this B&B makes me feel good all over. The interesting house is a haven, way up and away—with scenic surroundings—but in true B&B style, the hosts make the difference.

Arnold, recently retired from a split position as minister at two Unitarian Universalist churches, now edits the town (pop. 600) newsletter. With the help of his youngest (then college-age) son, he built most of the solar addition. Carolyn is responsible for the maple syrup, from the 350 taps to the sugarhouse and mail orders. Her organic garden has everything from asparagus to raspberries; the corn, carrots, and celery have been ribbon winners at regional fairs. Both Westwoods are concerned with ending the arms race and building community spirit.

Carolyn refers to their "joyous house." The active/passive solar addition rises from the foundation of the original (ca. 1815) cottage, retaining its pressed tin ceiling, paneled doors, and hand-hewn beams. It is of post-and-beam construction as is the connecting (ca. 1868) farmhouse, now reserved for guests, who have their own private entrance, and living and dining rooms. "It's like living in a sculpture. When we bought this place as a summer retreat in 1962, it was a mess. Our four children helped with some changes every summer. It became our year round residence in 1972. We live in the addition. B&B sort of evolved from the way we live. We thought it might be fun and it is."

**In residence:** Two dogs, Hui, an Irish setter/golden retriever born in Hawaii, and Pushamet, a mutt.
**Restrictions:** Children should be at least 12. No guests' pets. No smoking indoors. Winter guests should have snow tires!
**Bed and bath:** Two spacious corner bedrooms, "your castle as long as you're here." One with 1818 canopied double bed that belonged to Carolyn's great-great-great-grandmother. Queen-sized walnut bed

in other. Shared bath with club-foot tub, shower, and old-time barber's sink. Each room has a sitting area. Cot available.
**Breakfast:** "Announced to the strains of Mozart and Bach" at a prearranged time from 7:30 to 9. Homegrown organic produce, eggs, blueberries and raspberries in season. Pancakes, yogurt, maybe Irish oatmeal topped with granola, natural-grain homemade muffins or popovers, Windfields' low-sugar jams. Served in the guests' own dining room at an antique mahogany claw-footed table.
**Plus:** Cross-country skiing right here. Dinner served ($10 per person) if arranged well ahead of time. Your own kitchen for special weekends in winter or at change of season—solstice, equinox, May day. Spring-fed swimming pond with sandy beach, trails for hiking, wild blueberries for picking. A short walk to waterfall in the state forest. Cider or other beverages often served in late afternoon/evenings. Living room with piano, hi-fi, fireplace, and extensive library. Sun-dried towels. Tour of the solar addition and farm.
**Rates:** $35 single, $40 double. $10 cot. Special weekends payable in full in advance; $200 for two couples includes two nights, two breakfasts, and your own kitchen.

## Berkshire Bed & Breakfast Homes Host #PV20

Worthington, MA
**Location:** On the border of Berkshire County. Set back from the road. Surrounded by 50 acres of potato fields on the mountain. Two minutes from the village center. Less than a mile to Hickory Hill cross-country ski area.
**Reservations:** Available year round through Berkshire Bed & Breakfast Homes, page 346. Two-night minimum stay preferred.

The brown shingled colonial with stone fences, big old trees, and views in every direction is a photographer's dream. The "center of the town's social life" shortly after being built in 1780 and the site of county fairs during the 1800s was renovated in 1945 by William Gass, who also renovated Historic Deerfield. Opened as a B&B in 1985 by a young banker and his wife, the house, a recognized Massachusetts Historical Site, has 13 rooms, five fireplaces, wide board flooring, and many antiques.

This is maple-sugaring and apple-picking country, the home town of Sevenars Concerts, and there are several summer camps in the area. The host and hostess both race canoes, swim, and participate in triathlons.

**In residence:** Two children, ages one and five.
**Restrictions:** No guests' pets. Smoking allowed in designated areas.
**Foreign language spoken:** German.
**Bed and bath:** Four rooms. Two have private full baths. Two share a full bath. Double, twin beds, rollaway, and portacrib available.
**Breakfast:** Usually 7-9. Main dish could be eggs, crepes, blueberry pancakes, ham, bacon, sausage. Cheese, fresh fruit with real cream, popovers, pastries, homemade bread, fried bread dough. Served in fireplaced dining room or on stone porch.
**Plus:** Fireplace in living and dining rooms. TV room. Porches. Down comforters. Yard. Beverages. Babysitting may be arranged.
**Rates:** $60 ($75 one-night) for double bed or twins with private bath. $55 double, $50 ($60 one-night) twins with shared bath. Singles $50-$55.

*Can't find the community you are going to? Check with a reservation service described at the beginning of this chapter. Through the service, you may be placed (matched) with a welcoming B&B that is near your destination.*

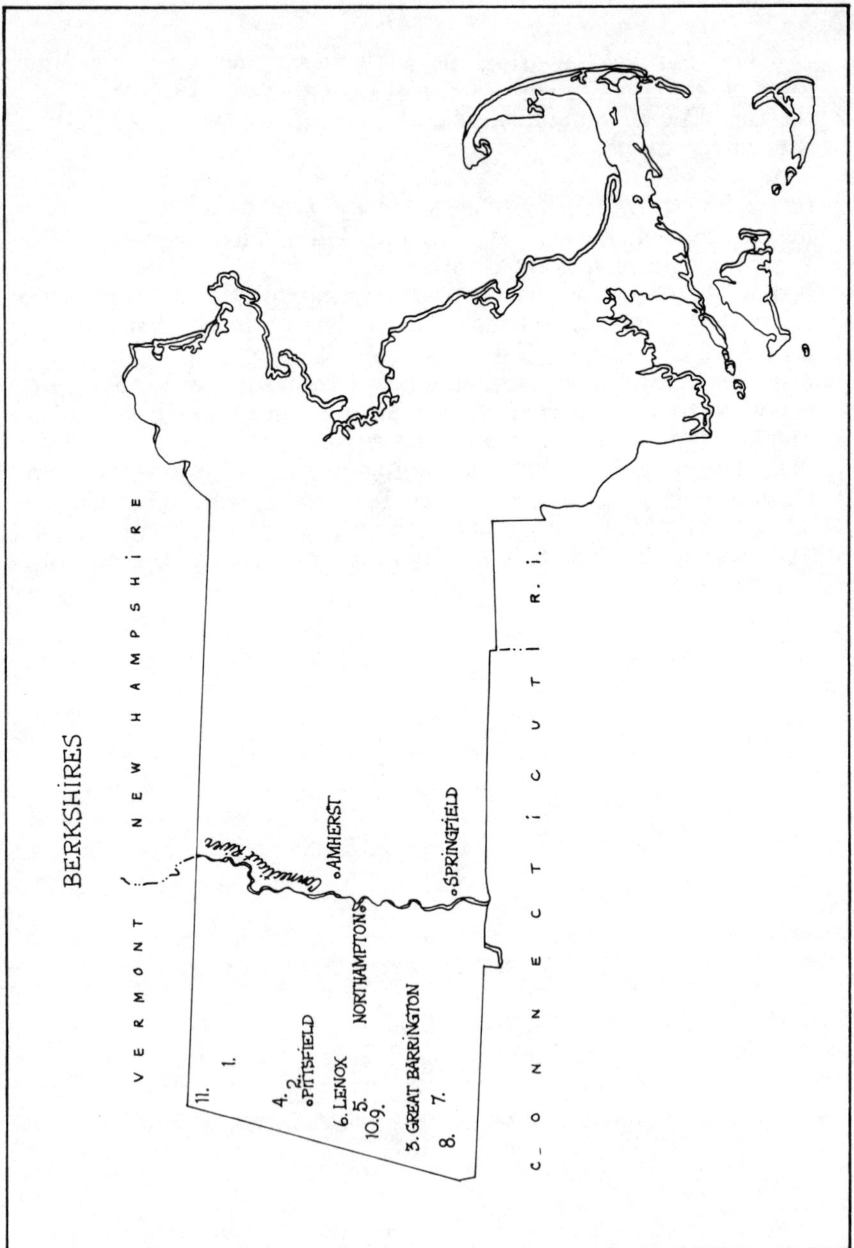


*The numbers on this map indicate the locations of B&Bs described in detail in this chapter.*

# BERKSHIRES

# Berkshires Reservation Services

## Berkshire Bed & Breakfast Homes

P.O. Box 211, Williamsburg, MA 01096
**Phone:** 413/268-7244. Monday through Friday, 9-7, Saturday 9-1. Closed December 24-January 2.
**Listings:** 50. Located throughout western Massachusetts. In the Sturbridge area, hosts are close to Brimfield and Sturbridge Village. In Hampshire Hills, close to the five-college area, with pastoral views. Springfield hosts are close to the Civic Center and Big E. Berkshires hosts are near Tanglewood and Williams College. Mostly hosted private residences. Three inns. Two unhosted residences. Directory ($3) includes individual rates.

When Eleanor Herbert took over the agency in 1986, she came with four years' (superb) hosting experience, a reputation for attending to detail, and many years as a professional librarian. She is aware of the importance of meeting the needs and expectations of hosts and guests. She knows what needs to be done and does it—well.

**Reservations:** Two weeks' advance notice is recommended. In the Berkshires, two-night minimum stays are often required on weekends or holidays and during Tanglewood season.
**Plus:** Short-term (several weeks) hosted and unhosted housing also available.
**Rates:** $25-$65 single, $30-$85 double. Family and weekly rates available. $6 booking fee. $5 surcharge for one night in a few cases. Twenty percent deposit required. If cancellation notice is received two weeks prior to arrival date, deposit less a $10 processing fee is refunded. No refund for cancellations with less than two weeks' notice.

Other services with B&Bs in the Berkshires:

The American Country Collection, page 135.
Covered Bridge Bed and Breakfast Reservation Service, page 390.
Pineapple Hospitality, page 214.

## Berkshires B&Bs

### Butternut Inn

6 East Street, Adams, MA 01220
**Phone:** 413/743-9394
**Location:** In a historic district, one minute from the center of town, at the junction of Routes 8 and 116. Twenty minutes from Tanglewood, Williamstown, and Pittsfield. Within 20 minutes of Brodie, Jiminy Peak, or Cummington Farms ski areas.
**Hosts:** Anita and Walter Avery
**Open:** Year round except Thanksgiving, Christmas, and Easter. Reservations required. Two-night minimum stay preferred during July, August, and fall foliage season.

The corner Victorian house with the spreading butternut tree has no B&B sign, but if you ring the bell, Anita will welcome you into a foyer of cherry woodwork and stained-glass windows.

"Adams is our home and we think the town and area are truly beautiful." After Anita had been a nurse in industry for 35 years—and mothered four children—she convinced Walt, electrical supervisor at Pfizer, that it was an opportune time to open a B&B.

They are the fifth private owners of the house, which was from 1939 to 1952 a church for Christian Scientists. Walt worked on renovations and Anita decorated with antiques. About the time they opened in 1984 they went to an auction at the First Congregational Church. Their treasure? "We are delighted to have guests play the Estey pump organ!"

Most guests write as much about the hosts as about their "immaculate lovely home." They speak of returning or sending their friends: "You can tell they love making people feel at home."

**In residence:** Maybe son Scott, a chef at 21, who caters for private families and sometimes bakes for breakfast here.
**Restrictions:** Children should be at least six. No guests' pets. Smoking not encouraged; restricted to certain areas.
**Bed and bath:** Three rooms, one with private bath. One small room is a favorite because of its balcony. Another room has five windows overlooking side yard and fountain and has a sitting area. The room

with private bath has two twin beds and a sitting area. Rollaway bed available. Oak floors and quilts in each room.
**Breakfast:** 8-9, but flexible. Hot cornbread, or apple or blueberry bread accompanied with warm spicy applesauce, maybe orange butter. Juice, beverage, porridge. Served by candlelight in formal dining room or in the sun room or on flagstone terrace. Special diets catered to. Music. ("Gershwin is our favorite.")
**Plus:** Beverages served upon arrival. Coal-burning cast iron fireplace in foyer. Turned-down beds. Bedroom window fans. Fresh flowers in season. Cards, games, and books. Front porch. Spacious yard with picnic table. Use of refrigerator. Loan of ice chest.
**Rates:** $45 double occupancy with shared bath, $50 with private bath. $5 discount per night for stays of two or more nights November-May 15. $5 less for single, if room available. $15 rollaway bed for adult, $10 child.

## The Dalton House

955 Main Street, Dalton, MA 01226
**Phone:** 413/684-3854
**Location:** On the main street of a small town that has a few basic stores and is home of the company that makes all the paper for U.S. currency. Close to Tanglewood, and skiing at Jiminy Peak and Brodie Mountain.
**Hosts:** Gary and Bernice Turetsky
**Open:** Year round. Two-night minimum reservation on summer and holiday weekends.

"I was a B&B before I knew there was a name for it," says transplanted Gary Turetsky. "It's really fun." Now that television has caught up with the idea, the hosts prompted a long-term winter guest who was a Bob Newhart look-alike to check in guests one weekend. More fun was had by all.

When the Turetskys came here from Freehold, New Jersey in 1971, it was the flower business in a quaint town that attracted them. Then a visit to innkeeper friends in Vermont provided the inspiration to think differently about their four-season Massachusetts location and their 1810 colonial home. The flower shop is still in business (some repeat guests even sell plants to customers if the hosts are out); but now they also offer hospitality in their meandering place (main house with wing, greenhouse, and converted carriage house) complete with fireplaced common room.

**In residence:** Three college-age daughters. When they are home, they host too. And they have a cat, Pumpkin.
**Restrictions:** Sorry, no guests' pets.
**Foreign languages spoken:** One daughter speaks French, another Hebrew.
**Bed and bath:** Nine carpeted rooms plus two suites with very large rooms and sitting areas. All with private baths. Four rooms each have two twin beds, five have doubles. Cots available.
**Breakfast:** Continental with muffins. Buffet style in dining room. Often part of the "experience" for a first-time B&B traveler not used to morning conversation with other guests.
**Plus:** Air conditioning and individual heat control in bedrooms. Living room with wood-lined walls, old beams, loft, piano, and TV. Patio. Greenhouse. Picnic area in the woods. Guided back-country touring and instruction in ice climbing.
**Rates:** Summer $58-$75, fall $48-$65, winter $42-$60, and spring $48-$65 double occupancy. Special midweek packages available.

From Massachusetts: ". . . superb host and hostess. The house is loaded with charm . . . comfortable and in excellent taste, and if you want a card table or an extra chair or two, the Turetskys get them for you almost before you think of it."

## Elling's Guest House B&B

RD 3, Box 6, Great Barrington, MA 01230
**Phone:** 413/528-4103
**Location:** On five acres of lawns, gardens, and wooded areas. One mile west of town on Route 23, 300 feet from the main road. Twenty minutes to Tanglewood. Minutes from Butternut Basin and Catamount ski area.
**Hosts:** Josephine and Raymond Elling
**Open:** Year round. Reservations required. Two-night minimum during July, August, and foliage season. Three-night minimum on long holiday weekends.

Through fourteen years of ownership the Ellings have noticed that the appeal of their kind of place has widened. "Younger people have discovered us." The hosts think that such accommodations should be reasonably priced and aim to keep things that way.

"Such accommodations" are in the second-oldest lived-in house in Great Barrington, built in 1746 for a woolen-mill owner. When Jo and Ray bought it as a summer house, they furnished it with family possessions. "Our pride is the 1820 tall clock which strikes each hour." It wasn't long before their summer address became a nonpaying guest house, so they decided that running a bed and breakfast in the Berkshires would be the thing to do.

Both are members of the local historical society. Ray is a do-it-yourself buff; Jo gardens, hooks rugs, and makes wreaths. Where will they send you? "Anywhere in the Berkshires is our favorite place, but we are partial to the small back roads. If you get lost, you'll enjoy it anyway."

**Restrictions:** Children should be in their teens. No pets please.
**Foreign language spoken:** Some Italian.
**Bed and bath:** Six rooms. The two with private baths (shower, no tub) have either a queen-sized bed or twin beds that can be made into a king. Four rooms, three with double beds and one with the twin/king option, share two large full baths. Cot available. Rooms have views of cornfields, mountains, or woodlands and grounds.
**Breakfast:** 8:30-10:30. Continental buffet including hot muffins or biscuits with homemade jam, fruit, juice, and a bottomless pot of coffee or tea. In summer, eat on the porch or lawns.
**Plus:** Porch with wicker furniture looking onto gardens. Private entrance for guests. Garden swing suspended from an old maple. Badminton, horseshoes. Common room with fireplace, TV, games, cards, checkers. Fans, if needed. Swimming three minutes away in river with a small pool and beach. Guest refrigerator. An invitation to see the original cooking fireplace and colonial carpentry in the Ellings' part of the house.
**Rates:** June-October and holidays $50 shared bath, $65 private bath. November-May $40 shared bath, $50 private bath. Singles $10 less Monday-Thursday. $15 for an extra person in a room.

From Seattle, Washington: "What a thrill it is to return to your former home and find it more beautiful than when you left! . . . But the best part is the warmth with which they welcome their guests."

## Seekonk Pines

142 Seekonk Cross Road, Great Barrington, MA 01230
**Phone:** 413/528-4192
**Location:** Just off Route 23, bordered with pine trees. Two miles west of town and Route 7, 15 minutes from three state forests, eight miles from Stockbridge, 16 miles from Tanglewood. Five miles to Butternut Basin and Catamount (snowmaking at both).
**Hosts:** Linda and Christian Best
**Open:** Year round except Thanksgiving. Two-day minimum stay on summer weekends. Three-day minimum on long holiday weekends.

They met while playing the lead roles in *Damn Yankees*. Both are paid soloists at a local church and they still study voice. Chris and Linda are the first to have paying guests in the 1830s house, a structure that expanded as several generations lived in it. The Bests "refinished, repaired, rebuilt, reinterpreted, and furnished comfortably and eclectically."

They live in the former servants' quarters and do everything themselves. Linda's watercolors exhibited in the house are for sale. Auction acquisitions emerge in a reconditioned state from Chris's barn workshop and they may be reupholstered or slipcovered by the professional seamstress-in-residence, Linda.

Chris loves his title of host and gets a kick out of telling about some of their first guests (in 1978) who eventually opened their own B&B. Linda enjoys telling about the daughter of a former president who, during a three-day stay, wasn't recognized until she emerged "looking like a queen" for dinner on the second night.

Blueberries are harvested from the nearby mountainside and the garden produces black raspberries, strawberries, rhubarb, and yellow squash (eventually cooked with apples) for breakfast jams and jellies. By popular demand, they are sold to guests (only).

**In residence:** College-age daughter during the summer. Bear is their shepherd/collie and Toby is a dachshund mix.
**Restrictions:** No smoking. No guests' pets.
**Foreign language spoken:** German.
**Bed and bath:** Seven rooms, many with Linda's stenciling. First floor room has a queen-sized bed, private bath and private entrance from porch. Second floor rooms, all with wide floorboards, have a double bed (one has a private half bath), two twin beds, or queen

plus a twin bed. Suite has double and a twin bed, private full bath. Handmade quilts on all beds. Cots available.
**Breakfast:** A leisurely meal in the formal dining room. Coffee/tea, homemade muffins or bread, fruit, juice, and sometimes a quiche.
**Plus:** Swimming pool. Large common room with fireplace, piano, chess, and puzzles. Wildflower meadow, huge lawn, picnic table. Unscheduled performances could include recitals with classical and popular music sung by Linda and Chris. Rental bicycles.
**Rates:** June-October and holidays \$60-\$62 twin or double with shared bath, \$65 with private half-bath, \$75 private bath downstairs, \$80 suite. Winter and spring \$48-\$50 twin or double with shared bath, \$55 private half-bath, \$60 private bath downstairs, \$65 suite. Singles, \$15 less on weekdays for shared bath. Crib \$8 one night, \$5 per night for two or more nights. \$15 extra person. Ten percent discount for stays of one week or more.

## Thornewood

453 Stockbridge Road, Great Barrington, MA 01230
**Phone:** 413/528-3828
**Location:** Beneath Monument Mountain on three acres that adjoin state forest. Set off Route 7, just minutes from Stockbridge, Lenox (Tanglewood), and the village of Great Barrington.
**Hosts:** Dave and Terry Thorne
**Open:** Year round. Reservations preferred. Two-day minimum stay on weekends in the summer and fall. Three-day minimum on some holiday and special weekends.

> From Massachusetts: "I first stayed there when my favorite inn was full and Thornewood was open just about three weeks . . . have returned every summer since then. . . . Terry and Dave are a warm, hospitable couple. . . . The inn is a wonderful old house which they have completely refurbished. It is immaculately kept, and beautifully decorated with antiques, but its warmth and coziness are the most outstanding characteristics. . . . The swimming pool is a bonus. . . . And if that's not enough . . . a hearty country breakfast, cooked with flair and served with grace."

Dave is a musician and song writer. Terry has had her own old-fashioned country ice cream parlor. They had talked of becoming innkeepers and, while living in Stockbridge, saw the potential of this neglected 1920 Dutch colonial when it was on the market four years ago. In stages they have added many baths, four bedrooms, a spacious dining room, a new kitchen—and a gracious entry, a cathedral-ceilinged foyer with arched window. Dave is now planning to build a studio for his writing.

"Some of our guests are adventurous and on the move constantly. Some come to get away from the fast pace and don't want to move at all. Some want to engage in conversation and others sometimes avoid that situation. We enjoy meeting different personalities."

**In residence:** Hosts' two teenage daughters, parents, and friends are likely to be around. Foxy Lady is their miniature fox terrier. Warlock is a Maine coon cat. Both animals are kept in hosts' quarters unless the guests want to visit with them.
**Restrictions:** Children should be at least 12. No guests' pets. No smoking, please.
**Bed and bath:** Nine rooms, each with private bath (three with showers only). One first-floor room. Four second-floor rooms with various bed sizes overlook pool. Another four rooms at back of house include a room with queen-sized canopied bed, two rooms with double beds, and one with two twin beds. Varied decor in Primrose Room, Violet Room, Blue Bow Room.
**Breakfast:** Usually at 9. Freshly squeezed orange juice, grapefruit, or fresh fruit cup. Cheddar quiche, apple pancakes, baked eggs and cheese in sour cream, eggs Benedict or various crepes, maybe sausage-tomato-egg scramble. Homemade sour-cream or raspberry coffee cake or apple crisp or muffins. Served in the bright dining room with view of pool and mountains.
**Plus:** Most bedrooms have air conditioning or fans. In-ground pool. Sitting room with fireplace, classical music, and library. Late-afternoon or evening beverages. Tour of house. Dinner offered occasionally ($9-$15) on Friday nights. Will meet guests at Great Barrington airport or bus stop. Will chill wine or store leftovers for guests. Hiking or cross-country trails right here—and through the adjoining Monument Mountain state reservation.
**Rates:** June 22-August 31 $85-$95 double occupancy. Foliage season $75-$85. Other months, $75 per room. $10 less for singles. Cots $15. MasterCard and VISA accepted.

## The Turning Point Inn

RD 2, Box 140, Great Barrington, MA 01230
**Phone:** 413/528-4777
**Location:** Fifteen minutes from Tanglewood, just down the road from Butternut Basin (snowmaking), on a well-traveled road.
**Hosts:** Irving and Shirley Yost
**Open:** Year round. Two-night minimum stay required during Tanglewood, foliage, and ski season weekends. Three-night minimum on holiday weekends.

The children, now all in their 20s, were the first Yost vegetarians. When it became a family style, there was thought of having a vegetarian summer restaurant. In 1976 Irv, an architect, and Shirley, a teacher, bought this place ("a mess then") to fulfill that goal. A restaurant permit wasn't allowed, so they established a B&B in July 1982. The match was right. In the fall of 1982 the Yosts moved from New Jersey so they could share their home with guests year round. In the summer of 1984, their son was married here.

While converting "the mess" into an inviting home they uncovered a beehive oven in the old kitchen and two Rumford fireplaces. The Yosts have traced the history of the house, have discovered on one of the chimneys the signature of the owner in its tavern/inn days, and can declare that Daniel Webster has slept here.

The Turning Point guest list includes honeymooners and family members who have come from opposite directions for a get-together. The couple mentioned in my first B&B book as having been here for their 50th anniversary have since celebrated their 51st, 52d, 53d, and 54th here too. (A year ago the husband was a member of a Witness for Peace group captured by the Nicaraguan Contras.) "He's 80 years old—and what a magnificent couple!"

**In residence:** One black cat, Cassandra, age 17. Eight-year-old granddaughter Alana visits frequently. And one of the junior Yosts ("all excellent cooks"), Jamie, occasionally takes over.
**Restrictions:** Children welcome as long as they sleep through the night and are well behaved. No guests' pets. No smoking.
**Bed and bath:** Seven rooms, moderate size, attractively furnished with "19th and 20th-century furniture." One room with private bath has two twin beds that can be a king. One single room, four double-bedded rooms, and a twin-bedded room share three baths. Cribs and cots available.

**Breakfast:** Two seatings, 8:30 and 9:30, but other arrangements can be made. Served in dining/common room. Menu could include Irv's special blend of whole-grain hot cereal; bran and whole-wheat pancakes; eggs with veggies; or Shirley's hot baked fruit, apple crisp, bran muffins, or zucchini-and-date bread. Tofu and tofu salad too.
**Plus:** Fresh fruit always available. Fireplaces in three common rooms. Piano. Babysitting. Library. TV and stereo. Refrigerator. Laundry facilities. Picnic tables, hammocks, outside swing. Nature trails on 11 acres. Appalachian Trail across the road.
**Rates:** Weekends $45 single, $65 double, $70 twin, $85 king (or twin) with private bath. Weekdays $5 less. One-night stay, if available, $5 extra. $5 crib. $10 cot for a child under 12, $15 if over 12.

## Townry Farm

Greylock Road, Lanesborough, MA 01237
**Phone:** 413/443-9285
**Location:** At the base of Mount Greylock state reservation, which surrounds the highest peak in Massachusetts. Just off Route 7 between Pittsfield and Williamstown, on a well-maintained road in an area of small farms. Three miles to Brodie Mountain and four miles to Jiminy Peak. Cross-country ski areas nearby. Twenty minutes from Tanglewood.
**Hosts:** Barbara and Cliff Feakes
**Open:** Year round except Thanksgiving and Christmas Day. Two-day minimum stay on weekends during Tanglewood season.

It may seem like a long way from the women's apparel business to a working farm, but there's no turning back now. As Barb and Cliff say, "Everyone wants to move to the Berkshires and live our lifestyle." Fifteen years ago they bought this 1750 farmhouse that had been owned by only one family. They have established a commercial sheep flock, and they also raise Labrador retrievers. Their thriving baking business includes Cliff's fudge and a mail-order arrangement. For some diversion, this enthusiastic couple enjoys classical music and dance skating.

Townry Farm is the source of my anecdote about the daughter home from school, working on a resume. Through a B&B guest who offered to help, the daughter got a fabulous job. A complete rundown on all the offspring includes a lawyer, a restaurant owner, a biochemist, a mother, and a farmer. Their former rooms, complete with 18-inch-wide floorboards, have been redecorated for guests, who say that they feel very much at home.

**In residence:** Four black Labrador retrievers (they produce yellow, black, and chocolate puppies). Breeding flock of 100 Dorset and crossbred ewes with varying quantities of growing lambs.
**Restrictions:** No guests' pets. Hosts do not smoke but do not object to smokers.
**Foreign language spoken:** Some French.
**Bed and bath:** Three first-floor guest rooms share one bath. One room has a double bed, the other two have both a double and a single bed.
**Breakfast:** Continental self-serve at dining room table set with lace tablecloth and fine china. Barbara's own breads—blueberry crunch, cranberry, peach, or maybe Irish soda.
**Plus:** Guest den with color TV. Coffee and tea always available. Tour of farm. Bread-making demonstrations. A suggestion for "the bargain of the century, the Clark Art Institute in Williamstown." In the nearby state reservation—hiking trails, blueberry picking, hunting in legal season, and cross-country skiing.
**Rates:** $25 single, $30 double. $10 additional person in room.

## 1777 Greylock House

58 Greylock Street, Lee, MA 01238
**Phone:** 413/243-1717
**Location:** About a mile north of town center. Three miles to Tanglewood. Eight miles to Jacob's Pillow. Within a twenty-mile radius of five major ski areas, both downhill and cross-country.
**Hosts:** Terry and Walt Parry
**Open:** Year round. Reservations recommended. Two-night minimum stay on weekends.

The Parrys are an energetic, flexible "retired" couple. When they sold their ten-year-old restaurant business to their son, they bought this 18th-century colonial house, one that had remained in the same family from 1777 until 1955. They started restoration in March of 1981 and together did everything, including a new kitchen, in time to receive their first guests three months later. It has antiques, stenciled walls, and the original wide floorboards—

yet first-timers and returnees alike always comment that the Parrys themselves make the 1777 house a home.

Restoration is a bit of a family avocation at this point. All the Parry children, including the one who lives across the street, have older homes in some state of restoration. And then there's always furniture refinishing to be done.

Previous careers include operating a snowmobile resort and growing potatoes (for potato chips) in seven states. Retirement does provide a little more time for cross-country skiing. Terry and Walt enjoy it together, with guests, and with their grandchildren too.

**Restrictions:** No guests' pets. Children should be at least five.
**Foreign language spoken:** Some French.
**Bed and bath:** Four rooms. First-floor suite has private bath, room with two twin beds, fireplaced living room with pull-out couch, TV. Air-conditioned second floor has one shared bath for two rooms with double beds and one room with two twin beds.
**Breakfast:** Continental, 8-10. On the porch overlooking 200-year-old maple trees and beautifully maintained lawn. When served in the dining room, guests sometimes move themselves into the homey kitchen. "Our guests seem to be sharers, and the kitchen is the focal point of activity in the house."
**Plus:** Fireplace in living room. Porches. Place to store skis.
**Rates:** July-September $65 double. Suite $85 for two. $10 extra person. October-May $45 suite, $35 other rooms.

## Kingsleigh 1840

32 Park Street, Lee, MA 01238
**Phone:** 413/243-3317
**Location:** In the center of Lee, next to the town park.
**Hosts:** Arthur and Linda Segal
**Open:** May through March. Reservations required. Two-night minimum stay on summer weekends.

"We wanted a change of career and to be away from the atmosphere of big city life. Arthur was a corporate executive. I am a free-lance artist and antique jewelry collector. Kingsleigh is historically registered and fully restored to its original splendor, thanks to the previous owners. . . . We like it because it's homelike—no stuffiness! Hosting is like having friends rather than paying guests. It is hard to accept money, but we do!"

Originally built in 1840, the house was expanded in 1870 and again in 1875. A great conversation point is the pictorial documentation in the library of the inn. As for the antiques throughout the house, "each piece has its own story." If you wish to own any of them, that could happen; most of them are for sale.

**In residence:** Son Morgan, age 15. Two dogs, Cindy, a female standard schnauzer, and Buttons, a female miniature poodle. One host, Linda, smokes.
**Restrictions:** Children should be at least 12. No guests' pets.
**Foreign language spoken:** Some Spanish.
**Bed and bath:** Four rooms, two with private baths. One honeymoon suite with queen-sized bed, Victorian furniture. Double or queen-sized bed in other rooms.
**Breakfast:** 8:30-10:30. Continental on weekdays. Weekends it's fruit, pancakes, French toast or eggs,and a specialty such as stuffed tomatoes and eggs and homemade jams and muffins. Served in the country kitchen at the counter or in dining area.
**Plus:** Cordial, tea, or wine in late afternoon or evening. Tour of the house. Bedroom window fans. Library reading room. Outside porch. Small backyard with gardens.
**Rates:** Double occupancy. Summer-fall weekdays $45 semiprivate bath, $65 private bath; weekends $65 semiprivate bath, $85 private bath. Winter-spring weekdays $40 semiprivate, $55 private bath; weekends semiprivate $55, private $70. MasterCard and VISA accepted.

From New Jersey: "We discovered the Kingsleigh late on a Sunday evening and were so pleased with our short visit that we returned several weeks later for a long weekend. Being interested in antiques, we felt at home. . . . Enjoyed the little touches that gave each room a distinct personality of its own."

From Connecticut: "We were fed until we were full. The coffee pot was never empty. . . . They made us feel like old friends of theirs."

## Berkshire Bed & Breakfast Host #SC2

Lenox, MA
**Location:** On a quiet road, one-half mile off Route 7. Five minutes from Lenox village and Tanglewood.
**Reservations:** Available year round through Berkshire Bed & Breakfast Homes, page 364. Two-night minimum on weekends.

"We wake to the songbirds here! After many years in the Berkshires I still enjoy Tanglewood and Jacob's Pillow. I bicycle about 50 miles a week, race canoes, downhill and cross-country ski. Guests are welcome to take my canoe for a lazy paddle down the Housatonic River, or in winter, to try the cross-country trails that lead from the back yard."

When her three children were in private schools, the hostess started B&B. Eleven years have passed, the children have grown, and more guests keep coming to the 1930s house that has country decor. The hostess is an expert on hidden spots as well as back-road routes.

**In residence:** A small black dog named "Tyler II and Tippie Canoe" is called "Tyler."
**Restrictions:** Children should be at least four and well behaved. Sorry, no guests' pets.
**Bed and bath:** Three rooms share a full bath. One room has king-sized bed, picture window overlooking the woods. A room with twin beds overlooking giant maples. The third room has a double bed, overlooks maple-tree deck and wooded back yard. Cot available.
**Breakfast:** Fresh fruit, homemade muffins and breads, juice, coffee, tea. Served with colorful table settings in a front sun room with wicker chairs or at pine table overlooking the back woods.
**Plus:** Welcoming beverage. Fans in bedrooms. Small pine grove with picnic table. Private country lake, three miles away, for swimming and sunning.
**Rates:** $50 double; $60 king, twins. November–mid-June, $5 less.

## East Country Berry Farm

830 East Street, Lenox, MA 01240
**Phone:** 413/442-2057
**Location:** In a peaceful country setting. Minutes from Herman Melville's home, Arrowhead; 6.5 miles from Tanglewood. Near horseback riding, two nature sanctuaries, and canoeing.
**Host:** Rita Fribush Miller
**Open:** Year round. Reservations required in July and August.

It was the back porch view of October Mountain that sold Rita on the property in 1983. One couple who had known each other for 15 years returned a month after their first visit here to be married on that very porch.

Romantics and families alike enjoy this relaxed comfortable B&B that consists of two houses, a 200-year-old colonial and a century old farmhouse. If you go berry picking and bring five filled cups back, Rita will make a pie. There are dolls and stuffed toys for children to play with. Summer midweek possibilities here include aerobics, aquaexercise, massages by a licensed professional. At other times there could be a special Melville theme weekend. The New Year's Day brunch lasts all day. For those who want to know "what the job is really like," there's a B&B apprentice program.

Who is implementing all these ideas? Rita is a lawyer who has taught in France, Africa, and New York. She has developed products for Milton Bradley and has been an executive producer for public and educational television in Georgia. She loves The Mount, "a fabulous home designed by Edith Wharton," Chesterwood, and the Lenox Library, formerly a courthouse. She added another layer to her adventures by opening this B&B. Now, after all the painting, papering, and preparing, she can say, "It is more fun than I expected. The ambiance comes from the guests' enthusiasm. . . . People come here for an experience."

**In residence:** College-age daughter during the summer. Finn, the dog, loves guests. "He's very polite and occasionally says 'hello.' "
**Restrictions:** Pets (no puppies or cats) with preapproval only.
**Foreign languages spoken:** French, Spanish.
**Bed and bath:** Ten rooms in July and August, four the rest of the year. The room with private bath has mountain views. Two rooms with fireplaces and color cable TV. Two rooms with a double and a single bed each have a sink in room. Cot and crib available.

**Breakfast:** 8:30-10:30. "Relaxed and too interesting to miss." Includes fruit salad, berry-filled muffins, freshly ground coffee, teas. Served family style in dining room or on the porch.
**Plus:** In-ground pool. Beverages. Summer wildflower arrangements in rooms. Tour of the house and farm. Surprises for special celebrations. Babysitting. Limited kitchen privileges. Porch hammock. Professional year-round horseback riding school next door plus public riding farther down the street. Walking trails on 23 acres. Hiking in adjacent mountains. Will meet guests at Lenox bus stop.
**Rates:** For doubles, July and August $65-$78 shared bath, $95 private bath. Off-season $50 shared bath, $65 private bath. Less for singles. Additional bed in room $10 if under 21, $25 adult. Midweek, weekly, and group rates are less. No charge for crib. MasterCard and VISA accepted.

## Walker House

74 Walker Street, Lenox, MA 01240
**Phone:** 413/637-1271
**Location:** On one of the main streets into Lenox, but set on three acres. Within walking distance of shops and restaurants. Buses from New York and Boston stop a block away. Brodie, Jiminy Peak, and Butternut mountains all within 25 minutes.
**Hosts:** Peggy and Richard Houdek
**Open:** Year round. Three-night minimum stay on July and August weekends and all holiday weekends. Two-night minimum for room with fireplace all other weekends.

They were a successful arts-oriented couple living in a Spanish-style house on a southern California hill and looking for adventure. Once the Houdeks decided on the Berkshires, they set out to establish a B&B that would give them the feeling of having some friends visit for a few days. And that's exactly what has happened since 1980. It is an ongoing open house, but still their new lifestyle affords the sought-after change. Peggy was managing editor of *Performing Arts Magazine*; Dick was director of public affairs at California Institute of the Arts, a contributing critic for the *Los Angeles Times*, a consultant for Long Beach Opera, and he found time to serve as president of Guild Opera of Los Angeles, a group that staged full productions for children.

The Houdeks have revitalized the vintage 1804 Walker House, one of the last remaining examples of Federal architecture in Lenox. It has eight fireplaces and is furnished with antiques. In true Houdek style the guest rooms are named after composers and furnished in a style suggesting the composer's work. " 'Debussy,' for example, looks impressionistic." Being people-oriented as well, Dick and Peggy have also collected much oral history—just about every local person has a tale about something that happened in the house.

**In residence:** Five cats, but only Elizabeth, a bobtailed cat, is allowed in the house.
**Restrictions:** Guests' pets permitted by approval. And children should be at least eight. Smoking not encouraged.
**Foreign languages spoken:** French and Spanish.
**Bed and bath:** Eight rooms, each with private bath. One with two double beds, two with twin beds, two with a double, and three with a queen-sized bed. Five have fireplaces, one also has a private veranda.
**Breakfast:** Continental, sort of. Includes fresh fruit (baked in winter), several kinds of muffins and croissants, freshly ground coffee. Served in dining rooms around large oak tables or on the plant filled veranda. Not before 8, but it can go beyond 10.
**Plus:** Lots of music around. Grand piano in the parlor is often the scene of a recital, either by a professional artist or in an impromptu performance by a guest. Occasionally, Peggy, a trained singer, is persuaded to join a pianist for a Mozart aria or Broadway hit song. Tours of unoccupied rooms given to guests and nonguests. Chess, checkers, and puzzles; refrigerator; large lawn for picnics; and a fleet of 10 bicycles. Special winter theme weekends—Scrabble, Trivial Pursuit, films—and on the first Sunday in December, a Handel's *Messiah* sing. Recommendations for an art museum, a "lesser known but really fine center for original music theater," and a nearby park for cross-country skiing.
**Rates:** Vary according to room and season. \$80-\$110 weekends, double occupancy, \$55-\$75 midweek. Weekly rates less 10 percent. Singles 10 percent less except July, August, and October.

From Pennsylvania: " A stay at Walker House is like a visit to relatives you like. The guest is greeted warmly and graciously by Peggy and Dick. . . . Breakfast is always a joy."

## The American Country Collection Host #019

New Marlborough, MA
**Location:** Ten minutes southeast of Great Barrington on a country road known as the Old Massachusetts Turnpike (Route 57), on ten acres of woodland and meadows. Five minutes to Butternut Basin.
**Reservations:** Available year round through The American Country Collection, page 135. Advance reservations preferred. Two-night minimum stay on weekends and holidays.

A guest wrote: "Lovely experience. Extremely gracious host and hostess. Everywhere there were special touches."

They bought the 1791 Federal Greek Revival house at the *completion* of (meticulous) restoration! That was in 1985 when the biology professor and tennis coach at Nassau Community College and his wife, an administrator in education, joined the hospitality field, a tradition established by their two adult New York City based children, managers of a five-star hotel and a large popular restaurant.

A tour of the former coach stop (now on the National Register of Historic Places) might focus on architectural details, but it's the total ambiance of warm colors and period antiques mixed with modern amenities that makes it so inviting. Sometimes musicians give spontaneous mini-concerts here. Artists, too, are inspired by the environment.

**Restrictions:** Sorry, no infants, no pets. Smoking limited to designated areas.
**Foreign language spoken:** Some Spanish.
**Bed and bath:** Five rooms. Three with private baths (shower only). A first-floor room with queen-sized bed, private entrance, library setting. On the second floor, one room with queen-sized bed and another with two twin beds and a fireplace. Of the two second-floor rooms sharing a full bath, one room has a double bed and the other two twin beds and a sink. Two rollaways available.
**Breakfast:** 8-10 but flexible. Orange and grapefruit juice, fruits of the season, granola, assorted pancakes, assorted jellies, preserves and conserves, freshly baked muffins and breads, croissants, herbal teas, freshly brewed coffee, and area specialties. Served in dining room or on screened porch.

**Plus:** Wine, tea, snacks. Library. Compact disc player and a collection of discs. Screened porch. Babysitting. Nature walks to brook and beaver pond. Croquet. Badminton. Volleyball. Will meet bus. Bedroom window fans. Flowers, mints, guest bathrobes.
**Rates:** $55-$75 single, $65-$85 double. Cot $10 per night.

## Unique Bed and Breakfast

Upper Mountain Road, P.O. Box 729, Sheffield, MA 01257
**Phone:** 413/229-3363
**Location:** On seven acres, at the foothills of Mount Everett. About 14 miles south of Tanglewood. Within ten miles of Butternut Basin and Catamount ski area.
**Host:** A. May Stendardi
**Open:** Year round. Reservations usually required. Two-night stay preferred May-August.

> From New York City: "Although not an old New England inn, there's open, friendly hospitality. It's spotless and tastefully decorated. Fresh flowers throughout. Breakfasts are excellent. And it is very secluded, away from crowds."

In 1985, May designed and decorated this "not overly rustic and quite different" 3,000-square-foot log house as a B&B, using wallpapers, soft colors, and carpeting. There are two skylights in the guest wing, and the lounge area also has a fireplace-type wood stove. The wood stove area is lined with blue flowered ceramic tiles.

Before moving to the Berkshires, the Stendardis lived in Dutchess County, New York, where May taught interior decorating. Her husband does home renovations and specialized carpentry.

**Restrictions:** "Children should be at least 13 and must occupy a separate room. Maximum of two guests per room." No smoking allowed indoors.
**Foreign languages spoken:** Some Italian and some Spanish.
**Bed and bath:** Three first-floor rooms, each with private full bath. Double or twin beds available.
**Breakfast:** 8:30. Juice, fresh (seasonal) fruit cocktail, blueberry pancakes and sausage, or omelet with bacon. Homemade baked goods, hot beverages. Served in the dining area or porch. How leisurely? "Sometimes guests talk among themselves for hours!"

**Plus:** Central air conditioning. Late-afternoon or evening beverages. Guest refrigerator. Color TV. Gazebo facing rock garden. Views of deer in pines.
**Rates:** January-April $60 double. May-December $75 double with deck $85. $5 less for singles.

## Historic Merrell Tavern Inn

Route 102, Main Street, South Lee, MA 01260
**Phone:** 413/243-1794
**Location:** On a main street in small village. A mile from Norman Rockwell's Stockbridge, three miles from I-90. Five miles to Tanglewood. Twenty five miles to Williamstown. Ten minutes to ski areas (with snowmaking).
**Hosts:** Charles and Faith Reynolds
**Open:** Year round. Three-night minimum stay on July and August weekends. Two-night minimum for all other weekends.

> From Connecticut: ". . . Captures the feeling of the 19th century while more than satisfying the expectations of 20th century travelers by anticipating all of their needs."

Authenticity, charm, and old-fashioned hospitality are evident from the moment you sign in at the only surviving circular colonial bar in America. The grandfather's clock in the central hallway dates from the late 1700s, when the building was constructed. Authentic colors, researched by Faith and Charles, are a background for their period Hepplewhite and Sheraton furniture collected over a period of 25 years. The inn is on the National Register of Historic Places and is under historic covenant with the Society for the Preservation of New England Antiquities.

Once a stagecoach stop, over time it has seen changes that include guest rooms made from an elegant front parlor and from the smokehouse, summer kitchen, and third-floor ballroom. The work of the innkeepers, two former Rochester, New York teachers, was recognized in 1982 when they received the Massachusetts Historical Society Preservation Award.

After five years of carrying on a tradition, the Reynoldses maintain enthusiasm along with commitment (and success). Improvements and additions are constant. Charles still does the cooking. Faith does the serving. Faith's 89-year-old mother makes beds "with the diligence and pride of an artist."

**In residence:** Two cats named Boots and Patches.
**Bed and bath:** Nine large rooms on three floors. All with private baths with showers (no tubs), air conditioning, wing chairs or Chippendale sofas. Three rooms have fireplaces. Bed sizes are double, twins, or double and twins; most are canopied. Cribs and cots available.
**Breakfast:** 8:30-10. Juice, hot beverage, and choice of cereal, ham or cheese omelets, or French toast and sausage, with toast or muffins. Served in fireplaced Tavern Room that has an 1817 birdcage bar.
**Plus:** Grounds with old stone walls, English garden, two acres of lawns to banks of Housatonic River.
**Rates:** Weekdays November-June $50-$65. Weekdays July-October $55-$65. Weekends $120-$210 for two nights, depending on the season. Single occupancy $10 less per night. Double occupancy with twin beds $10 additional per night. $15 third person in a room. MasterCard, VISA, and AMEX accepted.

## Stirling Moffat Guest House

Box 2105, Route 7, Stockbridge, MA 01212
**Phone:** 413/298-5539
**Location:** Two and a half miles from both Stockbridge and Lenox. On a hill surrounded by six acres of lawn and Kentucky-style horse fencing all around.
**Host:** Susan Crandall
**Open:** Year round. Three-night minimum stay on weekends, July through October. (Some bookings for summer made a year ahead.)

This is very much a family home, a center-hall colonial that Susan and Bill built themselves, with B&B in mind, in 1980. It's on the site of a mansion-turned-inn that Susan's parents owned for just a short time before it burned down many years ago. The decor is comfortable, furnished with some interesting pieces bought at area estate sales. On the grounds are the mature plantings that were part of the original estate, big old trees and perennial gardens; guests enter over a rustic bridge.

Most people learn to love this caring, sharing family very quickly. You might meet Susan's brother, who helps inside and out. Susan's mother often fills the house with the incredible aroma of her famous shortbread. And if you follow directions to Scottie's

Barber Shop in Lee, you'll meet Susan's dad, the barber in Norman Rockwell's "First Haircut." An uncle is a five-star chef and hotel owner "back home in Scotland." The newest family venture, opened in 1986, is the ten-room Stirling Moffat Inn, opposite the Red Lion Inn, run by Susan's mother, uncle, and brother.

Even the delivery men are part of the scene here. The milkman brings glass milk bottles with cream on the top. An entire local family arrives with maple syrup in gallon containers.

Guests are invited to visit the farm, Bridlewood Arabians Inc., in Hillsdale, New York, just 15 miles away, where Susan and Bill, her employer before he became her husband, train about 150 Arabian horses that they show all over the United States and Canada. It is one of the biggest stables on the east coast. In the winter, B&B guests get a sleigh ride around the farm. In the summer, guests bring a picnic lunch and enjoy the setting.

**In residence:** Husband, Bill; Susan's mother, Jessie. Laura, age six; Jess, age three. Two dogs, Bearshen and Lacey; Timothy the cat. Several Arabian horses. Maybe a sleigh horse and Welsh pony.
**Restrictions:** No guests' pets. Smoking in the sitting room and on porch only.
**Bed and bath:** Four rooms, each with private full bath. The first floor has double bed and sitting room. One room with queen-sized bed, bath with bidet and very deep tub. Twin or double beds in the other rooms. Each room has air conditioning, wall-to-wall carpeting, views of the horses and gardens. Cot and crib available.
**Breakfast:** 8-11. Fresh fruit, homemade croissants, muffins, juices, and freshly ground coffee. Omelets, French toast, fresh fruit pancakes. Eggs and milk come from a neighboring farm. Served on the porch overlooking horses or in the small dining room.
**Plus:** Air conditioning throughout the house. Swimming pool. Flower gardens. Tours of the house and farm. English "high tea" (extra charge) at 3 p.m. Winter Wonderland weekends include a Saturday candlelight dinner, sleigh ride at the farm, and an opportunity to watch training in indoor arena. Picnic baskets and dinner by request. Dairy farm visits two miles down the road.
**Rates:** July-October $105-$110 on weekends, $45-$65 weekdays. Off-season $55-$75 weekends, $45 weekdays. Special full-week and weekday rates available on request. MasterCard and VISA accepted.

## Steep Acres Farm B&B

520 White Oaks Road, Williamstown, MA 01267
**Phone:** 413-458-3774
**Location:** Two miles from the center of town, high on a hill with panoramic views of New York, Vermont, and Massachusetts. Adjacent to the Appalachian and Long Trails. Many downhill ski areas within a radius of 20 miles.
**Hosts:** Mary and Marvin Gangemi
**Open:** Year round.

"Our six children have grown. We're not ready to put our feet up yet. It was time for a new regime."

They sold their summer camp and bought this 52-acre site bordering Vermont with house, three barns, one-acre pond, and apple, cherry, peach, pear, and nut trees. The family never had farm animals before, but they learn everything as they go along. When you take a tour, you will see cows, calves, sheep, pigs, turkeys, geese, chickens, pheasants, and ducks—all signs of energetic people who are interested in self-sufficient farming.

Marvin is a teacher, Mary a nurse. Only their oldest son is home; he's the one who generally keeps things going. They have stocked the pond with trout. They have learned to shear sheep (the hostess knits), raise poultry and pheasant for eating, and deliver the many young of their animals. The honey you eat comes from the farm. There are more customers for fresh eggs than there are eggs. Their garden is very successful partly due to their newly installed greenhouse. And yes, B&B "just fits because we have the room and have found that every quest has been wonderful."

**In residence:** Two dogs plus. (They breed Labrador retrievers.)
**Restrictions:** No smoking. No guests' pets.
**Bed and bath:** Four rooms with two shared guest baths. One single room with antique bed, one twin-bedded room, and two rooms with antique oak double beds and marble-topped bureaus.
**Breakfast:** Continental with daily specials. Fresh fruits, milk, cream, butter ("put the plug in and the churn makes it in 20 minutes"), homemade breads, jams, and jellies. Eat by the fireplace in dining room or on the screened-in porch with its tri-state view.
**Plus:** Watch maple sugaring (they tap 85 trees) if you're there at the right time. Use of rowboat, canoes, and raft with diving board on the pond. Five kilometers of hiking and cross-country ski trails.
**Rates:** $30 single, $45 double or twin. $10 cot.

## KEY

Recipes shared, often for house specialties.

Inquiries welcomed about restoration and/or decorating. Symbol indicates that host is willing to share experiences with guests. Tips range from a before-and-after album to rebuilding advice, from furniture refinishing to curtain making. Expertise of hosts ranges from learn-by-doing to professional.

How-To B&B workshop, seminar or apprentice program offered.

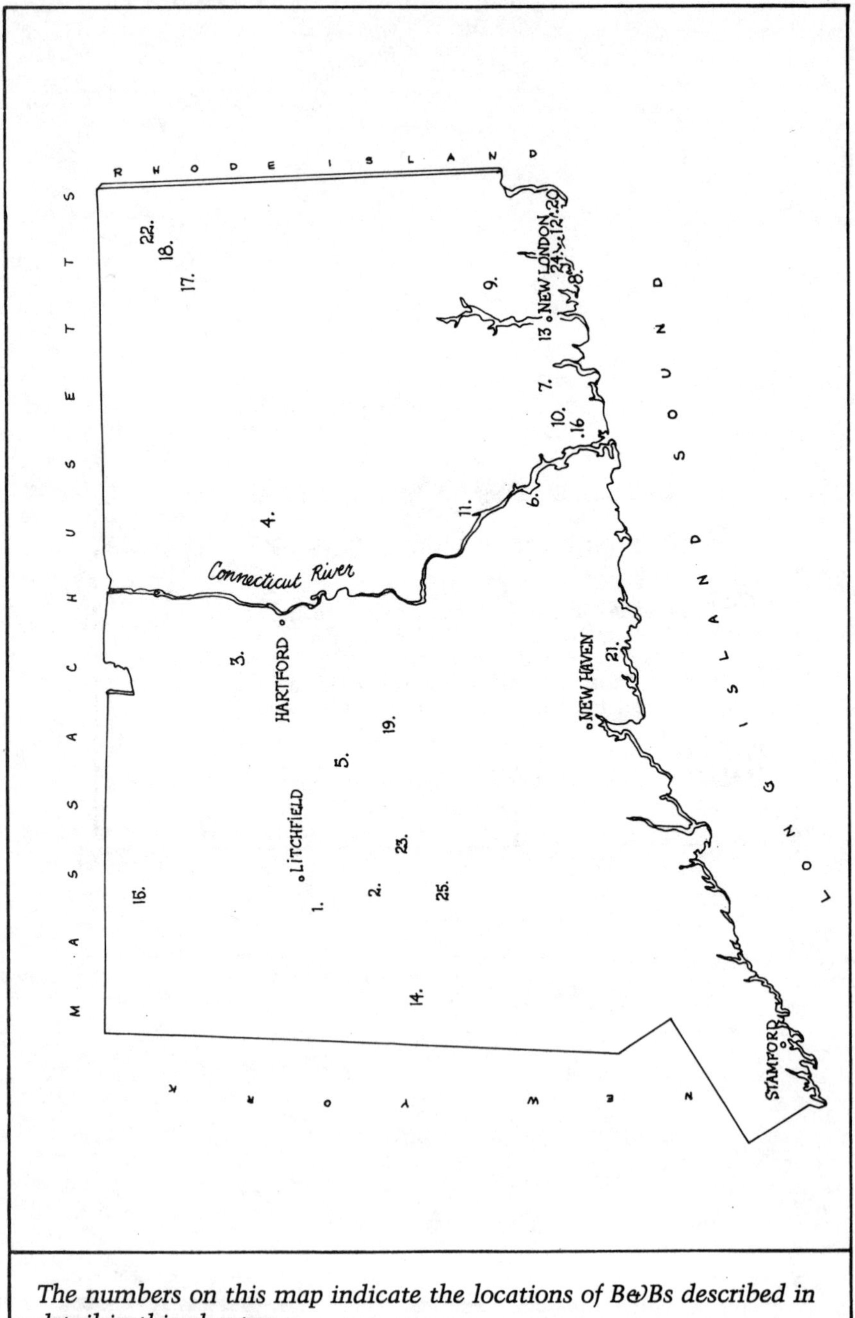


*The numbers on this map indicate the locations of B&Bs described in detail in this chapter.*

# CONNECTICUT

1. Bantam, Rockwood Farm Bed & Breakfast, 392
2. Bethlehem, Eastover Farm Bed & Breakfast, 393
3. Bloomfield, Nutmeg Bed & Breakfast Host #14, 394
4. Bolton, Jared Cone House, 396
5. Bristol, Chimney Crest Manor, 397
6. Deep River, Riverwind, 398
7. East Lyme, The Red House, 399
8. Groton Long Point, Shore Inne, 401
9. Ledyard, Applewood Farms Inn, 402
10. Lyme, Nutmeg Bed & Breakfast Host #20, 403
11. Moodus, The Fowler House, 404
12. Mystic: Noank, The Palmer Inn, 406
13. New London, The Queen Anne Inn, 407
14. New Milford, The Quid, 408
15. Norfolk, Manor House, 410
16. Old Lyme, Helen and Donald Janse, 411
17. Pomfret, Cobbscroft, 412
18. Putnam, The Felshaw Tavern, 414
19. Southington, Chaffee's B&B, 415
20. Stonington, Farnan House, 416
21. Stony Creek, Nutmeg Bed & Breakfast Host #23, 417
22. Thompson, Hedgerow House, 418
23. Watertown, The Clarks, 420
24. West Mystic, Leventhal B&B, 421
25. Woodbury, The Homestead, 422

# Connecticut Reservation Services

## Bed and Breakfast, Ltd.

P.O. Box 216, New Haven, CT 06513
**Phone:** 203/469-3260. During the academic year, 5-9 p.m. weekdays, anytime weekends; anytime during the summer.
**Listings:** Over 125. Located throughout Connecticut; new listings constantly added. Mostly private residences. A few inns and unhosted private residences.

Jack Argenio emphasizes variety—in types of homes as well as in price range. Many are historic residences filled with antiques. He selects knowledgeable and congenial hosts and tries to personalize matches to suit guests' needs and budget.

**Reservations:** Made for one day up to three months. Same-day service available in most cases. "A quick phone call encouraged to discuss availability and appropriate placement." Available through some travel agents.
**Plus:** In-ground pools, gourmet dinners, conference areas, arrangements for weddings. Some hosts will arrange to meet guests at airports or train stations.
**Rates:** $35-$40 singles, $40-$65 doubles. Some family and weekly rates. Deposit required: 20 percent. Cancellation policy: 48 hours' notice.

## Covered Bridge Bed and Breakfast Reservation Service

Maple Avenue, P.O. Box 701, Norfolk, CT 06058
**Phone:** 203/542-5944. 9 a.m.-8 p.m. daily.
**Listings:** 40. Located in northwest and shoreline Connecticut; in Shaftsbury, Vermont; in Hudson Valley of New York; and in the Berkshires of Massachusetts. All hosted private residences. Some short-term (two to three months) unhosted housing available. Di-

rectory (free with SASE) is a typed listing highlighting features of homes.

Hank and Diane Tremblay select their hosts so that they can provide guests "with a memorable B&B experience, an ideal getaway, at homes of distinction—in charming farmhouse with extensive acreage, Victorian estates, restored colonials, and Cape Cods." Hosts are also well traveled and appreciate the opportunity to share experiences with their guests.

**Reservations:** One to two weeks' advance notice preferred. Two-day minimum for holiday weekends and special events, e.g. Tanglewood. Also available through travel agents.
**Plus:** Many hosts offer concierge-type services and speak other languages. The Tremblays work with travelers on an individual basis to try to accommodate their needs.
**Rates:** $35-$120 single, $40-$120 double. Family, senior citizen, and weekly rates available. Prepayment in full is required. One-night surcharge of $5-$10 depending on holiday, special events. For cancellations, deposit refunded in full minus $10 service charge up to seven days before the reservation. VISA, MasterCard, and AMEX accepted only when it is too late to mail a deposit; room will be held but payment by check or cash is required.

## Nutmeg Bed & Breakfast

222 Girard Avenue, Hartford, CT 06105
**Phone:** 203/236-6698
**Open:** Monday through Friday, 9-5, year round.
**Listings:** 130. Located throughout Connecticut in every county in 60 towns and cities, near college campuses and hospitals, near private schools, along the shore, in the northwest hills. Mostly hosted private residences. A few inns and unhosted private residences. Directory ($2.50) has general characteristics of each area as well as house descriptions.

After four years of traveling all over the state to select hosts for tourists, Maxine Kates has expanded her service to assist relocating executives to find temporary and permanent housing. She also works with hospitals to provide lodging for visiting professionals and patients in private homes.

**Reservations:** One week's advance notice preferred. Same-day reservations sometimes possible. Available through some travel agents.
**Plus:** Short-term (from one month to a year) hosted and unhosted housing available. Can arrange excellent tours of the Hartford area.
**Rates:** $35-$75 single, $40-$85 double. Family and weekly rates available. Full payment in advance. $5 surcharge for a one-night stay. $10 cancellation fee at all times; full charge of one night's lodging if less than 48-hour notice. MasterCard, VISA, and AMEX accepted.

## Pineapple Hospitality

This service has hosts in Essex, and in the areas of Danbury, Mystic, and Stamford. Please see page 214.

# Connecticut B&Bs

## Rockwood Farm Bed & Breakfast

Bantam, CT
**Location:** "Sixty five acres of heaven for the guests' enjoyment." On a quiet undeveloped country road, five miles from historic Litchfield.
**Reservations:** Available May 1-October 31 through Covered Bridge Bed and Breakfast, page 390.

"After enjoying our European B&B travels, we thought that it would be wonderful to share our 11-room residence with others. And it is! We bought our 1750 colonial house seven years ago from a wonderful family that owned it for a century. It is filled with a sense of history—and our antiques. We are secluded; there is no traffic. People seem to really relax here."

The exquisite B&B, sometimes called "a resort for two," is the home of a couple who own a local retail establishment; they enjoy theater, cooking, and their horses.

**In residence:** Someone who smokes. Five dogs. Four outdoor cats. Five horses, not for riding, who appreciate a pat on the head.
**Restrictions:** Sorry, no guests' pets. No smoking in bedrooms.
**Bed and bath:** Accommodations for two people. Choice of two rooms. Either a first-floor room with twin/king bed option, fireplace, and private bath or second-floor room with double brass bed, private bath.
**Breakfast:** At guests' convenience. Fresh fruit, juice, freshly baked goods, cheese, coffee, tea. Fresh flowers on the table. China and antique linens from hosts' collection.
**Plus:** Guest quarters are a private wing with separate entrance with a very large fireplaced living room and air conditioning in bedroom. Swimming pool.
**Rates:** $95 single, $120 double.

From New York: "What guest wouldn't fall in love with this lovely place! . . . a memorable anniversary."

## Eastover Farm Bed & Breakfast

P.O. Box 275, Guilds Hollow Road, Bethlehem, CT 06751
**Phone:** 203/266-5740
**Location:** On 70 acres of hills and fields with grazing cows, long rolling rural road, two miles west of Bethlehem on Route 132 south. Five miles north of Woodbury. Near ski areas, antique shops, and the prep schools of Litchfield County. Five minutes from White Flower Farm.
**Hosts:** Erik and Mary Hawvermale
**Open:** September-June. As of 1988, open year round.

There's Granny's Room, The Pump Room, The Pine Room, The Cuckoo Room—and more, all named by Mary's grandmother after she and Mary's grandfather, a Manhattan dentist, bought the 1773 farm in 1929. As a child, Mary came here often on weekends and school vacations. In 1985, she and Erik declared that their days of talking about B&B were over. Erik, a physical education major who expanded a student job with the Chart House Restaurants to an eight-year career, helped develop Mary's long-held idea of sharing the country home as a B&B.

The real restoration took place about 50 years ago when the grandparents uncovered fireplaces, including the huge cooking hearth, originally part of the kitchen, now in the living room. Complete with beehive oven, crane, cooking pot, and pewter plates over the mantel, this is one of many rooms that gives a strong sense of history. All the family antiques are still in place—against a background, in many rooms, of fresh paint and paper.

Before Mary settled here, she owned a Boston art gallery. While working on her degree in biology, she has been involved in whale research on Cape Cod.

In addition to touring Eastover's grounds, many guests visit the nearby White Flower Farm, a nursery recognized nationally for its perennials and ornamental shrubs. Antique shops, too, abound in this area.

**In residence:** Jacob, one year old. Dogs and a cat in the Hawvermales' residence; none in guest house. Cows, chickens, rabbits, horses, a pony, ducks, and geese on the farm.
**Restrictions:** Children should be at least ten. Sorry, no guests' pets.
**Bed and bath:** Seven rooms, some with working fireplaces. Two private baths—for a room with two twin beds and another with a king-sized bed. Single, twin, and queen-bedded rooms share two full baths.
**Breakfast:** At 9, earlier if requested. Juice, fresh fruit, homemade muffins and bread, coffee, teas, or hot chocolate. Served in the dining room or, weather permitting, on the porches.
**Plus:** Three living areas. Glassed-in porches upstairs and down. Mints. Thick towels. Flowers in the rooms. Tennis court. Acres of lawns and gardens; woods and pine forest with trails, two ponds.
**Rates:** $45 single with shared bath. $65 double with shared bath, $75 double with private bath.

## Nutmeg Bed & Breakfast Host #14

Bloomfield, CT
**Location:** Five miles northwest of Hartford on a quiet road but a couple of miles to everything.
**Reservations:** Available year round through Nutmeg Bed & Breakfast, page 391.

"I love to have this wonderful house filled with happy people. I'm not much of a letter writer, so if everyone starts corresponding the way my early guests do, I don't know what I'll do." Since the hostess expressed those sentiments in my first B&B book, the happy guests keep coming.

A student of Frank Lloyd Wright designed the addition to the reproduction Federal residence. The glass walls bring the outside in. In the spring more than 200 varieties of daffodils bloom with 20,000 blossoms. The magnificent tulip tree is alleged to be the oldest and largest in the state. Pastures, two barns, and 11 pet goats (each will answer to its name) on over five magnificent acres make for a memorable setting.

The host is a crewel-embroidery designer who usually shows interested visitors the processes and an array of bird, flower, animal, and hobby designs on linen, cotton, and rayon, ready to become finished pillows, hangings, pocketbooks, or ties.

Who comes here? A young couple with two children walked in the extensive woodlands, picnicked, fed the goats, and generally relaxed. A group of women, conventiongoers, found time to "kibitz in the kitchen" while food was being prepared for a big party; they also enjoyed singing around the piano. The sharing possibilities go beyond bed and breakfast.

**In residence:** Two cats.
**Bed and bath:** Four rooms. Two, each with two twin beds and private bath. One room with king-sized bed, fireplace, private bath, private balcony. One with 3/4 bed, shared bath.
**Breakfast:** Orange juice, fruit, bacon or sausage with eggs, English muffins, jelly, hot beverages.
**Plus:** TV in smaller living room, piano in larger living room. Swimming pool.
**Rates:** $45-$65.

From Hong Kong: ". . . Like coming back home to a rediscovered relative. The beautiful house, the setting, the forest nearby—all in fall color—reflected the peace and elegance of the New England countryside which we hoped we would find, and did."

## Jared Cone House

25 Hebron Road, Bolton, CT 06040
**Phone:** 203/643-8538
**Location:** Fifteen miles east of Hartford in the country with farms and woodlands. In a community of 5,000 people. Fine cuisine nearby. Two miles from Bolton Lake. Five miles to Manchester, 15 miles to University of Connecticut.
**Hosts:** Jeff and Cinde Smith
**Open:** Year round. Reservations requested.

The Palladian window in the second-floor hallway is a dramatic introduction to the guest floor in this traditional post-and-beam center-hall Georgian colonial. Jeff and Cinde purchased their treasure in 1985 after living in Bolton for eight years. Built by a wealthy farmer in the late 1700s, and once the library and the town's post office, the house is now registered with the U.S. Department of the Interior Office of Archeology and Historic Preservations.

The Smiths refinished the wide board floors, painted, and cleaned. "Our first goal was to make it our home. Now we are really having fun with B&B."

Jeff is a machinist and furniture maker. The spacious rooms in their historic home have print wallpapers, antiques and reproductions, and a light, airy, uncluttered look. In the kitchen is a huge hearth. The Jared Cone House is a very pleasant overnight stop for those en route or a quiet getaway for big-city folks. This is the land of pick-your-own farms, the famous Caprilands Herb Farm seven miles to the east, hay and sleigh rides, and canoeing (with the hosts' canoe). Fall foliage is magnificent. Antiquing is popular.

**In residence:** Daughter Julie, age two. Goldie is a 12-year-old mixed-breed dog. Oliver, a 5-year-old tiger cat.
**Restrictions:** No guests' pets. Smoking allowed on the first floor.
**Bed and bath:** Two large second-floor sunny rooms, each with a queen-sized bed, share one full bath. Crib and twin-sized rollaway available.
**Breakfast:** Usually 8-10. Juice, fresh fruit in summer, homemade pumpkin and apple breads with cream cheese, eggs with toast, coffee or tea, jellies and marmalades. Served at a large table in the dining room or, by request, on the porch. Cinde and Jeff may join you for coffee.

**Plus:** Upstairs sitting area next to the Palladian window. Porch and patio. Use of canoe, bicycles, stroller, playpen.
**Rates:** $40 single, $55 double. $10 rollaway.

## Chimney Crest Manor

5 Founders Drive, Bristol, CT 06010
**Phone:** 203/582-4219
**Location:** On a hilltop overlooking Farmington Valley. In historic Federal Hill area, one-quarter mile from Bristol Clock Museum, 8 minutes from Hershey Park's Lake Compounce Amusement Park; 20 minutes west of Hartford, 15 minutes east of Waterbury.
**Hosts:** Dan and Cynthia Cimadamore
**Open:** Year round. Reservations preferred.

The television crew was outside filming this mansion from every possible angle for a B&B feature. They pointed the camera at the tile roof, arches, gardens, and multiflue chimneys. In the dining room with roaring blaze in huge fireplace and table set beautifully with ample fresh fruit compote and baskets of homemade breads, we waited (hungrily). Part of our conversation was about the history of the 32-room Tudor, built in 1930 by the Barnes family, known locally for specialty steels and springs. Since Cynthia's parents bought the house in the mid-1950s, it has seen use as a preparatory school. Today it is a sprawling residence for three generations and provides full huge suites for B&B guests. Much of the house is carpeted; furnishings are traditional.

After the second Cimadamore child was born, Cynthia found that she was ready for "something else" that she could do at home. Early Chimney Crest guests were business people who appreciated the relaxed quiet atmosphere. Soon honeymooners discovered the estate's private arrangements. By now, many travelers, including British royalty, have walked the 40-foot long arcade and seen some of the six handcrafted fireplaces and ornate plaster ceilings. A Texas family of 11 wrote to me about "being treated like family in this beautiful English-style manor house."

**In residence:** Diana, age ten, and Dante, age two. Their dog, Bootsie, is part beagle.
**Restrictions:** No guests' pets.

**Bed and bath:** Four units, each with private bath, three with full kitchens. Living room and queen-sized bed in each two- or three-room suite. One large single room has fireplace. Private guest entrance.
**Breakfast:** 7-9. Juice, fruit, a main course such as eggs and bacon or ham, or pancakes and sausage, coffee. Served with linen and china in the dining room. Sometimes Dan or Cynthia joins guests.
**Plus:** Air conditioning, fans, and television in each bedroom. Late-afternoon or evening tea and coffee. Library. Solarium. Garden. Large patio. Tour of the house. Laundry facilities (extra charge). Will meet guests at Bradley airport ($10 per person).
**Rates:** $55-$65 single or double occupancy. Weekly and monthly rates available. Corporate, senior citizen, and Lovers' Weekend (two-night stay) discounts.

## Riverwind

209 Main Street, Deep River, CT 06417
**Phone:** 203/526-2014
**Location:** Adjacent to the town green, in a small Connecticut River Valley village between Essex and Chester. Minutes to Goodspeed Opera House, Gillette Castle, Hammonasett Beach; half-hour drive to Mystic Seaport.
**Host:** Barbara Barlow
**Open:** Year round. Reservations preferred.

Just because Mrs. Barlow sometimes wonders how the North is treating her daughter, more than one guest has written to Mother about "charm, talents, graciousness and warm hospitality."

Still in her early thirties when she had had experience restoring her own small house in Virginia and two others, including one in nearby East Haddam, Connecticut, Barbara, on a sudden urge, took a week's leave from her junior high school learning-disabilities teaching position, came north, found, and bought the abandoned house by the town green. In just a year's time, she uncovered fireplaces, hand-sanded floors, wired, tiled, and stenciled the 1850 house. By the time the summer of 1984 arrived, she was ready to drive a truck from Smithfield, Virginia, with family and other country antiques "measured to fit and purchased at home especially for the inn." The result shows a love of folk art, a sense of display, imagination, and whimsy. Towels hang from antique carpenter's tools. The pig items acknowledge her growing up on a farm in the ham capital of the world. Quilts were the inspiration for the decor and color scheme of three guest rooms.

**In residence:** Miss Hickory is "a small affectionate tabby." The hostess smokes.
**Restrictions:** Children should be at least 12. Sorry, no guests' pets.
**Bed and bath:** Four rooms, each with a double bed and private bath. First-floor room—canopied four-poster bed, attached bath with claw-foot tub. Three second-floor rooms with high four-poster double bed, attached full bath; pine bed, hand-painted headboard, private unattached bath with shower only; carved oak furniture, attached full bath. Cot available.
**Breakfast:** Generally 8:30-10. A southern buffet of family recipes served by dining room fireplace. Smithfield ham from Barbara's hometown, pig-shaped biscuits, grapefruit and mandarin orange compote, two juices, coffee cake or sweet bread, jams, honey, coffee, tea.
**Plus:** Welcoming drink. Help-yourself coffee and tea for early risers. Sherry. Mints. Flowers. Thick towels. Bedroom ceiling fans. Game room filled with practical treasures. Living room. Piano and old sheet music. Guitar. Library. Plant- and wicker-filled wraparound (glassed-in) porch—with ceiling fans. Large back yard with bocci, badminton, and croquet, hibachis and picnic baskets. Will meet guests at Saybrook train.
**Rates:** $70 room with unattached bath, $75 room with claw-foot tub, $80 rooms with shower/tub. MasterCard and VISA accepted.

## The Red House

365 Boston Post Road, East Lyme, CT 06333
**Phone:** 203/739-5327
**Location:** A rural setting on three acres. On a two-lane road, 5 minutes from I-95, 3 minutes from the shore and 20 minutes to Essex and Mystic. Midway between New York City and Boston.
**Hosts:** Harlan and Joan Sturgis
**Open:** Year round. Reservations preferred.

From Rhode Island: "Great people. Harlan (justifiably) takes great pride in the berries he grows and serves for breakfast. . . . Joan's wonderful too. . . . Not to mention their 1760s house that's a real charmer."

A gem of a B&B is another way of putting it. Thank you, Holiday Inn! When Joan worked there, she noticed that there was often no room at the inn, just about the time Harlan had retired from his elementary school principalship. Their own B&B travels, grown children, and thoughts of a shared venture clinched the opening of The Red House.

Inside the 1760 center-chimney colonial you'll find wainscoting, small-print wallpapers, seven fireplaces (nonworking), and, in the living room, exposed ceiling beams and a beehive oven. Part of the family room is a greenhouse where most of the plantings are started. It also has a wood stove, and sliding doors to a wood deck. The Sturgises bought the house, all restored, in 1982.

Outside are thriving gardens, stone walls, root cellar, a mug, goose pen, and circular rock outcroppings, all with stories. When the house was a tavern years ago, the pen was used by farmers on their way to market. Archeologists think the outdoor cellar, the "mug," is similar to caves discovered nearby, carbon tested to circa 900 B.C.

Harlan, a selectman, has lived in the town for 40 years. Joan, a massage therapist, is a native. They can give good hints for interesting back roads to area attractions.

**In residence:** A large 11-year-old yellow cat "who answers to the name of 'Kat.' "
**Restrictions:** School-aged children preferred. Sorry, no guests' pets. No smoking, please.
**Bed and bath:** Two rooms. A first-floor room with twin beds has an adjoining bath, wide board floors, exposed beams. Second-floor room has heirloom double bed, next to full bath (shared with hosts). Cot available. Nonworking fireplaces in each room.
**Breakfast:** 6:30-9:30 weekdays, Sundays until 10. Harlan prepares blueberry pancakes with buttermilk and his blueberries. Served with sausages or bacon or French toast made from Joan's sourdough bread. Homemade jams. Unlimited coffee. Hosts usually join you in the sunny dining room or on the deck.
**Plus:** Afternoon or evening beverages and nut bread. Tour of house and gardens, and sometimes opportunities to pick raspberries. Family room with TV and wood stove. Window fans in bedrooms. Yard

and lawn furniture. Passes to private beach. Outdoor hot/cold shower. Laundry facilities (extra charge).
**Rates:** $40 single, $50 double. $5 for cot. Special rates for families using both rooms. MasterCard and VISA accepted.

## Shore Inne

54 East Shore Road, Groton Long Point, CT 06340
**Phone:** 203/536-1180
**Location:** Overlooking a tranquil harbor "where the sound of seagulls is the major attraction." Three beaches within walking distance; one has a diving dock and separate fishing pier. Half mile to area conservation lands for bird-watching and walking. Four miles to Mystic Seaport.
**Host:** Helen Ellison
**Open:** April 1 through November 1.

We arrived in time for a cool swim just down the road, followed by a tour of this quiet community of large older homes (and a very few newer ones). As usual, there was a full house. As usual, there were returnees who came just to sit and read and enjoy the ocean. Others were tourists who were about to see all of New England in two weeks.

The setting here gives guests the feeling of being residents rather than tourists. Even in the inn, there's no commercial feeling. You are visiting a grandmother in her comfortable old home that has an interesting origin. Around 1920, before the current zoning, vaudeville performers, owners of the summer home next door, had so many guests that they built this as an inn, using beach stones for the fireplace.

Helen hand-stenciled the library/sunroom walls, made quilts for all the guest rooms, and furnished the living room in white wicker. After eight years as a gracious hostess, she continues to enjoy this quiet place and her guests.

**Restrictions:** No smoking in the dining room. No pets. Sorry, no cribs or cots.
**Bed and bath:** Seven rooms, three with private full baths. Four share two baths.

**Breakfast:** 8-10. Juice, Helen's almost-famous buttermilk bran muffins, cold cereal, hot beverage. Served at several tables in the dining room, which faces the water.
**Plus:** Use of refrigerator, picnic table, lawn chairs, and lawn games.
**Rates:** Memorial Day weekend to closing $36-$42 shared bath, $50 rooms with private baths. Lower rates from April to Memorial Day. MasterCard and VISA accepted.

## Applewood Farms Inn

528 Colonel Ledyard Highway, Ledyard, CT 06339
**Phone:** 203/536-2022
**Location:** A colonial farm setting on 33 acres, 5 minutes to Mystic.
**Hosts:** Frankie and Tom Betz
**Open:** Year round. Two-day minimum stay on weekends.

> From New Hampshire: "This farm has been lovingly restored by a retired businessman (marine electronics) and his wife. . . . It is near many attractions and historic old towns, but the chief charm is the guest house, in a beautiful setting, surrounded by green pastures and bordering a breeding farm for prize Arabians (which you can visit). A cute dog named Milton is on the premises. All the rooms are different. . . . We were greeted by a pitcher of ice water and a basket of fruit and candies. Hosts were friendly and solicitous and made us a gourmet breakfast. Tom is training one of his horses to pull a sleigh and a real 'surrey with the fringe on top.' This B&B is a real discovery."

The farm features "pure unadulterated relaxation and philosophizing by the fire."

Until it became a horse farm in 1964, five generations of Gallups lived in the 1826 house. When the Betzes bought it in 1985, they restored everything—except the replacement joists and sills—themselves. Most walls are simulated whitewash. Stenciling abounds. Antiques, primitives, and a large pewter collection add to the charm.

Tom and Frankie lived in nearby Mystic for 20 years "and have been paying guests elsewhere for 30." The grandparents (of four) have linked their interests of horticulture, birding, and travel in a new career that is "a lot of fun work."

**In residence:** Both hosts smoke.

**Restrictions:** Smoking allowed in common rooms only. Polite pets welcomed; kennel and stable provided.
**Bed and bath:** Four rooms (with plans for three more) all with working fireplaces. Two on first floor, two on second. Two private baths, one shared. One king-sized bed (fashioned from two antique twin-sized beds). One room with a canopied four-poster double. Double beds in other rooms.
**Breakfast:** 8-10. Juice, tropical fruit dish with sherbet, eggs with bacon and toast. Hot beverages ("transfusions by the gallon"). At large table in the summer kitchen. Can last as long as two hours.
**Plus:** Beverages. Air conditioning in some bedrooms. Three common rooms. Parlor baby grand piano (three Betz children have music degrees). Seasonal wildflowers, fruit, and mints in rooms. Hiking or cross-country ski trails. Tour of house and farm. With advance notice, pickup at stations or Groton-New London Airport.
**Rates:** Double occupancy. $65-$95 large rooms. $50 smaller rooms. $25 cot for third person in room. MasterCharge or VISA accepted.

## Nutmeg Bed & Breakfast Host #20

Lyme, CT
**Location:** On 200 acres, eight miles from I-95. Within a half hour's drive of Essex, Goodspeed Opera House, Gillette's Castle, Connecticut River Valley.
**Reservations:** Available year round through Nutmeg Bed & Breakfast, page 391.

Genuine. Not fantasy. Not a museum. Good old-fashioned hospitality in a clean, friendly 1840 Federal farmhouse that has been in the family since 1917. All eight children are grown and gone and, at least for the moment, not showing any interest in carrying on their parents' lifestyle of self-sufficiency. However, one 200-pound ewe that was raised inside occasionally beckons for attention.

Both husband and wife run the farm. The host sells lumber here. The hostess spins, dyes, and weaves wool; yes, a demonstration for guests is quite possible. And as the hostess says, "This is a great place for kids, hikers, cross-country skiers, ice skaters or fishermen." A true getaway.

**In residence:** Sheep, lambs, cattle, and calves on the grounds.
**Restrictions:** Sorry, no guests' pets. No smoking.

**Bed and bath:** Four rooms on second floor share one full and one half guest baths. Double or twin-bedded rooms. Some with skylight. Crib available.
**Breakfast:** 8-9. Homemade juice, fruit, breads, jams, home-ground sausage and fresh eggs, bacon from their own smokehouse. Served in the dining room with French doors and hostess's loom, or in the welcoming kitchen by the fireplace, spinning wheels, bucksaws, and oxen yoke.
**Plus:** Rocking chairs on the front porch. Chess, checkers, books. Tour of the farm.
**Rates:** $40 single, $50 double. Crib is free.

## The Fowler House

Box 432, Plains Road, Moodus, CT 06469
**Phone:** 203/873-8906
**Location:** On the Moodus town green. Four miles north of antique shops, restaurants, shops, and Goodspeed Opera House in East Haddam. Half hour from Hartford and Wesleyan University, 40 minutes from Mystic Seaport.
**Hosts:** Penny Davidson and Barbara Ally
**Open:** Year round. Reservations recommended. Two-night minimum stay on holiday weekends.

"It's just as we pictured it would be. We're in a small town, offering country warmth and Victorian elegance. People who come here feel as though they have made a discovery."

Named for its first owner, a manufacturer of patent medicines, the house is endowed with wraparound porch, turret, six stained-glass windows, a stained-glass skylight, hand-carved woodwork, and eight working (coal-burning) fireplaces. It is furnished with period pieces and family antiques.

Since taking possession of the house in 1984, the two couples in their thirties have completely restored it inside and out. Shortly after opening in 1985 they organized a real Victorian Fair complete with high wheelers, barbershop quartet, and costumed guides. They have also hosted a Chocolate Lovers' Weekend and are a great resource for interesting crafts shops.

Barbara and Penny instinctively know how to host—to be there when you need them and to give guests in their home some privacy too. Barbara was an office manager in Hartford and Penny a pediatric nurse practitioner in Springfield. Although the husbands joined in the restoration work and are equally thrilled with their 1890 Victorian masterpiece, the running of inn is the project of the personable and imaginative women. Arnie is the owner of a furniture warehouse and Paul has his own appliance repair business.

**In residence:** Husbands Arnie Davidson and Paul Seals, and Ian Ally Seals, age eight. Boo-Boo, a dog, and one cat named Fluffy are not allowed in guest areas.
**Restrictions:** Children should be at least 12. No guests' pets. Smoking limited to common rooms. Check-in time, 2-9 p.m.; check-out at 11 a.m.
**Bed and bath:** Six large rooms. Of the four private baths, two have tub and shower; two, shower only. The first-floor room has a double bed, ceramic-tiled fireplace, private adjoining bath with claw-foot tub. Features of five second-floor rooms, including one in the turret, vary. One with queen-sized (brass) bed, three with a double bed in each, and one with two twin four-poster beds. Cot available. All beds have afghans made by Penny's mother.
**Breakfast:** 8:30-10. Fruit in season or homemade hot and cold fruit dishes, freshly squeezed juice, variety of home-baked goods with Fowler House jams. Homemade granola. Sometimes a feature such as cream cheese French toast or soufflelike apple pancakes. Coffee and teas. Served in the dining room (where it often lasts up to two hours) or, if preferred, in the guest's room.
**Plus:** Afternoon tea and/or welcoming glass of wine. Library with fireplace. Tour of the house. Occasional theme weekends. Turndown service; chocolates on the pillow. Bedroom window or ceiling fans. Complimentary champagne for special occasions. Dinner for house guests only on fall and winter Saturday nights ($40-$50 for two, advance reservations required). Guest refrigerator. Bicycles. Lawn chairs. Porch with hammocks. Volleyball. Will meet guests at Old Saybrook train; assist with car rental.
**Rates:** Spring/summer $60 double with shared bath, $65-$70 with private bath. Fall and winter $70 double with shared bath, $65-$85 double with private bath. Midweek specials. Seasonal packages. Ten percent discount for stays of one week or longer. MasterCard and VISA accepted.

*Can't find the community you are going to? Check with a reservation service described at the beginning of this chapter. Through the service, you may be placed (matched) with a welcoming B&B that is near your destination.*

## The Palmer Inn

25 Church Street, Noank, CT 06340
**Phone:** 203/572-9000
**Location:** In a quiet fishing village, two miles southwest of Mystic. One block to Long Island Sound beach; walk to tennis, art galleries, and a reknowned casual lobster-in-the-rough restaurant.
**Hosts:** Donald and Patricia W. Cornish
**Open:** Year round. Reservations suggested. Two-night minimum stay May-December weekends. Three-night minimum on holiday weekends.

Five steps up between 30-foot pillars and you're in the main hall with its 13-foot ceilings, mahogany beams, brass fixtures, and original wallcovering. At the turn of the century, this was the home of the Palmer family, owners of one of the largest shipyards on the east coast. It has nine stained-glass windows, a balcony looking out to the sea, family antiques, and, as an inn, some old traditions. For a full history of the unusually large (for Noank) Southern plantation-like home, located on just an acre of land, ask the innkeepers who began their work on this historical (sometimes they call it hysterical) structure in 1984. Although the total restoration and complete furnishing will take some time, guests are welcomed to a quiet relaxed atmosphere any time of the year. As a matter of fact, Pat, a former director of a nonprofit agency in Connecticut, and Don, an accountant, have dreamed up all sorts of package arrangements: Victorian Christmas with an 11-foot tree in the hall; Weekend Getaways; Cabin Fever Weekend; or St. Patti's Day. Each includes some activity, maybe a gift certificate to a restaurant, tea time, and, of course, breakfast.

Not only is there a menu book, but restaurant reviews are also collected. For suggestions of off-the-beaten-track highlights, try the Doll Museum, wineries, dinner sails, or hot-air ballooning. Mulled cider, a good book, and a crackling fireplace sound pretty good too.

**In residence:** Dickens, the official greeter, is a miniature dachshund, "a real charmer."
**Restrictions:** Children should be at least 16. Sorry, no accommodations for pets. Cigarette smoking only; limited to the first-floor parlor.
**Bed and bath:** Six (large, some huge) rooms. Some with water views; one with balcony. Three on the second floor with private full baths. One with private full bath on third floor; two with semipri-

vate full bath. King, queen, and twin-sized beds. Different antique furnishings in each room—oak, cherry, mahogany, wicker, walnut, and brass.
**Breakfast:** 8:30-9:30. Fresh fruit salad, juice, coffee, herbal tea, homemade muffins—especially banana walnut—and breads, homemade jellies, jams, and butters. Hosts usually join guests in the Grand Salon ("our parlor") for this family-style meal at table that seats 12.
**Plus:** Tea or sherry 4-6. Library. Board games. Fireplace in parlor. Fresh flowers in each room year round. Fans, if needed. Veranda. Bicycles.
**Rates:** $75-$85 shared bath, $80-$105 private baths, $105-$115 suites. Single occupancy is $5 less. MasterCard and VISA accepted.

## The Queen Anne Inn

265 Williams Street, New London, CT 06320
**Phone:** 203/447-2600
**Location:** In a residential neighborhood. Within walking distance of restaurants, Connecticut College, and the Coast Guard Academy. Ten-minute drive to Mystic Seaport, Eugene O'Neill Theater, Nautilus Museum. Five-minute drive to athletic facilities.
**Hosts:** Mary Piscitello and Captain Morgan Beatty
**Open:** Year round. Reservations required. Two- or three-night minimum stays on holiday weekends.

"Two books on historic homes have featured the Queen Anne. Business people have discovered us. We've had our first wedding here. (We can accommodate about 25 people at a reception.) Yes, my work is all over the inn, but it's not for sale! Yes, it is wonderful having a house full of people all the time. . . . I love cooking and talking to people."

Mary and Morgan, with the help of about ten friends, restored the 1880 Victorian over a year's time. Within a year after opening in the summer of 1985, the Queen Anne won a restoration award from the New London Landmarks Commission.

Many fireplaces, a paneled foyer, and stained-glass windows at the circular landing are some of the architectural features. Mary's artistic touches are everywhere—from the antiques and their placement to her hand-cut pierced lamp shades, reverse glass paintings, and more than 50 velvet theorems or tinsel paintings. (In the winter she conducts private and class lessons in early American arts.) The guest rooms are all bright and cheerful. There's lots of fabric—in swags on the windows, in dust ruffles, curtains, and canopies on the beds.

In addition to being a research scientist, Morgan is a charter boat captain. Arrangements can be made to charter his 43-foot sloop.

**Restrictions:** Children should be at least 12. No guests' pets. Smoking allowed in foyer and on porch.
**Bed and bath:** Eight rooms and a two-room suite, each with new private bath with shower or tub shower. Queen, king, double, or two twin-sized (brass or antique) beds. Bridal room features canopy bed, working fireplace, and balcony. The two-room suite has a kitchen. Rollaways available.

**Breakfast:** Usually 8-9:30 on weekdays, 9-10:30 on weekends. Earlier possible. Buffet of bacon and eggs, fresh fruit plate, juice, homemade bread and jellies and beverage. Can be a very social time.
**Plus:** All rooms are air conditioned. Afternoon fireside tea (includes cakes, breads, or fresh fruit) in winter; iced tea on the porch in warm weather. Free use of Waterford Racquet Club (Jacuzzi, sauna, nautilus, racquetball, and tennis). Four-day notice required to reserve court time. Tour of the house and, sometimes, Mary's studio.
**Rates:** Double occupancy. $95 with fireplace, $65 small double; others $75-$85. Singles $5 less. $10 for extra person in room. Corporate and midweek rates available. Discounts for extended stays. MasterCard, VISA, and AMEX accepted.

## The Quid

New Milford, CT
**Location:** In a rural setting, three miles out of town with no other house in sight. On 30 acres with lovely landscaping and beautiful views of woods, ponds, fields, and hills. Antiquing possibilities nearby.
**Reservations:** Available year round through Covered Bridge Bed and Breakfast, page 390.

"My favorite place is my home and its gardens. We even had resident bluebirds this spring. The original part of the house—it grew like Topsy—was built in 1939 from a tobacco barn that my parents tore down. . . . It's a unique blend of comfort, beauty and quiet elegance. My parents chose this location because they heard that the spring had never run dry. We still have fresh spring water."

Paneling from the barn was used in the living room, which has a cathedral beamed ceiling, walk-in stone fireplace, and huge picture window. Throughout there are English and American antiques, original art work, Polish rugs, fireplaces.

"B&B continually shows how small the world is. Often I find that we have mutual acquaintances—and even cousins!" The hostess has had considerable experience as a professional chef and enjoys preparing occasional dinners.

**In residence:** Hostess's parents live in a separate apartment at one end of the house. Ayliffe is a large and friendly golden retriever/ Newfoundland mix.

**Restrictions:** Pets must be well behaved and housebroken.
**Foreign language spoken:** Spanish
**Bed and bath:** Two rooms, one with private bath. A large first-floor room has two twins or one king-sized bed and a daybed, private bath with shower, outside entrance onto a deck. Upstairs, a very private room with two twin beds shares a bath (tub, no shower) with the hostess. A small room with a daybed may also be available. Handwoven or crocheted bedspreads.
**Breakfast:** Flexible hours. Homemade granola, jams, and jellies; seasonal fruits (homegrown blueberries, raspberries, and rhubarb), juice, muffins, breads, coffee, tea. Served in dining room, in sitting room with wood stove, or on terrace. Hostess often joins guests.
**Plus:** Late-afternoon or evening tea, cheese and crackers. Tour of house. Fresh flowers in rooms. Line-dried sheets. Turned-down beds. Bedroom fans. Outside deck. Hiking and cross-country ski trails. Tennis court (in fair condition). Swimming pool may be available. Dinner (fee charged) available with advance notice. Kitchen privileges by arrangement.
**Rates:** Shared bath $45 single, $50 double. $90 double with private bath. $95 three people in room with private bath. Add $5 for one-night stays. Rates may be slightly lower at some times of year.

## Manor House

Maple Avenue, Norfolk, CT 06058
**Phone:** 203/542-5690
**Location:** On a residential street, off of Route 44. Set on five landscaped acres, within walking distance of the village, historical society, and Yale chamber music concerts; 20 miles to Tanglewood.
**Hosts:** Diane and Hank Tremblay
**Open:** Year round. Reservations preferred. Two-day minimum stay on weekends in the summer, during the month of October and on holidays.

> A guest wrote, "Our return visit was certainly an endorsement. . . . Hank and Diane are thoughtful and gracious. . . . The house has perfect logistics for a B&B, plus it is loaded with interesting detail."

"It's a very different lifestyle, one that we consciously chose after working in the corporate world." Both hosts were executives with a large Connecticut-based insurance company. Their white stucco, brown-trimmed Manor House is "English Tudor with a Bavarian influence, large enough to invite socializing or to respect privacy." Built in 1898 by Charles Spofford, designer of London's underground system, it has until now been a private home with the original cherry paneling and Tiffany stained-glass windows and, for one room, a private elevator. The Tremblays have hung fresh wallpapers and furnished with Moroccan rugs and antiques.

Since their career change ("Not one regret!") the Tremblays have helped others to open a personalized quality B&B. Their commitment has gone yet another step with their reservation service, page 390, for private B&B homes in the area. Both Diane and Hank are active members of the Norfolk Early Music Society. They cycle, cross-country ski, and continue to go antiquing.

**In residence:** A calico cat named Rudy and her son, a gray and white angora named Ignatius, "both adored by guests."
**Restrictions:** For weekend stays, children should be at least 12. No guests' pets. No smoking, please.
**Foreign language spoken:** French.
**Bed and bath:** Eight rooms. Six on the second floor; four with private bath. Two on the third floor with semiprivate bath. King, queen, or two twin-sized beds available. A pineapple four-poster, a sleigh bed, or antique spool or brass bed among the antiques. Two rooms each have a private balcony.

**Breakfast:** 8:30-10, earlier by request. Blueberry pancakes, orange waffles, stuffed French toast, poached eggs with lemon chive sauce, homemade muffins and breads, honey from the Tremblays' hives, pure maple syrup from a local farm, vegetables, herbs, and berries from the garden, special teas and coffee brewed with spring water. Served in elegant dining room, on the porch, or in bed!
**Plus:** Piano in the living room. Library. Extensive collection of 78 rpm records. Flannel sheets in winter; down comforters in most rooms. Huge bath towels. Beverages. House tour. Flowers. Passes for the town lake. Sleigh rides and mulled cider at Christmas. Possible tour of harpsichord builder's studio. Will meet guests (fee charged) at the Bradley airport, Dover Plains train, or Canaan bus. Guest refrigerator. B&B apprentice program offered.
**Rates:** $50-$120 single, $60-$125 double. Off-season rates in March and April. Midweek discounts for seniors and families. MasterCard and VISA accepted. One-night surcharge.

## Helen and Donald Janse

11 Flat Rock Hill Road, Old Lyme, CT 06371
**Phone:** 203/434-7269
**Location:** On a parklike acre. On a quiet country road lined with stone walls and old maple trees. Ten minutes from I-95. Twenty minutes from Goodspeed Opera House, half hour west of Mystic Seaport.
**Open:** Year round. Reservations suggested.

> A guest wrote: "A pleasurable experience, the most comfortable one we have ever had at a B&B. The room was immaculate, spacious, and well-appointed. The breakfast was bountiful and delicious! We enjoyed the hosts' company and their suggestions of local points of interest."

Tradition reigns: The first guests came here as overflow from the local inn. Built just 13 years ago, the Williamsburg-style saltbox was designed for world travelers and antique collectors who were retiring. Since the Janses purchased the wonderful property nine years ago, they have developed extensive gardens that have become the basis for a mail-order business for their own crafts, foods, and how-to books. "Wreath making is our most popular one." Now they also have a shop in the garage with their own items, such as ornaments, preserves and wood products.

Inside, too, there's an unhurried gracious atmosphere with art work everywhere, Orientals, and antiques. Don is organist, church choir director, piano and vocal teacher, coach and composer. Helen was an executive secretary for Kodak and then IBM.

**In residence:** Twinkle, "a blond cocker, gentle, friendly, affectionate." A 17-year-old cat "who sleeps a lot but is an active hunter when awake."
**Restrictions:** Children should be at least seven. Sorry, no guests' pets.
**Bed and bath:** One room with double bed and private full bath. Four windows provide views of the grounds and adjacent woodlands. Rollaway available.
**Breakfast:** Juice or seasonal fruit, sausage, ham or bacon, eggs, toast, freshly baked muffins and homemade jams and coffee. Served in dining room or on the porch or patio.
**Plus:** Air conditioning. Beverages. Fireplaced living room. Library/den. Porch. Patio and grounds. Fresh bouquets. Tour of house and gardens.
**Rates:** $55 single, $60 double.

## Cobbscroft

P.O. Box 104, Routes 169 & 44, Pomfret, CT 06258
**Phone:** 203/928-5560
**Location:** On a hill 200 yards south of Pomfret School, 3/4 of a mile south of Rectory School. "In the quiet corner of northeast Connecticut." Near a small winery in town. Many antique shops in the area. Half-hour drive north to Old Sturbridge Village; 35 miles to Rhode Island beaches.
**Hosts:** Tom and Janet McCobb
**Open:** Year round. Reservations preferred.

Longevity and joie de vivre seem to come with the property. The house and barn were built in 1835 for a woman who loved horses; to this day you can see her stone mounting block at the front entrance. The wide Victorian porch was added in 1890, and in the early 1900s the house was purchased by a family with four daughters who served afternoon tea and Sunday dinners until the last daughter died at the age of 95. The McCobbs became owners in August 1985 in time to open with a full house the weekend of a hurricane. "We learned early that it helps to be flexible and to have a sense of humor in this business. . . . A good time was had by all, but we were glad to go back to hot water and electricity.

"For Cobbscroft, we have tried to use wallpapers and fabrics that reflect the ambiance of the era. Several rooms have been hand-stenciled in Early Victorian designs. . . . The comment we often hear is that the overall feeling is very comfortable and gracious."

The grandparents of seven came "to rural Connecticut at its best" because they wanted a new business. In Syracuse, New York Tom was a retired business executive and Janet ran a sheep farm. Their new lifestyle encompasses some of their many interests. Janet is a modern theoremist who cooks and gardens for a hobby. Tom is a full-time professional artist who also teaches painting. His studio was fashioned from a woodshed and its indoor privies. Your first introduction to Tom's work may be the charming watercolor of Cobbscroft on the brochure. Many of his original paintings are in the art gallery on the premises. From time to time they have special events such as an opera weekend featuring the New England Opera company.

**In residence:** Three spaniels—Oliver, a cocker; Valentine, a Brittany; and an English springer named Star.
**Restrictions:** No guests' pets. Smoking in designated areas. Boarding provisions can be made for pets.
**Bed and bath:** Five rooms on two floors. First-floor twin-bedded room shares an adjoining full bath with a single room. Upstairs, one room has a double bed (private half-bath), another has twin beds, and the third is a large suite with queen-sized bed, fireplace, huge full bath. Cot and crib available.
**Breakfast:** 7-9, earlier if necessary. Seasonal fruits, cooked apple crisp, sweet breads, coffee cakes, pastries, and muffins. A marvelous mushroom omelet made on request. Served in dining room.
**Plus:** Beverages. Tours of the area. Library, living room, antiques throughout. Bedroom fans if needed.
**Rates:** $55 double occupancy, $65 fireplaced room. $15 extra for children. $10 for crib. $10 less for single occupancy; 10 percent discount for seniors or businesses. MasterCard and VISA accepted.

## The Felshaw Tavern

Five Mile Road, Putnam, CT 06260
**Phone:** 203/928-3467
**Location:** In rural country, sometimes called " Connecticut's quiet corner." On Route 21, 3½ miles from Putnam, 1½ miles from Route 395, two miles from Route 44. Sturbridge is 30 miles away; Mystic, 50; Boston, 65. Within ten minutes of Pomfret, Rectory, and Marianapolis Schools.
**Hosts:** Herb and Terry Kinsman
**Open:** Year round.

With all the press attention showered on Felshaw Tavern, you might think it's a large B&B. At most, there are four guests at a time who appreciate the magnificent restoration that *is* worth a thousand pictures; still it is the hospitality that is remembered by many travelers, including business people, honeymooners, tourists—and travel writers.

This center-chimney colonial gem with five working fireplaces was built in 1742 as a tavern and converted to a private home in the 19th century. It had seen many changes by 1979, when Terry and Herb "fled east" after 30 years in Los Angeles. There he was "a professional rescuer of homes" and she wrote advertising copy.

The hosts greet you on the granite steps at the handsome mahogany-paneled front door made by Herb. Among the many rooms furnished with fine antiques is the Keeping Room (with beehive oven) where Revolutionary militia relaxed, drank ale, and smoked their pipes. The breakfast room and study are Herb's creations too. His craftsmanship extends to furniture making. It's hard for the untrained eye to tell that the slant-front mahogany desk or black walnut lowboy are reproductions. Outside, tons of bramble have been cleared—with thoughts of having a fountain. Now a high fence with perfectly scaled finials encloses the three acres.

What a setting for Terry to write copy for classical record liner notes! What a setting "for rediscovering oneself and each other"—and the Kinsmans with their global concerns.

**In residence:** "Outdoor terrace feeders are a magnet for blue jays, goldfinches, chickadees, woodpeckers, cardinals and grosbeaks."
**Restrictions:** No smoking in bedrooms; nonsmokers preferred. Sorry, no guests' pets and preferably no children.

**Bed and bath:** Two huge second-floor bedrooms, each with queen-sized four-poster bed, sitting area, working fireplace, private adjoining bath. One full bath; one shower bath.
**Breakfast:** A full meal served at guests' convenience in delightful greenhouse breakfast room overlooking meadow and woods. Perhaps eggs scrambled with cheese, beef sausages, homemade muffins, coffee or tea. Fresh flowers and classical music.
**Plus:** Afternoon or evening beverage. English oak-paneled study with books, periodicals, and television. A tour of the house. If you'd like, Herb's expertise, backed by examples of pitfalls and experiences. Suggestions for tour routes by foot, bicycle, or car, or for a lake in Woodstock or historic home in Canterbury.
**Rate:** $75 per room, includes tax.

## Chaffee's B&B

28 Reussner Road, Southington, CT 06489
**Phone:** 203/628-2750
**Location:** In a quiet residential area, two miles from I-84. Ten minutes from the Mount Southington (downhill) ski area and 15 from Hershey/Lake Compounce Amusement Park. Four large apple orchards are in Southington.
**Hosts:** Milton and Kay Chaffee
**Open:** Year round except Christmas. Reservations preferred.

> From Illinois: "Delightful! Comfortable beds, new sheets, bath all new, and morning awakening with the aroma of homemade muffins and delicious coffee cake. To add to that, a warm friendly visit with the Chaffees. I would highly rate it in your book as five star."

"Delightful" is the word the Chaffees also use to describe guests.

According to Milt and Kay, they used my first B&B book for their own travels, then came home and observed that the Southington area was lacking in personalized accommodations. Their family is grown, and Kay enjoys crafts, cooking, and baking. Milt, a retired banker, has been an active amateur radio operator for over half a century. Since 1985 they have been offering a relaxed environment in their six-room colonial ranch house located in an area that is "s-o-o quiet."

**Restrictions:** Adults preferred. No smokers or pets.

**Bed and bath:** First-floor room with two twin beds and private full bath.
**Breakfast:** 8:30 or time predetermined by guest and hostess. Juice, fruits, eggs any style, cereal, and Kay's specialty, muffins. Served in dining room overlooking the large yard, or on screened porch.
**Plus:** Central air conditioning. Hosts' living room with books, organ, cable television.
**Rates:** $35 single, $40 double.

## Farnan House

10 McGrath Court, Stonington, CT 06378
**Phone:** 203/535-0634
**Location:** On a cul-de-sac within walking distance of Stonington village. Eleven miles from Rhode Island beaches, 4 miles from Mystic Seaport, 16 from New London and Eugene O'Neill Theater.
**Host:** Mrs. Ann Farnan
**Open:** Year round. Reservations preferred.

> From Delaware: "A more warm and hospitable hostess you could not find. Her home is clean and nicely decorated and our bedroom was comfortable. Her kitchen is an antique lover's dream. In fact, on our first visit, breakfast was so good and all the guests so interesting, we spent at least an hour and a half before we could break away."

The family homestead was built by Mrs. Farnan's father-in-law in 1906. "When John and I restored (and redecorated) it in 1975, we took special care to retain the family antiques, diplomas, artifacts, and handcrafted needlework belonging to the family of nine children, all of whom were reared in the house by the first Mrs. Farnan, who lived here until she was 106 years old.

"In 1981 we opened the upper half as a B&B; ever since we have had the pleasure of meeting 'special' people. Periodically, I sleep in each room to check for lighting, drafts, and comfort of the bed and pillows. Many of our younger guests have commented, 'It's like grandma's house.' " (For nine between the ages of 6 and 21, this is grandma's house.)

**In residence:** Three cats, Baby, Punkins, and Peanuts, "all adorable and friendly to my guests." Occasionally grandchildren visit.
**Restrictions:** No pets or smoking.

**Bed and bath:** Four second-floor rooms. One with adjoining private half-bath. One shared full bath. Rooms have either a double bed or two twin beds. One daybed available.
**Breakfast:** 8-9. Juice, bagels, muffins, homemade Portuguese sweet bread, bread, rolls and marmalade, tea, freshly brewed coffee. Served in kitchen with open fireplace, oak floors, black "granny" stove (the logo for Farnan House), hooked rugs, beamed ceiling, gingham tablecloth and fresh flowers.
**Plus:** Guests' common room. Television in the kitchen. Thick towels. Potpourri in guest rooms. Window fans available. Access to refrigerator. Shaded back deck with water view.
**Rates:** \$40-\$45 single with shared bath, \$46-\$50 double with shared bath, \$52-\$55 private half-bath. \$10 daybed.

## Nutmeg Bed & Breakfast Host #23

Stony Creek, CT
**Location:** On a hilltop, two miles off I-95, in a popular and quaint area. Nine miles east of New Haven (18 minutes to Yale campus). On the shoreline, overlooking Long Island Sound and Thimble Island. Ten-minute drive to either Branford or Guilford, 45 to Mystic.
**Reservations:** Available year round through Nutmeg Bed & Breakfast, page 391. Two-day minimum stay on summer or holiday weekends.

Many hats. A flair. Joie de vivre.

Residents of the area for two years, the hosts have come from Kansas, Michigan, Indiana, and North Carolina. Retired from the air force, he is currently pilot and aviation manager for large corporations. She is a professional historian, genealogist and lecturer, a writer for the area newspaper and a published author, and does all her own interior decorating, including paperhanging and painting. In addition, she does counseling for preadoptive parents. Her collection of antique Victorian clothing includes outfits that she wears for fun whenever she is in the mood.

"When we started a second family, the lecture circuit was out. Having had company from all over the world most of my adult life, B&B was natural. It's like having friends of friends come to stay."

The seacoast manor Victorian is full of family memorabilia, antiques, Oriental rugs, dolls, and paintings. For a history of the 1897 house, inquire! Fascinating details include its half-century ownership by the NYNHRR. The other guests here are interesting too.

**In residence:** Three children under six. Two white cats, Gandolf and Munchkin, and two outdoor dogs.
**Restrictions:** Children not usually accepted. Guests' well-behaved cats are allowed. Please, no smoking indoors.
**Foreign languages spoken:** Hostess and children speak some Spanish. Host speaks some German.
**Bed and bath:** Four third-floor rooms share a full bath on the second floor and half-bath on the third floor. Two rooms with double beds, one with twin beds, and one with a double fold-out couch. One twin cot available. Three rooms overlook Long Island Sound. Victorian furnishings.
**Breakfast:** 7-9. Usually all guests manage to agree on a time for a single sitting. Juice, fresh fruits, French toast, pecan pancakes, sour cream/tomato omelet, homemade breads, rolls, assorted buns. Menu depends on the weather and where the guests are from. "Southerners get grits!" Served in the formal dining room.
**Plus:** Third-floor sitting room. The fourth-floor sitting room, originally a nursery/classroom, has spectacular views, Victorian furnishings, ceiling fan, and TV. Late-afternoon or evening beverages in cool weather. Tour of house. Bedroom ceiling fans. Two full porches that face the Sound.
**Rates:** $58-$65 double occupancy. $20 extra for the cot.

## Hedgerow House

1020 Quaddick Road, Thompson, CT 06277
**Phone:** 203/923-9073
**Location:** A quiet one, set back off the road, a few doors from the Thompson Green "in a parklike setting in a postcard New England village that's out in the country." Five hundred yards to an old coach stop restaurant. Half hour from Old Sturbridge Village or Worcester. Less than a mile from I-395.
**Hosts:** Harriett and Norman Macht
**Open:** Year round. Reservations required.

The first time Harriett saw Hedgerow House, she knew that the four-year search—for a B&B location in a New England village with a church spire, a green, and a quiet location close to a big city—was over. The first time Norman saw it was about 10 p.m., when he arrived with a U-Haul from Santa Rosa, California. "Sitting up on its knoll, this big white thing looked like a ship's prow. It was overwhelming."

It's that very scale that appealed to the hosts. They like to provide privacy for their guests, and at the same time, be sensitive to their needs. (One guest, a young mother, thanked Harriett for "time to ourselves as well as the mothering that I was ready for after a winter of caring for our sick child.")

The 1850 Italianate house was in pristine condition when the Machts bought it in 1984 from descendants of the original owners. Everything was perfect— the columns and fluting and even the canvas paintings installed in the dining room during the 1905 renovation. Although the new owners did some painting and papering, they consciously made very few changes. Throughout, they have furnished with Persian rugs, antiques, and original oil paintings.

Harriett runs an antique shop in the carriage house and teaches fine arts. Norman was a stockbroker and has taught financial management and economics. He has published numerous sports articles and is currently preparing a sports book.

**In residence:** Coriander, a Russian Blue cat.
**Restrictions:** Children should be at least 12. If there are no other guests, an infant will be accommodated. Sorry, no guests' pets. This is a nonsmoking residence.
**Bed and bath:** Three second-floor rooms. The one with private bath has two twin beds, overlooks the gardens. One full bath plus a half-bath on first floor shared by room that has two pineapple four-poster ¾-sized beds and a room that has an extra-long double bed and a working fireplace.
**Breakfast:** At a mutually agreed upon time. Fresh fruit, juice, homemade breads, muffins, souffles, quiches. Served in dining room copied from a Bavarian Castle, with hooded fireplace, rosewood paneling, and murals. Hosts often join guests for coffee.
**Plus:** Salt-water pool. Afternoon tea. Baby grand piano in hosts' living room. Guests' library with leather-covered walls, fireplace, and lots of books. No television. Hundred-foot front porch. Mints on the pillow. Down quilts. Huge bath towels. Dinners by prior arrangement ($15 per person, including wine).
**Rates:** $50 single, $60 double. Ten percent discount on stays longer than two nights.

## The Clarks

97 Scott Avenue, Watertown, CT 06795
**Phone:** 203/274-4866
**Location:** One block from the main street in Watertown. Three blocks from the Taft School; within a ten-minute drive of Route 8 and Route 84.
**Hosts:** Richard and Barbara Clark
**Open:** Year round except July.

This traditional B&B has filled a need. Taft School parents were having difficulty finding accommodations in the area, so the Clarks began hosting in 1983. Since then, others—particularly business people and those "passing through"—have also found the Cape-style home a convenient and comfortable stopping point.

Barbara is an elementary school teacher. Richard established his current home-improvement business after retiring from 33 years with Uniroyal. They are both active in community and church activities. As for B&B, "Each guest is different. We have been privileged to meet so many interesting people. It is fun!"

**In residence:** Sometimes their college-aged son is at home. Some of nine grandchildren, ages 3 to 13, drop in often but do not stay overnight.
**Bed and bath:** One first-floor room with two twin beds, studio couch, private half-bath, separate entrance, small porch. Second-floor shower shared with hosts.
**Breakfast:** 6-8 weekdays, 6-9 weekends. Usually a continental breakfast but eggs are also available. Served in the dining room.
**Plus:** Guest den adjoining guest room. Afternoon or evening beverages. Use of entire house including kitchen and laundry facilities, front and back porches, barbecue grill.
**Rates:** $30 single or double.

*Can't find the community you are going to? Check with a reservation service described at the beginning of this chapter. Through the service, you may be placed (matched) with a welcoming B&B that is near your destination.*

## Leventhal B&B

Box 105, 40 West Mystic Avenue, West Mystic, CT 06388
**Phone:** 203/536-1341
**Location:** In a historic district, on a main street with many old captains' houses. River view. Two miles off I-95. Ten-minute ride to Mystic Seaport, 15-minute walk to village. Ten minutes to Stonington, 20 minutes to New London.
**Hosts:** Bob and Natalie Leventhal
**Open:** Year round.

The house that was built by a boat builder in 1872 has become a home away from home for many who now come from all over the country to take a boat-building course offered at Mystic Seaport. When the boat-oriented Leventhals bought this house 25 years ago, it hadn't been lived in for 10 years and had to be completely refurbished.

Half hulls made by the original owner and found in the basement and attic are displayed on the walls. The family interest in crafts can be seen in their daughters' work, in Bob's airplane and train models, and in Natalie's newest interest, doll making.

In five years of hosting, they have met many people who appreciate the nonstandardized accommodations of a private home. A Pennsylvanian suggested that a dictionary definition of hospitality should be accompanied by a picture of the Leventhals. Bob and Nat, experienced travelers and former schoolteachers, sometimes take guests on a local tour and suggest other small seacoast communities for exploring.

**In residence:** One host smokes a pipe.
**Restrictions:** Well-behaved children are welcome. No pets.
**Foreign language spoken:** French.
**Bed and bath:** Two rooms share one full bath. One large room with a double bed and a cot. One single.
**Breakfast:** Continental with homemade muffins. Hosts usually join you in the family room or, weather permitting, out on the sun porch, which offers views of the Mystic River.
**Plus:** Air conditioning in large room; fan in smaller one.
**Rates:** $30 single, $35 double. $5 extra for a child in room with adults.

## The Homestead

Woodbury, CT
**Location:** Tranquil. On a three-acre setting that includes a two-acre field surrounded by hemlock hedges. Six miles north of Route 84. In "antique country." Near Taft and Westover Schools. Close to Litchfield.
**Reservations:** Available year round through Nutmeg Bed & Breakfast, page 391.

It's a beautiful 1741 farmhouse, purchased by the hosts from descendants of the original owners 20 years ago complete with barns that also date from the 1700s. Within a few hundred yards there's an eight-acre glacial kettle "pod," a geological phenomenon, a 150-foot lake with no inlet or outlet.

Everything is professionally done by the host, whose vocation is building and refinishing colonial furniture. The kitchen, pegged construction, has the original hand-hewn chestnut beams. Special touches include lovely old linens, flowers in profusion in the summer, and silver service. The hosts will gladly lead you to an antique lovers' paradise; not far from here there's a series of buildings with dozens of shops, filled with wonderful treasures.

**Restrictions:** School-age children welcome. Some guests' pets allowed.
**Bed and bath:** Three second-floor rooms; two with double beds can be a suite, share a bath. One single with private bath. Private guest entrance.
**Breakfast:** 6-9. Juice, seasonal fruit, homemade breads and jam, eggs or homemade blueberry pancakes or French toast, home-tapped maple syrup, coffee, tea, milk. Served either in the country kitchen or the formal dining room. Hosts join guests for a leisurely meal.
**Plus:** Late-afternoon or evening beverages. Tour of the house, farm, and area. Deck. Sitting room. Picnic area.
**Rates:** $60 double room, $45 single.

From North Carolina: "Fantastic. After 13 nights of B&B across New England and Nova Scotia, we thought we'd seen the best. Not so! [This was] super. Wish we could have stayed longer."

## KEY

 Recipes shared, often for house specialties.

 Inquiries welcomed about restoration and/or decorating. Symbol indicates that host is willing to share experiences with guests. Tips range from a before-and-after album to rebuilding advice, from furniture refinishing to curtain making. Expertise of hosts ranges from learn-by-doing to professional.

 How-To B&B workshop, seminar or apprentice program offered.

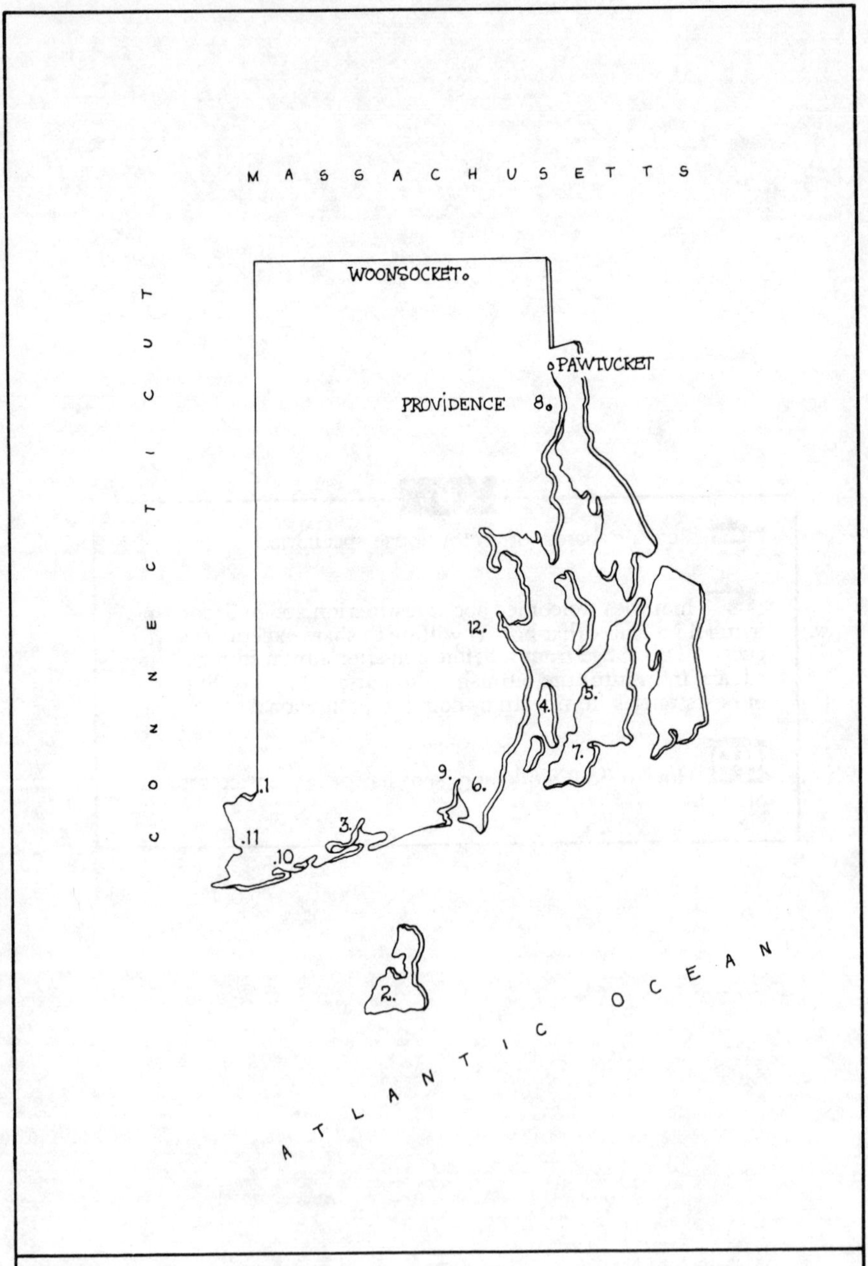


*The numbers on this map indicate the locations of B&Bs described in detail in this chapter.*

# RHODE ISLAND

# Rhode Island Reservation Services

## Bed & Breakfast of Rhode Island

P.O. Box 3291, Newport, RI 02840
**Phone:** 401/849-1298. Monday-Friday 9-5:30. During summer, also open 12-5 Saturdays.
**Listings:** 70+. Mostly hosted private residences; some inns and a few unhosted homes. A few on sailboats/yachts with bunk, board, and breakfast. Hosted and unhosted housing available for stays up to two months.

Although Joy Meiser and Ken Mendis have a roster that is concentrated in and around Newport, Providence, and Narragansett, about 20 other Rhode Island communities are represented in addition to a few over the Massachusetts border (in Attleboro, Rehoboth, Uxbridge, and Wrentham) and the Connecticut border (Mystic). In addition to establishing a professional organization that has sponsored B&B conferences and workshops, they offer assistance with travel plans to individual guests. More than half of their listings are in houses over 100 years old. Most are within two miles of a salt-water bay, cove, or the ocean. Directory ($2).

**Reservations:** Two weeks' advance notice is preferred; at least one day is required. Two-night minimum stay on summer weekends and three nights on holiday weekends required in most homes. Also available through travel agents.
**Plus:** Package weekends including historic tour and dining individually arranged with help of the hosts.
**Rates:** $30-$60 single, $40-$105 double. $10 surcharge for a one-night stay. Family and weekly rates available. Deposit of $20 per room per night required for rates up to $60; $30 per room per night for rates over $60; a few higher. Refund less $10 processing fee if cancellation is made at least two weeks in advance. No refunds within two weeks of arrival date. Return visits within 12 months to same host, 10 percent discount. MasterCard, VISA, and AMEX accepted.

## Pineapple Hospitality

This service has hosts in Newport, Providence, Tiverton, and Warwick. Please see page 214.

# Rhode Island B&Bs

## Pineapple Hospitality Host #RI216

Ashaway, RI
**Location:** Twelve minutes from Mystic Seaport, a half hour from New London, an hour from Newport and Providence. In the country, on a residential main road of a village that is part of the town of Hopkinton. About five minutes from Route 95. Seven miles from Rhode Island's south-shore beaches and Watch Hill.
**Reservations:** Available year round through Pineapple Hospitality, page 214.

As inviting as the pool looked, the day we were there, it was just too chilly to take a dip. We were visiting in the Mystic, Connecticut area, and this attractive white village colonial was in just the right place at the right time. Since then, the hostess, a grandmother to eight and retired secretary, has enrolled at the University of Rhode Island, just a half hour away.

She has hosted many guests, including one from England who came for one night, stayed for three, sent for his mother, returned for two more nights, and then called from England during the winter to "chat."

**In residence:** Emily, "a pretty but aloof cat."
**Restrictions:** Children should be at least four unless they come with their own sleeping accommodations, e.g. crib. Sorry, no guests' pets.
**Bed and bath:** Two rooms share a guest bath. One with twin beds that can be a king. One with pineapple four-poster twin beds. Cot available.

**Breakfast:** Usually at 8. Juice or fruit, homemade muffins, jams and jellies. Cereal available for children. Served in the dining room overlooking the patio.
**Plus:** In-ground swimming pool. Late-afternoon and evening beverages. Bedroom ceiling fans. Two patios and a screen house.
**Rates:** $33 single, $43 double. Cot $5 child, $10 adult.

## The Barrington

P.O. Box 90, Beach and Ocean Avenue, Block Island, RI 02807
**Phone:** 401/466-5510
**Location:** On a knoll overlooking the Great Salt Pond, with lovely views of surrounding waters. Three-quarters of a mile from Old Harbor, where the ferries dock; about 1/2 mile from the airport. Five-minute walk to beach.
**Hosts:** Joan and Howard Ballard
**Open:** Year round. Reservations required. Two-night minimum stay, three nights on holiday weekends (except in winter season).

Even though Howard's family had vacationed on the island since the turn of the century, he never had any idea that he would be doing what he is. As Joan says, "Through a series of happenings, we were thrown into this. I love it. It's easier than going to an office because it's a vacation atmosphere. For a while after we bought this house, Howard commuted to Newport where he was a shipyard manager, but now that he is here on the island full time, he's living his dream of being on his own. He's always repaired everything we ever had, and can even do wallpapering. He works for the water company and has a general home maintenance business."

After a year of hosting, the Ballards find that they have many returnees and referrals of all ages coming to a friendly, quiet place. Joan is on location full time and often hires students from a hotel management school as chambermaids, telling them that they are going to learn the business through what she considers an important part of running a B&B. Furnishings include some wicker, some antiques, some refinished, some from previous owners as well as what the Ballards brought. It is in keeping with a big old farmhouse—comfortable, "but we're constantly making changes." A picture of the original 1895 house is in the living room. Other photographs are Howard's work. On the grounds there's an old apple orchard favored by many colorful birds.

**Restrictions:** Sorry, no accommodations for pets.
**Bed and bath:** Eight rooms on three levels, many with private baths. A two-room suite with adjoining bath (shower, no tub) is on the ground level, has a private entrance and porch, is accessible to handicapped, and can accommodate up to five people. Four rooms on the second floor all have double beds and share a full bath and a half-bath. Two large rooms on the third floor have a double and single bed in each, private baths and sitting areas, and magnificent water views. Cot and crib available. Color-coordinated linens.
**Breakfast:** 8-9:30. At a predetermined time in winter. A leisurely breakfast of fresh fruit, juices, cereal, homemade muffins, coffee, tea, milk, and hot chocolate, served in the dining room.
**Plus:** Late-afternoon or evening beverages. Well water. Thick towels. Can usually arrange babysitting. Picnic table, barbecue grill, deck with tables and chairs, water view. Outside shower. Off-street parking. Will meet guests at ferry or airport during the off-season.
**Rates:** Summer weekends $65 single or double with shared bath, $90 with private bath, $5 less per room Monday-Thursday. About $15-$20 less September, October, May—except Memorial Day weekend—and early June; $20-$40 less November through April 16. $15 per night for third adult in a room, $10 for a child. MasterCard and VISA accepted.

## The Sea Breeze

Spring Street, P.O. Box 141, Block Island, RI 02807
**Phone:** 401/466-2275 (off-season: 212/724-4453)
**Location:** On the crest of a hill with full view of ocean and a swan pond. Three-minute walk from restaurants, shops, ferry landing.
**Hosts:** Robert and Mary Newhouse; daughters Alisa, Sarah, and Andrea
**Open:** Memorial Day weekend until late September. Reservations required. Two-night minimum, three nights on holiday weekends.

A daughter first suggested B&B, and ever since it has been a family project. Alisa is a glass artist; Sarah, an actress; and Andrea, a college student. Mary is an artist and her husband is a physician (in New York City).

The five cottages that were a boardinghouse compound in the first half of this century have been undergoing renovations since they were purchased—in a state of disrepair—in 1979. The Sea Breeze Gallery, known for its works by nationally and internationally recognized artists, opened in 1980. The B&B, designed to give the feeling of a seaside cottage, opened in 1984. Their own decorating service filled Sea Breeze with English chintzes, "early island furnishings, not a bit of plastic in the place," and, of course, contemporary art. "Beyond what we have created, the most important thing is to maintain an atmosphere that will be peaceful and relaxing."

Their gardens feature over a hundred varieties of perennials and flowering shrubs. Special spots for cycling, walking, swimming and picnicking are among the suggestions they share with guests.

**Restrictions:** Children should be at least five. Sorry, no guests' pets.
**Foreign languages spoken:** German, French, some Italian, depending on family members in residence.
**Bed and bath:** Five rooms with shared baths. Three first-floor rooms, two with double beds (one has an ocean view) and the third with twin beds, share a bath with shower. Upstairs, two rooms, each with a double bed, share a large bath with shower. Cot available.
**Breakfast:** 8:30-10. Viennese coffee or English tea, juice and fruit, freshly baked croissants or muffins, homemade preserves. Served on trays in the sitting room. May be taken to rooms or out onto the porch or lawns.
**Plus:** Sitting room on the first floor. Sitting and writing area on the second floor. Guest refrigerator, sink, and glasses provided. Porch, lawns, gardens. Fresh bouquets from perennial gardens.
**Rates:** $70-$80 double occupancy. Weekly rates $435-$495.

---

## The Sheffield House

High Street, P.O. Box 836, Block Island, RI 02807
**Phone:** 401/466-2494
**Location:** In historic district, one block from the ferry landing at Old Harbor. Two blocks from the beach.
**Hosts:** Steve and Claire McQueeny
**Open:** May-November, Reservations usually required. Two-night minimum stay on weekends.

"I feel like I am visiting Aunt Claire," said a young woman five minutes after arriving.

To Claire, that was the highest compliment. Her own enthusiasm and spontaneity are contagious. Sheffield House is a real home away from home. One major difference is that the cast of characters changes constantly. Among the returnees is a barbershop quartet. One year they gave a private "thank you" concert for Claire that attracted quite a crowd on the porch and lawn. Sometimes guests who meet here go out to dinner together. Sometimes they even help with the dishes. By the sound of things, the hostess could use a secretary to handle the personal winter correspondence.

In Wilton, Connecticut, she is a florist and Steve, a machinery broker. Their B&B is an 1888 Queen Anne, complete with turret, built as a summer cottage for a Providence doctor. The hall is hand-stenciled. Furnishings are as you might expect on Block Island, a combination of antiques, family pieces, and tag sale items, all freshened up to give a warm inviting feeling.

**In residence:** Maybe one or all of the three McQueenys (18 to 22 years old). Two "wonderful outdoor cats," Heather and Sylvester.
**Restrictions:** Children should be at least ten. No guests' pets.
**Foreign language spoken:** "Our daughters Molly and Ryan speak Spanish; I smile."
**Bed and bath:** Eight rooms. One full shared bath on each floor. Two with private baths. Two with twin beds; all others have double beds. Four first-floor rooms; four on second. Cot available.
**Breakfast:** Juices, coffee, herbal tea, fruit, homemade muffins. In the country kitchen. "Of course" Claire and Steve join guests. "It can go on forever."
**Plus:** Late-afternoon or evening beverages. Will meet guests at the airport or ferry. Babysitting usually available. TV, books, and games. Refrigerator, ice and glasses. Grill, picnic table, porch with rocking chairs. Bike rack. Suggestions for quieter, remote beaches and nature sanctuaries. "If convenient, will give a personalized island tour."
**Rates:** $65 double occupancy with shared bath, $85 with private bath. Senior citizen and midweek discounts (except in August). Spring and fall, 25 percent less. MasterCard and VISA accepted.

## The White House

Spring Street, P.O. Box 447, Block Island, RI 02807
**Phone:** 401/466-2653
**Location:** On top of rolling lawns overlooking the ocean. About a five-minute walk to town and the beaches.
**Hosts:** Joseph V. and Violette M. Connolly
**Open:** Year round. Reservations recommended. In July and August, two-night minimum stay required on weekends.

The hosts bring a strong sense of community to their B&B involvement. Joseph is a past president and a current board member of the Block Island Residents' Association. Violette is President of Block Island Gardeners, and founder/chairman of the Block Island House & Garden Tours, which benefit the Historical Society.

The Connollys' varied interests and experiences certainly make for lively conversation. When they started B&B in 1985, Joseph said that if he liked the guests, he would invite them for a drink. Violette reports, "So far, no one has gone dry." Joseph was brought up in a publishing family, studied drums with Gene Krupa and is still very much into big band jazz, and was a World War II navy pilot. He was Chairman of Synthetic Oil Corporation of America and is now retired. Violette had a long association with the Brooklyn Botanic Garden, has been media consultant to the Association of Junior Leagues of America and has just completed several special assignments for NBC.

Their house has seen many changes in its 200 years. From the late 1800s until World War I it was a successful B&B. Balconies were added after World War I. The wide board floors in the west wing are century-old planks found in the hayloft.

**Restrictions:** Smoking allowed downstairs. The Connollys are "old-fashioned about guests' marital status. Joseph says he's not square; he's a cube." Sorry, no pets, no children under 13.
**Bed and bath:** Two rooms share a bath with shower. In summer, Captain's Quarters (canopied four-poster double bed) and Oriental Room (two twin beds). Both with French doors to an ocean-facing balcony. In winter, Oriental Room and Louis Philippe Room with twin bed, collection of china, books, and accessories pertaining to royalty.
**Breakfast:** 8-9. Juices, cereals, bacon and eggs, muffins, fresh fruits, French toast. Hosts join you in Tavern Room facing the ocean.

**Plus:** Separate entrance, living/TV room, and staircase for guests. The 60-foot-long Tavern Room has a large fireplace. Garden flowers in the rooms. French Provincial antiques and collections. Possibility of island tours. Japanese garden. Dinner offered occasionally during the winter. Will meet guests at airport or ferry.
**Rates:** $110 for Captain's Quarters, $100 for Oriental, $75 for Louis Philippe. Weekly rate. Less off-season. MasterCard, VISA, and AMEX accepted.

## Fairfield-By-The-Sea

527 Green Hill Beach Road, Green Hill, RI 02879
**Phone:** 401/789-4717
**Location:** Between Westerly and Wakefield, in a secluded country setting, $\frac{3}{4}$ mile from ocean beach, two miles from Theater-By-The-Sea, 40 miles from Providence, 30 from New London, 10 from University of Rhode Island; 20 miles east of Mystic and 25 miles west of Newport. Near Block Island ferry and Yawgoo ski area.
**Host:** Jeanne Lewis
**Open:** Year round. Reservations recommended. Two-night minimum stay on weekends, three nights on most holiday weekends.

"My first season of hosting was just a whole summer of laughs. I am still meeting many different people, each one lovely, but now that I have retired from teaching (grades 5-8) I am here year round."

The contemporary country home on $3\frac{1}{2}$ acres was what Jeanne's husband always wanted to design and build. It is a lovely place filled with art, maps, family pictures, quilts, silhouettes, painted rocks, and books. The hostess, a creative home economist, has been a consumer consultant all over the country and has edited national publications. She is also a poet, an avid gardener, and a grandmother.

"Stress reduction" is the theme here. Even carless guests find this a good place to read, bird-watch, walk on the beach. Equipment is provided for catching blue crabs or harvesting mussels.

Jeanne is having a love affair with Rhode Island. "The resources of this state are rich and easily accessible. My newest career involves workshops here at home and in Providence—on food, crafts, and B&B too." Among the three dozen titles: stitchery, party planning, use of phyllo leaves, making an Easter egg tree, waiting on tables. The very latest development is "Elegant Obsessions," her small mail-order business that includes bouquets of chocolate roses. Zest, here art thou!

**In residence:** Mandy, a feisty Yorkie. Oreo, a Maine coon cat.
**Restrictions:** No guests' pets. Well-behaved children are welcome. Smokers should be considerate of other guests.
**Bed and bath:** Two rooms "in the treetops" reached by a spiral staircase in living room. One with twin beds, one with double. Shared full guest bath.
**Breakfast:** 8-10 but flexible. (Two young fishermen ate at 4 a.m.) Continental with fresh fruit and homemade breads. Eat in dining room or on an open deck. In fall and winter, hot blueberry soup may be ordered, served with cheese and Portuguese sweet bread.
**Plus:** Balcony. Living room with fireplace, library. Picnic area. Fans in rooms. Outdoor hot and cold shower. Sometimes Jeanne gives tours of Galilee, Watch Hill, and surrounding areas. Babysitting. Option of seafood feasts if preparation is a cooperative venture. "Mine is an equal opportunity kitchen." You are invited to be a guest at Jeanne's workshop, if one coincides with your visit.
**Rates:** In season $54 per room. Mid-October–April 1, midweek rate is $40 per room. Cot $7 for child under six, $12 over age six. Gift certificates available.

---

## The Calico Cat Guest House

14 Union Street, P.O. Box 634, Jamestown, RI 02835
**Phone:** 401/423-2641
**Location:** On a residential street one block from harbor with shops, restaurants, and view of Newport Bridge and Harbor. Ten-minute drive across bay to Newport.
**Hosts:** Joan and John Cicogna
**Open:** Year round. Reservations recommended. Two-day minimum stay on weekends May through October.

From Pennsylvania: "Our large family had a great time in this classic bed and breakfast . . . very friendly . . . gave good advice on where to eat and things to do in the area."

Other guests added, "Let's hope not too many people discover what we have, for we might not be able to reserve a room next time. . . . Residential area makes you feel private, quiet. . . . Good location for uncrowded small beach as well as others. . . . reasonable rates . . . a home away from home feeling."

After three years as an instructor at the Officers' Candidate School in Newport, John knew the area and decided, upon retirement, to stay here and open the kind of B&B that he and his wife knew from an extensive trip in England. The Cicognas, both brought up in large cities, had already done over three other old homes—in Washington, D.C.; Camden, Maine; and Springfield, Massachusetts. They especially appreciate New England and a particular kind of old home, one that is "in a small community near a big city, and one that has at least one floor-to-ceiling window."

After 30 years in the navy, John has plenty of sea stories "that get better with the passage of time." He's in real estate now—and thinking about redoing a fifth house some day, somewhere.

**In residence:** Host smokes. Daughter Hilary is sometimes around. Taylor is the resident calico cat and Daisy, the dog.
**Restrictions:** Small pets allowed. Smoking should be restricted to the common area.
**Bed and bath:** Eight rooms on the second and third floors, all air conditioned. One room has twin beds, the others have double beds. Third floor cozy rooms have stenciled floors, lots of angles. Roll-away beds available.
**Breakfast:** 8-9:30. Night owls and early birds can arrange for other hours. Homemade muffins, breads, toast, jams, fresh fruit, tea, coffee. A buffet, served in the closed-in porch, which looks out on the harbor. Hosts often join guests.
**Plus:** Late-afternoon beverages. Babysitting. ("Even for my one-year-old!" wrote a guest from Virginia.) Kitchen privileges for those with special needs. Guest lounge with TV, books, and games. Barbecue.
**Rates:** Memorial Day weekend and late June-September $45 single, $55 double, $70 triple. October 1-late June $35 single, $45 double and $60 triple. Special midweek packages and group rates available. Military and senior citizen discounts. No charge for children under 12. MasterCard, VISA, and AMEX accepted.

## Lindseys' Guest House

6 James Street, Middletown, RI 02840
**Phone:** 401/846-9386
**Location:** In a residential area. A ten-minute walk to Second Beach, several fine restaurants, Norman Bird Sanctuary and Sachuest Point Wildlife Refuge. Two miles to Newport's waterfront, 1½ to its mansions on Bellevue Avenue.
**Hosts:** Anne and Dave Lindsey
**Open:** Year round.

Twenty-five years as bed and breakfast hosts—and still going strong. "The more I meet different types of guests, the more I realize how much we as humans are alike."

Away from the hubbub is the Lindseys', a split-level house where conversation runs the gamut—from family to Newport attractions, from hints about bargain hours at good restaurants to stained-glass making, from gardening to shell collecting. However, you are not required to socialize! It is with the voice of experience that Anne says, "Even those who arrive as weary travelers are delightful over coffee in the morning."

Dave traveled the world over in his days with the navy. He and Anne have seven grown children and 13 grandchildren.

**Bed and bath:** Three rooms. One on street level with double bed has a private entrance, private bath with shower. Two rooms, each with twin beds, share a full bath. Rollaway and crib available.
**Breakfast:** 8-10; at other times by request. Orange juice, muffins and jam (often homemade), coffee cake or Danish, coffee or tea. Served in dining room at table set with linens, candles, and flowers with a color scheme of the month.
**Plus:** Ceiling fan in dining room. Off-street parking. Large yard.
**Rates:** $35 double with shared bath, $40 with private bath. $10 cot or crib. $5 less per room, November 1-May 1.

From Ohio: "The Lindseys' warm hospitality made us feel very much at home. . . . And it was very clean. . . . We intend to return."

From Florida: "We especially enjoyed being five minutes away from Newport without having to fight the crowds and congested parking!"

# Narragansett

Newport is just 20 minutes away from this community that has long been known for its beaches. In the 1980s, there are, as one host said, "people beaches, radio beaches, quiet beaches, surfing beaches"; and hosts can direct you accordingly. Watch Hill is only a half hour's drive. The fishing village of Galilee is just down the road. Block Island, reached by the ferry that leaves from Point Judith (10-minute drive), is a popular day trip. The University of Rhode Island is a 15-minute drive. Musical theater and restaurants make the list too. Cycling in this pocket of Rhode Island is scenic and pretty flat.

## The Four Gables

Pier Road, Narragansett, RI 02882
**Phone:** 401/789-6948
**Location:** One block off Route 1A, a major scenic route. On a main town road, one-half block from the ocean.
**Hosts:** Joyce and Peter Turco
**Open:** Year round.

"Where is that place in Rhode Island where a guest was introduced to a man who became her husband?" At least three interviewers have asked me that question after reading the bride's letter about her life being "turned around at The Four Gables" that appeared in my first B&B book. The Turcos report that the sequel to the story is that the couple, for whom they were best man and matron of honor, bought a home with an extra room that has been used by B&B guests.

The Four Gables was built in 1898 as a summer home with wonderful woodwork, four fireplaces, and interesting nooks and crannies. The Turcos, owners for 17 years, have furnished it with antiques and traditional pieces. In one room there's a huge countermarch loom. Just say the word and Joyce will give you a demonstration and, if you'd like, an opportunity to try it. She'll also share hints about stenciling as well as covering walls with fabric.

Peter is around at the ends of the day because his shopkeeping, especially in summer, is time-consuming. Joyce is a former airline stewardess. Son Matthew has been influenced by B&B enough to study hotel and restaurant management.

The family enjoys the area. In addition to the beaches, there's fishing right off the nearby dock. Their jogging route is along the seawall that borders the ocean. And they are familiar with a wide variety of restaurants—from seafood to Chinese to Italian.

**In residence:** College-aged sons, David and Matthew. Reuben, a lovable (and not shy) dachshund. Peter smokes.
**Bed and bath:** Two rooms share guest bath with shower and claw-foot tub. A double bed in one small cozy room with handmade quilt. A queen-sized bed in a room large enough for a cot too. Both have stenciled walls.
**Breakfast:** Available at your convenience. Choice of juices, fresh fruits, home-baked goods such as banana bread, zucchini bread, blueberry muffins; coffee and assorted teas. Eat in dining room with view of ocean or on balcony beyond sliding doors.
**Plus:** Bedroom fans. Patio. Backyard with badminton and croquet. Beach passes. Bicycles. Chocolates on the pillow. Flowers. Tray with liqueur in room. "Use of iron and most everything else."
**Rates:** $30 or $40 single. $35 or $45 double. $5 cot.

## Ilverthorpe Cottage

41 Robinson Street, Narragansett, RI 02882
**Phone:** 401/789-2392
**Location:** On a residential street in the historic district. Three blocks from the village shops, restaurants, and The Victorian Towers. Five-minute walk to beach.
**Hosts:** Chris, Rich, and Jill Raggio
**Open:** Year round. Reservations usually required from May through October. Minimum two-night stay on weekends June through August.

From Massachusetts: "A most gracious breakfast. Every bit of of the house artistically beautiful. Went with daughter and granddaughter (18 months). Even had an antique high chair with another little high chair with teddy bear at breakfast table."

After receiving that note, David and I arrived (without any children) and saw all the touches that Chris is responsible for—calligraphy, hats, small country prints on the walls. Rich, a former University of Rhode Island football player, was the one who put on an incredible spread for breakfast. It was very good and beautifully presented.

Since then, the Raggios have moved from Connecticut to Narragansett to live year round in the 2½-story hip-roofed Victorian. They are the second owners of the 1896 house, and if you'd like to see what kind of changes they have made since buying it in 1983, there is a before-and-after album. Chris has done all the stenciling and wallpapering and has displayed her collection of lace and other Victorian memorabilia. The wraparound porch has been restored. Jill has become a great assistant, often greeting guests and helping with breakfast. The vegetable and flower gardens are thriving. And the hosts find time for jogging, sailing, and golf.

More families have come as guests, but so has a young man who stayed here to train before he (successfully) swam the English channel. Who else? "The lovers, the quiet ones, the gregarious, the superfriendly, the apprehensive, the rich, the budget conscious—and the traffic stoppers, members of The Vintage Bentley Touring Club of America."

Chris gives workshops in basketry (her own are gorgeous) and she substitutes as a classroom teacher. Rich is a manufacturer's representative.

**In residence:** Jill, age nine.
**Restrictions:** No guests' pets. Smoking only on the first floor.
**Bed and bath:** Four rooms, two with private baths. One with twin beds and five windows shares a full bath with another room with a double bed. Room with king-sized bed has Victorian clothing decorating the walls. The other room with private bath has a canopied four-poster double bed. Cot and crib available.
**Breakfast:** "Meant to spoil each and every guest." Usually at 8:30. "Breakfast pizza is always requested by returning guests." Other possible dishes are cheese souffles, pocket omelets, baked eggs, blintzes. Served with fresh fruit, juices, coffee and regular, herbal, or English tea, and homemade breads—maybe fruit flan, French egg puff, poppy seed bread—in the dining room or on the wicker-furnished veranda. Chris always joins you for coffee.
**Plus:** Late-afternoon or evening wine. Will meet guests at the Greene airport, Kingston train station, or bus stop. Bus to Newport passes right by the street. Babysitting. Off-street parking. Use of

refrigerator, dishes and glassware. Wooden children's gym set in the yard. Games for adults and children. Front porch rockers.
**Rates:** $39-$45 double with semiprivate bath, $49-$60 with private bath.

---

## Mon Rêve

41 Gibson Avenue, Narragansett, RI 02882
**Phone:** 401/783-2846
**Location:** One mile to town beach. Ocean is three blocks away.
**Host:** Eva Doran
**Open:** Year round. Two-night minimum stay on weekends from May through September. Reservations requested.

A perfect blend at the right time. When the Narragansett Chamber of Commerce encouraged local homes to host B&Bs, they must have been thinking about places like this—a private home built for a New York financier in the 1890s and later owned by artist Florence Kane. It's now on the National Register of Historic Places and is filled with Victorian furnishings. For most of Eva Doran's 30 years here, there has been an ongoing open-house style. She has taught French at four Rhode Island colleges and universities, is a lecturer and writer, and now finds time for jogging and baking too. Her attention to detail includes concern about placing couples with wee babies "where crying won't disturb other guests."

> From Connecticut: "We are a young English couple staying here for two years. . . . We would like to thank you especially for introducing us to Jim and Eva Doran . . . a lovely house and the warmest of welcomes. We have returned with first my mother-in-law, then my brother-in-law and most recently, my parents."

> From Rhode Island: "It was the first vacation with our six-year-old son and three-year-old triplet daughters. We stayed for five days in an atmosphere of relaxation. . . . We enjoyed the front porch and loan of bicycles. . . ."

**In residence:** Husband, Jim. Shannon, a 16-year-old red Irish setter, "good natured in spite of his aches and pains."
**Restrictions:** No smoking in the bedrooms.
**Foreign languages spoken:** French and Italian.

**Bed and bath:** Four rooms. One second-floor room in a private wing with double bed, private full bath. Three third-floor rooms; one with double-sized antique brass and iron bed, the other with two twin beds. They share a large full bathroom (claw-foot tub) with a single that "has the cozy compactness of a ship's cabin."
**Breakfast:** 8, 9, and 10. Hearty and varied, "some dish you're apt not to have at home, with homemade breads, blueberries from nearby woods, and Mon Rêve's raspberries," in plant-filled sun porch.
**Plus:** Fans in bedrooms. Picnic table and grill. Free use of bicycles. Half-price tokens for Newport Bridge.
**Rates:** $25 single with shared bath, $30 double with shared bath, $40 double with private bath.

From New York: "Eva Doran is the quintessence of the perfect hostess. . . . Breakfasts are superb and beautiful to look at. . . . The bedrooms are clean and comfortable (I have stayed in all four bedrooms) with added touches of fresh flowers, turned-down sheets, mints at bedside, and vast amounts of reading material."

## Murphy's B&B

43 South Pier Road, Narragansett, RI 02882
**Phone:** 401/789-1824
**Location:** In a residential neighborhood one block from the ocean, small-boat launch site, and fishing pier. Ten-minute walk to beach.
**Hosts:** Martha and Kevin Murphy
**Open:** May-October.

What was built in 1894 as a summer home with a big fireplace in the living room has been the year-round home to the Murphys for about five years. Martha, a former travel agent who loves every aspect of B&B, has set the style here, featuring "a hearty welcome, a big wonderful breakfast, the feeling of being comfortable—and I'm fussy about cleanliness. We are both in our mid-thirties and find that one of the joys of running a B&B is meeting people of all ages from all over. Each 'mix' of guests is different and fascinating."

Kevin has his own lobster boat and also is a fisherman on draggers. He is home most summer evenings and often answers questions about his work. If you'd like to leave with some live or cooked lobsters, try to give a few days' advance notice.

The Murphys are restoring their old house—using prints, white woodwork, and "a simple, clean look" in the guest rooms. A parquet floor and Waterford crystal lamps make the dining room the most formal. "We have Victorian, early American, some antiques, some interesting old furniture. We are not a museum!"

Martha is an at-home "knotter," working mostly on necklaces, for a specialty company that makes exquisite handmade porcelain jewelry. She and Kevin snorkel, cycle, and swim.

**In residence:** Liza, an 11-year-old female German shepherd, "gentle and a good watchdog."
**Restrictions:** No guests' pets. No smoking, please.
**Foreign languages spoken:** Very little French and German.
**Bed and bath:** Three third-floor rooms share one full large guest bath. Two bedrooms and the bath have ocean views. Cot available.
**Breakfast:** 8-9, earlier on request. Fruit juice, fresh fruit salad; in season, homegrown raspberries and blueberries. Coffee cake, muffins, or sticky buns, bacon and eggs or pancakes, freshly ground coffee, assorted teas. Served in the dining room.
**Plus:** Seasonal beverages in late afternoon or evening. Living room with fireplace. Third-floor sitting area and large hallway with lots of sightseeing information. Much reading material. Front porch.
**Rates:** $40 single, $50 double. Discount for families who stay more than two nights.

## Narragansett Pier Inn

7 Prospect Avenue, Narragansett, RI 02882
**Phone:** 401/783-8090
**Location:** Set back from the main road on a two-acre corner lot with many trees. Less than a mile from beaches and Pier Village shops and dining.
**Hosts:** Robert and Judy Alexander
**Open:** Year round. Reservations suggested in summer. Busiest May-September.

This interesting couple "backed into B&B—happily." When Judy, a former nurse from Connecticut, and Bob, a Boston-based engineer and chemist, married five years ago, they wanted to settle near the sea where they could have design and office facilities. What they found in 1985 was an 1890s Victorian that had had much restoration and had recently become a B&B. The Alexanders have added and replaced furnishings, worked on the landscaping (Judy loves gardening), left the buried steamroller buried (the house was built by a road-construction contractor before the days of autos), and welcomed guests from around the world.

Impromptu concerts are welcomed on the antique baby grand piano. (Judy was an accomplished musician in her college days.) Bob's collection of dolls and his own photographs from his travels often are a source of conversation. The Alexanders enjoy fishing on their boat, which is moored in Galilee, and if you want to know about fine dining, they often recommend two out-of-the-way restaurants—one French and one featuring seafood.

When the current barn renovation is complete, guests will have the opportunity to tour Bob's workplace, a dream facility with exposed beams and floor-to-ceiling windows.

**In residence:** Hosts' grown children—they have nine between them—may be visiting. The Alexanders raise fancy guinea pigs, who reside in aquariums in the laundry room.
**Restrictions:** No guests' pets. Smoking allowed on the first floor and on the porches.
**Bed and bath:** Four large second-floor rooms share one full tiled bath. One room has four-poster double bed, one with cannonball double bed. One room with two twin beds. One room with thimble-style double bed. All rooms have color TV, closet, three large windows. Twin-size inflated mattresses used as extra beds.
**Breakfast:** 8:30-10, earlier by request. Three types of juice, fresh fruit, homemade breads and muffins. Side-dish possibilities—breakfast meats, hash brown potatoes, omelets, eggs Benedict, waffles, pancakes, French toast. Served in the dining room at small butcher-block tables or on the rear deck. In addition to coffee and coffee cake for those leaving too early for the full breakfast, the Alexanders provide sandwiches, fruit, and snacks to go.
**Plus:** Hot and cold outside shower. Electric blankets. Soaps and shampoos. Thick towels. Extensive library. Living room with color TV, VCR, books, wood stove. Use of dining room for bring-your-own lunches. Wraparound porch, one side fully screened. Deck with umbrella table and chairs and lighting. Grill.
**Rates:** In season $40 per room on weekdays, $45 on weekends. $8 cot. $5 less per room off-season. MasterCard and VISA accepted.

## The Phoenix

29 Gibson Avenue, Narragansett, RI 02882
**Phone:** 401/783-1918
**Location:** In a quiet residential area overlooking a green. A ten-minute walk to the beaches.
**Hosts:** Joyce and Dave Peterson
**Open:** Year round.

It was a rare 70-degree November weekend when we made last-minute reservations. After our stay we knew why it wouldn't be so easy to find an opening in season. Since then, "the season" for The Phoenix (featured on the cover of my first B&B book) has become spring through fall. Joyce's increased real estate activity made her wonder if she could continue B&B, but she pursued and now concludes, "It's a marvelous balance and for some reason, B&B guests are even better than ever!"

Some guests sit by the fire—for fun, to work on a thesis, or even to write a play. The porch can be the focal point for greeting and meeting and even an impromptu concert by visiting musicians. At least one wedding has taken place here.

The rambling house was built, kitchenless, in 1889 by Stanford White, as part of a compound for restauranteur Louis Sherry. It burned soon after and was rebuilt in 1912. When the Petersons first saw it about 15 years ago, it was much neglected. They did all the work—real work—by themselves. Their achievements have sagas that are related with a smile by a cheerful hostess. (Ask about the dramatic first—and extremely cold—winter when they realized they were *not* connected to a sewer line.) Today The Phoenix is on the State and National Historic Registers.

When Dave is home from his job as marketing manager for General Electric, he is host, chef's helper, builder, and active in politics. Joyce fits sports, photography, and Sunday school teaching into her days. Kim, too, wears many hats in the home filled with contagious joy.

**In residence:** Daughter Kim, a college student.
**Restrictions:** No guests' pets. Smoking only in the living room and on the porch.
**Bed and bath:** Five rooms. Private bath with third-floor double-bedded room. Second floor—three rooms with a double bed and one with a double and a single bed shared two baths. (One bath has a

wonderful deep long old tub on a marble stand.) European-style showers in all baths. Cots available.
**Breakfast:** Brunch. As Joyce's mother used to say, "Eat breakfast like a king, lunch like a prince, supper like a pauper." Maybe broiled grapefruit and homemade muffins and blueberry pancakes, eggs Benedict, cheese blintzes, or omelets filled with avocado and shrimp. Planned, cooked, and served by Joyce with timing that allows her to enjoy it with you.
**Plus:** Sherry in room. Maybe evening tea served as ours was, on a tray with a Russian doll-cozy. Wicker-furnished, flower-filled veranda overlooking private green. Fireplaced living room. Menus from restaurants that hosts have been to—this season. Newport Bridge half-price tokens. Lawn for sunbathing. Croquet.
**Rates:** $50 single, $60 double. Cots $10.

## Richards' Bed and Breakfast

144 Gibson Avenue, Narragansett, RI 02882
**Phone:** 401/789-7746
**Location:** On a quiet, private, dead-end road. (Coming soon: an access road off Ocean Road.) One-half mile from center of town. One-quarter mile from ocean; one mile to beach.
**Hosts:** Steven and Nancy Richards
**Open:** Year round. Two-night minimum weekends in July and August. Three-night minimum Memorial, July fourth, and Labor Day weekends.

"Nancy's dream." Ever since she saw this unusual (for this area) 2½ storied stone house 12 years ago, Nancy has been "in love" with it. Just as we went to press, the Richardses became the third owners of this gabled 1850 house that is on the National Register of Historic Places. The house has 11 fireplaces, a grand 40-foot-long entrance hall, and a two-person elevator. It is located on a 20-acre estate purchased by a developer who is building several mini-estates. From Richards', the only other house in sight is the former caretaker's cottage.

After seven years of hosting delighted travelers from around the world in their ten-room Narragansett Cape house, the Richardses are ready to welcome guests at their new Gibson Avenue address. Fresh paint and paper are in the place. Nancy is responsible for the flowers—inside and out (landscaping is coming), and she is making all the draperies. She is also a basketmaker and tennis player. Because of her culinary talents, Victoria and Kristina often hear, "Does your mother always make breakfasts like this?" Steven, co-chef on weekends, is still active in politics, having spent many years as director of a state legislature program, and is also involved in real estate sales and development.

**In residence:** Two teenaged daughters, Victoria and Kristina. Otis, the cat.
**Restrictions:** Sorry, no guests' pets. Children should be at least 12. No smoking indoors.
**Bed and bath:** Four large second-floor rooms, all with fireplaces "that may work when we get to them." One room with king-sized bed, private bath. Two double-bedded rooms with connecting bath. One room with two antique three-quarter sleigh beds, private hall bath. Cots available. Some baths may have shower arrangements.
**Breakfast:** 8:30. Gourmet breakfast of homemade muffins or bread and dishes from Nancy's long list of possible specialties—eggs Florentine, sausages, bacon or ham, baked apple pancakes or strudels, johnnycakes, cheese blintzes, and always, freshly ground coffees. Special diets accommodated.
**Plus:** Living room, dining room, even kitchen with "working, we hope" fireplaces. Outside hot/cold shower. Patio (to be surrounded by flowers). Badminton. Croquet. Half-price tokens for Newport Bridge. Guests may leave their things "at home" for the day, then shower and change before departing.
**Rates:** $40 single, $60 king, $45-$50 other rooms. October 15-May 15, $40 shared bath, $50 private.

---

## Wagon Wheel

16 Mathewson Street, Narragansett, RI 02882
**Phone:** 401/783-7178
**Location:** Five minutes from Route 1. One block to town beach, bus terminal, and town center.
**Hosts:** Diana and Marjorie Vogel
**Open:** Memorial Day-Labor Day. Reservations helpful; necessary on holidays. Two-night minimum stay on summer weekends.

"Having moved 29 times in 29 years of marriage (to a geologist), traveling in 26 countries and living in Africa, Norway, Philippines, I find that travel and all it entails is often part of the conversation here. As an artist, my work focuses on architectural renderings. . . . I have just completed drawings for the historical society of all the oceanfront hotels that were here in 1898. I always intend to do a drawing of my home and create a wonderful brochure, but haven't gotten to it yet!

"My 1822 house, painted red with white trim, was originally built on the site where the famous Towers now stands. Victorian touches were added. . . . The rooms for guests are nice, though not fancy, but appealing and cozy. . . . There are many touches—plenty of plants, and lace doilies, some antiques. In my small living room there are lots of books, a TV and piano. I call Wagon Wheel 'casual and comfortable.'

"Bed and breakfast is energizing! Sometimes we talk about history or architecture or I pull out old old area photos or we have spontaneous parties on the porch, the main gathering spot."

**In residence:** Poco, a small, black, very old border collie, "has a nice personality, but is shy and protective of her house."
**Restrictions:** Pets allowed only in rooms with private entrances. Ashtrays available upon request.
**Bed and bath:** Two second-floor rooms each with private baths. One with a double bed as well as a double sleep sofa and refrigerator; the other with a double four-poster bed and a view of the town beach. Cot available. Crib available with advance notice.
**Breakfast:** 8:30-10, earlier if necessary. "Full, but not fancy." Fruit dishes, croissants or Marjorie's coffee cake (blueberry in season), eggs, breakfast meats, pancakes or French toast. Special diets accommodated. Served on porch. "Table set with tablecloth, some antique dishes, flowers. . . . Kids seated at picnic table so parents don't have to worry about spills." Eat inside in inclement weather.
**Plus:** At night, the sound of the surf. Late-afternoon or evening beverages. Porch is large enough for several groups to be doing different things, including picnicking. With advance notice, champagne or wine for special occasions.
**Rates:** $45 double occupancy. Less for singles, seniors, and long stays. $5 cots.

## 1855 Marshall Slocum House

29 Kay Street, Newport, RI 02840
**Phone:** 401/841-5120 or 401/846-3787
**Location:** Canopied by a copper beech on a street of Victorian homes. Five-minute walk to waterfront, shops, beaches, and harbor.
**Host:** Joan Wilson
**Open:** Year round. Reservations preferred (and strongly recommended for summer). Two-night minimum stay on weekends during summer months.

"It's far more fun than I ever imagined. And it's certainly different from the rigors of running an orange grove in Florida for 13 years. (There was a short interlude as a travel agent.) All those experiences came in handy when the house was filled with an Australian film team covering the boats being developed for the Cup races. There are many times when I play tour guide here.

"When I planned to return to New England, I knew that I wanted to do this for my next career and feel fortunate to have found this Victorian that was beautifully restored and established as a B&B by the previous owners. The people who come here fit right in and make it their home away from home."

Joan's home is comfortably furnished with a mixture of antiques, collectibles, and family heirlooms. (Shared) favorite recipes are painted onto the kitchen tiles. It is a friendly place.

**In residence:** MaryAnn, "the ultimate housekeeper and right-hand lady." Buttons, the cat, "who has learned how to accept TLC from fellow kitty lovers."
**Restrictions:** No guests' pets. No smoking above the first floor.
**Foreign language spoken:** Kitchen Spanish.
**Bed and bath:** Five rooms on two floors share two guest baths. Four rooms with double bed, one with twin beds. Cot and crib available.
**Breakfast:** 8-10. Continental with embellishments. Fresh-baked breads, blueberry muffins, strawberry shortcake in season, popovers, fresh fruit, coffee, tea on backyard deck.
**Plus:** Off-street parking. Bedroom window fans. Front porch with rockers. Shaded backyard. Parlor with TV, VCR. Dinners and picnics (extra charge) by request. Jitney service to and from local transportation. Ice and use of refrigerator.
**Rates:** $60 per room, shared bath. $10 for a third person in a room. AMEX.

## Aboard Commander's Quarters

54 Dixon Street, Newport, RI 02840
**Phone:** 401/849-8393
**Location:** On a quiet narrow street one block from the harbor. Within walking distance of most attractions, including restaurants, shops, mansions, and the Tennis Hall of Fame. A five-minute ride to beaches.
**Hosts:** Joseph and Phyllis Tracy
**Open:** June-September. Two-night minimum stay on weekends. Three nights on holiday weekends.

From New Jersey: "We love the place because—it's a well-kept secret; very noncommercial and quiet; conveniently located; a very homey environment; comfortable rooms and beds. Phyllis's muffins are wonderful and the hosts are too."

It all started five years ago when Joe, an active commander in the Naval Reserve and a practicing school psychologist, and Phyllis, a teacher of fifth and sixth graders, chose B&B as their summer job. In order to retain their enthusiasm ("We love B&B!"), they set up an arrangement that really works. They get out every day; it's a time when guests are greeted by an assistant and a note from the hosts.

The flag- and flower-filled porch planters are the first signs of welcome to this rambling 14-room colonial. Built in 1885, it has seen many changes through several owners. Joe discovered some of them and, if you ask, he'll share a tale or two about their own efforts and challenges. The living room with braided rug, white curtains, and country furniture tells you that you are "home." Bouquets from Joe's garden are everywhere, including the bathrooms.

The Tracys' dining suggestions are based on an incredible feat: They have tried every eatery in town! For shopping, Joe suggests Phyllis as the ultimate source of every bargain in Newport.

**In residence:** College-age son, Thomas. Other sons, Michael and Paul, sometimes on weekends. Molly Pitcher of Bunker Hill, a gentle laid-back golden retriever, is a graduate of obedience school.
**Restrictions:** Children should be at least six. Sorry, no guests' pets.
**Foreign language spoken:** Some Spanish.
**Bed and bath:** Four rooms (including two that are part of suites). Three private baths. Twin beds or king-sized in first-floor rooms. Two twins or king-sized in cathedral-ceilinged second-floor suite that has a couch available for a third person and a refrigerator. The

other suite has two twin-sized beds, sitting room with single pull-out sofa, bath with shower, refrigerator, ceiling fan.
**Breakfast:** 8:30-10. Juice, seasonal fruit, freshly baked muffins and breads, toast and jelly, coffee, tea, or milk. Buffet in country kitchen or on outside deck. Phyllis and Joe usually join you.
**Plus:** Iced tea or lemonade upon arrival. Window or ceiling fans in bedrooms. Living room with wood stove. Large yard with flower gardens. Lawn chairs. Flower-laden deck with umbrella table. Shed for bicycles or camping equipment. Will meet bus. Parking.
**Rates:** Weekends and holidays $60 double occupancy, semiprivate bath; $70 with private bath; $85 suites. Weekdays $10 less. $10 for a third person in a room. MasterCard and VISA accepted.

## Blue Stone

33 Russell Street, Newport, RI 02840
**Phone:** 401/846-5408
**Location:** In a quiet residential area, a mile from downtown Newport.
**Hosts:** Cindy and Roger Roberts
**Open:** Year round. Advance registration preferred. Two-night minimum stay on weekends. Three nights on holiday weekends.

"After many years of collecting country antiques and refinishing furniture, we have found just the right place for them in this 1905 country Victorian that was owned by one family until we bought it in 1983. It has natural woodwork throughout. We have, as our son who is in the army in Kansas says, 'brought the house to life' with complete redecorating and accents of my herbal wreaths, cross-stitch samplers, and collections.

"I was involved in restaurant and hotel management work when we lived in Massachusetts. Now I'm at Blue Stone full time. Roger is an electrical lineman. We are Newport natives who moved back here with the idea of having a rooming house. When friends sent us our first (unplanned) B&B guests, we were hooked!"

**In residence:** Teenaged son, Sean. "Emergency" is a cat who was discovered one freezing January night outside the emergency room of the local hospital. Grandchildren ranging in age from 1 to 16 are occasional visitors.

**Restrictions:** No children. No guests' pets. Smoking allowed only on the first floor.
**Bed and bath:** Three rooms. One with double bed, private bath. One with queen-sized bed shares a full bath with a double-bedded room.
**Breakfast:** 8-10, earlier upon request. Continental. Varied. Could be blueberry buckle, strawberry muffins, cranberry or banana nut breads accompanied by seasonal fruits and a continuous cup of coffee. Assorted teas. Served in dining room with stoneware, samplers, baskets, plants, and quilts.
**Plus:** Beverages. Bedroom window fans. Guest refrigerator. Porch. Yard. Bicycle and surfboard storage. Will meet guests at bus.
**Rates:** March 15-November 15 private bath $75, shared bath $55-$65. November 15-March 15 private bath $50, shared bath $35-$50. $10 cot.

From Texas: "We wanted to sit in the wagon seat, but the teddy bears got there first . . . sewing machine with marble top used for coffee service . . . quilts upstairs . . . impeccable . . . a chance to relax in an 'at home' environment."

---

## Cliffside Inn

---

2 Seaview Avenue, Newport, RI 02840
**Phone:** 401/847-1811
**Location:** In a quiet residential area, one block from main entrance to Cliff Walk. Six blocks from the mansions on Bellevue Avenue, 15 minutes' walk from the waterfront. Five minutes from First Beach.
**Host:** Kathleen Russell
**Open:** May through October. Two-night minimum stay on weekends; three nights on three-day weekends.

Some guests call Cliffside one of Newport's best-kept secrets. At times, innkeeper Kay Russell calls it her "labor of love since 1981—now whipped into shape." She has decorated with color, wallpaper, and antiques. Since starting with 7 rooms (today there are 11), discovering three chimneys when redoing the kitchen, and adding baths, there has been time for the "fun part." The porch has an awning, painted canvas rugs, and wicker furniture. There's a little rose garden in the driveway circle, a perennial garden in the back. And the sea breezes keep coming. And so do guests—to this gracious and comfortable Victorian built in 1880 as a summer cottage by the governor of Maryland. Sometimes weddings are booked here too.

Mary, Laurie, Glenn, or Lynn handles the phone. On site, Kay is keenly aware of guests' needs and enjoys seeing those who have been in town for a couple of days become guides for new guests. "There seems to be a great combination of new people together with returnees who are like an extended family."

**In residence:** Two cats.
**Restrictions:** Children should be at least ten. Sorry, no guests' pets.
**Bed and bath:** Ten rooms plus an efficiency apartment on three floors. All private baths; some full, some with shower only—some large, some small. A double or queen-sized bed in most rooms. One on third floor has two twin beds. Suite has two double beds. One room has a wall of glass; another features an antique Lincoln-style bed. For a floor plan, request Cliffside's brochure.
**Breakfast:** Continental breakfast that includes (an endless supply of) homemade rolls or popovers. Special dietary needs can be accommodated. Buffet style in the living room.
**Plus:** Sitting room on the third floor with a TV and functional pump organ. Some rooms have window or ceiling fans. Parking.
**Rates:** Double occupancy. Late June through Labor Day $65-$88. Off-season $60-$82. $10.60 cots. Apartment $88, off-season $82. Tax included.

## Ellery Park House

44 Farewell Street, Newport, RI 02840
**Phone:** 401/847-6320
**Location:** About four blocks from waterfront in the quiet, historic Point section. A short walk to the bus and the airport shuttle.
**Host:** Margo Waite
**Open:** Year round.

"I really am a pure B&B with just two guest rooms in my three-bedroom house. After eight years of hosting, I still think of each arriving guest as a friend of a friend."

Travel stories abound here. When volunteer hosts were needed for participants in a sailboat race from England to Newport, Margo hosted a wonderful French family for ten days, and the idea of B&B was launched. Since then she has visited many of her guests from

Australia, France, and England, while traveling as general manager of *Cruising World*, an international sailing magazine. This year she is involved with a program that assists participants in a single-handed around-the-world race that starts and ends in Newport.

Many Americans, too, appreciate the hospitality in this 1889 Victorian cottage, one that was originally built to fit the lot so all four walls are different lengths.

**In residence:** Two cats, Furze, a long-haired yellow, and Fagin, a seven-toed tiger.
**Restrictions:** Children under two or over eight preferred. No smoking in bedrooms.
**Foreign languages spoken:** None (a very little French) but "I have had visitors who didn't speak English and it was fine."
**Bed and bath:** Two second-floor rooms with Oriental rugs and polished wood floors. One with a double bed and the other with two twins. Shared full guest bath.
**Breakfast:** Continental with homemade muffins and jam. Could be quite social or self-serve, depending on everyone's schedule.
**Plus:** Coffee and tea always available. TV in each bedroom. Bedroom fans. Many books. Patio. Several parks and wonderful walking in the Point area. Bicycle rental two blocks away.
**Rates:** $50 per room.

## Flower Garden Guests

Newport, RI
**Location:** In a residential neighborhood, less than two miles from Newport's mansions, beaches, waterfront, restaurants, shops. Five minutes to sightseeing/beach shuttle parking lot.
**Reservations:** Available year round through Bed & Breakfast of Rhode Island, page 426. Two-night minimum stay on weekends, three nights on holiday weekends.

Ever since a reporter covering a famous Newport trial in 1982 needed lodging, this hostess has loved sharing her home with travelers. What she calls "mellowed contemporary" (from the outside) is chock full of displayed collectibles—teddy bears, pottery, dollhouses, tinware. Everything has a story.

"I am definitely a 'Newporter.' My family has been here since the 1700s. I have lived in this house for 20 years. Living in Newport, you just always have company, so it was natural to become a B&B when the girls left for college. Now they kid about making reservations when they want to come home. . . . Once we had a power failure and guests took showers by candlelight and we made coffee on the gas grill. It was great! . . I love attending to detail. One surprise that I give guests is . . . but don't tell! [I won't.] Newport has it all—mansions, dining, boats, even a pond minutes from our door that has an excellent view of the ocean."

**In residence:** A tiny zebra finch, Leonard, holds court from his bamboo cage in the garden room; "sings along with the blue jays and cardinals outside his window and with any Barbra Streisand tape."
**Restrictions:** Couples only. No children. No pets. Smoking is not allowed in the bedrooms.
**Bed and bath:** Three second-floor rooms, each with an antique double bed, share one full bath. Each room has TV and radio.
**Breakfast:** 7:30-9:30. Served in the country kitchen or on the deck overlooking the garden. Fresh fruit (strawberries from garden), assorted bread and pastries, freshly squeezed juice, coffee, assorted teas. Tends to be quite leisurely.
**Plus:** Late-afternoon wine. Glass-enclosed cozy wicker garden room, "the great gathering place." VCR. Fans in bedrooms. Toiletries provided. Guest garden for relaxing, sunbathing or croquet. Four free tennis courts are a two-minute walk away. Good area for jogging and walking. "And sometimes I take guests to an antiques flea market." Fireplace and hot chocolate in winter.
**Rates:** $65 per room. $10 surcharge for one-night stay.

## Ivy Lodge

12 Clay Street, Newport, RI 02840
**Phone:** 401/849-6865
**Location:** One block from Bellevue Avenue, Newport's mansion area. Quiet, residential estate setting, about a 15-minute walk to waterfront, restaurants, shops, and beaches.
**Hosts:** Cris and Jerry Harrington
**Open:** Year round. Reservations preferred. Two-night minimum stay on weekends from May through October.

Guests say that it's delightful, lovely, a beautiful place. "I think it was harder to restore than to build!" exclaims Cris about this B&B, which opened just because Cris and Jerry fell in love with the hallway of the seven-bedroom house. That happened in 1984, almost a century after it was built. The *Newport Mercury* of July 31, 1886, commented that "with its vine covered piazza [it's] one of the prettiest cottages in Newport." The report also speaks of the huge rooms, the cherry library, the mahogany study, and the enormous hall with paneled walls from floor to ceiling and elegant staircase. To this day, the foyer offers a dramatic introduction to the house that is now on the National Register of Historic Places.

The Harringtons' personalized approach is appreciated. After a group of doctors stayed here while attending a course conducted in Newport, the program director wrote, "Late arrivals, irregular hours, unannounced assignments, unexpected children, you took it all in your stride and made our people feel at home with your graciousness and flexibility."

A real bonus for Ivy Lodge guests is the 90-minute taped tour of Newport that you can borrow for use in your car. And what about some secret place that the natives know about? Yes, the Harringtons have a favorite. "Come and find out!"

Jerry is an accountant who likes the worlds of real estate and sports and cars. Cris owned and operated a card and gift shop and has a penchant for music, magazines and catalogues, and shopping.

**In residence:** Erin, age four. Cats named Tiger and Missy, and a golden retriever named Nikki.
**Restrictions:** Sorry, no guests' pets.
**Bed and bath:** Four rooms on two floors. All have private bath with shower. Two rooms on the second floor each with queen-sized brass bed, one with oak furnishings, the other with wicker. One third-floor room has twin beds and a comfortable sitting area. Also on the third floor, a two-room combination with bath ideal for a family. One room has a queen-sized bed and wicker furnishings; the other, designed with children in mind, has twin beds. Cot available.
**Breakfast:** 8:30-10 weekdays, 9-11 weekends. Juice, fruits, muffins or pastry, coffee, tea, in newly carpeted and draped dining room.
**Plus:** Tour of house. Books on Newport's past and present. Bedroom window fans. Thick towels. Beach towels. Refrigerator, ice. Wraparound porches. Parking. Potential babysitters. The tour tape.
**Rates:** In season $75-$125 per room. Off-season $50-$65. $10 rollaway bed. MasterCard and VISA accepted.

## Queen Anne Inn

16 Clarke Street, Newport, RI 02840
**Phone:** 401/846-5676
**Location:** In the historic district, on a street that is one block long, just two blocks from the waterfront.
**Host:** Peg McCabe
**Open:** At least April through early November. Two-night minimum for summer weekdays, two nights on weekends year round, three nights on holiday weekends. Phone reservations, to clarify room selection, preferred. (You'll also arrive feeling that you already know Peg.)

"That great woman with a great place! When I arrived 'home' after the marathon, I was greeted with congratulatory signs and a bottle of champagne that we all shared from my prize, a Paul Revere bowl."

Peg is always doing things like that. Whether you're in town because you just sailed across the Atlantic or for your honeymoon or for touring, this B&B seems to attract "people, all wonderful, who have the choice of much more than they expected; yet they can relax in the garden and not feel they *have* to go someplace."

The house is done just exactly as Peg envisioned it when she lived across the street about ten years ago. Now the Victorian house has an uncluttered light and airy look, with wallpaper on many ceilings, lovely lamps, and many touches including old crocheted pieces that have been framed by one of Peg's daughters. The 150-year-old brass beds were a find in Italy just a couple of years ago. There's an armoire in one room, and, in season, cut flowers in the common rooms.

Where are you going for dinner? "Restaurants are my passion!" As a "people person" and a former librarian, Peg shares and ferrets out *all* kinds of information about her adopted city. In New York she was "a suburban housewife and mother to four." Here she is constantly reminded about just how small the world is—and how much of a real community Newport is.

**In residence:** A hostess who, at the time this book went to press, said, "I'm still trying to stop smoking."
**Restrictions:** No pets please. No incoming or outgoing phone service is available between 11 p.m. and 8 a.m.
**Foreign language spoken:** The most rudimentary French.

**Bed and bath:** Twelve rooms and seven shared baths. One single, four rooms with twin beds, seven with double beds. Cot or futon available.
**Breakfast:** 8:30-10:30. "The happy hour in the morning," according to one guest. Continental. Portuguese sweet bread and selection of breakfast biscuits, coffee and tea. In reception room or in garden.
**Plus:** Off-street parking. Flower garden.
**Rates:** $30 single, $40-$60 double. $10 for cot or futon (available only in the $60 rooms). Rate varies according to size of room and its location. MasterCard and VISA accepted.

## The Willows of Newport

8 Willow Street, Newport, RI 02840
**Phone:** 401/846-5486
**Location:** On a quiet residential street in the historic Point section among pre-Revolutionary houses, just three blocks from the downtown waterfront. Five-minute walk to shops, restaurants, tours, night life.
**Host:** Pattie Murphy
**Open:** Year round. Reservations required.

> A guest wrote: "We are greedily planning our next escape to The Willows for fun, fantasy and rest. You're keeping dreams alive."

Fantasy in a historic house. Romantic getaways an ongoing feature. Style adapted from the Gilded Age. All created by a woman who in eight years has restored (with the help of lots of contractors) three houses as inns on the same street. Pattie grew up in the elegant Bellevue Avenue mansion, Chateau sur Mer, as the daughter of the nurse to the aging mistress. Her Willows is a combination of two small adjacent town houses, one built in 1740 and the other 100 years later. Today they are connected and on the National Register of Historic Places.

Pampering. Breakfast in bed served on bone china and silver service. Waiter in black tie and tails. Pattie muses, "I have a love of design and imagination. The Willows fulfills something I always wanted to do since childhood. My guests are a special breed. They ask about fine dining. They stroll hand in hand by the sea." Some go home and write odes to "The Penguin."

**Restrictions:** Not appropriate for children. No guests' pets. Smoking in parlor only.

**Bed and bath:** Five rooms. All private baths, some full, some with showers only. Double, queen, or king-sized beds. Matching comforters and draperies on high dust-ruffled beds, wall-to-wall carpeting, dimmers on lights. The Captain's Loft has a cathedral ceiling and a skylight plus three other windows. Nonworking fireplaces in two rooms.
**Breakfast:** At 9. Freshly squeezed orange juice, hot muffins or croissants, coffee and tea.
**Plus:** Fireplaced Victorian parlor decorated in soft pink. Wet bar. Air conditioning in each bedroom. Mints on the pillow. Turned-down beds. Flowers. Champagne glasses and silver ice buckets. Concierge service 3-5 p.m. Tours of the house. Backyard. Fenced and garage parking.
**Rates:** $98-$125 summer, $68-$88 winter.

## The Yellow Cottage

82 Gibbs Avenue, Newport, RI 02840
**Phone:** 401/847-6568 or 849-4483
**Location:** In residential area. Five-minute ride to town or beaches.
**Host:** Nancy A. Rubeck
**Open:** Year round. Two-night minimum stay on weekends.

How have the children fared with all the coming and going? Nancy always answers, "Good indeed! At this point I think I could run a B&B training course for children."

The Yellow Cottage, built as a summer home about 1900, has been the Rubeck residence for 15 years. Nancy comes from a big family and is used to having numbers of people around. For many years, as military wife, she lived in several states, Hawaii, Barbados, and Panama. So it was natural for her to turn to B&B as a way to work and stay home with her children. She started six years ago, "in my grandmother's style of 'clean, courteous, and kind.' "

"Because I am a psychic medium, often we get talking about it, sometimes over lots of good Swedish coffee. I try to take pictures of guests and enjoy sending them copies. When guests return, we renew acquaintances. I enjoy my B&B."

**In residence:** One who smokes. Trina, age 20; James II, 17; and Amy, 9. Three cats.
**Bed and bath:** Four guest rooms (and family) share one and one-half baths. Two rooms have queen-sized beds and two each have a double bed.
**Breakfast:** Flexible. Has been as early as 3 a.m. for one family that had plans to leave for a long drive. Fresh orange juice, fruit, and homemade breads.
**Plus:** Half-price tokens for the Newport Bridge sent to you if time permits. Postcards with stamps. If you should be unhappy with a local restaurant, Nancy will follow up.
**Rates:** $40 single, $70 double in summer. $35 and $50 other months.

## Bed & Breakfast of Rhode Island Host #122

Providence, RI
**Location:** Quiet residential area on street of historic homes. Near Brown University. Five-minute bus ride or ten-minute walk to center city.
**Reservations:** Available late August-early June through Bed & Breakfast of Rhode Island, page 426.

> From England: "Delightful hosts. Excellent breakfast. Very homey atmosphere. Could not be bettered altogether. We were treated like relatives."

"Our office is wallpapered in maps. Visitors enjoy showing us where they came from and where they are going."

They come from all over the world, from London, Japan, Princeton, New Jersey, and the west coast. They come for Brown University, the Rhode Island School of Design, historic house tours, interviews, or performances (sometimes their own). The bonus is the opportunity to stay with the caring voice teacher/music director and sculptor/consultant who live in a gracious 1883 Victorian furnished with "comfortable antiques and reproductions."

**In residence:** Three cats. Pippa, a female calico; her brother Nehi (short for Nehemiah); and a recently acquired stray Persian-tiger named Sam.
**Restrictions:** No smoking. Children should be at least eight.

**Foreign languages spoken:** French and some Italian.
**Bed and bath:** Two large second-floor rooms, each with two twin beds, desk, private full bath. Cot available.
**Breakfast:** Usually 8-9. Juice, cereal, eggs, sausage or ham, croissants or homemade muffins or coffee cake, hot beverages. Special diets accommodated. Served in large formal dining room with many plants and flowers, silver service, lace cloth.
**Plus:** Will meet guests at transportation points. Bedroom fans. Library/TV room filled with books. Music/living room (when lessons not being given) that has a grand piano. Parking. Guests' deck overlooking secluded backyard.
**Rates:** $40-$50 single, $55-$60 double. $10 cot. $10 surcharge for one-night stay.

## Isaac Peck House

Providence, RI
**Location:** In the restored East Side historic district. Five to ten minutes' walk to Brown University and Rhode Island School of Design and Museum, and to free loop downtown bus transportation. Less than a mile from center city attractions and restaurants. Three blocks from I-195.
**Reservations:** Available year round through Bed & Breakfast of Rhode Island, page 426.

Guests' quarters are a picture come to life in this city house that was built as a two-family structure in 1812 but restored by the present owners in 1980 as a one-family. Since then, it has been featured on a historic house tour. What was intended as a third-floor suite for grown children has become guests' home away from home because the children are indeed very far away from home. Early 19th-century antiques and exposed beams enhance the ambiance. Outside there's an oasis in the city: a charming terrace garden that uses brick, stone, and wood as borders for plantings and eating areas. The hostess is a historic preservation consultant on interior decoration and her husband is a business executive.

**Restrictions:** Sorry, no guests' pets. No smoking.

**Bed and bath:** A suite (bedroom with double bed, living room with single sofa bed, kitchen, private bath) plus another room one flight down with two twin beds available to the same party. Crib available.
**Breakfast:** Until 9. Freshly squeezed orange juice and fruit, coffee, regular and herbal teas, homemade muffins, coffee cakes, rolls and breads. Served in the Federal-style formal dining room or, weather permitting, in garden.
**Plus:** Off-street parking. Telephone in suite. Private terrace garden. Bedroom window fans. Color TV. Babysitting.
**Rates:** $65 double. $10 third adult. $5 child. Extra room, $50 per night. Weekly rates. $10 surcharge for one-night stay.

## William M. Read House

Providence, RI
**Location:** In historic district, near Brown University and Rhode Island School of Design. Ten-minute walk to downtown. Two-block walk to bus.
**Reservations:** Available year round September-May through Bed & Breakfast of Rhode Island, page 426.

On the host's side of the family, there have been four generations of innkeepers. He is a commercial banker and his wife one of the organizers of the annual Providence Festival of Historic Houses. They have been carrying on the tradition by sharing their 1849 Greek Revival home with overnight guests as well as with one who stayed two nights a week while working on her doctoral thesis. Their house was moved to its present site in 1947 when Pembroke College expanded. Since the couple bought it in 1983, they have done much of the restoration themselves, blending contemporary and traditional ideas.

**In residence:** Two children, ages three and five.
**Restrictions:** No guests' pets. No smoking.
**Bed and bath:** Up two steep flights of steps to a third-floor room with two twin beds, private bath, guest sitting room with daybed for extra guest, view of Brown campus and the city. Crib available.
**Breakfast:** 7-9. Orange juice, homemade muffins, bread or coffee cake, coffee or tea. Served in breakfast area of the contemporary kitchen or, weather permitting, on private terrace.

**Plus:** Air-conditioned bedroom. A notebook of restaurant reviews. On-street parking.
**Rates:** $50 single, $60 double. $10 daybed. $5 crib for child under three. $10 surcharge for one-night stay.

Guests wrote: "A nice family. Charming, quaint, delightful place."

## Blueberry Bush

128 South Road, Wakefield, RI 02879
**Phone:** 401/783-0907
**Location:** A quiet suburban setting. Fifteen minutes from I-95; 10 minutes to beautiful beaches, 25 minutes to Newport, 15 to Block Island ferry, 10 to the University of Rhode Island, 45 to Mystic, Connecticut.
**Hosts:** June and Pete Nielsen
**Open:** Year round. Two-day minimum stay on three-day holiday weekends.

From New Jersey: "The perfect hosts. Their home is charming, comfortable and very inviting. Our bedrooms were immaculate and beautifully decorated. Mrs. Nielsen shared her recipe for blueberry muffins—the best we ever tasted!"

Those blueberry muffins *are* "the best ever" according to many others who have written about the "friendly but never intrusive hosts who are knowledgeable about the area."

Pete calls June the "people person," one who also makes Oriental rugs and enjoys knitting. Pete, too, even though he doesn't call himself that, is a "people person." He is an executive with a textile firm and enjoys woodworking. Their inviting Cape Cod–style home is traditionally furnished and has some lovely antique and refinished pieces. After six years of hosting bed & breakfast they say, "We still find each new guest interesting, informative, and fun."

**In residence:** One "pussy cat," Smudge.
**Restrictions:** Sorry, no guests' pets.
**Bed and bath:** Two rooms. One full bath. One room with twin beds can accommodate two more. One double-bedded room with rollaway. Crib available.

**Breakfast:** Available 7-9:30. Full. Fresh fruit (maybe homegrown blueberries and peaches). Homemade bread or muffins, jams or jellies. Choice of specialties.
**Plus:** Use of yard, cookout facilities, outdoor table and chairs. High chair available. Laundry facilities available if stay is three days or longer. Attic fan cools the whole house.
**Rates:** $45 single, $50 double. $10 for an extra adult. $7.50 for a child under 14. Special rates for extended stays.

## Highland Farm

4145 Tower Hill Road, Wakefield, RI 02879
**Phone:** 401/783-2408 (if no answer, keep trying)
**Location:** On a 28-acre farm, on a main road two miles north of Wakefield center. Five minutes to beaches, 20 minutes to Galilee (fishing village and charter boats), 30 minutes to Newport, 20 minutes to the Block Island ferry.
**Hosts:** Richard and Edith Sumner
**Open:** May through October. Reservations required.

> Dear Bernice: I sent my overflow to Edith and Richard all last summer and had glowing feedback. Touring the farm and visiting the rec room where quilts and rugs are always in progress were things people raved about. Their charming old house is so comfortable and is filled with things they have made or refinished. They are both good cooks and serve wholesome all-American goodies. They are caring and friendly. . . . I do hope you'll include Highland Farm in your new book.
> Warmly,
> Jeanne [Lewis of Fairfield-By-The-Sea in Green Hill, R.I.]
> P.S. The flower gardens are exquisite!

"We will never be natives as we came from Maine 41 years ago. We talk 'different.' We talk about everything with guests—fishing or boat trips, farming, Theater-By-The-Sea. Richard was a rubber mechanic and he is a retired farmer. Now we have a full-time job maintaining the house, lawns, vegetable and flower gardens. We treat guests like family. Some of them like to shell peas or snap beans. Some play the piano. They all have their special interests and we have maps, brochures about historical places and things to do, restaurant menus."

At one time, the Sumners' one-and-a-half–story farmhouse, built in the early 1800s, had a store in one room. The garage was a one-room schoolhouse moved from across the road.

**In residence:** Benny, a white toy poodle. Four cats—Chub, Chet, Flash, and Muffin.
**Restrictions:** Smoking permitted outdoors only.
**Bed and bath:** Two cozy upstairs rooms with shared full bath. Shower on first floor also available. Crib available.
**Breakfast:** Whenever; anytime from 6 to 12. Farm-fresh eggs poached, scrambled, or fried; cereal, pancakes, French toast, muffins, homemade jelly, molasses cookies (both from old Maine recipes), juice and hot beverages. Served on the deck or in the kitchen.
**Plus:** Large living room with fireplace and baby grand piano. Bedroom window fans. Rec room with Edith's projects—braided and hooked rugs, quilting and smocking. Bring your own coolers for picnics in the yard and on the deck.
**Rates:** $25 single, $35 double. Crib free for children under one year.

## J. Livingston's Guest House By The Sea

39 Weekapaug Road, Weekapaug, RI 02891
**Phone:** 401/322-0249
**Location:** Less than a half-mile from the ocean and beach. Directly across the street from Breachway with year-round fishing. Bordered in back by wildlife preserve with geese, swans, herons, and songbirds. Three miles from Center for the Arts in Westerly. Three miles from state park.
**Host:** Peg Cloutier
**Open:** Year round. Reservations preferred.

> "If you have never been to the J. Livingston House, you really must go! Peg has it decorated so quaintly with stenciling throughout the house. . . . I did plenty of reading in between long walks along deserted beaches and salt ponds. . . . Each morning a generous and delicious breakfast. . . . I guess what I appreciated most though, was the good conversations we had. Peg has a knack of making a guest feel like a long-time friend."

The setting and the name of this B&B reflect Peg's concern for pace and environment. Before coming here in 1985, she owned a craft shop, and before that she was a registered nurse. She is a leading fiber artist and designer, has many patterns in print, and is a member of the Society of Craft Designers. Seven times a year she offers craft workshops and creative reflective seminars here.

She brought much interior-design and restoration experience to her efforts with J. Livingston; before this she gutted an old mill! Originally built as a guesthouse in the 1800s, J. Livingston was rebuilt in 1939, after having been washed nearly a mile away during the hurricane of 1938.

The long list of memorable guests includes a violinist who practiced each day when others went to the beach.

**In residence:** Daughter Carrie, age 19. Son Christopher, when home on college vacations. Raz is a black Lab retriever restricted to Peg's apartment or his own run.
**Restrictions:** Children should be well behaved. No guests' pets.
**Bed and bath:** Nine rooms. The seven second-floor small rooms—with a double or two twin beds—share three baths. All have individual electric thermostats, Priscilla curtains, ruffled bedspreads, and stenciled walls. A narrow staircase to third floor leads to two spacious rooms that can sleep up to five; one large shared bath with shower. Many rooms have water views.
**Breakfast:** 8-10. Juice, fresh fruit, hot and cold cereals, croissants, homemade breads, homemade whole-grain muffins or Danish, bagels, jams, cream cheese, butter, coffee, tea, and milk. Buffet style in dining room.
**Plus:** Late-afternoon or evening beverages. Living room with library and finely tuned piano. Charcoal grills in summer. Umbrella tables. Yard and lawn chairs. Screened porch. Seven theme weekends/workshops per year. Will meet guests at Westerly airport or train.
**Rates:** Double occupancy. July-September weekdays/weekends \$45/\$50 double rooms, \$50/\$55 studio, \$60/\$65 efficiency. Less in other seasons. \$10 additional person in room. Fishing, golf, tennis, and theater packages available.

## Woody Hill Guest House B&B

RR3, Box 676E, Woody Hill Road, Westerly, RI 02891
**Phone:** 401/322-0452
**Location:** Just off busy Route 1, but really in the country. Two miles from wonderful ocean beaches. Minutes from Mystic Seaport and Newport.
**Host:** Ellen Madison
**Open:** Year round.

" 'How old *is* this house?' I live for that question, for it means that I have successfully fooled my questioner. The only old structural details are the bricks in the fireplaces and, in the addition, the doors from the ancestral 1857 'homestead' next door."

Ellen's family has lived within a two-mile radius of her home since 1636. She designed and did much of the finishing work on this gambrel-roofed colonial reproduction built on the "family farm." It has wide floorboards; weathered shingles; and large, airy, welcoming rooms—each one different and filled with inherited furniture, crafts, and some wonderful handmade (by Ellen) quilts. The 1986 addition carries out her attention to detail and love of nooks and crannies. The Library, a guest room, has four walls of books, shuttered windows, and window seats. The Great Room, with atrium door and furniture made by her father from leftover pine flooring, overlooks a meadow in one direction, the gardens in another.

Since being in my first B&B book, Woody Hill has become a year-round haven, with winter guests coming to sit by the fire or walk the beaches. In the early fall the ocean is still warm enough for swimming and the roads practically trafficless.

Cooking and gardening are fun for Ellen. She currently teaches English to high school students and has taught on the university level. The year of her house addition was also the year she completed her doctoral dissertation. Her inspiration for hosting is deep-rooted. "My parents took tourists in their home while I was growing up and I saw what treasured friendships they made."

**In residence:** Two cats. "Treasure is a fat happy lazy black cat who cozies up to anyone and molds himself to that person. Lady is aloof and skittish."
**Restrictions:** No smoking. No guests' pets. Only well-behaved children, please.

**Bed and bath:** Four rooms on two floors with two shared full baths. The very large Great Room has canopied double bed and a private outside entrance. One room with double bed. One with a double and a 3/4 bed. The Library has a double sofa bed.
**Breakfast:** 8-9. Homegrown raspberries year round. Homemade muffins—maybe strawberry nut or blueberry ginger, seasonal fruit—with interesting sauces. In winter you may be served warm applesauce and waffles. Huge repertoire from hundreds of cookbooks. Served artistically in the cozy dining room with harvest table, Windsor chairs, braided rug, and wainscoting.
**Plus:** Living room with fireplace. One second-floor room has a pump organ (and music) just waiting to be played. Yard with gardens, privacy, "and sometimes mosquitoes."
**Rates:** $50 for two (Great Room slightly higher). $10 rollaway. $5 under age five, $10 for child over five or extra adult in a room. One night free for a week's stay.

## The Sparrow's Nest

470 Annaquatucket Road, Wickford, RI 02852
**Phone:** 401/295-1142
**Location:** On 2½ acres, set back on a quiet road. One mile from the center of the "unpretentious" coastal village of Wickford with its numerous 18th- and 19th-century homes, some small shops and antique dealers, and in July, the Wickford Art Festival. Fifteen minutes to University of Rhode Island, Newport, or beaches; 30 minutes to Providence.
**Hosts:** Mary Worobec and Peter Doering
**Open:** Year round. Reservations required. Two-day minimum stay preferred in summer. Three-day minimum required on Memorial Day, July 4, and Labor Day weekends.

> From Texas: "A delightful experience—immaculate, lovely, restored antiques, fresh wildflowers everywhere. . . . A warm, gracious and talented couple who made us feel very much at home."

Since 1985 guests from all over the world have stayed here. Some from Virginia, Washington, D.C., New York, and Maryland were among those who wrote to me about "the lovable Labrador" and the hosts who made "room in their barn for our vintage Daimler Saloon that we drove for a Jaguar car festival in Newport." One letter concludes, "We could have stayed for weeks."

## Wickford

This is a picture-book colonial surrounded by a picket fence, stone walls, barns, and beautiful gardens. Once part of a working farm, the original section of the house was brought here by oxcart in the 1700s. The main house dates from 1854. Completely redone inside and out by Mary and Peter, both oceanographers, it has been decorated (all by the hosts themselves) with country antiques, wicker, some Oriental rugs and lots of contemporary folk art—sculpture, quilts, patchwork items, tin snips, and folk dolls. Mary designs, sews, and quilts, and has, since becoming a full-time mother, developed her own line of children's clothing.

Yes, of course these terrific hosts can direct you to beaches, but you might be tempted to try their suggestions of nature or bird walks, of rocky or marsh areas to explore, or even organized environmental programs for adults and/or children.

**In residence:** Caitlin (Katie), "our sweetheart," aged two. Peter smokes, but "only outside or up the chimney." Gus, a black Lab, "has been known to entertain the guests with his bat imitation and 'rocket dog.' "
**Restrictions:** Well-behaved children only. Sorry, no pets and no smoking indoors.
**Foreign language spoken:** Peter can converse in French (un peu).
**Bed and bath:** Three rooms on the second floor share a full guest bath. Two rooms have double beds and one room has two twins. One cot available.
**Breakfast:** 8:30-9:30. Juice, fresh fruit, homemade muffins and coffee cake—Scandinavian apple cake, Sue's pumpkin bread, Swedish tea cake, banana-cranberry-nut bread, blueberry bread—herbal and regular teas and coffee. Different menu and settings every day. Served in the dining room on pewter, on china, or on individual trays ready to carry outside to the apple trees or picnic bench.
**Plus:** Fans in bedrooms. Picnic table under the apple tree. Imaginative and traditional suggestions for things to do.
**Rates:** Mid-May–mid-October $40-$45 double bed, $45 twin beds. Off-season $35-$40. $10 extra for cot.

*Can't find the community you are going to? Check with a reservation service described at the beginning of this chapter. Through the service, you may be placed (matched) with a welcoming B&B that is near your destination.*

# NORTH AMERICAN RESERVATION SERVICES

## Reservation Services: What They Are and How to Use Them

**A reservation service is a business that is organized to match host and guest.** Although it is considered to be part of a rapidly growing cottage industry that can be seasonal, in some areas the service is a full-time job for an individual, a couple, partners, or a small group. The service could be very small—and almost waiting to be discovered. Others have become quite professional and even computerized.

**Listings may be in communities where there are no overnight lodging facilities, or they may provide an alternative to hotels or motels.** Although most services feature private homes, others include B&B inns, small public lodging places that are usually owner-occupied with 10 or 12 guest rooms.

**Beyond homes with a host in residence, some services now offer stays in unhosted homes.** Other expanded services might include car rentals, sightseeing tours, and theater tickets.

**Each service determines its own area.** They may cover just one community, a metropolitan area, or an entire region. Because some services network with others, in some cases you can make one call and the service will book you into its own area, into another region, or even into another country.

**Write for printed information or maybe, better yet, call.** The printed information is usually a brochure together with application form that asks you about your needs, preferences, purpose of trip, and perhaps special interests. It may also ask you about your driver's license and/or place of employment. If you choose to write, please include a self-addressed, stamped business-sized envelope.

A directory, when published by a serivce, rarely has addresses and phone numbers of hosts. The directory may have a few sample listings on a single sheet or complete listings in a booklet or, occasionally, in a spiral-bound book. Directory prices are usually in the $2–$5 range. You can use a service and its judgment without obtaining the directory.

A call can save a tremendous amount of time even if you reach an answering service or machine. (Return long-distance calls are usually made collect.) When you speak to the service, you can get a sense of the kind of personalized service offered while conveying your thoughts about price range, location, amenities, ambiance, and just how much hospitality you would like. Before placing the call think about bed and bath arrangements, parking, smoking, pets, children, air conditioning—whatever is important to you. And if you tell the service a little about yourself, it could help toward making a more appropriate match.

**Advance notice is preferred and, with many services, required.** If you can provide enough information and references, and if a host is available that very night or "tomorrow," some services will flex and accommodate you on the spot.

**Length of stay requirements vary.** One night may be fine. If so, there may be a one-night surcharge. Two nights may be the minimum. Short-term (interim) lodging for weeks or months may also be available.

**Rates are usually much less than area hotels and motels.** Depending on the area, rates may average $40–$50 a night for two—including breakfast. The range may cover everything from "budget" to "luxury"—from homes that are "clean, neat, and reasonably priced" to antique-filled mansions that are more expensive. *Deposits are usually required.* Refund policies differ; inquire.

**Fee arrangements vary.** Autonomy reigns. Many services include their commission in the quoted nightly rate—period. For public inns (in contrast to private homes with one to three rooms) the quoted rate may be the same as what the inn charges or it could be a total of the inn's rate plus a booking fee. Some services have a standard booking fee, perhaps $5, $10, or $15, for any reservation. A few services now have a membership fee, perhaps $25, that entitles you to book through the service for a year.

**Guests receive name and address of host only after being booked.** Only a handful of services distribute printed lists of hosts' names, addresses, and telephone numbers to allow you to book your own B&B.

**Generally, reservation service hosts are screened and homes are inspected.** Most services are concerned with quality and high standards. Prospective guests' questions about screening procedures should be welcomed. And if a service requests an evaluation from you as guest, give it! (Even if they don't ask you, think about giving one.) Guests' comments can be helpful to everyone. The (predominantly) complimentary ones are often treasured by hosts.

**A reservation service acts as a clearinghouse and frequently provides an opportunity to stay at a B&B that would not be available any other way.**

# U.S. B&B Reservation Services

Reservation services are listed alphabetically by home state. Within each state, services are organized according to the communities in which they are based.

## Alabama

Bed & Breakfast Birmingham, Inc.
P.O. Box 31328
Birmingham, AL 35222
205/591-6406

Bed & Breakfast Montgomery
P.O. Box 886
Millbrook, AL 36054
205/285-5421

Bed & Breakfast Mobile
P.O. Box 66261
Mobile, AL 36606
205/473-2939

## Alaska

Alaska Private Lodgings
1236 West 10th Avenue
Anchorage, AK 99501
907/258-1717

Stay With A Friend
3605 Arctic Boulevard—Box 173
Anchorage, AK 99503
907/344-4006

Alaska Bed & Breakfast Association
P.O. Box 1018
Douglas, AK 99824
907/586-2959

Fairbanks Bed & Breakfast
P.O. Box 74573
Fairbanks, AK 99707
907/452-4967

Ketchikan Bed & Breakfast
P.O. Box 3213
Ketchikan, AK 99901
907/225-8550

Kodiak Bed & Breakfast
P.O Box 1729
Kodiak, AK 99615
907/486-5367

## Arizona

Bed & Breakfast in Arizona
P.O. Box 8628
Scottsdale, AZ 85252
602/995-2831

Bed & Breakfast Scottsdale
P.O. Box 624
Scottsdale, AZ 85252
602/998-7044

Valley 'O the Sun Bed & Breakfast
P.O. Box 2214
Scottsdale, AZ 85252
602/841-1281

Mi Casa—Su Casa Bed & Breakfast
P.O. Box 950
Tempe, AZ 85281
602/990-0682

Barbara's Bed & Breakfast
P.O. Box 13603
Tucson, AZ 85732
602/790-2399

## Arkansas

Bed & Breakfast of the Arkansas Ozarks
Route 1, Box 38
Calico Rock, AR 72519
501/297-8764

## California

Eye Openers Bed & Breakfast Reservations
P.O. Box 694
Altadena, CA 91001
213/684-4428 or 818/797-2055

Digs West and Bed & Breakfast Inland Empire
8191 Crowley Circle
Buena Park, CA 90621
714/739-1669

Bed & Breakfast Homestay
P.O. Box 326
Cambria, CA 93428
805/927-4613 or 1-800-447-6667 (in California)

Travelers Bed & Breakfast
P.O. Box 1368
Chino, CA 91710
714/627-7971

Carolyn's Bed & Breakfast Homes of San Diego
416 Third Avenue #25
Chula Vista, CA 92010
619/435-7009

Bed & Breakfast Homes Directory—West Coast
(book-your-own reservations)
P.O. Box 591
Cupertino, CA 95015
408/996-0668

American Historic Homes Bed & Breakfast
P.O. Box 336
Dana Point, CA 92629
714/496-6953

Bed & Breakfast of Southern California
1943 Sunny Crest Drive, Suite 304
Fullerton, CA 92635
714/738-8361 or 525-8695

Rent-A-Room
11531 Varna Street
Garden Grove, CA 92640
714/638-1406

Bed & Breakfast International
151 Ardmore Road
Kensington, CA 94707
415/525-4569

Napa Valley Bed & Breakfast
1834 First Street
Napa, CA 94559
707/257-1051

Bed & Breakfast Hospitality
P.O. Box 2407
Oceanside, CA 92054
619/722-6694

Bed & Breakfast Exchange
P.O. Box 88
Saint Helena, CA 94574
707/963-7756

San Diego Bed & Breakfast
P.O. Box 22948
San Diego, CA 92122
619/560-7322

American Family Inn/Bed & Breakfast
San Francisco
P.O. Box 349
San Francisco, CA 94101
415/931-3083

BayHosts
1155 Bosworth Street
San Francisco, CA 94131
415/334-9632

University Beds & Breakfasts
1387 Sixth Avenue
San Francisco, CA 94122
415/661-8940

Christian Bed & Breakfast of America
P.O. Box 388
San Juan Capistrano, CA 92693
714/496-7050

Hospitality Plus
P.O. Box 388
San Juan Capistrano, CA 92693
714/496-7050

Megan's Friends
1768 Royal Way
San Luis Obispo, CA 93401
805/544-4406

Wine Country Bed & Breakfast
P.O. Box 3211
Santa Rosa, CA 95403
707/578-1661

California Houseguests International, Inc.
18653 Ventura Boulevard #190
Tarzana, CA 91356
818/344-7878

Bed & Breakfast Approved Hosts
10890 Galvin
Ventura, CA 93004
805/647-0651

Bed & Breakfast of Los Angeles
32074 Waterside Lane
Westlake Village, CA 91361
818/889-7325 or 889-8870

CoHost, America's Bed & Breakfast
P.O. Box 9302
Whittier, CA 90608
213/699-8427

Bed & Breakfast California Sunshine
22704 Ventura Boulevard, Suite 1984
Woodland Hills, CA 91364
818/992-1984 or 213/274-4494

## Colorado

Bed and Breakfast Colorado
Box 6061
Boulder, CO 80306
303/442-6664

Bed & Breakfast—Rocky Mountains
P.O. Box 804
Colorado Springs, CO 80901
303/630-3433 or 303/989-4296 (in Metro Denver)

Bed & Breakfast, Vail Valley
P.O. Box 491
Vail, CO 81658
303/949-1212

## Connecticut

Nutmeg Bed & Breakfast
222 Girard Avenue
Hartford, CT 06105
203/236-6698

Bed and Breakfast, Ltd.
P.O. Box 216
New Haven, CT 06513
203/469-3260

Covered Bridge Bed & Breakfast Reservation Service
Maple Avenue, P.O. Box 701
Norfolk, CT 06058
203/542-5944

## Delaware

Bed and Breakfast of Delaware
Box 177, 3650 Silverside Road
Wilmington, DE 19810
302/479-9500

## District of Columbia

The Bed & Breakfast League, Ltd.
3639 Van Ness Street
Washington, DC 20008
202/363-7767

Bed 'n' Breakfast Ltd. of Washington, D.C.
P.O. Box 12011
Washington, DC 20005
202/328-3510

Sweet Dreams & Toast, Inc.
P.O. Box 4835-0035
Washington, DC 20008
202/483-9191

## Florida

Tropical Isles Bed & Breakfast
P.O. Box 490382
Key Biscayne, FL 33149
305/361-2937

Bed & Breakfast, Inc. of the Florida Keys
5 Man-O-War Drive
Marathon, FL 33050
305/743-4118

B&B Accommodations of Orlando
8205 Banyan Boulevard
Orlando, FL 32819
305/352-9157

Central Florida Bed and Breakfast Reservation Service
719 S.E. Fourth Street
Ocala, FL 32671
904/351-1167

B&B Suncoast Accommodations
8690 Gulf Boulevard
St. Pete Beach, FL 33706
813/360-1753

Bed & Breakfast Co.
P.O. Box 262
South Miami, FL 33243
305/661-3270

A&A Bed & Breakfast of Florida, Inc.
P.O. Box 1316
Winter Park, FL 32790
305/628-3233

## Georgia

Atlanta Hospitality
2472 Lauderdale Drive N.E.
Atlanta, GA 30345
404/493-1930

Bed & Breakfast Atlanta
1801 Piedmont Avenue N.E., Suite 208
Atlanta, GA 30324
404/875-0525

Bed & Breakfast Hideaway Homes
P.O. Box 300
Blue Ridge, GA 30513
404/632-2411 or 632-3669

Savannah Historic Inns & Guest Houses
1900 Lincoln Street
Savannah, GA 31401
912/233-7666 (in Savannah)
1-800-722-4667 (in Georgia)
1-800-262-4667 (outside Georgia)

Quail Country Bed & Breakfast, Ltd.
1104 Old Monticello Road
Thomasville, GA 31792
912/226-7218 or 226-6882

## Hawaii

Pacific-Hawaii Bed & Breakfast
19 Kai Nani Place
Kailua, Oahu, HI 96734
808/262-6026 or 263-4848

Go Native . . Hawaii
130 Puhill Street
Hilo, HI 06720
808/961-2080 (Hawaii)
517/349-9598 (Lansing, Michigan)

Bed & Breakfast Honolulu
3242 Kaohinani Drive
Honolulu, HI 96817
808/595-6170 or
1-800-367-8047, ext. 35
(from continental U.S.)

Bed & Breakfast Hawaii
Box 449
Kapaa, HI 96746
808/822-7771

## Idaho

Bed & Breakfast of Idaho
P.O. Box 7323
Boise, ID 83707
208/336-5174

## Illinois

Bed & Breakfast/Chicago, Inc.
P.O. Box 14088
Chicago, IL 60614-0088
312/951-0085

Prairie Hospitality
P.O. Box 3035
Oak Park, FL 60303
312/386-8620

## Indiana

Amish Acres, Inc.
1600 West Market Street
Nappanee, IN 46550
219/773-4188

## Iowa

Bed & Breakfast in Iowa, Ltd.
P.O. Box 430
Preston, IA 52069
319/689-4222

## Kansas

Kansas City Bed & Breakfast
P.O. Box 14781
Lenexa, KS 66215
913/268-4214

## Kentucky

Ohio Valley Bed & Breakfast
6867 Taylor Mill Road
Independence, KY 41051
606/356-7865

Kentucky Homes Bed & Breakfast
1431 St. James Court
Louisville, KY 40208
502/635-7341 or 452-6629

Bluegrass Bed & Breakfast
Route 1, Box 263
Versailles, KY 40383
606/873-3208

## Louisiana

Southern Comfort Bed & Breakfast
Reservation Service
2856 Hundred Oaks
Baton Rouge, LA 70808
504/346-1928 or 928-9815

Bed & Breakfast, Inc.
1360 Moss Street, Box 52257
New Orleans, LA 70152-2257
504/525-4640 or
1-800-228-9711/dial tone/184

Bed, Bath & Breakfast
P.O. Box 15843
New Orleans, LA 70175
504/897-3867

New Orleans Bed & Breakfast/Bed & Breakfast of Louisiana Tours
P.O. Box 8163
New Orleans, LA 70182
504/822-5038 or 822-5046

## Maine

Bed & Breakfast Down East, Ltd.
Box 547, Macomber Mill Road
Eastbrook, ME 04634
207/565-3517

Bed & Breakfast of Maine
32 Colonial Village
Falmouth, ME 04105
207/781-4528

## Maryland

Amanda's Bed & Breakfast
1428 Park Avenue
Baltimore, MD 21217-4230
301/225-0001

The Traveller In Maryland, Inc.
33 West Street
Annapolis, MD 21401
301/269-6232 or 261-2233 (in D.C. metro area)

## Massachusetts

Bed & Breakfast Marblehead and North Shore
54 Amherst Road
Beverly, MA 01915
617/921-1336

Bed & Breakfast Associates Bay Colony, Ltd.
P.O. Box 166
Boston, MA 02157
617/449-5302

Bed & Breakfast Agency of Boston, Inc.
47 Commercial Wharf
Boston, MA 02110
617/720-3540

Folkstone Bed & Breakfast
P.O. Box 931
Boylston, MA 01505-0931
617/869-2687

University Bed & Breakfast, Ltd.
12 Churchill Street
Brookline, MA 02146
617/738-1424

Greater Boston Hospitality
P.O. Box 1142
Brookline, MA 02146
617/277-5430

Bed and Breakfast, Brookline/Boston
Box 732
Brookline, MA 02146
617/227-2292

Bettina's Bed & Breakfast
P.O. Box 585
Cambridge, MA 02238
617/497-9166
1-800-624-6654 (outside Massachusetts)

Bed & Breakfast à la Cambridge & Greater Boston
P.O. Box 665
Cambridge, MA 02140
617/576-1492

Bed and Breakfast Exchange
332 Washington Avenue
Chelsea, MA 02150
617/884-6087

B&B House Guests, Cape Cod
Box AR
Dennis, MA 02638
617/398-0787

Christian Hospitality Bed and Breakfast of New England
636 Union Street
Duxbury, MA 02332
617/834-8528

Bed and Breakfast in Minuteman Country
8 Carriage Drive
Lexington, MA 02173
617/861-7063

Pineapple Hospitality, Inc.
100 Cottage Street
New Bedford, MA 02740
617/990-1696

Host Homes of Boston
P.O. Box 117
Newton, MA 02168
617/244-1308, TELEX:136575

Boston Bed and Breakfast, Inc.
16 Ballard Street
Newton, MA 02159
617/332-4199

New England Bed & Breakfast, Inc.
1045 Center Street
Newton Center, MA 02159
617/244-2112 or 498-9819

Orleans Bed & Breakfast Associates
P.O. Box 1312
Orleans, MA 02653
617/255-3824

Be Our Guest, Bed & Breakfast, Ltd.
P.O. Box 1333
Plymouth, MA 02360
617/837-9867

Greater Springfield Bed and Breakfast
25 Bellevue Avenue
Springfield, MA 01108
413/739-7400

Bed & Breakfast Cape Cod
P.O. Box 341
West Hyannisport, MA 02672
617/775-2772

The Bed & Breakfast Folks
73 Providence Road
Westford, MA 01886
617/692-3232

Berkshire Bed & Breakfast Homes
P.O. Box 211
Williamsburg, MA 01096
413/268-7244

## Michigan

Betsy Ross Bed & Breakfast of Michigan
P.O. Box 1731
Dearborn, MI 48121-1731
313/561-6041

Frankenmuth Area Bed & Breakfast Reservation Service
337 Trinklein Street
Frankenmuth, MI 48734
517/652-8897 or 652-6747

Bed & Breakfast of Grand Rapids
344 College S.E.
Grand Rapids, MI 49503
616/451-4849 or 456-7121

Dutch Country Bed & Breakfast
339 East 16th Street
Holland, MI 49423
616/396-3344

B & B in Mid-Michigan League
1251 North Shiawassee
Owosso, MI 48867
517/723-4890, 723-4708

Capital Bed & Breakfast
5150 Corey Road
Williamston, MI 48895
517/468-3434

## Minnesota

Bed & Breakfast Registry
P.O. Box 8174
St. Paul, MN 55108-0174
612/646-4238

## Mississippi

Natchez Pilgrimage Tours
Canal Street Depot, P.O. Box 347
Natchez, MS 39120
601/446-6631 or 1-800-647-6742

Lincoln, Ltd. Bed and Breakfast
P.O. Box 3479
Meridian, MS 39303
601/482-5483

## Missouri

Ozark Mountain Country Bed & Breakfast Service
Box 295
Branson, MO 65616
417/334-4720 or 334-5077

Truman Country
424 North Pleasant
Independence, MO 64050
816/254-6657

Bed & Biscuits Home Lodging
Box 10107
Kansas City, MO 64111
816/931-2716 or 316/896-7880

Bed & Breakfast in St. Louis
4418 West Pine Street
St. Louis, MO 63108
314/533-9299

Bed & Breakfast of St. Louis, River Country of Missouri & Illinois Inc.
1 Grandview Heights
St. Louis, MO 63131
314/965-4328

## Nebraska

Bed and Breakfast of Nebraska
1464 28th Avenue
Columbus, NE 68601
402/564-7591

Swede Hospitality Bed & Breakfast
1617 Avenue A
Gothenburg, NE 69138
308/537-2680

Bed & Breakfast of the Great Plains
P.O. Box 2333
Lincoln, NE 68502
402/423-3480

## Nevada

Nevada Bed and Breakfast Guild
Capitol Complex
Carson City, NV 89701
702/885-4322

## New Hampshire

New Hampshire Bed & Breakfast
RFD #3, Box 53
Laconia, NH 03246
603/279-8348

## New Jersey

Northern New Jersey Bed & Breakfast/Temporary Lodgings for Transferees
11 Sunset Trail
Denville, NJ 07834
201/625-5129

Bed & Breakfast of New Jersey, Inc.
103 Godwin Avenue, Suite 132
Midland Park, NJ 07432
201/444-7409

## New Mexico

Bed & Breakfast of Santa Fe
436 Sunset Street
Santa Fe, NM 87501
505/982-3332

New Mexico Bed & Breakfast Association
(book-your-own-list)
P.O. Box 2925
Santa Fe, NM 87504-2925

## New York

Bed & Breakfast U.S.A., Ltd.
P.O. Box 606
Croton-on-Hudson, NY 10520
914/271-6228

Alternate Lodging Inc.
P.O. Box 1782
East Hampton, NY 11937
516/324-9449

Hampton Bed & Breakfast
P.O. Box 378
East Moriches, NY 11940
516/878-8197

Bed & Breakfast Rochester
P.O. Box 444
Fairport, NY 14450
716/223-8510 or 223-8877

Bed & Breakfast—Leatherstocking, Central New York Reservation Service
389 Brockway Road
Frankfort, NY 13340
315/733-0040

Mid-Island B&B Reservation Service
518 Mid-Island Plaza
Hicksville, NY 11801
516/931-1234

At Home in New York
P.O. Box 407
New York, NY 10185
212/956-3125 or 265-8539

Bed & Breakfast (& Books)
P.O. Box 20366
New York, NY 10025
212/865-8740

Bed & Breakfast Network of New York
134 West 32nd Street, Suite 602
New York, NY 10001
212/645-8134

City Lights B&B, Ltd.
P.O. Box 20355, Cherokee Station
New York, NY 10028
212/737-7049

Urban Ventures
P.O. Box 426
New York, NY 10024
212/594-5650

New World Bed & Breakfast Ltd.
150 5th Avenue, Suite 711
New York, NY 10011
212/675-5600 (in New York state)
1-800-443-3800 (outside New York state)

Rainbow Hospitality
9348 Hennepin Avenue
Niagara Falls, NY 14304
716/283-4794 or 754-7788

Bed & Breakfast of Long Island
P.O. Box 392
Old Westbury, NY 11568
516/334-6231

A Reasonable Alternative
117 Spring Street
Port Jefferson, NY 11777
516/928-4034

The American Country Collection
984 Gloucester Place
Schenectady, NY 12309
518/370-4948

Bed & Breakfast of the Greater Syracuse Area
143 Didama Street
Syracuse, NY 13224
315/446-4199

## North Carolina

Charlotte Bed and Breakfast
1700–2 Delane Avenue
Charlotte, NC 28211
704/366-0979

Bed and Breakfast in the Albemarle
P.O. Box 248
Everetts, NC 27825
919/792-4584

Bed & Biscuits Reservations
5316 Belsay Drive
Raleigh, NC 27612
919/787-2109

## North Dakota

The Old West B&B
Box 211
Regent, ND 58650
701/563-4542

## Ohio

Private Lodgings, Inc.
P.O. Box 18590
Cleveland, OH 44118
216/321-3213

Columbus Bed & Breakfast
769 South Third Street
Columbus, OH 43206
614/444-8888 or 443-3680

Buckeye Bed & Breakfast
P.O. Box 130
Powell, OH 43065
614/548-4555

## Oklahoma

Redbud Reservations/B&B for Oklahoma
P.O. Box 23954
Oklahoma City, OK 73123
405/720-0212

Bed & Breakfast Oklahoma Style
P.O. Box 32045
Oklahoma City, OK 73123
405/946-2894

## Oregon

Bed & Breakfast Accommodations—Oregon Plus
5733 S.W. Dickinson Street
Portland, OR 97219
503/245-0642

Northwest Bed and Breakfast Travel Unlimited
610 S.W. Broadway, Suite 609
Portland, OR 97205
503/243-7616

## Pennsylvania

Bed & Breakfast of Southeast Pennsylvania
Box 278, RD 1
Barto, PA 19504
215/845-3526

Bed & Breakfast of Philadelphia
P.O. Box 630
Chester Springs, PA 19425
215/827-9650

Hershey Bed & Breakfast Reservation Service
P.O. Box 208
Hershey, PA 17033-0208
717/533-2928

Bed & Breakfast of Chester County
P.O. Box 825
Kennett Square, PA 19348
215/444-1367

Bed & Breakfast of Lancaster County
P.O. Box 19
Mountville, PA 17554
717/285-7200

Bed & Breakfast in Pennsylvania
(referrals for book-your-own)
P.O. Box 162
Oreland, PA 19075
215/885-0991

Harvest Time
Box 48, RD 3
Parker, PA 16049
412/791-2061

Rest & Repast Bed & Breakfast Service
P.O. Box 126
Pine Grove Mills, PA 16868
814/238-1484

Pittsburgh Bed & Breakfast
2190 Ben Franklin Drive
Pittsburgh, PA 15237
412/367-8080

Bed & Breakfast of Valley Forge
P.O. Box 562
Valley Forge, PA 19481
215/783-7838

Guesthouses
RD 9
West Chester, PA 19380
215/692-4575

## Rhode Island

Bed & Breakfast of Rhode Island
P.O. Box 3291
Newport, RI 02840
401/849-1298

Castle Keep
44 Everett Street
Newport, RI 02840
401/846-0362

## South Carolina

Charleston Society Bed and Breakfast
84 Murray Boulevard
Charleston, SC 29401
803/723-4948

Historic Charleston Bed & Breakfast
43 Legare Street
Charleston, SC 29401
803/722-6606

Charleston East Bed & Breakfast
1031 Tall Pine Road
Mount Pleasant, SC 29464
803/884-8208

## South Dakota

South Dakota Bed & Breakfast
P.O. Box 80137
Sioux Falls, SD 57116
605/528-6571 or 339-0759

## Tennessee

Bed & Breakfast in Memphis
P.O. Box 41621
Memphis, TN 38174
901/726-5920

Host Homes of Tennessee
P.O. Box 110227
Nashville, TN 37222-0227
615/331-5244

## Texas

Bed & Breakfast Society of Austin
1702 Graywood Cove
Austin, TX 78704
512/441-2857

Sand Dollar Hospitality
3605 Mendenhall
Corpus Christi, TX 78415
512/853-1222

Bed & Breakfast Texas Style
4224 West Red Bird Lane
Dallas, TX 75237
214/298-8586 or 298-5433

Bed & Breakfast of Fredericksburg
102 South Cherry Street
Fredericksburg, TX 78624
512/997-4712

Be My Guest Lodging Service
330 West Main Street
Fredericksburg, TX 78624
512/997-7227

Gästehaus Schmidt
501 West Main Street
Fredericksburg, TX 78624
512/997-5612

Bed & Breakfast Society of Houston
921 Heights Boulevard
Houston, TX 77008
713/868-4654

Bed and Breakfast Hosts of San Antonio
166 Rockhill
San Antonio, TX 78209
512/824-8036

King William Bed & Breakfast Registry
201 East Rische Street
San Antonio, TX 78204
512/227-1190

Bed & Breakfast Society of San Marcos
326 West Hopkins
San Marcos, TX 78666
512/396-3739

Bed & Breakfast of Wimberley Texas
P.O. Box 589
Wimberley, TX 78676
512/847-9666

## Utah

Bed 'n Breakfast Homestay of Utah
P.O. Box 355
Salt Lake Cty, UT 84110
801/532-7076

## Vermont

Green Mountain Bed & Breakfast
Stage Road
Benson, VT 05731
802/537-2081

Vermont Bed & Breakfast
P.O. Box One
East Fairfield, VT 05448
802/827-3827

American Bed & Breakfast in New England
(book-your-own list)
P.O. Box 983
St. Albans, VT 05478

## Virginia

Princely Bed & Breakfast, Ltd.
819 Prince Street
Alexandria, VA 22314
703/683-2159

Blue Ridge Bed & Breakfast
Rocks & Rills, Route 2, Box 3895
Berryville, VA 22611
703/955-1246

Shenandoah Valley Bed & Breakfast Reservations
P.O. Box 305
Broadway, VA 22815
703/896-9702

Rockbridge Reservations
Sleepy Hollow, P.O. Box 76
Brownsburg, VA 24415
703/348-5698

Guesthouses Bed & Breakfast, Inc.
P.O. Box 5737
Charlottesville, VA 22905
804/979-7264 or 979-8327

Military Bed & Breakfast
P.O. Box 2347
Falls Church, VA 22042
703/847-5211

Sojourners Bed and Breakfast
P.O. Box 3587
Lynchburg, VA 24503-0587
804/384-1655

Bed and Breakfast of Tidewater Virginia
P.O. Box 3343
Norfolk, VA 23514
804/627-1983

Bensonhouse
P.O. Box 15131
Richmond, VA 23227
804/648-7560

The Travel Tree
P.O. Box 838
Williamsburg, VA 23187
804/253-1571

## Washington

BABS—Bed & Breakfast Service
P.O. Box 5025
Bellingham, WA 98227
206/733-8642

Bed & Breakfast Associates
Route 2, Box 126
Cheney, WA 99004
509/299-3973

Travellers' Bed & Breakfast (Pacific Northwest)
P.O. Box 492
Mercer Island, WA 98040
206/232-2345

Pacific Bed & Breakfast
701 N.W. 60th Street
Seattle, WA 98107
206/784-0539

Spokane Bed & Breakfast Reservation Service
627 25th Street
Spokane, WA 99203
509/624-3776

## West Virginia

Martindale Bed and Breakfast Reservation Service
P.O. Box 1308
Lewisburg, WV 24901
304/647-4777

## Wisconsin

Bed & Breakfast Guest Homes
Route 2
Algoma, WI 54201
414/743-9742

Bed & Breakfast Information Service—Wisconsin
458 Glenway Street
Madison, WI 53711
608/238-6776

Bed & Breakfast of Milwaukee
P.O. Box 1822
Waukesha, WI 53187-1822
414/544-0060

# Canadian B&B Reservation Services

The following information sources are mostly reservation services that arrange bookings. All are wonderful clearing houses for B&Bs (mostly private homes—some include B&B inns or farm vacations). The toll-free 800 numbers are for the provincial tourist offices.

The provinces are listed alphabetically.

**Reminder: Allow several weeks for round-trip mail.**

## Alberta

Provincial Tourism Information
10025 Jasper Avenue, 15th floor
Edmonton, Alberta, T5G 323, Canada
1-800-661-8888

Bed & Breakfast Bureau—Canadian Care Inc.
Box 7094, Station "E"
Calgary, Alberta, T3C 3L8, Canada
403/242-5555 (Calgary) and
403/762-5070 (Banff)

Welcome West Vacation Ltd.
1320 Kerwood Crescent, S.W.
Calgary, Alberta, T2V 2N6, Canada
403/258-3373

Calgary Bed & Breakfast—AAA Bed West Ltd.
Box 7094, Station "E"
Calgary, Alberta, T3C 3L8, Canada
403/242-5555

Alberta Bed and Breakfast
4327 86th Street
Edmonton, Alberta, T6K 1A9, Canada
403/462-8885

## British Columbia

Born Free Bed & Breakfast of B.C. Ltd.
4390 Frances Street
Burnaby, British Columbia, V5C 2R3, Canada
604/298-8815

Vancouver Bed & Breakfast Ltd.
1685 Ingleton Avenue
Burnaby, British Columbia, V5C 4L8, Canada
604/291-6147

TCS Bed & Breakfast Registry
937 Delestre Avenue
Coquitlam, British Columbia, V3K 2G7, Canada
604/324-2930 or 926-0004

Canada West Accommodations Bed & Breakfast Registry
1383 Mill Street
North Vancouver, British Columbia, V7K 1V5, Canada
604/987-1088

Royal West Bed & Breakfast Registry, Ltd.
Box 86818
North Vancouver, British Columbia, V7L 4L3, Canada
604/276-2144

Western Comfort Bed & Breakfast Registry
180 East Carisbrooke Road
North Vancouver, British Columbia, V7N 1M9, Canada
604/985-2674

Royal West Bed & Breakfast Registry Ltd.
P.O. Box 416—8155 Park Road
Richmond, British Columbia, V6Y 3C9, Canada
604/276-2144

Family Care Ltd.
6104-172 A Street
Surrey, British Columbia, V3S 5M3, Canada
604/573-3113

A Home Away From Home
4228 Windsor Street
Vancouver, British Columbia, V5V 4P4, Canada
604/873-4888

Cottage Bed and Breakfast Registry
3524 West King Edward Avenue
Vancouver, British Columbia, V6S 1M5, Canada
604/738-7561

Town & Country B&B in British Columbia, Canada
P.O. Box 46554, Station "G"
Vancouver, British Columbia, V6R 4G6, Canada
604/731-5942

All Season Bed & Breakfast Agency
Box 5511, Station B
Victoria, British Columbia, V8R 6S4, Canada
604/595-2237 (604/595-BEDS)

Traveller's Bed & Breakfast
1840 Midgard Avenue
Victoria, British Columbia, Z8P 2Y9, Canada
604/477-3069

Host International B&B Reservations
1478 Gordon Avenue
West Vancouver, British Columbia, V7T 1R5, Canada
604/926-0004

## Manitoba

Provincial Tourism Information
Room 101, Legislative Building
450 Broadway
Winnipeg, Manitoba, R3C 0U8, Canada
1-800-665-0040

B&B of Manitoba
7 Sandale Drive
Winnipeg, Manitoba, R2N 1A1, Canada
204/256-6151

## New Brunswick

New Brunswick Department of Tourism
P.O. Box 12345
Fredericton, New Brunswick, E3B 5C3, Canada
1-800-561-0123

## Newfoundland/Labrador

Newfoundland Tourism Information
Government of Newfoundland
P.O. Box 2016
St. John's, Newfoundland, A1C 5R8, Canada
1-800-563-6353

## Nova Scotia

Provincial Tourism Information
136 Commercial Street
Portland, ME 04101
1-800-341-6096
1-800-492-0643 (in Maine)

South Shore Bed & Breakfast Association
P.O. Box 82
Bridgewater, Nova Scotia, B4V 2W6, Canada
902/543-5391

Halifax–Metro Bed & Breakfast
P.O. Box 1613, Station M
Halifax, Nova Scotia, B3J 2Y3, Canada
902/434-7283

Farm and Country Vacation Association
Newport Station, Hants County
Nova Scotia, B0N 2B0, Canada
902/798-5864

Cape Breton Bed and Breakfast
P.O. Box 1750
Sydney, Nova Scotia, B1P 6T7, Canada
902/564-3600

## Ontario

Provincial Tourism Information
77 Bloor Street West, 9th floor
Toronto, Ontario, M7A 2R9, Canada
1-800-268-3735

## Ontario: Eastern Region

Beachburg and Area Bed & Breakfast
Box 146
Beachburg, Ontario, K0J 1C0, Canada
613/582-3585

South Renfrew County Bed & Breakfast Association
Box 67
Calabogie, Ontario, K0J 1H0, Canada
613/752-2201

Seaway Valley Bed & Breakfast
Box 884
Cornwall, Ontario, K6J 1Z3, Canada
613/932-0299

Kingston Area Bed & Breakfast
10 Westview Road
Kingston, Ontario, K7M 2C3, Canada
613/542-0214 or 542-6058

Capital Bed & Breakfast Association of Ottawa, "Canada-Wide Accommodations"
2071 Riverside Drive
Ottawa, Ontario, K1H 7X2, Canada
613/737-4129

Ottawa Area Bed & Breakfast
44 Hampton Avenue
Ottawa, Ontario, K1Y 0N2, Canada
613/563-0161

Ottawa Centretown Bed & Breakfast
253 McLeod Street
Ottawa, Ontario, K2P 1A1, Canada
613/234-7577

## Ontario: Central Region

Brighton Area Bed & Breakfast Association
c/o Applecrest House
61 Simpson Street, Box 1106
Brighton, Ontario, K0K 1H0, Canada
613/475-0538

Durham East Bed and Breakfast Assocation
RR2
Newcastle, Ontario, L0A 1H0, Canada
416/987-4096

Bed and Breakfast Prince Edward County
P.O. Box 160
Picton, Ontario, K0K 2T0, Canada
613/393-3046

Prince Edward County Bed & Breakfast Independents
P.O. Box 502
Wellington, Ontario, K0K 3L0, Canada
613/399-2569

## Ontario: Metropolitan Toronto

All Seasons Bed and Breakfast
383 Mississauga Valley Boulevard
Mississauga, Ontario, L5A 1Y9, Canada
416/276-4572

Country Host
R.R. #1
Palgrave, Ontario, L0N 1P0, Canada
519/941-7633

The Downtown Toronto Association of Bed & Breakfast Guest Houses
P.O. Box 190, Station B
Toronto, Ontario, M5T 2W1, Canada
416/598-4562 or 977-6841

Metropolitan Bed & Breakfast Registry of Toronto
72 Lowther Avenue
Toronto, Ontario, M5R 1C8, Canada
416/964-2566 or 928-2833

Toronto Bed and Breakfast
P.O. Box 74, Station M
Toronto, Ontario, M6S 4T2, Canada
416/233-3887 or 233-4041 (both numbers evenings and weekends only)

## Ontario: Georgian Lakelands

Muskoka Bed and Breakfast Association
Box 1431
Gravenhurst, Ontario, P0C 1G0, Canada
705/687-4395

Orillia Area Bed & Breakfast Association
RR2 Hawkestone
Orillia, Ontario, L0L 1T0, Canada
705/326-7743 or 487-3135

Grey Bruce Bed & Breakfast Association
R.R. 5
Owen Sound, Ontario, N4K 5N7, Canada
519/371-2071 or (in Ontario) 1-800-265-3127

Country Host
R.R. 1
Palgrave, Ontario, L0N 1P0, Canada
519/941-7633

Penetanguishene Bed & Breakfast
Centre d'Activités Français
C.P. 1270, 63 Main Street
Penetanguishene, Ontario, L0K 1P0, Canada
705/549-3116

## Ontario: Festival Country in Niagara and Mid-Western Ontario

Alma, Elmira, Elora Bed & Breakfast
Washa Farm, RR #2
Alma, Ontario, N0B 1A0, Canada
519/846-9788

Bed & Breakfast Burlington
5435 Stratton Road
Burlington, Ontario, L7L 2Z1, Canada
416/637-0329

Fergus/Alora Bed & Breakfast
500 St. Andrew Street
Fergus, Ontario, N1M 1R6, Canada
519/854-2584

Niagara Region Bed & Breakfast
2631 Dorchester Road
Niagara Falls, Ontario, L2J 2Y9, Canada
416/358-8998

Niagara-on-the-Lake Bed & Breakfast
P.O. Box 1515
Niagara-on-the-Lake, Ontario, L0S 1J0, Canada
416/358-8988

## Ontario: Southwestern Region

Home Suite Home Bed & Breakfast Association
115 Erie Street South
Leamington, Ontario, N8H 3B5, Canada
519/326-7169

London and Area Bed and Breakfast Association
720 Headley Drive
London, Ontario, N6H 3V6, Canada
519/471-6228

Southwestern Ontario Countryside Vacation Association
Honey Brook Farm, R.R. 1
Millbank, Ontario, N0K 1L0, Canada
519/595-4604

Country House
R.R. 1
Palgrave, Ontario, L0N 1P0, Canada
519/941-7633

Pelee Island Bed & Breakfast
Pelee Island, Ontario, N0R 1M0, Canada
519/724-2068

Sarnia-Lambton Bed & Breakfast Association
131 Maria Street
Sarnia, Ontario, M7T 4S6, Canada
519/337-6984

Stratford and Area Visitors' and Convention Bureau
38 Albert Street
Stratford, Ontario, N5A 3K3, Canada
519/271-5140

## Ontario: Northwestern Region

The Thunder Bay Area Bed & Breakfast
The Unicorn Inn, R.R. #1
South Gilles, Ontario, P0P 2V0, Canada
613/752-2201

## Prince Edward Island

Visitor Services of Prince Edward Island
P.O. Box 940
Charlottetown, P.E.I., C1A 7M5, Canada
902/892-2457 or 1-800-565-9060

## Quebec

Provincial Tourism Information
CP 20000
Quebec, G1K 7X2, Canada
1-800-443-7000 (most of eastern U.S.) or 514/873-2015

Montreal Bed & Breakfast
4912 Victoria
Montreal, Quebec, H3W 2N1, Canada
514/738-9410 or 738-3859

Gîte Québec
3729, Ave. LeCorbusier
Ste-Foy, Quebec, G1W 4R8, Canada
418/651-1860

A Downtown Bed and Breakfast Network
3458 Laval Avenue at Sherbrooke Street
Montreal, Quebec, H2X 3C8, Canada
514/289-9749

## Saskatchewan

Tourism Saskatchewan
2103 11th Avenue, 2nd floor
Regina, Saskatchewan, F.K., S4P 3V7, Canada
1-800-667-7191

## Yukon

A & P Bed & Breakfast Agency
102, 302 Steele Street
Whitehorse, Yukon, Y1A 2C5, Canada
403/668-2999

# INDEX

## Connecticut



## Maine

## Massachusetts

## New Hampshire

## Rhode Island



## Vermont

## Vermont